Western Civilizations

Their History & Their Culture

Joshua Cole

Carol Symes

Western Civilizations

Their History & Their Culture

EIGHTEENTH EDITION

VOLUME A

W. W. NORTON & COMPANY ▪ NEW YORK ▪ LONDON

W. W. Norton & Company has been independent since its founding in 1923, when William Warder Norton and Mary D. Herter Norton first published lectures delivered at the People's Institute, the adult education division of New York City's Cooper Union. The firm soon expanded its program beyond the Institute, publishing books by celebrated academics from America and abroad. By midcentury, the two major pillars of Norton's publishing program—trade books and college texts—were firmly established. In the 1950s, the Norton family transferred control of the company to its employees, and today—with a staff of four hundred and a comparable number of trade, college, and professional titles published each year—W. W. Norton & Company stands as the largest and oldest publishing house owned wholly by its employees.

Editor: Jon Durbin
Associate editor: Justin Cahill
Editorial assistant: Penelope Lin
Project editor: Melissa Atkin
Managing editor, College: Marian Johnson
Copyeditor: Jude Grant
E-media editors: Steve Hoge, Tacy Quinn
Ancillary editor: Lorraine Klimowich
Assistant editor, E-media: Stefani Wallace
Photo editor: Evan Luberger
Photo research: Rona Tucillo
Marketing manager, History: Sarah England
Production manager, College: Sean Mintus
Design director: Rubina Yeh
Book designer: Judith Abbate / Abbate Design
Composition: Jouve
Cartographers: Mapping Specialists
Manufacturing: Transcontinental

Library of Congress has catalogued the one-volume edition as follows:

Cole, Joshua, 1961–
    Western civilizations : their history & their culture / Joshua Cole and Carol Symes. —Eighteenth edition.
        pages cm
    Includes bibliographical references and index.

    ISBN 978-0-393-92213-4 (hardcover)
    1. Civilization, Western—Textbooks.   2. Europe—Civilization—Textbooks.   I. Symes, Carol.   II. Title.
    CB245.C56 2013
    909'.09821—dc23

                                                        2013029952

This edition:
ISBN: 978-0-393-92216-5 (pbk.)

W. W. Norton & Company, Inc., 500 Fifth Avenue, New York, N. Y. 10110
wwnorton.com

W. W. Norton & Company Ltd., Castle House, 75/76 Wells Street, London W1T 3QT

2 3 4 5 6 7 8 9 0

To our families:

Kate Tremel, Lucas and Ruby Cole
Tom, Erin, and Connor Wilson

with love and gratitude for their support.
And to all our students, who have also been
our teachers.

JOSHUA COLE (Ph.D., University of California, Berkeley) is Associate Professor of History at the University of Michigan, Ann Arbor. His publications include work on gender and the history of the population sciences, colonial violence, and the politics of memory in nineteenth- and twentieth-century France, Germany, and Algeria. His first book was *The Power of Large Numbers: Population, Politics, and Gender in Nineteenth-Century France* (Ithaca, NY: Cornell University Press, 2000).

CAROL SYMES (Ph.D., Harvard University) is Associate Professor of History and Director of Undergraduate Studies in the history department at the University of Illinois, Urbana-Champaign, where she has won the top teaching award in the College of Liberal Arts and Sciences. Her main areas of study include medieval Europe, the history of information media and communication technologies, and the history of theater. Her first book was *A Common Stage: Theater and Public Life in Medieval Arras* (Ithaca, NY: Cornell University Press, 2007).

Brief Contents

Contents

Chapter 12 ■ INNOVATION AND EXPLORATION, 1453–1533　389

Maps

Primary Sources

This new edition of *Western Civilizations* sharpens and expands the set of tools we have developed to empower students—our own and yours—to engage effectively with the themes, sources, and challenges of history. It presents a clear and vigorous narrative, supplemented by a compelling selection of primary sources and striking images. At the same time, as the authors of this book's previous edition, we have worked to develop a unified program of pedagogical elements that guide students toward a more thorough understanding of the past, and of the ways that historians reconstruct that past. This framework helps students to analyze and interpret historical evidence on their own, encouraging them to become active participants in the learning process.

Moreover, the wide chronological scope of this book offers an unusual opportunity to trace central human developments (population movements, intellectual currents, economic trends, the formation of political institutions, the power of religious belief, the role of the arts and of technologies) in a region of the world whose cultural diversity has been constantly invigorated and renewed by its interactions with peoples living in other places. Students today have a wide selection of introductory history courses to choose from, thanks to the welcome availability of introductory surveys in Latin American, African, and Asian history, alongside both traditional and innovative offerings in the history of the United States and Europe. Global history has also come into its own in recent years. But our increasing awareness that no region's history can be isolated from global processes and connections has merely heightened the need for a richly contextualized and broad-based history such as that represented in *Western Civilizations*.

As in previous editions, we have attempted to balance the coverage of political, social, economic, and cultural phenomena with extensive treatment of material culture, daily life, gender, sexuality, art, science, and popular culture. And following the path laid out by the book's previous authors, Judith Coffin and Robert Stacey, we have insisted

that the history of European peoples must be understood through their interactions with peoples in other parts of the world. Our treatment of this history is accordingly both deep and dynamic, attentive to the latest developments in historical scholarship.

Given the importance of placing human history in a global context, those of us who study the histories of ancient, medieval, and modern Europe are actively changing the ways that we teach this history. For good reasons reflected in the title of this book, few historians today would uphold a monolithic vision of a single and enduring "Western civilization" whose inevitable march to domination can be traced chapter by chapter through time. This older paradigm, strongly associated with the curriculum of early twentieth-century American colleges and universities, no longer conforms to what we know about the human past. Neither the "West" nor "Europe" can be seen as distinct, unified entities in space or time; the meanings attributed to these geographical expressions have changed in significant ways. Moreover, historians now agree that a linear notion of any civilization persisting unchanged over the centuries was made coherent only by leaving out the intense conflicts, extraordinary ruptures, and dynamic changes that took place at the heart of the societies we call "Western." Smoothing out the rough edges of the past does students no favors; even an introductory text such as this one should present the past as it appears to the historians who study it—that is, as complex panorama of human effort, filled with possibility and achievement but also fraught with discord, uncertainty, accident, and tragedy.

We know that current and future users of our text will be enthusiastic to see the efforts made in this new edition to update and reorganize the Late Medieval and Early Modern periods in order to place them in a larger Atlantic World context. The major highlight of this reorganization is a brand new chapter, entitled "Europe in the Atlantic World, 1550–1650." It places the newly integrated space of the Atlantic at the center of the story, exploring the ways, that religious warfare, economic developments, population movements, and cultural trends shaped—and were shaped by—historical actors on this dynamic frontier. Another significant result of the reorganization of these two periods is to provide a clearer chronological framework for the narrative, so that the students can better see how major topics and events emerge from their historical contexts. This, of course, was part of a larger effort begun across the entire text in the previous edition. These revisions demonstrate our dual commitment to keep the book current and up-to-date, while striving to integrate strong pedagogical features that help students build their study and history skills.

New and Revised Pedagogical Features

In our ongoing effort to shape students' engagement with history, this book is designed to reinforce your course objectives by helping students to master core content while challenging them to think critically about the past. In order to achieve these aims, our previous edition augmented the traditional strengths of *Western Civilizations* by introducing several exciting new features. These have since been refined and revised in accordance with feedback from student readers and teachers of the book. The most important and revolutionary feature is the pedagogical structure that supports each chapter. As we know from long experience, many students in introductory survey courses find the sheer quantity of information overwhelming, and so we have provided guidance to help them navigate through the material and to read in meaningful ways.

At the outset of each chapter, the *Before You Read This Chapter* feature offers three preliminary windows onto the material to be covered: *Story Lines*, *Chronology*, and *Core Objectives*. *Story Lines* allow the student to become familiar with the primary narrative threads that tie the chapter's elements together, and the *Chronology* grounds these *Story Lines* in the period under study. *Core Objectives* provide a checklist to ensure that the student is aware of the primary teaching points in the chapter. The student is then reminded of these teaching points upon completing the chapter, in the *After You Read This Chapter* section, which prompts the student to revisit the chapter in three ways. The first, *Reviewing the Core Objectives*, asks the reader to reconsider core objectives by answering a pointed question about each one. The second, *People, Ideas, and Events in Context*, summarizes some of the particulars that students should retain from their reading, through questions that allow them to relate individual terms to the major objectives and story

lines. Finally, *Thinking about Connections*, new to this edition, allow for more open-ended reflection on the significance of the chapter's material, drawing students' attention to issues that connect it to previous chapters and giving them insight into what comes next. As a package, the pedagogical features at the beginning and end of each chapter work together to enhance the student's learning experience, by breaking down the process of reading and analysis into manageable tasks.

A second package of pedagogical features is designed to capture students' interest and to compel them to think about what is at stake in the construction and use of historical narratives. Each chapter opens with a vignette that showcases a particular person or event representative of the era as a whole. Within each chapter, an expanded program of illustrations and maps has been enhanced by the addition of *Guiding Questions* (following these illustrations' and maps' captions) that urge the reader to explore the historical contexts and significance of these features in a more analytical way. The historical value of images, artifacts, and material culture is further emphasized in another feature we introduced in our previous edition, *Interpreting Visual Evidence*. This section provides discussion leaders with a provocative departure point for conversations about the key issues raised by visual sources, which students often find more approachable than texts. Once this conversation has begun, students can further develop their skills by *Analyzing Primary Sources*, through close readings of primary texts accompanied by cogent interpretive questions. The dynamism and diversity of Western civilizations are also illuminated through a look at *Competing Viewpoints* in each chapter, in which specific debates are presented through paired primary-source texts. The bibliographical *Further Readings*, located at the end of the book, has also been edited and brought up-to-date.

In addition to these features, which have proven successful, we are delighted to introduce an entirely new segment with this eighteenth edition. The new *Past and Present* features in the main text prompt students to connect events unfolding in the past with the breaking news of our own time, by taking one episode from each chapter and comparing it with a phenomenon that resonates more immediately with our students. To bring this new feature to life for students, we have also created a new series of **Author Videos**, in which we describe and analyze these connections across time and place. There are a number of illuminating discussions, including, "Spectator Sports," which compares the Roman gladiatorial games with NFL Football; "The Reputation of Richard III," which shows how modern forensics like those we see used on numerous TV shows were recently used to identify the remains of Richard III;

"The Persistence of Monarchies in a Democratic Age," which explains the origins and evolution of our ongoing fascination with royals like Louis XIV and Princess Diana; and "The Internet and the Enlightenment Public Sphere," which compares the kinds of public networks that helped spread Enlightenment ideas to the way the Internet can be used today to spread political ideas in movements such as the Arab Spring and Occupy Wall Street. Through this new feature, not only do we want to encourage students to recognize the continuing relevance of seemingly distant historical moments, but also we want to encourage historically-minded habits that will be useful for a lifetime. If students learn to see the connections among their world and the past, they will be more apt to place unfolding developments and debates in a more informed and complex historical context.

A Tour of New Chapters and Revisions

Our previous edition of *Western Civilizations* featured significant changes to each of the book's first five chapters, and this process of revision has continued in the present edition. In Chapter 1, the challenge of locating and interpreting historical evidence drawn from nontextual sources (archaeological, environmental, anthropological, mythic) is a special focus. Chapter 2 further underscores the degree to which recent archeological discoveries and new historical techniques have revolutionized our understanding of ancient history, and have also corroborated ancient peoples' own understandings of their past. Chapter 3 offers expanded coverage of the diverse polities that emerged in ancient Greece, and of Athens' closely related political, documentary, artistic, and intellectual achievements. Chapter 4's exploration of the Hellenistic world includes an unusually wide-ranging discussion of the scientific revolution powered by this first cosmopolitan civilization. Chapter 5 emphasizes the ways that the unique values and institutions of the Roman Republic are transformed through imperial expansion under the Principate.

With Chapter 6, a more extensive series of revisions has resulted in some significant reshaping and reorganization, so that the book's narrative reflects recent scholarship. The story of Rome's transformative encounter with early Christianity has been rewritten to ensure clarity and also to emphasize the fundamental ways that Christianity itself changed through the Roman Empire and in contact with peoples from northwestern Europe. Chapter 7, which examines Rome's three distinctive successor civilizations, now offers more extensive coverage of the reign of Justinian

and emergence of Islam. Balanced attention to the interlocking histories of Byzantium, the Muslim caliphates, and western Europe has carried forward in subsequent chapters. Chapters 8 contains an entirely new section, "A Tour of Europe around the Year 1000," with coverage of the Viking diaspora, the formation of Scandinavian kingdoms and the empire of Cnute, early medieval Rus' and eastern Europe, and the relationship among Mediterranean microcosms. It also features greatly expanded coverage of economy, trade, and the events leading up to the First Crusade. Chapter 9, which now covers the period 1000–1250, features a new segment on the Crusader States and crusading movements within Europe.

Chapter 10's treatment of the medieval world between 1250 and 1350 is almost wholly new, reflecting cutting-edge scholarship on this era. It includes a fresh look at the consolidation of the Mongol Khanates, new images and maps, some new sources, and a new *Interpreting Visual Evidence* segment on seals and their users. Chapters 11 and 12 have been thoroughly reorganized and rewritten to ensure that the narrative of medieval Europeans' colonial ventures (from the western Mediterranean to the eastern Atlantic and Africa, and beyond) is integrated with the story of the Black Death's effects on the medieval world and the impetus for the intellectual and artistic innovations of the Renaissance. In previous editions of the book, these concurrent phenomena were treated as separate, as though they took place in three separate periods (the later Middle Ages, the Renaissance, and the Age of Exploration). This made the connections among them almost impossible to explain or appreciate. In this eighteenth edition, therefore, the voyages of Columbus are firmly rooted in their historical contexts while the religious, social, and cultural upheavals of the Reformation (Chapter 13) are more clearly placed against a backdrop of political and economic competition in Europe and the Americas.

This program of revisions sets the stage for the most significant new chapter in the book: Chapter 14, "Europe in the Atlantic World, 1550–1650." This chapter, the hinge between the book's first and second halves, resulted from a close collaboration between us. It is designed to function either as the satisfying culmination of a course that surveys the history of Western civilizations up to the middle of the seventeenth century (like that taught by Carol Symes) or to provide a foundation for a course on the history of the modern West (like that taught by Joshua Cole). The chapter illuminates the changing nature of Europe as it becomes fully integrated into the larger Atlantic world that dramatically impacts all of its internal political, social, cultural, and economic development. In addition to greatly enhanced treatment of the transatlantic slave trade and the Columbian

Exchange, it also features new sections on the different models of colonial settlement in the Caribbean and the Americas, as well as expanded coverage of the Thirty Years' War.

The new emphasis on the emergence of the Atlantic world carries over to Chapter 15, which covers the emergence of powerful absolutist regimes on the continent and the evolution of wealthy European trading empires in the Americas, Africa, and Asia. This material has now been reorganized to clarify developments over time, as the early successes of the Spanish empire are gradually eclipsed by the successes of the Dutch, the French, and the British empires. A new document on the Streltsy rebellion, meanwhile, allows students to better understand the contested nature of power under the Russian tsars during the absolutist period. We have retained the emphasis on intellectual and cultural history in Chapter 16, on the Scientific Revolution, and in Chapter 17, on the Enlightenment. In Chapter 16 we have enhanced our treatment of the relationship between Christian faith and the new sciences of observation with a new primary-source document by Pierre Gassendi. In Chapter 17, meanwhile, we have sought to set the Enlightenment more clearly in its social and political context, connecting it more explicitly to the theme of European expansion into the Americas and the Pacific. This helps, for example, in connecting a document like the American Declaration of Independence with the ideas of European Enlightenment thinkers.

Chapters 18–19 cover the political and economic revolutions of the late eighteenth and early nineteenth centuries. Chapter 18 covers the French Revolution and the Napoleonic empires in depth, while also drawing attention to the way that these central episodes were rooted in a larger pattern of revolutionary political change that engulfed the Atlantic world. Chapter 19 emphasizes both the economic growth and the technological innovations that were a part of the Industrial Revolution, while also exploring the social and cultural consequences of industrialization for men and women in Europe's new industrial societies. The *Interpreting Visual Evidence* feature in Chapter 19 allows students to explore the ways that industrialization created new perceptions of the global economy in Europe, changing the way people thought of their place in the world.

Chapters 20–21 explore the successive struggles between conservative reaction and radicals in Europe, as the dynamic forces of nationalism unleashed by the French Revolution redrew the map of Europe and threatened the dynastic regimes that had ruled for centuries. Here, however, we have sought to clarify the periodization of the post-Napoleonic decades by focusing Chapter 20 more clearly on the conservative reaction in Europe after 1815, and the ideologies of conservatism, liberalism, republicanism, socialism,

and nationalism. By setting the 1848 revolutions entirely in Chapter 21 (rather than split between the two chapters as in previous editions) instructors should be able to demonstrate more easily the connection between these political movements and the history of national unification in Germany and Italy in subsequent decades. While making these changes in the organization of the chapters, we have retained our treatment of the important cultural movements of the first half of the nineteenth century, especially Romanticism.

Chapter 22 takes on the history of nineteenth-century colonialism, exploring both its political and economic origins and its consequences for the peoples of Africa and Asia. The chapter gives new emphasis to the significance of colonial conquest for European culture, as colonial power became increasingly associated with national greatness, both in conservative monarchies and in more democratic regimes. Meanwhile, Chapter 23 brings the narrative back to the heart of Europe, covering the long-term consequences of industrialization and the consolidation of a conservative form of nationalism in many European nations even as the electorate was being expanded. The chapter emphasizes the varied nature of the new forms of political dissent, from the feminists who claimed the right to vote to the newly organized socialist movements that proved so enduring in many European countries.

Chapters 24 and 25 bring new vividness to the history of the First World War and the intense conflicts of the interwar period, while Chapter 26 uses the history of the Second World War as a hinge for understanding European and global developments in the second half of the twentieth century. The *Interpreting Visual Evidence* feature in Chapter 24 allows for a special focus on the role of propaganda among the belligerent nations in 1914–1918; and the chapter's section on the diplomatic crisis that preceded the First World War has been streamlined to allow students to more easily comprehend the essential issues at the heart of the conflict. In Chapter 25 the *Interpreting Visual Evidence* feature continues to explore the theme touched on in earlier chapters, political representations of "the people," this time in the context of fascist spectacles in Germany and Italy in the 1930s. These visual sources help students to understand the vulnerability of Europe's democratic regimes during these years as they faced the dual assault from fascists on the right and Bolsheviks on the left.

Chapters 27–29 bring the volumes to a close in a thorough exploration of the Cold War, decolonization, the collapse of the Soviet Union and the Eastern Bloc in 1989–1991, and the roots of the multifaceted global conflicts that beset the world in the first decade of the twenty-first century. Chapter 27 juxtaposes the Cold War with decolonization, showing how this combination sharply diminished the ability of European nations to control events in the international arena, even as they succeeded in rebuilding their economies at home. Chapter 28 explores the vibrancy of European culture in the crucial period of the 1960s to the early 1990s, bringing new attention to the significance of 1989 as a turning point in European history. Finally, extensive revisions to Chapter 29, add to the issues covered in our treatment of Europe's place in the contemporary globalized world. The chapter now includes a new section on efforts to deal with climate change, as well as expanded discussion of the impact of global terrorism, and recent developments in the Arab-Israeli conflict. The discussion on the financial crisis of 2008 and the presidency of Barack Obama has been brought up to date, and two new sections have been added to allow students to think about the Arab Spring of 2011 and the European debt crisis of recent years in connection with the broader history of European democracy, nation building, and colonialism in the modern period.

Media Resources for Instructors and Students

LMS COURSEPACKS WITH STRONG ASSESSMENT AND LECTURE TOOLS

- **Dynamic Author Videos (55 total)** in which the authors discuss two of the main topics or themes in each chapter. New to this edition, illustrations, maps, and other types of media are integrated into the interviews to make them richer and more dynamic. These segments can serve as lecture launchers or as a preview tool for students before and after they read a chapter. (Available in PowerPoint and on Norton StudySpace.)
- **NEW *Past and Present* Author Videos (29 total)** that connect topics across time and place and show why history is relevant to understanding our world today (see further explanation above). Examples include "Spectator Sports," "Medieval Plots and Modern Movies," "Global Pandemics," and "The Atlantic Revolutions and Human Rights" (Available in PowerPoint and on Norton StudySpace.)
- **NEW Guided Reading Exercises** by Scott Corbett (Ventura College) are designed to help students learn how to effectively read a textbook. The reading exercises, which are keyed to each chapter's *People, Ideas, and Events in Context*

questions, instill a three-step Note-Summarize-Assess pedagogy. Exercises are based on actual passages from the textbook (three exercises per chapter). Feedback will provide model responses with direct page references. (Available only in the Norton Coursepack.)
- **NEW 36 Map Exercises** can be assigned for assessment. These activities ask students a series of questions about historical events that must be answered by clicking on the map to record the answer. (Available only in the Norton Coursepack.)
- **NEW Chrono-Quiz** improving on the ever-popular Chrono-Sequencer, the Chrono-Quiz is now available as an assessment activity that will report to the school's native LMS. (Available only in the Norton Coursepack.)
- **NEW *StoryMaps*** break complex maps into a sequence of four to five annotated screens that focus on the *story* behind the *geography*. There are ten StoryMaps that include such topics as The Silk Road, The Spread of the Black Death, and Nineteenth-Century Imperialism. (Available only on wwnorton .com/web/westernciv18/instructors.)

INSTRUCTOR'S MANUAL
Bob Brennan (Cape Fear Community College)
Bruce Delfini (Rockland Community College)
Christopher Laney (Berkshire Community College)
Alice Roberti (Santa Rosa Community College)

The Instructor's Manual for *Western Civilizations*, Eighteenth edition, is designed to help instructors prepare lectures and exams. The Instructor's Manual contains detailed chapter outlines, general discussion questions, document discussion questions, lecture objectives, interdisciplinary discussion topics, and recommended reading and film lists. **This edition has been revised to include sample answers to all of the student-facing comprehension questions in the text.**

TEST BANK
Geoffrey Clark (SUNY Potsdam)
Donna Trembinski (St. Francis Xavier University)

The Test Bank contains over 2,000 multiple-choice, true/false, and essay questions. This edition of the Test Bank has been completely revised for content and accuracy. All test questions are now aligned to Bloom's Taxonomy for greater ease and effectiveness of assessment.

FOR STUDENTS

⊚ wwnorton.com/web/westerncivl8
Free and open to all students, Norton StudySpace includes

- **Author Videos (over 80 in all)** for every chapter, including the new *Past and Present* segments that connect topics. Examples include
  - "Medieval Plots and Modern Movies"
  - "Controlling Consumption" (the legalization of controlled substances, from sixteenth-century regulations to contemporary marijuana policy)
  - "The Internet and the Enlightenment Public Sphere"
- **Chapter Outlines and Quizzes.** Quiz feedback is aligned to student learning outcomes and core objectives, along with page references.
- **World History Tours,** powered by Google Earth™, now operate from within the browser, eliminating the need to download third-party applications or files.
- **iMaps** allow students to view layers of information on each map.
- **Map Worksheets** provide each map without labels for offline re-labeling and quizzing.
- **Flashcards** align key terms and events with brief descriptions and definitions.
- Over **400 primary-source documents and images**
- **Ebook links** tie the online text to all study and review materials.

A FEW WORDS OF THANKS

Our first edition as members of *Western Civilizations'* authorial team was a challenging and rewarding one. Our second edition has been equally rewarding in that we have been able to implement a number of useful and engaging changes in the content and structure of the book, which we hope will make it even more student- and classroom-friendly. We are very grateful for the expert assistance and support of the Norton team, especially that of our editor, Jon Durbin. Melissa Atkin, our fabulous project editor, has driven the book beautifully through the manuscript process. Justin Cahill has provided good critiques of the illustrations and the new *Past and Present* features in addition to all the other parts of the project he has handled so skillfully. Evan Luberger and Rona Tucillo did an excellent job finding many of the exact images we specified. Lorraine Klimowich did an expert job developing the print ancillaries. Sean Mintus has efficiently marched

us through the production process. Steve Hoge has done a great job developing the book's fantastic emedia, particularly the new *Past and Present* Author Videos, the new Guided Reading Exercises, and the new StoryMaps. Jude Grant and John Gould were terrific in skillfully guiding the manuscript through the copyediting and proofreading stages. Finally, we want to thank Sarah England for spearheading the marketing campaign for the new edition. We are also indebted to the numerous expert readers who commented on various chapters and who thereby strengthened the book as a whole. We are thankful to our families, for their patience and advice, and to our students, whose questions and comments over the years have been essential to the framing of this book. And we extend a special thanks to, and hope to hear from, all the teachers and students we might never meet—their engagement with this book will frame new understandings of our shared past and its bearing on our future.

REVIEWERS

17th Edition Consultants
Paul Freedman, Yale University
Sheryl Kroen, University of Florida
Michael Kulikowski, Pennsylvania State University
Harry Liebersohn, University of Illinois, Urbana-Champaign
Helmut Smith, Vanderbilt University

17th Edition Reviewers
Donna Allen, Glendale Community College
Ken Bartlett, University of Toronto
Volker Benkert, Arizona State University
Dean Bennett, Schenectady City Community College
Patrick Brennan, Gulf Coast Community College
Neil Brooks, Community College of Baltimore County, Essex
James Brophy, University of Delaware
Kevin Caldwell, Blue Ridge Community College
Keith Chu, Bergen Community College
Alex D'Erizans, Borough of Manhattan Community College, CUNY
Hilary Earl, Nipissing University
Kirk Ford, Mississippi College
Michael Gattis, Gulf Coast Community College
David M. Gallo, College of Mount Saint Vincent
Jamie Gruring, Arizona State University
Tim Hack, Salem Community College
Bernard Hagerty, University of Pittsburg
Paul T. Hietter, Mesa Community College

Paul Hughes, Sussex County Community College
Kyle Irvin, Jefferson State Community College
Llana Krug, York College of Pennsylvania
Guy Lalande, St. Francis Xavier University
Chris Laney, Berkshire Community College
Charles Levine, Mesa Community College
Michael McKeown, Daytona State University
Dan Puckett, Troy State University
Dan Robinson, Troy State University
Craig Saucier, Southeastern Louisiana University
Aletia Seaborn, Southern Union State College
Victoria Thompson, Arizona State University
Donna Trembinski, St. Francis Xavier University
Pamela West, Jefferson State Community College
Julianna Wilson, Pima Community College

18th Edition Reviewers
Matthew Barlow, John Abbott College
Ken Bartlett, University of Toronto
Bob Brennan, Cape Fear Community College
Jim Brophy, University of Delaware
Keith Chu, Bergen Community College

Geoffrey Clark, SUNY Potsdam
Bill Donovan, Loyola University Maryland
Jeff Ewen, Sussex County Community College
Peter Goddard, University of Guelph
Paul Hughes, Sussex County Community College
Michael Kulikowski, Penn State University
Chris Laney, Berkshire Community College
James Martin, Campbell University
Derrick McKisick, Fairfield University
Dan Puckett, Troy University
Major Ben Richards, US Military Academy
Bo Riley, Columbus State Community College
Kimlisa Salazar, Pima Community College
Sara Scalenghe, Loyola University Maryland
Suzanne Smith, Cape Fear Community College
Bobbi Sutherland, Dordt College
David Tengwall, Anne Arundel Community College
Pam West, Jefferson State Community College
Julianna Wilson, Pima Community College
Margarita Youngo, Pima Community College

Western Civilizations

Their History & Their Culture

STORY LINES

- Historians gather and interpret evidence from a diverse array of sources, many of them environmental, visual, and archaeological.

- All civilizations emerge as the result of complex historical processes specific to a time and place, yet all share certain defining features.

- Prominent individuals can come to power through the use of force, but maintaining power requires legitimacy.

- Those individuals wielding power in ancient Mesopotamia and Egypt responded in different ways to the challenge of establishing legitimacy.

CHRONOLOGY

11,000 B.C.E.	Neolithic Revolution begins
7500–5700 B.C.E.	Çatalhöyük flourishes
6800–3000 B.C.E.	Jericho flourishes
4300–2900 B.C.E.	The rise of Uruk in Sumer
c. 3200 B.C.E.	Development of writing
c. 3100 B.C.E.	King Narmer unites Upper and Lower Egypt
2900–2500 B.C.E.	Early Dynastic Period in Sumer
c. 2700 B.C.E.	Reign of Gilgamesh
c. 2686–2160 B.C.E.	Old Kingdom of Egypt
c. 2650 B.C.E.	Imhotep engineers the Step Pyramid for King Djoser
c. 2350 B.C.E.	Sargon of Akkad consolidates power in Sumer
2160–2055 B.C.E.	First Intermediate Period in Egypt
2100–2000 B.C.E.	Ziggurat of Ur constructed
2055–c. 1650 B.C.E.	Middle Kingdom of Egypt
c. 1792–1750 B.C.E.	Reign of Hammurabi

Early Civilizations

CORE OBJECTIVES

- **UNDERSTAND** the challenges involved in studying the distant past.

- **DEFINE** the key characteristics of civilization.

- **IDENTIFY** the factors that shaped the earliest cities.

- **EXPLAIN** how Hammurabi's empire was governed.

- **DESCRIBE** the main differences between Mesopotamian and Egyptian civilizations.

T here was a time, the story goes, when all the peoples of the earth shared a common language and could therefore accomplish great things. They developed new technologies, made bricks, and aspired to build a fortified city with a tower reaching to the sky. But their god was troubled by this, so he destroyed their civilization by making it hard for them to understand one another's speech.

We know this as the legend of Babel. It's a story that probably circulated among peoples of the ancient world for thousands of years before it became part of the Hebrew book we call by its Greek name, Genesis, "the beginning." The story lets us glimpse some of the conditions in which the first civilizations arose, and it also reminds us of the ruptures that make studying them hard. We no longer speak the same languages as those ancient peoples, just as we no longer have direct access to their experiences or their beliefs.

Such foundational stories are usually called *myths*, but they are really an early form of history. For the people who told them, myths helped to make sense of the present by explaining the past. The fate of Babel conveyed a crucial message: human beings are powerful when they share a common goal,

3

and what enables human interaction is civilization. To the peoples of the ancient world, the characteristic benefits of civilization—stability and safety, government, art, literature, science—were always products of city life. The very word *civilization* derives from the Latin word *civis*, "city." Cities, however, became possible only as a result of innovations that began around the end of the last Ice Age, about 13,000 years ago, and that came to fruition in Mesopotamia 8,000 years later. The history of civilization is therefore a short one. Within the study of humanity, which reaches back to the genus *Homo* in Africa, some 1.7 million years ago, it is merely a blip on the radar screen. Even within the history of *Homo sapiens*, the subspecies to which we all belong and which evolved about 40,000 years ago, civilization is a very recent development.

The study of early civilizations is both fascinating and challenging. Historians still do not understand why the first-known cities should have developed in the region between the Tigris and the Euphrates Rivers, in what is now Iraq. Once developed, however, the basic patterns of urban life quickly spread to other parts of the Near East, both by imitation and by conquest. A network of trading connections linked these early cities, but intense competition for resources made alliances among them fragile. Then, around the middle of the second millennium B.C.E. (that is, "Before the Common Era," equivalent to the Christian dating system B.C., "Before Christ"), emerging powers began to shape these fiercely independent cities into empires. How this happened—and how we know that it happened—is the subject of Chapter 1.

BEFORE CIVILIZATION

More than 9,000 years ago, a town began to develop at Çatalhöyük (*CHUH-tal-hih-yik*) in what is now south-central Turkey. Over the next 2,000 years, it grew to cover an area of thirty-three acres, within which some 8,000 inhabitants lived in more than 2,000 separate houses. If this seems small, consider that Çatalhöyük's population density was actually twice that of today's most populous city, Mumbai (India). It was so tightly packed that there were hardly any streets. Instead, each house was built immediately next to its neighbor and generally on top of a previous house. People entered their houses by walking across their neighbors' rooftops and climbing down ladders into their own living spaces.

The people of Çatalhöyük developed a highly organized and advanced society. They wove wool cloth; they made kiln-fired pottery; they painted elaborate hunting scenes on the plaster-covered walls of their houses; they made weapons and tools from razor-sharp obsidian imported from the nearby Cappadocian mountains. They honored their ancestors with religious rites and buried their dead beneath the floors of their houses. As settled agriculturalists, they grew grains, peas, and lentils and tended herds of domesticated sheep and goats. But they also hunted and gathered fruits and nuts, like their nomadic ancestors, and their society was egalitarian—another feature common to nomadic societies: both men and women did the same kinds of work. But despite their relatively diverse food supply, their life spans were very short. Men died, on average, at the age of thirty-four. Women, who bore the additional risks of childbirth, died around age thirty.

The basic features of life in Çatalhöyük are common to all early civilizations. But how, when, and why did such settlements emerge? And how do we have access to information about this distant past? The era before the appearance of written records, which begin to proliferate around 3100 B.C.E., is of far greater duration than the subsequent eras we are able to document—and no less important. But it requires special ingenuity to identify, collect, and interpret the evidence of the very distant past. In fact, historians have only just begun to explore the ways that climatology, neuroscience, and evolutionary biology can further illuminate this period, augmenting the older findings of paleontology, archaeology, and historical anthropology. The following summary of our knowledge may need to be radically revised in the next few years.

Societies of the Stone Age

Primates with human characteristics originated in Africa 4 to 5 million years ago, and toolmaking hominids—species belonging to the genus *Homo*, our distant ancestors—evolved approximately 2 million years ago. Because these early hominids made most of their tools out of stone, all human cultures flourishing before the fourth millennium B.C.E. (that is, the thousand years ending in 3000 B.C.E.) are designated as belonging to the Stone Age. This vast expanse of time is divided into the Paleolithic ("Old Stone") and the Neolithic ("New Stone") Eras, with the break between them falling around 11,000 B.C.E.

Long before modern humans made their appearance, then, recognizable human traits had already begun to leave traces on the landscape. Hominids in Africa were kindling and controlling fire as early as 164,000 years ago, and using it to make tools. The Neanderthals, a hominid species that flourished about 200,000 years ago, made

CAVE PAINTINGS FROM LASCAUX. These paintings, which date to between 10,000 and 15,000 B.C.E., show several of the different species of animals that were hunted by people of the Ice Age. The largest animal depicted here, a species of long-horned cattle known as the *auroch,* is now extinct.

jewelry, painted on the walls of caves, and buried their dead in distinctive graves with meaningful objects such as horns (blown to make music) and, in one case, flowers. Could these hominids speak? Did they have a language? At present, there is no way that archaeology can answer such questions.

However, archaeology has shown that in the last phase of the Paleolithic Era, around 40,000 B.C.E., the pace of human development began to accelerate dramatically. Human populations in Africa expanded, suggesting that people were better nourished, perhaps as a result of new technologies. In Europe, the subspecies *Homo sapiens sapiens* began to produce finely crafted and more effective tools such as fishhooks, arrowheads, and sewing needles made from wood, antler, and bone. The most astonishing evidence of this change was produced by these new tools: cave paintings like those at Lascaux and Chauvet (France)—those at Chauvet were discovered only in 1994—some of which may be 30,000 years old. These amazing scenes were purposefully painted in recesses where acoustic resonance is greatest, and were probably intended to be experienced as part of multimedia musical ceremonies. (Flutes made from bone and ivory, dating to around 33,000 B.C.E., were found in a cave in southern Germany in 2008.) This is almost certain evidence for the development of language.

Despite these extraordinary changes, the basic patterns of human life altered very little during this era. Virtually all human societies consisted of hunter-gatherers, bands of a few dozen people who moved incessantly in search of food. As a result of this constant movement, these groups have left no continuous archaeological record. Yet we can discern some of the social, economic, and political structures that make these subsistence societies different from those that can be called "civilizations." Early humans had no domestic animals to transport goods, so they could have no significant material possessions aside from basic tools. And because they could not accumulate goods over time, the distinctions of rank and status created by disparities in wealth could not develop. Hierarchical structures were therefore uncommon. When conflicts arose among members of a group or resources became scarce, the solution was probably to divide and separate.

Although scholars once assumed that men did the hunting and women the gathering, such gendered presumptions do not reflect the complex realities of modern hunter-gatherer societies and they are probably not applicable to the Paleolithic Period, either. It is more likely that all members of a band (except for the very young and very old) engaged in the basic activity of acquiring food.

THE BUILDING BLOCKS OF CIVILIZATION

What changes allowed some hunter-gatherer societies to settle and build civilizations? Around 11,000 B.C.E., very evident developments brought about by changes in the climate led to the development of managed food production, which in turn fostered settlements that could trade with one another, both locally and over long distances. For the first time, it became possible for individuals and communities to accumulate and store wealth on a large scale. The results were far-reaching. Communities became more stable, and human interactions more complex. Specialization developed, along with distinctions of status and rank. Both the rapidity and the radical implications of these changes have given this era its name: the Neolithic Revolution.

The Neolithic Revolution

The artists who executed the cave paintings at Lascaux and Chauvet were conditioned to survive in harsh climatic conditions. Between 40,000 and 11,000 B.C.E., daytime temperatures in the Mediterranean basin averaged about 60° F (16° C) in the summer and about 30° F (–1° C) in the winter. These are very low compared to today's temperatures in the city of Marseilles, not far from Lascaux, which average about 86° F (30° C) in summer and 52° F (11° C) in winter. Cold-loving reindeer, elk, wild boars, bison, and mountain goats abounded in regions now famous for their beaches and vineyards. But as the glaciers receded northward with the warming climate, these species retreated with them, all the way to Scandinavia. Some humans moved north with the game, but others stayed behind to create a very different world.

Within a few thousand years after the end of the Ice Age, the peoples living in the eastern Mediterranean accomplished the most momentous transformation in human

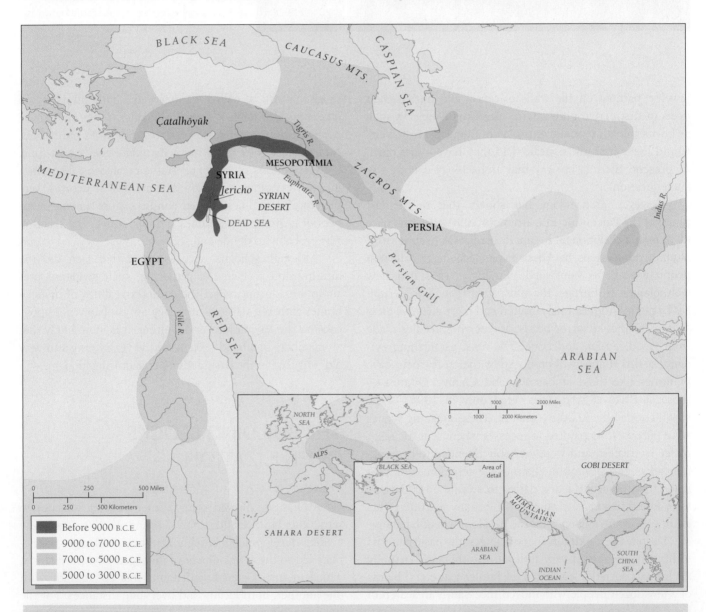

THE GROWTH OF AGRICULTURE. Examine the chronology of agriculture's development in this region. ▪ *What areas began cultivating crops first, and why?* ▪ *In what period did agriculture spread the most rapidly, and why?* ▪ *How might rivers have played a crucial role in the spread of farming technologies?*

history: a switch from food-gathering for subsistence to food production. The warmer, wetter climate allowed wild grains to flourish, geometrically increasing the food supply and making settlements possible. People then began to domesticate animals and cultivate plants. Stable settlements grew into cities. This process took several thousand years, but it still deserves to be called "revolutionary." In a relatively short time, people living in this area fundamentally altered patterns of existence that were millions of years old.

This revolution produced new challenges and new inequalities—a salutary reminder that not all attributes of a civilization are positive. For example well-nourished women in sedentary communities can bear more children than women in hunter-gatherer groups, and so the women of this new era became increasingly sequestered from their male counterparts, who in turn gave up an equal role in child care. The rapid increase in population was also countered by the rapid spread of infectious diseases, while dependence on carbohydrates resulted in earlier deaths than were typical among hunter-gatherers.

Eventually, increased fertility and birthrates outweighed these limiting factors, and by about 8000 B.C.E. human populations were beginning to exceed the wild food supply. They therefore had to increase the food-growing capacity of the land and to devise ways of preserving and storing grain between harvests. Some peoples had learned how to preserve wild grain in storage pits as early as 11,500 B.C.E., and eventually they discovered that they could use this seed to produce even more grain the following year. The importance of this latter discovery cannot be overstated: once humans began deliberate cultivation, they could support larger populations and could also compensate for disasters (such as flooding) that might inhibit natural reseeding. Even more important, intensified seeding and storage provided humans with the stable and predictable surpluses needed to support domestic animals. This brought a host of additional benefits, not only guaranteeing a more reliable supply of meat, milk, leather, wool, bone, and horn but also providing animal power to pull carts and plows and to power mills. But it also resulted in a pattern of environmental engineering that could have devastating and unsustainable effects.

The Emergence of Towns and Villages

The accelerating changes of the Neolithic Revolution are exemplified by towns like Çatalhöyük and by the simultaneous rise of trade and warfare—sure signs of increased specialization and competition among human societies. Hundreds, and probably thousands, of settlements grew up in the Near East between 7500 and 3500 B.C.E. Some of these can be classified as cities: that is, centers of administration and commerce with a relatively large and diverse population, often protected by walls. Among the earliest of these was Jericho, in the territory lying between modern Israel and Jordan. Jericho emerged as a seasonal, grain-producing settlement, but by 6800 B.C.E. its inhabitants were undertaking a spectacular building program to protect their stored surplus of food. Many new dwellings were built on stone foundations, and a massive dressed stone wall was constructed around the western edge of the settlement. It included a circular tower whose excavated remains still reach to a height of thirty feet, a powerful expression of its builders' wealth, technical prowess, and political ambitions.

This wall and its tower served a growing and now permanent population: Jericho eventually covered at least eight acres and supported 3,000 people, so it was even more densely settled than Çatalhöyük. It was sustained by the intensive cultivation, made possible by irrigation, of recently domesticated strains of wheat and barley. Jericho's inhabitants also produced some of the earliest-known pottery, which allowed them to store grain, wine, and oils more effectively. Pottery's most important benefits, however, were in cooking. For the first time, it was possible

EARLY POTTERY. This ceramic bowl, with its lovely depiction of dancing figures, was fashioned sometime between 5000 and 1700 B.C.E. Although it cannot be dated precisely, distinctive design features such as these make it possible to track the shipment of commodities throughout the ancient world.

to produce nourishing stews, porridges, and ales. (The capacity to produce beer is a sure sign of civilization.) Pottery production was not only vital to ancient civilizations, it is vital to those who study them: as the techniques for making pottery spread throughout the Near East and Asia, identifiable regional styles also developed. By studying the different varieties, archaeologists can construct a reasonably accurate chronology and can also trace the movements of goods and people.

Jericho and Çatalhöyük illustrate the impact that stored agricultural surpluses have on human relations. In these settled societies, significant differences began to arise in the amount of wealth individuals could stockpile for themselves and their heirs. Dependence on agriculture also made it more difficult for individuals to split off from the community when disputes and inequities arose. The result was the emergence of a much more stratified society, with more opportunities for a few powerful people to become dominant. The new reliance on agriculture also meant a new dependence on the land, the seasons, and the weather, which led to new speculations about the supernatural. Different life forces were believed to require special services and gifts, and the regular practice of ritual and sacrifice ultimately produced a priestly caste of individuals or families who seemed able to communicate with these forces. Such spiritual leadership was allied to more worldly forms of power, including the capacity to lead war bands, to exact tribute from other settlements, to construct defenses, and to resolve disputes. Through their command of the community's religious, military, economic, and political structures, certain clans could establish themselves as a ruling class.

Trade was another important element in the development of early settlements. Local trading networks were already established around 9000 B.C.E., and by 5000 long-distance routes linked settlements throughout the Near East. Exotic goods and luxury items were the most frequent objects of exchange, including marine shells and semiprecious stones like turquoise and lapis lazuli. Long-distance trade also accelerated the exchange of ideas and information, and it further increased social stratification: because status was enhanced by access to high-prestige goods, local elites sought to monopolize trade by organizing and controlling the production of commodities within their own communities and by regulating their export. Certain people could now devote at least a portion of their labor to pursuits other than agriculture: making pottery or cloth, manufacturing weapons or tools, building houses and fortifications, or facilitating trade. The elites who fostered and exploited the labor of others eventually became specialized themselves, as full-time speculators and organizers,

with the leisure and resources to engage in intellectual, artistic, and political pursuits. The building blocks of civilization had been laid.

URBAN DEVELOPMENT IN MESOPOTAMIA

The Greeks called it Mesopotamia, the "Land between Rivers." It was a land that received only about eight inches (20 cm) of rainfall per year. Its soils are sandy and summer temperatures exceed 110° F (44° C). The two rivers supplying water—the Tigris and Euphrates—are noted for their violence and unpredictability. Both are prone to flooding, and the Tigris was liable to jump its banks and change its course from year to year. It was in this challenging environment that the first urban society, the civilization of Sumer, flourished.

The Ubaid Culture

The earliest cities of Mesopotamia were founded by the Ubaid peoples, so called because of their settlement at al-Ubaid (now in Iraq), which dates from around 5900 B.C.E. In this era, the headwaters of the Persian Gulf extended at least 100 miles farther inland than they do today, so some Ubaid settlements bordered on fertile marshlands, which enabled them to develop irrigation systems. Although these began as relatively simple channels and collection pools, Ubaid farmers quickly learned to build more sophisticated canals and to line some pools with stone. They also constructed dikes and levees to control the seasonal flooding of the rivers and to direct the excess water into irrigation canals. Despite the hostility of the environment, Ubaid communities were soon producing surpluses sufficient to support specialists in construction, weaving, pottery making, metalwork, and trade: the typical attributes of Neolithic village life.

Yet there is also evidence of something quite new in Ubaid culture: central structures that served religious, economic, and administrative functions, something not found in Çatalhöyük. Starting out as shrines, these structures soon became impressive temples built of dried mud brick, like the bricks described in the story of Babel—and unlike the plentiful stone used at Jericho; the scarcity of stone meant that builders in this region had to be more resourceful. Each large settlement had such a temple, from which a

THE WHITE TEMPLE AT URUK, c. 3400 B.C.E. This temple may have been dedicated to the sky god, An, or designed to provide all the region's gods with a mountaintop home in a part of the world known for its level plains.

priestly class acted as managers of the community's stored wealth and of the complex irrigation systems that would make the civilization of Sumer possible.

Urbanism in Uruk, 4300–2900 B.C.E.

After about 4300 B.C.E., these Ubaid settlements developed into larger, more prosperous, and more highly organized communities. The most famous of these sites, Uruk, is considered the first Sumerian city-state. Its sophistication and scale is exemplified by the White Temple at Uruk, built between 3500 and 3300 B.C.E. This massive sloping platform looms nearly forty feet above the surrounding flatlands, and its four corners are oriented toward the cardinal points of the compass. Atop the platform stands the temple proper, dressed in brick and originally painted a brilliant white.

Such temples were eventually constructed in every Sumerian city, reflecting the central role that worship played in civic life. Uruk in particular seems to have owed its rapid urban growth to its importance as a religious center. By 3100 B.C.E. it encompassed several hundred acres, enclosing a population of 40,000 people within its massive brick walls. The villages and towns of Sumer were also growing rapidly, their teeming economic activity attracting immigrants just as the great cities did. Grain and cloth production grew tenfold. Trade routes expanded dramatically, binding the peoples of Mesopotamia to the Mediterranean and bringing foods from as far away as Scandinavia and China. To manage this increasingly complex economy, the Sumerians invented the technology on which most historians rely: writing.

The Development of Writing

In 4000 B.C.E., the peoples of Mesopotamia were already using clay tokens to keep inventories. Within a few centuries, they developed a practice of placing tokens inside hollow clay balls and inscribing, on the outside of each ball, the shapes of all the tokens it contained. By 3300 B.C.E., priests (or their scribes) had replaced these balls with flat clay tablets

CUNEIFORM WRITING. The image on the left shows a Sumerian clay tablet from about 3000 B.C.E. Here, standardized pictures are beginning to represent abstractions: notice the symbol *ninda* (food) at the top. On the right, carvings on limestone from about 2600 B.C.E. reveal the evolution of cuneiform into more abstract forms. ▪ *Why would such standardized pictograms have been easier to reproduce quickly?*

on which they inscribed symbols representing the tokens. These tablets made keeping the tokens themselves unnecessary, and they could also be archived for future reference or sent to other settlements as receipts or requests for goods.

Writing thus evolved as a practical recording technology to support economic pursuits. And because it existed to represent real things, its system of symbols—called pictograms—was also realistic: each pictogram resembled the thing it represented. Over time, however, a pictogram might be used not only to symbolize a physical object but to evoke an idea associated with that object. For example, the symbol for a bowl of food, a *ninda*, might be used to express something more abstract, such as "nourishment" or "sustenance." Pictograms also came to be associated with particular spoken sounds, or *phonemes*. Thus when a Sumerian scribe needed to employ the sound *ninda*, even as part of another word or name, he would use the symbol for a bowl of food to represent that phoneme. Later, special marks were added to the symbol, so that a reader could tell whether the writer meant it to represent the object itself, or an abstract concept, or a sound used in a context that might have nothing to do with food.

By 3100 B.C.E., Sumerian scribes also developed a specialized tool suited to the task of writing, a durable stylus made of reed. Because this stylus leaves an impression shaped like a wedge (in Latin, *cuneus*), this script is called *cuneiform* (*kyoo-NAY-i-form*). With it, cuneiform symbols could be impressed more quickly into clay. But because the new stylus was not suited to drawing pictograms that accurately represented things, the symbols became even more abstract; eventually they barely resembled the original pictograms at all. Meanwhile, symbols were invented for every

possible phonetic combination in the Sumerian language, reducing the number of necessary pictograms from about 1,200 to 600. Whereas the earliest pictograms could have been written and read by anyone, writing and reading now became specialized, powerful skills accessible only to a small and influential minority who were taught in designated scribal schools.

Despite the complicated nature of the script, cuneiform proved remarkably durable. For over 2,000 years it remained the principal writing system of the ancient Near East, even in societies that did not speak the Sumerian language. Documents using the script were still being produced as late as the first century C.E. ("Common Era," equivalent to the traditional Christian practice of designating dates by A.D., for *Anno Domini,* "in the Year of the Lord"). By about 2500 B.C.E., Sumerians were using writing for a wide variety of economic, religious, political, and artistic purposes. Tens of thousands of clay tablets still survive and this makes it possible for us to know a great deal more about the Sumerians than we do about any other human society before this time. We can better understand the social structures that shaped their lives, their attitudes toward their gods, and their changing political circumstances.

THE CULTURE OF SUMER

The great centers of Sumerian civilization—the cities of Uruk, Ur, Lagash, Eridu, and Kish—shared a common culture and a common language. They also shared a set of beliefs. However, this common religion did not produce

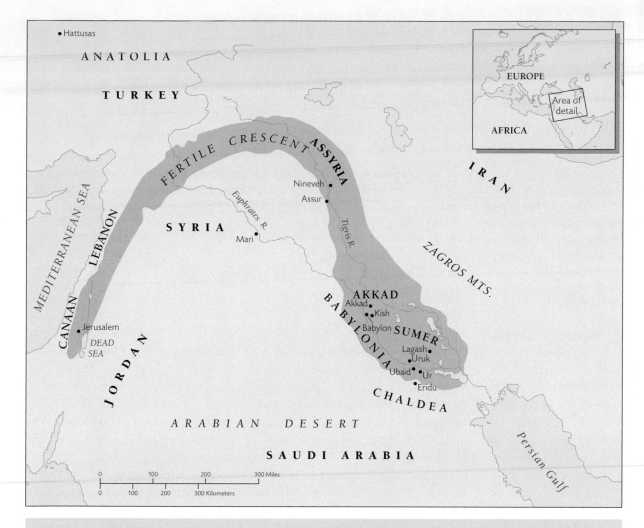

THE FERTILE CRESCENT. Notice the proximity of Sumerian cities to rivers; consider the vital role played by the Tigris and Euphrates in shaping the Mesopotamian civilizations. ▪ *How many Sumerian city-states can you identify on the map?* ▪ *Why would Sumerian city-states have been clustered so closely together?* ▪ *What challenges and opportunities did this present?*

peace. The residents of each city considered themselves to be the servants of a particular god, whom they sought to glorify by exalting their own city above others. The result was intense competition that frequently escalated into warfare. There was also an economic dimension to this conflict, since water rights and access to arable land and trade routes were often at stake.

Much of the economic production of a city passed through great temple warehouses, where priests redistributed the city's produce. During the third millennium, these great temples also began to control the production of textiles, employing thousands of servile women and children. Temple elites also played a key role in long-distance trade, as both buyers and sellers of goods. So for any city-state to surrender its independence would not only offend the conquered city's god, it would jeopardize its entire economy and the power of its ruling class.

Each Sumerian city therefore had its own aristocracy, the group from which priests were drawn. As much as half the remaining population consisted of free persons who held parcels of land sufficient to sustain themselves; but the rest were dependents of the temple who worked as artisans or as agricultural laborers on its lands. Many of these dependents were slaves. Most were prisoners of war from other Sumerian city-states whose bondage was limited to three years, after which time a slave had to be released. But non-Sumerians could be held indefinitely, although a few might manage to buy their freedom. In either case, slaves were the property of their owners. They could be beaten, branded, bought, and sold like any other form of merchandise. Perhaps the only positive thing to say about slavery in antiquity is that it was egalitarian: anyone could become a slave. It was not until the beginning of the modern era that slavery became linked to race (see Chapter 14).

Competing Viewpoints

The Flood: Two Accounts

One of the oldest stories in the world tells of a great flood that decimated the lands and peoples of the earth, an event that can be traced to the warming of the earth's climate at the end of the last Ice Age. Many ancient cultures told versions of this story, and two of these are excerpted below. The first, included in the Epic of Gilgamesh, *was written down during the first half of the third millennium* B.C.E., *making it at least 1,500 years older than the similar account in the Hebrew Bible. But both are probably the products of much older storytelling traditions. The hero of the Sumerian story is Utnapishtim. The Hebrew story's hero is Noah.*

The Epic of Gilgamesh

Utnapishtim spoke to Gilgamesh, saying: "I will reveal to you, Gilgamesh . . . a secret of the gods. . . . The hearts of the Great Gods moved them to inflict the Flood. Their Father Anu uttered the oath (of secrecy). . . . [But the god] Ea . . . repeated their talk [to me, saying]: 'O man of Shuruppak, son of Ubartutu: Tear down the house and build a boat! . . . Spurn possessions and keep alive living beings! Make all living beings go up into the boat. The boat which you are to build, its dimensions must measure equal to each other: its length must correspond to its width. Roof it over like the Apsu.' I understood and spoke to my lord, Ea: 'My lord, thus is the command which you have uttered. I will heed and will do it.' . . . On the fifth day I laid out her exterior. It was a field in area, its walls were each 10 times 12 cubits in height. . . . I provided it with six decks, thus dividing it into seven (levels). . . . Whatever I had I loaded on it. . . . All the living beings that I had I loaded on it. I had all my kith and kin go up into the boat, all the beasts and animals of the field and the draftsmen I had go up.

I watched the appearance of the weather—the weather was frightful to behold! I went into the boat and sealed the entry. . . . All day long the South Wind blew . . . , submerging the mountain in water, overwhelming the people like an attack. . . . Six days and seven nights came the wind and flood, the storm flattening the land. When the seventh day arrived . . . [t]he sea calmed, fell still, the whirlwind and flood stopped up. . . . When a seventh day arrived, I sent forth a dove and released it. The dove went off, but came back to me, no perch was visible so it circled back to me. I sent forth a swallow and released it. The swallow went off, but came back to me, no perch was visible so it circled back to me. I sent forth a raven and released it. The raven went off, and saw the waters slither back. It eats, it scratches, it bobs, but does not circle back to me. Then I sent out everything in all directions and sacrificed (a sheep). I offered incense in front of the mountain-ziggurat. . . .

The gods smelled the savor . . . and collected like flies over a sacrifice. . . . Just then Enlil arrived. He saw the boat and became furious. . . . 'Where did a living being escape? No man was to survive the annihilation!' Ea spoke to Valiant Enlil, saying . . . How, how could you bring about a Flood without consideration? Charge the violation to the violator,

The Early Dynastic Period, 2900–2500 B.C.E.

Around 2900 B.C.E., conflicts among the growing Sumerian city-states became more acute. Competition for resources intensified and warfare became more frequent and destructive, leading to the eradication of many urban centers. During this period, a new type of military leadership began to emerge and eventually evolved into a form of kingship. Historians refer to this phase as the Early Dynastic Period because it was dominated by powerful clans, each headed by a war leader known as a *lugal*, "big man." Unlike the priestly rulers of the Uruk Period, lugals did not see themselves as humble servants of a city's god. Rather, they believed that success in battle had earned them the right to exploit the city's wealth for their own glory. This gave them a new and frightening degree of influence.

charge the offense to the offender, but be compassionate lest (mankind) be cut off, be patient lest they be killed.' Enlil went up inside the boat and, grasping my hand, made me go up. He had my wife go up and kneel by my side. He touched our forehead and, standing between us, he blessed us. . . ."

Source: Maureen Gallery Kovacs, trans., *The Epic of Gilgamesh*, Tablet XI (Stanford, CA: 1985, 1989), pp. 97–103.

The Book of Genesis

The Lord saw that the wickedness of humankind was great in the earth and . . . said "I will blot out from the earth the human beings I have created . . . for I am sorry I have made them." But Noah found favor in the sight of the Lord. . . . God saw that the earth was corrupt and . . . said to Noah, "I have determined to make an end to all flesh. . . . Make yourself an ark of cypress wood, make rooms in the ark, and cover it inside and out with pitch. . . . Make a roof for the ark, and put the door of the ark in its side. . . . For my part I am going to bring a flood on the earth, to destroy from under heaven all flesh. . . . But I will establish a covenant with you, and you shall come into the ark, you, your sons, your wife, and your sons' wives with you. And of every living thing you shall bring two of every kind into the ark, to keep them alive with you. . . . Also take with you every kind of food that is eaten." . . . All the fountains of the great deep burst forth, and the windows of the heavens were opened. . . . The waters gradually receded from the earth. . . . At the end of forty days, Noah opened a window of the ark . . . and sent out the raven, and it went to and fro until the waters were dried up from the earth. Then he sent out the dove from him, to see if the waters had subsided from the face of the ground, but the dove found no place to set its foot, and it returned. . . . He waited another seven days, and again sent out the dove [which] came back to him . . . and there in its beak was a freshly plucked olive leaf, so Noah knew the waters had subsided from the earth. Then he . . . sent out the dove, and it did not return to him anymore. . . . Noah built an altar to the Lord . . . and offered burnt offerings. And when the Lord smelled the pleasing odor, the Lord said in his heart, "I will never again curse the ground because of humankind . . . nor will I ever again destroy every living creature as I have done." . . . God blessed Noah and his sons.

Source: Genesis 6:5–9:1, *The New Oxford Annotated Bible* (Oxford: 1994).

Questions for Analysis

1. What are the similarities and differences between these two accounts?

2. What do these differences or similarities reveal about the two societies that told these stories? Does one seem to derive from the other? Why or why not?

3. How did the geography and climate of Mesopotamia affect the Sumerian version of the story?

The most striking expression of this development is the *Epic of Gilgamesh*, a series of stories recited over many generations and eventually written down on cuneiform tablets: the first literary monument in world history. It recounts the exploits of a lugal named Gilgamesh, who probably lived in Uruk sometime around 2700 B.C.E. Gilgamesh earns his legendary reputation through military conquest and personal heroism, particularly in campaigns against uncivilized—that is, nonurban, non-Sumerian—tribes. But he becomes so powerful that he ignores his own society's code of conduct: we hear at the start of the epic that his people complain about him because he keeps their sons away at war and shows no respect for the nobles, carousing with their wives and compromising their daughters; he also disrespects the priesthood and commits acts of sacrilege. So the people of Uruk pray to the gods for retribution, and the gods fashion a wild man named Enkidu to challenge Gilgamesh.

The confrontation between Gilgamesh and Enkidu reveals the core values of Sumerian society. Gilgamesh is a creature of the city; Enkidu is a creature of the past, a hunter-gatherer. But then Enkidu has a sexual encounter with a beguiling woman and is unable to return to the wilderness: his urban initiation has civilized him, and this allows him to befriend the lord of Uruk. Together they have many adventures. But Enkidu is eventually killed by the goddess Inanna, who punishes the friends for mocking her powers. Gilgamesh, distraught with grief, searches for a magical medicinal plant that will revive his friend. He finds it at the bottom of a deep pool, only to have it stolen from him by a water snake. In the end, he is forced to confront the futility of all human effort. He becomes "The One Who Looked into the Depths," the name by which his story was known to Sumerians. The larger message seems to be that not even civilization can shield humans from the forces of nature and the inevitability of death.

Sumerian Religion

In the Uruk Period, the Sumerians identified their gods with the capricious forces of the natural world. In the Early Dynastic Period, however, they came to imagine their gods as resembling the lugals who now lorded over their city-states. Like these dynastic rulers, the gods were imagined as having the desire to live in the finest palaces and temples, to wear the costliest clothing and jewels, and to consume the tastiest foods. According to this new theology, which clearly reflects changes in Sumerian society, humans exist merely to provide such luxuries for their gods. This was, indeed, why the gods had created people in the first place; for if humanity ever ceased to serve the gods, the gods themselves would starve. There was thus a reciprocal relationship between humanity and divinity. The gods depended on their servants to honor and sustain them; and in return, the gods occasionally bestowed gifts and favors on humans.

As the gods' representatives on earth, lugals who reigned as kings bore special responsibilities and also enjoyed special privileges. They were believed to rule by divine sanction and were thus set apart from all other men, including priests. But kings were also obliged to honor the gods through offerings, sacrifices, festivals, and massive building projects; their obligations were greater, just as their power was greater. Kings who neglected these duties, or who exalted themselves at the expense of the gods, were likely to bring disaster on themselves and their people. And even kings could not evade death, when the human body returned to clay and the soul crossed into the underworld, a place of silent darkness.

Science, Technology, and Trade

The Sumerians' worldview was colored by their adversarial relationship with their capricious surroundings. Precisely because neither their gods nor their environment were trustworthy, Sumerians cultivated a high degree of self-reliance and ingenuity. These qualities made them the most technologically innovative people of the ancient world.

For example, despite the fact that their land had no mineral deposits, the Sumerians became skilled metallurgists. By 6000 B.C.E., a number of cultures throughout the Near East and Europe had learned how to produce weapons and tools using copper. Mesopotamia itself has no

SUMERIAN WAR CHARIOTS. The earliest-known representation of the wheel, dating from about 2600 B.C.E., shows how wheels were fashioned from slabs of wood. (For a later Mesopotamian wheel with spokes, see the illustration on page 42.)

copper, but by the Uruk Period (4300–2900 B.C.E.), trade routes were bringing this raw element into Sumer, where it was processed into weapons and tools. Shortly before 3000 B.C.E., perhaps starting in eastern Anatolia (now Turkey), people also discovered that copper could be alloyed with arsenic (or later, tin) to produce bronze. Bronze is almost as malleable as copper, and it pours more easily into molds; when cooled, it also maintains its rigidity and shape better than copper. For almost 2,000 years, until about 1200 B.C.E. and the development of techniques for smelting iron (see Chapter 2), bronze was the strongest metal known to man—the most useful and, in war, the most deadly. Following the ancient Greeks, we call this period the Bronze Age.

Alongside writing and the making of bronze, the invention of the wheel was a fundamental technological achievement of the era. The Sumerians were using potter's wheels by the middle of the fourth millennium B.C.E. and could produce high-quality clay vessels in greater quantity than ever before. By around 3200 B.C.E., the Sumerians were also using two- and four-wheeled chariots and carts drawn by donkeys. (Horses were unknown in the Near East until sometime between 2000 and 1700 B.C.E.). Chariots were another new and deadly military technology, giving warriors a tremendous advantage over armies on foot: the earliest depiction of their use, dating from 2600 B.C.E., shows one trampling an enemy. At the same time, wheeled carts dramatically increased the productivity of the Sumerian workforce.

The use of the wheel in pottery making may have suggested its use for vehicles, but such a connection is not inevitable. The ancient Egyptians, too, were using the potter's wheel by at least 2700 B.C.E., but they did not use the wheel for transport until a millennium later, when they learned the technique from Mesopotamia. In the Western Hemisphere, wheeled vehicles were unknown until the sixteenth century C.E., although the Incas had a sophisticated system of roads and probably used iron rollers to move huge blocks of stone for use in building projects. These two points of comparison help to explain why the wheel was probably invented by nomadic peoples living on the steppes of what is now Russia: sedentary civilizations that can rely on the manpower of thousands, or that can transport heavy cargo by water, do not feel the same necessity for invention.

The Sumerians can also be credited with innovations that made the most of their scarce resources. An example is the seed drill, in use for two millennia before it was depicted on a stone tablet of the seventh century B.C.E. Strikingly, this was a technology unknown to any other Western civilization until the sixteenth century C.E., when Europeans adopted it from China, and it would not be in general use until the nineteenth century of our era. Other impressive Sumerian inventions derived from the study of mathematics. In order to construct their elaborate irrigation systems, the Sumerians had developed sophisticated measuring and surveying techniques as well as the art of mapmaking. Agricultural needs may also lie behind the lunar calendar they invented, which consisted of twelve months, six lasting 30 days and six lasting 29 days. Since this produced a year of only 354 days, the Sumerians eventually began to add a month to their calendars every few years in order to predict the recurrence of the seasons with sufficient accuracy. The Sumerian practice of dividing time has lasted to the present day, not only in our notions of the 30-day month (which corresponds approximately with the phases of the moon) but also in our division of the hour into sixty minutes, each comprising sixty seconds. Mathematics also contributed to Sumerian architecture, allowing them to build domes and arches thousands of years before the Romans would adopt and spread these architectural forms throughout the West.

Sumerian technology depended not only on ingenuity but also the spread of information and raw materials

A SUMERIAN PLOW WITH A SEED DRILL. Seed drills control the distribution of seed and ensure that it falls directly into the furrow made by the plow. By contrast, the method of sowing seed practiced elsewhere in the world—and as late as the nineteenth century in Europe and the Americas—was to broadcast the seed by throwing it out in handfuls. Such plows were developed during the third millennium B.C.E. and were still being used in the seventh century B.C.E., when this black stone tablet was engraved.
■ *Based on what you have learned about the Sumerians and their environment, why would they have developed this technology?*

through trade. Because their homeland was almost completely devoid of many natural resources, Sumerian pioneers traced routes up and down the rivers and into the hinterlands of Mesopotamia, following the tributaries of the Tigris and Euphrates. They blazed trails across the deserts toward the west, where they interacted with and influenced the Egyptians. By sea, they traded with the peoples of the Persian Gulf and, directly or indirectly, with the civilizations of the Indus Valley (modern Pakistan and India). And, along with merchandise, they carried ideas: stories, art, the use of writing, and the whole cultural complex that arose from their way of life. The elements of civilization, which had fused in their urban crucible, would thus come together in many other places throughout the world.

THE FIRST EMPIRES

Evidence shows that competition among Sumerian city-states reached a new level around 2500 B.C.E., as ambitious lugals vied to magnify themselves and their kingdoms. This aggrandizement of royal power was made possible by the growing complicity of the aristocracy and the priesthood, and also by the growing marginalization of commoners, whose lives and property were increasingly exploited.

It was also facilitated by the new technologies discussed above.

The Royal Tombs of Ur showcase the wealth of the city's ruling families during this period. The dazzling armor and jewelry uncovered by excavations also reveal a shift in Sumerian ideas about the afterlife, since they presuppose a belief that one could enjoy such goods in perpetuity. The tombs further demonstrate how powerful the lugals had become. Still, it seems that no Sumerian lugal ever attempted to create an empire by imposing centralized rule on the cities he conquered. As a result, Sumer remained a collection of interdependent but mutually hostile states whose rulers were unable to forge any lasting structures of authority. This pattern would ultimately make the people of Sumer vulnerable to a new style of imperial rulership imposed on them from the north, in the person of Sargon the Akkadian.

Sargon and the Akkadian Empire, 2350–2160 B.C.E.

The Akkadians were the predominant people of central Mesopotamia. Their Sumerian neighbors to the south had greatly influenced them, and they had adopted cuneiform script along with many other elements of Sumerian culture.

OBJECTS FROM THE ROYAL TOMBS AT UR. On the left is a helmet made from an alloy of gold and silver. Its cloth lining would have been attached through the holes visible around the edges of the helmet. On the right is a queen's headdress made of gold leaf, lapis lazuli, and carnelian.

Yet the Akkadians preserved their own Semitic language, part of the linguistic family that includes Hebrew, Arabic, Aramaic, Ethiopic, and Assyrian. Sumerians tended to regard these peoples as uncivilized, but in the case of the lugal whom the Akkadians called "great king," this probably meant that Akkadians were not bound by the conventions of Sumerian warfare. For Sargon initiated a systematic program of conquest designed to subject all the neighboring regions to his authority. By 2350 B.C.E., he had conquered the cities of Sumer and then moved to establish direct control over all of Mesopotamia.

From his capital at Akkad, Sargon installed Akkadian-speaking governors to rule the cities under his control, ordering them to pull down existing fortifications, collect taxes, and impose his will. Sargon thus transformed the independent city-states of Sumer and Akkad into a much larger political unit: the first-known empire, a word derived from the Latin *imperium*, "command." This enabled him to manage and exploit the network of trade routes crisscrossing the Near East. So although his political influence was felt only in Mesopotamia, his economic influence stretched from Ethiopia to India. Sargon's capital became the most splendid city in the world, and he exercised unprecedented power for a remarkable fifty-six years.

Sargon's imperialism also had an effect on Sumerian religion. To unite the two halves of his empire, Sargon merged the Akkadian and Sumerian divinities, so that (for example) the Akkadian fertility goddess Ishtar became identified with the Sumerian goddess Inanna. He also tried to lessen the rivalry of Sumerian cities by appointing a single Akkadian high priest or priestess, often a member of his own family, to preside over several temples. His own daughter Enheduanna (*en-he-doo-AH-nah*) was high priestess of both Uruk and Ur, and her hymns in honor of Ishtar/Inanna are the earliest surviving works by a named author in world history. The precedent she and her father established would continue even after their Sargonid dynasty finally fell: for several centuries thereafter, the kings of Sumer continued to appoint their daughters as high priestesses of Ur and Uruk.

Sargon's successor, his grandson Naram-Sin, extended Akkadian conquests and consolidated trade, helping to stimulate the growth of cities throughout his dominion and binding them more closely together. By 2200 B.C.E., most people in central and southern Mesopotamia would have been able to converse in the language of either the Sumerians or the Akkadians. Indeed, the two civilizations became virtually indistinguishable except for these different languages.

The Dynasty of Ur and the Amorites, 2100–1800 B.C.E.

After Naram-Sin's death, Akkadian rule faltered. For a brief period, evidence shows that invaders from the Iranian plateau gained control of the region, which once again

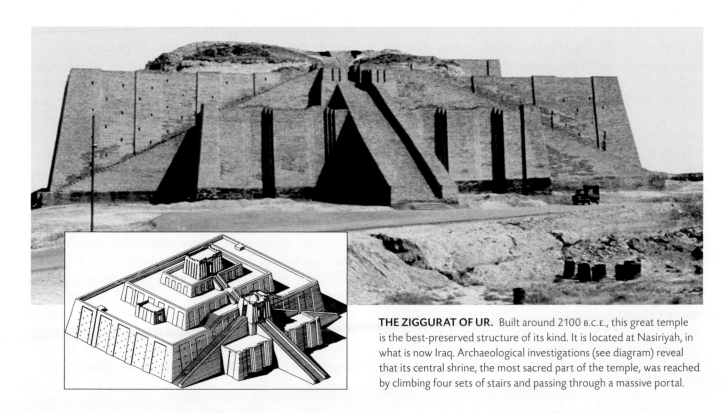

THE ZIGGURAT OF UR. Built around 2100 B.C.E., this great temple is the best-preserved structure of its kind. It is located at Nasiriyah, in what is now Iraq. Archaeological investigations (see diagram) reveal that its central shrine, the most sacred part of the temple, was reached by climbing four sets of stairs and passing through a massive portal.

dissolved into a collection of rival city-states. Around 2100 B.C.E., however, a new dynasty came to power in Ur under a king called Ur-Nammu and his son Shulgi. Ur-Nammu was responsible for the construction of the great ziggurat at Ur, which originally rose seventy feet above the surrounding plain, and for many other architectural marvels. Shulgi continued his father's work, subduing the lands up to the Zagros Mountains northeast of Ur and demanding massive tribute payments from them; one collection site accounted for 350,000 sheep per year. Shulgi built state-run textile-production facilities to process the wool. He promulgated a code of law, calling for fair weights and measures, the protection of widows and orphans, and limitations on the death penalty for crimes. He also pursued military conquests, the centralization of government, commercial expansion and consolidation, and the patronage of art and literature.

Shulgi established a pattern of rule that influenced the region for centuries to come, and that could even survive the much less competent rule of his grandson, Ibbi-Sin, who was eventually deposed by his own general. This man, Ishbi-Irra, was a chieftain of Amorite descent. The Amorites, like the Akkadians, were a Semitic people. Until this period they had largely been nomads and warriors, but now they came to control the ancient cities of Mesopotamia. For the next 200 years, they used these cities as bases for the wars they fought among themselves.

The Empire of Hammurabi

In 1792 B.C.E., a young Amorite chieftain named Hammurabi (*hah-muh-RAH-bee*) became the ruler of Babylon, an insignificant city in central Mesopotamia. By this time, Babylon was precariously wedged among a number of powerful Amorite kingdoms. Its site on the Tigris and Euphrates had great potential; but it was also dangerous, because it lay in the path of mighty antagonists.

Hammurabi turned this situation to advantage. Indeed, he may have been the first ruler in history to understand that power need not be based on force. He recognized that military intelligence, diplomacy, and strategic planning might accomplish what his small army could not. A rich archive of tablets found at the city of Mari (which eventually fell under his rule) testifies to his talents and cleverness, for Hammurabi used writing itself as a weapon. He did not try to confront his mightier neighbors directly. Rather, through letters and embassies, double-dealing and cunning, he induced his stronger counterparts to fight each other. While other Amorite kings exhausted their resources

in costly wars, Hammurabi fanned their mutual hatred and skillfully portrayed himself as a friend and ally to all sides. Meanwhile, he quietly strengthened his kingdom, built up his army, and, when the time was right, fell on his depleted neighbors. By such policies, he transformed his small state into what historians call the Old Babylonian Empire.

Under Hammurabi's rule, Mesopotamia achieved an unprecedented degree of political integration. Ultimately, his empire stretched from the Persian Gulf into Assyria. The southern half of the region, formerly Sumer and Akkad, would henceforth be known as Babylonia. To help unify these territories, Hammurabi introduced another innovation, promoting the worship of the little-known patron god of Babylon, Marduk, and making him the ruler-god of his entire empire. Although he also paid homage to the ancient gods of Sumer and Akkad, Hammurabi made it clear that all his subjects now owed allegiance to Marduk.

The idea that political power derives from divine approval was nothing new, but Hammurabi's genius was to use Marduk's supremacy over all other gods to legitimate his own claim to rule, in Marduk's name, because he was king of Marduk's home city. Hammurabi thus became the first-known ruler to launch wars of aggression justified in the name of his primary god. This set a precedent for colonial expansion that would become a characteristic feature of Near Eastern politics, as we will see in Chapter 2—and that lies behind nearly all imperial ventures down to the present day.

Yet Hammurabi did not rely solely on religion to bind his empire together. Building on the precedents of past rulers, he also issued a collection of laws, copies of which were inscribed on stone and set up in public places throughout his realm. The example that survives is an eight-foot-tall *stele* (*STEH-leh*) made of gleaming black basalt, erected in the central marketplace of Babylon. The upper portion shows Hammurabi consulting with Shamash, the god of justice. The phallic form on which the laws were inscribed would have been immediately recognizable as a potent symbol of Hammurabi's authority, obvious even to those who could not read the laws themselves. (It still makes a strong impression on visitors to the Louvre museum in Paris.)

It is impossible to overemphasize the importance of Hammurabi's decision to become a lawgiver. By collecting and codifying legal precedents, like those of Shulgi, Hammurabi declared himself to be (as he stated in the code's preamble) "the shepherd of the people, the capable king"—not a lugal ruling through fear and caprice. This was setting a new standard of kingship, and expressing a new vision of empire as a union of peoples subject to the same laws.

WOMEN AND TEXTILES. Women were the predominant producers of textiles throughout the ancient world. Even upper-class women were almost continuously engaged in spinning thread and weaving cloth for their households. Here, a servant fans an elegant lady at work with her spindle.

Law and Society under Hammurabi

The code of Hammurabi reveals a great deal about the structure and values of Babylonian society. The organization of its 282 pronouncements offers insight into the kinds of litigation that Hammurabi and his officials regularly handled, and also suggests the relative importance of these cases. It begins with legislation against false testimony (fraud or lying under oath) and theft; followed by laws regulating business deals; laws regulating the use of public resources, especially water; laws relating to taverns and brothels, most of which appear to have been run by women; laws relating to debt and slavery; many laws dealing with marriage, inheritance, divorce, and widows' rights; and finally laws punishing murder, violent assault, and even medical malpractice. What emerges is a fascinating picture of a complex urban society that required more formal legislation than the accumulated customs of previous generations.

Most of these laws appear to be aimed at free commoners, who made up the bulk of the population. Above them was an aristocratic class, tied to the king's court and active in its bureaucracy, who controlled a great deal of the community's wealth: these were the palace officials, temple priests, high-ranking military officers, and rich merchants. Indeed, even legally free individuals were probably dependents of the palace or the temple in some way, or leased land from the estates of the powerful. They included laborers and artisans, small-scale merchants and farmers, and the minor political and religious officials. At the bottom of Babylonian society were the slaves, and these were far more numerous than they had been in the older civilizations of Sumer or Akkad. Many, indeed, had become slaves not because of war but through trade: either sold as payment for debts or to the profit of a family with too many children, or because they had been forced to sell themselves on the open market. Others had been enslaved in punishment for certain offenses. Slaves in the Old Babylonian Empire were treated much more harshly than in previous civilizations and were more readily identifiable as a separate group: whereas free men in Babylonia wore long hair and beards, male slaves were shaved and branded.

The division among classes in this society was marked. As Hammurabi's code indicates, an offense committed against a nobleman carried a far more severe penalty than did the same crime committed against a social equal or against a dependent or slave; nobles were also punished more severely than were commoners for crimes they committed against other nobles. Marriage arrangements also reflected class differences, with bride-prices and dowries depending on the status of the parties involved. That said, Hammurabi's code also provides evidence as to the status of women in Babylonian society, and shows that they enjoyed certain important protections under the law, including the right to divorce abusive or indigent husbands. If a husband divorced a wife "without cause," he was obliged to

The Code of Hammurabi

The laws of Hammurabi, published on the authority of this powerful king and set up in central places throughout Old Babylonian Empire, were influenced both by the needs of an urban society and by older ideas of justice and punishment common among Semitic peoples. In its entirety, the code comprises 282 laws, beginning and ending with statements of Hammurabi's devotion to the gods, his peacekeeping mission, and his sense of his duties as king. The following excerpts are numbered so as to show the order in which these provisions appear on the stele that publicizes them.

When the god Marduk commanded me to provide just ways for the people of the land in order to attain appropriate behavior, I established truth and justice as the declaration of the land. I enhanced the well-being of the people.

* * *

1. If a man accuses another man and charges him with homicide but cannot bring proof against him, his accuser shall be killed.

2. If a man charges another man with practicing witchcraft but cannot bring proof against him, he who is charged with witchcraft shall go to the divine River Ordeal, he shall indeed submit to the divine River Ordeal; if the divine River Ordeal should overwhelm him, his accuser shall take full legal possession of his estate; if the divine River Ordeal should clear that man and should he survive, he who made the charge of witchcraft against him shall be killed; he who submitted to the divine River Ordeal shall take full legal possession of his accuser's estate.

   If a man comes forward to give false testimony in a case but cannot bring evidence for his accusation, if that case involves a capital offense, that man shall be killed.

* * *

6. If a man steals valuables belonging to the god or to the palace, that man shall be killed, and also he who received the stolen goods from him shall be killed.

7. If a man should purchase silver, gold, a slave, a slave woman, an ox, a sheep, a donkey, or anything else whatsoever, from a son of a man or from a slave of a man without witnesses or a contract—or if he accepts the goods for safe-keeping—that man is a thief, he shall be killed.

8. If a man steals an ox, a sheep, a donkey, a pig, or a boat—if it belongs either to the god or to the palace, he shall give thirtyfold; if it belongs to a commoner, he shall replace it tenfold; if the thief does not have anything to give, he shall be killed.

* * *

15. If a man should enable a palace slave, a palace slave woman, a commoner's slave, or a commoner's slave woman to leave through the main city-gate, he shall be killed.

* * *

53. If a man neglects to reinforce the embankment of the irrigation canal of his field and then a breach opens and allows the water to carry away the common irrigated area, the man in whose embankment the breach opened shall replace the grain whose loss he caused.

* * *

104. If a merchant gives a trading agent grain, wool, oil, or any other commodity for local transactions, the trading agent shall collect a sealed receipt for each payment in silver that he gives to the merchant.

* * *

128. If a man marries a wife but does not draw up a formal contract for her, she is not a wife.

129. If a man's wife should be seized lying with another male, they shall bind them and throw them into the water; if the wife's master allows his wife to live, then the king shall allow his subject (i.e., the other male) to live.

* * *

142. If a woman repudiates her husband, and declares, "You will not have marital relations with me"—her circumstances shall be investigated by the authorities of her city quarter, and if she is circumspect and without fault, but her husband is wayward and disparages her greatly, that woman will not be subject to any penalty; she shall take her dowry and she shall depart for her father's house.

Source: Martha T. Roth, ed., *Law Collections from Ancient Mesopotamia and Asia Minor* (Atlanta, GA: 1995), pp. 76–135 (excerpted).

THE CODE OF HAMMURABI.
The laws of Hammurabi survive on an eight-foot column made of basalt. The top quarter of the column depicts the Babylonian king (standing, at left) being vested with authority by Shamash, the god of justice. Directly below one can make out the cuneiform inscriptions that are the law code's text.
■ *How would the very format of these laws send a powerful message about Hammurabi's kingship?*

Questions for Analysis

1. Based on these excerpts, what conclusions can you draw about the values of Old Babylonian society? For example, what types of crimes are punishable by death, and why?

2. In what ways does the code of Hammurabi exhibit the influences of the urban civilization for which these laws were issued? What are some characteristics and consequences of urbanization? What, for example, do we learn about economic developments?

3. Examine the photographs of the *stele* preserving the code. What is the significance of the image that accompanies the laws, Hammurabi's conference with the enthroned god Marduk? What is the significance of the *stele* itself as the medium that conveyed these laws to the people?

provide financial support for her and their children. However, a wife who went around the city defaming her spouse was subject to severe punishment; and a woman would risk death, as would her lover, if she were caught in adultery. The sexual promiscuity of husbands, by contrast, was protected under the law.

Hammurabi's Legacy

Hammurabi died around 1750 B.C.E. Although some contraction of the Babylonian Empire followed under his successors, his administrative efforts created a durable state in Mesopotamia. For another two centuries, the Old

Babylonian Empire played a significant role in the Near East, until invaders from the north sacked the capital and occupied it. But even for another thousand years thereafter, Babylon remained the region's most famous city.

Hammurabi's legacy also extended well beyond the borders of his own kingdom. His success in achieving political stability was instrumental in shaping conceptions of kingship in the ancient world. After Hammurabi, unifying state religions would play an increasingly important role in the techniques that kings used to annex and subjugate diverse territories and peoples. Hammurabi had also demonstrated the effectiveness of writing as a political tool. Diplomacy and the keeping of archives would be essential to all subsequent empires. So too would the claim that rulers should be the protectors of the weak and the arbiters of justice.

THE DEVELOPMENT OF CIVILIZATION IN EGYPT

At about the same time that Sumerian civilization was transforming Mesopotamia, another civilization was taking shape in a very different part of the world and in very different ways. Unlike the Sumerians, the Egyptians did not have to wrest survival from a hostile and unpredictable environment. Instead, their land was renewed every year by the flooding of the Nile River. The fertile black soil that was left behind every summer made theirs the richest agricultural region in the entire Mediterranean world.

The distinctiveness of Egyptian civilization rests on this fundamental ecological fact. It also explains why ancient Egypt was a narrow, elongated kingdom, running along the Nile north from the First Cataract (a series of rocks and rapids near the ancient city of Elephantine) toward the Mediterranean Sea for a distance of more than 600 miles (1,100 km). Outside this narrow band of territory—which ranged from a few hundred yards to no more than 14 miles (23 km)—lay uninhabitable desert. This contrast—between the fertile Black Land along the Nile and the dessicated Red Land beyond—deeply influenced the Egyptian worldview, in which the Nile itself was the center of the cosmos and the lands beyond were hostile and beyond the pale of habitation.

In many respects, ancient Egyptian civilization enjoyed a remarkable continuity. Its roots date back to 5000 B.C.E. at least, and Egypt would continue to thrive as an independent and distinctive entity even after it was conquered

by Alexander the Great in 331 B.C.E. (see Chapter 4), until its assimilation into the Roman Empire after 30 B.C.E. (see Chapter 5). From about 3000 B.C.E., the defining element of this civilization would be the pervasive influence of a powerful, centralized, bureaucratic state headed by pharaohs who were regarded as living gods. No other civilization in world history has ever been governed so steadily, for so long, as ancient Egypt.

For convenience, historians have traditionally divided ancient Egyptian history into distinctive "kingdoms" and "periods." Following ancient Egyptian chroniclers, modern historians have also tended to portray these Old, Middle, and New Kingdoms as characterized by unity and prosperity, punctuated by chaotic interludes when central authority broke down: the so-called Intermediate Periods. Like all attempts at periodization, these divisions do not capture the complexities of human experience or even the real pace of historical development. In essence, the periodization still used by historians reflects the conservative perspective of the ancient Egyptian state, which prized continuity and feared change. As we will see, though, the "First Intermediate Period" in particular looks like a positive development if viewed from the perspective of individual communities and commoners, rather than from the viewpoint of the pharaoh's court.

Predynastic Egypt, c. 10,000–3100 B.C.E.

The phrase *Predynastic Egypt* refers to the period before the emergence of the pharaohs and their royal dynasties, an era for which archaeological evidence is difficult to find and interpret. Many predynastic settlements were destroyed long ago by the waters of the Nile and are now buried under innumerable layers of silt. Furthermore, the very abundance of naturally occurring foodstuffs in the Nile Valley made the need for settlement and cultivation less pressing than in the Fertile Crescent, where (as we have seen) Mesopotamian peoples were already living together in villages during the eighth millennium B.C.E. In Egypt, by contrast, a growing population was able to sustain itself by hunting and gathering until the fifth millennium B.C.E.

The first-known permanent settlement in Egypt, situated at the southwestern edge of the Nile Delta (near the modern town of Merimde Beni Salama) dates to approximately 4750 B.C.E. It was a farming community that may have numbered as many as 16,000 residents, and this number (based on burial remains) suggests that some Egyptian communities were much larger than those of a comparable period in Mesopotamia. Thereafter, evidence shows that

ANCIENT EGYPT AND THE NEAR EAST. Notice the peculiar geography of ancient Egypt and the role played by the Nile River. Identify the Nile on the map. ▪ *In what direction does the Nile flow?* ▪ *How did the lands on either side help to isolate Egyptian culture from outside influences?* ▪ *Consider how the Nile helped forge Egypt into a unitary state under a powerful centralized government. Yet how might Egypt's relationship to the Nile be potentially hazardous as well as beneficial?*

the Egyptian economy rapidly became more diversified: by around 3500 B.C.E. the residents of Ma'adi, just three miles away from Merimde Beni Salama, had extensive commercial contacts with the Sinai Peninsula, the Near East, and the upper reaches of the Nile some several hundred miles to the south. Copper was a particularly vital import, since it enabled residents to replace stone tools with metal ones.

Many other Neolithic farming centers have also been discovered in or near the Nile Delta, where a degree of cultural cohesiveness was already developing, fostered by shared interests and trade. In later centuries, this northern area would be known as Lower Egypt, so called because

it was downstream. Comparable developments were also occurring upstream. By the end of this Predynastic Period, Egyptian culture was more or less uniform from the southern edge of the delta to the First Cataract, a vast length of the Nile known as Upper Egypt.

Although towns in Lower Egypt were more numerous, it was in Upper Egypt that the first Egyptian cities developed. By 3200 B.C.E.—when the Sumerian city of Uruk had been thriving for a thousand years—important communities such as Nekhen, Naqada, This, and Abydos had all developed high degrees of occupational and social specialization. They had encircled themselves with sophisticated

Past and Present

Engineering Nature

Humans have been manipulating our planet's environment since the Neolithic Revolution. The image on the left shows the irrigation canals that enabled ancient Egyptians to channel the Nile's life-giving waters into the desert. The image on the right shows a storm-surge barrier in the Netherlands, which protects reclaimed land from rising sea levels (ironically) caused by the cumulative results of man-made climate change.

 Watch related author interview on StudySpace
wwnorton.com/web/westernciv18

fortifications and had begun to build elaborate shrines to honor their gods. Indeed, the establishment of permanent sites of public worship may be key to explaining the growth of these towns into cities. As in Mesopotamia, a city's role as the center of a prominent religious cult attracted travelers and encouraged the growth of industries. Yet travel in Upper Egypt was relatively easy compared to Mesopotamia. The Nile bound cities together, and the lack of competition for resources fostered peace.

It was due to the Nile, therefore, that the region south of the delta was able to forge a cultural and eventually a political unity, despite its enormous length. The Nile fed Egypt and was a conduit for people, goods, and ideas. Centralizing rulers could project their power quickly and effectively up and down its course. Within a remarkably short time, just a century or two after the first cities' appearance in Upper Egypt, they had banded together in a confederacy under the leadership of This. The pressure

exerted by this confederacy in turn forced the towns of Lower Egypt to adopt their own form of political organization. By 3100 B.C.E., the rivalry between these competing regions had given rise to the two nascent kingdoms of Upper and Lower Egypt.

The Power of the Pharaoh, c. 3100–c. 2686 B.C.E.

With the rise of powerful rulers in these two kingdoms, Egyptian history enters a new phase, one that can be chronicled with unusual precision. The system for numbering the ruling dynasties that emerged in this era—known as the Archaic Period—was actually devised nearly 3,000 years later by an historian named Manetho (*mahn-EH-thoh*), who wrote in the third century B.C.E. By and large, Manetho's

work has withstood the scrutiny of modern historians and archaeologists, although recent research has added a "Zero Dynasty" of early kings who were instrumental in bringing about the initial unification of Egypt.

Manetho did not record these rulers because he didn't know about them; we know them almost exclusively from archaeological evidence. Among them was an Upper Egyptian warlord known to us as King Scorpion, because the image of a scorpion accompanies engravings that assert his authority over most of Egypt. Another warlord, King Narmer, appears to have ruled both Upper and Lower Egypt. His exploits, too, come down to us in powerful pictures (see **Interpreting Visual Evidence** on page 26). Both of these kings probably came from Abydos in Upper Egypt, where they were later buried. Their administrative capital, however, was at Memphis, the capital city of Lower Egypt and an important center for trade with the Sinai Peninsula and the Near East.

Following the political unification of Upper and Lower Egypt, the basic features of Egypt's distinctive centralized kingship took shape along lines that would persist for the next 3,000 years, down to Manetho's own day. The title used to describe this kingship was *pharaoh*, a word that actually means "great household" and thus refers not only to an individual king but to the whole apparatus that sustains his rule. This fact, in turn, helps to explain the extraordinary stability and longevity of Egyptian civilization, which could survive even a dynastic takeover by Macedonian Greeks in the century before Manetho wrote his chronicle. Indeed, it is comparable to some modern forms of government—none of which has yet lasted nearly so long. As we have seen, kingship in Mesopotamia tended to be a form of personal rule, dependent on the charisma of a particular individual; the empires of Sargon and Ur-Nammu scarcely survived another generation or two after their deaths. But in Egypt, the office of the pharaoh was durable enough to survive the deaths of many individual successors, facilitating the peaceful transition of power to new rulers and withstanding the incompetence of many.

This was accomplished, as we shall see, by the efficiency of palace bureaucracy, but it was also a function of the pharaoh's close identification with the divine forces credited with renewing Egypt every year. Like the seasons, the pharaoh died only to be born again, renewed and empowered. Egyptian rulers thus laid claim to a sacred nature quite different—and much more benign—than that governing Sumeria. And they were more powerful than any Sumerian lugal, who was never more than a mortal who enjoyed (an all too temporary) divine favor.

How the earliest kings of Egypt came to be distinguished as pharaohs and to establish their claims to divinity is still not well understood. We do know, however, that legitimating their rule over Egypt was difficult. Local civic and religious loyalties remained strong, and for centuries Lower Egyptians would continue to see themselves as distinct in some respects from their neighbors to the south. Efforts to create a united Egyptian identity began very early, however, as the Narmer Palette may indicate. Indeed, it seems probable that the centralization of government in the person of the pharaoh, and his association with divinity, were related approaches to solving the problem of political unity. Together, they had astonishing success. By the end of the Second Dynasty, which coincides with the end of the Archaic or Early Dynastic Period (2686 B.C.E.), the pharaoh was not just the ruler of Egypt, he *was* Egypt: a personification of the land, the people, and their gods.

The Old Kingdom, c. 2686–2160 B.C.E.

Because so few written documents of the Old Kingdom survive, historians have to rely on surviving funerary texts from the tombs of the elite in order to reconstruct the achievements of particular individuals. These sources are hardly representative, and they have tended to convey the impression that Egyptians were obsessed with death; they also tell us little about the lives of ordinary people. Further complicating the historian's task is the early Egyptians' own belief in the unchanging, cyclical nature of the universe. In this early period, there appears to have been little interest in maintaining a record of key events arranged in chronological order. This makes it difficult for us to reconstruct ancient Egyptian history in detail.

However, the surviving inscriptions, papyri, and art of the Third Dynasty (c. 2686–2613 B.C.E.) do tell us a great deal about the workings of the "great household" that undergirded individual rulers' power. This power was vast because the pharaoh, as the embodiment of Egypt, was considered to be the intermediary between the land, its people, and their gods. Hence, all the resources of Egypt belonged to him. Long-distance trade was entirely controlled by the pharaoh, as were systems for imposing taxation and conscripting labor. To administer these, the pharaohs installed provincial governors, known to the Greeks as *nomarchs*, many of whom were members of the pharaoh's own family.

Old Kingdom pharaohs kept tight control over the nomarchs and their armies of lesser officials, in order to prevent them from establishing local roots in the territories they administered. Writing was therefore critical to internal

Interpreting Visual Evidence

The Narmer Palette

The Narmer Palette (c. 3100 B.C.E.) is a double-sided carving made of green silt-stone. Palettes were used to grind pigments for the making of cosmetics, but the large size (63 cm, over 2 feet) of this one is unusual. It was discovered in 1897 by archaeologists excavating a temple dedicated to the god Horus at Nekhen, the capital of Upper Egypt. Found nearby were other artifacts, including the so-called Narmer Macehead, thought to depict the marriage of Narmer, king of Upper Egypt, to a princess of Lower Egypt.

On the left, dominating the central panel, Narmer wears the White Crown of Upper Egypt (image A). He wields a mace and seizes the hair of a captive kneeling at his feet. Above the captive's head is a cluster of lotus leaves (a symbol of Lower Egypt) and a falcon representing the god Horus, who may be drawing the captive's life force (ka) from his body. The figure behind Narmer is carrying the king's sandals; he is depicted as smaller because he is an inferior. The two men in the lower panel are either running or sprawling on the ground, and the symbols above them indicate the name of a defeated town. On the right, the other side of the palette shows Narmer as the chief figure in a procession (image B). He now wears the Red Crown of Lower

A. Namer wearing the White Crown of Egypt.

B. Namar wearing the Red Crown of Egypt.

Egypt and holds a mace and a flail, symbols of conquest. Behind him is the same servant carrying his sandals, and in front of him are a man with long hair and four standard-bearers. There are also ten headless corpses. Below, the entwined necks of two mythical creatures (serpopards, leopards with serpents' heads) are tethered to leashes held by two men. In the lowest section, a bull tramples the body of a man whose city he is destroying.

Questions for Analysis

1. This artifact has been called "the first historical document in the world," but scholars are still debating its meanings. For example, does it represent something that actually happened, or is it political propaganda? In your view, is this proof that Narmer has united two kingdoms? Why or why not?

2. Do the two sides of the palette tell a coherent story, and if so, on which side does that story begin?

3. What might be significant about the site where the palette was found? Should the palette be interpreted as belonging with the mace, found nearby? If so, how might that change your interpretation of the palette's significance?

communication and the management and exploitation of Egypt's vast wealth. This gave rise to a whole class of scribal administrators who enjoyed the power, influence, and status that went along with literacy, a skill few people could command—especially in Egypt, since few could master the intricacies of hieroglyphic reading or writing. Even a child just beginning his scribal education was considered worthy of great respect because the training was so difficult. But it carried great rewards. Indeed, the scribal author of a document from the Middle Kingdom called "The Satire of the Trades" exhorted the beginning student to persevere by reminding him how much better off he would be than everyone else.

The Power of Writing

Among the many facets of Egyptian culture that have fascinated generations of scholars is the Egyptian system of pictographic writing. Called *hieroglyphs* (HI-eroh-glifs) or "sacred carvings" by the Greeks, these strange and elaborate symbols remained completely impenetrable and mysterious to modern scholars until the nineteenth century, when a Frenchman named Jean François Champollion deciphered them with the help of history's most famous decoding device, the Rosetta Stone. This *stele* preserves three versions of the same decree issued by one of the Ptolemaic rulers of Egypt in 196 B.C.E. (see Chapter 3), written in ancient Greek, demotic (a later Egyptian script), and hieroglyphics—still in use after more than three thousand years. Because he could read the text in Greek, Champollion was eventually able to translate the demotic and hieroglyphic texts as well. From this beginning, generations of scholars have added to and refined the knowledge of ancient Egyptian language.

The development of hieroglyphic writing in Egypt dates to around 3200 B.C.E., about the time when pictograms begin to appear in Mesopotamia. But the two scripts are so different that they probably developed independently; and the uses of writing for government and administration developed far more quickly in Egypt than in Sumer. But unlike Sumerian cuneiform, Egyptian hieroglyphics never evolved into a system of phonograms. Instead, the Egyptians developed a faster, cursive script for representing hieroglyphics, called *hieratic*, which they employed for the everyday business of government and commerce. They also developed a shorthand version of hieratic that scribes could use for rapid note taking. Little of this hieratic script remains, however, owing to the perishable nature of the medium on which it was usually written: papyrus. Produced by hammering, drying, and processing river reeds, papyrus was much lighter, easier to write on, and more transportable than the clay tablets used by the Sumerians. When sewn together into scrolls, papyrus also made it possible to record and store large quantities of information in very small packages. Production of this versatile writing material remained one of Egypt's most important industries and exports throughout antiquity and into the Middle Ages. Yet even in the arid environment of Egypt, which has preserved so many ancient artifacts that would have perished in wetter, colder climates, papyrus is fragile and subject to decay.

THE ROSETTA STONE. This famous stone, carved in 196 B.C.E., preserves three translations of a single decree in three different forms of writing: hieroglyphs (top), demotic Egyptian (middle), and classical Greek (bottom). ▪ *Why would scholars be able to use the classical Greek text to decipher the hieroglyphic and demotic scripts?*

EGYPTIAN WRITING. Egyptian scribes used a variety of scripts: hieroglyphs for inscriptions and religious texts (top), a cursive hieratic script for administrative documents (middle), and a more informal shorthand for note taking (bottom). ▪ *What are the relationships among these three forms of writing?*

Compared to the huge volume of papyrus documents that would have been produced, therefore, the quantity that survives is small, and this significantly limits our understanding of Old Kingdom Egypt.

The origins of the ancient Egyptian language in which these texts were written has long been a matter of debate, and it can be plausibly linked to both the Semitic languages of the Near East and a number of African language groups. Some historical linguists have postulated that early Egyptian might represent the survival of a root language from which the other languages of the Afro-Asiatic group evolved. The movements of people through the Nile Valley makes this theory a distinct possibility. Whatever its origins, the Egyptian language has enjoyed a long history. Eventually, it became the tongue known as Coptic, which is still used today in the liturgy of the Coptic Christian church in Ethiopia.

STEP PYRAMID OF KING DJOSER. This monument to the pharoah's power and divinity was designed by the palace official Imhotep around 2650 B.C.E.

Imhotep and the Step Pyramid

One of the greatest administrative officials in the history of Egypt exemplifies both the skills and the possibilities for advancement that the consummate scribe could command. Imhotep (*im-HO-tep*) rose through the ranks of the pharaoh's administration to become a sort of prime minister, the right-hand man to Djoser (*ZOH-ser*), a pharaoh of the Third Dynasty (c. 2686–2613 B.C.E.). Imhotep's expertise embraced medicine, astronomy, theology, and mathematics; but above all, he was an architect. Earlier pharaohs had already devoted enormous resources to their burial arrangements at Abydos. It was Imhotep, however, who designed the Step Pyramid, the first building in history constructed entirely of dressed stone. It was not only to be the final resting place of Djoser but an expression of his transcendent power as pharaoh.

Built west of the administrative capital at Memphis, the Step Pyramid towers over the desert to a height of 200 feet. Its design was based on an older form of burial monument, the *mastaba*, a low rectangular structure built entirely of brick with a flat top and sloping sides. Imhotep probably began with the mastaba pattern in mind, but he radically altered it by stacking one smaller mastaba on top of another and constructing each entirely of limestone. Surrounding this structure was a huge temple and mortuary complex, perhaps modeled after Djoser's palace. These buildings served two purposes. First and foremost, they would provide Djoser's *ka*, his spirit or life force, with a habitation and sustenance in the

afterlife. Second, the design of the buildings, with their immovable doors and labyrinthine passageways, would (it was hoped) thwart tomb robbers, a chronic problem as pharaonic burials became more elaborate and more tempting to thieves.

Imhotep set a precedent to which all other Old Kingdom pharaohs would aspire. The pyramids on the plain of Giza, built during the Fourth Dynasty (2613–2494 B.C.E.), are a case in point. The Great Pyramid itself, built for the pharaoh Khufu (*KOO-foo*, called Cheops by the Greeks), was originally 481 feet high and 756 feet along each side of its base, constructed from more than 2.3 million limestone blocks and enclosing a volume of about 91 million cubic feet. In ancient times, the entire pyramid was encased in gleaming white limestone and topped by a gilded capstone, as were the two massive but slightly smaller pyramids built for Khufu's successors. During the Middle Ages, the Muslim rulers of nearby Cairo had their builders strip off the pyramid's casing stones and used them to construct and fortify their new city. (The gold capstones had probably disappeared already.) But in antiquity these pyramids would have glistened brilliantly by day and glowed by night, making them visible for miles in all directions. The Greek historian Herodotus (*heh-RAH-duh-tuhs*), who toured Egypt more than 2,000 years after the pyramids were built, estimated that it must have taken 100,000 laborers 20 years to build the Great Pyramid. This is probably an exaggeration, but it is a measure of the impression these monuments made.

Once thought to have been the work of slaves, the pyramids were in fact raised by tens of thousands of peasant

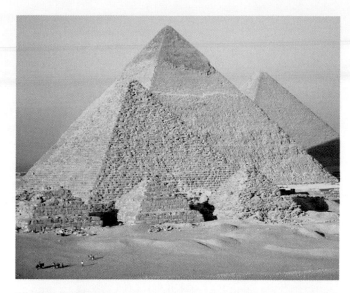

PYRAMIDS AT GIZA. The Great Pyramid of Khufu (Cheops) is in the center and was completed c. 2560 B.C.E.

workers, who labored most intensively on the pyramids while their fields were under water during the Nile's annual flood. Some workers may have been conscripts, but most probably participated willingly, since these projects glorified the living god who served as their link to the cosmic order. Still, the investment of human and material resources required to build the great pyramids put strains on Egyptian society. Control over the lives of individual Egyptians increased and the number of administrative officials employed by the state grew ever larger. So too did the contrast between the lifestyle of the pharaoh's splendid court at Memphis and that of Egyptian society as a whole. At the same time, a gap was opening between the pretensions of the pharaohs and the continuing loyalties of Egyptians to their local gods and local leaders.

The End of the Old Kingdom

For reasons that are not entirely clear, the Fifth and Sixth Dynasties of the Old Kingdom (2494–2181 B.C.E.) witnessed the slow erosion of pharaonic power. Although pyramid construction continued, the monuments of this period are less impressive in design, craftsmanship, and size, perhaps mirroring the diminishing prestige of the pharaohs who ordered them built. Instead, the priesthood of Ra at Nekhen, which was the center of worship for the god Horus and the place where Narmer's unification of Egypt was memorialized, began to assert its own authority over that of the pharaoh. Ultimately, it declared that

the pharaoh was not an incarnation of Horus or Ra, but merely the god's earthly son. This was a blow to the heart of the pharaoh's political theology. More practically threatening was the growing power of the pharaoh's nomarchs, whose increased authority in the provinces allowed them to become a hereditary local nobility: precisely what the vigorous kings of earlier dynasties had refused to permit. These nobles became so influential that one Sixth Dynasty pharaoh, Pepy I, even married into their ranks and produced half-caste successors by these marriages.

Scholars are uncertain as to how certain priests and local officials were able to take power away from the pharaonic center. It may be that the extraordinarily costly building efforts of the Fourth Dynasty had overtaxed the economy, while the continued channeling of resources to the royal capital at Memphis increased shortages and resentments in the provinces. Other evidence points to changing climatic conditions that may have disrupted the regular inundations of the Nile, leading to famine in the countryside. Meanwhile, small states were beginning to form to the south in Nubia, perhaps in response to Egyptian aggression. With better organization and equipment, the Nubians may have restricted Egyptian access to precious metal deposits in and around the First Cataract, further crippling the Egyptian economy.

As a result of these developments, the pharaoh's power diminished. Local governors and religious authorities began to emerge as the only effective guarantors of stability and order. By 2160 B.C.E., which marks the beginning of what historians call the First Intermediate Period, Egypt had effectively ceased to exist as a united entity. The central authority of the pharaoh in Memphis collapsed, and a more ancient distribution of power reemerged: a northern center of influence based at Herakleopolis was opposed by a southern regime headquartered at Thebes, with families from each region claiming to be the legitimate pharaohs of all Egypt.

Compared to the centralized authority of the Old Kingdom, this looks like chaos. But redistribution of power always leads to the opening of new opportunities in any society. In Egypt, wealth became much more widely and evenly diffused than it had been, as did access to education, means for the creation of art, and possibilities for personal advancement. Resources that the pharaoh's court at Memphis had once monopolized now remained in the provinces, enabling local elites to emerge as both protectors of society and as patrons of local artisans. The result was a much wider and more rapid dispersal of cultural forms and goods throughout Egyptian society than had been possible under the old regime. Many of these arts and luxuries—including elaborate rites for the dead—had been developed originally at the pharaoh's court, and limited to it. Now, however, they became available to Egyptian society at large.

EGYPTIAN CULTURE AND SOCIETY

As we noted above, the special environment of Egypt and the special benefits it conferred on its inhabitants were construed as divine gifts, renewed each year through the mediation of the pharaoh. From what we can discern, this meant that Egyptians saw themselves as superior to all other civilizations. A person was either an Egyptian or a foreigner, and the lines between the two were absolute. For Egyptians, it was simply self-evident that their country—nurtured by the Nile and guarded by the deserts and seas that surrounded it—was the center of the universe.

Religion and Worldview

Although the Egyptians told a variety of stories that dealt with the creation of their world, these were not greatly concerned with how humanity came to exist. Rather, what mattered was the means by which all life was created and re-created in an endless cycle of renewal. Unlike the peoples of Mesopotamia, who were constantly faced by new and terrible challenges, both environmental and political, Egyptians experienced existence as predictably repetitive, and this was mirrored in their perception of the cosmos. At the heart of Egyptian religion lay the myth of the gods Osiris and Isis, not only brother and sister but husband and wife, two of the gods most fundamental to Egyptian belief. Osiris was, in a sense, the first pharaoh: the first god to hold kingship on earth. But his brother, Seth, wanted the throne for himself. So Seth betrayed and killed Osiris, sealing his body in a coffin. But his loyal sister Isis retrieved the corpse and managed to revive it long enough to conceive her brother's child, the god Horus. Enraged by this, Seth seized Osiris's body and hacked it to pieces, spreading the remains all over Egypt. (All of Egypt could therefore claim to be part of Osiris, a belief witnessed by shrines dedicated to him throughout the land.) Still undeterred, Isis sought the help of Anubis, the god of the afterlife. Together, they found, reassembled, and preserved the scattered portions of Osiris's body, thus inventing the practice of mummification. Then Horus, with the help of his mother, managed to

PHARAOH MENKAURE AND HIS QUEEN, KHAMERERNEBTY II. A sculpture from the Fourth Dynasty, c. 2500 B.C.E., shows this queen as her husband's royal partner.

defeat Seth. Osiris was avenged and revived as god of the underworld. Like Egypt itself, he could not be killed, and the cycle of his death, dismemberment, and resurrection was reflected in the yearly renewal of Egypt itself.

Life and Death in Ancient Egypt

In addition to embodying Egypt's continual regeneration, Osiris exemplified the Egyptian attitude toward death, which was very different from the Sumerians' rather bleak view. For the Egyptians, death was a rite of passage, a journey to be endured on the way to an afterlife that was more or less like one's earthly existence, only better. To be sure, the journey was full of dangers. After death, the individual body's ka would have to roam the Duat, the underworld, searching for the House of Judgment. There, Osiris and

Analyzing Primary Sources

The Instruction of Ptah-Hotep

Egyptian literature often took the form of "instructions" to or from important personages, offering advice to those in public life. This document declares itself to be the advice of a high-ranking official of the Old Kingdom to his son and successor, perhaps composed around 2450 B.C.E. However, the earliest surviving text dates from the Middle Kingdom period.

Be not arrogant because of your knowledge, and be not puffed up because you are a learned man. Take counsel with the ignorant as with the learned, for the limits of art cannot be reached, and no artist is perfect in his skills. Good speech is more hidden than the precious greenstone, and yet it is found among slave girls at the millstones.

. . . If you are a leader commanding the conduct of many seek out every good aim, so that your policy may be without error. A great thing is *ma'at*, enduring and surviving; it has not been upset since the time of Osiris. He who departs from its laws is punished. It is the right path for him who knows nothing. Wrongdoing has never brought its venture safe to port. Evil may win riches, but it is the strength of *ma'at* that endures long, and a man can say, "I learned it from my father." . . . If you wish to prolong friendship in a house which you enter as master, brother, or friend, or anyplace that you enter, beware of approaching the women. No place in which that is done prospers. There is no wisdom in it.

A thousand men are turned aside from their own good because of a little moment, like a dream, by tasting which death is reached. . . . He who lusts after women, no plan of his will succeed. . . . If you are a worthy man sitting in the council of his lord, confine your attention to excellence. Silence is more valuable than chatter. Speak only when you know you can resolve difficulties. He who gives good counsel is an artist, for speech is more difficult than any craft.

Source: Nels M. Bailkey, ed., *Readings in Ancient History: Thought and Experience from Gilgamesh to St. Augustine*, 5th ed. (Boston, MA: 1995), pp. 39–42.

Questions for Analysis

1. According to Ptah-Hotep, what are the most important attributes of a man engaged in public life? What are the most dangerous pitfalls and temptations he will encounter?

2. Why does Ptah-Hotep emphasize the importance of acting in accordance with *ma'at*? How does this idea of *ma'at* compare to that in "the Prophecies of Neferty"?

3. Based on what you have learned about the changes in Egyptian politics and society, what might indicate that Ptah-Hotep lived during the time of the prosperous Fifth Dynasty of the Old Kingdom? How might these instructions have resonated differently with later readers of the Middle Kingdom?

---

forty-two other judges would decide the ka's fate. Demons and evil spirits might try to frustrate the ka's quest to reach the House of Judgment, and the journey might take some time. But if successful and judged worthy, the deceased would enjoy immortality as an aspect of Osiris.

Egyptian funerary rites aimed to emulate the example set by Isis and Anubis, who had carefully preserved the parts of Osiris's body and enabled his afterlife. This is why the Egyptians developed their sophisticated techniques of embalming, whereby all of the body's vital organs were removed and then treated with chemicals—except for the heart, which played a key role in the ka's final judgment.

A portrait mask was then placed on the mummy before burial, so that the deceased would be recognizable despite being wrapped in hundreds of yards of linen. To sustain the ka on his or her journey, food, clothing, utensils, weapons, and other items of vital importance would be placed in the grave along with the body.

"Coffin texts," or books of the dead, also accompanied the body and were designed to speed the ka's journey. They contained special instructions, including magic spells and ritual incantations, that would help the ka travel through the underworld and prepare it for the final test. They also described the "negative confession" the ka would

FOOD FOR THE JOURNEY OF THE KA. These wooden models show peasants plowing, grinding grain, baking bread, brewing beer, and slaughtering a steer. Bread and beer were the staple foods of ancient Egypt; beef was too expensive for ordinary consumption, but cattle were frequently sacrificed as funeral offerings. Such models were placed in Middle Kingdom tombs to provide food for the afterlife.

make before the court of Osiris, a formal denial of offenses committed in life. The god Anubis would then weigh the deceased's heart against the principle of *ma'at*: truth, order, justice. Because ma'at was often envisioned as a goddess wearing a plumed headdress, a feather from this headdress would be placed in the scales, along with the heart, at the time of judgment; only if the heart was light (empty of wrongdoing) and in perfect balance with the feather would the ka achieve immortality.

Throughout the era of the Old Kingdom, the privilege of undergoing these preparations (and thus of ensuring immortality) was reserved for the royal family alone. By the time of the Middle Kingdom, however, it was becoming possible for most Egyptians to ensure that their bodies would participate in these rituals, too.

As noted above, this careful manner of confronting death has often led to the erroneous assumption that ancient Egyptians were pessimistic, but in actuality their practices and beliefs were inherently life affirming, bolstered by confidence in the resilience of nature and the renewal of creation. Binding together this endless cycle was ma'at, the serene order of the universe with which the individual must remain in harmony, and against which each person's ka would be weighed after death. And embodying ma'at on earth was the pharaoh, the earthly manifestation of all gods. For most of the third millennium, thanks to a long period of successful harvests and peace guaranteed by Egypt's geographic isolation from the outside world, the Egyptians were able to maintain their belief in this perfectly ordered paradise and the pharaoh that ensured it. But when that order broke down, so too did their confidence in the pharaoh's power.

Egyptian Science

Given the powerful impression conveyed by their monumental architecture, it may seem surprising that the ancient Egyptians lagged far behind the Sumerians and Akkadians in science and mathematics, as well as in the application of new technologies. Only in the calculation of time did the Egyptians make notable advances, since their close observation of the sun for religious and agricultural reasons led them to develop a solar calendar that was far more accurate than the Mesopotamian lunar calendar. Whereas the Sumerians have bequeathed to us their means of dividing and measuring the day, the Egyptian calendar is the direct ancestor of the Julian Calendar adopted for Rome by Julius Caesar in 45 B.C.E. (see Chapter 5) and later corrected by Pope Gregory XIII in 1582 C.E.: this is the calendar we use today. The Egyptians also devised some effective irrigation and water-control systems, but they did not adopt such labor-saving devices as the wheel until much later than the Sumerians, perhaps because the available pool of peasant manpower was virtually inexhaustible, so that the necessity for such innovations was not felt.

The Social Pyramid

The social pyramid of Old Kingdom Egypt was extremely steep. At its apex stood the pharaoh and his extended family, whose prestige and power set them entirely apart from all other Egyptians. Below them was a class of nobles, whose primary role was to serve as priests and officials of the pharaoh's government; scribes were usually recruited and trained from among the sons of these families. All of these Egyptian elites lived in considerable luxury. They owned extensive estates, exotic possessions, and fine furniture. They kept dogs and cats and monkeys as pets, and hunted and fished for sport.

Beneath this tiny minority was everyone else. Most Egyptians lived in crowded conditions in simple mudbrick dwellings. During a period of prosperity, master craftsmen—jewelers, goldsmiths, and the like—could improve their own conditions and those of their families by fulfilling the needs of the wealthy, but they did not constitute anything like a middle class. Other skilled professionals—potters, weavers, masons, bricklayers, brewers, merchants, and schoolteachers—also enjoyed some measure of respect as well as a higher standard of living. The vast majority of Egyptians, however, were peasants who provided the labor for agriculture and construction. Beneath them were slaves, typically captives from foreign wars rather than native Egyptians.

Yet despite the enormous demands the pharaohs placed on Egypt's wealth, this Egyptian social hierarchy does not appear to have been particularly oppressive. Commoners' belief in the pharaoh's divinity made them willing subjects, as did the material benefits of living in a stable, well-governed society. Even slaves had certain legal rights, including the ability to own, sell, and bequeath personal property.

Unfortunately, though, the written laws and other documentary practices produced by the lugals of Mesopotamia do not have any Old Kingdom parallels. The Egyptians of this era apparently had no need for written laws beyond what was customary in their communities or what was proclaimed as law by their pharaoh. This makes it difficult for historians to reconstruct their lives in any detail.

The Status of Women

Despite the absence of formal law codes, there is evidence that Egyptian women enjoyed unusual freedoms by the standards of the ancient world. Female commoners were recognized as persons in their own right and were allowed to initiate lawsuits (including suits for divorce), to defend

FUNERARY PAPYRUS. This scene, inscribed on a papyrus scroll dating from the Twenty-First Dynasty (c. 1000 B.C.E.), shows the heart of the princess for whom this book was prepared being weighed in a balance before the god Osiris. On the other side of the balance are the symbols for life (the *ankh*) and the feather of the goddess Ma'at.

themselves and act as witnesses, to possess property of their own, and to dispose of it: all without the sanction of a male guardian or representative, as was typically required in other ancient societies—and in most modern ones until the twentieth century. Women were not allowed to undergo formal scribal training, but surviving personal notes exchanged between high-born ladies suggest that some could read and even write.

Normally, women were barred from holding high office, apart from that of priestess and also, importantly, queen. Indeed, queens are often represented as the partners of their royal husbands and were certainly instrumental in ruling alongside them: note the proud, confident bearing of Queen Khamerernebty II (*kah-mehr-en-EB-tee*, see image on page 30). And occasionally, a woman from the royal family might assume pharaonic authority for a time, as did Queen Khasekhemwy (*kah-sehk-KEM-wee*, d. 2686 B.C.E.) on behalf of her son Djoser before he came of age. Some women may even have ruled in their own right; this was certainly the case under the New Kingdom (see Chapter 2).

Among the peasantry, gender divisions were less clearly defined. Peasant women often worked in the fields during the harvest alongside men and carried out a number of vital tasks in the community. The limitations of our sources, however, means that we can only glimpse the lives of these people through the eyes of their social superiors. Whatever their status, it seems that women did not enjoy sexual equality. While most Egyptians practiced monogamy, wealthy men could and did keep a number of lesser wives, concubines, and female slaves; and any Egyptian man, married or not, enjoyed freedoms that were denied to women, who would be subject to severe punishments under the law if they were viewed as guilty of any misconduct.

The Widening Horizons of the Middle Kingdom (2055–c. 1650 B.C.E.)

After the disruption of Old Kingdom authority around 2160 B.C.E., warfare between two competing pharaonic dynasties would continue for over a century. Then, in 2055 B.C.E., the Theban king Mentuhotep (*men-too-Ho-tep*) II conquered the northerners and declared himself the ruler of a reunited Egypt. His reign marks the beginning of Egypt's Middle Kingdom and the reestablishment of a central government—but this time based in Thebes rather than Memphis. The head of this new government was Men-

tuhotep's chief supporter, Amenemhet (*ah-meh-NEHM-het*), who actually seized power after the king's death and established himself and his descendants as Egypt's Twelfth Dynasty.

This succession of remarkable pharaohs remained in power for nearly 200 years, and under them Egyptians began to exploit more thoroughly the potential for trade. They secured their border with Nubia and began to send mounted expeditions to the land they called Punt, probably the coast of Somalia. By the middle of the nineteenth century B.C.E., Nubia was firmly under Egypt's control. Meanwhile, diplomatic relations with the smaller states and principalities of Palestine and Syria led to decisive Egyptian political and economic influence in this region. Yet these lands were not incorporated into Egypt; instead, Amenemhet constructed the Walls of the Prince in Sinai to guard against incursions from the Near East.

The huge fortifications built along Egypt's new frontier demonstrate the great resourcefulness of the Twelfth Dynasty and their very different ways of allocating resources and expressing ambition. As such, they also dis-

SESOSTRIS III (1870–1831 B.C.E.). This powerful Twelfth Dynasty pharaoh led military campaigns into Nubia, constructed massive, garrisoned fortresses along the Nile, and dug new waterways near Aswan. More than a hundred portrait busts of Sesostris survive, all with similar features. His overhanging brow, deep-set eyes, and drawn-down mouth are intended to communicate the enormous burden of responsibility the pharaoh bore as the ruler of all Egypt.

Analyzing Primary Sources

The Prophecies of Neferty

This text presents itself as a prophecy foretelling the disasters that would strike Egypt during the First Intermediate Period. In fact, it was composed during the Middle Kingdom, shortly after the death of the pharaoh Amenemhet I, the founder of the Twelfth Dynasty. By contrasting the disorders that preceded Amenemhet's reign with the peace that he established, the document seeks to justify Amenemhet's usurpation of the throne and perhaps to legitimize his son's succession.

rise, oh my heart! Weep for this land wherein you were born! Falsehood is as the flood, and behold, evil is spoken with impunity.... The land perishes, and there is no one who cares for it. There is no one who speaks out, no one who makes lament.... Perished and gone are those joyful places, the fish ponds where dwell fish-eating birds, ponds alive with fish and fowl. All joy has been driven out, and the land is plunged into anguish by those voracious Asiatics who rove throughout the land. Foes have appeared in the east, Asiatics have entered Egypt. We have no (border) fortress, for foreigners now hold it, and there is no one to heed who the plunderers are. One may expect attack by night, the fortress will be breached and sleep driven from all eyes.... The land is destitute, although its rulers are numerous, it is ruined, but its taxes are immense. Sparse is the grain, but great is the measure, for it is distributed as if it were abundant.

But then there shall come a king from the south. His name will be Ameny, justified. He will be the son of a woman of Ta-Sety [Nubia], an offspring of the royal house of Nekhen. He shall receive the White Crown, he shall wear the Red Crown, he shall unite the Two Powers.... The people of his time will rejoice, for this son of a man will establish his name for ever and eternity.... The Asiatics will fall before his sword, the Libyans will fall before his fire, rebels will fall before his wrath, and enemies will fall through awe of him....

Then Ma'at will return to her throne, and Chaos will be driven off. Joyful will he be who will see (these things), he who will serve the king.

Source: William Kelly Simpson, ed., *The Literature of Ancient Egypt: An Anthology of Stories, Instruction, Stelae, Autobiography, and Poetry*, 3rd ed. (New Haven, CT: 2003), pp. 214–220.

Questions for Analysis

1. In what ways does the "Prophecies of Neferty" highlight the anxieties felt by Middle Kingdom Egyptians? What caused these anxieties?

2. Why would the author of this document choose to present it as a prophecy about the future, rather than as a description of current events?

play a marked shift in the Egyptian outlook on the world. The placid serenity epitomized by ma'at, and the shared devotion to the pharaoh that had built the pyramids, had been challenged. Egyptians could no longer be dismissive of outsiders or disregard the world beyond their borders. Unlike their Old Kingdom ancestors, the Egyptians of the Middle Kingdom were not turned inward. Their attitude to the pharaoh also seems to have changed. Although he continued to enjoy a special position as a divine representative, his authority did not derive solely from this source. Rather, the pharaohs of the Middle Kingdom represented themselves in a new light, as good shepherds, tenders of their flock. Only by diligently protecting Egypt from a hostile outside world could a pharaoh provide the peace,

prosperity, and security desired by his subjects; his alignment with ma'at was now clearly conditional, and it had to be earned.

Portraits of the great pharaohs of the Twelfth Dynasty mirror this anxious outlook on the world. The literature of the Middle Kingdom also expresses the general change in attitude. Among the most popular of the new literary forms were manuals ostensibly written by or for kings, detailing the duties and perils of high office and offering advice for dealing with difficult situations. These include the *Instruction of Amenemhet*, which purports to be life lessons handed down by this pharaoh to his son from beyond the grave, and *The Instruction of Ptah-Hotep* (see **Analyzing Primary Sources** above), an example of Egyptian "wisdom literature" attributed to a court official of the Old Kingdom, which achieved a wider readership in this new era—much as Machiavelli's *The Prince* (see Chapter 12) has become a "self-help" book for business executives and politicians in our own time. Ptah-Hotep's teaching is upbeat and practical; by contrast, the examples of this genre produced under the Middle Kingdom are bleakly pragmatic. A pharaoh must trust no one: not a brother, not a friend, not intimate companions. He must crush the ambitions of local nobles with ruthless ferocity. He must always be on the lookout for potential trouble. In return for his exertions on behalf of his people, he should expect neither gratitude nor reward; he should expect only that each year will bring new dangers and more pressing challenges. Reading between the lines, we discern

that Egyptians' sense of their own superiority—a product of their former isolation and their comparatively benign environment—had been shattered. They saw themselves being drawn into a much wider world, and in the course of the next millennium they would become more fully a part of it.

CONCLUSION

While the story of Babel records the legendary loss of a shared language, this chapter shows that people of the distant past can still communicate with us. The marks they have left on the landscape, the remains of their daily lives, their written

After You Read This Chapter

Visit StudySpace for quizzes, additional review materials, and multimedia documents. **wwnorton.com/web/westernciv18**

- The study of the distant past is challenging because written sources are rare. What other sources of information do historians use?
- All civilizations require the same basic things and share certain characteristics. What are they?
- The cities of Mesopotamia remained largely independent from one another yet shared a common culture. Why was this the case?
- Hammurabi's empire created a new precedent for governance in Mesopotamia. How did he achieve this?
- The civilizations of ancient Mesopotamia and Egypt differ in profound ways. What were the major causes of their differences?

records, and their very bodies make it possible for historians to piece together evidence and to make sense of it. And every year new sources come to light, meaning that we have to be ready to revise—constantly—our understanding of what happened in the past.

Although this chapter has emphasized the differences between the early civilizations of Mesopotamia and Egypt, it is worth noting some significant similarities. Both developed the fundamental technologies of writing at about the same time, and this facilitated political alliances, long-distance trade, and the transmission of vital information to posterity. During the third millennium, both underwent a process of political consolidation, an elaboration of religious ritual, and a melding of spiritual and political leadership. Both engaged in massive building and irrigation projects, and both commanded material and human resources on an enormous scale. At the same time, each of these civilizations cultivated an inward focus. Although they had some contact with each other, and some transfers of information and technology probably took place, there were few significant political or cultural interactions. For the most part, they inhabited separate worlds. This relative isolation was about to change, however. The next millennium would see the emergence of large-scale, land-based empires in the Near East that would transform life in Mesopotamia, Egypt, and the lands that lay between them. These are the developments we examine in Chapter 2.

PEOPLE, IDEAS, AND EVENTS IN CONTEXT

- What fundamental changes associated with the **NEOLITHIC REVOLUTION** made early civilizations possible?
- What new technologies allowed the **SUMERIANS** to master the environment of **MESOPOTAMIA**, and how did these technologies contribute to the development of a new, urbanized society?
- By contrast, why did the Nile River foster a very different civilization and enable the centralized authority of the **PHARAOH**?
- How do the differences between **CUNEIFORM** and **HIEROGLYPHS** reflect the different circumstances in which they were invented and the different uses to which they were put?
- In what ways are the *EPIC OF GILGAMESH* and the *CODE OF HAMMURABI* rich sources of information about the civilizations of Sumer and **BABYLON**?
- How do the **ZIGGURATS** of Mesopotamia and the pyramids of Egypt exemplify different forms of power, different ideas about the gods, and different beliefs about the afterlife?
- Why was the worldview of ancient Egyptians, which was strongly reflected in the concept of **MA'AT** during the **OLD KINGDOM**, altered in significant ways by the time of the **MIDDLE KINGDOM**?

THINKING ABOUT CONNECTIONS

- How do the surviving sources of any period limit the kinds of questions that we can ask and answer about the distant past? In your view, are there sources for this early era that have been undervalued? For example, if writing had not been developed in Mesopotamia and Egypt, what would we still be able to know about the civilizations of these two regions?
- What features of ancient civilizations do modern civilizations share? What might be the implications of these shared ideas, social structures, and technologies?
- In particular, what lessons could we draw from humans' tendency to manipulate their environment? How should knowledge of the distant past influence current debates over sustainability and climate change?

Before
You
Read
This
Chapter

Peoples, Gods, and Empires: 1700–500 B.C.E.

CORE OBJECTIVES

- **DESCRIBE** the impact of new migrations and settlements on the ancient Near East.

- **DEFINE** the differences between Egypt's New Kingdom and the previous Old and Middle Kingdoms.

- **EXPLAIN** the workings of transnational networks in the late Bronze Age.

- **IDENTIFY** the new empires and kingdoms that emerged in the Iron Age.

- **UNDERSTAND** the historical importance of monotheism.

According to Hesiod, a Greek poet who flourished during the eighth century B.C.E., all of human history falls into five ages. The dawn of time was a golden age, when men lived like gods. Everything was good then, food was plentiful, and work was easy. The next age was silver, when men took gods for granted, killed one another, and lived in dishonor. So the gods destroyed them, sending a mighty flood that spared only the family of Deucalion, the son of wily Prometheus, who built an ark. Then came the age of bronze, when everything was made of bronze—houses and armor and weapons and tools—and giants fought incessantly from huge strongholds, causing destruction so great that no man's name survives. The time following was short but bright, a heroic age, the time of men who ventured with Theseus and fought with Achilles and sailed with Odysseus, men whose names will live forever. But Hesiod's own age was iron—a dull age, a time of tedium and strife and bickering and petty feuds.`

Hesiod's periodization captures an understanding of history that had evolved with humanity itself and that reflects actual developments. The stories he knew told of a time before cities and the need for agriculture. They recalled a time when

39

the harmony between gods and men broke down, and the human race was saved by one man's ingenuity: the Sumerian Utnapishtim, the Hebrew Noah, or the Greek Deucalion. These stories chronicled the wars of the age we still call Bronze, when the enormous abandoned palaces still visible in Hesiod's day were built. And they remembered the race of heroes whose glory was measured by their abiding fame, and who bequeathed to us a further round of stories. Thanks to new archaeological finds, new linguistic discoveries, and new efforts at decoding the historical record, we can both confirm and correct Hesiod's perspective on the past.

In the second millennium B.C.E., the ancient Near East was transformed by the arrival of new peoples and by the emergence of extensive land-based empires built up through systematic military conquest. These migrations and conquests caused upheaval, but they also led to cultural contact and economic integration that encompassed not only the Mediterranean but even extended from Scandinavia

to China. The last few centuries of the Bronze Age (1500–1200 B.C.E.) were a period of intense diplomacy, trade, and exchange. By the thirteenth century B.C.E., peoples from the southern Balkans to the western fringes of Iran had been drawn into a wide-ranging web of relationships.

Yet this extraordinary system proved more fragile than its participants could have imagined. Around 1200 B.C.E., a wave of mysterious invasions led to the destruction of nearly every established Mediterranean civilization. As a result, around the turn of the first millennium B.C.E., we enter a world organized along profoundly different lines. In this Iron Age, iron would slowly replace bronze as the primary component of tools and weapons. New and more brutal empires would come to power, while new ideas about the divine and its relationship to humanity would emerge. Two of the Western world's most enduring religious traditions—Judaism and Zoroastrianism (*zoh-roh-AHS-tree-nism*)—were born, fundamentally altering conceptions

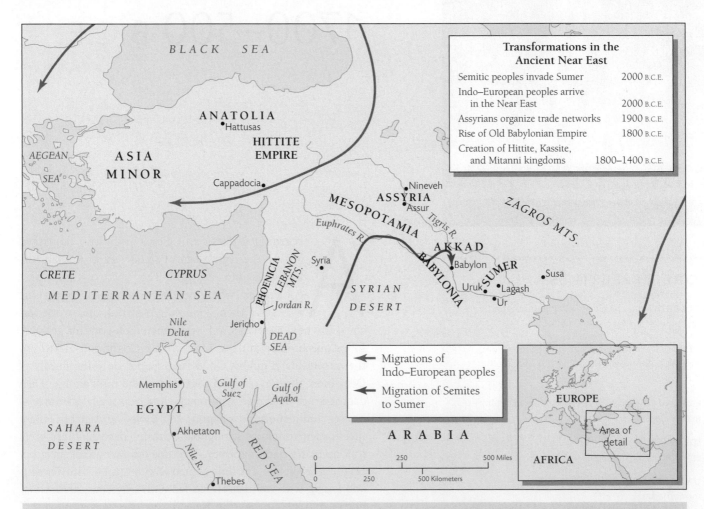

THE BRONZE AGE NEAR EAST, 2000–1400 B.C.E. Notice the geographical relationship among the older centers of Mesopotamia and Egypt, and among newer civilizations such as Babylonia, Assyria, Phoenicia, and the Hittite Empire. ▪ *Which of these emerging cultures would be most likely to come into contact with Egypt, and why?* ▪ *Where did the Indo-European peoples come from?* ▪ *What was the impact of Indo-European settlements?*

of ethics, politics, and the natural world. This age would prove a fateful historical crossroads, as elements both old and new combined to reconfigure the ancient world.

INDO-EUROPEAN LANGUAGES AND PEOPLES

In 1786, a British judge serving in India made a discovery that transformed the prevailing understanding of history. Turning his spare time to the study of Sanskrit, the ancient language of South Asia, Sir William Jones discovered that it shares the same grammar and vocabulary as ancient Greek and Latin, to an extent inexplicable by sheer coincidence. His interest piqued, he then examined the early Germanic and Celtic languages of Europe and the Old Persian language of the Near East and found that they also exhibit marked similarities. He concluded that all of these languages must have evolved from a common source. Within another generation, the ancient language whose existence Jones had hypothesized, and the later languages derived from it, would be labeled Indo-European, reflecting a wide distribution from India to Ireland. The biblical story of mankind's shared language, the story of Babel, turns out to be partly true.

Since then, scholars have greatly enlarged our understanding of Indo-European languages and their speakers. Yet much remains controversial. Was an original form of the language spoken by a single population at some point in time? If so, when and where? How did it spread? Can the diffusion of its speakers be determined archaeologically, by tracing characteristic pottery types and burial rites, or are such practices distinct from language? At the moment, we have no clear answers to any such questions. It is certain, however, that Indo-European linguistic forms began to appear in the Near East and eastern Mediterranean shortly after 2000 B.C.E. Around this same time, a group of Indo-European speakers also moved into the Aegean basin, where the resulting language became an early form of Greek. Other Indo-European speakers went east; some may have reached western China.

These were not the only new peoples moving into the Near East. As we noted in Chapter 1, Semitic-speaking peoples were also making their mark, beginning with the Akkadians and the Amorites, from whose ranks Hammurabi came. The Assyrians, the Phoenicians, and the Canaanites would also become prominent. These newcomers did not wipe out existing cultures; rather, they built on established patterns of urban life and organization. But their collective impact was enormous.

New Settlers in Anatolia

By 1900 B.C.E., the nomadic Assyrians had become caravan merchants whose extensive trade networks stretched across Anatolia and Mesopotamia. They did not seek military dominance over the region; instead, they relied on the protection of local rulers and, in turn, they made these rulers rich. They also served as advisers and officials, and married into important urban families. In the process, they carried Mesopotamian civilization and its trappings into far-flung regions of the world.

In the wake of Assyrian-assisted urbanization, new population groups were attracted to Anatolia, northern Syria, and Mesopotamia. The most formidable of these were the Hittites, an Indo-European-speaking people who arrived around 2000 B.C.E. In contrast to the Assyrians, the Hittites were military conquerors and colonists who imposed themselves and their language on the peoples they vanquished. By 1700 B.C.E., they had integrated many Hittite-dominated city-states into a larger kingdom. About fifty years later, they captured a strategic mountain stronghold, Hattusas, from which their king took a new name, Hattusilis.

Under Hattusilis and his successors, the Hittites' warrior aristocracy fielded the most fearsome army of the Bronze Age. They were quick to adopt the latest technologies, including the chariot and (eventually) the use of iron for weaponry. But the Hittites also adopted the more peaceful practices of those they conquered, using cuneiform to record their own language and laws. They also sought to control trade routes, particularly the overland trade in copper and arsenic, the raw materials for making bronze. By 1595 B.C.E., they had moved southeastward into Mesopotamia, capturing and sacking Babylon.

A century later, the Kassites, another new people, moved into the devastated city and took control of it. For the next 500 years, they presided over a largely peaceful and prosperous Babylonian realm. The Hittites, however, continued to destabilize the region, until they were themselves checked by the arrival of a people known as the Mitannians, who moved into Syria around 1550 B.C.E. The Mitannians' initial advantage was their use of horses, hitherto unknown outside the steppes of Asia. Their light, horse-drawn chariots became terrifying death-machines, transporting archers rapidly around the battlefield. The Mitannians also pioneered cavalry tactics which devastated the foot soldiers of their rivals. Eventually, however, the Mitannians' opponents borrowed these same technologies, and the Hittites once again achieved the advantage. By the mid-fourteenth century, they had subjugated the Mitannians and were turning their attention to Egypt.

A NEAR EASTERN WAR CHARIOT. A light, spoke-wheeled chariot, developed for warfare, is here being used for lion hunting by the Assyrian king Assurnasirpal II (883–859 B.C.E.), whose reign is discussed on page 59.

THE NEW KINGDOM OF EGYPT

As we have seen, Egypt's Middle Kingdom had been reshaped by the many internal changes of the First Intermediate Period, chiefly the redistribution of wealth and power. Now it was further transformed by external forces, through the dynamic movement of new peoples from western Asia and Nubia. Some of these came to Egypt as immigrants; others were hired as mercenaries. And for a while, a strategy of accommodation preserved Egypt from large-scale armed attack and fostered commercial exchange with neighboring regions. But around 1700 B.C.E., Egypt was invaded for the first time since the unification of the Upper and Lower Kingdoms. The invaders' origins and identity remain mysterious; the Egyptians called them simply Hyksos (*HIHK-sohs*), "rulers of foreign lands." From their power base in the eastern delta of the Nile, the Hyksos began to project their authority over most of Lower Egypt.

With this conquest, the central authority of the pharaoh once again dissolved and Egypt entered what historians call the Second Intermediate Period (c. 1650–1550 B.C.E.). Significantly, however, the Hyksos did not destroy the machinery of pharaonic government in Lower Egypt but took steps to legitimize their rule in accordance with Egyptian precedents. Some Hyksos rulers even incorporated the name of the sun-god Ra into their own names. In Upper Egypt, by contrast, Hyksos power was weak. Here, a native pharaonic regime maintained a tenuous independence at the traditional capital of Thebes, although it sometimes had to acknowledge the suzerainty of the foreigners to the north.

This relatively short period of Hyksos domination was regarded by later Egyptians as the greatest shame of their history. Although the Hyksos established Lower Egypt as the most significant power in the Near East, filling the temporary power vacuum left by the Hittites, their conquest also weakened the dominion of Upper Egypt over the Nubians, who eventually founded an independent kingdom called Kush. This Nubian kingdom posed a much greater threat to the native dynasty at Thebes than to the Hyksos in Lower Egypt—but it also provided an additional incentive to southern pharaohs determined to oust the Hyksos usurpers and reunify Egypt. Ultimately, they succeeded. By the end of the sixteenth century B.C.E., the pharaoh Ahmose had driven out the Hyksos, establishing the Eighteenth Dynasty and the New Kingdom of Egypt.

The Pharaohs of the Eighteenth Dynasty

Under the Eighteenth Dynasty, Egyptian civilization reached the height of its magnificence and power, which it now exercised more widely than ever before. Although many Egyptian traditions were renewed and strengthened, the dynamism of the New Kingdom—particularly its new focus on imperial expansion—changed the very fabric of Egyptian life, which had never before looked beyond the narrow world of the fertile Nile Valley.

The Eighteenth Dynasty ruled Egypt for more than two and a half centuries, and striking developments took place during this period. Most important was the rise of an aristocracy whose wealth was acquired through warfare and the winning of lands (with slaves to work them) which they received from the pharaoh as rewards for service. The Eighteenth Dynasty itself was forged in battle, something that had not been true of a ruling family since the time of King Narmer, over a millennium and a half earlier (see Chapter 1). Ahmose, the man who expelled the Hyksos, had been reared by the warrior queen Ahhotep, who had ruled Upper Egypt in her own right. His eventual successor, Thutmose I (c. 1504–1492 B.C.E.), was the son of an unknown warrior who married Amhose's daughter.

Under Thutmose's leadership, the Egyptians subdued the Nubians to the south, seizing control of their gold mines and securing the wealth needed to finance expanded commerce in the Near East. They also penetrated beyond their northeastern frontier, driving deep into Palestine and Syria.

By the time of his death, Thutmose could claim to rule the land from beyond the Nile's Fourth Cataract in the south to the banks of the Euphrates in the north. Never had Egypt held sway over so much territory, or so clearly declared its imperial ambitions. Nor was this success fleeting. The Egyptians would sustain a strong military presence in the Near East for the next 400 years, using the new horse-powered battle chariots to devastating effect against their enemies.

The Legacy of Hatshepsut

The early death of Thutmose's son and successor could have resulted in a crisis for the Eighteenth Dynasty. Instead, it led to one of the most remarkable reigns in Egypt's history, for Thutmose II (1492–1479 B.C.E.) passed the power of

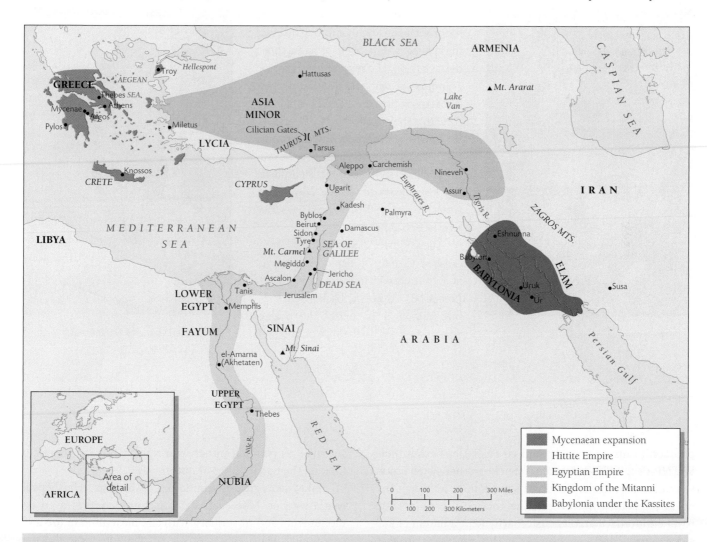

EGYPT AND ITS NEIGHBORS, C. 1400 B.C.E. ▪ *What is the major change on this map compared to the previous map of the Bronze Age Near East (page 40)?* ▪ *What factors appear to shape patterns of conquest and settlement in the Mediterranean?* ▪ *What developments would have enabled trade to flourish during this period?*

Interpreting Visual Evidence

Remembering Hatshepsut

The pharaohs of Egypt's New Kingdom were obsessed with self-representation and they carefully controlled their public images. The visual language they used was highly symbolic, an iconogra-phy (vocabulary of images) intended to make each successive pharaoh look as much like his royal predecessors as possible: godlike, steadfast, virile, authoritative—even when the pharaoh was a woman, Hatshepsut (1479–1458 B.C.E.). So many statues and portraits of her survive that nearly every major museum in the world has at least one (the Metropolitan Museum of Art in New York has a whole room set aside for them). But many of these images show signs of having been defaced during the reign of her successor, Thutmose III, who was also her nephew and stepson (images A and B). Until very recently, scholars assumed that Hatshepsut must have usurped his powers, and that this was his revenge. Yet the evidence clearly shows that Hatshepsut was Egypt's legitimate ruler. Why, then, would Thutmose III or his heirs have tried to efface to her memory?

These two unblemished *steles* (images C and D) depict Hatshepsut and Thutmose III. In the *stele* on the left (image C), they sit back-to-back on matching thrones, under the protection of the gods. In the *stele* on the right (image D), Thutmose III wears a warrior's crown, while Hatshepsut wears the double crown of Upper and Lower Egypt and wields a mace.

A. Defaced head of Hatshepsut.

B. Undefaced statue of Hatshepsut.

pharaoh to his sister, wife, and co-ruler Hatshepsut (*haht-SHEHP-soot*, 1479–1458 B.C.E.). Such brother-sister unions were common in the Egyptian royal family, although they do not appear to have been the routine way to produce royal children: pharaohs customarily kept a harem of sub-sidiary wives and concubines for this purpose. However, Thutmose II and Hatshepsut did conceive at least one child together, Neferure (*neh-feh-RUH-reh*); in fact, she may have been their designated heir. For twenty-one years, Hatshep-sut ruled as pharaoh in her own right, while her daughter took on the usual duties of queen.

Like her great-grandmother, Ahhotep, Hatshepsut was a warrior. Moroever, she was routinely protrayed on monuments and in statuary with the masculine figure and ceremonial beard characteristic of pharaohs. She did not pretend to be a man; inscriptions almost always indicate her gender, and she herself claimed to be the most beautiful woman in the world. But it was important to Egyptians that

Questions for Analysis

1. Bearing in mind that few Egyptians could read the hieroglyphs accompanying these images, how might they have "read" the relationship between these two royal relatives? Does this evidence support the hypothesis that Thutmose was slighted by Hatshepsut?

2. What can these images tell us about gender roles? What else would we need to know before making a judgment about masculine and feminine characteristics in ancient Egypt?

3. Given that Hatshepsut was Egypt's legitimate pharaoh, what might have motivated either Thutmose III or his son Amenhotep II to deface her image many years after her death?

C. *Stele* of Hatshepsut and Thutmose.

D. *Stele* of Thutmose and Hatshepsut from the Red Chapel at Karnak.

she use the conventional iconography of power to locate herself firmly within a long history of dynastic rule.

Hatshepsut's statecraft proved crucial to the continuing success of Egypt. With her stepson/nephew, Thutmose III (son of one of her brother's lesser wives), she launched several successful military campaigns and extended trade and diplomacy. The arts also flourished, setting standards that would be emulated for a thousand years. Indeed, Hatshepsut was one of the most ambitious builders in Egyptian history, which is saying something. Her own mortuary temple, which housed the remains of her father and herself, was probably the first tomb constructed in the Valley of the Kings, the New Kingdom's answer to the pyramids.

Yet after Hatshepsut's death in 1458 B.C.E. her legacy was called into question. At some point late in her nephew's reign, attempts were made to remove her name from inscriptions and to destroy her images (see ***Interpreting***

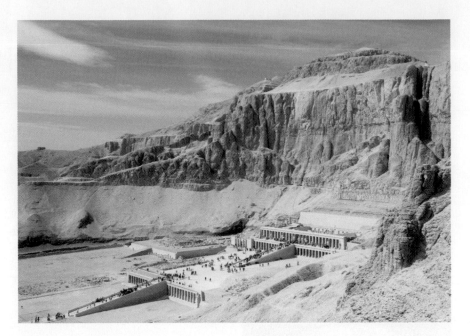

THE MORTUARY TEMPLE OF HATSHEPSUT.
Unlike the pharaohs of the Old Kingdom, those of the Eighteenth Dynasty chose to be buried in specially built temples rather than in separate pyramids. The innovative architecture of Hatshepsut's temple, which was built into a hillside and set off by rows of columns, was widely imitated by her successors.

Visual Evidence on pages 44–45). Scholars used to assume that Thutmose himself was responsible, because he resented his stepmother/aunt's power over him. But more recent research has suggested that the culprit was his son, Amenhotep II (1427–1400 B.C.E.), who was thereby blocking the claims of royal rivals, possibly the descendants of Hatshepsut or her daughter Neferure. In either case, the near erasure of Hatshepsut's legacy caused her to be neglected by historians until the late twentieth century.

Religious Change and Political Challenge

The great conquests of the Eighteenth Dynasty brought mind-boggling riches to Egypt. Much of this wealth went to the glorification of the pharaoh in the form of grand temples, tombs, and other monuments, including the thousands of steles that provide us with so much information about this era. Another significant portion of the plunder went to the military aristocracy that made such conquests possible. But the lion's share went to the gods as offerings of thanks for Egypt's success. As the temples became wealthy and powerful, so too did their priests. But no temple complex was so well endowed as that of Amon at Thebes.

Thebes was not only the capital of New Kingdom Egypt, it was also the capital of the Eighteenth Dynasty and the place most sacred to Amon (or Amun), the god of creation.

He therefore played an important role in the dynasty's self-image, and he is evoked in the dynastic name Amenhotep ("Amon Is Pleased"). But Amon was more than a local god. He had come into prominence when the political center of gravity shifted to Thebes during the Middle Kingdom, and his cult had steadily increased in status and popularity. By 1550 B.C.E., he had become identified as another manifestation of the sun god Ra, and as Amon-Ra he was believed to be the divine force behind the Eighteenth Dynasty's triumph over the Hyksos. This accounts for the favor shown to his priests at Thebes, who became a formidable political and economic force. Eventually, the priesthood of Amon surpassed even the military aristocracy in importance and influence. And since the dynasty's prestige was intertwined with that of Amon, the priests had seemingly gained the controlling voice in Egypt.

The Reign of Akhenaten (1352–1336 B.C.E.)

All of these factors are important when we consider the reign of Amenhotep IV, who inherited the vast, well-governed kingdom assembled by his predecessors. This young pharaoh showed an early inclination toward the worship of the sun—but not as an aspect of Amon. Instead, Amenhotep exalted Ra as a discrete divinity and he laid aside the traditional iconography of this god as a falcon (or a falcon-headed man), replacing it with the symbol *Aten*, the hieroglyph representing the sun's rays. He then went further, changing his own name to Akhenaten (*AH-keh-NAH-ton*), "He Who Is Profitable to the Aten," and building a new capital to honor the god. Located halfway between Memphis in the north and Thebes in the south, it was called Akhetaten ("The Horizon of the Aten").

Although the priesthood of Amon exalted Amon-Ra, it had continued to recognize all the other gods of the Egyptian pantheon. Akhenaten's theology, by contrast, was closer to monotheism: unlike traditional Egyptian deities, the Aten could not be imagined as taking on human or animal form. As if this were not controversial enough, Akhenaten also celebrated his new religion by representing himself in a very unconventional way. In a complete departure from the divine virility of his ancestors—which even his ancestor Hatshepsut had emulated—Akhenaten had himself pictured as a normal human being with distinctive features and as a family man enjoying the company of his wife, Nefertiti, and their children. This emphasis on his own humanity might have been an extension of his theology, which honored the life force within every being. But it was very dangerous to the ideology of royal power. The pharaoh was not supposed to be approachable and affable, a man with quirky personality. He was supposed to be god's son on earth.

Akhenaten's spiritual revolution therefore had enormous political implications. Indeed, some scholars have suggested that it was part of a cunning attempt to undermine the influence of Amon's priests, to the pharaoh's benefit. Whatever the motives behind it, Akhenaten did not succeed in converting many Egyptians to his new religion. Not surprisingly, the priesthood of Amon also put up strenuous resistance. To make matters worse, Akhenaten did not balance his theological enthusiasm with attention to Egypt's security or interests abroad. This cost him the support of his nobility and may even have led to his deposition. He was ultimately succeeded by one of his younger sons, Tutankhaten ("Living Image of Aten"), a child of nine whose name was quickly changed to reflect his advisers' rejection of Akhenaten's beliefs and the restoration of the god Amon and his priesthood to a position of power. He thus became Tutankhamun (1333–1324 B.C.E.), the famous boy king whose sumptuous tomb was discovered in 1922. After his early death, he was succeeded by a general called Horemheb, a man unrelated to the royal family who nonetheless reigned as the last pharaoh of the Eighteenth Dynasty and managed to maintain stability for nearly three decades. When he died, he passed his office to another general. This was Ramses, the founder of the Nineteenth Dynasty, who would restore Egypt to glory in the Near East.

AKHENATEN, HIS WIFE NEFERTITI, AND THEIR CHILDREN. The Aten is depicted here as a sun disk, raining down power on the royal family. ▪ *What messages might this image have conveyed to contemporary Egyptians?* ▪ *How does this depiction of the pharaoh differ from earlier precedents?*

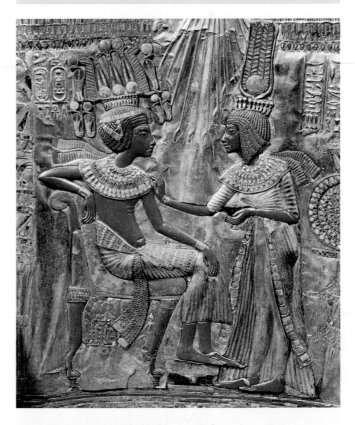

THRONE OF TUTANKHAMUN. Dating from about 1330 B.C.E., this relief in gold and silver is part of the back of the young pharaoh's throne. Although the reign of the boy king marked the rejection of Akhenaten's theology, the informal artistic style favored by his father is still detectable here in the relaxed, lounging position of the pharaoh and the intimate, confiding gesture of his queen, Ankhesenamen.

TRANSNATIONAL NETWORKS OF THE LATE BRONZE AGE

After 1500 B.C.E., Bronze Age history must be understood within the context of what we might call international relations. Yet it is more accurate to call the political and economic networks of this period *transnational*, because this web of alliances and relationships transcended any idea of national identity or national boundaries.

This Late Bronze Age was an age of superpowers. The great pharaohs of the Eighteenth Dynasty had transformed Egypt into a conquering state, and the Hittites had created an empire out of the disparate city-states and kingdoms of Anatolia. The Assyrians controlled Near Eastern trade, and the Kassite kingdom of Babylonia remained a significant force in economic and military relationships. In addition to these imperial entities, numerous smaller states also flourished and extended their influence westward into the Mediterranean. Holding it all together was a network of trade routes that created an interdependent Afro-Eurasian world.

Transnational Diplomacy

Although warfare remained the fundamental mode of interaction in the late Bronze Age, a balance of power among the larger empires gradually helped to stabilize the region and encourage trade. The archives discovered by archaeologists at Akhenaten's abandoned capital of Akhetaten (modern el-Amarna) provide us with a clear picture of this process. By the fourteenth century B.C.E., a wide-ranging correspondence was forging alliances and promoting a set of mutual goals and understandings among rulers and elites. This is reflected in the letters' vocabulary: the most powerful rulers address one another as "brother," while lesser princes and chieftains show their deference to the pharaoh, the Hittite king, and other sovereigns by using the term "father." Breach of this protocol could cause great offense. When a thirteenth-century Assyrian king presumed to address the Hittite ruler as "brother," he received a stern rebuke: "What is this you keep saying about 'brotherhood'? Were you and I born of the same mother? Far from it! Just as my father and grandfather were not in the habit of writing about 'brotherhood' to the king of Assyria, so should you stop writing to me about 'brotherhood!'"

Rulers of this period also exchanged lavish gifts and entered into marriage contracts with each other. Professional envoys journeyed back and forth between the centers of power, conveying gifts and handling politically sensitive missions. Some of these emissaries were also merchants, sent to explore the possibility of trading opportunities as well as to cement alliances.

Transnational Trade

Indeed, it was trade that allowed smaller communities to become integral parts of this transnational network. Seaside centers became powerful merchant city-states and centers for the exchange of dazzling commodities. A single vessel's cargo might contain scores of distinct items originating anywhere from the interior of Africa to the Baltic Sea, as demonstrated by the contents of a merchant ship discovered at Uluburun off the Turkish coast in 1982. At the same time, the region was supplied with goods brought in over land, via contacts reaching into India and the Far East.

Long-distance trade was not only the basis for a new economy but also the conduit for art, ideas, and technology. In the past, such influences had spread slowly and unevenly; now, though, the societies of the late Bronze Age could keep abreast of all the latest developments. Egyptians delighted in Canaanite glass, Greeks prized Egyptian amulets, and the merchants of Syria admired Greek pottery and wool. Examples of avid desire for the products of other cultures could be endlessly enumerated.

This trend was particularly marked in large coastal towns. At Ugarit, on the coast of modern-day Syria, the swirl of commerce and the multiplicity of languages spoken by traders even propelled the development of a simpler form of written communication than the cuneiform still current throughout most of the Near East. The Ugaritic alphabet consisted of about thirty symbols representing the sounds of consonants. (Vowels had to be inferred.) This system was far more easily mastered and more flexible than cuneiform, and it would become the model for the development of all modern alphabets.

The search for markets, resources, and trade routes also promoted greater understanding among cultures. After a great battle between Egyptians and Hittites near Kadesh (c. 1275 B.C.E.), the pharaoh Ramses II realized that more was to be gained through peaceful relations with his northern neighbors than through warfare. The treaty he established with the Hittites fostered geopolitical stability in the region and allowed further economic exchanges to flourish. But greater integration also meant greater mutual dependence. If one economy suffered, the effects of that decline were sure to be felt elsewhere. And the farther this transnational system spread, the more fragile it became. Many of the new markets depended on emerging societies in regions far less stable, where civilization was new.

AEGEAN CIVILIZATION: MINOAN CRETE, MYCENAEAN GREECE

Like Hesiod, many ancient Greek poets described a heroic age when great men mingled with gods and powerful kingdoms contended for wealth and glory. For a long time, modern scholars dismissed these stories as fables. Tales of Theseus and the Minotaur, the Trojan War, and the wanderings of Odysseus were not regarded as reflecting any historical reality. Greek history was assumed to begin in 776 B.C.E., when the first recorded Olympic Games occurred. Greece in the Bronze Age was considered a primitive backwater that played no significant role in the Mediterranean world or in the later, glorious history of classical Greece.

But in the late nineteenth century, an amateur archaeologist named Heinrich Schliemann became convinced that these legends were really historical accounts. Using the epic poems of Homer as his guide, he found the site of Ilium (Troy) near the coast of northwest Anatolia. He also identified a number of once-powerful citadels on the Greek main-

land, including the home of the legendary king Agamemnon at Mycenae (*MY-seh-nee*). Soon afterward, the British archaeologist Sir Arthur Evans took credit for discovering the remains of a great palace at Knossos (*Kuh-NAHS-ohs*) on the island of Crete, a vast complex that predated any of the major citadels on the Greek mainland. He dubbed its magnificent culture—which no modern person had known to exist—"Minoan," after King Minos, the powerful ruler whom the ancient Greeks had described as dominating the Aegean, and the man for whom the legendary engineer Daedalus had designed the Labyrinth. Although some of their conclusions have proven false, the discoveries of Schliemann and Evans forced scholars to revise, entirely, the early history of Western civilizations. It is now clear that Bronze Age Greece—or, as it is often termed, Mycenaean Greece—was an important player in this integrated Mediterranean world during the second millennium B.C.E.

The Minoan Thalassocracy

In the fifth century B.C.E., the Athenian historian Thucydides wrote that King Minos of Crete had ruled a *thalassocracy*, an empire of the sea. We now know that he was correct, that a very wealthy civilization began to flourish on the island of Crete around 2500 B.C.E. Thereafter, for about a millennium, the Minoans controlled shipping around the central Mediterranean and the Aegean and may have exacted tribute from many smaller islands. At its height between 1900 and 1500 B.C.E., Minoan civilization was the contemporary of Egypt's Middle Kingdom and the Hittite Old Kingdom. And unlike them, it was virtually unassailable by outside forces, protected by the surrounding sea. Astonishingly, neither the great palace at Knossos nor the other palaces on the island were fortified so secure were they from attack.

Thanks to its strategic position, Crete was not only a safe haven but also a nexus of vibrant economic exchange. In this it resembled its counterparts in the Near East because it acted as a magnet for the collection of resources which were then redistributed by its rulers and their emissaries. Knossos was also a production center for textiles, pottery, and metalwork. Minoan merchants traded these with Egypt, southwest Anatolia, and Cyprus for a range of exotic goods. Through Cyprus, the Minoans had further contacts with the Levantine coast of modern-day Lebanon and Syria. Artistic influences also traveled along these routes; among much else, Minoan-style paintings from this period appear regularly in the Nile Delta and the Levant.

Traces of the bright colors and graceful lines of these paintings are still evident on the ruined walls of the palace

MYCENAEAN DEATH MASK, C. 1550–1500 B.C.E. When the archaeologist Heinrich Schliemann discovered this gold funeral mask in a burial shaft at Mycenae, he immediately declared it to be that of Agamemnon. Although it is certainly royal, this mask is too old to have been made for that legendary king, who would have lived several centuries later.

MINOAN FRESCO, C. 1500 B.C.E. A stylized representation of bull-leaping, painted into the plaster of a wall at Knossos. ▪ *Is this likely to represent real practices?* ▪ *Why or why not?*

at Knossos. Endowed with indoor plumbing, among other luxuries, it covered several acres and comprised hundreds of rooms joined by an intricate network of winding hallways that surely inspired the famous story of the Labyrinth, where the terrible Minotaur lurked in the center. These legends, too, reflect historical evidence: the Minoans probably worshiped a god in the form of a bull or bull-man, and they appear to have devised an elaborate ritual sport known as bull-leaping, similar to bull-fighting but involving an element of athletic dance. There is also some evidence that they practiced human sacrifice (possibly facilitated by the dangers of bull-dancing) as a religious rite.

Despite all these fascinating remains, Minoan culture remains mysterious because its language has yet to be decoded. Its script is called Linear A, to distinguish it from Linear B, used in Mycenaen Greece—a script that *has* been deciphered. Although Linear A and Linear B represent different languages, the formal relationship between them reflects the fact that Minoan commercial activity engaged the mainland of Greece. The presence of a wide variety of Minoan objects on the Greek mainland corroborates this.

Yet the dynamics of the relationship between Minoans and Mycenaeans remains debatable. Before 1600 B.C.E., the Minoans were clearly much more sophisticated and may have dominated their Greek neighbors. One story told of Theseus describes how the young hero was sent to Crete as a hostage, intending to free Athens from the heavy tribute imposed by King Minos. Given what we have already learned about the close relationship between myth and history, it is probable that this story preserves ancient memory, just as the story of Daedalus, the brilliant inventor and engineer, is an attempt to explain the technological marvels of the palace at Knossos.

Mycenaean Greece

In the early 1950s, the Englishmen Michael Ventris and John Chadwick joined their linguistic skills to expertise gained during the Second World War, when many classically trained scholars were employed in cracking enemy codes. Their efforts resulted in the decoding of Linear B. Analysis of the texts written in this script forced scholars to reconsider the history of ancient Greece, and proved that it stretched well back into the Bronze Age. Since then, new

LINEAR B TABLET FROM KNOSSOS. Unlike cuneiform, whose characters are formed using the wedge-shaped tip of a reed, the scripts of Linear B used a sharp stylus that incised fine lines in clay or soft stone.

research shows that the Indo-Europeans whose language became Greek entered the region in several waves after the turn of the second millennium, dominating and displacing the indigenous inhabitants. By 1500 B.C.E., huge citadels dotted the Greek landscape, ruled by warriors whose epitaphs boast of their martial prowess and who were buried with their weapons. The power of these rulers was based on their leadership and their ability to reward followers with plunder. The most successful of them gained control of strategic sites from which they could exploit major trade routes, engaging in both trade and piracy. (The line between these two pursuits has always been fine.)

Over time, and perhaps under the influence of Minoan culture, the Mycenaean citadels developed into complex societies. They served as both centers of government and warehouses for the storage and redistribution of goods and agricultural surpluses, of which they kept careful records. (Thousands of Linear B tablets have survived to testify to this.) By the thirteenth century B.C.E., some rulers had carved out territorial kingdoms with as many as 100,000 inhabitants, dwarfing the city-states of the later classical age; Hesiod imagined them to have been built by giants.

Indeed, these palace centers were adapted from Near Eastern models and their massive size was not ideally suited to the Greek landscape. In war also, Mycenaean imitation of Near Eastern examples had its limits. For example, Mycenaean kings cherished the chariots used by their contemporaries on the plains of Anatolia, yet such chariots were highly impractical on Greece's rocky terrain.

Despite these and other differences from their Mediterranean neighbors, the Mycenaean Greeks played a central role in Bronze Age networks. By about 1400 B.C.E., they had subjugated Crete, taking over Knossos and making it as a Mycenaean center. When the pharaoh Amenhotep III mentions a place called "Keftiu" in his correspondence, he is probably negotiating with Crete's Mycenaean conquerors. In western Anatolia, not far from fabled Troy, at least one Mycenaean king exercised enough influence for a Hittite ruler to address him as "my brother." This evidence suggests that the Mycenaeans earned prestige as warriors and mercenaries, just as the Greeks' heroic poems attest.

The basic political and commercial unit of the Mycenaean world—a powerful king and war leader, a warrior aristocracy, a palace bureaucracy, a complex economy, large territorial kingdoms—differs markedly from the tiny, self-contained Greek city-state of the later classical age (see Chapter 3). However, we can trace some features

AN ARTIST'S RECONSTRUCTION OF THE GREAT HALL AT PYLOS. Located on the western coast of the Greek Peloponnesus, Pylos was excavated in 1952 by the archaeologist Carl Blegen and his team. The principal feature of its Bronze Age palace was a large, brightly painted "great room" (*megaron*) with a central hearth.

of this later civilization back to the Mycenaeans, including the Greek language. Linear B tablets speak of a social group with considerable economic and political rights, the *damos*; this may be the precursor of the *demos*, the urban population that sought political empowerment (*democracy*) in many Greek cities. The tablets also preserve the names of several gods familiar from the later period, such as Zeus, Poseidon, and Dionysus. Indeed, the later Greeks believed themselves to be descended from these legendary forebears, whom they credited with superhuman achievements. Although later Greeks like Hesiod knew little about these Mycenaean ancestors in fact, the impact of what they imagined about them was considerable.

The Sea Peoples and the End of the Bronze Age

The civilization of Mycenaean Greece seems to have collapsed around the end of the thirteenth century B.C.E. What triggered this cannot be determined with any certainty: drought, famine, disease, and social unrest have all been posited. But the consequences of the collapse are clear. Because Mycenaean Greece was an integrated part of a transnational network, the effects of its demise were felt throughout the Near East. Thereafter, a wave of devastation swept from north to south, caused by a group of people so

The Diplomacy of the Mycenaeans and the Hittites

Around 1260 B.C.E., the powerful Hittite king Hattusilis III sent the following letter to a "King of Ahhiyawa," identifiable as a leader of the Mycenaean Greeks, who often called themselves Akhaiwoi, Achaeans. This fascinating document exemplifies the tangle of close ties that bound powerful men together within the transnational system of the Late Bronze Age, as well as the problems and misunderstandings that could arise from the misbehavior of men under their command. The events referenced here all occur in western Anatolia (Turkey), a region controlled partly by the Hittites and partly by the Greeks, the same region in which Troy (Ilium) was located. (See the map on page 52.)

have to complain of the insolent and treacherous conduct of one Tawagalawas. We came into contact in the land of Lycia, and he offered to become a vassal of the Hittite Empire. I agreed, and sent an officer of most exalted rank to conduct him to my presence. He had the audacity to complain that the officer's rank was not exalted enough; he insulted my ambassador in public, and demanded that he be declared vassal-king there and then, without the formality of an interview. Very well: I order him, if he desires to become a vassal of mine, to make sure that no troops of his are found in Iyalanda when I arrive there. And what do I find when I arrive in Iyalanda?—the troops of Tawagalawas, fighting on the side of my enemies. I defeat them, take many prisoners . . . scrupulously leaving the fortress of Atriya intact out of respect for my treaty with you. Now a Hittite subject, Piyamaradus by name, steals my 7,000 prisoners, and makes off to your city of Miletus. I command him to return to me: he disobeys. I write to you: you send a surly message unaccompanied by gift or greeting, to say that you have ordered your representative in Miletus, a certain Atpas, to deliver up Piyamaradus. Nothing happens, so I go fetch him. I enter your city of Miletus, for I have something to say to Piyamaradus, and it would be well that your subjects there should hear me say it. But my visit is not a success. I ask for Tawagalawas: he is not at home. I should like to see Piyamaradus: he has gone to sea. You refer me to your representative Atpas: I find that both he and his brother are married to daughters of Piyamaradus; they are not likely to give me satisfaction or to give you an unbiased account of these transactions. . . . Are you aware, and is it with your blessing, that Piyamaradus is going round saying that he intends to leave his wife and family, and incidentally my 7,000 prisoners, under your protection while he makes continual inroads on my dominion? . . . Do not let him use Achaea [in Greece] as a base for operations against me. You and I are friends. There has been no quarrel between us since we came to terms in the matter of Ilios [the territory of Troy]: the trouble there was my fault, and I promise it will not happen again. As for my military occupation of Miletus, please regard it as a friendly visit. . . . [As for the problems between us], I suggest that the fault may not lie with ourselves but with our messengers; let us bring them to trial, cut off their heads, mutilate their bodies, and live henceforth in perfect friendship.

Source: Adapted from Denys Page, *History and the Homeric Iliad* (Berkeley, CA: 1959), pp. 11–12.

Questions for Analysis

1. Reconstruct the relationship between Hattusilis III and the Achaean king, based on the references to people and places in this letter. What picture emerges of their interactions and of the connections between the Hittite Empire and Mycenaean Greece?

2. Why is Hattusilis so concerned about the disrespect shown to him by the Achaeans? Reading between the lines, what do you think he wanted to accomplish by sending this letter?

3. Based on this letter, what you can you deduce about the standards of behavior expected of civilized participants in the transnational system of the Late Bronze Age? Within this code of conduct, what sanctions or penalties could be imposed on individuals or their nations?

thoroughly destructive that they obliterated everything in their path.

We might know nothing at all about them were it not for a narrow victory by the pharaoh Ramses III around 1176 B.C.E. In the *stele* set up to commemorate his triumph near the modern city of Luxor on Egypt's West Bank, Ramses III referred to these invaders as the "Sea Peoples" and named several groups as part of a coalition. Some were familiar to the Egyptians, who had employed them as mercenaries. From Ramses' description of their battle gear, it seems that many were from the Aegean. Most notable were the Philistines who, after their defeat, withdrew to populate the coast of the region named after them: Palestine.

Because the Sea Peoples' arc of annihilation started in the north, it may have been one of the factors contributing to the collapse of Mycenaean Greece. Disruption of northern commercial networks would have devastated the Mycenaean kingdoms, which could not support their enormous populations without trade. Suddenly faced with an apocalyptic combination of overpopulation, famine, and violence, bands of desperate refugees would have fled the Aegean basin. Meanwhile, the damage to commerce had a domino effect and devastated the economy of the Hittites, whose ancient kingdom rapidly disintegrated. Along the Mediterranean coast we find other clues. The king of Ugarit wrote a letter to a "brother" king on the island of Cyprus, begging for immediate aid because he had sent all his own warriors to help the Hittites. Poignantly, however, we have his letter only because the clay tablet on which it was written baked hard in the fire that destroyed his palace. The letter was never sent.

In the end, the Sea Peoples destroyed the civilizations that had flourished in the Near East and Mediterranean for over two thousand years. The devastation was not total; not all cities disappeared, and trade did not cease entirely. But the Hittite Empire was eradicated, leaving behind it many weak, short-lived principalities. The great cosmopolitan cities of the eastern Mediterranean lay in ruins, and new groups—sometimes contingents of Sea Peoples like the Philistines—populated the coast. The citadels of Mycenaean Greece were depopulated by as much as 90 percent over the next century, and Greece entered into a period of cultural and economic isolation that would last for 250 years.

The victorious Egyptians survived; but with their major trading partners diminished or dead, their civilization suffered. The Assyrians, the original architects of the networks that had undergirded the transnational system, had to fight for their very existence. In Babylon, the peaceful and prosperous rule of the Kassites withered. In the vacuum left behind, new political configurations took shape and a new metallurgical technology began to supplant the use of bronze. Out of the ashes arose the culture of the Iron Age.

THE STATES OF THE EARLY IRON AGE

With the destruction of transnational networks, the geopolitical map of the Near East changed significantly. In Anatolia, a patchwork of small kingdoms grew up within the territories once controlled by the Hittites. Similar developments took place in the Levant: the eastern Mediterranean coastline that today comprises Israel, Lebanon, and parts of Syria. For centuries, this region had been controlled either by the Egyptians or the Hittites. With the collapse of these empires, new states began to emerge there, too. They were small, but they had a huge impact on the history of Western civilizations.

The Phoenicians

One of the most influential peoples of this period are usually called by their name: the Greek Phoenicians. They are also known as Canaanites, and were speakers of a Semitic language closely related to Hebrew, Amorite, and Ugaritic. Each Phoenician city on the coast of the Levant had its own hereditary royal government, and every Phoenician's first loyalty was to his or her own city. In the Phoenicians' overseas colonies, however, a new type of political system emerged in which power was shared among a handful of elite families. This aristocratic form of government would become a model for many other Western societies, including those of classical Greece and Rome (see Chapters 3 and 5).

During the late Bronze Age, most Phoenician cities had been controlled by Egypt. But the erosion of Egyptian imperial power after 1200 B.C.E. gave these cities the opportunity to forge a new independence and to capitalize on their commercial advantages. One Phoenician city, Gubla, was a clearing house for papyrus, the highly prized Egyptian writing material. This explains why the Greek name for this city, Byblos, became the basis for the Greek word *biblion*, meaning "book." (The Bible is so called from the plural *biblia*, "the books.") Another valuable commodity came to be associated with the Phoenicians and gave them their name a rare purple dye derived from the shells of snails culled from seabeds off the Levantine coast. As far as the Greeks were concerned, those who supplied this rich dye were *phoinikeoi*, "purple people." Phoenician textiles commanded a high price everywhere. So did timber from the Levant, especially cedar, and Canaanite glass. The Phoenicians also became expert metalworkers, ivory carvers, and shipbuilders.

Phoenician Colonies and Cultural Influence

The Phoenicians became famous as merchants and sea-farers, but they were also aggressive colonists. By the end of the tenth century B.C.E., they had planted settlements from one end of the Mediterranean to the other and their merchants had begun to venture out into the Atlantic Ocean. We have good evidence that they traveled as far as Cornwall (southwest Britain) during this period. The Greek historian Herodotus later claimed that Phoenician merchant-explorers even circumnavigated Africa. At the end of the ninth century B.C.E., Phoenicians from the city of Tyre established Carthage in modern-day Tunisia (North Africa). Carthage would ultimately become the preeminent power in the western Mediterranean, bringing it into conflict with Rome centuries later (see Chapter 5).

The widespread colonial and mercantile efforts of the Phoenicians meant that they influenced cultures across the Mediterranean. Among their early overseas trading partners were the Greeks, and the Phoenicians may have played an important role in reintroducing urban life to Greece after the collapse of the Mycenaean citadels. They also brought with them a number of Near Eastern artistic and literary influences. Without question, however, the most important contribution of the Phoenicians was their alphabet.

As we noted earlier, a thirty-character alphabet had evolved at Ugarit by the end of the Bronze Age. Around 1100 B.C.E., the Phoenicians refined this writing system to twenty-two characters. This simpler system further facilitated trade and accounting, and the Phoenicians may have wanted to encourage similar practices among their partners, to safeguard their own interests. The Greeks certainly remained aware of their debt to the Phoenicians: their legends ascribe the invention of the alphabet to Cadmus, a Phoenician who settled in Greece. Their debt is also clear in the close relationship between the names of letters in Greek (alpha, beta, gamma, delta . . .) and Phoenician letter names (aleph, bayt, gimel, dalet . . .), and from the obvious similarities in letter shapes.

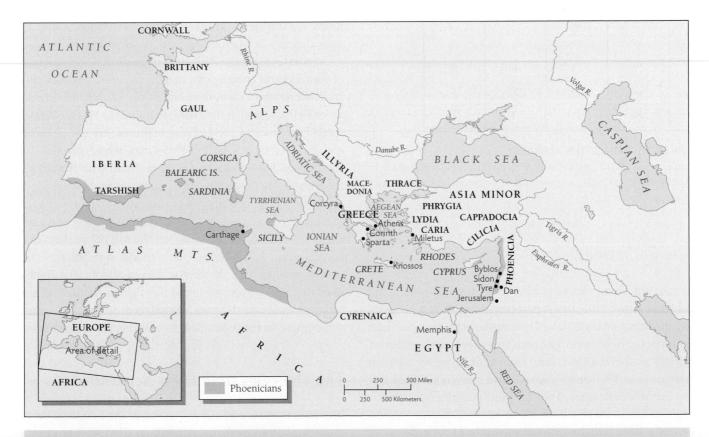

PHOENICIAN COLONIZATION. Compare this map to the more detailed one of the Hebrew kingdoms on page 59. ■ *What part of the Mediterranean serves as the homeland for the Phoenician city-states, and where did Phoenicians establish colonies?* ■ *Why would overseas colonization be of such crucial importance to Phoenician city-states?* ■ *What does their westward colonization imply about the Phoenicians' aims and about the different opportunities available in the western Mediterranean, as compared to the New East?*

Phoenician	Hebrew	Classical Greek	Modern Alphabetic
𐤀	א	A	A
𐤁	ב	B	B
𐤂	ג	Γ	G
𐤃	ד	Δ	D
𐤄	ה	E	E
𐤅	ו	Y	V
𐤆	ז	Z	Z
𐤇	ח	H	H
𐤈	ט	Θ	T
𐤉	י	I	Y
𐤊	כ	K	K
𐤋	ל	Λ	L
𐤌	מ	M	M
𐤍	נ	N	N
𐤎	ס	Ξ	S
𐤏	ע	O	O
𐤐	פ	Π	P
𐤑	צ		TZ
𐤒	ק		Q
𐤓	ר	P	R
𐤔	ש	Σ	S
𐤕	ת	T	T

THE EVOLUTION OF THE ALPHABET. This table shows how the shapes of letters changed as the Phoenician alphabet was adapted by the Hebrews, the Greeks, and eventually the Romans (from whom our modern alphabet derives).

The Philistines

Southward along the Levantine coast from Phoenicia lay the land of the Philistines, descendants of the Sea Peoples defeated by Ramses III. Their reputation is the result of their dominance over their pastoral neighbors, the herdsmen known as the Hebrews, who used writing as an effective weapon: the Philistines thus became the great villains of the Hebrew scriptures, and the word *philistine* has accordingly come to mean a boorish, uncultured person. Unfortunately, the Philistines do not appear to have made use of the same powerful technology to record their own outlook on the world, and almost everything we know about them comes from the work of archaeologists, or has to be sifted through the bad press of their detractors.

The Philistines occupied a unique position in the Levant and retained a separate identity for several generations; each new archaeological discovery roots this identity more firmly in their Aegean past. We know little about their language, but their material culture, behavior, and organization all exhibit close affinities with Mycenaean Greece. For example, the Philistines introduced grapevines and olive trees to the Levant from the Aegean basin. With the profits from these industries, they created powerful armies that dominated the region in the twelfth and eleventh centuries B.C.E. They also established a monopoly over metal smithing, making it virtually impossible for their enemies to forge competitive weaponry.

Philistine power was based in five great strongholds, the so-called Pentapolis (Greek for "five cities"): Gaza, Ashkelon, and Ashdod on the coast, and the inland cities of Ekron and Gath. (Again, these citadels are strikingly similar to the fortified palaces of Mycenaean civilization, and they appear to have served many of the same functions). From these strongholds, the Philistines dominated the surrounding countryside by organizing agricultural production and controlling trade routes. An independent lord ruled over each citadel, and no doubt tensions and rivalries existed among them. But much like the heroes of Greek epic, the Philistines could set aside differences when facing a common enemy.

Because we see the Philistines primarily through the eyes of their Hebrew enemies, we must be careful about drawing conclusions about them from the stories of Goliath's brutality or Delilah's sexual treachery, to name the two most infamous Philistines of the Hebrew sciptures. Yet the Hebrews had good reason to fear the Philistines, whose pressure on the Hebrew hill country was constant and who threatened the Hebrews' holy sanctuary at Shiloh, where the sacred Ark of the Covenant was said to contain the original tablets of the law given to Moses on Mount Sinai. In Hebrew tradition, the tribes of Israel had once carried the Ark before them into battle against the Philistines, only to lose it in the fray and to witness thereafter the destruction of Shiloh. The Philistines then established garrisons throughout the land of the Hebrews and exacted tribute, denied them access to weapons, and engaged in the typical abuses of an occupying people.

The Hebrews and Their Scriptures

The central feature of Hebrew culture, their conception of and relationship to their god, will be discussed at greater length toward the end of this chapter. In this section, we focus our attention on the development of Hebrew society in the Iron Age Levant—while at the same time acknowledging that religion is always related to politics, as well as to economic conditions and the concerns of everyday life. Indeed the Hebrews, like all ancient peoples and many people today, could not have distinguished among these phenomena.

In reconstructing the early history of the Hebrews, we are indebted to an unusual textual source already mentioned: a series of scriptures (literally "writings") that comprise mythology, laws and ritual practices, genealogical records, books of prophecy, proverbs, poetry, and royal chronicles. These are collectively known as the Hebrew Bible or (among Christians) as the Old Testament. These books are full of information about cultural practices and key events, and they are also a guide to the intellectual unfolding of the most influential religious tradition of the West. They do not, however, constitute a unified history. The books of the Bible were assembled over many centuries, mostly by unknown authors, copyists, and editors. Like other historical sources, they have to be treated as artifacts produced by particular historical circumstances, which also governed the way that certain texts were preserved and put together.

The first five books of the Hebrew Bible are traditionally attributed to the Hebrew leader Moses, but most of the materials in these books were borrowed from other Near Eastern cultures, including the stories of the creation and the flood, which parallel those of Sumer (as we saw in Chapter 1). The story of Moses's childhood draws on a legend told about the Akkadian king Sargon the Great. The laws and rituals of the patriarchs can be found in other traditions, too. Meanwhile, the story of the exodus from Egypt is fraught with contradictions. Although the later Book of Joshua claims that the Hebrews who returned from Egypt conquered and expelled the native Canaanites, archaeological and linguistic evidence suggests that the Hebrews were essentially Canaanites themselves. They may have merged with scattered refugees from Egypt in the aftermath of the Sea Peoples' invasions, but for the most part they had been continuously resident in Canaan for centuries. In sum, the first five books of the Bible constitute a retrospective history whose purpose was to justify Hebrew traditions and claims to power.

Among the other writings included in the Hebrew Bible are a group of texts which record events of the more recent past, those of the period we are considering now. These "historical books" are more straightforwardly verifiable, even if many details are difficult to confirm. According to the Book of Judges, the Hebrews were herdsmen who had just begun to establish permanent settlements around the time of the Philistines' arrival in the Levant. They had organized themselves into twelve tribes—extended clan units whose families owed one another mutual aid and protection in times of war, but who frequently fought over cattle and grazing rights. Each tribe was ruled by a patriarch known as a judge, who exercised the typical functions of authority in a clan-based society: war leadership, high priesthood, and dispute settlement. By the middle of the twelfth century B.C.E., these tribes occupied two major territories, with those settled in the south calling themselves the tribes of Judah, and those in the north the tribes of Israel.

The Struggle for Hebrew Identity

The Hebrew tribes of this period had few occasions to work together as a group and little experience of organized activity. This made them highly vulnerable, especially when the Philistines conquered the Levantine coast, around 1050 B.C.E. Faced with the threat of extinction, the Hebrews appear to have put up desperate resistance from their bases in the hilly interior. To counter the Philistine threat effectively, however, they needed a leader. Accordingly, around 1025 B.C.E., an influential tribal judge called Samuel selected a king to lead the Hebrew resistance against the Philistines. His name was Saul. However, Saul proved to be an ineffective war-leader. Although he blocked Philistine penetration into the hill country, he could not oust the Philistines from the valleys or coastal plains. So Samuel withdrew his support from Saul and threw it behind a young warrior in Saul's entourage, Saul's son-in-law David. Waging his own independent military campaigns, David achieved one triumph after another over the Philistines. By contrast, the armies of Saul met frequent reverses—that is, according to the chroniclers responsible for the historical books of the Bible, who wrote their accounts under David's patronage.

These same books reveal that David was not initially motivated by patriotism. He was a man on the make; and when Saul finally drove him from his court, he became an outlaw on the fringes of Hebrew society and then a mercenary in Philistine service. It was as a Philistine mercenary, in fact, that David fought against Saul in the climactic battle in which Saul was killed. Soon thereafter, David himself became king, first over the tribes of Judah, his home territory, and later over Saul's territory of Israel as well.

The Consolidation of the Hebrew Kingdom

After David's victory around 1000 B.C.E., he strove to strengthen his authority within and beyond his kingdom. He took advantage of the opportunity afforded by Egypt's decline to expand his territory southward, eventually confining the Philistines to an inconsequential strip of coastal land. David also defeated the neighboring Moabites and Ammonites, extending his control to the Dead Sea. By the time of his

The Fragility of Global Networks

In the late Bronze Age, the destruction of transnational commercial networks had a domino effect on the interlocking civilizations of the West, plunging many into a "dark age" of isolation and impoverishment. The global economic crisis of our own day was caused by a similar phenomenon: the collapse of mutually dependent financial systems that proved more fragile than anyone had anticipated.

 Watch related author interview on StudySpace
wwnorton.com/web/westernciv18

death in 973 B.C.E., his kingdom stretched from the middle Euphrates in the north to the Gulf of Aqaba in the south, and from the Mediterranean coast eastward into the Syrian deserts. Israel was now a force to be reckoned with, although it owed that status to the temporary weakness of its imperial neighbors, Egypt and Assyria.

As David's power and prestige grew, he was able to impose on his subjects a highly unpopular system of taxation and forced labor. His goal was to build a glorious capital at Jerusalem, a Canaanite settlement that he designated as the central city of his realm. It was a shrewd choice. As a newly conquered city, Jerusalem had no previous affiliation with any of Israel's twelve tribes and so stood outside the ancient rivalries that divided them. Geographically, too, Jerusalem was a strategic choice, lying between the southern tribes of Judah (David's people) and the northern tribes of Israel. David also took steps to exalt the city as a religious center by making Jerusalem the resting place of the sacred Ark of the Covenant and elevating the priesthood of the Hebrew god, Yahweh. By these measures, he sought to forge a new collective identity centered on his own family and its connections to Yahweh. To this end, he also encouraged the writing of histories and prophecies that would affirm this identity and his central role in forging it.

The Reign of King Solomon (973–937 B.C.E.)

Continuing his father's policies, but on a much grander scale, David's son Solomon built a great temple complex at Jerusalem to house the Ark. Such visible support of Yahweh's cult was approved by the chroniclers whose works

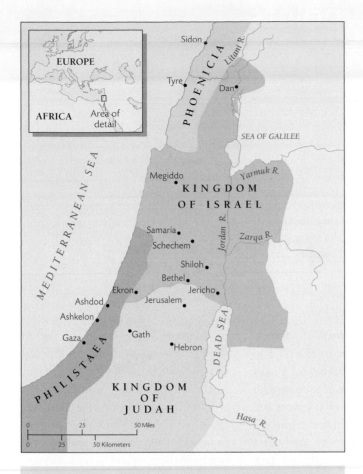

Israel's new wealth was bought at a high price. Solomon maintained a large standing army of unwilling conscripts from his own people, equipped with chariot and cavalry squadrons and powered by horses purchased abroad. To undertake his ambitious building projects, Solomon also required many of his subjects to perform forced labor four months out of every year. This level of oppression was too much for many Israelites, and the northern tribes seethed with rebellion against the royal capital. Within a decade or so of Solomon's death, in fact, the fragile monarchy split in two. The dynasty descended from David continued to rule the southern kingdom of Judah with its capital at Jerusalem, but the ten northern tribes banded together as the kingdom of Israel, with their capital at Shechem. Archaeology combined with other accounts included in the Bible reveal that the cult of Yahweh was not yet dominant in either the north or the south, so major religious differences made reunification even more difficult. In the meantime, the changing political situation of the Near East made the Hebrew kingdoms increasingly vulnerable.

THE REVIVAL OF THE ASSYRIAN EMPIRE

As we have already seen, the Assyrians had long played an important role in spreading trade and promoting urban settlements. But like the other great powers of the Near East, their civilization had been devastated by the Sea Peoples. For several centuries afterward they struggled for survival. Then, in the ninth century B.C.E., a brilliant but brutal ruler laid the foundations of what historians call the Neo-Assyrian Empire. Under the leadership of Assurnasirpal II (*ah-sur-NAH-sur-PAHL,* 883–859 B.C.E.), the Assyrians began to conduct aggressive military campaigns against their neighbors on an annual basis. Those whom they defeated either had to pay tribute or face the full onslaught of the Assyrian war machine, which under Assurnasirpal acquired a deserved reputation for savagery.

Despite their military successes, Assurnasirpal and his son, Shalmeneser III (*SHAHL-meh-NEE-zehr,* 853–827 B.C.E.), also inspired stiff resistance. The northern kingdom of Israel formed an alliance with other small states to halt Assyrian expansion. This coalition ultimately forced Shalmeneser III to settle for smaller victories against the Armenians to his northwest and the Medes to his northeast, until a great revolt within Assyria itself ended his reign. Thereafter, a usurper named Tiglath-Pileser III seized the Assyrian throne in 744 B.C.E. and immediately demanded

are included in the Bible, and which portray Solomon's reign as a golden age. Despite his proverbial wisdom, however, Solomon was a ruthless and often brutal ruler whose promotion of Yahweh coincided with a program of despotism. According to his own histories, Solomon kept an enormous harem of some 300 wives and 700 concubines, many of them drawn from subject or allied peoples. His palace complex—of which the Temple was a part—allowed him to rule in the grand style of ancient Near Eastern potentates. To finance his expensive tastes and programs, Solomon instituted oppressive taxation and imposed customs duties on the lucrative caravan trade that passed through his country. With the help of the Phoenician king of Tyre, Solomon constructed a commercial fleet whose ships plied the waters of the Red Sea and beyond, trading—among other commodities—the gold and copper mined by Solomon's slaves.

Two Accounts of Saul's Anointing

> *When the charismatic judge Samuel chose Saul as the first king of the Hebrews, he opened a new chapter in the political history of Israel. But Saul's kingship was not a success, and Samuel ultimately turned against him, supporting Saul's rival (and son-in-law), David. These two quite different accounts of Samuel's anointing of Saul reflect the tensions that later arose between them—and were probably written down during the later kingship of David, Saul's challenger and successor. The first account also suggests the ambivalence some Hebrews felt about having a human king at all, doubts which may have been shared by Saul himself.*

1 Samuel 8:4–22, 10:20–25

All the elders of Israel gathered together and [said to Samuel]: "You are old and your sons do not follow in your ways; appoint for us, then, a king to govern us, like other nations." But the thing displeased Samuel [who] prayed to the Lord, and the Lord said to Samuel, "Listen to the voice of the people in all that they say to you; for they have not rejected you, but they have rejected me from being king over them. Just as they have done to me, from the day I brought them up out of Egypt to this day, forsaking me and serving other gods, so they are also doing to you. Now then, listen to their voice; only—you shall solemnly warn them, and show them the ways of the king who shall reign over them." So Samuel reported all the words of the Lord to the people who were asking for a king. "These will be the ways of the king who will reign over you: he will take sons and appoint them to his chariots . . . he will take your daughters to be perfumers and cooks and bakers . . . he will take one-tenth of your grain and your vineyards and give it to his officers and courtiers . . . and one-tenth of your flocks, and you shall be his slaves." But the people refused to listen, and Samuel said to the people, "Each of you return to his home."

Then Samuel brought all the tribes of Israel near, and the tribe of Benjamin was chosen by lot. He brought the tribe of Benjamin near, [organized] by its families . . . and Saul the son of Kish was chosen by lot. But when they sought him, he could not be found. So they inquired again of the Lord . . . and the Lord said, "See, he has hidden himself among the baggage." Then they ran and brought him from there. When he took his stand among the people, he was head and shoulders taller than any of them. Samuel said, "You see the one whom the Lord has chosen? There is no one like him among the people." And the people all shouted, "Long live the king!" Samuel told the people the rights and duties of the kingship; and he wrote them in a book and laid it up before the Lord.

tribute from various kingdoms that had not paid up for generations. Those who refused fell victim to his armies.

When Tiglath-Pileser III died in 727 B.C.E., many of these recently conquered states rebelled, but Tiglath-Pileser's son, Shalmeneser V, energetically crushed them. When he died in battle, he was quickly replaced by one of his military commanders, who took the name Sargon II (722–705 B.C.E.) and claimed to be the direct successor of Sargon of Akkad, the great king of Sumer and the first great king in Mesopotamian history, nearly 1,500 years earlier (see Chapter 1). Like the Hebrews, then, Sargon and his successors skillfully deployed history as a political tool. Eventually, they extended the frontiers of the Assyrian Empire from western Iran to the shores of the Mediterranean. Briefly, they even subjugated parts of Egypt. Sargon himself put an end to the kingdom of Israel in 722, enslaving and deporting most of the population, and he terrified the southern kingdom of Judah into remaining a loyal and quiet vassal. The ancient kingdom of Elam on the Iranian plateau—a civilization almost as old as Sumer— also fell during this period. By the seventh century B.C.E., Assyria was the unrivaled power of the ancient Near East.

1 Samuel 9:1–10:1

There was a man of Benjamin whose name was Kish . . . [who] had a son whose name was Saul, a handsome young man . . . he stood head and shoulders above everyone else. Now the donkeys of Kish had strayed. So Kish said to his son Saul, "Take one of the boys with you; go and look for the donkeys." . . . As they were entering [a] town, they saw Samuel coming out toward them on his way up to the shrine. Now the day before Saul came, the Lord revealed to Samuel, "Tomorrow about this time I will send you a man from the land of Benjamin, and you shall anoint him to be ruler over my people Israel. He shall save my people from the hand of the Philistines; for I have seen the suffering of my people, because their outcry has come to me." . . . Saul approached Samuel inside the gate and said, "Tell me please, where is the house of the seer?" Samuel answered Saul, "I am the seer, go up before me to the shrine. . . . As for your donkeys that were lost three days ago, give no further thought to them, for they have been found. And on whom is all Israel's desire fixed, if not on you and your ancestral house?" Saul answered, "I am only a Benjaminite, from the least of the tribes of Israel, and my family is the humblest of all the families of the tribe of Benjamin. Why then have you spoken of me this way?" . . . As they were going down to the outskirts of town, Samuel said to Saul, "Tell the boy to go on before us . . . that I may make known to you the word of God." Samuel took a vial of oil and poured it on [Saul's] head and kissed him; he said: "The Lord has anointed you ruler over his people Israel. You shall reign over the people of the Lord and you will save them from the hand of their enemies all around."

Source: *The New Oxford Annotated Bible* (Oxford: 1994) (slightly adapted, source for both documents).

Questions for Analysis

1. Do these two accounts fit together? How do they differ? Why would both have been preserved in the Book of Samuel?

2. What view of kingship emerges in the first account? What are the attributes of a king, and what is the relationship between the king, his god, and the priest anointing him? What is the role of the people in his selection?

3. The writers of Jewish scripture judged kings by their observance of the law, their zeal in fighting against competing religious cults, and their support of centralized worship at the temple in Jerusalem. How did this form of theocracy in ancient Israel compare to that in Egypt and Mesopotamia?

Neo-Assyrian Government and Administration

The Neo-Assyrian Empire was a military dictatorship, built on the ability of its army to spread terror and oppress both enemies and subjects alike. At its head was a hereditary monarch regarded as the earthly representative of the Assyrians' patron god, Assur. When his army was not in the field, the king's time was taken up with elaborate sacrifices and rituals to appease the "great god." Divination and the consultation of oracles were central features of this religion, because the Neo-Assyrian king—as chief priest—had to be able to discern the will of Assur through the portents of nature.

Supporting the empire's centralized authority was an extensive bureaucracy of governors, high priests, and military commanders—professions by no means mutually exclusive. These administrators formed the highest class in Neo-Assyrian society and exercised local authority on

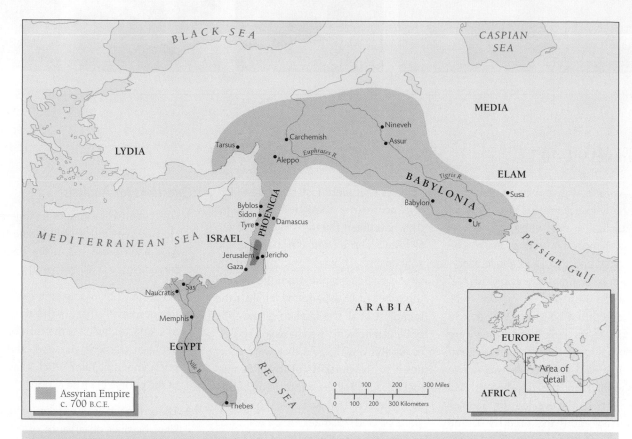

THE NEO-ASSYRIAN EMPIRE, C. 700 B.C.E. ▪ *What were the territorial boundaries of the Neo-Assyrian Empire?* ▪ *Why would the Assyrians concentrate their efforts in the river valleys and along the coast, neglecting the Syrian interior?* ▪ *Notice the location of the Neo-Assyrian capitals of Nineveh and Assur; how was their situation in Mesopotamia likely to affect the Assyrians' sense of their own historical identity?* ▪ *Consider the position of Egypt. Why might the Assyrians find it difficult to subjugate Egypt permanently?*

behalf of the king. They maintained lines of transport and communication, which were the engines of imperial hegemony, and they oversaw construction of an extensive network of roads across the Near East that served these needs for centuries. The Neo-Assyrian state also deployed a system of spies and messengers to report to the royal court on the activities of subjects and provincial governors.

These provincial governors collected tribute, recruited for the army, and administered the king's law. Not surprising for a people so mindful of historical precedent, the Assyrians modeled their laws on the code of Hammurabi, though many of their penalties were more severe. The harshest punishments were reserved for practices deemed detrimental to human reproduction; the penalties for homosexuality and abortion were particularly harsh. Neo-Assyrian law was also rigidly patriarchal, which entailed substantial revision of Hammurabi's code: now only husbands had the power of divorce, and they were legally permitted to inflict a variety of penalties on their wives, ranging from corporal punishment to mutilation and death.

The Assyrian Military-Religious Ethos

The Assyrians' new religious, political, and military ideology had taken shape during the long centuries when they fought for survival, and it then became the foundational ethos for their empire's relentless conquests. Its two fundamental tenets were the waging of holy war and the exaction of tribute through terror.

The Neo-Assyrians were convinced that their god demanded the constant expansion of his worship through military conquest. Essentially, their army belonged to Assur, and all who did not accept Assur's supremacy were, by that fact alone, enemies of Assur's people. Ritual humiliation of a defeated city's gods was therefore a regular feature of conquest. Statues of conquered gods would be carried off to the Neo-Assyrian capital, where they would remain as hostages at the court of Assur. Meanwhile, an image of Assur himself—usually represented as a sun disk with the head and shoulders of an archer—would be installed in the defeated city, and the conquered people would be required to worship him. Although conquered peoples did not have to abandon their previous gods altogether, they were made to feel their gods' inferiority. The Assyrians were therefore strict henotheists, meaning that they acknowledged the existence of other gods but believed that one god should be the supreme deity of all peoples.

For the Neo-Assyrians, "receiving tribute" meant the taking of plunder. Rather than defeating their foes once and imposing formal obligations, the Assyrians raided even their vanquished foes each year. This strategy kept the Neo-Assyrian military machine primed for battle, but it did little to inspire loyalty among subject peoples, who often felt that they had nothing to lose through rebellion. Moreover, annual invasions toughened the forces of the Neo-Assyrians' subjects. To counter them, imperial battle tactics became notoriously savage—even by the standards of ancient warfare, which regarded the mutilation of prisoners, systematic rape, and mass deportations as com-

monplace. Neo-Assyrian artwork and inscriptions often celebrate the butchering and torture of their enemies. Smiling archers are shown shooting fleeing enemies in the back while remorseless soldiers impale captives on stakes.

The Neo-Assyrian army was not a seasonal army of part-time warriors or peasant conscripts, but rather a massive standing force of more than 100,000 soldiers. Because the Assyrians had mastered iron-smelting techniques on a large scale, they could equip their fighting men with high-quality steel weapons that overwhelmed opponents still reliant on bronze. The organization of this army also contributed to its success. At its core were heavily armed and armored shock troops, equipped with a variety of thrusting weapons and bearing tall shields for protection. They were the main force for crushing enemy infantry in the field and for routing the inhabitants of an enemy city once inside. To harass enemy infantry and break up their formations, the Assyrians deployed light skirmishers with slings and javelins, and they combined archery and chariotry as never before. They also developed the first true cavalry force in the West, with individual warriors mounted on armored steeds, wielding bows and arrows or heavy lances. They even trained a highly skilled corps of combat engineers to undermine city walls and to build catapults, siege engines, battering rams, and battle towers.

The Legacy of Neo-Assyrian Power

The successors of Sargon II continued these military policies while devoting great energy to promoting an Assyrian cultural legacy. Sargon's immediate successor Sennacherib (*sen-AH-sher-ib*, 704–681 B.C.E.) rebuilt the ancient Assyrian city of Nineveh, fortifying it with a double wall for a circuit of nine miles. He constructed an enormous palace there, raised on a giant platform decorated with marble, ivory, and exotic woods; and he ordered the construction of a massive irrigation system, including an aqueduct that carried fresh water to the city from thirty miles away. His son rebuilt the conquered city of Babylon along similar lines, and was also a patron of the arts and sciences. His grandson Assurbanipal (*ah-sur-BAHN-en-pahl*, r. 669–627 B.C.E.) was perhaps the greatest of all the Neo-Assyrian kings. For a time, he ruled the entire delta region of northern Egypt. He also enacted a series of internal reforms, seeking ways to govern his empire more peacefully.

By Neo-Assyrian standards, Assurbanipal was an enlightened ruler, and one to whom we owe a tremendous debt. Like Sargon II before him, he had a strong sense of the rich traditions of Mesopotamian history and laid claim

NEO-ASSYRIAN ATROCITIES. Judean captives whose city has fallen to the Neo-Assyrian king Sennacherib (704–681 B.C.E.) are shown being impaled on stakes. This triumphal carving comes from the walls of Sennacherib's palace at Nineveh. ■ *What would be the purpose of advertising these captives' fates?*

ASSURBANIPAL FEASTING WITH HIS WIFE IN A HANGING GARDEN. Even in this peaceful, domestic scene, the severed head of the king's recently defeated enemy, the king of Elam, can be seen hanging from the pine tree on the left.

to it. But he did this much more systematically: he ordered the construction of a magnificent library at the great capital of Nineveh, where all the cultural monuments of Mesopotamian literature were to be copied and preserved. This library also served as an archive for the correspondence and official acts of the king. Fortunately, this trove of documentation has survived. Our knowledge of history, not to mention all modern editions of the *Epic of Gilgamesh*, derive from the library at Nineveh.

When Assurbanipal died in 627 B.C.E., the Neo-Assyrian Empire appeared to be at its zenith. Its borders were secure, the realm was largely at peace with its neighbors, its kings had adorned their capitals with magnificent artwork, and the hanging gardens of Babylon were already famous: these were artificial slopes whose cascading flowers and trees were fed by irrigation systems that pumped water uphill, an amazing marriage of engineering and horticulture. The collapse of this empire is therefore all the more dramatic for its suddenness. Within fifteen years of Assurbanipal's reign, Nineveh lay in ruins. An alliance had formed between the Indo-European Medes of Iran and the Chaldeans, a Semitic people who controlled the southern half of Babylonia. By 605 B.C.E., the Chaldeans had occupied Babylon and destroyed the last remnants of Neo-Assyrian power on the upper Euphrates, becoming the predominant imperial power in Mesopotamia and the Levant. In 586 B.C.E., they captured Jerusalem, destroyed the Temple, and deported the population of Judea to Babylon. Meanwhile, the Medes retired to the Iranian Plateau to extend their suzerainty there.

THE RISE OF THE PERSIANS

In the sixth century B.C.E., the Persian Empire emerged as the successor state to the Neo-Assyrian kings. This was after the region had been ruled for a few decades by the Chaldean Empire (612–539 B.C.E.) and the Lydian kingdom. Once the Persians had thrown off the Chaldeans' dominance, they would in turn construct the largest empire known to the world until that time.

The Persian Empire of Cyrus the Great

The Persians came to power relatively suddenly, under an extraordinary prince named Cyrus who succeeded to the rule of a single Persian tribe in 559 B.C.E. Shortly thereafter, Cyrus made himself ruler of all the Persians and then, around 549 B.C.E., challenged the lordship of the Medes and began to claim dominion over lands stretching from the Persian Gulf to the Halys River in Asia Minor.

This brought the Persians into close contact with the kingdom of Lydia. The Lydians had attained great prosperity as producers of gold and silver specie and as intermediaries for overland commerce between Mesopotamia and the Aegean. Most important, they were the first people in the ancient Near East to use precious-metal coinage as a medium of exchange for goods and services. When Cyrus came to power, their king was Croesus (*CREE-suhs*), a man whose reputation as the possessor of untold riches survives in the expression "rich as Croesus." Distrusting his new neighbor, Croesus decided to launch a preventive strike against the Persians in order to preserve his own kingdom from conquest. According to the Greek historian Herodotus, he took the precaution of asking the oracle of Apollo at Delphi whether this strategy was a good one, and was told that if he attacked the Persians he would destroy a great nation. The oracle's pronouncement was both ambiguous and true: the nation Croesus destroyed was his own. Cyrus defeated his forces in 546 B.C.E.

Cyrus then invaded Mesopotamia in 539 B.C.E., striking so quickly that he took Babylon without a fight. Once he was in Babylon, the entire Chaldean Empire was his for the taking, though his own imperial policies proved very different from those of his predecessors in that region. Cyrus freed the Hebrews who had been held captive in Babylon since 586 B.C.E. and sent them back to Jerusalem, helping them to rebuild their temple and allowing them to set up a semi-independent vassal state. Cyrus also allowed other conquered peoples considerable self-determination, especially with respect to cultural and religious practices—a marked reversal of Neo-Assyrian and Chaldean policies. When Cyrus died in battle in 530 B.C.E., Persian expansion continued and his son even conquered Egypt in 525 B.C.E. Two hundred years later, a young Macedonian king, Alexander, would emulate many of Cyrus's policies and build an empire sustained by many of the same strategies (see Chapter 4).

AN EARLY LYDIAN COIN. Probably struck during the reign of Croesus, this coin was one of many that facilitated long-distance trade by making wealth portable.

The Consolidation of Persian Rule

Cyrus's son Cambyses II was a warrior king like his father, but after his death he left the Persian Empire a cumbersome and poorly organized collection of rapid conquests. After a short period of civil war, the aristocratic inner circle that had served both him and his father settled on a collateral member of the royal family as the new king. This was Darius, whose long reign of thirty-five years (521–486 B.C.E.) consolidated his predecessors' military gains by improving the administration of the Persian state. Darius divided the empire into provinces, each of which was administered by an official called a *satrap*. Although satraps enjoyed extensive powers and considerable political latitude, they owed fixed tributes and absolute loyalty to the central government, as did vassal states such as the technically autonomous Hebrew kingdom.

Adhering to the tolerant policy of Cyrus, Darius allowed the various peoples of the empire to retain most of their local institutions while enforcing a standardized central currency and a system of weights and measures. Beyond this, he had little interest in imposing onerous taxes, martial law, or the Persians' own religious practices on subject peoples. After centuries of Neo-Assyrian and Chaldean tyranny, the light hand of Persian rule was welcomed throughout the empire's far-reaching lands.

Darius was also a great builder. He erected a new royal residence and ceremonial capital which the Greeks called Persepolis ("Persia City"). He ordered a canal dug from the Nile to the Red Sea to facilitate trade with the Egyptian interior, and installed irrigation systems on the Persian plateau and on the fringe of the Syrian desert to increase agricultural production. Darius also expanded the existing Assyrian road system to enhance trade and communications throughout his huge realm. The most famous artery was the Royal Road, stretching 1,600 miles from Susa, near the Persian Gulf, to Sardis (the former Lydian capital) near the Aegean. Government couriers along this road constituted the first postal system, carrying messages and goods in relay stages from one post to another. Each post was a day's horseback ride from the next, where a fresh horse and rider would be ready to carry the dispatches brought by the postman before him. An extensive imperial spy network also used this postal system and was famed throughout Persia as "the eyes and ears of the king."

Darius was an extraordinarily gifted administrator, but as a military strategist he made an enormous mistake when he attempted to extend Persian hegemony into Greece. Cyrus's conquest of Lydia had made Persia the ruler of some long-established Greek-speaking cities on the western coast of Asia Minor, a region called Ionia. But these cities resisted

THE PERSIAN EMPIRE UNDER DARIUS I, 521–486 B.C.E. Consider the location of the Persian heartland and the four administrative centers of Persepolis, Susa, Ecbatana, and Sardis. ▪ *What older kingdoms and empires did the Persian Empire contain?* ▪ *Why is the Royal Road especially noted on this map?* ▪ *How did Darius I successfully rule such a large and complex empire?*

even the easy terms of Persian rule, desiring instead to model themselves on the self-governing city-states that had come into being across the Aegean. Consequently, between 499 and 494 B.C.E., the Greeks of Asia waged a war for independence and briefly gained the support of troops from Athens, who joined the Greeks of Ionia in burning the Persian administrative center at Sardis. Darius quelled this uprising and then decided to send a force to punish Athens and serve notice of Persian dominion over all Greek states. But at the battle of Marathon in 490 B.C.E., the Athenians dealt Darius the only major setback of his reign. And when his son and successor, Xerxes (*ZEhRK-zees*), attempted to avenge this humiliation in 480 B.C.E., a resistance led by both Athens and Sparta forced him to retreat and abandon his plans a year later. (We will discuss these events at greater length in Chapter 3.)

The Persians were thus compelled to recognize that they had reached the westward limits of their expansion. Thereafter, they concentrated on their Asian possessions and used money and diplomacy to keep the Greeks in check. This was not difficult, because the Greeks' hasty union in the face of Persian hegemony was short-lived, and they were too

embroiled in wars with one another to pose any threat to Persia.

The richness of their culture and the general tolerance they exhibited served the Persians well in maintaining their enormous empire. Unlike the Neo-Assyrian or Chaldean rulers, the Persians could count on the loyalty and even the affection of their subjects. In fact, their imperial model— the accommodation of local institutions and practices, consistent administration through a trained bureaucracy, and rapid communications between center and periphery— would be the one adopted by the great and lasting empires of all subsequent Western civilizations.

The Legacy of Zoroastrianism

The Persians' political and cultural achievements were paralleled by a spiritual one: Zoroastrianism. This important religion was one of the three major universal faiths known to the world before Christianity and Islam, along with Buddhism and Judaism. Its founder was Zarathustra, known

A CYLINDRICAL SEAL OF DARIUS THE GREAT (522–486 B.C.E.). Seals were used in place of signatures to authenticate documents and correspondence. The cylindrical matrix (right) was rolled in soft wax to create an impression. This finely wrought example shows the king in a chariot, hunting lions with a bow. A winged representation of the god Ahura-Mazda rises above the scene.

to the Greeks as Zoroaster, a Persian who probably lived shortly before 600 B.C.E. Zarathustra sought to reform the traditional customs of the Persian tribes by eradicating polytheism, animal sacrifice, and magic. That is, he wanted to redefine religion as an ethical practice common to all people, rather than a set of rituals and superstitions that caused divisions among people.

Zoroastrianism teaches that there is one supreme god in the universe, whom Zarathustra called Ahura-Mazda, "Wise Lord." Ahura-Mazda is the essence of light, truth, and righteousness; there is nothing wrathful or wicked about him, and his goodness extends to everyone, not just to one people or tribe. How, then, can there be evil and suffering in the world? Because, Zarathustra posited, there is a counter-deity, Ahriman, treacherous and malignant, who rules the forces of darkness. Yet Zarathustra also posited that Ahura-Mazda must be vastly stronger than Ahriman. Later teachers and priests of Zoroastrianism, the magi, placed greater emphasis on the dualism of these divine forces: they insisted that Ahura-Mazda and Ahriman are evenly matched, engaged in a desperate and eternal struggle for supremacy. According to them, light will not triumph over darkness until the Last Day, when the forces of Ahura-Mazda vanquish those of Ahriman forever. This vision of the universe would prove enormously influential, informing the developing theologies of Christianity and Islam—not to mention the plots of much modern science fiction, fantasy literature, and film.

The devotion of the Persian imperial dynasty to Zarathustra's teachings made Zoroastrianism important to the conduct of Persian government and helps to explain the tolerance of Persian rule. Unlike the Neo-Assyrians, the Chaldeans, or even the Egyptians, the Persian kings saw themselves as presiding over an assemblage of different nations whose customs and beliefs they were prepared to tolerate. Whereas Mesopotamian potentates characteristically called themselves "true king," Persian rulers took the title "king of kings" or "great king," implying that they recognized the legitimacy of other kings who ruled under their canopy. This same spirit is reflected in Persian architecture, which drew freely and creatively on Sumerian, Babylonian, Assyrian, Egyptian, and Greek influences yet nonetheless created a distinctively Persian style.

Unlike other ancient religions, then, Zoroastrianism did not exalt the power of a godlike king or support any particular political regime. It was a personal religion, making private, spiritual demands as opposed to public, ritual ones. Its Wise Lord supports neither tribes nor states but only individuals who serve the cause of truth and justice. These individuals possess free will and can choose to sin or not to sin; they are not compelled by an array of conflicting gods to act in particular ways. Zoroastrianism thus urges its adherents

Competing Viewpoints

Two Perspectives on Imperial Rule

> *These two inscriptions exemplify two very different attitudes toward imperial power and two very different methods of achieving it. The first glorifies the victories of the Assyrian king Esarhaddon in Syria and is one of the most important records of his reign (681–669 B.C.E.). The second commemorates the taking of Babylon by the Persian king Cyrus the Great (c. 559–530 B.C.E.), whose empire came to encompass and surpass that of the Assyrians.*

The *Stele* of King Esarhaddon at Senjirli, c. 680 B.C.E.

To Assur, father of the gods, lover of my priesthood, Anu mighty and preeminent, who called me by name, Ba'al, the exalted lord, establisher of my dynasty, Ea, the wise, all-knowing . . . Ishtar, lady of battle and combat, who goes at my side . . . all of them who determine my destiny, who grant to the king, their favorite, power and might . . . the king, the offering of whose sacrifices the great gods love . . . their unsparing weapons they have presented him as a royal gift . . . [he] who has brought all the lands in submission at his feet, who has imposed tribute and tax upon them; conqueror of his foes, destroyer of his enemies, the king, who

as to his walk is a storm, and as to his deeds, a raging wolf; . . . the onset of his battle is powerful, he is a consuming flame, a fire that does not sink: son of Sennacherib, king of the universe, king of Assyria, grandson of Sargon, king of the universe, king of Assyria, viceroy of Babylon, king of Sumer and Akkad. . . . I am powerful, I am all-powerful, I am a hero, I am gigantic, I am colossal, I am honored, I am magnified, I am without an equal among all kings, the chosen one of Assur . . . the great lord [who], in order to show to the peoples the immensity of my mighty deeds, made powerful my kingship over the four regions of the world and made my name great.

. . . Of Tirhakah, king of Egypt and Kush, the accursed . . . without cessation I slew multitudes of his men, and him I smote five times with the point of my javelin, with wounds, no recovery. Memphis, his royal city, in half a day . . . I besieged, I captured, I destroyed, I devastated, I burned with fire. . . . The root of Kush I tore up out of Egypt and not one therein escaped to submit to me.

Source: Daniel David Luckenbill, ed., *Ancient Records of Assyria and Babylonia*, Vol. 2 (Chicago: 1926–27), pp. 224–27.

Inscription Honoring Cyrus, c. 539

He [the god Marduk] scanned and looked (through) all the countries, searching for a righteous ruler who would lead him. (Then) he pronounced the name of Cyrus, king of Anshan [Persia], declared him to be the leader of the world. . . . And he (Cyrus) did always endeavor to treat according to justice the black-headed [people] whom he (Marduk) made him conquer. Marduk, the great lord, a protector of his people/worshipers, beheld with pleasure his good deeds and his upright mind, (and therefore) ordered

him to march against his city Babylon. He made him set out on the road to Babylon, going at his side like a real friend. His widespread troops—their number, like the water of a river, could not be established—strolled along, their weapons packed away. Without any battle, he made them enter his town Babylon, sparing Babylon any calamity. He delivered into his hands Nabonidus, the king who did not worship him. All the inhabitants of Babylon as well as of the entire country of Sumer and Akkad, princes and governors (included), bowed to him

and kissed his feet, jubilant that he (had received) the kingship, and with shining faces. Happily they greeted him as a master through whose help they had come (again) to life from death (and) had all been spared damage and disaster, and they worshiped his name.

I am Cyrus, king of the world, great king, legitimate king, king of Babylon, king of Sumer and Akkad, king of the four rims (of the earth), son of Cambyses, great king, king of Anshan, grandson of Cyrus, great king, king of Anshan, descendent of Teipes, great king, king of

Anshan, of a family (which) always (exercised) kingship; whose rule Bel and Nebo love, whom they want as king to please their hearts.

When I entered Babylon as a friend and (when) I established the seat of the government in the palace of the ruler under jubilation and rejoicing. . . . My numerous troops walked around Babylon in peace, I did not allow anybody to terrorize (any place) of the (the country of Sumer) and Akkad. I strove for peace in Babylon and in all his (other) sacred cities. . . . I abolished the . . . [yoke] which was against their (social) standing, I brought relief to their dilapidated housing, putting (thus) an end to their (main)

complaints. . . . All the kings of the entire world from the Upper to the Lower Sea, those who are seated in throne rooms, (those who) live in other (types of buildings as well as) all the kings of the West living in tents, brought their heavy tributes and kissed my feet in Babylon.

Source: Excerpted from James B. Pritchard, ed. *Ancient Near Eastern Texts Relating to the Old Testament*, 3rd ed. (Princeton, NJ: 1969), pp. 315–16.

Questions for Analysis

1. Both of these inscriptions constitute propaganda, but of different kinds.

How do they differ? What audience(s) are they addressing? What function(s) does each inscription serve?

2. Each of these rulers claims to have a close relationship with the divine. How do those relationships differ, and what do those differences reveal about their attitudes to kingship and its sources of power?

3. Both of these kings boast of their royal lineage and their connections to past rulers. How different or similar are these perspectives? What do they reveal about these kings' awareness of history?

to choose good over evil, to be truthful, to love and help one another to the best of their powers, to aid the poor, and to practice generous hospitality. Those who do so will be rewarded in an afterlife, when the dead are resurrected on Judgment Day and consigned either to a realm of joy or to the flames of despair. In the scriptures of the Zoroastrian faith, known as the Avesta (compiled, like the Bible, over the course of many centuries), the rewards for righteousness are great but not immediate. They are spiritual, not material.

THE DEVELOPMENT OF HEBREW MONOTHEISM

Of all the important developments that we have traced in our study of the Iron Age Near East, perhaps none is of greater significance than monotheism: the belief in a single god, the creator and ruler of all things. This development is traditionally associated with the Hebrews, but even the Hebrews were not always monotheists. Those who argued for the exclusive worship of Yahweh were a minority within

Hebrew society, albeit a vocal and assertive one. How the Hebrews came to regard Yahweh as the only divine being in the universe, and to root their identity in such an exclusive religious outlook, is a phenomenon that can only be understood within its historical context.

From Monolatry to Monotheism

For those who later advocated the exclusive worship of Yahweh, the early history of the Hebrews was full of embarrassments. Even the Hebrew scriptures reveal their propensity for the worship of many gods. Yahweh himself, in commanding that his people "have no other gods before me," clearly acknowledged the existence of other gods. The older, polytheistic Hebrew religion honored nature spirits such as Azazel and the Canaanite deity El, whose name is an important element in many Hebrew place-names (for example, Bethel) and soon became a synonym for "god." The temple built by Solomon at Jerusalem had even included altars dedicated to Ba'al and his wife Asherah, a fertility goddess. Later Hebrew kings continued such practices, overriding the protests of religious purists devoted to Yahweh.

By the beginning of the first millennium, however, the Hebrews living under the rule of David began to promote monolatry, meaning that they exalted one god without denying the existence of others. Although the legendary prophet Moses is often credited as the first promoter of Yahweh's cult, sometime around the middle of the second millennium B.C.E., the ascendancy of Yahweh really took place much later, under the influence of the Levites, a tribe who claimed unique priestly authority over Yahwah's worship and sought to enhance their own power and prestige by discrediting other gods.

The success of their campaign rested on the Levites' access to writing. As we have frequently noted, the written word was especially potent in the ancient world because the skills necessary for its mastery were rare. In an age of constant threats to Hebrew religious and political sovereignty, the literacy of the Levites thus helped to preserve and promote Yahweh's worship. So did the political supremacy of David's dynasty, which bolstered its own legitimacy by allying itself with the Levites. The result was a centralized cult situated in the new royal capital of Jerusalem, which attempted to link the political and the religious identity of the Hebrews to the acknowledgment of Yahweh as the supreme god.

Nevertheless, the worship of other Hebrew gods actually increased in the eighth and seventh centuries B.C.E., perhaps in reaction to the austere morality demanded and imposed by the Yahwists. One of these, Jeremiah (c. 637–587 B.C.E.), railed against "foreign" cults and warned of the disastrous consequences that would arise if Yahweh's people did not remain faithful to him. For the Yahweh of this era was still imagined as a conventional god. He was understood as possessing a physical body and was often portrayed as capricious and irascible. Further, he was not omnipotent; his power was largely confined to the territory occupied by the Hebrews.

Still, some of the Hebrews' most important contributions to subsequent Western religions crystallized during this period. One was a theology of Yahweh's transcendence: the teaching that God is not part of nature but exists outside of it. God can therefore be understood, in purely intellectual or abstract terms, as entirely separate from the operations of the natural world. Complementing this principle was the belief that Yahweh had appointed humans to be the rulers of nature by divine mandate. In the book of Genesis, when Yahweh orders Adam and Eve to "replenish the earth and subdue it, and have dominion over . . . every living thing," his injunction stands in striking contrast to other accounts of creation in which humans are made to serve the gods. Finally, Hebrew religious thought was moving in this period toward the articulation of universal ethics—a universal theory of justice and righteousness. According to the Babylonian flood story, for example, a particularly petulant god destroys humanity because their noise deprives him of sleep.

In Genesis, by contrast, Yahweh sends a flood in punishment for human wickedness but saves Noah and his family because "Noah was a just man."

The Hebrews honored Yahweh during this era by subscribing to certain moral precepts and taboos. The Ten Commandments as they now appear in Exodus 20:3–17 may not yet have existed in that exact form, but they certainly reflect earlier ethical injunctions against murder, adultery, lying, and greed. In addition, the Hebrews observed an array of ritual practices unusual in the ancient world, such as infant circumcision, adherence to strict dietary laws, and refraining from labor on the seventh day of the week.

Yet the moral standards imposed by Yahweh on the Hebrew community were not binding when the Hebrews dealt with outsiders. Lending at interest, for example, was not acceptable among Hebrews but was quite acceptable between a Hebrew and a non-Hebrew. Such distinctions applied also to more serious issues, such as the killing of

THE GODDESS ASHERAH. The Canaanite fertility goddess, Asherah, was the wife of the god Ba'al (or his father, El), but she also figures in some inscriptions as the wife of the Hebrew god Yahweh. One Hebrew king placed an image of her in the temple of Yahweh at Jerusalem. ■ *Why would this be viewed as controversial?*

civilians in battle. When the Hebrews conquered territories in Canaan, they took "all the spoil of the cities, and every man they smote with the sword . . . until they had destroyed them." Far from having any doubts about such a brutal policy, the Hebrews believed that Yahweh had inspired the Canaanites to resist so that the Hebrews could slaughter them: "For it was the Lord's doing to harden their hearts that they should come against Israel in battle, in order that they should be utterly destroyed, and should receive no mercy but be exterminated" (Joshua 11:20).

With the political fragmentation of the Hebrew kingdoms after Solomon's death, important regional distinctions arose within Yahweh's cult. As mentioned above, the rulers of the northern kingdom discouraged their citizens from participating in ritual activities at Jerusalem, thereby earning the disapproval of the Jerusalem-based Yahwists who shaped the biblical tradition. The erosion of a cohesive Hebrew identity was further accelerated by the Neo-Assyrians, who under Sargon II absorbed the northern kingdom as a province and enslaved nearly 28,000 Hebrews. The southern kingdom of Judah survived, but political collaboration with the Neo-Assyrians also meant acceptance of the god Assur.

This Neo-Assyrian threat was the whetstone on which the Yahwist prophets sharpened their demands for an exclusive monotheism that went beyond monolatry. Hebrew prophets were practical political leaders as well as religious figures, and most of them understood that military resistance to the Neo-Assyrians was futile. So if the Hebrews were to survive as a people, they had to emphasize the one thing that separated them from everyone else in the known world: the worship of Yahweh and the denial of all other gods. The prophets' insistence that Yahweh alone should be exalted was thus an aggressive reaction to the equally aggressive promotion of Assur by the Neo-Assyrians.

The foremost Hebrew prophets of this era were Amos and Hosea, who preached in the kingdom of Israel before it fell to the Neo-Assyrians in 722 B.C.E.; Isaiah and Jeremiah, who preached in Judah before its fall in 586 B.C.E.; and Ezekiel and the "second Isaiah" (the Book of Isaiah had at least two different authors), who continued to preach "by the waters of Babylon" during the Hebrews' exile there. Despite some differences in emphasis, these prophets' messages consistently emphasize three core doctrines.

RECONSTRUCTION OF THE ISHTAR GATE. This is a reconstruction of one of the fifty-foot-high entrance gates built into the walls of Babylon by King Nebuchadnezzar around 575 B.C.E. About half of this reconstruction in the Pergamon Museum of Berlin, is original.

1. Yahweh is the ruler of the universe. He even makes use of peoples other than the Hebrews to accomplish his purposes. The gods of other nations are false gods. There has never been and never will be more than this one god.
2. Yahweh is exclusively a god of righteousness. He wills only the good, and evil in the world comes from humanity, not from him.
3. Because Yahweh is righteous, he demands ethical behavior from his people. Over and above ritual and sacrifice, he requires that his followers "seek justice, relieve the oppressed, protect the fatherless, and plead for the widow."

The prophet Amos summarized these teachings when he expressed Yahweh's resounding warning in the eighth century B.C.E.:

I hate, I despise your feasts, and I take no delight in your solemn assemblies. Even though you offer me your burnt offerings and cereal offerings, I will not accept them, and the peace offerings of your fatted beasts I will not look upon. Take away from me the noise of your songs; to the melody of your harps I will not listen. But let justice roll down like waters, and righteousness like an ever-flowing stream. (Amos 5:21–24)

Judaism Takes Shape

Through their insistence on monotheism as the cornerstone of Hebrew identity, the Yahwists made it possible for the Hebrews to survive under Neo-Assyrian domination. And as this threat receded in the late seventh century B.C.E., so the Yahwists triumphed religiously and politically. The king of Judah during the waning years of the Neo-Assyrian Empire, Josiah (621–609 B.C.E.), was a committed monotheist whose court employed prominent prophets, including Jeremiah. With his own power increasing, Josiah found himself in a position to pursue significant reforms. He presided over the redrafting and revision of the "Law of Moses" to bring it into line with current policies, and it was during his reign that the Book of Deuteronomy was "discovered" and hailed as Moses's "Second Law." Deuteronomy is the most stridently monotheistic book of the Hebrew Bible, and it lent weight to this new political program.

But within a generation of King Josiah's death, the Chaldeans under Nebuchadnezzar conquered Jerusalem, destroyed the Temple, and carried thousands of Hebrews off to Babylon in 587/586 B.C.E. This Babylonian Captivity brought many challenges, paramount among them the maintenance of the Hebrews' hard-won religious identity. The leading voices in defining that identity continued to be the patriotic Yahwists, the same people who would later spearhead the return to Palestine after Cyrus captured Babylon and liberated the Hebrews two generations later. Among the Yahwists, the prophet Ezekiel stressed that salvation could be found only through religious purity, which meant ignoring all foreign gods and acknowledging only Yahweh. Kingdoms and states and empires came to nothing in the long run, Ezekiel said. What mattered for those living in exile was the creature God had made in his image—man—and the relationship between God and his creation.

This period of captivity and exile was therefore decisive in forging a universal religion that transcended politics. Just as Yahweh existed outside creation, so the people who worshiped him could exist outside of a Hebrew kingdom. In Babylon, the worship of Yahweh therefore became something different; it became Judaism, a religion that was not tied to any particular political system or territory—for after 586 B.C.E., there was neither a Hebrew ruling class nor a Hebrew state. Outside of Judah, Judaism paradoxically flourished. This was an unparalleled achievement in the ancient world: the survival of a religion that had no political power to back it and no holy place to ground it.

After 538 B.C.E., when Cyrus permitted the Hebrews of Babylon to return to their lands and to rebuild the Temple, Jerusalem became once again the central holy place of Hebrew religious life. But the new developments that had fashioned Judaism during captivity would prove lasting, despite the religious conflicts that soon erupted. These conflicts led to ever more specific assertions about the nature of Judaism, and to religious teachings that focused on ethical conduct as an obligation owed by all human beings toward their creator, independent of place or political identity. The observance of ritual requirements and religious taboos would continue,

After You Read This Chapter

Visit StudySpace for quizzes, additional review materials, and multimedia documents. wwnorton.com/web/westernciv18

REVIEWING THE OBJECTIVES

- The settlement of Indo-European peoples in the Near East had marked effects on the older civilizations there. What were some major consequences?
- Egypt's New Kingdom differed profoundly from the Old and Middle Kingdoms that preceded it. Why was this the case?
- The civilizations of the late Bronze Age were bound together by transnational networks. What were the strengths and fragilities of these relationships?
- What kingdoms and empires emerged in the Near East after the devastation caused by the Sea Peoples?
- Monotheism was a significant historical development of the first millennium B.C.E. Why is it so important?

but not as the essence of religious life; rather, they would be symbolic of the special relationship binding Yahweh to the Hebrews. Eventually, the transcendental monotheism that emerged from these historical processes would become common to the worldview of all Western civilizations.

CONCLUSION

The centuries between 1700 and 500 B.C.E. were an epoch of empires. While the two great powers of the second millennium were New Kingdom Egypt and the Hittite Empire in Anatolia, a host of lesser empires also coalesced during this period, including Minoan Crete, Mycenaean Greece, and the trading empire of the Assyrians. All were sustained by a sophisticated network of trade and diplomacy. But between 1200 and 1000 B.C.E. the devastation wrought by the Sea Peoples destroyed this integrated civilization. These invasions cleared the way for the emergence of many new, small states, including those of the Phoenicians, the Philistines, the Hebrews, and the Lydians. Many crucial cultural and economic developments were fostered by these small states, including alphabetic writing, coinage, mercantile colonization, and monotheism. But the dominant states of the Iron Age continued to be great land empires centered in western Asia: first that of the Neo-Assyrians, then briefly the Chaldeans, and finally the Persians.

Yet the empires of the early Iron Age were quite different from those that had dominated the Near East a thousand years before. These new empires were much more highly unified. They had capital cities, centrally managed systems of communication, sophisticated administrative structures, and ideologies that justified their aggressive imperialism. They commanded armies of unprecedented size, and they demanded from their subjects a degree of obedience impossible for any Bronze Age emperor to imagine or enforce. Their rulers declared themselves the chosen instruments of their god's divine will.

At the same time, we can trace the emergence of more personalized religions. Zoroastrian dualism and Hebrew monotheism added an important new emphasis on ethical conduct, and both pioneered the development of authoritative written scriptures that advanced religious teachings. Zoroastrianism, despite its radical re-imagining of the cosmos, proved fully compatible with imperialism and became the driving spiritual force behind the Persian Empire. Judaism, by contrast, was forged in the struggle to resist the imperialism of the Neo-Assyrians and Chaldeans. Both systems of belief would exercise enormous influence on future civilizations. In particular, they would provide the models on which Christianity and Islam would ultimately erect their own traditions, just as models of imperial governance forged in this period would become the template for future empires. In Chapter 3, we will look at the ways in which the city-states of ancient Greece both built on and departed from these models.

PEOPLE, IDEAS, AND EVENTS IN CONTEXT

- How did the Hittite Empire integrate the cultures of **INDO-EUROPEANS** with the older civilizations of this region?
- What do the reigns of **HATSHEPSUT** and **AKHENATEN** tell us about the continuities and limitations of pharaonic power?
- What factors produced the transnational networks of the Late **BRONZE AGE**?
- How did the civilizations of **MINOAN CRETE** and **MYCENAEAN GREECE** differ from one another and from the neighboring civilizations of the Near East?
- In what ways do the **PHOENICIANS**, the **PHILISTINES**, and the **HEBREWS** exemplify three different approaches to state-building at the beginning of the first millennium B.C.E.?
- What was new about the **NEO-ASSYRIAN EMPIRE**? How do its methods of conquest and its military-religious ethos compare to the **PERSIAN EMPIRE** that followed it?
- How and why did monotheism develop in the Hebrew kingdoms? In what ways might **JUDAISM** have been influenced by **ZOROASTRIANISM**?

THINKING ABOUT CONNECTIONS

- In the religions of Akhenaten, the Persians, and the Hebrews, we see a rejection of polytheism. What cultural factors may have contributed to this? What would you consider to be the long-term effects of montheism as a motivating force in history?
- What patterns of success or failure appear to be emerging when we consider the empires that flourished in the Iron Age, particularly those of the Assyrians and the Persians? Are similar patterns visible in other periods of history, including our own?

STORY LINES

- The emergence of democracy was dependent on the historical circumstances of the ancient Greek world, which included reliance on slavery and the exclusion of women from public life. It therefore differs markedly from the political system(s) described as democratic today.

- The Greeks were united only through a shared language and culture. The lack of a common political structure thus made it difficult for them to work toward a common goal except when faced with annihilation.

- The Athenians' leadership in the Persian Wars enabled them to dominate the Mediterranean and also, through the use of writing, to influence our understanding of their role in history.

- The cultural achievements of the fifth century B.C.E. glorified the individual male and his role in the community. Again, they valorized Athenian imperial ambitions.

CHRONOLOGY

800–400 B.C.E.	Rise of the polis
c. 750 B.C.E.	Homeric epics transcribed
725–650 B.C.E.	Hoplite tactics become standard
c. 600 B.C.E	Militarization of Sparta
600–500 B.C.E.	Emergence of the Milesian School (pre-Socratic philosophy)
594 B.C.E.	Solon's reforms in Athens
546 B.C.E.	Cyrus of Persia conquers Lydia and controls the Greek cities of Ionia
510 B.C.E.	Overthrow of the Peisistratid tyrants in Athens
499–494 B.C.E.	Ionian Revolt
490 B.C.E.	Battle of Marathon
480 B.C.E.	Battles of Thermopylae and Salamis
479 B.C.E.	Battle of Plataea
478 B.C.E.	Formation of the Delian League
431 B.C.E.	Peloponnesian War begins
404 B.C.E.	Defeat of Athens by Sparta
399 B.C.E.	Death of Socrates

Before
You
Read
This
Chapter

The Civilization of Greece, 1000–400 B.C.E.

CORE OBJECTIVES

- **DESCRIBE** the factors that led to the emergence of the Greek polis.

- **EXPLAIN** the importance of hoplite warfare and its effects on democracy.

- **DEFINE** the key differences among the poleis of Athens, Sparta, and Miletus.

- **IDENTIFY** the ways in which Athenian culture, philosophy, and art reflect democratic ideals.

- **UNDERSTAND** the impact of the Persian and Peloponnesian Wars on Greek civilization.

I n the fifth century B.C.E., a Greek-speaking subject of the Persian Empire began to write a book. He had been to Egypt and along the African coast, to the Greek colonies of Italy, the cities of Persia, the wilds of Thrace and Macedonia, and all over the Aegean. He had collected stories about peoples and places even farther afield: Ethiopia, India, the Black Sea. We have already met this intrepid traveler, Herodotus (c. 484–c. 425 B.C.E.), who marveled at the pyramids of Giza (see Chapter 1) and who told how the king of Lydia lost his power to the Persians (see Chapter 2). His reason for compiling this information was timely: he wanted to write a history of recent events. As he put it, "Herodotus of Halicarnassus here sets forth the results of his research, with the aim of preserving the remembrance of what men have done, and of preventing the great and wonderful deeds of both Greeks and barbarians from losing their glory; and in particular to examine the causes that made them fight one another."

Herodotus's fascination with the Persians, Phoenicians, and Egyptians underscores the extent to which all Greek-speakers regarded themselves as different from other ancient peoples.

75

THE ACROPOLIS OF ATHENS AND THE PARTHENON. Many Greek cities were built upon mountain strongholds, but the most famous of these is the acropolis of Athens. First settled in the Neolithic Period, it was a fortified palace during the Bronze Age—allegedly that of the hero Theseus—and then a precinct sacred to the goddess Athena, for whom the city was named. The Parthenon, its most important surviving structure, was built on the site of an older temple after the Athenian victory over the Persians at Marathon in 490 B.C.E. It was then rebuilt after the Persians sacked Athens ten years later. Most of the damage it sustained thereafter occurred during modern wars. ▪ *Why was this site the focal point of so much activity?* ▪ *What does its longevity tell us about the relationship between place and identity in Greece?*

Indeed, they had responded very differently to the Bronze Age collapse. While they struggled to cooperate politically, they were able to forge a common language and culture, and they cherished values that were distinct from those of the people they called *barbarians*: peoples whose speech, to Greek ears, sounded like jibberish ("bar-bar-bar"). They celebrated individual liberty, participatory government, artistic innovation, scientific investigation, and confidence in the creative powers of the human mind. Although the practical implementation of these ideals would prove problematic—and continues to be so—our own civilization would be unimaginable without the political experiments and cultural achievements of ancient Greece.

FROM CHAOS TO POLIS

By the end of the twelfth century B.C.E., Mycenaean civilization had vanished. Except at Athens, the great citadels that had crowned the heights of mainland kingdoms were destroyed. But even at Athens the population steadily declined, with severe effects on the economy and on social organization. Settlements shrank in size and moved inland, away from vulnerable coastlines, thus cutting themselves off from trade and communication. Indeed, the use of writing declined to such an extent that the knowledge of the system known as Linear B disappeared (see Chapter 2). Archaeological evidence suggests a world in stasis, isolated from the centers of civilization that were re-emerging in the Near East.

The material realities of life in this era profoundly shaped the civilization that emerged from it. This civilization would emphasize political equality and modest display, the importance of domestic economy and self-sufficiency: these were the principles that formed the basis of early democracies. At the same time, this new historical reality had similar long-term effects on religion and philosophy; the hardships of daily life, which contrasted sharply with the stories of a heroic and opulent past, made the Greeks suspicious of their gods. They came to rely far more on the power of individual human beings than on divine intervention in human affairs. They also developed an awareness that excessive pride in one's own accomplishments could be dangerous, because such *hubris* attracted the adverse attention of the gods. While the gods favored those who showed initiative and daring, they would punish the hubris of those who failed to acknowledge their own limitations.

Homer and the Heroic Tradition

By the year 1000 B.C.E., the chaotic conditions that had contributed to the isolation of Greece were alleviated by a period of relative peace. The standard of living improved, artisans developed their crafts, and increased contact among individual settlements fostered trade. Greek pottery, in particular, became a sophisticated and sought-after commodity, which Greek merchants could exchange for luxury goods from abroad.

As trade became an increasingly important feature of the new economy, the personal fortunes of those who engaged in trade increased accordingly, leading to a new kind of social stratification based on wealth. The men who controlled that wealth were aware that their status was not founded on warfare or noble birth, as had been the case in the distant past. Instead, they began to justify their preeminence as a reflection of their own superior qualities as "best men" (*aristoi*). Wealth was one sign of this superiority, but it was not sufficient in itself as a claim to aristocracy, which literally means "the rule of the best." Those who aspired to this status were also expected to emulate, as far as possible, the heroes of old, whose stories lived in the prodigious memories and agile voices of the singers of tales.

These singers, the guardians of a rich oral history that had never been written down, were part poets in their own right and part *rhapsodes*, "weavers of songs." The most famous of these is Homer, the poet credited with having woven together the mesh of stories that we know as the *Iliad* and the *Odyssey*. They appear to have crystallized around 800 B.C.E., at about the same time that Hesiod was working on a series of much shorter lyrics that capture a more contemporary perspective (see Chapter 2). By contrast, the epics ascribed to Homer are vast encyclopedias of lore set at the end of the Bronze Age, the time Hesiod called "the Age of Heroes." These were the days when Agamemnon had ruled in Mycenae and launched a vast expedition to conquer Troy, where the prince Paris had taken Helen, the ravishing wife of Agamemnon's brother, Menalaus; it was the age of Achilles and his Trojan rival, Hector; it was the age of Odysseus.

Like the much older epic of *Gilgamesh* (see Chapter 1), these epics preserve long-standing traditions. But over centuries of retelling, the social and political relationships portrayed in the poems changed to reflect the assumptions and agendas of later ages. As a result, the Homeric epics are of tremendous value to historians. They also offer significant analytical challenges. For although the great events and many of the material objects described in them date from the late Bronze Age, the society they reflect is that of Homer's contemporaries, half a millennium later. Treating these epics as historical sources, therefore, requires the historian to work like an archaeologist, carefully peeling back layers of meaning and sifting through the accumulated sediment of generations.

For example, Homer depicts a world in which competition and status are of paramount importance to the warrior elite, just as they were of vital concern to the aristocrats of his own day. Through the exchange of expensive gifts and hospitality, men aspiring to positions of power sought to create strong ties of guest friendship (*xenia, zeh-NEE-ah*) with one another, and thus to construct networks of influence that would support their economic, social, and political ambitions. Indeed, it is almost impossible to overestimate the importance of guest friendship as a sacred institution, something that is well illustrated by the encounter between the Trojan warrior Glaucus and the Greek Diomedes in the *Iliad* (see page 78). It suggests that aristocrats in the Greek world conceived of themselves as having more in common with each other than they did with the local societies they dominated, something that is also reflected in the essential similarity of Trojans and Greeks in the *Iliad* and the lack of perceived differences among various Greek tribes.

However, the practice of guest friendship and the shared sense of a common culture among artistocratic households did not lessen the competition that frequently led to violence. (The Trojan War, after all, is supposed to have begun when Paris violated the holy ties of hospitality by seducing the wife of Menalaus while he was a guest of the Spartan king.) It also led to competition over the epic past, as fledgling aristocratic clans vied to claim descent from one or another legendary hero. A hero cult might begin when an important family claimed an impressive Mycenaean tomb as that of their own famous ancestor, someone named in the *Iliad* and said to come from that place. They would then develop a pious tradition of practicing dutiful sacrifices and other observances at the tomb. This devotion would extend to their followers and dependents; eventually, an entire community might come to identify itself with the famous local hero. The heroic ideal thus became a deeply ingrained feature of Greek society, as did the stories that the epics preserved and propagated.

Analyzing Primary Sources

Greek Guest Friendship and Heroic Ideals

Before the emergence of the Greek poleis, relations among communities depended largely on the personal connections made among leading families of different settlements. Often founded on the exchange of gifts or hospitality, the resulting bonds of guest friendship imposed serious obligations on those involved in such relationships—and on their heirs. Honoring these ties was an important part of the heroic ideal, even among those fighting on opposing sides. In this episode from the Iliad *(Book VI), the fierce Greek warrior Diomedes encounters Glaucus of Lykia, fighting for Troy, on the field of battle.*

 hen Glaucus, son of Hippolochus,
Met Diomedes in no-man's-land.
Both were eager to fight, but first Tydaeus' son
Made his voice heard above the battle noise:
"And which mortal hero are you? I've never seen you
Out here before on the fields of glory,
And now you're here ahead of everyone,
Ready to face my spear. Pretty bold.
I feel sorry for your parents . . ."
And Glaucus, Hippolochus' son:
"Great son of Tydaeus, why ask me about my lineage? . . .
But if you really want to hear my story,
You're welcome to listen. Many men know it.
Ephyra, in the heart of Argive horse country,
Was home to Sisyphus, the shrewdest man alive,
Sisyphus son of Aeolus. He had a son, Glaucus,
Who was the father of faultless Bellerophon,
A man of grace and courage by the gift of the gods. . . .
[Here, Glaucus relates the adventures of his grandfather, Bellerophon, and how he came to Lykia and fought many battles for its king.]
When the king realized that Bellerophon had divine blood,

He kept him there and gave him his daughter,
And half his royal honor. . . .
His wife, the princess, bore him three children,
Isander, Hippolochus, and Laodameia. . . .
His son Isander was slain by Ares,
As he fought against the glorious Solymi,
And his daughter was killed by Artemis
Of the golden reins. But Hippolochus
Bore me, and I am proud he is my father.
He sent me to Troy with strict instructions
To be the best ever, better than all the rest,
And not to bring shame on the race of my fathers. . . .
This, I am proud to say, is my lineage."
Diomedes grinned when he heard all this.
He planted his spear in the bounteous earth
And spoke gently to the Lykian prince:
"We have old ties of hospitality!
My grandfather Oeneus long ago
Entertained Bellerophon in his halls
For twenty days, and they gave each other
Gifts of friendship. Oeneus gave
A belt bright with scarlet, and Bellerophon
A golden cup, which I left at home.
I don't remember my father Tydeus,
Since I was very small when he left for Thebes

In that great war that killed so many Achaeans.
But that makes me your friend and you my guest
If ever you come to Argos, as you are my friend
And I your guest whenever I travel to Lykia.
So we can't cross spears with each other. . . .
And let's exchange armor, so everyone will know
That we are friends from our fathers' days."
With this, they vaulted from their chariots,
Clasped hands, and pledged their friendship.

Source: Excerpted from the *Iliad* of Homer, trans. Stanley Lombardo (Indianapolis, IN: 1997), pp. 115–18 (vv. 120–241).

Questions for Analysis

1. Why would Glaucus and Diomedes place such emphasis on lineage and on the stories of their ancestors?

2. What are the attributes of heroism in this passage? Why is respect for the sacred ties of hospitality so important?

3. Why do these two men exchange armor? What might be the symbolic significance of this action? What might be its consequences on the battlefield?

The Rise of the Polis

The ninth century B.C.E. saw dramatic changes throughout the Aegean basin. Contacts between Greeks and Phoenicians intensified. Most crucially, the Greeks adopted the Phoenician alphabet, which replaced the forgotten Linear B of the Myceneans (Chapter 2). Indeed, the Greeks adopted this alphabet to better serve their own language by assigning some unneeded consonantal symbols to vowels. They also incorporated into their culture many artistic and literary traditions of the Near East, reshaping them to suit their own purposes.

At the same time, the example of the Phoenicians pointed the way to the revival of a lost art among the Greeks: seafaring. After the devastation of the late Bronze Age, Greek vessels no longer ventured out into the Mediterranean, but hugged the shoreline and traveled only short distances. Most Greek traders waited at home for the Phoenicians to come to them. By the tenth century, however, Greeks were copying Phoenician designs for merchant vessels, which allowed them to launch trading enterprises of their own. As commercial activity increased, significant numbers of Greeks began to move back to the shores of the mainland, to outlying islands, and to the coast of Anatolia.

These developments were accompanied by a dramatic expansion of the Greek population. Around Athens, the population may have quadrupled during the ninth and early eighth centuries. Such rapid growth placed heavy demands on the resources of Greece, a mountainous country with limited agricultural land. As smaller villages grew into towns,

THE ATTIC PENINSULA. This map highlights the numerous poleis that dotted the Attic peninsula. It also shows the surrounding territories of Euboea, Boeotia, and Megaris. Consider the scale of the map and the geography of the peninsula.
■ *Where is Athens located?* ■ *How do natural boundaries appear to affect patterns of settlement?* ■ *Why would citizens of the other Attic poleis be regarded as citizens of Athens also, even though they did not live in the city itself?*

inhabitants of rival communities came into more frequent contact with each other. Soon, some degree of economic, political, and social cooperation among the inhabitants of these towns became necessary. But the values that had developed during centuries of isolation did not make such cooperation easy. Each local community treasured its autonomy and independence, celebrated its own rituals, and honored its own heroes. On what basis could such communities unite?

The Greek solution to this challenge was the *polis*, the root from which we derive the words *politics* and *political*. Yet Greeks considered the polis to be a social collectivity, first and foremost—not a state. For this reason, our sources speak of groups of people—"the Athenians," "the Spartans," or "the Thebans"—rather than places (Athens, Sparta, Thebes). The formation of *poleis* (the plural of *polis*) came to be considered so essential to Greek identity that Aristotle would later define man as "a political animal," someone who participates in the life of the polis and who cannot survive outside it.

Most poleis combined both formal legal institutions and informal social and cultural customs that could differ widely according to the size of the population and its material and historical circumstances. They were usually organized around a social center known as the *agora* ("central marketplace"), where markets and meetings were held and where the business of the polis was conducted in the open air. Surrounding this was the urban settlement, the *asty*, and beyond this was the *khora*, "land." The khora of a large polis might support several other towns or smaller poleis, as well as numerous villages; for example, all the residents of the entire territory of Attica were considered to be citizens of Athens. Thus the vast majority of Athenian citizens were farmers, who might come to the asty only at certain times of the year to participate in the affairs of their polis or to exchange goods in the agora.

The Greeks described this early process of urbanization as the "bringing together of dwellings" (*synoikismos*, synoecism). Polis formation could come about through the conquest of one settlement by another and/or through the gradual alliance of neighboring communities. Some poleis took shape around fortified hilltops, such as the Athenian acropolis, which suggests that the initial impetus may have been defensive. Other communities may have borrowed a Near Eastern (and particularly Phoenician) practice of orienting the urban center around a temple precinct. In Greece, however, the main temple of a polis was not always located within the city's walls; at Argos, for example, the massive temple to Hera was located several miles away from any sizable settlement. In many Greek cities, moreover, temple building may have been a consequence of polis formation rather than a cause, as elites competed with one another to exalt their poleis and glorify themselves.

THE CULTURE OF ARCHAIC GREECE, 800–500 B.C.E.

Scholars date the Archaic Period of Greek history to the emergence of the polis and the return of writing, which the Greeks would put to a wide variety of practical, artistic, intellectual, and political uses. The Athenians, in particular, used writing as a way of establishing their cultural dominance over other Greek poleis, by controlling the inscription of the Homeric canon, promoting the work of contemporary poets, and fostering the writing of prose histories, which allowed them to pass on a narrative of Greek history in which they themselves played the central role. It is therefore important to bear in mind that much of what we know about this early period derives from the work of later authors who wrote from this Athenian perspective: these include the Ionian-born Herodotus, who spent much of his later life in Athens; the historians Thucydides (c. 460–c. 395 B.C.E.) and Xenophon (430–354); and the philosophers Plato (c. 428–348) and his pupil Aristotle (384–322).

Colonization and Panhellenism

In the eighth and seventh centuries B.C.E., small-scale Greek trading ventures and settlements had gradually developed into a full-fledged colonial enterprises which, like their mercantile efforts, followed the example of the Phoenicians. Many larger poleis competed with one another to establish colonies that functioned as trading posts, with Athens and Corinth being particularly successful. Although each new colony was technically an independent entity, it sustained familial and emotional ties to its mother polis; so even if it had no formal obligations to that city, it was often called upon to support the polis and could become entangled in the political and military affairs of the mainland. At the same time, these scattered Greek colonies were united by their shared language and heritage, which was being exported to far-flung reaches of the known world, eventually creating a Panhellenic ("all-Greek") culture that stretched from the Black Sea (parts of modern Romania, Ukraine, and Russia) to the southern coastlines of modern France and Spain.

This process of Greek colonization permanently altered the cultural geography of the Mediterranean world. The western shores of Anatolia (modern Turkey) would remain a stronghold of Greek culture for the next 2,000 years (see Chapter 12). So many Greeks settled in southern Italy that later Romans called the region Magna Graecia, "Greater Greece"; Greek-speaking enclaves would survive there into

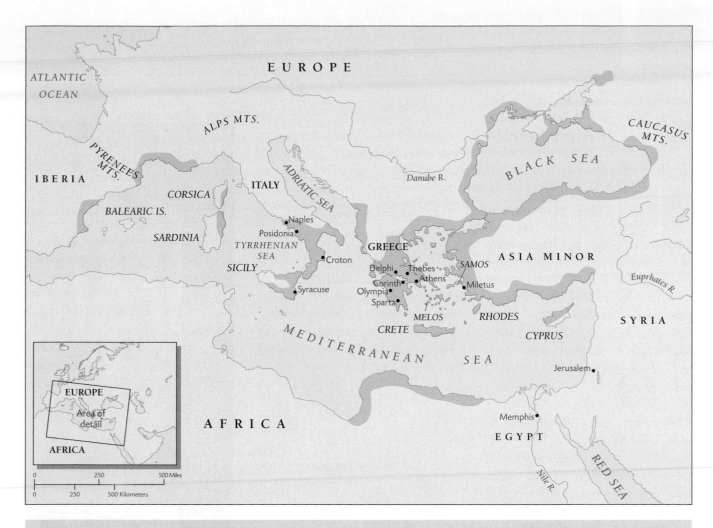

GREEK COLONIZATION, C. 550 B.C.E. Compare this map with that on page 55. ▪ *How do you account for the differences in Greek and Phoenician patterns of colonization?* ▪ *Were Greek colonies likely to compete with Phoenician colonies?* ▪ *Where were such conflicts most likely to erupt?*

the twentieth century of our era. By the fourth century B.C.E., more Greeks lived in Magna Graecia than in Greece itself.

Motives for colonization varied. A polis such as Corinth was blessed by its strategic location on the land bridge between Attica and the Peloponnesus (*pel-oh-poh-NEE-suhs*; the large peninsula of mainland Greece) but cursed by the poverty of its land. Trade therefore became the lifeblood of this polis and of the ruling aristocracy who bankrolled the ambitious planting of colonies up the coast of the Adriatic and into Sicily during the eighth century B.C.E. Other poleis, confronted by the pressures of growing populations and political unrest, sponsored new colonies as outlets for undesirable elements or unwanted multitudes. These colonial projects parallel, in many ways, those of modern nation-states.

Colonial expansion intensified Greek contacts with other cultures. Phoenician pottery brought new artistic motifs and mythological figures into Greece, while Egyptian artists profoundly influenced early Greek sculptural representations of the human form (see ***Interpreting Visual Evidence*** on page 82). However, intensified contact with other cultures also sharpened Greeks' awareness of their own identity as Hellenes (the Greeks' name for themselves). Such self-conscious Hellenism did not necessarily lead to greater political cooperation, but it did encourage the establishment of Panhellenic festivals, such as the Olympic Games, and holy sites. The most important of these was the temple of Apollo at Delphi, home to the oracle of the sun god and situated on the slope of the sacred mountain of Parnassus. People from all over the Greek world (and beyond) came to seek advice from the prophetic spirit embodied in Apollo's priestess, who lived in a state of trance induced by fumes rising from a fissure in the earth and enhanced by the chewing of eucalyptus leaves. Suppliants who sought

The Ideal of Male Beauty

The Greek word *kouros* ("young man" or "youth") is now applied to a whole series of life-sized statues from the Archaic Period. The one shown here comes from Anavyssos in Attica, and was made between 540 and 515 B.C.E. (It is now in the National Archaeological Museum of Athens.) Although scholars used to believe that such statues were meant to represent the god Apollo, further research has shown that most were made to commemorate the dead, especially young warriors who had fallen in battle. This one appears to be walking forward, smiling, but his eyes are closed. The accompanying inscription reads: "Stop and show your pity here for Kroisos, now dead, who once fighting in the foremost ranks of battle was destroyed by raging Ares."

Questions for Analysis

1. What aspects of the body does the kouros emphasize? If this is intended to be a model of Greek manhood, what values would it convey to contemporary youths?

2. Is this a representation of the young man as he was when living or in death? How do your conclusions about the ideal of male beauty change if this is a glorification of death?

3. Compare this image to the values expressed in the verses by Tyrtaeus of Sparta on "The Beautiful and the Good" (page 84). How do these two perspectives complement one another?

to have their questions answered by the oracle would offer gifts to the shrine and then wait while the god spoke through the priestess, whose mysterious answers would be translated by an attending priest into enigmatic Greek verse. The resulting advice was essentially a riddle that called for further interpretation on the part of the recipient—who often misconstrued it: as we noted in Chapter 2, Croesus of Lydia thought that he was following the advice of the oracle when he attacked the Persians, but the great nation he destroyed turned out to be his own.

At the Olympic Games, Greeks honored the king of the gods, Zeus, near the giant temple dedicated to him at Olympia. The Greeks took great pride in these athletic competitions, and Greek historians dated events by Olympiads, the four-year periods between games, traditionally believed to have begun in 776 B.C.E. Only Hellenes were

permitted to participate in these sacred contests, and all wars among Greeks ceased while they took place. A victory in the games brought great prestige to the victor, who could be catapulted to a position of social and political power within his polis. These games did little to alleviate rivalry among the poleis; in fact, they often increased it. Yet they further strengthened the Greeks' awareness of their common culture, an awareness that could be harnessed when they faced a common threat.

Hoplite Warfare

In the centuries immediately following the calamities of the late Bronze Age, the defense of surviving Greek communities rested with the few elite warriors who had the

HOPLITE INFANTRY ADVANCING INTO COMBAT. This Corinthian vase, dating from around 650 B.C.E., displays the earliest-known depiction of hoplites fighting in a phalanx formation.

resources to invest in armor, chariots, and weaponry—and the leisure to emulate the heroic ideals of the past. Commoners fighting on foot played a very secondary role. This monopoly on military prowess gave the aristocracy tremendous political and social leverage. As a result, aristocrats dominated political offices and priesthoods in the poleis, as well as economic life.

But during the Archaic Period, a revolution in military tactics brought aristocratic military dominance to an end. It came about because the effective defense of a polis increasingly required that it be able to call on a standing militia, not just an ad hoc band of elite warriors. Accordingly, able-bodied citizens began to equip themselves for battle and to train alongside one another. These citizen-soldiers became known as *hoplites*, from the large round shield (*hoplon*) carried by each, which was the chief element in a panoply (*hoplite outfit*) weighing as much as seventy pounds, which also consisted of spear, short sword, breastplate, helmet, and sometimes leather greaves and wrist-guards. In battle, hoplites stood shoulder to shoulder in a close formation called a *phalanx*, several columns across and several rows deep, with each hoplite carrying his shield on the left arm to protect the unshielded right side of the man standing next to him. In his right hand, each hoplite carried a thrusting weapon, a spear or sword, so that an approaching phalanx presented a nearly impenetrable wall of armor and weaponry to its opponents. If a man in the front rank fell, the one behind him stepped up to take his place; indeed, the weight of the entire phalanx was literally behind the front line, with each soldier aiding the assault by leaning with his shield into the man in front of him.

This tight formation required only one shared skill: the ability to stay together. As long as the phalanx remained intact, it was a nearly unbeatable formation. But like the polis itself, it could fall apart if its men were not committed to a common goal. The "hoplite revolution" was therefore bound up with a parallel revolution in politics. As a polis came increasingly to draw upon the resources of more and more citizens, it was forced to offer them a larger share in political power. By the seventh century B.C.E., every polis needed a hoplite force to protect its independence, so any town-dweller or farmer who could afford the requisite panoply became a man with political and social standing. Together, these citizen-soldiers formed a new hoplite class, which could demand a share in decision making and thereby challenge the dominance of old elites. Sometimes, though, they could be co-opted by an aristocratic faction or persuaded to throw support behind an aspiring tyrant.

Aristocracy, Tyranny, and Democracy

For the better part of the seventh and sixth centuries B.C.E., aristocrats continued to control the Greek poleis. Struggles for influence among competing families were commonplace, and factions often attempted to checkmate rivals by passing new laws which favored their interests, or by sponsoring building projects or colonial expeditions. These rivalries affected polis government at every level, not least because aristocrats were the only members of society who

"The Beautiful and The Good"

The poet known as Tyrtaeus of Sparta flourished during the middle of the sixth century B.C.E. He may originally have come from Athens, but whatever his origins he expressed ideas of honor, beauty, and virtue that were universal among the hoplite warriors of the new poleis. The key terms he uses in the following verses cannot be adequately translated into English, since these short Greek adjectives are freighted with ancient meanings: kalos (beautiful, honorable), agathos (good, brave, manly). They stand in opposition to the term aischros (shameful, ugly, mean).

 alos it is for an *agathos* warrior to die, fallen among the foremost fighters, in battle for his native land; but to leave his polis and rich fields and beg—that is most painful of all, as he wanders with his dear mother and aged father, his small children and his wedded wife. Detested he will be in the eyes of all those to whom he comes, constrained by need and hateful poverty. He shames his birth and belies his glorious appearance; dishonor and misery are his companions. If no account is taken of a warrior who is a wanderer, if there is no respect for him or his family in the future, then let us fight with all our hearts for this land and die for our children, no longer hesitating to risk our lives. Young men, stand firm beside each other and fight. Do not begin shameful flight or fear. Rather, cre-

ate a mighty, valorous spirit in your breasts, and show no love for your lives when you are fighting. Do not flee, abandoning the older men, whose knees are no longer nimble. For *aischros* it is for an older warrior to fall among the foremost fighters and lie out ahead of the young men—a man whose hair is already white and his beard grey—as he breathes out his valorous spirit in the dust, holding his bloody guts in his own hands, his body laid bare. *Aischros* is this to the eyes, and a cause of resentment to look upon. But to the young men all is seemly, while the glorious flower of lovely youth is theirs. To men the young man is admirable to look upon, and to women lovable while he lives and *kalos* when he lies among the foremost fighters. So let a man take a firm stance and stand fast, with both feet planted upon the ground, biting his lip with his teeth.

Source: Excerpted and modified from *The Greek Polis*, eds. W. H. Adkins and Peter White (Chicago: 1986), pp. 23–24.

Questions for Analysis

1. How does Tyrtaeus characterize defeat? How does this poem exemplify the values and tactics of hoplite warfare?

2. Why is so much emphasis placed on physical beauty and youth? What other qualities are associated with the word *kalos*? Why is old age potentially *aischros*?

3. How does this ideal of male beauty compare with that made visible in the kouros of Anavyssos (page 82)? How does it compare to the heroic ideal expressed in the exchange between Diomedes and Glaucus (page 78)?

could afford to hold unpaid and time-consuming political offices.

The aristocrats of this period pursued not only wealth, power, and fame; they also cultivated a distinctive lifestyle. Participating in politics and holding office was part of this lifestyle. So too was the *symposium*, literally a "drinking party," an intimate gathering at which elite men would enjoy wine, poetic competition performances by trained dancers and acrobats, and the company of *hetaeras* (courtesans) who provided witty conversation, music, and the promise of sex. Respectable women were excluded from such meet-

ings, as they were from most other aspects of social and political life (see below). So too were non-aristocratic men. The symposium was thus an arena for the display of aristocratic masculinity.

The glorification of male sexuality was another important aspect of this homosocial aristocratic culture and was regulated by social custom. Typically, a man in his late twenties to late thirties, who had just begun to make his career in political life, would take as his lover and protégé an aristocratic youth in his early to mid-teens. The two would form an intimate bond in which sexual intercourse played a role. This personal and social intimacy benefited both partners and their families and allowed the younger partner to learn the workings of politics while making valuable connections and alliances. Many later philosophers, including Plato, argued that true love could exist only between two such lovers, because only within such a relationship could a man find a partner worthy of his affections. Other types of sexual relationships were considered illicit, including those between men of unequal social status.

A complex system of values, ideas, practices, and assumptions thus shaped aristocratic identity in this era. As a result, it was difficult for those outside this elite world to participate fully in the public life of the polis. Eventually, in many poleis, the circle of the aristocratic elite tightened further as smaller and smaller groups came to dominate higher offices. This meant that even many aristocrats were left on the outside of their own culture, looking in.

For these men, one remedy lay close at hand: they could form an alliance with the rising class of hoplites, who had complaints of their own about exclusion from political power. And occasionally, a single aristocrat with the backing of the hoplites would succeed in setting up an alternative form of government, a *tyranny*. The word *tyrannos* was actually foreign to the Greeks, and had been borrowed from the Lydians; it signified someone who ruled outside the traditional framework of the polis.

But a tyrant in Archaic Greece was not necessarily an abusive ruler. Indeed, tyranny often led the way to wider political enfranchisement. This is because a would-be tyrant who had sought the support of the hoplite class would then have to appease that class by extending further rights of political participation, while all the time striving to keep the reins of power in his own hands. This was an inherently unstable state of affairs, because after the original tyrant had fulfilled the wishes of the hoplites, the continuance of tyranny became an obstacle to even greater power for this segment of the population, which would work to overthrow it. For this reason, tyrannies rarely lasted for more than two generations and could drive a transition from aristocracy to a more broadly participatory form of government: democracy.

It is important to stress that our notion of democracy is quite different from that of the Greeks. In fact, the philosopher Aristotle denigrated this form of government as "mob rule," because it gave too much power to the *demos*, a word meaning "neighborhood" or "affinity group." He saw it as a system too easily controlled by a particular faction. Our ideal of democracy is closer to what Aristotle would have called a polity, governance by the polis as a whole.

The Power of Poetry

Although the aristocracies of this period were deeply invested in the heroic ideals enshrined in the epics of an earlier age, they also strove to express their unique culture and outlook in newer poetic forms. The most characteristic of these is the lyric, a series of rhythmic verses sung to the music of the lyre. Because these songs would have been composed orally, or even improvised, relatively few survive. But those that do are valuable historical sources because they concentrate on themes of immediate interest to poets and their audiences: beauty, love, sorrow, ambition, or important life events. And because they were the focus of entertainment at gatherings, lyrics are often politically charged, sexually explicit, or daringly subversive of accepted norms. For example, the poet Archilochus of Paros (c. 680–640 B.C.E.) flouts the conventions of epic poetry by mocking his own failures on the battlefield: "Some barbarian hefts my shield, since I had to abandon it / . . . but I escaped, so it scarcely matters / . . . I can get another just as good." So much for the heroic ideal of returning either with one's shield or on it! In another lyric, Archilochus castigates his faithless (female) lover and his even more faithless (male) lover with whom she has an affair.

AN ARISTOCRATIC MAN AND HIS YOUNG LOVER. An illustration from a red-figure drinking cup, c. 480 B.C.E. ▪ *As suggested by this image, what are the differences between these two male lovers?* ▪ *What relationship(s) are being depicted here?*

Songs of Sappho

Although Sappho of Lesbos (c. 620–550 B.C.E.) was a prolific poet and skilled musician, we know very little about her life, and only a few examples of her extraordinary verse survive. Of the nine books collected in the third century B.C.E., we now have just one complete lyric and a series of fragments, some consisting of only two or three words, often preserved because they were quoted admiringly by other authors. Astonishingly, though, a papyrus scroll containing a previously unknown part of a poem was identified as recently as 2004.

Fragment 16

Some say thronging cavalry, some say
   foot soldiers,
others call a fleet the most beautiful of
sights the dark earth offers, but I say it's
   whatever you love best.

And it's easy to make this understood by
everyone, for she who surpassed all
   human
kind in beauty, Helen, abandoning her
   husband—that best of

men—went sailing off to the shores of
   Troy and
never spent a thought on her child or
   loving
parents: when the goddess seduced her
   wits and left her to wander,

she forgot them all, she could not
   remember
anything but longing, and lightly straying
aside, lost her way. But that reminds me
   now: Anactória,

she's not here, and I'd rather see her
   lovely

step, her sparkling glance and her face
   than gaze on
all the troops in Lydia in their chariots
   and glittering armor.

Source: Translated by Jim Powell, *The Poetry of Sappho* (New York: 2007), pp. 6–7.

The New Fragment (2004)

Live for the gifts the fragrant-breasted
   Muses
send, for the clear, the singing, lyre, my
   children.
Old age freezes my body, once so lithe,
rinses the darkness from my hair, now
   white.
My heart's heavy, my knees no longer
   keep me
up through the dance they used to
   prance like fawns in.
Oh, I grumble about it, but for what?
Nothing can stop a person's growing
   old.
They say that Tithonus was swept away
in Dawn's passionate, rose-flushed arms
   to live

forever, but he lost his looks, his youth,
failing husband of an immortal bride.

Source: Translated by Lachlan Mackinnon, *Times Literary Supplement*, July 15, 2005.

Questions for Analysis

1. How does Sappho use stories from the older tradition she has inherited to address her own concerns? How does the perspective of the female poet transform masculine ideas about heroism, beauty, warfare, aging?

2. What are the challenges of working with such fragmentary sources as these? If these were the only pieces of evidence to survive from Archaic Greece, what conclusions could you draw about the society and its values?

    Given the male domination of Greek culture, it is surprising that the most famous poet of this age was not a man. Rather, it was Sappho (*SAF-foh*, c. 620–550 B.C.E.), who lived in the polis of Mytilene on the island of Lesbos. Revered by her contemporaries as the Tenth Muse, Sappho composed songs for a wide array of occasions and a range of moods: songs of courtship and marriage, longing and desire, loss, old age, and death. Sometimes her lyrics seem to be addressed to men, but more often they are passionately dedicated to women: both the women whom Sappho loved and the historical women who occupy the margins of masculine epic. Frequently, her verses take some image or incident from that inherited tradition and give it a distinctive spin. In one song, Sappho compares herself to Agamemnon, who was only able to return from Troy after he prayed to Hera, a goddess worshiped at Lesbos; Sappho now prays that her beloved will arrive safely with the goddess's help. In another, she imagines a scene not included in the *Iliad*, the joyous wedding of the Trojan Hector and his bride, Andromache. Like later tragedies, the poignancy of this bridal song (just like the ones Sappho herself would have sung at the marriage feasts of her friends) derives from the listeners' foreknowledge of the legendary couple's terrible fate: Hector's death at the hands of Achilles, Andromache's enslavement at the hands of the victorious Greeks, and the murder of their infant son. The intimacy of lyric thus reveals something that few other sources from antiquity are able to convey: the distinctive feelings and desires of individuals who were often at odds with the dominant culture of their time.

OSTRACISM. This political practice takes its name from the pot shards (in Greek, *ostraka*) on which the names of candidates for political exile were scratched. Many of the ballots have survived. Here we see the names of Aristeides, Kimon, and Themistocles: prominent citizens of the fifth century B.C.E. who had fallen out of favor.

PORTRAITS OF THREE POLEIS

The poleis of the Archaic Period developed in very different ways. To illustrate this diversity, we examine three particularly interesting examples: Athens, Sparta, and the Ionian city of Miletus. None of these, however, can be considered typical. There were approximately 1,000 poleis in Greece, and about most of them we know almost nothing. But at least we can survey some of the features that, with variations, made each polis unique—and yet comparable, in some ways, to its neighbors.

Athens

The Athenians liked to boast that their city had been a great metropolis since the Bronze Age described by Hesiod: a claim integral to their identity and their sense of self-importance within the larger Greek world. But although Attica had long been a populous and prosperous region, Athens itself was of no great significance during the Mycenaean Era. Moreover, it continued throughout the Archaic Period to be overshadowed by Corinth, the leading commercial city; Sparta, the preeminent military power; and the leading cultural centers of the Aegean islands and the coast of Anatolia.

When Athenians first came together to form a polis, theirs was a distinctly agricultural economy. Whatever profits aristocrats acquired through trade, they reinvested in land on the Attic Peninsula. Indeed, Athenian elites came to regard commerce as a disreputable means of earning a living, a mentality that persisted even when the city's excellent harbors and orientation toward the Aegean made Athens famous as a mercantile polis.

In the Archaic Period, aristocratic dominance over the polis rested on monopolization of elected offices and control of the city's council, the Areopagus (*ah-ree-OP-ah-guhs*), which was composed of former office-holders. It took its name from the rocky outcrop where the council met, just below the Acropolis, a site that afforded a panoramic view of the whole city. By the early seventh century B.C.E., an even smaller group of aristocratic officials wielded executive authority in Athens: the *archons* or "first men." Ultimately, nine archons presided over the entire governance of the polis, including its military, judicial, and religious affairs. Although each served for only one year, all became lifetime members of the Areopagus. And because the Areopagus appointed the archons, it could therefore control its own future membership. It also served as a kind of high court, with tremendous influence over the hearing of cases.

As power was consolidated by this small group, deep economic and social divisions developed in Athenian society. A significant proportion of the population fell into slavery through debt, while struggles among aristocratic families destabilized the government and fomented cycles of revenge killings. This situation eventually inspired Athenians' first attempt to promulgate a set of written laws. In 621 B.C.E., an aristocrat named Drakon was charged with this task, and he sought to control civic violence through harsh punishments: hence our term *draconian* to describe

THE ATHENIAN PNYX, WITH A VIEW OF THE ACROPOLIS. The Athenian assembly, the *ekklesia*, met on the sloping hill of the Pnyx. A speaker standing on the *bema* ("stepping-stone," to the right) would have to make himself heard by all the citizens gathered in front of this platform, and all proceedings would have been plainly visible to noncitizens and foreigners in the agora at the foot of the hill (to the left). Overlooking it all was the temple of the city's patron goddess, Athena, on the crest of the Acropolis. ▪ *How is the relative openness and accessibility of Athenian democracy symbolized by this chosen site?*

any severe penalty, policy, or regime. Drakon's attempt failed, but its effects ultimately led both aristocrats and hoplites to an agreement. In 594 B.C.E., they elected one man, the poet Solon, as the sole archon for one year, and they gave him broad legislative powers. Solon was an aristocrat, but he had made his fortune as a merchant and did not hold that vocation in contempt; this meant that he was not allied with any single interest.

Solon's legendary political and economic reforms laid the foundations for the later development of Athenian democracy. He forbade the practice of debt slavery and set up a fund to buy back Athenian slaves who had been sold abroad. He encouraged the cultivation of olives and grapes, thus spurring cash-crop farming and urban industries such as oil and wine production, and the manufacture of pottery storage jars and decorative drinking cups. He also broadened rights of political participation and set up courts in which a range of citizens served as jurors and to which any Athenian might appeal. He based eligibility for political office on property qualifications, thus making it possible for someone not born into the aristocracy to gain access to power. Moreover, he convened an Athenian assembly, the *ekklesia* (*eh-KLAY-see-a*) and gave it the right to elect archons. Now all free-born Athenian men over the age of eighteen could participate in government. Even those who were not eligible for citizenship were able to see the workings of government for themselves, since the assembled citizens met on the slopes of the Pnyx (*pNIX*), a hill visible from the central marketplace and overlooked by the sacred precincts of the Acropolis.

However, Solon's reforms were not immediately accepted. The aristocracy thought them too radical; the people of the demos, not radical enough. In the resulting generation of turmoil, an aristocrat named Peisistratos (*pi-SIS-trah-tohs*) succeeded in establishing himself as tyrant in 546 B.C.E. Somewhat ironically, Peisistratos then proceeded to institute Solon's reforms, and he also launched a massive campaign of public-works projects, including the collection and codification of Homer's epics. But the apparent mildness of his rule was undergirded by the quiet, persistent intimidation of Athenian citizens by foreign mercenaries and the ruthlessness with which he crushed any dissent. Still, by enforcing Solon's laws, he strengthened the political role of the demos and remained a popular ruler until his death. His sons, however, were less able to control the various factions that threatened their rule. One was assassinated and the other was ousted with the help of the Spartans in 510 B.C.E.

The following period of Spartan-sponsored oligarchy ("rule of the few") was very brief. Two generations of increasing access to power had left the Athenian demos with a taste for self-government, and for the first time in recorded history, a group of commoners can be credited with the overthrow of a regime: they rallied behind Cleisthenes (CLIE-sthen-ees), an aristocrat who championed the cause of the demos. Once voted in as archon in 508/7 B.C.E., Cleisthenes took steps to limit aristocratic power. By reorganizing the Athenian population into ten voting districts, he suppressed traditional loyalties tied to certain aristocratic families. He further strengthened the Athenian assembly and extended the machinery of democratic government to the local level throughout Attica. He also introduced the practice of ostracism, whereby Athenians could decide each year whether they wanted to banish someone for a decade and, if so, whom. With this power, Cleisthenes hoped that the demos could prevent the return of a tyrant and quell factional strife if civil war seemed imminent.

By 500 B.C.E., the political struggles of the sixth century had given Athens a far more populist character than any other Greek polis and had strengthened its institutions of government. In the meantime, Athens had become the principal exporter of olive oil, wine, and pottery in the Greek world. It was poised to assume the role it would claim for itself during the fifth century B.C.E. as the exemplar of Greek culture and the proponent of democracy.

Sparta

Located in the southern part of the Peloponnesus, the polis of the Spartans represented everything that Athens was not. Athens was sophisticated, outward looking, and creative; Sparta was practical, defensive, and conservative. Depending on one's point of view, either set of adjectives might indicate admiration or criticism.

Sparta took shape when four villages (and ultimately a fifth) combined to form a single polis. Perhaps as a relic of the unification process, Sparta retained a dual monarchy throughout its history, with two royal families and two lines of succession. Although seniority or ability usually determined which of the two ruling kings had more influence, neither was technically superior to the other, a situation that often led to political in-fighting among their respective supporters.

According to traditional accounts, Spartan control over the surrounding region of Laconia began with the conquest of Messenia, one of Greece's few agriculturally rich territories. Around 720 B.C.E., the Spartans subjugated and enslaved the indigenous people there, the *helots*, who now became an unfree population forced to work under Spartan lordship. Around 650 B.C.E., however, the helots revolted, gaining support from several neighboring poleis and briefly threatening Spartan hegemony with annihilation. Eventually, Sparta triumphed; but the shock of this rebellion brought about a permanent transformation.

Determined to prevent another uprising and to protect its superior position, Sparta became the most militarized polis in Greece. Within a few generations, everything was oriented to the maintenance of its hoplite army—a force so superior that Spartans confidently left their city unfortified. At a time when Athenian society was becoming more democratic and when citizens spent more time legislating than fighting, Spartan society was becoming increasingly devoted to an older aristocratic ideal of perpetual warfare, with personal freedom mattering less than the collective honor and security of the polis.

The Spartan system made every male citizen a professional soldier of the phalanx. At birth, every Spartiate child was therefore examined by officials who determined whether it was healthy enough to raise; if not, the infant was abandoned in the mountains. This was a custom observed elsewhere in the ancient world, but only in Sparta was it institutionalized by the state. If deemed worthy of upbringing, the child was placed at age seven in the polis-run educational system. Boys and girls trained together until age twelve, participating in exercise, gymnastics, and other physical drills and competitions. Boys then went to live in barracks, where their military training would commence in earnest. Girls continued their training until they became the mates of eligible Spartiate males, usually when the girls were around the age of eighteen and the men were often much older. This was not a domestic partnership: no such thing was possible under the Spartiate system, or even desirable, for such a marriage would merely create a new set of loyalties and interests that would compete with the Spartan state.

THE PELOPONNESUS. Located on the Peloponnesian peninsula, the highly militarized society of Sparta dominated the region known as Laconia. ▪ *Where is Sparta located?* ▪ *How might Sparta's location have influenced its outlook on foreign affairs?* ▪ *Did geography make conflict between Athens and Sparta inevitable?*

Barracks life was rigorous, designed to accustom youths to physical hardship. At age eighteen, the young man who survived this training would try for membership in a brotherhood whose sworn comrades lived, ate, and fought together. Failure to gain acceptance would mean that the young man could not become a full Spartiate and would lose his rights as a citizen. If accepted, however, he remained with his brotherhood until he was thirty years of age. Between the ages of twenty and thirty he was also expected to mate with a Spartiate woman—but occasions for this were few, a fact that partially accounts for the low birthrate among Spartan citizens. After age thirty, a Spartiate male could opt to live with his family, but he was still required to remain on active military duty until he was sixty.

All Spartiate males over the age of thirty were members of the citizens' assembly, the *apella*, which voted on matters proposed to it by a council consisting of twenty-eight elders (the *gerousia*, "assembly of elders") and the two kings. This gerousia (*gher-oo-SEE-ah*) was the main policy-making body of the polis and also its primary court. Its members were elected for life but had to be over the age of sixty before they could stand for office. Meanwhile, five *ephors* (overseers), elected annually, supervised the educational system and acted as guardians of Spartan tradition. In the latter role, ephors could even remove an ineffectual king from command of the army while on campaign. The ephors also supervised the Spartan "secret service," the *krypteia*, recruiting agents from among the most promising young Spartiates. Agents spied on citizens, but their main job was to infiltrate the helot population and identify potential troublemakers.

This Spartan polity hinged on the precarious relationship with the helots, who outnumbered the Spartiates ten to one. Messenia routinely seethed with revolt. In wartime, helots accompanied the Spartans on campaign as shield bearers, spear carriers, and baggage handlers. At home, however, the helots were a constant security concern. Every year the Spartans ritually declared war on them as a reminder that they would not tolerate dissent. Moreover, the constant threat of unrest at home meant that the polis was notoriously reluctant to commit its army abroad. So helot slavery made the Spartan system possible, but Sparta's reliance on a hostile population of slaves was also a serious limitation.

This system also limited Spartans' contact with the outside world. Spartiates were forbidden to engage in trade or commerce, because wealth might distract them from the pursuit of martial glory. Nor did Spartiates farm their own lands, as many Athenians did. Economic activity in the Spartan state fell either to the helots or to the free residents of other Peloponnesian cities who were known as *perioikoi*, "those dwelling round about." The perioikoi (*per-ee-OY-koi*) enjoyed certain rights and protections within Spartan society, and some grew rich handling its business concerns. But unlike the residents of Attica, in the hinterland of Athens, the perioikoi exercised no political rights within the Spartan polis. Spartiates who lost their rights as citizens also became perioikoi.

The Spartans self-consciously rejected innovation or change. They styled themselves as the protectors of the "traditional customs" of Greece, by which they meant aristocratic regimes and a strict observance of older heroic ideals. In this role, Sparta tried to prevent the establishment of tyrannies in neighboring states and moved to overthrow them

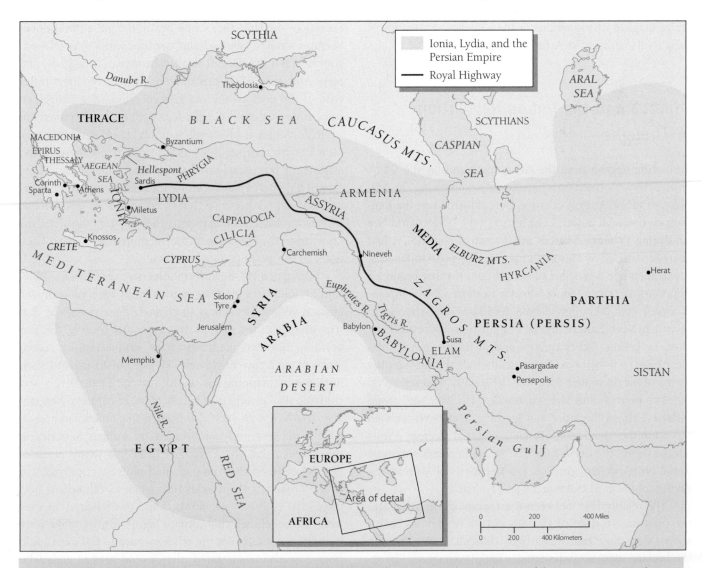

IONIA, LYDIA, AND THE PERSIAN EMPIRE. During the seventh and sixth centuries B.C.E., the Greek cities of the Ionian coast were the cultural and commercial leaders of Greece. But during the fifth century B.C.E., after the Persians conquered Lydia, they lost this position to Athens. ▪ *Where are Ionia, Lydia, and Miletus on this map?* ▪ *How does Ionia's geographical position help to explain the change in its fortunes?* ▪ *How might this change have influenced Ionian attitudes toward the Persian Empire?*

when they arose: hence their willing intervention in the affairs of Athens under the Peisistratids. Indeed, Sparta's stern defense of tradition made it an object of admiration throughout the Greek world, even though few Greeks had any desire to live as the Spartans did.

The fatal flaw in the Spartan system was demographic. There were many ways to fall from the status of Spartiate, but the only way to become one was by birth—and the Spartan birthrate simply could not keep pace with the demand for trained warriors. As a result, the number of full Spartiates declined from perhaps as many as 10,000 in the seventh century to only about 1,000 by the middle of the fourth century B.C.E. Another flaw is historical: because the Spartans placed little value on the written record of their traditions, almost everything we know about them (including the summary offered here) must be gleaned from archaeological investigations or the negative propaganda of their rivals notably the Athenians.

Miletus and the Ionian Revolution in Thought

Across the Aegean from the Greek mainland lay the Greek cities of Ionia, located on a narrow strip dominating the central part of the Anatolian coast. Here, Miletus was the foremost commercial power. Long a part of the Greek world (see **Analyzing Primary Sources** in Chapter 2, page 53), it had also been shaped by Mesopotamian and Egyptian influences. It was therefore a crucible of hybrid cultures that produced important art forms. Ionia was, for example, the birthplace of Greek epic, although debate continues over the extent to which Near Eastern models might have influenced the Homeric poems. Other creative endeavors certainly exhibit Near Eastern influences. Fantastic animals, a long-standing theme of the decorative arts, were frequently represented on Milesian pottery; and Milesian intellectuals were well aware of Near Eastern literature and learning. Some even echoed the vaunting rhetoric of Persian imperial decrees ("thus speaks Darius the Great King. . . .") to make their own, more ironic observations ("thus speaks Hecataeus of Miletus: the sayings of the Greeks are many and foolish").

The relationship between the Ionians of the coast and the interior kingdom of Lydia—and its Persian successor state—were close but increasingly difficult. It was through the Ionians that the Lydian invention of coinage was introduced to the Greek world, where it revolutionized trade, made wealth portable for the first time there, and introduced a host of new philosophical and ethical problems. The Ionians, in turn, played a crucial role in Hellenizing

Asia Minor while at the same time insisting on their independence from it. Under the pressure of the Lydians—who sought the excellent ports of the Anatolian coast for themselves—the major cities of Ionia ultimately banded together to form the Ionian League, a political and cultural confederation of poleis pledged to support each other. This was the first such organization known in the Greek world.

The Milesians founded many colonies, especially in and around the Black Sea. They were also active in Egypt, where the main Greek trading outposts were Milesian foundations. These colonial efforts, combined with its advantageous position for trade with the rest of Asia Minor, brought Miletus extraordinary wealth. At the same time, it also became a center for speculative thinking, what the Greeks called *philosophia*, "the love of wisdom." Beginning in the sixth century B.C.E., a series of intellectuals now known as the pre-Socratics—because they came before the great philosopher Socrates—raised new and vital questions about the relationship between the natural world (the *kosmos*), the gods, and men. And often, their explanations moved the direct influence of the gods to the margins or removed it altogether, something that other Greeks regarded as blasphemous. For example, Milesian philosophers built on older traditions of Near Eastern learning, such as Babylonian mathematics and astronomy, but complicated many older conclusions. They sought physical explanations for the movements of the heavens, and did not presume that heavenly bodies were divine. By making human observations the starting point for their knowledge, they began to formulate more scientific explanations for the working of the universe.

Stimulated by the cultural diversity of their city, Milesian philosophers also began to rethink their place in the cosmos. When Hecataeus (*heck-ah-TAY-us*) remarked that "the sayings of the Greeks are many and foolish," he was deriding his own contemporaries' unquestioning acceptance of a narrow worldview. He set out to expand their horizons by mapping the world, traveling extensively and studying the customs and beliefs of other cultures. Xenophanes (*zee-NOFF-uh-nees*) also posited that all human knowledge is relative and conditioned by human experience: he observed that the Thracians (a people living north of Greece) believed that the gods had blue eyes and red hair as the Thracians themselves did, whereas Ethiopians portrayed the gods as dark skinned and curly haired, as they were. He concluded that human beings always make gods in their own image, not the other way around. If oxen could pray, Xenophanes declared, they would pray to gods who looked like oxen.

Such theories would become a distinctive strand in later Greek philosophy, yet they would continue to be regarded as disturbing and dangerous—dangerous enough to warrant the execution of Socrates in Athens, where the struggle between religion and philosophy would ultimately be fought more than a hundred years after Xenophanes' bold proclamation. By that time, the Persian conquest of Lydia had made Miletus and its sister cities subject to that great empire. Indeed, Ionian resistance to Persian rule would ultimately trigger the greatest clash the Greek world had yet known.

A MODERN REPLICA OF AN ATHENIAN TRIREME. These versatile warships were much more powerful than the old 50-oared pentakonters that had been in use for centuries. As the name suggests, a trireme featured three banks of oars on each side, 170 oars in total. These were manned by citizen rowers seated on benches at three different levels in the vessel's hold. In battle, rowers could help power a ship forward, turn it, and keep it on course in a chase, even when sailing into the wind. In favorable winds, sails could be used to add speed. ▪ *How does this new military technology build on some of the same strategies as hoplite warfare?*

THE CHALLENGE OF THE PERSIAN WARS

The two major wars fought between the uneasily unified Greeks and the vast empire of the Persians were construed as defining events by those who witnessed and looked back on them. From the first, the contest was unequal. Persia was the largest and most efficient state the world had ever seen, capable of mustering over a million armed men. The Greeks, by contrast, remained a collection of disparate communities, fiercely competitive and suspicious of one another. An exceptionally large polis, such as Athens or Sparta, might put 10,000 hoplites in the field; but the vast majority of Greek states could only provide a few hundred each. So the threat of Persian conquest loomed large on the Greek horizon, after which the experience of international warfare changed the Greek world immeasurably.

The Ionian Revolt (499–494 B.C.E.)

For the first time in the history of Western civilizations, we can follow the unfolding of these events through the narrative of a contemporary historian: Herodotus, the first person who self-consciously set out to write an account of his own times in careful, unambiguous prose—rather than in the form of heroic poetry or the boastful language of victorious inscriptions. And luckily for us, Herodotus was uniquely qualified to probe the long-term and more immediate causes of the Persian Wars. Raised in the Ionian polis of Halicarnassus, he was a product of the hybrid culture discussed above. He was also a keen observer of human nature and human diversity. He regarded both the Greeks and the Persians as great peoples. Yet, as a Greek himself—albeit one born within the Persian dominion—he was not impartial. Indeed, his surviving account reflects many of the intellectual currents of mid-fifth-century Athens, where he spent the better part of his career, as well as many Athenian prejudices. This is something that must be borne in mind when reading his work.

Herodotus wanted to show that the war between the Persians and Greeks had ancient roots and could be traced back to long-standing cultural differences, but his narrative also shows that the catalyst was a political conflict in Miletus. In 501 B.C.E., the city was governed by Aristagoras (*EHR-is-STAG-or-uhs*), a tyrant who owed his power to the backing of the Persian emperor, Darius (Chapter 2). But apparently, Aristagoras came to believe that his days as the emperor's favorite were numbered. So he turned abruptly from puppet to patriot, rousing the Milesians and the rest of Ionia to revolt against Persian rule. As a safeguard, he also sought military support from the sympathetic poleis on the Greek mainland. The Spartans refused to send their army abroad, but Athens and Eretria (*er-eh-TREE-uh*), on

Past and Present

Political Satire

In the fifth century B.C.E., the playwright Aristophanes took an older form of comedy, the satyr play, and turned it into a vehicle for what we still call satire. Instead of gently mocking the gods, he lampooned the politics, popular culture, and current events of his own day—and so made his fellow citizens take a fresh look at themselves. If he were alive today, he might be working for *The Daily Show*.

 Watch related author interview on StudySpace
wwnorton.com/web/westernciv18

the island of Euboea (*you-BOY-ah*), agreed to send twenty-five ships and crews. This small force managed to capture the old Lydian capital of Sardis (by then a Persian administrative center) and burn it to the ground. Then the Athenians and Eretrians went home, leaving the Ionians to their own devices. In 494 B.C.E., the rebellious poleis were finally overwhelmed by the vastly superior might of Persia.

Darius realized, however, that so long as his Greek subjects in Asia Minor could cast a hopeful eye to their neighbors across the Aegean, they would forge alliances with them. He therefore decided to launch a preemptive strike against Athens and Eretria, to teach these upstart poleis a lesson. In the summer of 490 B.C.E, a punitive expedition of 20,000 soldiers under two of Persia's finest generals crossed the Aegean and landed on the coast of Euboea. Their forces sacked and burned Eretria to the ground, sending its population into captivity in Persia. They then crossed the narrow strait to Attica, landing on the plain of Marathon, approximately twenty-six miles from Athens.

Marathon and Its Aftermath

When the Persians landed in Attica, the Athenians quickly sought help from the only polis that could conceivably help them forestall annhilation: Sparta. But the Spartans responded that they were unable to assist—they were celebrating a religious festival. Only the small, nearby polis of Plataea offered the Athenians aid. The Athenian and Plataean hoplites would have to engage the mighty Persians on their own.

Heavily outnumbered and without effective cavalry to counter that of the Persians, the Athenian phalanx took a position between two hills blocking the main road to the polis. After a standoff of several days, the Athenian general Miltiades (*mil-TIE-uh-dees*) received word that the Persians were watering their horses and that the Persian infantry was vulnerable to attack. So Miltiades led a charge that smashed the Persian force and resulted in crippling losses. Almost unbelievably, the Athenians had defeated the world's major imperial power, and they had done it without Spartan help. It was a vindication of hoplite tactics and a tremendous boost to Athenian confidence.

Yet the Athenian politician Themistocles (the-MIS-toh-klees) warned that the Persians would not suffer such humiliation quietly and that they would retaliate with an even larger force. So when the Athenians discovered a rich vein of silver ore in the Attic countryside a few years later, Themistocles persuaded them not to divide the windfall among themselves (the customary practice) but to finance a fleet of 200 triremes, state-of-the-art warships. Athens thereby transformed itself into the preeminent naval power of the Greek world, just in time to confront a new Persian onslaught.

Xerxes' Invasion

Darius the Great died in 486 B.C.E. and was succeeded by his son Xerxes, who almost immediately began preparing a massive overland invasion of Greece designed to conquer the entire territory, thus eradicating any future threats to Persian imperial expansion while avenging his father's shame. Supported by a fleet of 600 ships, this grand army (which numbered at least 150,000 men and may have been as large as 300,000) set out from Sardis in 480 B.C.E., crossing the Hellespont (literally "bridge to Greece"), the narrow strait separating Europe from Asia. Unlike his father, who had dispatched talented generals against Athens, Xerxes led this campaign himself.

THE PERSIAN WARS WITH GREECE. Imagine that you are the Persian emperor Xerxes, planning the conquest of Greece in 480 B.C.E.
- *What are the two possible routes that you could take to attack Greece?* - *What geographical considerations would dictate your military strategy?* - *Bearing in mind that Xerxes' attempt failed, what would you do differently?*

Many Greek poleis capitulated immediately. But Athens, Sparta, Corinth, and some thirty others refused to surrender. Instead, they hastily formed the Hellenic League, an unprecedented alliance in the face of an unprecedented external threat. In August of 480, a major Persian offensive was held at bay when the outnumbered Greek allies, under the military leadership of Sparta, confronted Xerxes at the mountain pass of Thermopylae (ther-MO-puh-lie). For three days, they valiantly held off the Persian multitude, whose way through the narrow pass was effectively blocked. Meanwhile, a Greek fleet led by Athens and guided by Themistocles engaged a Persian flotilla off the Attic coast. The Spartans' defense of Thermopylae ultimately failed, but their sacrifice allowed the new Athenian warships to inflict heavy losses on the Persians.

However, these engagements left Athens without any men to defend the city. Themistocles therefore persuaded the entire population to abandon Athens for the island of Salamis. From there, the Athenians watched the Persians torch their city. Time, however, was on their side. Xerxes' massive army depended on his damaged fleet for supplies, and the Persians' military tactics—which included a heavy reliance on cavalry and chariots—were not adapted for the rocky terrain of Greece. Bad weather also made sailing the Aegean in autumn a risky business; the Persians were now desperate to force a decisive battle and return home before the season turned against them.

In late September, the numerically superior Persian fleet sailed into the straits of Salamis, believing that the Athenians were preparing to flee the island. The report turned out to be false, but so confident was Xerxes that he had a throne placed on the headland above the bay, where he would have a good view of his victory. Instead, he watched as the battle-ready Athenian triremes demolished the Persian fleet. This was the turning point of the war. Xerxes retreated with the majority of his army to Persia, while an elite force stayed behind. But when the allied Greek army met the Persians on favorable terrain the next spring—an open plain near Plataea, which had been razed the year before—the Greeks prevailed. Against all odds, the small, fractious poleis had defeated the mightiest army of the known world.

THE GOLDEN AGE OF CLASSICAL GREECE

In the half century after the Persian Wars, Athens enjoyed a meteoric rise in power and prestige, becoming the premier naval power of the eastern Mediterranean and the military rival of Sparta. Athens also emerged as leader of the Delian League, a group of poleis whose representatives met on the sacred island of Delos and pledged to continue the war against Persia, which was now being fought in the Aegean. As the league's leader, Athens controlled its funds and resources. This era simultaneously witnessed the greatest achievements in Athenian culture and politics. These were complicated, however, by the increasingly awkward relationship of Athens with its allies, who began to feel more like Athenian subjects than free poleis.

Periclean Athens

In the decades before the Persian Wars, political reforms in Athens had continued to encourage further experiments in democracy, including the practice of selecting major officeholders by lot. Only one key position was now filled by traditional voting: the office of *strategos*, or general. And because a man could be elected strategos year after year, this office became the career goal of Athens' most ambitious figures. Themistocles had been strategos, as was Cimon (KEY-mohn), who led the Delian League to victories over Persia in the 470s and 460s B.C.E. But Cimon also used the league

GREEK FORCES DEFEAT PERSIANS. This detail from a bowl commemorating the defeat of Xerxes' army depicts an Athenian hoplite poised to strike a death-blow to his Persian opponent. The artist has carefully delineated the differences between the enemies' dress and weaponry. To the Greeks, the Persian preference for trousers over short tunics seemed particularly barbaric and effeminate.

to punish poleis who tried to opt out of membership, even suppressing revolts in these cities by force of arms and so turning the league into an instrument of Athenian policy.

By then, the political mood in Athens was changing. New voices were demanding a greater role in government; most prominent were the *thetes* (*THAY-taes*), the lowest class of free men and the class that provided the triremes' rowers: the backbone of the all-important Athenian fleet. Like the hoplites of the Archaic Period, who had achieved citizenship because they were indispensable to the defense of the poleis, the thetes wanted higher status and equal representation. The man who emerged to champion their cause was Pericles (*PEHR-eh-klees*), an aristocrat from one of Athens' most prestigious families.

Pericles made the enfranchisement of the thetes the main plank of his political platform, and also advocated a foreign policy that was oriented away from cooperation with Sparta. In 462–461 B.C.E. he was elected strategos and immediately used his position to secure the ostracism of his rival, Cimon. He then pushed through reforms that gave every Athenian citizen the right to propose and amend legislation, not just to vote yes or no in the citizen assembly. And by paying an average day's wage for attendance, he made it easier for poorer citizens to participate in the assembly and in courts of justice. Through such measures, the thetes and other free men of modest means became a dominant force in politics—and loyal to the man who had made that dominance possible.

In keeping with the ambitions of Pericles, this populist program glorified Athens through an ambitious scheme of public building and lavish festivals honoring the gods, especially Athena. Personally, too, Pericles was a generous patron of the arts and sciences, attracting the greatest minds and talents of the day to Athens. His popularity, combined with his charisma and his promotion of the Athenians' sense of superiority, ensured his reelection as strategos for the next three decades. During these years Athens flourished, but it also alienated much of the Greek world by its arrogance and aggression.

Athenian Literature and Drama

Athens was not the only city to produce great works of art during this period, but our knowledge of classical Greek culture is dominated by the dramas produced at its great religious festivals. The most important of these was the Dionysia, a great spring feast devoted to the god Dionysus, which became a celebration of Athenian exceptionalism and democratic ideals. From the beginning, therefore, drama was closely connected to the political and religious life of the state that sponsored it. Indeed, the very format of classical tragedy replicates the tensions of democracy, with its complex cast of characters and its conflict among opposing perspectives. This format was perfected under the great tragedian Aeschylus (*AY-skihl-uhs*, 525–456 B.C.E.) and his younger contemporary, Sophocles (496–406 B.C.E.). Their dramas made use of two or eventually, three professional actors, each of whom could play numerous roles, and a chorus of Athenian citizens which represented collective opinion and could comment on the action.

Although Aristotle would later declare that the purpose of tragedy was to inspire pity and fear and so to purge these emotions through a process called *katharsis* ("purification"), this definition does not capture either the variety or impact of Athenian tragedy. Tragedies were almost always set in the distant or mythical past, but they were intended to address the cutting-edge issues of their day. Indeed, the very earliest of all surviving tragedies, Aeschylus' *The Persians*, represents events of the playwright's own lifetime; we know for certain that he fought at Marathon, because he had this fact proudly recorded on his tomb. Performed for the first time in 472, this contemporary tragedy tells the story of the great Athenian victory at Salamis—but through the eyes of the defeated Xerxes, who thus becomes its tragic hero.

Even when its subject matter was derived from the epics of Homer, the fundamental themes of tragedy—justice, the conflicting demands of personal desire and public duty, the unforeseen consequences of human actions, the brutalizing effects of power—addressed problems of immediate concern to Athenians. For example, Aeschylus' trilogy the *Oresteia* (458 B.C.E.) is ostensibly about the legendary family of the Mycenaean king Agamemnon, and traces the long-term consequences of the king's sacrifice of his daughter, Iphigenia; his subsequent murder at the hands of his grieving wife, Clytemnestra; and the vengeance taken by the couple's son, Orestes, on his own mother. But the court of law which eventually tries Orestes is actually that of Periclean Athens, and the plays' debates over the rational application of law are debates that resonated with Aeschylus' contemporaries. *Oedipus at Colonus*, one of Sophocles' later tragedies, used the story of the mythical king of Thebes to comment bitterly on Athens' disastrous war with Sparta (see below). Similarly, the *Trojan Women* of Euripides (485–406 B.C.E.), presented in 415, marks the tragic turning point in the Athenians' march toward defeat in this war. By looking back at the capture, rape, and enslavement of Troy's defeated women, Athenians were forced to look at the dreadful consequences of their own imperial policies.

Comedy was even more obviously a genre of political commentary and social satire, and could deal openly with the absurdities and atrocities of current events. Not

THE THEATER AT EPIDAUROS. Greek dramas were invariably presented in the open air, usually at dawn. Since these were civic spectacles, theaters had to be large enough to accommodate all citizens. Most, like this one at Epidauros (right), took advantage of the natural slope of a hill. The plan for the theater is shown above (left). The acting area would have been backed by a high wall, the *skene*, which housed stage machinery and enhanced the acoustics. A trained actor standing in the *orchestra* would have been plainly audible even to those seated in the top tier. ▪ *How would the size and setting of such a theater enhance the political character of the plays performed within it?*

only was it unconstrained by any formal poetic framework, comedy—then as now—could be effectively and safely deployed to deal with issues that were too hot to handle in any other medium: sexual scandals, political corruption, moral hypocrisy, intellectual pretension, popular fads. Aristophanes (*EHR-ih-STOFF-ah-nees*, c. 446–386 B.C.E.), the greatest of the Athenian comic playwrights, lampooned everything from the philosophy of Socrates to the tragedies of his contemporary Euripides, and was an especially outspoken critic of Athenian warmongers and their imperialist aims. He regularly savaged the powerful figures whom he saw as leading Athens to its doom, and he was repeatedly dragged into court to defend himself against the demagogues he attacked. But the power and popularity of comic theater was such that politicians never dared to shut it down for long. It was too much an expression, and outcome, of Athenian ideals.

Periclean Athens was also fertile ground for the development of new literary forms. Even though the Greeks of this age were becoming more dependent on writing for legal and commercial transactions, they valued highly the arts of memory and oral debate; and intellectuals had long been used to expressing themselves through poetry, which was always intended to be sung and enjoyed in performance, not to be read. (The Milesian philosophers had conveyed their ideas in verse, and Solon had used poetry in justifying his political reforms). In the course of this century, though, the rise of functional literacy in Athens encouraged the emergence of prose as a distinct literary form. Herodotus found

a ready market for his histories in Athens. His younger contemporary Thucydides (*thoo-SID-ih-dees*) followed suit, using his time in exile to write a masterful—and scathingly critical—history of the war between his polis and Sparta, in which he himself had unsuccessfully fought.

Between them, these two historians developed a new approach to the study of the past, emphasizing the need to collect and interpret multiple sources and focusing on human agency as the driving force of history (rather than divine intervention or divine will). Although in different ways, both conceived the historian's role as distinct from that of a storyteller. The word *historia* would continue to mean both "story" and "history" in Greek, but for Herodotus and Thucydides the historian's task was to investigate and critically reflect on the events of his own time, as well as to illuminate those of the past. These methods and goals would increasingly come to inform other prose genres, including the philosophical writings of Plato and Aristotle (see Chapter 4).

Art and Architecture

The visual artists of fifth-century B.C.E. Greece revealed the same range of talents in the visual arts as poets did in their dramas. Their comic gift is exhibited in vessels made for festive use at symposia, which often depict the delights of sensuality, sexual encounters, and scenes from bawdy tales. By contrast, the heroic but humane mode of tragedy corresponds to the marble statues and sculptured reliefs made for temples and public places. Athenian sculptors in particular were drawn to the challenges of representing the human form accurately, while at the same time celebrating an ideal of physical beauty.

Perhaps the most striking development in fifth-century Greek sculpture was the new attention paid to the crafting of naturalistic figures, both clothed and nude. This happened first in Athens. Nothing like it had ever been seen before, although it is a trend already discernible in the figure of the kouros examined on page 82 and in the successive refinements of the sculptor's art made in the previous century. What hastened the acceptance of naturalism in art is a matter of intense debate, but scholars have long wanted to link this innovation to the triumphant victories over the Persians in those key decades. Greeks tended to

regard the Persian male's modesty of dress, preference for trousers, fondness for jewelry, and luxurious long hair as proofs of effeminacy (see the bowl on page 96), whereas Greek men took pride in sculpting their physiques, exercising and participating in athletic contests in the nude. A Greek might have said that only barbarians bowed down to their rulers like slaves and covered their shameful bodies in constricting clothes; free men celebrate their individuality not only in politics but in the care of the body and its representation.

The Athenians also made exceptional contributions to architecture in this period. All Greek temples sought to create an impression of harmony, but the Parthenon of Athens, built between 447 and 438 B.C.E., is generally considered the finest example. Construction of this stunning, expensive, and structurally ambitious building was urged on the

APOLLO OF TENEA, APOLLO OF PIOMBINO, AND THE CRITIAN BOY. These three statues, dating from about 560, 500, and 480 B.C.E., respectively, display the development of Greek statuary art. The first rather stiff and symmetrical statue (left) is imitative of Egyptian sculpture. Roughly a half century later, the second representation (middle) of Apollo begins to display motion, not unlike the kouros on page 82. The last figure (right), showing a boy standing in a relaxed posture with his weight resting on one leg, displays even greater naturalism.

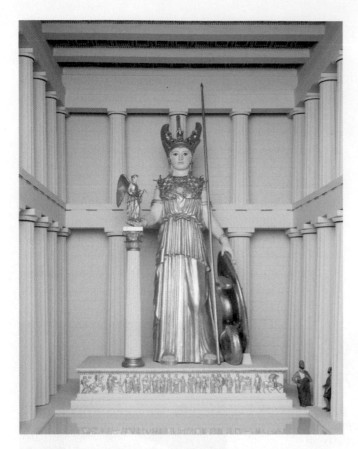

THE SHRINE OF ATHENA IN THE PARTHENON. This is a replica of the statue of Athena that once stood inside the Parthenon dedicated to her (see also the image on page 76). Made of gold and ivory and designed by the great sculptor Phidias, who was updating a more archaic style, the statue stood forty feet high and was visible to viewers oustide the temple and some distance away. Its image would have been reflected in a shallow pool of water located in front of the statue.

Athenians by Pericles as a tribute to their patron goddess, Athena Parthenos ("Athena the Virgin"), and as a symbol of their own power, confidence, and genius.

The Daily Life of Athens: Men, Women, and Slaves

Toward the end of his famous funeral oration, which Thucydides quotes in his history, Pericles addresses only a few brief remarks to the women of Athens who mourn their fallen fathers, husbands, and sons at the end of the first year of the disastrous war with Sparta. He urges them to do three things: rear more children for the support of Athens and its wars, show no more weakness than is "natural to their sex," and attract no attention to themselves. For as he says, the greatest glory of a woman is not to be spoken of at all, whether for good or ill. His remarks reveal widely held attitudes toward women in classical Greece, although they may not reflect complex historical realities.

The growth of democracy did not lead to greater equality between the sexes; in fact, it had the opposite result. In the Bronze Age of Mycenaean Greece, women were viewed as possessing extraordinary funds of courage and wisdom, as well as beauty and virtue. They were prized for their shrewd advice on political and military matters, and they played an active role in the world. Sometimes, elite women ruled kingdoms in their own right. Indeed, this was still the case in the northern territories of Macedon and Epirus, as we shall see (Chapter 4), as well as in some Ionian poleis.

But as aristocratic ideals gave way to more democratic ones, Greek women increasingly spent their lives in the confinement of the home. On the one hand, the importance of the hoplite infantry and its spirit of shared purpose encouraged men to train together and to develop close relationships, something that was also sanctioned by the political system. On the other hand, that spirit of equality discouraged the political agency of women. Instead, the production of children to supply the infantry became the female imperative. Public spaces were largely restricted to male activities, while domestic spaces were reserved for female endeavors, such as child care and weaving. Respectable women lived largely in the seclusion of a house's inner courtyard, rarely venturing forth from their homes.

In Athens, girls could be legally married at age fourteen to husbands more than twice their age. (Younger men were supposed to devote themselves to war.) A girl's father arranged her marriage and provided a dowry that her husband could use for her support. Shortly after a wife entered her new home, a regular schedule of childbirth would begin. Typically, the interval between births was two to four years, meaning that the average young wife would bear between four and six children before she died, usually around the age of thirty-five. Her place might then be taken by another, younger woman.

Because women seldom went out of doors or ventured beyond their immediate neighborhood, since it was thought immodest for them to be seen by men other than those in their families, slaves did whatever shopping or marketing the household required. Even at home, women were expected to withdraw into private rooms if visitors arrived. But they were not supposed to sit around idly, and their main occupation—this was true of all women, from royalty to slaves—was the spinning and weaving of cloth. And since women's work was basically menial, men looked down on them for it, even though their own livelihoods and comfort depended on it. Some evidence even suggests that husbands were not encouraged to form emotional attachments to their wives, although many certainly

WOMEN AND WEAVING. Wool-working and weaving were gender-specific activities throughout the ancient world, in which women of all social ranks were expected to participate. On this red-figure vase, dating from 460–450 B.C.E., we see the woman on the left carding wool, and the two women on the right preparing fibers for spinning into threads, which could then be woven into cloth.

did. In a revealing passage, Herodotus reports of a certain Lydian king that he "fell in love with his own wife, a fancy that had strange consequences." By contrast, an Athenian orator remarked that "we have prostitutes for pleasure, concubines for daily physical needs, and wives to bear us legitimate children and be our faithful housekeepers." But these perspectives are offset by a range of archaeological and material evidence that testify to women's valued social roles, the affection of their husbands and children, and even their wider economic and legal powers.

In addition to depending on the labor and fertility of women, Athenians were as reliant on slaves as Spartans were on helots. Without slavery, none of the Athenian accomplishments in politics, thought, or art would have been possible. The Athenian ideal of dividing and rotating governmental duties among all free men depended on slaves who worked in fields, businesses, and homes while free men engaged in politics. In fact, the Athenian democratic system began to function fully only with the expansion of Athenian mining and commerce around 500 B.C.E., which enabled the Athenians to buy slaves in larger numbers. Freedom and slavery were thus an inescapable contradiction of this democracy—much as they would be many centuries later in the United States, prior to the Civil War.

Although widespread, Athenian slavery was modest in scale. Slaves did not ordinarily work in teams or in factories; the only exceptions were the state-owned silver mines, where large numbers of slaves toiled in miserable conditions. Most slaves were owned in small numbers by a wide range of Athenian families, including the relatively poor. As domestic servants and farm laborers, slaves might even be considered

trusted members of the household, although their masters were legally empowered to beat them or abuse them; concubines were often drawn from among this class of slaves. Yet slaves could never be entirely dehumanized, as they were in modern slaveholding societies: the misfortune of becoming a slave through debt was a reality of Athens' recent past, and the real possibility of being enslaved in war would become a widespread consequence of Athens' overreaching ambitions.

"THE GREATEST WAR IN HISTORY" AND ITS CONSEQUENCES

In more ways than one, Athenian freedom rested on the servitude of others. Slaves performed much of the labor at home, while Athens' allies in the Delian League provided the resources that supported Athenian greatness. Without the surplus wealth flowing into Athens from the league, none of the projects Pericles undertook—pay for political participation, massive building projects, the patronage of Athenian drama—would have been possible. These projects kept Athens rich, its democracy vibrant, and Pericles in power. But ultimately, Athens' foreign policy and imperial ambitions undermined these achievements.

Since the 470s, as we noted above, Athens had begun crushing those allies who attempted to break from its control. By the early 440s, its only rival for supremacy in the Greek world was Sparta. Rather than attempting to maintain a balance of power, however, Pericles determined on a more aggressive policy. In order to ensure that available military resources would be directed toward any future Spartan opposition, he made formal peace with Persia. Yet this undermined the sole purpose of the Delian League, which had been the defense of Greece against Persian aggression. Athens now had no justification for compelling its members to maintain their allegiance. Many remained loyal nonetheless, paying their contributions and enjoying the economic benefits of warm relations with Athens. Others, however, did not, and Athens found itself increasingly having to force its reluctant allies back into line, often installing Athenian garrisons and planting Athenian colonists—who retained their Athenian citizenship—to ensure continued loyalty.

In the context of recent history and longstanding Greek values, such behavior was disturbing. The Delian League had been established to preserve Greek independence. Now Athens itself was becoming an oppressive, imperial power. Foremost among its critics were the Corinthians, whose own economic standing was threatened by Athenian dominance. The Corinthians were close allies of the Spartans, who in turn were the dominant power in what historians call the Peloponnesian League. (The Greeks called it simply the "Spartans and their allies.") When war finally erupted between Athens and Sparta, Thucydides—himself an Athenian—ascribed it to the growing power of Athens and the anxiety this inspired in other poleis. No modern historian has improved on Thucydides' thesis. Yet for the Athenians and their leaders, there could be no question of relinquishing their empire, or the dream of dominating the Mediterranean world. For Sparta and its allies, meanwhile, the prospect of relinquishing their own culture and independence was equally unthinkable. Two very different ideas of Greek superiority were about to fight to the death.

The Peloponnesian War Begins

When the Athenians and Spartans found themselves at war with one another in 431 B.C.E., both sides believed a conclusion would come quickly—a delusion common to many of history's pivotal wars. Instead, the war dragged on for twenty-seven years. Thucydides, writing about it in exile, recalled that he knew from the time of its outbreak that it was going to be "the greatest war in history," amounting to the first world war, because by the time it was over it would involve the entire Mediterranean. He also meant that it was the worst, so devastating to both sides that it partially destroyed the Greeks' proud heritage of freedom. By the time Athens was forced to concede defeat, all the poleis were weakened to such an extent that they would never again be able to withstand outside threats.

From the beginning, Athens knew that it could not defeat Sparta on land; and neither Sparta nor its allies had a fleet capable of facing the Athenians at sea. Pericles therefore developed a bold strategy: he would pull the entire population of Attica within the walls of Athens and its harbor, and not attempt to defend the countryside against Sparta. For sustenance, Athens would rely on supplies shipped in by its fleet, which would also be deployed to ravage the coasts of the Peloponnesus.

The Spartans duly plundered the farms and pastures of Attica, frustrated that the Athenians would not engage them in battle. Meanwhile, the Athenians inflicted significant destruction on Spartan territory in a series of raids and by successfully encouraging rebellion among the helots. The advantage appeared to be on Athens' side, but in 429 B.C.E. the crowded conditions of the besieged city gave rise to a typhus epidemic that killed over a third of the population, including the aged Pericles. Pericles' death revealed that he had been the only man capable of managing the political forces he had unleashed. His successors were mostly dema-

gogues, ambitious men who played to the worst instincts of the demos. The most successful of these was Cleon, a particular target of Aristophanes' ridicule, who refused a Spartan offer of peace in 425 B.C.E. and continued the war until his own death in battle four years later. It was under Cleon that Thucydides was given the impossible task of liberating a city under Spartan control; his failure in 423 led to his exile.

After the death of Cleon, a truce with Sparta was negotiated by an able Athenian leader named Nikias. But Athenians continued to pursue a "dirty war" by preying on poleis that it feared might support the Spartans. This led to atrocities like the destruction of Melos, an island that had been colonized by the Spartans but had maintained its neutrality since the beginning of the war. When the inhabitants of Melos refused to compromise this position by accepting Athenian rule, Athens had the entire male population slaughtered and every woman and child sold into slavery. Thereafter, Athens' policy of preemptive warfare proved destructive to itself. In 415 B.C.E., a charismatic young aristocrat named Alkibiades (al-kih-BY-uh-dees) convinced the Athenians to attack the powerful Greek city of Syracuse in Sicily, which was allegedly harrying Athenian allies in the western Mediterranean. The expedition failed disastrously, ending with the death or enslavement of thousands of Athenian warriors.

News of the Syracusan disaster shattered the Athenians. Many political leaders were driven from the polis as scapegoats, and in 411 B.C.E. a hastily convened assembly of citizens voted democracy out of existence, replacing it with an oligarchy ("rule of the few") consisting of 400 members, many of whom had been present at this vote. The remains of the Athenian fleet, then stationed at Samos on the Ionian coast, responded by declaring a democratic government in exile under the leadership of none other than Alkibiades. The oligarchy proved to be brief, and democracy was restored to Athens by 409. But a pattern of self-destruction had been established, making it difficult for anyone in Athens or outside it to believe in the possibility of restored greatness.

THE FAILURE OF ATHENIAN DEMOCRACY

The Spartans, too, despaired of bringing the war to an end. Even in its weakened condition, the Athenian fleet was still invincible. Finally, Sparta turned to the Persians, who were glad to avenge themselves on Athens and agreed to supply the gold and expertise necessary to train an effective

THE PELOPONNESIAN WAR. This map shows the patchwork of colonies and alliances that bound together the supporters of Sparta and Athens at the outbreak of the Peloponnesian War. ▪ *Which side had the geographical advantage?* ▪ *Which neutral powers might have been able to tip the balance by entering the war on one side or the other?* ▪ *What strategic and military choices did geography impose on the two combatants and their allies?*

Spartan navy. Meanwhile, Athenians were turning against each other and making the Spartans' task easier. In 406, a rare Athenian naval victory at Arginusae (*ar-geh-NOO-si*) ended in a sudden storm, which prevented Athenian commanders from rescuing the sailors whose ships had been wrecked. A firestorm of protest was fanned by demagogues who insisted on making an example of those generals brave enough to return to Athens. One of these was Pericles' son Pericles, who was executed, thereby dying a victim of his father's policies. Through such measures, the Athenians killed or exiled the last of their able commanders.

The result was tragic. The poorly led Athenian fleet was destroyed in 404 B.C.E. Without ships, the Athe-

nians could neither feed themselves nor defend their city. The Spartans sailed the Aegean unopposed, installing pro-Spartan oligarchies to rule former Athenian allies. Finally, they besieged Athens, which surrendered. Corinth and Thebes, remembering the ruthless treatment of Melos, called for Athens' annihilation. The Spartans refused, but imposed harsh terms: the dismantling of Athens' defensive walls, the scrapping of its fleet, and the acceptance of an oligarchy under Spartan supervision. These so-called Thirty Tyrants confiscated private property and murdered their political opponents. Their excesses drove committed democrats to plan a desperate coup, a bloodbath averted only through the intervention of the Spartan kings. By the end

Two Views of Socrates

Socrates as a Sophist

Most people regard Socrates as the sage thinker who challenged the prevailing prejudices of his day. During his own time, however, he was not so universally admired. In Aristophanes' comedy The Clouds, *the protagonist, Strepsiades, goes to Socrates and his "Thought Shop," asking that Socrates make him and his son, Pheidippides, orators capable of winning lawsuits and growing rich. Aristophanes implies throughout that Socrates is a charlatan who teaches word games and tricks for hire.*

STREPSIADES: See that he [Pheidippides] learns your two Arguments, whatever you call them—oh yes, Right and Wrong—the one that takes a bad case and defeats Right with it. If he can't manage both, then at least Wrong—that will do—but that he must have.

SOCRATES: Well, I'll go and send the Arguments here in person, and they'll teach him themselves.

STREPSIADES: Don't forget, he's got to be able to argue against any kind of justified claim at all.

RIGHT: This way. Let the audience see you. . . .

WRONG: Sure, go wherever you like. The more of an audience we have, the more soundly I'll trounce you.

RIGHT: What sort of trick will you use?

WRONG: Oh, just a few new ideas.

RIGHT: Yes, they're in fashion now, aren't they, [*to the audience*] thanks to you idiots. . . . [*to Pheiddipides*] You don't want to be the sort of chap who's always in the agora telling stories about other people's sex lives, or in the courts arguing about some petty, filthy little dispute. . . .

WRONG: People here at the Thought Shop call me Wrong, because I was the one who invented ways of proving anything wrong, laws, prosecutors, anything. Isn't that worth millions—to have a really bad case and yet win? . . . Suppose you fall in love with a married woman—have a bit of fun—and get caught in the act. As you are now, without a tongue in your head, you're done for. But if you come and learn from me, then you can do

whatever you like and get away with it . . . and supposing you do get caught with someone's wife, you can say to him. . . . "What have I done wrong? Look at Zeus; wasn't he always a slave of his sexual passions? And do you expect a mere mortal like me to do any better than a god?" . . .

STREPSIADES [*to Socrates*]: I wonder if you'd accept a token of my appreciation? But my son, has he learned that Argument we were listening to a moment ago?

SOCRATES: Yes, he has.

STREPSIADES: Holy Fraud, how wonderful!

SOCRATES: Yes, you'll now be able to win any case at all.

Source: Aristophanes, *The Clouds*, trans. Alan H. Sommerstein (New York: 1973), pp. 148–50, 154, 159–60 (slightly revised).

Socrates and the Laws of Athens

According to his pupil Plato, Socrates spent the last days of his life in conversation with his friends and followers, some of whom urged him to escape from captivity and live in exile. In the dialogue Crito, *a young aristocrat of that name argues that the very laws that have condemned Socrates are unjust, and that by choosing to obey them Socrates is giving them a legitimacy they do not deserve. Halfway through the debate, Socrates turns the tables on him.*

SOCRATES: I should like you to consider whether we are still satisfied on this point: that the really important thing is not to live, but to live well.

CRITO: Why, yes.

SOCRATES: And that to live well means the same thing as to live honorably, or rightly?

CRITO: Yes.

SOCRATES: Then in light of this agreement we must consider whether or not it is right for me to try to get away without an official pardon. If it turns out to be right, we must make the attempt; if not, we must let it drop. . . .

CRITO: I agree with what you say, Socrates. . . .

SOCRATES: Well, here is my next point, or rather question. Ought one to fulfill all one's agreements, provided they are right, or break them?

CRITO: One ought to fulfill them.

SOCRATES: Then consider the logical consequence. If we leave this place without first persuading the polis to let us go . . . are we or are we not abiding by our just agreements?

CRITO: I can't answer your question, Socrates. I am not clear in my mind.

SOCRATES: Look at it this way. Suppose that while we were preparing to run away (or however one should describe it), the Laws of Athens were to come and confront us with this question: "Now, Socrates, what are your proposing to do? Can you deny that by this act which you are contemplating you intend, so far as you have the power, to destroy us, the Laws, and the whole polis as well? Do you imagine that a city can continue to exist and not be turned upside down, if the legal judgments which are pronounced in it have no force but are nullified and destroyed by private persons?"—How shall we answer this question, Crito, and

others of the same kind? . . . Shall we say, "Yes, I do intend to destroy the laws, because the polis has wronged me by passing a faulty judgment at my trial"? Is this to be our answer, or what?

CRITO: What you have just said, by all means, Socrates.

SOCRATES: Then supposing the Laws say, "Was there provision for this in the agreement between you and us, Socrates? Or did you pledge to abide by whatever judgments the polis pronounced? . . . [I]f you cannot persuade your country you must do whatever it orders, and patiently submit to any punishment it imposes, whether it be flogging or imprisonment. And if it leads you out to war, you must comply, and it is right that you should do so; you must not give way or retreat or abandon your position. Both in war and in the law courts you must do whatever your city and your country commands."

Source: Plato, *Crito*, excerpted (with modifications) from *The Last Days of Socrates*, trans. Hugh Tredennick (New York: 1969), pp. 87–91.

Questions for Analysis

1. Socrates actually refused to teach the art of "making the weaker argument defeat the stronger." But in *The Clouds*, Aristophanes shows him teaching how "to win any case at all." Why were the powers of persuasion considered potentially dangerous in democratic Athens? Why would Aristophanes choose to represent Socrates in this way?

2. How do the arguments of Plato's Socrates compare to those of Aristophanes' character?

3. How does Socrates' sense of honor and his duty toward the polis compare to that of Tyrtaeus of Sparta (page 84)?

---

of 401 B.C.E., Athens had restored a semblance of democratic governance, but it was never more than a shadow of its former self.

With its victory, Sparta succeeded Athens as the arbiter of the Greek world. But this was a thankless job, made worse by the losses the Spartans themselves had suffered during the war, and by the fact that they were even more aggressive in their control of the Aegean than the Athenians had been. In fact, the Spartans found themselves in a position they had avoided throughout their history, because their far-flung interests now sapped their manpower and undermined their control over the helots. They also faced a reinvigorated Persian Empire, which took advantage of the Greeks' fratricidal struggles to increase its naval presence in the Aegean.

These were the circumstances in which the Athenian philosopher Socrates (469–399 B.C.E.) attempted to reform

his city's ethical and political traditions. To understand something of his accomplishments, and to assess the reasons for his tragic death, we must trace briefly the history of philosophical speculation in the half century before his birth.

The Pythagoreans and the Sophists

After the Persian conquest of Ionia, many Milesian philosophers fled to southern Italy. Philosophical speculation thus continued in the Greek "far west." A major proponent was Pythagoras, who founded a philosophical community in the Italian city of Croton. Pythagoras and his followers regarded the speculative life as the highest good, but they believed that one must be purified of fleshly desires in order to achieve this. Just as the essence of life lay in the mind,

SOCRATES. According to Plato, Socrates looked like a goatman but spoke like a god.

other words, values are not moral imperatives, established by the gods. Instead, Protagoras declared that no one could know whether the gods existed or, if they did, what they wanted. He thus concluded that there could be no absolute standards of right and wrong. Empirical facts, established by the perception of the senses, were thus the only source of knowledge. And because each man experienced the world in a different way, there could be only individual truths valid for the individual knower.

Such teachings struck many Greeks as dangerous. Sophists like Protagoras made everyday life a subject for philosophical discussion, but their relativism could too easily degenerate into a conviction that the wise man (or the wise state) is the one best able to manipulate others and gratify individual desires. Both personally and collectively, this conviction could rationalize monstrous acts of brutality—like those committed by Athens in the case of Melos. Indeed, the lessons of the Peloponnesian War went a long way toward demonstrating the disastrous consequences of this self-serving logic: if justice is merely relative, then neither individual morality nor society can survive. This ethical conviction led to the growth of a new philosophical movement grounded on the theory that absolute standards do exist, and that human beings can determine what these are through the exercise of reason. The initiator of this trend was Socrates.

The Life and Thought of Socrates

Socrates was not a professional teacher, as the Sophists were. He may have trained as a stonemason, and he certainly had some sort of livelihood that enabled him to maintain his status as a citizen and hoplite. Having fought in three campaigns as part of the Athenian infantry during the war with Sparta, he was both an ardent patriot and a sincere critic of Athenian policy. His method of instruction was conversation: through dialogue with passers-by, he submitted every presumed truth to rigorous examination in order to establish a firm foundation for further inquiry. Everything we know about Socrates' teachings comes from the writings of younger men who considered themselves his pupils, and who participated in these conversations. The most important of these followers was Plato.

According to Plato, Socrates sought to show that all supposed certainties are merely unexamined prejudices inherited from others. Socrates always said that he himself knew nothing, because this was a more secure place from which to begin the learning process. He sought to base his speculations on sound definitions of key concepts—justice, virtue,

they believed that the essence of the universe was to be found not in the natural world but in the study of abstracts, and so they concentrated on mathematics and musical theory. The Pythagoreans established the key properties of odd and even numbers and also proved an old Babylonian hypothesis in geometry, known today as the Pythagorean theorem. Even though they shunned the material world, they still exhibited the characteristic Greek quest for regularity and predictability in that world.

Meanwhile, philosophy as it developed in mainland Greece was more attuned to questions of ethics and politics than mathematics. The increasing power of individual citizens begged the question of how a man should conduct himself, in public and private life, so as to embrace "the beautiful and the good"—or at least to advance himself by the use of his wits. To answer this latter need were a new group of teachers known as Sophists, a term simply meaning "wise men."

Unlike the Milesian philosophers or the Pythagoreans, however, the Sophists made a living by selling their knowledge. Their teachings are best exemplified by Protagoras (*pro-TAG-or-ahs*), an older contemporary of Socrates. His famous dictum, "man is the measure of all things," means that goodness, truth, and justice are relative concepts, adaptable to the needs and interests of human beings. In

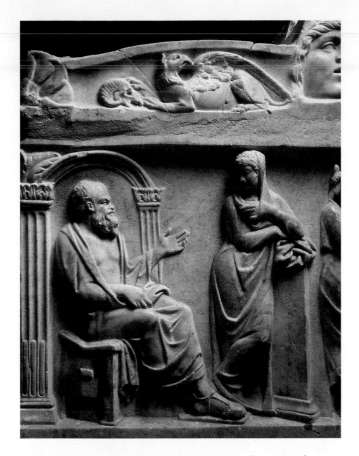

SOCRATES AS THE IDEAL EDUCATED MAN. This image of Socrates features a Roman funerary monument known as the Sarcophagus of the Muses, made in the second century C.E. The Sarcophagus advertises its owner-occupant's desire to be viewed (even in death) as a highly cultivated man: the companion of the Nine Muses of Greek mythology and the companion of Socrates, who taught that the practice of philosophy helped to prepare the soul for immortality.

ing the youth." Although his friends made arrangements for him to flee the city and thus evade punishment, Socrates insisted on abiding by the laws and remaining in prison, thus proving himself true to his own principles and setting an example for future citizens. He died calmly by the prescribed method, self-administered poison.

According to Socrates, the goal of philosophy is to help human beings understand and *apply* standards of absolute good, rather than to master a series of mental tricks that facilitate personal gain at the expense of others. The circumstances of his death, however, show that it is difficult to translate this philosophy into principles that can be widely accepted. This would be the task of Plato, who would lay the groundwork for all subsequent Western philosophy (see Chapter 4).

CONCLUSION

There are many striking similarities between the civilization of ancient Greece and our own—and many stark differences. Perhaps the most salient example of both is the concept of democracy, which the people of ancient Greece would have defined as rule by a class of privileged male citizens supported by slavery. In theory and in practice, this amounted to only a small percentage of the population in Athens, whereas in Sparta the vast majority were subject to the rule of an even smaller class of Spartiates. Moreover, the growth of Athenian power meant, increasingly, the exploitation of other poleis and the spread of imperialism, a ruinous policy of preemptive warfare, and increased intolerance and paranoia. Socrates was not the only man put to death for expressing his opinions. Finally, the status of women in this "golden age" was lower than it had been in earlier periods of Greek history, and women had fewer personal rights than in any of the ancient societies we have studied so far.

And yet the profound significance of Greek experiments with new forms of governance and new ideas about the world is undeniable. This can be seen with particular clarity if we compare the Greek poleis with the empires and kingdoms of the Bronze Age. The typical political regime of the ancient Near Eastern world was, as we have seen, that of a monarch supported by a powerful priesthood. In this context, cultural achievements were mainly instruments to enhance the prestige of rulers, and economic life was controlled by palaces and temples. By contrast, the core values of the Greeks were the primacy of the human male and the principles of competition, individual achievement, and human freedom and responsibility. (The very word for freedom—*eleutheria*—cannot be translated into any ancient Near Eastern language, not even Hebrew.) In his history,

beauty, love—which he and his pupils could arrive at only by investigating their own assumptions. And he focused his attention on practical ethics rather than the study of the physical world (as the Milesians did) or mathematical abstractions (like the Pythagoreans). He urged his listeners to reflect on the principles of proper conduct, both for their own sakes and for that of society as a whole. One should consider the meaning and consequences of one's actions at all times, he taught, and be prepared to take responsibility for them. According to one of his most memorable sayings, "the unexamined life is not worth living."

It is bitterly ironic that such a man, the product of Athenian democracy, should have been put to death by democratic processes. Shortly after the end of the Peloponnesian War, in 399 B.C.E., when Athens was reeling from both the shock of defeat and violent internal upheavals, a democratic faction decided that Socrates was a threat to the state. A democratic court agreed, condemning him to death for denying the gods, disloyalty to the polis, and "corrupt-

Herodotus records a conversation between a Greek (in this case a Spartan) and a Persian, who expresses surprise that the Greeks should raise spears against the supposedly benign rule of his emperor. The Spartan retorts, "You understand how to be a slave, but you know nothing of freedom. Had you tasted it, you would advise us to fight not only with spears but with axes." How the Greeks came to turn those spears on one another within a few generations of their united victory is a story worthy of one of their own tragedies.

Another way of appreciating the enduring importance of Greek civilization is to recall the essential vocabulary we

After You Read
This Chapter

Visit StudySpace for quizzes, additional review materials, and multimedia documents. **wwnorton.com/web/westernciv18**

REVIEWING THE OBJECTIVES

- The Greek polis was a unique form of government. What factors led to its emergence?
- Hoplite warfare had a direct effect on the shaping of early democracy. Why?
- Poleis could develop in very different ways. What are some of the reasons for this?
- In what ways did Athenian culture, philosophy, and art reflect democratic ideals?
- The Persian and Peloponnesian Wars affected Greek civilization in profound ways. Describe some of the consequences of Athens' victory in the former and its defeat in the latter.

have inherited from it: not only the word *democracy* but *politics, philosophy, theater, history*. How would we think without these concepts? The very notion of humanity comes to us from the Greeks. For them, the fullest development of one's potential should be the aim of existence: every free man is the sculptor of his own monument. This work of growing from childishness to personhood is what the Greeks called *paideia,* from which our term *pedagogy* is derived; the Romans called it *humanitas.* How this and other ideas came to be disseminated beyond Greece, to be adopted by the peoples and places of a much wider world, is the subject of Chapter 4.

PEOPLE, IDEAS, AND EVENTS IN CONTEXT

- How did the epics of **HOMER** transmit the values of the Bronze Age to the **ARISTOCRACY** of the new Greek **POLEIS**?

- How did the spread of Greek culture transform the Mediterranean, even as the adoption of **HOPLITE** military tactics transformed Greek politics?

- Compare and contrast the historical circumstances that led to the development of **ATHENS**, **SPARTA**, and **MILETUS**. What were the main differences among them?

- What were the different motives for the invasions of **DARIUS** and **XERXES**? By what methods did the Greek poleis manage to emerge victorious from the **PERSIAN WARS**?

- What were the triumphs and limitations of **DEMOCRACY** in **PERICLEAN ATHENS**?

- How did the **PELOPONNESIAN WAR** transform Athens and affect the balance of power in the Mediterranean?

THINKING ABOUT CONNECTIONS

- The trial and execution of Socrates can be seen as a referendum on the relationship between the individual and the state. What does this incident reveal about the limitations of personal power and individual rights? To what degree was this incident a product of Athenian losses during the Peloponnesian War? To what extent does it reflect long-term trends in the Greek world?

- We like to think that we can trace our democratic ideals and institutions back to Athens, but does this mean that the failings of Athenian democracy also mirror those of our own? What parallels can you draw between the cultures of fifth-century Athens and today's United States? What are some key differences?

STORY LINES

- After the Peloponnesian War, divisions within and among the Greek poleis eventually made them vulnerable to the imperial ambitions of King Philip II of Macedonia and his son, Alexander the Great.

- Alexander's conquest of the Persian Empire and Egypt united the civilizations of antiquity under Greco-Macedonian rule. Even after his untimely death, a shared language and culture continued to bind these civilizations together in a new Hellenistic ("Greek-like") world.

- Ease of travel, trade, and communication throughout this Hellenistic world fostered urbanization on an unprecedented scale. The resulting cosmopolitan culture challenged traditional social, economic, and political norms, giving rise to new social classes, forms of wealth, and technological innovations.

- The unique art forms and intellectual inquiries of Greece were thus disseminated throughout this world, and transformed by it.

CHRONOLOGY

404 B.C.E.	Sparta defeats Athens in the Peloponnesian War
401 B.C.E.	Xenophon and the Ten Thousand begin their Persian expedition
395–338 B.C.E.	The struggle for Greek dominance (Thebes, Athens, Sparta)
371 B.C.E.	Epaminondas of Thebes defeats the Spartans at Leuctra
356 B.C.E.	Philip II becomes king of Macedonia
338 B.C.E.	Macedonia defeats Thebes and Athens at Chaeronea
336–323 B.C.E.	Reign and campaigns of Alexander
323–c. 275 B.C.E.	Formation of the Hellenistic kingdoms
323–c. 225 B.C.E.	The Greek diaspora
c. 300 B.C.E.	Formation of the Aetolian and Achaean Leagues
300–270 B.C.E.	Rise of Stoicism and Epicureanism
c. 300–200 B.C.E.	The Hellenistic scientific revolution
203–120 B.C.E.	Lifetime of the historian Polybius

Before You Read This Chapter

The Greek World Expands, 400–150 B.C.E.

CORE OBJECTIVES

- **EXPLAIN** the reasons for Macedonia's rise to power and its triumph over the Greek poleis.

- **DESCRIBE** Alexander's methods of conquest, colonization, and governance.

- **IDENTIFY** the three main Hellenistic kingdoms and their essential differences.

- **DEFINE** the main characteristics of the Hellenistic world.

- **UNDERSTAND** how new philosophies and artistic movements reflect historical changes.

When the young Alexander of Macedonia set out for Persia in 334 B.C.E, he brought along two favorite books. The first was a copy of the *Iliad*, which his teacher Aristotle had given him. The second was the *Anabasis*, "The Inland Expedition," by an Athenian called Xenophon (*ZEN-oh-fon*, 430–354 B.C.E). Both choices are significant. The *Iliad* recounts the story of a much earlier Greek assault on Asia, and its protagonist is the hero Achilles—a figure with whom Alexander identified: consummate warrior, favorite of the gods, a man who inspired passionate loyalty. It is also full of information useful to someone planning a long campaign in foreign lands against a formidable enemy, with a fractious army drawn from all parts of Greece and little prospect of bringing them home safely or soon. The *Anabasis* was an even more practical choice. Its author had been one of 10,000 Greek mercenaries hired by a Persian prince to overthrow his older brother, the Great King. The attempted coup failed, but Xenophon's book made the prince, Cyrus, another role model for Alexander. It also told, in detail, how Persians fought, how they lived, how they were governed, and what the terrain of their vast empire was like. Moreover, it showed what

111

a dedicated army of hoplites could accomplish on Persian soil. This book would be Alexander's bible for the next ten years as he cut a victorious swath through the ancient civilizations of the Near East.

An avid student of history, Alexander recognized that the golden age of the Greek polis had ended in the war of attrition between Athens and Sparta (discussed in Chapter 3). The fifty years prior to his own birth in 356 B.C.E. had merely continued this trend on a smaller scale, as the dominant poleis—first Sparta, then Thebes, then Athens—jockeyed for prominence. Meanwhile, social and economic problems were mounting. Faith in the old ideals of democracy were compromised by the vast gulf which now opened up between the rich and the poor. Increasingly, the wealthy withdrew from politics altogether, while free citizens were reduced to debt slavery. As the values of the polis decayed, a new generation of intellectuals argued about what had gone wrong, and they tried to imagine how Greece could be saved. One of these philosophers was Aristotle, pupil of Plato and Alexander's own tutor.

Under the circumstances, no one would have been able to predict that the era of greatest Greek influence lay ahead. For rather suddenly, the stalemate of the weakened poleis was shattered by the rise to prominence of a tiny kingdom on their northern borders. Beginning in the reign of King Philip II, Macedonia came to control the Greek mainland. Then, under Philip's remarkable son, a united Greek and Macedonian army extended Greek culture and Greek governance from Egypt to the frontiers of India.

This personal empire, the empire of Alexander, could not last. But a cultural empire built upon it did. For a thousand years, a Hellenistic ("Greek-like") civilization united the disparate lands and peoples of a vast region, forming the basis of the more lasting Roman Empire and mirroring, in uncanny ways, the cosmopolitan world of our own time. How this happened is the subject of Chapter 4.

THE DOWNFALL OF THE GREEK POLIS

The Peloponnesian War had left Sparta as the dominant power in the Greek world, but the Spartans showed little talent for their new preeminence. At home, Spartan politicians remained deeply divided over the wisdom of sending forces beyond their frontiers; abroad, Spartan armies showed even less restraint than the Athenians had done in subduing cities that should have been their allies. In 395, a significant portion of Greece—including such sworn enemies as Athens, Argos, Corinth, and Thebes—accordingly aligned themselves against Sparta in the so-called Corinthian War (395–387 B.C.E.). After years of stalemate, the Spartans could win the war only by turning once again to Persia, as they had done in the final stages of the Peloponnesian War. The Persians brokered a peace which they were also prepared to enforce, one which left Sparta in control of Greece. This pattern of Greek-on-Greek violence, temporarily halted by the intervention of Persia, was repeated time and again over the next fifty years, during which the advantage shifted steadily toward Persia.

The Struggle for Dominance

After the Corinthian War, the Spartans punished the most dangerous of their rivals, Thebes, by occupying the city for four years. This subjugation to a military garrison was intended and received as an act of humiliation, and when

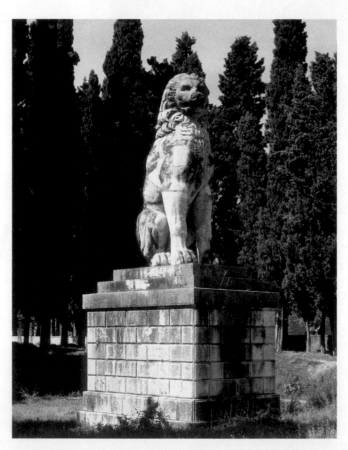

HONORING THE THEBAN SACRED BAND. According to ancient historians, all 300 of the Band's sworn lovers fell at the Battle of Chaeronea in 338 B.C.E., when Thebes was defeated by Macedonian forces led by King Philip II and his son, Alexander. An excavation undertaken at this site in 1890 uncovered the remains of only 254 warriors, but it is possible that some were buried elsewhere. This monument is a modern reconstruction of the one originally erected by the citizens of Thebes toward the end of the fourth century B.C.E.

the Thebans regained their autonomy they elected as their leader a fierce patriot who was also a military genius, Epaminondas (*eh-pa-min-OHN-das*, c. 410–362 B.C.E.).

For decades, various poleis had been experimenting with the basic form of the hoplite phalanx, adding light skirmishers and archers to enhance its effectiveness. Epaminondas now went further. In imitation of the Spartan system, he formed an elite hoplite unit known as the Theban Sacred Band, made up of 150 male couples, sworn lovers who had pledged to fight to the death for their polis and for each other's honor. Epaminondas also trained a corps of lighter-armed, fast-moving infantry. By the early 370s, he was ready for another trial of strength with the Spartans.

The Theban and Spartan armies met at Leuctra in 371 B.C.E. Epaminondas defied convention by placing his best troops (the Sacred Band) on the left-hand side of his formation, and by stacking this phalanx fifty rows deep, making

a narrow wedge of ten men abreast whose hidden depth of strength he further disguised under a cover of arrows and javelin attacks. When the two sides met, the weight of the Theban left drove through the Spartan right flank, breaking it in two and collapsing it. Epaminondas followed his victory by marching through Messenia and freeing the helots. Spartan power—and the unique social system that had supported it—was at an end. Almost overnight, Epaminondas had reduced Sparta to a small, provincial polis and launched what has often been called the Theban Hegemony.

But as Theban power grew, so did the animosity of the other Greek poleis. In 371, Athens had supported Thebes against Sparta, its ancient enemy, but when the Thebans and Spartans squared off again in 362 at the Battle of Mantinea, the Athenians allied themselves with the weaker Spartans. Although the Theban army again carried the day, the brilliant Epaminondas fell in battle, crippling Thebes'

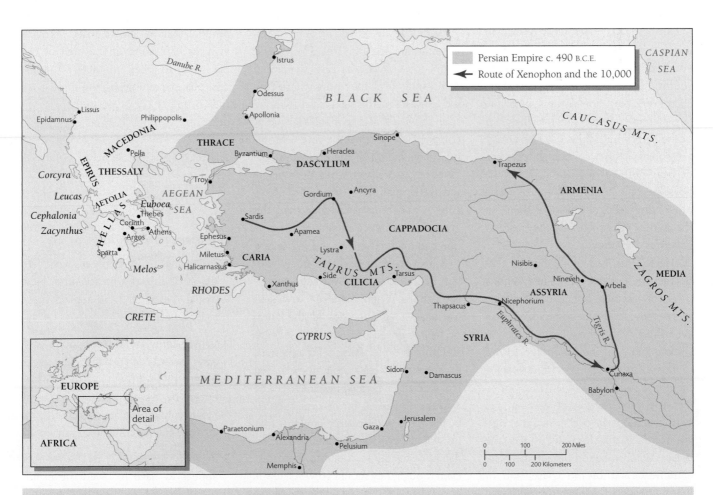

THE INLAND EXPEDITION OF THE TEN THOUSAND. This map shows the route taken by Xenophon and his fellow Greek mercenaries during their Persian campaigns, when they supported the failed coup of Cyrus against his brother Artaxerxes II and then fought their way home through enemy territory (as the *Anabasis* records). Follow Xenophon's route with your finger. ▪ *Where did it start and end?* ▪ *Compare this route with that of Alexander on page 125. How closely was Alexander following it?* ▪ *When and how did he diverge from it?* ▪ *Why would this journey of Greek mercenaries have provided Alexander with an important model?*

Xenophon Describes an Ideal Leader

In his history of "The Inland Expedition" undertaken by the Ten Thousand, Xenophon (430–354 B.C.E.) mourns the death of Cyrus the Younger, whom he believes would have made a better Great King of Persia than the brother he challenged, Artaxerxes II. The following description of the prince's character and leadership became very famous in its time, often circulating as a separate booklet. It is likely to have influenced the young Alexander.

hus then died Cyrus, a man who, of all the Persians since Cyrus the elder, was the most princely and the most worthy of rule, as is agreed by all who appear to have had personal knowledge of him. In the first place, while he was yet a boy, and when he was receiving his education with his brother and other youths, he was thought to surpass them all in everything. For all the sons of the Persian nobles are educated at the gates of the king, where they may learn many a lesson of virtuous conduct, but can see or hear nothing disgraceful. Here the boys see some honored by the king, and others disgraced, and hear of them, so that in their very childhood they learn to govern and to obey.

Here Cyrus, first of all, showed himself most remarkable for modesty among those of his own age, and for paying more ready obedience to his elders than even those who were inferior to him in station; and next, he was noted for his fondness for horses, and for managing them in a superior manner. They found him, too, very desirous of learning, and most assiduous in practicing, the warlike exercises of archery, and hurling the javelin. When it suited his age, he grew extremely fond of the chase, and of braving dangers in encounters with wild beasts. On one occasion, he did not shrink from a she-bear that attacked him, but, in grappling with her, was dragged from off his horse, and received some wounds, the scars of which were visible on his body, but at last killed her. The person who first came to his assistance he made a happy man in the eyes of many.

When he was sent down by his father, as satrap of Lydia and Great Phrygia and Cappadocia, and was also appointed commander of all the troops whose duty it is to muster in the plain of Castolus, he soon showed that if he made a league or compact with anyone, or gave a promise, he deemed it of the utmost importance not to break his word. Accordingly the states that were committed to his charge, as well as individuals, had the greatest confidence in him; and if anyone had been his enemy, he felt secure that if Cyrus entered into a treaty with him, he should suffer no infraction of the stipulations. When, therefore, he waged war against Tissaphernes, all the cities, of their own accord, chose to adhere to Cyrus in preference to Tissaphernes, except the Milesians; but they feared him, because he would not abandon the cause of the exiles; for he both showed by his deeds and declared in words that he would never desert them, since he had once become a friend to them, not even though they should grow still fewer in number, and be in a worse condition than they were.

Whenever anyone did him a kindness or an injury, he showed himself anxious to go beyond him in those respects; and some used to mention a wish of his that he desired to live long enough to outdo both those who had done him good, and those who had done him ill, in the requital that he should make. Accordingly to him alone of the men of our days were so great a number of people desirous of committing the disposal of their property, their cities, and their own persons.

Source: Excerpted from Xenophon, *Anabasis*, ed. M. I. Finley in *The Portable Greek Historians* (New York: 1959), pp. 383–84.

Questions for Analysis

1. According to Xenophon, what are the attributes of a great leader? How would Alexander have applied these to his own situation?

2. What seems to be Xenophon's attitude toward the Persians? How might his portrayal of them have been influenced by his travels among them? How might it have been colored by his attitude toward his own countrymen?

3. In what ways does Cyrus the Younger appear to have followed the example of his ancestor, Cyrus the Great (Chapter 2, page 64)?

leadership. Athens then attempted to fill the vacuum by establishing a naval confederacy, organized more equitably than the Delian League had been. But the Athenians quickly reverted to manipulating and abusing their allies, and the confederacy dissolved in rebellions. Greece was thus reduced to a constellation of petty warring states, increasingly debilitated by their struggles with one other.

Social and Economic Crises

Meanwhile, individual poleis were also riven by internal turmoil. Athens was spared the political revolutions many other cities suffered, mostly because the memory of the Thirty Tyrants had discredited the cause of oligarchy there; but elsewhere in the Greek world, strife between democrats and oligarchs worsened. Incessant warfare, combined with these political struggles, profoundly affected the Greek world's economic and social infrastructures. Many ordinary people were driven from their homes or reduced to slavery. Country towns had been ravaged, some repeatedly, as had farmlands throughout Greece. The destruction of orchards and vineyards was particularly devastating because of the long time it takes grapevines and olive trees to mature: 40 or 50 years in the latter case. So when an invading army cut down an olive grove, it was destroying a staple crop for two generations. Even arable land was exhausted and less productive than it had been earlier. As a result, prices rose around 50 percent while standards of living declined because wages remained more or less stagnant. Taxes increased. In Athens, the wealthiest private citizens now became the sponsors of public theaters and buildings, as well as the patrons who maintained roads and warships. Even so, the kind of ambitious civic spending undertaken by the tyrants or by Pericles was unknown in the fourth century B.C.E.

Unemployment was also widespread, especially among the growing population of the cities, which were swollen with refugees from the political collapse of the countryside and overseas colonies. During wartime, men might find employment as rowers or soldiers in the service of their city; but when their city was at peace, many turned instead to mercenary service. The Greek states of Sicily and Italy began to hire mercenaries from the mainland, as did Sparta to supplement its own campaigns. As we have already noted, the brother of the Persian emperor Artaxerxes II, Cyrus, even hired a Greek mercenary force of 10,000 men in an attempt to seize the throne in 401 B.C.E.—although he did not reveal this aim until the army was deep in Persian territory and suddenly confronted with an enemy far more formidable than the tribal bands it had originally agreed to fight. Cyrus was killed in battle, and shortly thereafter, the Ten Thousand's Spartan general was murdered by agents of Artaxerxes. The army—marooned in a hostile country—had to fight its way out under elected leaders, one of whom was Xenophon, who later wrote his account of these adventures. Finally, the veterans reached the Black Sea and made their way back to Greece, where many (including Xenophon) settled in Sparta. Despite all these hardships, this episode was a stunning demonstration of what a professional Greek army could achieve, and it would fire the imagination of Alexander.

REIMAGINING THE POLIS: THE ARTISTIC AND INTELLECTUAL RESPONSE

399 B.C.E., the year of Socrates' execution, might be taken to mark the end of an era: that of the polis. This basic engine of Greek life had continued to drive innovation and cultural production even during the Peloponnesian War, both in support of the war and in opposition to it. In Athens alone, the historians Herodotus (in his final years) and Thucydides were at work, as were the tragic poets Sophocles and Euripides, the comic playwright Aristophanes, and scores of talented statesmen, poets, sculptors, and artisans. But it's hard not to see the death of Socrates as symbolic of democracy's failure. Thereafter, the evident breakdown of society during the fourth century had a profound impact on the arts, philosophy, and political thought.

The Arts of the Fourth Century

As we observed in Chapter 3, the painters and sculptors of the fifth century B.C.E. were already working to achieve a heightened appearance of realism. This experimentation continued in the fourth century, especially in the relatively new art of portraiture. In this era, painters and sculptors tried to render both objects and people as they actually looked—for better or for worse—and to convey the illusion of movement, trends that would continue in subsequent centuries. They also grew bolder in their use of tricky techniques, like the casting of full-size statues in bronze, a technology that combined high levels of artistry with sophisticated metallurgy. This was a medium in which the era's most famous sculptor, Praxiteles, excelled. Praxiteles (*prak-SIT-el-ees*) was bold, too, in his choice of subjects, and he is widely regarded as the first artist to create full-size

Reconstructing an Ideal of Female Beauty

The lost statue known as the Aphrodite of Knidos was considered the most beautiful in the ancient world, but we can only study it by looking at later copies. It was the work of the fourth century's most renowned sculptor, Praxiteles, who was reputed to have modeled it after the Athenian courtesan known as Phryne, a renowned beauty who inspired several contemporary artists and a whole series of apocryphal stories. The most reliable of these tales concerns the riches she accrued: apparently she became so wealthy that she offered to finance the rebuilding of Thebes in 336—on the condition that the slogan "destroyed by Alexander, restored by Phryne the Courtesan" be prominently displayed on the new walls. (Her offer was rejected.)

Praxiteles' original statue is thought to have been the first monumental female nude fashioned in antiquity. According to one authority, Praxiteles had initially received a commission from the island of Kos, for which he fashioned both clothed and naked versions of Aphrodite. Apparently, the scandalized citizens approved only the draped version and refused to pay for the nude. It was purchased instead by the city of Knidos on Cyprus, where it was displayed in an open-air temple so that it could be seen from all sides. It quickly became a tourist attraction and was widely copied and emulated. Two of the more faithful replicas, made by later artists working in Rome, are pictured here.

Questions for Analysis

1. As we have seen, the male nude was a favorite subject of Greek artists from the Archaic Period onward. Based on your knowledge of contemporary Greek culture and society, why was it only in the fourth century B.C.E. that a life-size female nude could be publicly displayed? Are there any precedents for statues like this?

2. Compare and contrast the ideal of female beauty suggested by the Knidian Aphrodite with the male ideals discussed in Chapter 3. What can you conclude about the relationship between these ideals and the different expectations of male and female behavior in Greek society? Why, for example, would ancient sources insist that the model for this statue was a courtesan?

3. Among the Romans, a statue like the Knidian Aphrodite was called a *Venus pudica*, a "modest Venus" (image A). Yet the citizens of Kos were allegedly shocked by its indecency, while old photographs of the copy in the Vatican Museum (image B) show that it was displayed until 1932 with additional draperies made of tin. How do you account for these very different standards of decency? To what degree do they suggest that concepts of "beauty" or "modesty" are historically constructed?

A. Roman copy of the Aphrodite of Knidos.

B. Second century C.E. copy of the Aphrodite of Knidos.

female nudes, an innovation that sparked controversy in his own day and in other eras as well (see **Interpreting Visual Evidence** on page 116).

The forms and functions of drama also changed considerably. In large part, this was because tragedy and comedy were no longer mounted as part of publicly funded festivals but were instead paid for by private individuals who could exercise greater control over the content of performances. As a result, fourth-century playwrights did not have the freedom to use drama as a vehicle for political and social critique. Nor did the comic genius of Aristophanes have any true fourth-century successors. His biting, satirical wit gave way to a milder, less provocative style that bears some resemblance to early

BRONZE YOUTH. This lithe statue, dating from the years 340–330 B.C.E., was found in the sea near Marathon and has been identified as a work by the master sculptor Praxiteles (or one of his pupils). Compare this male nude to those discussed in Chapter 3. ■ *How might changes in the style of sculpture parallel cultural changes in society at large?*

television sitcoms. It was this "New Comedy" that laid the groundwork for comedy as it developed over the next several centuries: it came to rely more and more on mistaken identities, tangled familial relationships, humorous misunderstandings, and breaches of etiquette. The most famous comic playwright of this age was Menander (c. 342–292 B.C.E.), whose work survives today only in fragments but who directly inspired the comedians of the Roman theater, who in turn inspired medieval and then early modern playwrights like Shakespeare. Similar trends toward escapism and frivolity are also apparent in a new literary genre that emerged during the fourth century: the prose novel, in which star-crossed lovers undergo extraordinary trials and perilous adventures before reuniting happily after a long separation. These pleasant fictions targeted an increasingly literate audience, including (like modern romance novels) an audience of women.

Philosophy after Socrates: The Schools of Plato and Aristotle

The intellectual and political work undertaken by Socrates was carried forward by his most talented student, Plato. Born in Athens to an aristocratic family around 429 B.C.E., Plato joined Socrates' circle as a young man and witnessed at first hand the persecution, trial, and death of his mentor. For the next fifty years, to the time of his own death around 349 B.C.E., he usually shunned direct political involvement and strove instead to vindicate Socrates by constructing a philosophical system based on his teacher's unwritten precepts. Socrates had taught through dialectical conversation and by example; he mistrusted writing and resisted developing a coherent set of principles. Plato's mission was therefore to transmit his legacy in a way that captured the liveliness and charm of the Socratic method but within a more structured framework.

He did this in two ways: first by founding an informal school called the Academy (which had no tuition or set curriculum) and later by writing a series of dialogues that wrapped weighty philosophical content in a witty and accessible dramatic format, with Socrates as the central character. Most dialogues are known by the names of Plato's contemporaries, the original students who had engaged Socrates in discussion (such as Crito, whose imagined dialogue with Socrates is excerpted in Chapter 3). One dialogue, the *Symposium*, actually re-creates the conversation at a drinking party, where a tipsy Socrates, the comedian Aristophanes, and other Athenian worthies debate the nature of love.

PLATO AND ARISTOTLE. Although many artistic representations of Plato and Aristotle were made in antiquity, the image that best captures the essential difference between their philosophies is this one, the focal point of a fresco by the Renaissance painter Raphael Sanzio (1483–1520 c.e., to be discussed further in Chapter 12). Plato is the older man to the viewer's left, who points with his right hand to the heavens; Aristotle is the younger man, gesturing with an open palm to the earth. ■ *How does this double portrait reflect these philosophers' teachings and perspectives?*

The longest and most famous of Plato's dialogues is now known by its Latin title, the *Republic*. In Greek, it is the *Politeía* ("Polis-governance" or even "Policy"), the first treatise on political philosophy written in the West. In it, Plato argues—through the character of Socrates—that social harmony and order are more important than individual liberty or equality. He imagines an ideal polis in which most of the people—farmers, artisans, traders—are governed by a superior group of "guardians" chosen in their youth for their natural attributes of intelligence and character. These prospective guardians would serve the polis first as soldiers, living together without private property. Those found to be the wisest would then receive more education, and a few would ultimately become "philosopher-kings." These enlightened rulers would in turn choose the next generation of guardians.

This utopian system actually bears an intriguing resemblance to the social order of Sparta, as well as containing elements of a benign tyranny, and is clearly a response to the failures of Athenian democracy in Plato's youth. But whether Plato himself believed in this system—he never voices his own opinion—is open to interpretation. Indeed, the students of Socrates who are represented as discussing it with him voice many objections. The most obvious of these is "Who will guard the guardians?" For such a system presumes that properly educated rulers will never be corrupted by power or wealth: a proposition that has yet to be sustained in practice.

The more practical applications of philosophy would be the preoccupation of Plato's own student, Aristotle (384–322 B.C.E.). Aristotle, the son of a physician, learned from his father the importance of observing natural phenomena. Although receptive to Plato's training, Aristotle's own philosophical system was geared toward understanding the workings of the world through the rational analysis of empirical knowledge—that is, information gained through sensory experience. In contrast to Plato, who taught that everything we see and touch is an untrustworthy reflection of some intangible ideal, Aristotle advocated the rigorous investigation of real phenomena, in order to uncover the natural order of the universe and of human beings' place within it. His method of instruction was also different. Unlike Socrates and Plato, whose dialogues were often playful, Aristotle delivered lectures on which his students took detailed notes, and eventually these notes became the basis of separate but interrelated treatises on politics, ethics, logic, metaphysics, and poetics. Aristotle also established rules for the syllogism, a form of reasoning in which certain premises inevitably lead to a valid conclusion, and he developed precise categories that could be used to further philosophical and scientific analysis.

With respect to ethics, Aristotle taught that the highest good consists in the harmonious functioning of the individual human mind and body. Since humans differ from animals by virtue of their rational capacities, he argued, they find happiness by exercising these capacities appropriately. Good conduct is therefore rational conduct, and consists in acting moderately: showing courage rather than rashness or cowardice, temperance rather than excessive indulgence or self-denial. And whereas Plato conceived of politics as a means to an end which could never be achieved in this life, Aristotle thought of politics as an end in itself: the collective exercise of moderation.

But Aristotle also took it for granted that some people—like barbarians—are not fully human, and so are intended by nature to be slaves. He also believed that women were not endowed with a full measure of humanity and so could never achieve the good life, either as individuals or as participants in the public sphere of the polis. So when Aristotle asserted that "man is by nature a political animal" (or, to be more faithful to the Greek, "a creature of the polis"), he meant only Greek males of privileged status. Nor did he believe that the best form of government is a democracy. Like Plato, Aristotle saw that as a "debased" form of government. What he preferred was the polity, in which monarchical, aristocratic, and democratic elements are combined by means of checks and balances. Only this form of government, he posited, would allow free men to realize their rational potential.

Men of Thought and Action

For all their brilliance and originality, Plato and Aristotle offered few prescriptions for reforming their own societies. Both imagined the perfect polis as one made up of a few thousand households, largely engaged in agriculture and living together in a single community. Although Greek civilization had begun in such a world, the realities of fourth-century political life were very different. Plato and Aristotle recognized this, to an extent, yet for both the answer was a reorganization of existing institutions, not something entirely new.

But there were other intellectuals at this time who were considering more radical alternatives. One was Xenophon, that veteran of the Ten Thousand, who was actually another product of the Socratic tradition and an exact contemporary of Plato. After his return from Persia, he went on to fight for the Spartan king Agesilaus (*ah-geh-si-LA-uhs*), who became a trusted friend. Thoroughly disillusioned by the failures of Athenian democracy, Xenophon spent most of his adult life in exile, and it is mostly thanks to his admiring account that we know anything about the Spartiate system described in Chapter 3. He intended his description to be a rebuke to Athens. We also have his own view of Socrates' teaching, which he related in a series of memoirs and treatises on kingship and household management (the *Oikonomikos*, the root of our word *economics*). He also loved horses and dogs, and wrote a treatise on training them for the hunt. All the while, he watched as the Theban leader Epaminondas crippled the state he so admired, Sparta. (Xenophon hated him so much that he refused to mention his name in the history he was compiling).

The Athenian orator Isocrates (436–338 B.C.E.) was another direct contemporary of Plato and was also convinced that something had gone horribly awry as a result of the Peloponnesian War. Rather than imagining that a solution lay in the reform of the polis, he proposed instead that the Greeks rediscover their lost unity by staging a massive invasion of Persia. This assault, he prophesied, would be led by a man of vision and ability, someone who could unite the Greek world behind his cause. Isocrates spent most of his life casting about to find such a leader. Finally, he began to think that the man for the job was someone whom most Greeks considered no Greek at all: the king of Macedonia, Philip II.

THE RISE OF MACEDONIA

Iscocrates had a point. By the middle of the fourth century, the Greek poleis had become so embroiled in military, political, and socioeconomic turmoil that they barely noticed the powerhouse on their northern frontier. Until the fourth century, Macedonia (or Macedon) had been a weak kingdom, regarded as a throwback to the "dark ages" before the

Aristotle's Justification of Slavery

Like The Republic *of his teacher, Plato, Aristotle's treatise on* Politics *attempts to define and rationalize various methods of governance. Early in this work, Aristotle must grapple with the fact that all ancient societies were highly dependent on slave labor, and he must answer objections that the forcible subjugation of some men to the will of others goes against the laws of nature and the ideals of his own society.*

But is there anyone thus intended by nature to be a slave, and for whom such a condition is expedient and right, or rather is not all slavery a violation of nature? There is no difficulty in answering this question, on grounds both of reason and of fact. For that some should rule and others be ruled is a thing not only necessary, but expedient; from the hour of their birth, some are marked out for subjection, others for rule. . . .

But that those who take the opposite view have in a certain way right on their side, may be easily seen. For the words *slavery* and *slave* are used in two senses. There is a slave or slavery by law as well as by nature. The law of which I speak is a sort of convention—the law by which whatever is taken in war is supposed to belong to the victors. But this right many jurists impeach, as they would an orator who brought forward an unconstitutional measure: they detest the notion that, because one man has the power of doing violence and is superior in brute strength, another shall be his slave and subject.

Even among philosophers there is a difference of opinion. The origin of the dispute, and what makes the views invade each other's territory, is as follows: in some sense virtue, when furnished with means, has actually the greatest power of exercising force; and as superior power is only found where there is superior excellence of some kind, power seems to imply virtue, and

the dispute to be simply one about justice (for it is due to one party identifying justice with goodwill while the other identifies it with the mere rule of the stronger). If these views are thus set out separately, the other views have no force or plausibility against the view that the superior in virtue ought to rule, or be master. Others, clinging, as they think, simply to a principle of justice (for law and custom are a sort of justice), assume that slavery in accordance with the custom of war is justified by law, but at the same moment they deny this. For what if the cause of the war be unjust?

And again, no one would ever say he is a slave who is unworthy to be a slave. Were this the case, men of the highest rank would be slaves and the children of slaves if they or their parents chance to have been taken captive and sold. Wherefore Hellenes [Greeks] do not like to call Hellenes slaves, but confine the term to barbarians. Yet, in using this language, they really mean the natural slave of whom we spoke at first; for it must be admitted that some are slaves everywhere, others nowhere.

The same principle applies to nobility. Hellenes regard themselves as noble everywhere, and not only in their own country, but they deem the barbarians noble only when at home, thereby implying that there are two sorts of nobility and freedom, the one absolute, the other relative. . . .

We see then that there is some foundation for this difference of opinion, and that all are not either slaves by nature or

freemen by nature, and also that there is in some cases a marked distinction between the two classes, rendering it expedient and right for the one to be slaves and the others to be masters: the one practicing obedience, the others exercising the authority and lordship which nature intended them to have. The abuse of this authority is injurious to both; for the interests of part and whole, of body and soul, are the same, and the slave is a part of the master, a living but separated part of his bodily frame. Hence, where the relation of master and slave between them is natural they are friends and have a common interest, but where it rests merely on law and force the reverse is true.

Source: Excerpted from Aristotle, *Politics*, Book I: v–vi, trans. Benjamin Jowett (Oxford: 1920), pp. 32–37.

Questions For Analysis

1. According to Aristotle, how does one become a slave? Why is the question of slavery's justice related to that of the just war?

2. Aristotle posits that some people are slaves by nature, others by some unfortunate circumstances (such as being captured in battle). For example, he says that Hellenes (Greeks) do not admit that they can be slaves; that is possible only for barbarians. What are the implications of this argument?

emergence of enlightened poleis, ruled by a royal dynasty barely strong enough to control its own nobility and beset by intrigue and murderous ambition. As recently as the 360s, Macedonia had teetered on collapse, nearly succumbing to the even smaller kingdoms and predatory tribes that surrounded it.

Despite the efforts of a few Macedonian kings to add a gloss of Hellenic culture to their court—one had successfully invited Euripides and Sophocles to his palace—the Greeks considered them nearly as barbaric as their northern neighbors. It is still not known whether the ancient Macedonians were Greek-speaking during this period, although the royal family and nobility would at least have spoken Greek as a second language; and Macedonians seem to have participated in the Olympic Games, which were open only to Greeks. But they were definitely perceived as dangerous outsiders. Therefore, when a young and energetic king named Philip consolidated the southern Balkans under his rule, many Greeks saw it as a development no less troubling than the approach of the Persians in the fifth century.

The Reign of Philip II (359–336 B.C.E.)

Philip II of Macedonia was not supposed to be its ruler. Born in 382, he was the third and youngest son of King Amyntas III, and was considered so dispensable that he was sent to Thebes as hostage when he was fourteen, at the time of the Theban Hegemony. This turns out to have been the making of him: he became the protégé of the brilliant Epaminondas and may even have trained alongside the general Pelopidas (*pel-OH-pi-das*) in the Theban Sacred Band. By the time he returned to the Macedonian capital of Pella in 364, three years later, he had received a more thorough education in Greek culture and military tactics than any Macedonian before him.

He was also ambitious, and may already have laid great plans for the future. So when both of his older brothers died in battle, one after the other, Philip was not content with the role of regent for an infant nephew. By 356, he had supplanted this nephew and was reigning as king, the same year that his queen, Olympias, bore him an heir. The boy was given the dynastic name Alexandros, meaning "a leader of men."

The first problem of Philip's reign was the fragility of Macedonia's northern borders. Through a combination of warfare and diplomacy, he subdued the tribes of the southern Balkans and incorporated their territory into his kingdom—losing an eye in the process. His success in this had much to do with his reorganization of Macedonian warriors into a hoplite infantry along Theban lines. The mineral resources to which he now had access also helped, since Philip used that new wealth to pay and equip

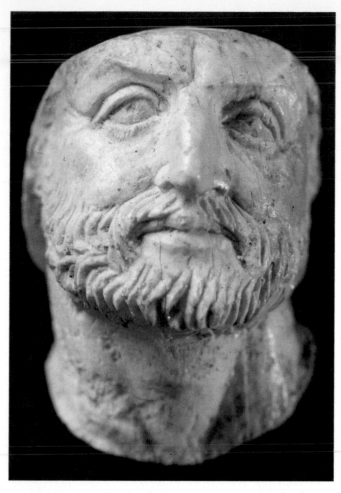

PHILIP II OF MACEDONIA. This tiny ivory head was discovered in a royal tomb at Vergina and is almost certainly a bust of the king himself. Contemporary sources report that Philip the Great had his right eye blinded by a catapult bolt, a deformity visible here—and testimony to the unflinching realism of Greek portraiture in the fourth century B.C.E.

a standing professional army; just one of his gold mines produced as much in one year as the Delian League at its height had collected annually.

Philip also organized an elite cavalry squad—the Companions—who fought with and beside the king, an innovation that may have been designed to emulate the esprit de corps of the Sacred Band, and was further intended to counter the Persian reliance on cavalry. These young men were drawn exclusively from the nobility, and Philip thereby hoped to inspire their deeper loyalty; in fact, under the guise of recruiting future Companions, he gained valuable young hostages to ensure the good conduct of aristocratic rivals. Their sons were now being brought up alongside Alexander and sharing his lessons with Aristotle, who had arrived at the Macedonian court in 343 B.C.E. Through a series of strategic marriages, Philip also managed to gain the good will and alliance of many neighboring kingdoms—although his frank polygamy was, in Greek eyes, another barbarity that called to mind the harems of Persia.

Eventually, the increasing strength of Macedonia began to impinge on the consciousness of some Greeks, most notably the Athenians. But whereas Isocrates saw in Philip a potential savior of Greece, many Athenians believed that Philip's ultimate aim was to conquer and subjugate them. They may have misunderstood Philip's goals: his northward expansion was designed to secure his frontiers and the resources necessary to support an invasion of Persia, not of Greece. From 348 B.C.E. on, he was actually trying to forge an alliance with Athens, whose fleet could facilitate such an invasion by sea; in return, Philip promised to support Athens' old claim to hegemony over Greece. But the Athenians took the advice of an orator called Demosthenes, and refused to cooperate with Philip.

This miscalculation would prove disastrous. Philip's inability to reach a peaceful understanding with Athens, despite strenuous diplomatic efforts, ultimately led to war, which sent the Athenians scrambling to ally with their former enemy, Thebes, and a number of smaller poleis. Their fate was sealed at the battle of Chaeronea (*kie-ROH-nee-ah* in 338 B.C.E., when an army led jointly by Philip and Alexander (aged eighteen) won a narrow victory, decimating the Athenian forces and destroying the Theban Sacred Band. In the aftermath, Philip called delegates from around mainland Greece to Corinth, where he established a new political federation. The main purpose of this federation, the League of Corinth, was to provide forces for the invasion of Persia and to maintain peace among the rival poleis.

Philip never realized his dream of Persian conquest. Two years later, in 336 B.C.E., he was assassinated during a festival at Pella, purportedly by a vengeful favorite. The kingship now fell to Alexander. Among the Greeks, he would be known as Alexander, the Sacker of Cities. To the Romans, impressed by his ruthless military genius, he was Alexander the Great.

MACEDONIAN PHALANX. Philip of Macedonia's hoplite infantry—the model for Alexander's—was armed with two-handed pikes of graduated lengths, from thirteen to twenty-one feet, and was massed in squares sixteen rows deep and wide. Members of the phalanx were trained to wheel quickly in step formation and to double the width of their front rank as needed, by filing off in rows of eight. The reach of their spears, called *sarissas*, extended the phalanx's fighting range.

THE CONQUESTS OF ALEXANDER (336–323 B.C.E.)

By the time of Alexander's early death at the age of thirty-two, a monumental legend had already built up around him. This makes it all the more ironic and frustrating that no contemporary account of his life and achievements survives. The great library assembled in his capital of Alexandria in Egypt—the repository of all ancient Greek learning and literature—was destroyed centuries later, and with it a great portion of assembled knowledge. So when we try to reconstruct the history of Alexander, we are depending on the writings of men who lived and worked under the Roman Empire, notably Plutarch (46–120 C.E.) and Arrian (c. 86–160 C.E.), both of whom were separated from their subject by a distance of 400 years. Luckily, there is good reason to believe that they were basing their histories on sources derived from two firsthand accounts, one written by Alexander's general (and alleged half brother) Ptolemy (*TOHL-eh-mee*, c. 367–c. 284 B.C.E.), who founded a new dynasty of Egyptian pharaohs, and another by Æschines Socraticus (c. 387–322 B.C.E.), an Athenian statesman. Nevertheless, it is a salutary reminder of how fragile the historical record of antiquity is, that sources for the life of the era's most famous man are so hard to come by.

The Conquest of Persia

When Alexander succeeded his father in 336 B.C.E., he could not begin to carry out his plans of conquest until he had put down the revolts that erupted immediately after Philip's death—notably at Thebes, an uprising that he punished by destroying its famous walls. Two years later, he was crossing the Hellespont at the head of a hoplite army to challenge the Great King of Persia, Darius III.

From the beginning, Darius was no match for Alexander. He was a minor member of the royal family who had taken the dynastic name when he was placed on the throne after a palace coup, at the relatively old age of forty-five, in the same year that Alexander himself became king at age twenty. Darius and his advisers failed to take the Macedonian threat seriously, despite the Persians' past history of defeat at the hands of Greek armies—even on Persian soil and within living memory. Perhaps they assumed that the enormous forces they could rally in defense of their empire would easily overwhelm a comparatively small army of 42,000; perhaps they misunderstood Alexander's aims, which would reveal themselves over time to be far-reaching indeed. In any event, the Persian army of Darius III was made up of mercenaries or poorly paid conscripts under the command of inexperienced generals.

Alexander achieved a series of extraordinary victories, beginning in northwest Anatolia, near the epic field of Troy, and continuing down the Ionian coastline. In 333 B.C.E., Darius was persuaded to engage Alexander personally, at the head of a force that significantly outnumbered that of his opponent. But the chosen site, on the banks of a river near Issus, favored Alexander's fast-moving infantry, not the heavy cavalry and chariots of the Persians, which had no room to maneuver and were hampered by mud. No warrior himself, Darius disrespectfully fled the battlefield, abandoning not only his army but his entire household, which included his wife and his mother. They were captured by Alexander's troops, and treated by him with great respect.

Darius spent the remainder of his life running from Alexander's advancing army, until his decisive defeat at Gaugamela (near Mosul in modern Iraq) in 331, when he was killed by a local chieftain who hoped to win Alexander's favor. Instead, Alexander—acting as the new Great King—had the chieftain executed for treason against his former enemy and predecessor. The next spring, Alexander destroyed the royal capital of Persepolis, lest it serve as a rallying point for Persian resistance.

Meanwhile, in the two years that had passed since Darius's humiliation at Issus, Alexander had completed his conquest of Asia Minor. One by one, the cities of Syria and Palestine surrendered after Alexander made a powerful statement by destroying the wealthy Phoenician capital at Tyre. Following the example of Cyrus the Great, whose tactics he came increasingly to emulate, Alexander developed a policy of offering amnesty to cities that submitted peacefully—but dealing mercilessly with those that resisted. The forti-

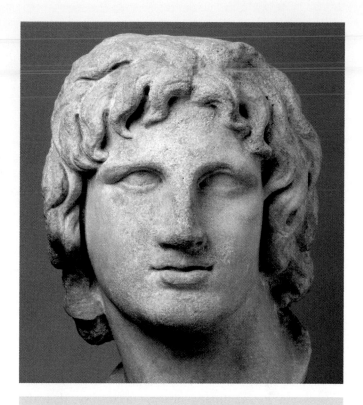

MARBLE HEAD OF ALEXANDER. Alexander the Great was reported to have been very striking in appearance, although sources vary in their assessment of his physical beauty. This portrait bust was made in 180 B.C.E., about 150 years after his death. ■ *Given the trends in sculpture during that period (see page 139), is this likely to have been an accurate portrait?*

fied city of Gaza, the last Persian stronghold on the Egyptian border, provides an example: its commander, Batis, not only refused to surrender but seemed determined to fight to the death, inflicting severe losses on the troops besieging his city and seriously wounding Alexander himself. When the fortress was finally taken, Alexander's troops slew all the adult

ALEXANDER DEFEATS KING DARIUS OF PERSIA AT THE BATTLE OF ISSUS (333 B.C.E.). This Roman mural, discovered at Pompeii, shows Darius fleeing from the battlefield in his chariot (right), pursued by Alexander, the mounted figure on the far left. Note the reflection of Alexander and his horse in Darius's large round shield.

males and enslaved the women and children. According to a later Roman historian, Alexander also dragged the body of Batis around the city's walls behind his chariot, imitating Achilles' treatment of his fallen rival Hector.

Alexander in Egypt

After this, Alexander marched into Egypt unopposed. In fact, he was welcomed as a liberator: Egypt had been governed as a Persian satrapy (principality) since 525 B.C.E., when Cambyses, son of Cyrus the Great, had deposed the last pharaoh of the reigning dynasty (see Chapter 2). Now Alexander himself was hailed as pharaoh and given the double crown of Upper and Lower Egypt, becoming the latest in a succession of rulers reaching back 3,000 years to the time of King Narmer (see Chapter 1).

Something about this feat seems to have amazed even Alexander himself. The "barbarian" chieftain of a backwater kingdom in the Balkan foothills had become pharaoh of the oldest civilization on earth and heir to its immense riches and extraordinary history—a history that the Greeks knew, thanks to the writings of Herodotus. While the Persians and (before them) the Medes had long been the Greeks' traditional enemies, the Egyptians had always been too far away to pose a threat; indeed, they were an object of awe and source of inspiration.

This may help to explain Alexander's response to the oracle of Ammon, the name the Greeks gave to the Egyptian sun god Amun-Ra, whom they identified with Zeus. At the oracle's desert oasis of Siwa, Alexander was reportedly told that he was "son of Ammon" and a god himself, a pronouncement that gave weight to a story already in circulation among his men, that he had been fathered not by Philip but by Zeus. Alexander, ever mindful of historical precedent and the historical significance of his own actions, seems to have decided at this point that Egypt should be the capital of his new empire. Persia had been the goal, and it still remained to be conquered, piece by piece; but it was in Egypt that he would build his shining new city of Alexandria. In the end, he had time only to lay out a plan for the streets and central spaces before he marched north to the reckoning with Darius at Gaugamela. When he finally returned, he was in his sarcophagus.

Alexander's Final Campaigns

Over the ensuing five years, Alexander campaigned in the far reaches of the Persian Empire, in the mountainous regions that had been only loosely yoked together with

ALEXANDER'S WORLD. This view of the world, modeled on maps made in antiquity, represents what intellectuals of Alexander's own time knew about geography. ▪ *Comparing it to the map of Alexander's campaigns on page 125, how do you think this worldview affected the planning of his route?* ▪ *Based on available knowledge, why would he have traveled down the Indus river (near the marking* **India***) and traveled overland to Susa?* ▪ *What similarities and differences do you find more generally, comparing this ancient map with the other maps that appear in this book?*

the more settled lands of Mesopotamia. This is the region encompassed today by Afghanistan, a terrain famous for defeating every attempt at conquest or control. There, in the mountains of Bactria, Alexander and his army experienced the hardest fighting of their long campaign. Indeed, they never succeeded in getting more than a tenuous hold on the territory, despite Alexander's marriage to Roxane, daughter of a local Bactrian chieftain. Thereafter, Alexander moved down through what is now Pakistan to the Indus Valley, meeting stiff resistance from its warlords but eventually defeating their leader, Porus, at the Battle of Hydaspes (*heed-AH-spes*) in 326 B.C.E.

This was to be the last major battle of his career, and the one in which his famous warhorse, Bucephalus, was killed. (He was buried nearby, and a city was founded in his name.) And it was here in India that Alexander's exhausted army refused to go on, thousands of miles and eight years from home. He was forced to turn back, and

THE CAMPAIGNS OF ALEXANDER. The conquests of Alexander the Great brought Greek culture to the vast expanse of the former Persian Empire, as far east as the Indus River. Trace Alexander's route with your finger. ▪ *Where did he start and end?* ▪ *What was the farthest point east that he traveled on his conquests?* ▪ *Why might Alexander have chosen to found so many cities named after him, and what can you conclude about the purposes of these cities, based on their locations?*

rather than attempting to recross the mountains of the Hindu Kush or the foothills of the Himalayas, he pressed southward to the shores of the Arabian Sea—what was then known as Ocean, and the end of the world. The ensuing march through the Gedrosian Desert, combined with a decade of continuous fighting, weakened him and his army considerably.

But Alexander still had great plans for the future, and when he reached the royal palace of Susa he took steps that indicate how he would have tried to combine his Greco-Macedonian Empire with that of Persia, had he lived. He announced that he would begin training Persian youths to fight alongside Greeks and Macedonians, so as to begin an integration of the two armies. He arranged a mass marriage between hundreds of his officers and a corresponding number of Persian noblewomen, and he made

an example of men who had been caught desecrating the nearby tomb of Cyrus the Great. Most controversially, he showed respect for his Persian subjects by adopting Persian dress—considered by Greeks to be symbolic of their enemies' barbarism—and by encouraging those around him to perform the ritual of *proskynesis* (*pros-kin-EE-sis*).

According to Herodotus, who gave the practice its Greek name, this was a gesture of bodily submission performed by those of lesser social standing when they met their superiors, and by all Persians—even those of royal rank—to honor the Great King. The person paying homage would bow deeply and kiss his hand to the emperor, in some cases prostrating himself entirely. To the Greeks, this practice was not only humiliating but blasphemous: it suggested that the Persians worshiped their emperor as a god. To Alexander and his close advisers, *proskynesis* may

LESSER KINGS OF PERSIA APPROACH THE GREAT KING TO PERFORM THE *PROSKYNESIS.* ■ *Why would Alexander's Greek and Macedonian soldiers have balked at the suggestion that they show their solidarity with Persians by performing this ritual?*

have seemed an appropriate tribute to his status as "son of Ammon," but it was more likely intended to level cultural differences between Persians and Greeks. In any case, it was not a success, and it fueled a mutiny among the Macedonians, which Alexander himself had to quell.

Alexander's Death

Apart from these attempts to create cross-cultural cohesion, which he was not able to pursue fully, Alexander took no realistic steps to create an administration for his vast empire. How he planned to govern it effectively and bequeath it intact remains a mystery; he seems to have fixed his sights more clearly on further conquests, perhaps in Arabia, perhaps toward "Greater Greece"—Italy and Sicily. We will never know. In late May of 323 B.C.E., he began to show signs of what may have been malarial fever. Some ancient sources suggest he was poisoned; his closest friend and longtime lover, Hephaistion, had died the year before at Ecbatana, leaving Alexander without his most able and vigilant bodyguard. (Emulating Achilles' passionate grief at the death of Patroclus, the mourning Alexander is reported to have built an enormous funeral pyre and "sacrificed" the residents of a nearby town to appease Hephaistion's ghost.) But Alexander ignored the advice of his doctors and continued to play the part of a Homeric hero, drinking late into the night and exerting himself

incautiously. His condition worsened, and he died on June 10 or 11, 323 B.C.E., in the palace built by the Chaldean king Nebuchadnezzar in Babylon, the ancient capital of Hammurabi. He was not yet thirty-three years old.

THE HELLENISTIC KINGDOMS

According to one account—by a later Roman historian—Alexander's friends and officers gathered around his bed as he lay dying and asked to whom he wished to leave his empire. He had replied, "To the strongest." According to Plutarch and Arrian, though, he was actually incapable of speech. According to still other late sources, he silently gave his signet ring to a Macedonian general called Perdiccas, the leader of his cavalry.

It was certainly Perdiccas who attempted to arrange a settlement among all the possible claimants to Alexander's imperial power, albeit unsuccessfully. Alexander's own son and heir was born to Roxane after his death, and eventually it was decided that the baby, Alexander IV of Macedonia, should rule jointly with Alexander's half brother, Philip, the son of Philip II by one of his lesser wives, who may have been both mentally and physically disabled. This solution proved impractical, and eventually both the child and his uncle were murdered, as was Perdiccas.

Alexander Puts Down a Mutiny

The following account comes from the history of Alexander's campaigns by the Greek-speaking Roman historian Arrian (c. 86–160 C.E.), who lived in the Roman province of Bythinia in northern Anatolia. This is the closest thing we have to a primary source, since histories written by Alexander's own contemporaries have not survived. The following passage describes Alexander's response to a mutiny among his troops after his return from India, in 324 B.C.E.

 y countrymen, you are sick for home—so be it! I shall make no attempt to check your longing to return. Go wherever you will; I shall not hinder you. But if go you must, there is one thing I would have you understand—what I have done for you, and in what coin you have repaid me. . . .

"[M]arching out from a country too poor to maintain you decently, [I] laid open for you at a blow, and in spite of Persia's naval supremacy, the gates of the Hellespont. My cavalry crushed the satraps of Darius, and I added all Ionia and Aeolia, the two Phrygias and Lydia to your empire. . . . I took them and gave them to you for your profit and enjoyment. The wealth of Egypt and Cyrene, which I shed no blood to win, now flows in your hands; Palestine and the plains of Syria and Mesopotamia are now your property; Babylon and Bactria and Susa are yours; you are the masters of the gold of Lydia, the treasures of Persia, the wealth of India—yes, and the seas beyond India, too. You are my captains, my generals, my governors of provinces.

"From all this that I have labored to win for you, what is left for me myself except the purple and the crown? I keep nothing for my own. . . . Perhaps you will say that, in my position as your commander, I had none of the labors and distress which you had to endure to win me what I have won. . . . Come now—if you are wounded, strip and show your wounds, and I will show mine. There is no part of my body but my back which does not have a scar; not a weapon a man may grasp or fling, the mark of which I do not carry on me . . . and all for your sakes: for your glory and your gain. Over every land and sea, across river, mountain, and plain, I led you to the world's end, a victorious army. I marry as you marry, and many of you will have children related by blood to my own. . . . But you all wish to leave me. Go then! And when you reach home, tell them that Alexander your king, who vanquished the Persians and Medes and Bactrians . . . tell them, I say, that you deserted him and left him to the mercy of barbarian men, whom you yourselves conquered. . . ."

On the Macedonians, the immediate effect of Alexander's speech was profound. . . . But when they were told [three days later that] . . . command was being given to Persian officers, foreign troops drafted into Macedonian units, a Persian corps of Guards called by a Macedonian name, Persian infantry units given the coveted title of Companions . . . every man of them hurried to the palace . . . and [they] swore they would not stir from the spot until Alexander took pity on them.

Source: Arrian, *The Campaigns of Alexander*, trans. Aubrey de Selincourt (New York: 1958), pp. 360–65 (slightly modified).

Questions for Analysis

1. What qualities of leadership does Alexander display in this speech? How do these qualities compare to those of Cyrus the Younger, in Xenophon's description of him (page 114)?

2. Given the circumstances that precipitated this mutiny, why does Alexander use the term *barbarians* to describe the Persians and other conquered peoples? What does he hope to convey by using this word and then by reorganizing his forces to replace Macedonians with Persians?

3. Histories written well into the nineteenth century of our era feature speeches that were allegedly spoken by historical characters on momentous occasions. How closely do you think Arrian's reconstruction of this speech reflects historical reality? How might you go about arguing that it is, in fact, an accurate reflection of what Alexander actually said?

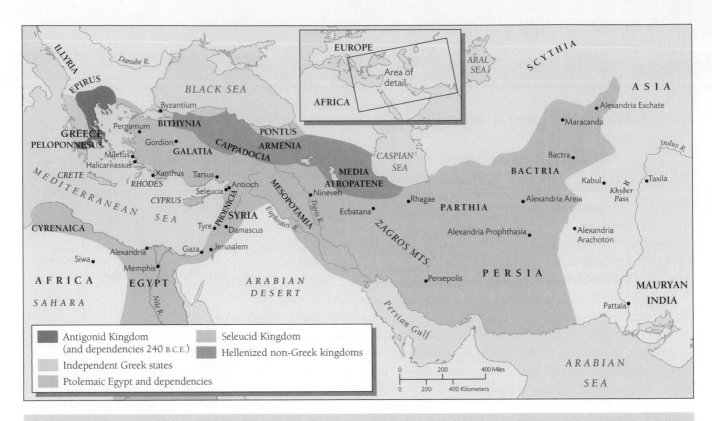

THE HELLENISTIC WORLD. Each of the three successor kingdoms to Alexander's empire was based in one of the three major civilizations we have studied so far: Egyptian, Mesopotamian, and Greek. ▪ *Based on the map above, what were the names of the three main successor states and where were they located?* ▪ *What might the division of Alexander's empire along such lines suggest about the lasting cultural differences among these regions?* ▪ *What might it suggest about the likelihood of forging a united empire, had he lived?*

Meanwhile, the Persian satrapies that had been alloted to various leaders of Alexander's armies became the bases from which they attempted to seize control. The turmoil lasted for two generations. By about 275 B.C.E., however, three separate axes of military and political power had emerged, each with a distinctive character but all headed by a Greco-Macedonian ruling class that shared a similar background. Indeed, a striking feature of this period is the renewal of ancient political patterns. But more striking is the fact that a common culture continued to unite Alexander's fragmented empire, which is why the era after his death is called Hellenistic, "Greek-like."

Ptolemaic Egypt

By far the most stable of the three successor states was Egypt, thanks in large part to the canny governance of Alexander's former general Ptolemy, possibly an illegitimate son of Philip II and certainly one of Alexander's most trusted advisers. Ptolemy decided to withdraw from the contest over the larger empire and asked only to be given Egypt as his satrapy. This might have been construed as a

modest request by potential rivals, but Ptolemy had ulterior motives. Clearly, he recognized Egypt's virtual invulnerability to attack. He also seems to have appreciated, as Alexander did, its historical cachet. And he may already have been planning to make Egypt an independent monarchy and a shrine to Alexander's memory.

It was thanks to Ptolemy, in fact, that Alexander's embalmed body was returned to Egypt in 323 B.C.E. It was supposed to have gone to the royal burial ground of Aigai in Macedonia, but Ptolemy hijacked the funeral cortege and brought it to the holy city of Memphis. Later, his son Ptolemy II moved the sarcophagus to a tomb in Alexandria, where it became a pilgrimage site and an object of veneration, especially by Romans with imperial ambitions of their own (see Chapter 5).

The Ptolemies ruled for the next 300 years, until Egypt became a Roman province in 30 B.C.E. This dynasty, the thirty-second since the unification of the Upper and Lower Nile in the fourth millennium B.C.E., would be the last. The male heirs of the line all took the name Ptolemy (hence the term Ptolemaic Egypt). Many of their sisters were called Cleopatra, the name of Alexander's own sister and a dynastic name among Macedonian royal women.

Beginning in the reign of Ptolemy II Philadelphus ("sibling-lover"), the Ptolemies even began to follow ancient Egyptian custom by marrying their siblings. And in many other ways, they showed reverence for the culture of their kingdom while at the same time bringing it within the ambit of the wider Hellenistic world.

TWO PORTRAITS OF PTOLEMY I OF EGYPT. The Ptolemaic rulers of Egypt represented themselves as pharaohs to their Egyptian subjects (as in this bust) and as Greeks to their Macedonian and Greek subjects (as on this gold coin). ▪ *Why would it have been important to project these two very different images?*

They achieved this, in part, by ruling from the new city of Alexandria on the Mediterranean coast, rather than from the older pharaonic capitals. In Alexandria, they acted as Macedonian kings toward their Greek and Macedonian citizens; outside of Alexandria, they played the role of pharaohs, surrounding themselves with the trappings and symbols of Egypt's heritage. But only the last Ptolemaic ruler, Cleopatra VII (69–30 B.C.E.), bothered to learn the Egyptian language—although, as the Rosetta Stone attests (see Chapter 1), the Ptolemies surrounded themselves with able administrators who could communicate effectively with their multilingual and multicultural subjects.

For the Ptolemies, as for the ancient pharaohs, all of Egypt was basically crown land, to be exploited for the benefit of the royal house. Supporting this tradition was the Macedonian idea that conquered land—land won by the spear—was plunder, to be used for personal enrichment and glorification. Accordingly, the Ptolemies exploited the wealth of the Egyptian countryside to the fullest. Most of this wealth ended up in Alexandria, which became the dazzling hub of the Hellenistic world. But there was little interest in improving the lives of the Egyptian peasantry whose bread-winning labors made their rulers rich. So although the third century was a prosperous and relatively peaceful one in Egypt, future pharaohs would face regular and dangerous revolts from the native populations of the countryside.

Nevertheless, Ptolemaic Egypt remained the most successful of the Hellenistic kingdoms. It was also the most influential, not only in its own day but for posterity, because of its key role in preserving and transmitting the accumulated heritage of the civilizations that had preceded it: Egyptian, Mesopotamian, and Greek. The Ptolemies used their wealth to patronize science and the arts, and they established a great Museum ("home of the Muses") and library, which attracted the greatest minds of the Hellenistic world and eventually displaced Athens as an intellectual and artistic center. Many breakthroughs in astronomy, mechanical engineering, and physics occurred in Alexandria. In particular, the study of medicine advanced greatly under Ptolemaic rule: freed from the taboos of their homeland, Greek researchers were permitted to perform autopsies on the bodies of dead criminals and vagrants, making it possible for anatomy to become a scientific discipline in its own right. It was also here that the texts of Greek poetry, drama, history, and philosophy were copied and preserved in the forms in which we know them, and here that the Hebrew scriptures were translated into Greek for a wider audience.

Seleucid Asia

The vast possessions that Alexander had accumulated in Asia—both within the Persian Empire and outside of it—eventually fell to another Macedonian, Seleucus (seh-LOO-kus). Seleucus had not been a senior officer during Alexander's lifetime, but he had navigated the turmoil after Alexander's death successfully and cleverly exploited the connections he made through his Persian wife. At his death in 281 B.C.E., his half-Persian son Antiochus (an-TYE-oh-kuhs) inherited an expansive realm; but despite his best efforts he could not extend it beyond the city named after him, Antioch, into Egypt.

Throughout its history, the Persian dynasty founded by Seleucus (known as the Seleucids) struggled with the problem of keeping the disparate parts of their realm together. Their hold on the easternmost provinces was especially tenuous, but Seleucus solved part of this problem by ceding much of the Indus Valley to the great Indian warrior-king Chandragupta, in exchange for peace and a squad of war elephants. By the middle of the third century B.C.E., the Seleucids had also lost control of Bactria, where a series of Indo-Greek states were emerging with a uniquely complex culture of their own. (One Greco-Bactrian king, Menander, is memorialized in Buddhist tradition. The Seleucid heartland became northern Syria, parts of Anatolia, Mesopotamia, and the western half of Persia: still a great, wealthy kingdom but far less than what Alexander had left.

Like the Ptolemies, the Seleucids presented two faces to their subjects, one looking to ancient Near Eastern tradition, another looking to Greece. In his proclamations, Antiochus used terms reminiscent of Sargon, Hammurabi, and Cyrus: "I am Antiochus, Great King, legitimate king . . . king of Babylon, king of all countries." But on his coins, he wore his hair short in the fashion of the Greeks and styled himself *basileus*, the Greek word for "king." Although the Seleucids' bureaucracy was less organized than that of the Ptolemies, even haphazard tax collection could reap huge rewards in an empire of 30 million inhabitants. However, the Seleucids did not convert their gains into public-works projects or capital investments. Instead, they hoarded their wealth in great state treasuries. All the same, they had more than enough cash to defend their borders through the third century, a period of regular warfare with Egypt. It was not until the second century, when Antiochus III lost a costly war with the Romans, that he had to plunder temples and private wealth to pay off the indemnity imposed on him.

Antigonid Macedonia and Greece

The Macedonian homeland did not possess the vast wealth of the new kingdoms carved from Alexander's conquests in Egypt and the Near East. It also remained highly unstable from the time of Alexander's death until 276 B.C.E., when a general named Antigonus (an-TIG-on-uhs) was finally able to establish his rule over the area and his own dynasty (known as the Antigonids). Thereafter, Macedonia drew its strength from considerable natural resources and from its influence over Aegean trade, as well as its status as overlord of Greece. The Macedonians also continued to field the most effective army of any of the successor states, and these warriors had coveted bragging rights as the heirs of Alexander's unconquered army.

Antigonus was influenced by a philosophical outlook called Stoicism (discussed later in this chapter) and viewed kingship as a form of noble servitude, an office to be endured rather than enjoyed. This perspective, combined with his modest resources, convinced him not to compete with the Seleucids and Ptolemies for dominance. Instead, Antigonid policy was to keep these other two powers at war with one another and away from the Macedonian sphere of influence. Antigonus and his successors thus pursued a strategy more reminiscent of Philip II than of his son. They secured the northern frontiers, maintained a strong, standing army, and kept the divided Greeks at heel.

The Greeks, however, were restive under the Antigonids, and two emergent powers within the Greek world served as rallying points for those who resented "barbarian" rule. These two forces, the Aetolian League and the Achaean League, represent a new form of Greek political organization. Unlike the defensive alliances of the classical period, each of these two leagues constituted a real political unification, with some centralization of governance. Citizens of the member poleis participated in councils of state that dealt with foreign policy and military affairs, trials for treason, and the annual election of a league general (also the chief executive officer) and his deputy. New members were admitted on an equal footing with existing members, and all citizens of the various poleis enjoyed joint citizenship throughout the league. The same laws, weights and measures, coinage, and judicial procedures also applied throughout each federation. So impressive was this degree of cooperation that James Madison, John Jay, and Alexander Hamilton employed the Achaean League as one of their models in advocating federalism in the United States.

FROM POLIS TO COSMOPOLIS

So what became of the polis, that building block of classical Greek civilization? As we have seen, the changes of the fourth century B.C.E. were already disrupting the traditional patterns of social and political life well before Alexander's conquests. But these conquests hastened the process of transformation, and they also opened up a wider world—a world that, within a few generations, came to admire all things Greek. By 300 B.C.E., a common Hellenistic culture encompassed the eastern Mediterranean and western Asia, transcending political and geographical boundaries. It was fueled by the hundreds of thousands of adventurers who joined the Greek *diaspora* ("dispersion") and whose emigration reduced the population of the Greek mainland by as much as 50 percent in the century between 325 and 225 B.C.E.

This exciting, urbane world was made up of interconnected cities whose scale dwarfed anything imaginable in Periclean Athens. In the fifth century B.C.E., direct participation in government had meant that every male citizen of a Greek polis had some share and stake in his society, its institutions, its gods, its army, and its cultural life. If we transpose this outlook onto the cosmopolitan Hellenistic city, which would have been at least three times larger, we can appreciate the magnitude of the change: two centuries later, all these ways of defining oneself were no longer rele-

Past and Present

Assimilation and Difference

The Greek diaspora ("dispersion") that bound the Hellenistic kingdoms together would eventually lead to the emergence of distinctive new hybrid cultures. The mosaic on the left comes from an ancient synagogue and shows Jewish ritual objects (including a menorah and a shofar) accompanied by a Greek inscription. The image on the right shows one manifestation of the modern Turkish diaspora: a clothing store in a district of Berlin called "Little Istanbul," where many German "guest workers" settled in the 1960s.

 Watch related author interview on StudySpace
wwnorton.com/web/westernciv18

vant. The individual male's intimate connection with the political life of the state was broken, as was his nexus of social and familial relationships. An average Greek in one of the Hellenistic cities might have only his immediate family to rely on, if that. Very often, he was alone. What resulted was a traumatic disjunction between the traditional values and assumptions of Greek life and the social and political realities of the day—and a host of entirely new opportunities.

Commerce and Urbanization

The Hellenistic world was prosperous, owing to the freedom of long-distance trade, the development of financial networks, and the enormous growth of cities. Alexander's conquests had opened up a vast trading area stretching from Egypt to the Persian Gulf, dominated by Greek-speaking

rulers and well-established merchant communities. These conquests also stimulated the economy by putting into circulation hoards of Persian gold and silver coins, jewelry, and other commodities acquired through plunder. Industries also benefited, because autocratic rulers found manufacturing to be a further means of increasing their revenues through trade and taxation.

New trading ventures were particularly encouraged in Ptolemaic Egypt and the area of western Asia ruled over by the Seleucid monarchs, the heartland of which was Syria. Every facility was provided by the Ptolemies and the Seleucids for the encouragement of commerce. Harbors were improved, warships were sent out to police the seas, roads and canals were built. The Ptolemies even employed geographers to discover new routes to distant lands and thereby opened up valuable markets. As a result of such methods, Egypt developed a flourishing commerce in the widest

HELLENISTIC EARRINGS. These exquisite pieces of jewelry illustrate the enormous wealth and extraordinary craftsmanship available to the elites of the Hellenistic world.

variety of products obtainable. Into the port of Alexandria came spices from Arabia, gold from Ethiopia and India, tin from Britain, elephants and ivory from Nubia, silver from Spain, fine carpets from Asia Minor, and even silk from China. Profits for the government and for some of the merchants were often as high as 20 or 30 percent.

The rapid growth of cities had both political and economic causes. Greek rulers imported Greek officials and especially Greek soldiers to maintain their control over non-Greek populations, making many new Greek settlements necessary. Alexander himself had founded some 70 cities as outposts of imperial domination; in the next two centuries, his successors founded about 200 more. Urbanization also increased due to the expansion of commerce and industry, as well as the proliferation of government offices.

But the most significant factors contributing to urban expansion were the Greek diaspora and the migration of workers from rural areas. Population growth in some centers was explosive. At Antioch, the population quadrupled during a single century. Seleucia on the Tigris grew from nothing to a metropolis of several hundred thousand in less than two centuries. Alexandria in Egypt had a half-million inhabitants. Only imperial Rome would have surpassed it in size, and it would not be until the eighteenth century of our era that European cities like London and Paris were as large. Alexandria was not only populous, it was magnificent and spacious—which Rome never was. Its wide streets were paved and laid out in an orderly grid. It had splen-

did public buildings and parks, the great museum, and the famous library containing a half-million books. It was the storehouse and showcase of Greek culture.

Despite the overall growth of the Hellenistic economy, not everyone enjoyed prosperity. Agriculture remained the major occupation and primary source of wealth, and small farmers in particular suffered severely from exploitative taxation. Although industrial production increased, it continued to be based on manual labor by individual artisans, most of whom lived in poverty. Among the teeming populations of Hellenistic cities, unemployment was a constant concern. Those who could not find work were forced to beg, steal, or prostitute themselves to survive.

Even those who prospered in the new economy were often subject to drastic fluctuations in their fortunes, owing to the precarious nature of mercantile endeavors. A trader who did very well selling a luxury cloth might invest heavily in it, only to find that tastes had changed or that a ship full of his wares had sunk. Merchants were also vulnerable to the boom-and-bust syndrome all too familiar to us today: an investor, thinking he could make a fortune during an upward price spiral, might go into debt to take advantage of the trend, only to find that supply in the commodity he traded suddenly exceeded demand, leaving him nothing with which to pay back his creditors. The economic landscape of the Hellenistic world was therefore one of contrasting extremes. In many ways, this was also the case with respect to its culture.

HELLENISTIC WORLDVIEWS

Life in the Hellenistic boomtowns produced new perspectives on the world and new philosophies that differed significantly from those of Plato and Aristotle. Two opposing trends ran almost parallel with one another. The first, exemplified by Stoicism (*STOH-iss-ism*) and Epicureanism (*eh-pi-CURE-ee-an-ism*), promoted rational thought as the key to alleviating the anxieties of modern life. This trend was a manifestation of Greek influence, although a major departure was the new separation of philosophy from scientific inquiry, which now became its own field of study. The second trend, exemplified by the Skeptics and various religious cults, tended to deny the possibility of attaining truth through the exercise of human reason alone and in some cases turned toward mysticism and reliance on divine revelation. Despite these stark differences, however, both philosophers and religious teachers were motivated by the same thing: the need to make human existence meaningful in a new age that lacked traditional civic structures and social values.

Two Paths to Tranquility: Stoicism and Epicureanism

The two strains of philosophy that dominated the Hellenistic world both originated in Athens around 300 B.C.E. Their promoters were Epicurus (c. 342–270 B.C.E.) and Zeno (fl. after 300 B.C.E.), and their teachings had several features in common. Both were concerned with the well-being of the individual, not with the welfare of society as a whole. Both were also firmly rooted in the material world, denying the existence of any purely spiritual phenomena; even the soul was considered to be part of the mortal body. Stoicism and Epicureanism also responded to the new cosmpolitan age by promoting universal values: both taught that people are the same the world over, and both recognized no distinctions between Greeks and the peoples hitherto known as "barbarians."

But in other ways the two systems were radically different. The Stoics who followed Zeno of Citium (c. 335–c. 263 B.C.E.)—they took their name from the *stoa* ("colonnade") in which he regularly taught—believed that the cosmos is an ordered whole in which all contradictions are resolved for ultimate good. Evil is not absolute but relative; this means that the particular misfortunes that befall individual human beings are merely incidents that will lead to the final perfection of the universe. Everything that happens is therefore predetermined, which means that no individual is master of his or her fate. People are free only in the sense that they can accept fate or rebel against it; that is, one is free to choose *how to respond* to adversity or prosperity. By freely submitting to the workings of the universe, and by acknowledging that whatever happens must be for the best, one can attain true happiness: tranquility of mind. Through the exercise of reason and emotional restraint, Stoics strove to adjust their expectations to the workings of fate and to purge their souls of all bitterness or regret.

The Stoics' theory of ethics and social responsibility grew out of this personal philosophy. Believing that the highest good is serenity of mind, they emphasized self-discipline and the fulfillment of one's duties. They taught tolerance and forgiveness, and they also urged participation in public affairs as a special responsibility for those with able minds. They condemned slavery and violence, although they took no real actions against these evils because they saw them as inevitable—and because extreme social change might be worse.

With some later modifications, Stoic philosophy became the driving force behind the values of the Roman Republic and even influenced early Christianity; it can be considered one of the most important products of the Hellenistic Age. Even today, those who do not consciously embrace its tenets or its perspective may find that they have been influenced by its egalitarian and humanitarian ethos.

The second main philosophical trend in this era derives from teachings of Epicurus (341–270 B.C.E.). Epicurius, in turn, was influenced by the atomic theory of an earlier Greek philosopher called Democritus (*dem-OH-kree-tuhs*), who lived in the latter part of the fifth century B.C.E. and who is often called "the father of modern science." According to his central thesis, the universe is made up entirely of atoms, infinite in number, indestructible, and indivisible. Every individual object or organism is therefore the product of a combination of atoms.

Studying Democritus's writings, Epicurus and his followers reached a conclusion exactly opposite to that of the Stoics: they interpreted the atomic theory to mean that there is no ultimate purpose in the workings of the universe, that these workings are entirely random. So the highest good cannot come of submitting oneself stoically to the endurance of hardship, because no hardship is part of a larger plan; it is merely the chance by-product of random atomic actions. The highest good, then, must be pleasure: the moderate satisfaction of bodily appetites, the intellectual pleasure of contemplating excellence and remembering past enjoyments, and serenity in the face of death. Indeed, an individual who understands that the soul itself is material and will not survive the death of the body, that the universe operates at random, and that no gods intervene in human affairs should have no fear of death or any other supernatural phenomena. The Epicureans thus came by a very different route to the same general conclusion as the Stoics: nothing is better than tranquility of mind.

The moral teachings and political goals of the Epicureans reflected this worldview. In contrast to the Stoics, however, they did not insist on virtue as an end in itself or on the fulfillment of one's duties. For an Epicurean, the only duty a person has is to the self, and the only reason to act virtuously is to increase one's own happiness. Similarly, Epicureans also denied that there is any such thing as justice: laws and political institutions are "just" only insofar as they contribute to the welfare of the individual. Yes, certain rules have been found necessary in every society for the maintenance of order, but these rules should be obeyed solely because that is to one's advantage. The state is, at best, a mere convenience, and the wise man should take no active part in politics. Instead, he should withdraw to study philosophy and enjoy the fellowship of a few congenial friends. Modern libertarian movements share many characteristics with Epicureanism.

Extreme Doubt: Skepticism

The most pessimistic philosophy generated by the Hellenistic era was propounded by the Skeptics, whose name derives from a Greek word meaning "those on the lookout" or "the spies." Skepticism reached the zenith of its popularity in the second century under the influence of Carneades (*kar-NEE-ah-dees*, c. 214–129 B.C.E.), a man born in the Greek city of Cyrene, in North Africa, who spent his youth in Athens. The chief source of his inspiration was the teaching (filtered through Aristotle) that all knowledge is based on sense perception and is therefore limited and relative. From this, the Skeptics concluded that no one can truly know or prove anything. Because the impressions of our senses can deceive us, we cannot even be certain about the truth of whatever empirical knowledge we think we have gained by observation of the world. All we can say is that things *appear* to be such and such; we do not know that they really *are* that way. It follows, furthermore, that we can have no definite knowledge of the supernatural, of the meaning of life, or of right and wrong.

The only sensible course for the Skeptic is therefore to suspend judgment: this alone can lead to happiness. If a person abandons the fruitless quest for truth and ceases to worry about good conduct and the existence of evil, he can at least attain a certain peace of mind—the highest satisfaction that an uncertain life affords. Needless to say, the Skeptics were even less concerned than the Epicureans with political and social problems, from which they felt wholly alienated. Their ideal was one of escape from an incomprehensible world. In some key respects they anticipated modern existentialism and nihilism.

The Varieties of Religion

Like Epicureanism and Skepticism, Hellenistic religion tended to offer vehicles of escape from political commitments. When we think back to how close was the link between Greek selfhood and politics down to the middle of the fourth century B.C.E.—"man is a creature of the polis"—we can begin to appreciate what a radical change had occurred in just a few generations. In the classical age of the polis, as in all the societies we have studied so far, religion was wholly interconnected with politics. Divine worship centered on the gods who protected a community and furthered its interests. Hence, the most serious of the charges brought against Socrates was that he had "denied the gods of the polis" and thus committed treason. Religious crimes were political crimes, and piety was the same as patriotism.

Although this sense of a vital connection between a place and its gods persisted to a certain extent during the Hellenistic period, civic-oriented worship was compromised by the rootless multiculturalism of the third and second centuries B.C.E. In its place, some elite members of society gravitated toward one of the philosophies discussed above. Ordinary people, though, were more likely to embrace religious cults that offered emotional gratification or the diversion of colorful rituals, as well as some assurance of an afterlife, which the new philosophies did not.

In Greek-speaking communities especially, cults that stressed extreme methods of atonement for sin, ecstatic mystical union with the divine, or contact with supernatural forces attracted many followers. Among these mystery religions—so called because their membership was select and their rites secret—one of the most popular was the cult of Dionysus, which celebrated the cyclical death and resurrection of that Greek god. The Egyptian cult of Isis, drawing on the story of Osiris (see Chapter 1), also revolved around rituals of death and rebirth. So too did Zoroastrianism (see Chapter 2), which became increasingly dualistic: its magi taught that the material world was entirely evil and urged believers to adopt ascetic practices that would purify their souls and prepare them for ethereal joy in the afterlife.

Like the peoples who worshiped them, the gods of the Hellenistic world were often immigrants from other lands. Temples to Greek gods and goddesses were dedicated throughout the Near East and Egypt; conversely, temples to Near Eastern divinities were constructed in the cities of the Greek homeland. In Alexandria, scholars of religion collected Egyptian and Near Eastern mythologies, which were recorded and reformulated for Greek-speaking audiences. Throughout the Hellenistic world, there was a dazzling variety of religious choices.

Even among the Jews of Palestine, who resisted assimilation and the adoption of foreign customs, Hellenistic culture put down deep roots. This was especially true among Jewish elites and Jews living outside Palestine, who outnumbered the Palestinian population by a considerable margin by the end of the second century B.C.E. To meet the needs of these Greek-speaking Jews, and to satisfy the curiosity of Gentiles interested in Jewish beliefs, scholars working in Alexandria produced a Greek version of the Hebrew scriptures. It is still known as the Septuagint, from the Greek word meaning "the seventy": legend has it that seventy scribes, each working independently, produced individual translations from Hebrew to Greek that were identical in every respect. This story conveyed the message that the Septuagint was no less a product of divine inspiration than the original books that made up the Hebrew Bible, and could be treated as an authoritative text in its own right. For Jews concerned about their social and cultural standing vis-à-vis their Greek neighbors, it was also proof of their cultivation and their acceptance of Hellenistic values—although, ironically, many of the Jewish scriptures that were now written in Greek disapproved strongly of those values.

A Jewish Response to Hellenization

Greek culture became a powerful force throughout the Hellenistic world, even in Israel. In the second century B.C.E., the Hellenized ways of the Jewish elites in Jerusalem led to a revolt by a native Hebrew dynasty known as the Maccabees, who decried the effects of Hellenization on Jewish life. These events are recorded in two apocryphal books of the Hebrew Bible. In the passage that follows, note that even the High Priest of the Temple bears a Greek name, Jason.

n those days, lawless men came forth from Israel and misled many, saying, "Let us go and make a covenant with the Gentiles [Greeks] round about us, for since we separated from them many disasters have come upon us." . . .

[This happened when] Antiochus [IV, 175–164 B.C.E.] who was called Epiphanes had succeeded to the kingdom, [and] Jason the brother of Onias obtained the high priesthood by corruption. . . . [H]e at once shifted his countrymen over to the Greek way of life . . . and he destroyed the lawful ways of living and introduced new customs contrary to the law. For with alacrity he founded a gymnasium right under the citadel, and he induced the noblest of the young men to wear the Greek hat [and not the traditional head covering]. There was such an extreme of Hellenization and increase in the adoption of foreign ways . . . that the priests were no longer intent upon the services of the altar. Despising the sanctuary and neglecting the sacrifices, they hurried to take part in the unlawful proceedings in the wrestling arena after the signal for the discus-throwing, disdaining the honors prized by their ancestors and putting the highest value upon Greek forms of prestige. . . . When the quadrennial games were being held at Tyre and the king was present, the vile Jason sent envoys . . . to carry three hundred silver drachmas for the sacrifice to Heracles. . . .

Not long after this, the king sent an Athenian senator to compel the Jews to forsake the laws of their fathers and cease to live by the laws of God, and also to pollute the temple in Jerusalem and call it the temple of Olympian Zeus. . . . Harsh and utterly grievous was the onslaught of evil. For the temple was filled with debauchery and reveling by the Gentiles, who dallied with prostitutes and had intercourse with women within the sacred precincts, and besides brought in things for sacrifice that were unfit. The altar was covered with abominable offerings that were forbidden by the laws. A man could neither keep the Sabbath nor observe the feasts of his fathers, nor so much as confess himself to be a Jew.

Source: Excerpted from 1 Maccabees 1:11; 2 Maccabees 4:10–18 and 6:1–6, in *The New Oxford Annotated Bible* (Oxford: 1973).

Questions for Analysis

1. Given the history of the Hebrew kingdoms (see Chapter 2), why would Hellenistic culture be particularly threatening to the Jews?

2. What, specifically, are the offensive actions and activities described here? Why, for example, would the building of a gymnasium (a Greek academy and athletic facility) in Jerusalem be problematic?

THE SCIENTIFIC REVOLUTION OF ANTIQUITY

The Hellenistic period was the most brilliant age in the history of science before the seventeenth century of our era. There are three major reasons for this. First, there was the enormous stimulus to intellectual inquiry caused by the fusion of Mesopotamian and Egyptian science with the philosophical methods of the Greeks. Second, as in the more famous scientific revolution of modernity (see Chapter 16), the use of a common language (in the seventeenth century it was Latin) and the ease of communication facilitated by quick, affordable travel also made the circulation of knowledge and sharing of ideas easier (in the seventeenth century, ease of communication was increased by the printing press and an international postal system). Finally, as in the seventeenth century, the competition among patrons of science was intense, which ensured the availability of ample funding. Every Hellenistic autocrat wanted to be thought enlightened

Competing Viewpoints

Debating the Education and Role of Women

The drastic political, social, and economic changes of the fourth century led philosophers to reimagine the traditional structures of the polis and to debate the proper role of women within these structures. Meanwhile, the cosmopolitan culture of the expanding Hellenistic world made it increasingly difficult to limit women's access to public spaces. The following excerpts represent two philosophical responses to these problems. The first comes from Plato's treatise on "Polis-matters" (Politeía), known to us as The Republic, *the longest of his philosophical dialogues and the most influential work of political thought in history. Its conceptual narrator and protagonist is Socrates, who engages in a series of debates with his pupils. The second excerpt is taken from a philosophical treatise attributed to a female follower of Pythagoras (see Chapter 3), but it was really written around 200 B.C.E. in Hellenistic Italy, and by a man.*

Plato, *The Republic*, c. 380 B.C.E.

SOCRATES: For men born and educated like our citizens, the only way, in my opinion, of arriving at a right conclusion about the possession and use of women and children is to follow the path on which we originally started, when we said that the men were to be the guardians and watchdogs of the herd.

GLAUCON: True.

SOCRATES: Let us further suppose the birth and education of our women to be subject to similar or nearly similar regulations; then we shall see whether the result accords with our design.

GLAUCON: What do you mean?

SOCRATES: . . . The education which was assigned to the men was music and gymnastic[s].

GLAUCON: Yes.

SOCRATES: Then women must be taught music and gymnastic[s] and also the art of war, which they must practice like the men?

GLAUCON: That is the inference, I suppose.

SOCRATES: I should rather expect . . . that several of our proposals, if they are carried out, being unusual, may appear ridiculous.

GLAUCON: No doubt of it.

SOCRATES: Yes, and the most ridiculous thing of all will be the sight of women naked in the palaestra, exercising with the men, especially when they are no longer young; they certainly will not be a vision of beauty, any more than the enthusiastic old men who in spite of wrinkles and ugliness continue to frequent the gymnasia. . . . . [Yet] not long ago, as we shall remind them, the Hellenes were of the opinion, which is still generally received among the barbarians, that the sight of a naked man was ridiculous and improper; and when first the Cretans and then the Lacedaemonians [Spartans] introduced the custom, the wits of that day might equally have ridiculed the innovation.

GLAUCON: No doubt. . . .

SOCRATES: First, then, whether the question is to be put in jest or in earnest, let us come to an understanding about the nature of woman: Is she capable of sharing either wholly or partially in the actions of men, or not at all? And is the art of war one of those arts in which she can or cannot share? That will be the best way of commencing the enquiry, and will probably lead to the fairest conclusion. . . .

GLAUCON: I suppose so. . . .

SOCRATES: And if . . . the male and female sex appear to differ in their fitness for any art or pursuit, we should say that such pursuit or art ought to be assigned to one or the other of them; but if the difference consists only in women bearing and men begetting children, this does not amount to a proof that a woman differs from a man in respect of the sort of education she should receive; and we shall therefore continue to maintain that our guardians and their wives ought to have the same pursuits.

GLAUCON: Very true.

SOCRATES: Next, we shall ask . . . how, in reference to any of the pursuits or arts of civic life, the nature of a woman differs from that of a man? . . .

GLAUCON: By all means.

SOCRATES: . . . [W]hen you spoke of a nature gifted or not gifted in any respect, did you mean to say that one man will acquire a thing easily, another with difficulty; a little learning will lead the one to discover a great deal; whereas the other, after much study and application, no sooner learns than he forgets? Or again, did you mean, that the one has a body which is a good servant to his mind, while the body of the other is a hindrance to him? Would not these be the sort of differences which distinguish the man gifted by nature from the one who is ungifted?

GLAUCON: No one will deny that.

SOCRATES: And can you mention any pursuit of mankind in which the male sex has not all these gifts and qualities in a higher degree than the female? Need I waste time in speaking of the art of weaving, and the management of pan-cakes and preserves, in which woman-kind does really appear to be great, and in which for her to be beaten by a man is of all things the most absurd?

GLAUCON: You are quite right ... in maintaining the general inferiority of the female sex: although many women are in many things superior to many men, yet on the whole what you say is true.

Source: Excerpted from Plato, *The Republic*, Book V, trans. Benjamin Jowett (New York: 1982), pp. 170–76.

Treatise attributed to Phintys, Third/Second Century B.C.E.

Now some people think that it is not appropriate for a woman to be a philosopher, just as a woman should not be a cavalry officer or a politician. . . . I agree that men should be generals and city officials and politicians, and women should keep house and stay inside and receive and take care of their husbands. But I believe that courage, justice, and intelligence are qualities that men and women have in common. . . . Courage and intelligence are more appropriately male qualities because of the strength of men's bodies and the power of their minds. Chastity is more appropriately female.

Accordingly, a woman must learn about chastity and realize what she must do quantitatively and qualitatively to be able to obtain this womanly virtue. I believe that there are five qualifications: (1) the sanctity of her marriage bed, (2) the cleanliness of her body, (3) the manner in which she chooses to leave her house, (4) her refusal to participate in secret cults . . . , (5) her readiness and moderation in sacrificing to the gods.

Of these, the most important quality for chastity is to be pure in respect of the marriage bed, and for her not to have affairs with men from other house-holds. If she breaks the law in this way she wrongs the gods of her family and provides her family and home not with its own offspring but with bastards. . . .

She should also consider the following: that there is no means of atoning for this sin; no way she can approach the shrines or the altars of the gods as a pure woman. . . . The greatest glory a freeborn woman can have—her foremost honor—is the witness her own children will give to her chastity toward her husband, the stamp of the likeness they bear to the father whose seed produced them. . . .

As far as adornment of her body is concerned . . . [h]er clothes should not be transparent or ornate. She should not put on silken material, but moderate, white-colored clothes. In this way, she will avoid being over-dressed or luxurious or made-up, and not give other women cause to be uncomfortably envious . . . She should not apply imported or artificial coloring to her face—with her own natural color-ing, by washing only with water, she can ornament herself with modesty. . . .

Women of importance leave the house to sacrifice to the leading divin-ity of the community on behalf of their husbands and their households. They do not leave home at night nor in the evening, but at midday, to attend a reli-gious festival or to make some purchase, accompanied by a single female servant or decorously escorted by two servants at most. . . . They keep away from secret cults . . . particularly because these forms of worship encourage drunkenness and ecstasy. The mistress of the house and head of the household should be chaste and untouched in all respects.

Source: From Mary R. Lefkowitz and Maureen B. Fant, eds. *Women's Life in Greece & Rome: A Source Book in Translation*, 2nd ed. (Baltimore, MD: 1992), pp. 163–64.

Questions for Analysis

1. Follow the steps of the argument made by Socrates. How does he go about proving that women and men are different and should have differ-ent roles in society? Are there flaws in this argument? What are they?

2. How does the author of the treatise seem to define "chastity," and why does she (or he) say that it corre-sponds to more masculine qualities of courage and intelligence? Why would this author have wanted to attribute these reflections to female members of the community founded by the phi-losopher Pythagoras (c. 570–c. 495), three centuries earlier? How might this treatise be responding to the changes brought about by the expan-sion of the Greek world in the fourth and third centuries B.C.E?

3. What are main points on which these two perspectives agree? How might ideas like those expressed here have influenced contemporary ideas of female beauty (see **Interpreting Visual Evidence**, page 116)?

and to be associated with new discoveries. And it might even be profitable to subsidize research that led to the development of new technologies, especially ones with military applications. But most of all, the rulers who financed scientific endeavors did so primarily for motives of prestige and competition: they could show off a scientific gadget just as they could show off a sculpture. Even purely theoretical advances were so much admired that a Hellenistic prince who had bankrolled such a breakthrough would share the glory of it.

The arts were also transformed by the economic and political conditions of the Hellenistic world. Writers and artists working in various media strove to demonstrate their mastery of difficult techniques and so to attract the notice of potential patrons. New markets for art also changed *what* was being made, how, and for whom. In all of the civilizations we have studied so far, artists worked directly for royal or civic patrons, who were often very particular in their demands. In the Hellenistic world, art became commodified. Sometimes a piece would be made expressly for a particular patron, but many works of art were fashioned for the open market. They were also designed to suit the tastes and lifestyles of urbane men and women, especially those of the merchant classes and the elite who had disposable income and wanted to increase their social standing through conspicuous consumption. This was as true of literature as of sculpture or the decorative arts: we know the names of over a thousand Hellenistic authors, either because their work survives in multiple copies sold in bookshops, or because they are mentioned in other writings (letters, pamphlets) as being in fashion. Indeed, the number of texts and *objets d'art* that exist from this period is huge compared to earlier eras.

Measuring and Mapping: Astronomy, Geography, and Mathematics

Hellenistic scientists took a major interest in measurements and mapmaking, whether of the heavens (astronomy) or the earth (geography) and the forms occuring in nature (geometry). The most renowned—and most wronged—of the Hellenistic astronomers was Aristarchus of Samos (310–230 B.C.E.), whose major discovery anticipated that of Copernicus by 1,700 years: he deduced that the earth and other planets revolve around the sun. Unfortunately, however, his heliocentric model was not accepted by many of his contemporaries or successors because it conflicted with the teachings of Aristotle and with the Greek conviction that humanity, and therefore the earth, must be at the center of the universe.

The sad fate of his discovery was sealed in the second century C.E., when the Alexandrian scholar Claudius Ptol-

emaeus (also known as Ptolemy) published an astronomical treatise called the *Almagest*, which unequivocally argued that Aristotle was correct, and that all heavenly bodies revolve around the earth. This misinformative book was then handed down to posterity as the authoritative work of ancient astronomy. It would not be overturned until a much later scientific revolution occurred two-thousand years later—and after the condemnation of theories advanced by Copernicus and Galileo that were identical to that of Aristarchus.

Closely allied with astronomy were geography and mathematics, especially geometry. The most influential Hellenistic mathematician was Euclid, whose *Elements of Geometry* (c. 300 B.C.E.) codified the work of others, including pre-Socratic philosophers like Pythagoras (see Chapter 3). It remained the basic textbook for the study of that subject until the twentieth century of our era. Euclid's successor Hipparchus (second century B.C.E.) then laid the foundations of both plane and spherical trigonometry.

In the field of geography—and in a host of other pursuits, too—the most original thinker was Eratosthenes of Alexandria (*air-ah-TOS-then-ees*, c. 276–c. 196 B.C.E.). Not only did he accurately calculate the circumference of the earth (within a tiny margin of error, less than 200 miles), he also developed a system of latitude and longitude, and he was the first to suggest the possibility of reaching eastern Asia by sailing west. In addition, he founded the science of chronology by attempting to establish the dates of major events reaching back to the siege of Troy. Students of history are forever in his debt.

Medicine and Mechanics: The Sciences of Physiology and Physics

Before the third century B.C.E., physics had been a branch of philosophy. It became a separate, experimental science thanks to the single-handed genius of one man, Archimedes of Syracuse (*ar-ki-MEE-dees*, c. 287–212 B.C.E.). It was he who discovered the law of floating bodies, or specific gravity, now known as "Archimedes' principle." According to legend, the idea came to him quite suddenly when he was in his bath, pondering possible theories. The stunning insight so excited him that he leaped from the water and dashed out naked into the street, shouting *"Eureka!"* ("I found it!"). He also established the principles of the lever, the pulley, and the screw, and he invented both a compound pulley and a propeller. All of these discoveries had numerous practical uses in the construction of buildings, ships, and military machinery.

Other extaordinary advances of Hellenistic science were made in the field of medicine. Especially significant was the work of the Alexandrian scholar Herophilus of Chalcedon (c.335–c.280 B.C.E.), the greatest anatomist of antiquity and probably the first to practice human dissection. Many of his discoveries directly challenged the orthodoxy of Aristotelian teaching—and rightly, since Aristotle's understanding of physiology (like his knowledge of astronomical and natural science) has not stood the test of time so well as his grasp of logic and politics. Herophilus's achievements included a detailed description of the brain, which allowed him to prove that the brain was the engine of human intellect (Aristotle thought this was the heart), as well as the discovery that the arteries contain blood alone (not a mixture of blood and air, as Aristotle had taught), and that their function is to carry blood from the heart to all parts of the body. He also understood the significance of the pulse and its use in diagnosing illness.

His colleague Erasistratus (*ehr-ah-sis-STRAH-tus*) made allied discoveries, establishing that the heart was a pump and not an organ of emotion, explaining the working of its valves, and distinguishing between motor and sensory nerves. Erasistratus also rejected the widely held theory of the physician Hippocrates (c. 460–c. 370), who had posited that the body consists of four "humors" which need to be kept in balance through bloodletting and other invasive practices. Unfortunately, this discovery went the way of the heliocentric universe posited by Aristarchus: another encyclopedist of the second century C.E., Galen, preferred the erroneous theory of Hippocrates. His baleful influence, and the practice of bloodletting, thus persisted into the nineteenth century of our era.

SURGICAL INSTRUMENTS. Tools like these were used by both Hellenistic and Roman doctors to perform surgical procedures, but they also had a variety of nonmedical uses. Shown here are a grinding stone, spoons, probes, depressors, and tongs. The large, flat-headed tool may have been used for cauterizing wounds. The inscription visible on the stone in the upper left-hand corner is probably a recipe for eye medicine.

Urban Architecture and Sculpture

Hellenistic architecture drew on Greek models, but it was also influenced by standards and tastes more characteristic of Egypt and Persia. Two examples (both of which no longer survive) are the great lighthouse of Alexandria, which rose to a height of nearly 400 feet and which was daringly composed of three diminishing stories topped by eight slender columns supporting the light; and the citadel of Alexandria, built of stone and covered with blue-tinted plaster, described by a contemporary as seeming to float in mid-air. The best-surviving example, though, comes from Pergamon, a city on the coast of Anatolia that became the capital of a new kingdom wrested from the control of the Seleucids in the second century B.C.E. It boasted an enormous altar dedicated to Zeus that crowned the heights of the city, below which an open-air theater was built into the steep slope of the hill. In Ephesus, not far away, the streets were not only paved, but paved with marble.

Perhaps the most influential of all Hellenistic arts was sculpture, which represents a further movement away from classical ideals and even more emphasis on realism than the fourth-century sculptures discussed earlier in this chapter. Sculptors now prided themselves on faithfully reproducing facial furrows, muscular distensions, and complex folds of drapery. Awkward human postures offered the greatest technical challenges, to the degree that sculptors might prefer to show people stretching themselves or balancing on one leg in ways that hardly ever occur in real life.

Because monumental sculpture of this kind was executed for wealthy private patrons, it is clear that the goal was to create something unique in both conception and craftsmanship—something a collector could show off as the only one of its type. It is not surprising, therefore, that complexity came to be admired for its own sake, and extreme naturalism sometimes teetered on the brink of distortion. To our eyes, such works frequently appear familiar because of the influence they exerted on later sculptors like Michelangelo (see Chapter 12) and Auguste Rodin. Three of the most famous examples are pictured here, each exhibiting different aesthetic qualities and artistic techniques: the *Dying Gaul*, made in Pergamon around 220 B.C.E.; the *Winged Victory of Samothrace*, dating from around 200 B.C.E.; and the *Laocoön* group, from the first century B.C.E.

Literary Fantasy and Historical Reality

In the sixth century B.C.E. it was the lyric, in the fifth century it was tragedy, and in the fourth century it was the novel; but in the Hellenistic era, the new literary genre was pastoral verse.

THE CITADEL OF PERGAMON. An artist's reconstruction of Pergamon in the second century B.C.E., based on the work of nineteenth-century German archaeologists. High atop the hill is the massive altar of Zeus (now in the Pergamon Museum in Berlin) and below it slope the tiers of the theater. Other features include fortifications, terraces, and artificial landscaping for public gardens. ■ *How does this complex of buildings compare to that of another citadel, the Acropolis of Athens (see page 76)?*

These poems tapped into a strong vein of nostalgia for rural pastimes and simple pleasures, a make-believe world of shepherds and wood nymphs. The most important pastoral poet of the age was Theocritus (*thee-AW-krit-uhs*), who flourished around 270 B.C.E. in the big-city environment of Alexandria. Theocritus was a merchant of escapism. In the midst of urban bustle and within sight of overcrowded slums, he celebrated the charms of country life and lazy summer afternoons, putting into the mouths of his rustic characters unlikely sentiments expressed in ornate language. He thereby founded an enduring tradition that would be taken up by poets from the Roman Virgil to the Englishman (and classical scholar) A. E. Housman, and that has continuously provided a wealth of themes for the visual arts. Musical composers like Beethoven and Debussy also owe a debt to Theocritus.

By contrast, Hellenistic prose literature was dominated by historians and biographers who consciously modeled their work on earlier pioneers, especially Thucydides. By far

the most important was Polybius (*pol-LIB-ee-uhs,* c. 203–120 B.C.E.), a well-born Greek from the mainland whose father was a prominent politician active in the Achaean League. Polybius himself was trained as a horseman and cavalry officer, and both his vocation and his family connections gave him ample opportunity to observe the workings of government, diplomacy, and military strategy. This was at a time when the Achaean League was trying to position itself favorably in ongoing wars between the rising republic of Rome and the various warring kingdoms of northern Greece, notably Macedonia and Epiros. In 168 B.C.E., the Romans became suspicious of the Achaeans' declared neutrality and demanded that a thousand noble hostages be sent from Greece to Rome as a guarantee of the League's good behavior.

Polybius was one of those hostages, and he spent the next seventeen years living in Rome. There, he became a fervent admirer of Roman customs and especially of Rome's unique form of government. He also formed warm friendships with

THE MARBLE STREETS OF EPHESUS. Ephesus was already a splendid city when it was incorporated into the Persian Empire, along with other Greek settlements in Ionia. In the Hellenistic era, it became more splendid still.

high-ranking Roman families, including the descendants of Scipio Africanus, a prominent Roman general. He kept up these contacts after his release, traveling to North Africa during the Third Punic War and witnessing firsthand the destruction of Carthage in 146 B.C.E. (see Chapter 5).

The result of this colorful career was a series of histories that glorified the achievements of Rome and its political system. Polybius also attempted to account for the patterns that he discerned in the history of Greece since the Peloponnesian War. He argued that historical developments follow regular cycles, and that nations pass inevitably through stages of growth and decay. Hence, it should be possible to predict exactly where a given state is heading if one knows what has happened to it in the past. Yet he also argued that the special character of Rome's constitution would allow it to break free from this cycle, because it combined all of the different forms of government that Aristotle had outlined in his *Politics*. This view of history galvanized the framers of the U.S. Constitution, directly influencing their conception of our own political institutions.

CONCLUSION

Judged from the perspective of classical Greece, Hellenistic civilization seems strange. The autocratic governments of the age that followed Alexander's conquests would probably appear repugnant to a staunch proponent of Athenian democracy, and the Hellenistic love of extravagance and

display can contrast strikingly with the more austere tastes of the fifth century B.C.E. Yet Hellenistic civilization had its own achievements that the classical age could not match, achievements that make it in some ways more familiar to us. Most Hellenistic cities offered a greater range of public facilities than any Greek cities of the previous period, and the numerous advances in science and technology are astonishing when compared to anything that came before or even after.

But the most important contribution of the Hellenistic era to subsequent historical developments was its role as an intermediary between the nascent empire of Rome and the older civilizations of Mesopotamia, Egypt, and Greece. The example set by Alexander, in particular, was one that the Romans would emulate, and the economic and political infrastuctures that were put in place after his conquests would form the framework of Roman imperial government. The Romans would also take advantage of the common language and cultural expectations that bound the far reaches of the Greek-speaking world together. Their own Latin language would only become acceptable for cultivated conversation and literary expression toward the

DYING GAUL. The original (now lost) statue on which this Roman copy was based was sculpted in Pergamon around 220 B.C.E. The sculptor clearly wished to exhibit skill in depicting an unusual subject: the Gauls were a Celtic people about whom very little was known in this era. ▪ *How does this sympathetic representation of a "barbarian" express the new values of Hellenistic philosophy?*

***THE WINGED VICTORY OF SAMOTHRACE* (left).** This marble sculpture of the goddess Nike (Victory) may originally have been displayed on the prow of a monumental ship. It formed part of a temple complex on the island of Samothrace in the northern Aegean, and dates to around the year 200 B.C.E. It is now in the Louvre museum, Paris. ***LAOCOÖN AND HIS SONS* (right).** In sharp contrast to the serene and confident *Winged Victory* is this famous sculpture group from the first century B.C.E. According to legend, Laocoön warned the Trojans not to accept the wooden horse sent by the Greeks and was accordingly punished by the sea-god Poseidon, who sent two serpents to kill him and his sons. The intense physicality of this work was an important influence on Michelangelo, a millennium and a half later. It is now in the Vatican museum, Rome.

After You Read This Chapter

Visit StudySpace for quizzes, additional review materials, and multimedia documents. **wwnorton.com/web/westernciv18**

REVIEWING THE OBJECTIVES

- Macedonia's successful conquest of the Greek poleis can be attributed to several factors. What are they?

- Alexander the Great's imperial policies were influenced by his own upbringing, the different cultures he encountered, and some key historical precedents. Give at least one example of each type of influence.

- Explain how the three Hellenistic kingdoms reflect the differences among the three main civilizations we have studied so far.

- Why is the Hellenistic world described as "cosmopolitan"? How did this urban culture differ from that of the Greek poleis?

- The philosophies of Plato and Aristotle both derive from the teachings of Socrates, but they diverge in some important ways. What are those main differences?

very end of the first century B.C.E., and it would never supplant Greek as the preeminent language of scholarship and administration in the eastern portions of their empire.

The Hellenistic era must also be recognized as the bridge that connects us to the earlier ages of antiquity: most of what is contained in the first four chapters of this book is known to us only because older texts and inscriptions and artifacts were collected and copied by the scholars of Alexandria and other Hellenistic cities. This era also bridges the gap between the tastes and ideals and customs of classical Greece and those that would be more characteristic of Rome. It was Hellenistic art and architecture, Hellenistic city planning and civic culture that the Romans strove to emulate and export to their own colonies, not those of Periclean Athens. The same can be said of drama and poetry.

For us, two further aspects of Hellenistic culture deserve special mention: its cosmopolitanism and its modernity. The word *cosmopolitan* itself comes from a Greek word meaning "universal city," and it was the Greeks of the Hellenistic period who came closest to turning this ideal of globalization into reality. Around 250 B.C.E. a Greek tourist could have traveled from Sicily to the borders of India—the two known ends of the earth—and never have found himself among people who did not speak his language or share his basic outlook. Nor would this tourist have identified himself in ethnic or nationalist terms, or felt any exclusive loyalty to a city-state or kingdom. He would have considered himself a citizen of the world. He would also have considered himself a modern man, not bound by the old prejudices and superstitions of the past. It is for these reasons that Hellenistic civilization seems so closely related to our own. It was a world of stark contrasts and infinite possibilities, where economic instability, extremism, and authoritarian regimes existed side by side with unprecedented prosperity, rational inquiry, and extraordinary freedoms. In Chapter 5, we will see how this world adapted itself to the dominion of a single Italian city.

PEOPLE, IDEAS, AND EVENTS IN CONTEXT

- In what ways were the military strategies of **PHILIP II** variations on older forms of hoplite warfare? How did the rise of mercenary armies and of Thebes further change military strategies in the fourth century?
- How did the philosophies of **PLATO** and **ARISTOTLE** respond to the crisis of the polis?
- To what degree did the conquests of **ALEXANDER THE GREAT** unite Mesopotamia, Egypt, and Greece?
- Why and how did the three **HELLENISTIC KINGDOMS** emerge? How were the **AETOLIAN AND ACHAEAN LEAGUES** new models for governance and cooperation in Greece?
- In what ways were **STOICISM**, **EPICUREANISM**, and other new philosophies a response to **COSMOPOLITANISM** and the breakdown of traditional societies and values?
- What were the driving forces behind the **SCIENTIFIC REVOLUTION OF ANTIQUITY**? What were its main achievements?
- What are some essential characteristics of **HELLENISTIC ART**? In what ways did it differ from that of the fifth century B.C.E. (see Chapter 3)?

THINKING ABOUT CONNECTIONS

- "The history of the world is but the biography of great men": so the Scottish historian Thomas Carlyle (1795–1881) summarized the impact of figures like Alexander the Great. How would you construct an argument in support of this proposition, using what you've learned in this chapter? How would you refute it?
- In what ways do Alexander's actions demonstrate his own knowledge of history as well as a capacity to apply that knowledge to his own circumstances? Can you identify leaders of our own day who have mobilized their understanding of history in similar ways?
- In your view, which civilization more resembles our own: classical Athens or the Hellenistic world? Why? What characteristics make an era seem "modern"?

Before You Read This Chapter

STORY LINES

- Romans were proud of their unique history, especially the legend that they had overthrown their kings. They clung to this story even when individual men came to wield kingly powers.

- Roman identity, religion, and politics were intimately bound up in the worship of ancestors, especially male ancestors. As a result, fathers (living and dead) wielded extraordinary power in early Rome.

- Roman women enjoyed many more freedoms than women of ancient Greece, but they were still subject to the authority of their male relatives.

- Paradoxically, the Romans celebrated their farming heritage even as they built a highly urbanized society. At the same time, they regarded Greek culture as both superior and dangerous.

- The Roman army had unprecedented strength and importance in this civilization, but the army's relationship to Roman politics and society changed drastically as Rome's empire grew.

CHRONOLOGY

753 B.C.E.	Legendary founding of Rome
c. 509 B.C.E.	Roman Republic established
c. 450 B.C.E.	Law of the Twelve Tables
287 B.C.E.	"Struggle of the Orders" ends
264–146 B.C.E.	Punic Wars
134–104 B.C.E.	Slave revolts in Sicily
133–122 B.C.E.	Reforms of the Gracchi
107–86 B.C.E.	Consulship of Marius
82–79 B.C.E.	Dictatorship of Sulla
73–71 B.C.E.	Rebellion of Spartacus
52–48 B.C.E.	Struggle of Pompey and Caesar
48–44 B.C.E.	Dictatorship of Casaer
44–30 B.C.E.	Rivalry of Octavian and Antony
27 B.C.E.–14 C.E.	Principate of the Emperor Augustus
27–180 C.E.	Flowering of the *Pax Romana*
79 C.E.	Eruption of Mount Vesuvius destroys (and preserves) Pompeii
117 C.E.	Roman Empire reaches its greatest territorial extent under Trajan

5

The Civilization of Ancient Rome

CORE OBJECTIVES

- **IDENTIFY** the factors that influenced the formation of the Roman Republic.

- **UNDERSTAND** the basic elements of Roman identity.

- **DEFINE** the classes of people who struggled for power in Rome.

- **DESCRIBE** the impact of territorial expansion on Roman society.

- **TRACE** the events leading up to the establishment of the Principate.

"Could anyone be so indifferent or slow-witted as not to care how, and under what system of government, the Romans managed to bring nearly the whole inhabited world under their rule? Can anything be more important than understanding this?" So the Greek soldier Polybius (c. 203–120 B.C.E.) addresses Greek readers in a history celebrating the achievements of the Roman Republic. Polybius had witnessed some of these firsthand: on the battlefield, in Rome itself as a hostage and a guest, and on a visit to newly conquered Carthage. What better testament could there be to the success of a small Italian city than the admiration of a cultivated Greek aristocrat who, having been subjected to Roman authority, wholeheartedly embraced it? None, unless we cite the equally enthusiastic endorsement of the same Jews who had rebelled against Greek influence in 164 B.C.E. They, too, could not say enough in praise of the Romans, and they willingly placed themselves under Roman protection:

> Those whom they wish to help and to make kings, they make kings, and those whom they wish they depose; and they have been greatly exalted. Yet for all that, not one of

145

them has put on a crown or worn purple as a mark of pride, but they have built for themselves a senate chamber and every day three hundred and twenty senators constantly deliberate concerning the people, to govern them well. (1 Maccabees 8:12–15)

The only people who could say more in praise of Rome were the Romans themselves. To them, the enormous success of their empire meant that they were divinely chosen to colonize the world. This was the message conveyed by the poet Virgil (70–19 B.C.E.), commissioned by the emperor Augustus to tell the story of Rome's rise to glory in a manner imitating the epics of Homer. In one key passage of this monumental poem, the father of Aeneas, Virgil's epic hero, "foretells" the future and addresses posterity: "Remember, Roman, you whose power rules / all peoples, that these are your arts: plant peace, / make law, spare subjects, and put down the proud" (*Aeneid*, Book VI, lines 851–53).

While the Greeks struggled against the Persians and against each other, a new civilization had emerged beyond the far fringes of the Greek world, on the banks of the river Tiber in central Italy. By 300 B.C.E., Rome was the dominant power on the Italian peninsula. Two centuries later, it had conquered Greece itself. For the next three centuries after that—an unprecedented period of sustained expansion—its power steadily increased. In the first century of our era, it ruled the former Hellenistic kingdoms as well as a vast region that Greek culture had never touched: northwestern Europe. Eventually, Rome's empire united the entire Mediterranean world and most of Asia Minor, while at the same time embracing provinces that are now parts of France, Spain, Portugal, Britain, Belgium, Germany, Switzerland, and the Balkan states. Rome thus built a historical arch that enabled Europe to share in a rich heritage reaching back to ancient Mesopotamia and Egypt, and which gives meaning to the concept of "western civilization." Without Rome, European culture as we know it would not exist, and neither would the political and legal institutions that formed the United States. To echo Polybius: "Can anything be more important than understanding this?"

THE TIME OF THE KINGS

Romans looked back uneasily on their early history, for this was the time when they were ruled by kings. It may have been necessary in those days: Romans had never been peaceful settlers, and their land did not yield an easy living. Although Italy had sizable forests and much more fertile land than Greece, it has few mineral resources aside from excellent supplies of marble. Its extensive coastline boasts only a few good harbors, and most of these are on the western side, away from the commercial hubs of Greece and the Near East. Nor does the length of this coastline offer secure natural defenses. In short, Italy was rich enough to be attractive but not rich enough to be easily defended. So the Romans were a warlike people from the first, continually forced to defend their hard-won lands against other invaders and needing strong leaders to spearhead their efforts.

Early Influences

When the Romans arrived in Italy, the dominant inhabitants of the peninsula were a people whom the Greeks called Tyrrhenians. To the Romans, they were Etruscans; and to us they remain mysterious, despite the rich archaeological record they left behind. This is because their language (not a branch of Indo-European) has never been fully deciphered, even though the Etruscans used an alphabet borrowed from the Greeks, with whom they were in frequent contact. By the sixth century B.C.E., the Etruscans had established a confederation of independent city-states in north-central Italy. They were skilled metalworkers, artists, and architects, from whom the Romans later took their knowledge of the arch and the vault, among much else, including the bloody sport of gladiatorial combat and the practice of foretelling the future by studying the entrails of animals and the flight of birds.

The two most important foundation myths told by the Romans were also derived from Etruscan tradition: the story of Aeneas's escape from Troy, which became the basis of Virgil's *Aeneid*; and also the story of the infant twins Romulus and Remus, abandoned at birth and then raised by a maternal wolf, afterward founding a city on the slopes of the Palatine Hill. Both legends would be mined by Rome's politicians and historians for their metaphorical significance, and further details would be added to increase their relevance for a changing audience. For example, the story of Aeneas's seduction and abandonment of Dido, queen of Carthage, reflected Rome's defeat of that powerful North African civilization. And for many Roman commentators, the murder of Remus at the hands of his brother Romulus encapsulated an all-too-familiar pattern in Roman politics.

One aspect of Etruscan culture was of more limited influence. In marked contrast to Greek society, Etruscan women enjoyed a very high status and played important roles in public life. They participated in politics and sporting events, they attended dramatic performances and athletic competitions (forbidden to Greek women), and they danced

The Romans also borrowed ideas from the Greek settlers who had begun to colonize southern Italy and Sicily in large numbers during the eighth century B.C.E. From them, Romans derived their alphabet, many of their religious beliefs, and much of their art. But the Romans downplayed Greek influence in their founding mythology, preferring to emphasize their alleged descent from Trojans and also tracing their ancestry back to an Italic people called the Sabines, from whom (according to legend) Romulus and his men had forcibly abducted their women. This was a practice Romans would continue, in one form or another, as the legions planted new colonies and intermarried with indigenous populations from the Persian Gulf to the lowlands of Scotland.

The Founding of Rome

The real founders of Rome were a tribe called the Latins, descendants of a cluster of Indo-European-speaking peoples who crossed the Alps into Italy during the second millennium B.C.E. Recent archaeological research has pushed the origins of the city back to at least the tenth century, several centuries earlier than 753 B.C.E., which the Romans themselves calculated as the year of their city's foundation.

Rome's position on the Tiber was advantageous. Trading ships (but not large war fleets) could navigate the river as far as the city, but no farther; Rome could thus serve as a commercial port but was not threatened by attack from the sea. Rome also sat astride the first good ford across the Tiber, making it a major crossroads. This was particularly important in its early years, when all roads did *not* lead to Rome and the city was just a trading post on the frontier between Latium (the territory of the Latins) and Etruria (the Etruscan homeland). There were also strategic advantages to the seven hills that ringed the settlement, among which Rome was nestled. Eventually, its central marketplace—the *forum* or "open space"—would become the beating heart of the world's most populous and powerful city, with approximately a million people crowded into an area of five square miles.

The topography of Latium—a broad, flat plain with few natural obstacles—also influenced the way the Romans dealt with neighboring communities, because it was not a terrain with defensible natural boundaries. At an early date, they negotiated a series of agreements with their neighbors which were collectively known as the Latin Right: a trading pact called the *commercium*, provisions for intermarriage called the *connubium*, and the *migratio* that allowed a Latin resident of one settlement to emigrate to another and, after a year's residence, to have the full rights of a citizen there. These privileges contrast strongly with the rigid isolationism and mutual suspicion that divided the city-states of

AN ETRUSCAN COUPLE. This sarcophagus lid dates from the middle of the fourth century B.C.E. and depicts a deceased couple as they lie together in bed, emphasizing by their intimate embrace the closeness of their marital bond.

in ways that shocked both Greeks and Romans. Etruscan wives also ate meals with their husbands, another departure from both Greek and Roman custom, and reclined with them on the same couch at banquets. After death, these devoted couples were buried together in the same mortuary vaults, and their tombstones and sarcophagi often emphasize their mutual affection. Etruscan families even traced their descent through the female line. Some of these practices certainly affected the Romans, since Roman women were less sequestered than their Greek counterparts. Yet they did not enjoy the same freedoms as Etruscan women until very late in Roman history, and by then these freedoms were condemned as signs of Rome's decadence.

ancient Mesopotamia or Greece. Indeed, the Romans' later willingness to extend the Latin Right far beyond Latium was a key factor in the success of their empire.

According to their own legends, the Romans' early government was a monarchy that mirrored the structure of Roman households, with a patriarchal king who exercised power that was checked only by a council of elders, the Senate (a word derived from the Latin *senex*, "old man"). Seven kings, including Romulus, are said to have ruled in succession. The last, Tarquinius Superbus (Tarquin the Arrogant), is reputed to have been an Etruscan who paved the way for Rome's imperial expansion by dominating Latium and the agriculturally wealthy district of Campania to the south. But his power came at the price of Roman freedom and dignity, as was made clear when Tarquin's son allegedly raped a virtuous Roman wife, Lucretia, around 510 B.C.E. When she committed suicide to avoid dishonor, the Romans—led by Lucretia's kinsman, Lucius Junius Brutus—rose up in rebellion, overthrowing not only the Etruscan dynasty but rejecting the very idea of monarchy as a legitimate form of government. Henceforth, any claim to royal authority in Rome was considered anathema, and the very word *rex* ("king") was a term of insult. The Brutus who would be instrumental in the assassination of Julius Caesar nearly five centuries later was a descendant of that same Brutus who had driven out the Tarquin kings, something he and his contemporaries never forgot.

THE TRIUMPH OF THE EARLY REPUBLIC

The story of Lucretia's defilement and death, whether or not it occurred as it was remembered, remained a rallying theme of patriotic myth and was also a potent statement of Roman attitudes toward female chastity and family honor. And it coincided with a radical change in Roman governance. This change was so radical, in fact, that it did not match any of Aristotle's political categories (see Chapter 4), but instead combined elements of them all. The Romans themselves didn't know what to call their political system: they spoke of it merely as *res publica*, "the public thing."

The Territorial Expansion of Rome

The early Roman republic was marked by almost constant warfare, initially defensive but soon aimed at stitching together a patchwork of valuable territories that could sup-

port Rome's growing population. Gradually, Romans came to control all of the Latin hinterland and the valuable port of Ostia at the mouth of the Tiber, about twenty miles from their city. They also pushed northward toward Etruscan territory, and southward to Naples, another good port. By 300 B.C.E., Romans had absorbed or allied themselves with all of central Italy and had begun to look even further south, to the wealthy Greek colonies of Sicily.

Their rapid success is remarkable when compared to the patterns familiar to us from our study of classical Greece, the only corollary (and not a close one) being Philip II of Macedonia's subjugation of the poleis earlier in that same century. What was the secret of it? For one thing, the Romans did not impose heavy burdens of taxation and tribute on the settlements they conquered. More often, they demanded that their allies contribute only soldiers to the Roman army. Rome also extended the Latin Right to many of these conquered territories, giving them a further stake in its continued political and military expansion.

Rome thus gained for itself nearly inexhaustible reserves of fighting men. By the middle of the third century B.C.E., its army may have counted as many as 300,000—a huge force even by modern standards, and all the more formidable due to the soldiers' rigorous training. As we have seen, the Greeks had eventually turned to paid soldiering out of economic necessity, but they fought in smaller numbers; Xenophon's army was 10,000 and Alexander's 100,000. The Great King of Persia, at the height of his powers, could claim to muster a million men, but these were private or tribal armies commanded by his satraps, not a standing army loyal to him. The Romans, by contrast, devoted themselves to the discipline of warfare in ways the Greeks (except for the Spartans) and the Persians did not. In this, although not in their tactics, they resemble the Hittites of the late Bronze Age and the Neo-Assyrians of the eighth century B.C.E. (see Chapter 2).

Although the Romans originally used the phalanx formation borrowed from the Greeks, they quickly replaced it with smaller, more flexible divisions that could adjust to the varied geographical conditions of central Italy. While the major unit of the Roman army was always the legion (5,000 men), the basic combat unit was the *maniple* ("handful"), a group of about 120 infantrymen who trained together and who often performed specialized tasks or used special weaponry. The Greek Polybius could not say enough in praise of this system, which made the army adaptable to climate, terrain, and the deployment of new military technologies.

The republic's early history reinforced not only the military character of the Roman state but its commitment to agriculture as the only proper peacetime employment for a Roman. The acquisition of new lands made it possible

ROMAN EXPANSION TO 218 B.C.E.

- Roman and Latin territory in 298 B.C.E.
- Roman allies in 298 B.C.E.
- Roman and Latin acquisitions from 298–263 B.C.E.
- Roman allies from 298–263 B.C.E.
- Roman acquisitions from 241–218 B.C.E.
- Roman acquisitions from the Second Punic War 218–201 B.C.E.
- Kingdom of Syracuse
- Allies of Syracuse

ROMAN EXPANSION IN ITALY, 485–265 B.C.E. This map illustrates early Roman expansion in the peninsula. ▪ *What is the geographical relationship between Roman and Etruscan territory?* ▪ *What seem to have been the most attractive avenues for Roman expansion?* ▪ *What powers might have threatened Rome after its transformation into the dominant power on the peninsula after 265 B.C.E.?*

for needy citizens to maintain themselves as farmers in the new colonies around Rome. By accommodating an increasing population in this way, Romans were able to remain staunchly agricultural for a surprisingly long time. As a result, they developed an interest in shipping and commerce fairly late when compared with the Greeks or Phoenicians. And they would continue—even at the height of their empire—to valorize rural life over that of the city.

The paragon of Roman heroism in this era was Lucius Quinctius Cincinnatus (519–c. 430 B.C.E.), a stout-hearted citizen-farmer who reluctantly accepted political office when Rome was threatened by attack. According to legend, he

The Constitution of the Early Republic

During this period of expansion, Rome's political system evolved accordingly. Initially, the overthrow of the monarchy had resulted in only moderate changes; instead of a king, the government was headed by two elected officers called *consuls*. Although the consuls of the infant republic were supposedly chosen by all citizens, the Roman assembly of this period actually voted in affiliated blocs with shared interests, economic or territorial. And since groups consisting of the wealthiest citizens voted first, a majority could be reached even before the votes of the poorer groups were cast.

Consequently, the consuls were inevitably members of aristocratic families, known in Rome as *patricians* because they traced descent from a famous ancestor or "father" (*pater*). During his term of office, which lasted for one year, each consul exercised essentially the same power as a king: dealing justice, making law, and commanding the army. The only limit on consular power was the right of each consul to veto the actions of the other, which often led to stalemate or violent conflict. In such cases, the Senate might have to arbitrate. In times of grave emergency (like that resulting in Cincinnatus's election), a dictator might be appointed for a term not longer than six months.

Within a generation after the establishment of the republic, patrician dominance of the government began to be challenged by the *plebs* ("people"). This was the first stage in a centuries-long contest known as the Struggle of the Orders. The plebeian classes made up nearly 98 percent of the Roman population, and they were a diverse group. Some had grown wealthy through trade or agriculture, but most were smallholding farmers, artisans, or the urban poor. Their causes for grievance were numerous. Although they were forced to serve in the army, they were nevertheless excluded from holding office. They were also the victims of discriminatory decisions in judicial trials, which were judged by patricians. They did not even know what legal rights they were supposed to enjoy, because Rome had as yet no established laws: there were only unwritten customs and practices whose meaning was interpreted by the patricians to their own advantage. The plebeians were also, like the poorer citizens of Greek poleis, threatened with debt slavery.

These wrongs prompted a rebellion in the early fifth century B.C.E., when plebeians refused to join in the military defense of Rome and instead seceded from the city, camping out on the Aventine hill (see the map of Rome on page 174). This general strike of military labor forced the patricians to allow the people to elect their own officers, who were known as *tribunes* (tribal leaders). The job of each tribune was to protect his constituents from patrician injustice. Moreover, the plebeians guaranteed the safety of these

CINCINNATUS THE STATESMAN-FARMER. This bronze statue of Cincinnatus is prominent in Cincinnati, Ohio, which was named after the Roman hero (and in honor of George Washington) in 1790. In his right hand he holds the *fasces,* symbolizing his powers as dictator. In his left, he grasps the handle of a plow. ▪ *Why would this figure have fired the imagination of Americans after their War of Independence?*

was found plowing his fields when a delegation of senators arrived to bring him to Rome. Arriving in the city, he found that he had been named *dictator*: a word that originally (like *tyrant* in Greece) had neutral connotations. This was a position of power to which the Romans elected one man during times of crisis. And as the term implies, the dictator's job was to tell everyone what they should do in a tough situation requiring decisive leadership. As legend has it, Cincinnatus dutifully performed this role, led Rome in its wars with hostile neighbors—and then went back to his farm. If Lucretia was the Roman epitome of matronly fortitude, Cincinnatus was the paradigm of manly virtue: willing to put his hand to politics or warfare, but preferring to put it to the plow. George Washington was frequently compared to him, to his own satisfaction.

officers by vowing to kill any person who hindered them in the exercise of their powers.

The plebs' victory led to the codification of the Law of the Twelve Tables, issued around 450 B.C.E. and inscribed on wooden tablets (hence "tables"). Although this law would be regarded by later Romans as a charter of liberties, it was really a perpetuation of ancient custom. Nevertheless, the fact that the law was now *defined* made it a significant improvement. Plebeians were also made eligible to hold elected offices and they gradually gained access to the Senate. A further victory came in 287 B.C.E., when the plebeians succeeded in passing a law that made decisions enacted in their own assembly, the *concilium plebis*, binding on the Roman government—whether the Senate approved them or not. It was at this time that the phrase *Senatus Populusque Romanum* came into regular use, abbreviated *SPQR* and designating any decree or decision made by "the Senate and People of Rome." (Visitors to Rome will still find *SPQR* emblazoned on everything from public buildings to the manhole covers of Rome's sewers.)

These reforms had several important consequences over the long term. Successful plebeians could now work their way into the upper reaches of Roman society, which loosened the hold of patrician families on the exercise of power. At the same time, laws preventing wealth from becoming a controlling factor in Roman politics barred senators from engaging directly in commerce. This restriction had the effect of creating a new social order, that of the equestrians ("horsemen" or knights): men who chose a life of business rather than politics and whose wealth made it possible for them to own and equip warhorses and thus to provide Rome's cavalry. But the equestrians and the senators were never wholly distinct. Often, some members of an important family would stay aloof from politics while underwriting the political careers of their brothers and cousins. Those families who managed to win election by such means, generation after generation, became increasingly prestigious and influential. Meanwhile, patricians who chose politics over wealth became impoverished and resentful. By the first century B.C.E., many such men felt excluded from political influence and were tempted to pursue their private agendas by styling themselves champions of the people (see below).

Later Roman patriots would regard this as a golden age of shared government, but Rome was never a democracy. A republic differs from a monarchy only because power is exercised by officers who are in some way responsible to citizens and whose offices are not (at least in theory) hereditary. It is essentially a system for reserving power to an oligarchy or privileged group. This is what the republic had been founded to achieve: kings were driven out, but patricians reigned. The constitution that emerged in these key centuries therefore broadened and stabilized oligarchy by the balance it struck between competing governmental institutions: the assembly, the Senate, and executive officeholders. Thanks to this distribution of powers, no single individual or clique could become overwhelmingly strong; but neither could direct expressions of the popular will (that is, democracy) affect Roman policy.

For the Greek historian Polybius, this was an ideal system because it combined elements of a monarchy (executive officeholders, the consuls), an aristocracy (the Senate), and a polity (the people's assembly and the tribunes). For the framers of the U.S. Constitution, it was a model for the three branches of a new government designed to *prevent* the vast majority of Americans from participating directly in politics, while allowing some citizens (originally, white men with sufficient property) a say in choosing their representatives. Polybius prophesied that such a system would break the political cycle that had destroyed the Greek poleis and that it would last forever. He was wrong.

SENATUS POPULUSQUE ROMANUM. The proud stamp of "the Senate and People of Rome" can be found even on public works and buildings in modern Rome. It is displayed here on a manhole cover.

THE ESSENCE OF ROMAN IDENTITY

The slow unfolding of the early republic ensured, in part, its success: Romans were conservatives who accepted new things reluctantly but then preserved them fiercely. The prevailing principle behind their institutions was the *mos maiorum* (MOHSmy-OR-um), "the code of the elders" or "the custom of the ancestors" or even—to use the word derived from the Latin *mos*—"morality." This unwritten code was sacrosanct and essential to Roman identity. It accounts for the remarkable coherence of Roman culture, religion, and law, all of which rested on ancestor worship. The Latin word *pietas* ("piety") meant reverence for family traditions and for one's fathers—living and dead. What made the legendary Aeneas "pious Aeneas" was his devotion to his father, Anchises (*an-KIE-sees*), whom he carried to safety on his back while Troy burned. Metaphorically, this meant that Aeneas was the carrier of tradition, a man willing to shoulder the burdens of his ancestors and carry them forever.

This helps to explain why the Romans, in the ensuing centuries of their world domination, continued to identify so strongly with their homeland and its customs. To a Roman, "going native" in a foreign place was a terrible betrayal of the *mos maiorum*; patriotism, after all, is dedication to the fatherland. It also explains the extraordinary maxim of *patria potestas* (*PAH-tree-apoh-TEST-as*, "fatherly power") upheld by the Twelve Tables. A Roman father, no matter what his social class, had absolute authority within his household, including the powers of life and death. If he was too poor to raise a child, he could expose it (leaving it to perish or to charity) or sell it into slavery. If his wife or child dishonored him, he could kill with impunity. It was upheld in theory and in legends like that of Lucretia: had she not killed herself, her father could have killed her with his own hands.

These values set the Romans apart from everyone in the Hellenistic world. The Greeks, for example, never condoned anything like *patria potestas*: when fathers kill their children in Greek mythology, they are inevitably killed in revenge by another member of their own family or by the gods. And while pride in one's ancestry is a very human attribute, and patriarchy common to every known civilization, the Romans' contemporaries were awed by their extreme devotion to these principles. It was one of the things that made the Romans so admirable in the eyes of those Jews disgusted by the loose morals of Hellenistic civilization (see Chapter 4). For the Greek Polybius, it was the key to Roman success. In addition to describing the workings of the Roman government and army in minute detail, he reports (with anthropological interest) on the conduct of Roman funeral processions and the Romans' practice of wearing the death-masks of their ancestors, which on other days would be hung in special household shrines.

In some respects, Rome's public religion resembled that of the Greeks: Jupiter corresponded to Zeus as god of the skies, Neptune to Poseidon as god of the seas, Venus to Aphrodite as goddess of beauty and sexuality, Mars to Ares as god of war. But in keeping with the Roman equation of religion with family, this entire pantheon functioned

A ROMAN PATRICIAN OF THE FIRST CENTURY B.C.E. This man, who wears the toga of an aristocrat, displays his piety by holding the busts of his ancestors. Busts, like the funerary masks described by Polybius (see page 153), commemorated the dead and served as the focus for family worship in household shrines. ■ *How does the Roman attitude toward age and death differ from that of the Greeks (see the image on page 82)?* ■ *What do these differences suggest about the broader values of these two societies?*

Analyzing Primary Sources

Polybius Describes the Romans' Worship of Their Ancestors

The Law of the Twelve Tables forbade excessive display at funerals, especially displays of wealth and grief on the part of women. Instead, funerals were supposed to be occasions for the display of family piety. In the following passage, the Greek historian Polybius—who had spent a formative fourteen years of his life in Rome—describes Roman burial customs and these rites' relationship to the strength of republican ideals.

I quote just one example to illustrate the pains taken by the Roman state to produce men who will endure anything to win a reputation for valor in their country. Whenever one of their celebrated men dies . . . his body is carried with every kind of honor into the Forum, . . . sometimes in an upright position so as to be conspicuous, or else, more rarely, recumbent. The whole mass of the people stand round to watch, and his son, if he has one of adult age who can be present, or if not some other relative, then . . . delivers an address which recounts the virtues and successes achieved by the dead man during his lifetime. By these means the whole populace . . . are involved in the ceremony, so that when the facts of the dead man's career are recalled . . . their sympathies are so deeply engaged that the loss seems . . . to be a public one which affects the whole people. Then, after the burial of the body and the performance of the customary rites, they place the image of the dead man in the most conspicuous position in the house, where it is enclosed in a wooden shrine. This image consists of a mask which is fashioned with extraordinary fidelity . . . to represent the features of these dead men. On occasions when public sacrifices are offered, these masks are displayed and decorated with great care. And when any distinguished member of the family dies, the masks are taken to the funeral, and are worn by men who are considered to bear the closest resemblance to the original, both in height and their general appearance and bearing. . . .

It would be hard to imagine a more impressive scene for a young man who aspires to win fame and practice virtue. For who could remain unmoved at the sight of the images of all these men who have won renown in their time, now gathered together as if alive and breathing? What spectacle could be more glorious than this?

Source: Polybius, *The Rise of the Roman Empire*, trans. Ian Scott-Kilvert (New York: 1979), pp. 346–47.

Questions for Analysis

1. Why does Polybius place so high a premium on the Romans' conduct at funerals? How can such rites be related to republican ideals?

2. Compare this analysis of Roman funerary rites to the image of a Roman patrician and his ancestors on page 152. How do they complement one another?

---

as family gods of the Roman state. The republic was essentially a giant, timeless household run by "elders" (senators) and "father figures" (patricians), some of whom traced their ancestry back to gods; the mother of Aeneas was Venus. Like a Roman household, the Roman state could flourish only if these father- and mother-gods lent their continuing and active support to its enterprises. Committees of priests therefore functioned as branches of the government and tended to the worship of the city's temples. And in stark contrast to other ancient societies, these priests were not full-time professionals who formed a special caste, but prominent men who rotated in and out of office while serving as leaders of the Senate. Their dual roles made religion even more integral to political life in Rome than it had been in Greece—similar in some ways to the integration of religion and politics in ancient Mesopotamia (see Chapter 1).

The Roman man's primary duty to honor his ancestors also bolstered the prestige of the Roman army, because soldiers were supposed to sacrifice themselves for the public good and to fear disgrace above all things. The all-important sense of ancestral duty is further reflected in Roman naming practices, another custom that separated them from other ancient cultures. Most free men in antiquity were known by a given name and their father's name only: Alexander, before he was "the Great," was "son of Philip." A free-born Roman, by contrast, had at least two names. The name by which he was known—the name that mattered—was the name of his earliest ancestor, the man from whom his family descended. Gaius Julius Caesar, to take a famous example, would have entered public life as Julius, a member of the family of the Julii, who claimed ancestry from Iulus, the son of Aeneas. His forename, Gaius, was the most common name in Rome, the equivalent of "Joe" or "John," and he would never be addressed by this name in public, except perhaps by very intimate friends or family members. His third name, Caesar, was a nickname he acquired in the course of his career: "Hairy" (probably a joke). And because it was the most distinctive of his names—the name he didn't share with an ancestor or with average Romans—it became the name by which he was universally known. The same goes for Marcus Tullius Cicero (Cicero means "chickpea"). The illustrious Cincinnatus was actually "Curly."

What's in a name? Everything, if you were a Roman man. And nothing, at least nothing of personal significance, if you were a Roman woman. Lucretia's name was not her own but her father's—or forefather's: the feminine version of Lucretius. If she had a sister, they would both be called Lucretia, differentiated only as Major and Minor ("big/elder" and "little/younger") Lucretia. If there were two more girls, they would be Tertia and Quarta ("Third" and "Fourth") Lucretia, and so on. The only people in Rome who had personal names were slaves (who were named by their masters, like pets) or very low-born Romans and immigrants who had no lineage that mattered.

FROM REPUBLIC TO EMPIRE

For more than two centuries after the founding of the republic, warfare and agriculture remained the chief occupations of most Romans. A few artisans could be found in cities, and some minor attempts were made to establish trading networks. But the fact that Rome had no standard system of coinage until 289 B.C.E suggests strongly that commerce was an insignificant component of its economy. Apparently, Romans didn't rely on portable wealth; when they weren't fighting, they wanted to be home on the farm, not gadding about the world. If they had money, they put it into real estate: land or slaves.

All of this changed rapidly when Romans began to look beyond Italy. In 265 B.C.E., they completed their absorption of Etruscan territory and could claim to control most of the peninsula. A year later, they were already embroiled in a war overseas. For a home-loving people who had now secured ample resources for their own support, this seems paradoxical. Indeed, historians continue to argue about the motives for Roman expansion. Did Rome constantly seek to extend its rule as a matter of policy, to feed a collective appetite for warfare and plunder? Or was it an accidental empire, built up in a series of reactions to changing pressures at home as well as in response to threats—real and imagined—from abroad? No definitive answer is yet possible, but it is in this crucial period that the Roman Republic began to transform Western civilizations and to transform itself into the Roman Empire.

The Punic Wars, 264–146 B.C.E

In 265 B.C.E., Roman territory extended to the tip of Italy's "boot," but there it ended. Just off its coast, the large islands of Corsica and Sardinia and the western half of Sicily were part of another state, much older and far wealthier. This was the great maritime empire of Carthage, which stretched along the northern coast of Africa from modern-day Tunisia through the Straits of Gibraltar and into modern Spain. Carthage itself was a vital port city at the northeastern tip of Africa, founded around 800 B.C.E. as a Phoenician colony (see Chapter 2) but now independent and powerful. It had the largest and most effective navy of its day, and it commanded the vast resources of commercial networks that reached as far north as Britain and deep into Egypt and the Near East. In almost every respect but one it was far superior to Rome. Yet that one factor was decisive: while the Carthaginian fleet was unrivaled, Carthage had no standing army. It relied on mercenaries bankrolled by the enormous profits of its merchants.

The epic struggle between Rome and Carthage for dominance of the Mediterranean lasted well over a century. It crystallized in three periods of concentrated warfare known as the Punic Wars, because the Romans called their enemies Poeni, "Phoenicians." The first of these wars began in 264 B.C.E., when Rome sent a garrison to occupy the independent city of Messina (originally a Greek colony) on the eastern tip of Sicily, directly across from the Italian mainland. Carthage, in response, took advantage of the local enmity between Messina and Syracuse, another Greek city, and sent warships to protect Syracuse from what it saw as Roman aggression. Twenty-three years of bitter fighting ensued, protracted because the Carthaginians only needed to suffer one defeat in a land battle before resolving to engage the Romans solely at sea. There, they had the advantage—until the Romans built their own navy, virtually from scratch. In 241 B.C.E., Carthage was beaten down and forced to cede all of her Sicilian lands to Rome and to pay a large indemnity. Sicily thus became Rome's first overseas province. It was shortly followed by Corsica and Sardinia, which the Roman Senate contrived to seize on the grounds that Carthage had defaulted on the payment of reparations.

Thereafter, the Carthaginians had ample reason to harbor resentment against Rome, while the Romans were determined not to let Carthage revive its maritime power. So when Carthage attempted to expand its presence in Spain, leaders of the Senate intepreted this as a threat to Roman interests and declared a new war that lasted for sixteen years: the Second Punic War. This time, however, Rome was thrown entirely off its guard by the brilliant exploits of the Carthaginian commander Hannibal (247–183 B.C.E), who very nearly defeated the Romans at their own game and on their own soil. No one had imagined that a Carthaginian attack could come by land, from the north. But daringly, Hannibal raised an army in Spain, heavily manned by cavalry in order to counter the superior infantry of Rome, and equipped it with dozens of war elephants and siege engines. He then led this entire force across the Pyrenees into Gaul (now southern France) and then over the Alps into Italy. There, he harried Roman forces in their own territories for nearly sixteen years, from 218 to 202 B.C.E.

In the end, Hannibal was challenged more by the rigors of campaigning and the difficulty of supplying his army in hostile terrain than by the Romans themselves (he had lost many of his elephants and some important equipment in the icy mountain passes of the Alps). He also seems to have counted on winning the support of the Italian territories that Rome had conquered, but Rome's generous treatment of its Latin allies kept them loyal. As a result, Rome could call on vast human resources while Hannibal had only his exhausted army, and no reserves forthcoming from Carthage. Nevertheless, he won several amazing victories in Italy before retreating—technically undefeated—in 202 B.C.E. He also won the admiration of the Romans themselves, whose own histories frankly acknowledge his tactical genius. Indeed, this phase of warfare ended only when a Roman general, Publius Cornelius Scipio, took a leaf out of Hannibal's book. He had been campaigning in Spain against the army of Hannibal's brother, Hasdrubal, and having seized a number of key Carthaginian strongholds he crossed into Africa and met Hannibal at Zama, near Carthage, in 201 B.C.E. Scipio's victory ended the Second Punic War and won him a new name, "Africanus," in honor of his conquest.

Carthage was now compelled to abandon all of its possessions except the city itself and its immediate hinterlands, and to pay an indemnity three times greater than the already crippling reparations demanded after the First Punic War. Yet Roman suspicion of Carthage remained obsessive, and warmongers in the Senate read every sign of its recovery as a threat. By the middle of the second century, some hardliners were urging a preemptive strike. Among the most vocal was an elderly patrician called Marcus Porcius Cato, famous for his stern obedience to Roman custom and his virulent xenophobia. Cato ended every speech he gave—no matter what the topic—with the words: "And furthermore, I strongly advise that Carthage be destroyed." This won him the nickname Cato the Censor, from the Latin verb meaning "to advise."

Eventually, the Senate was persuaded. In 149 B.C.E., it seized on a minor pretext to demand that the Carthaginians abandon their city and settle at least ten miles from the coast, where they would have no access to the sea. Of course, this absurd mandate amounted to a death sentence for a city dependent on commerce, and it was refused—as the Romans knew it would be. The result was the Third Punic War and the siege of Carthage, which ended in 146 B.C.E. when the Romans breached the walls and butchered the population.

CARTHAGINIAN COIN. This coin was issued by Hannibal's family around 230 B.C.E. and circulated in the Carthaginian colonies of Spain. Its face shows the Carthaginian god Melqart in the guise of Hercules (notice the club over his shoulder). The reverse features a war elephant with a mounted rider, like the ones that would be used by Hannibal against Rome.

Those who survived the massacre were sold into slavery, and their once-magnificent city was razed to the ground. The legend that the Romans sowed the land with salt (to make it infertile) is not a real tactic but a poetic way of describing the successful eradication of an entire civilization. It would stand as a warning to Rome's other potential enemies.

Roman Control of the Hellenistic World

Rome's victories over Carthage enormously increased Roman territory, leading to the creation of new colonial provinces in Sicily, North Africa, and Hispania (Spain).

This not only brought Rome great new wealth (above all, access to Sicilian and African grain supplies and to the silver mines of the Iberian Peninsula), but it was also the beginning of the westward expansion that became Rome's defining influence on the history of Europe.

At the same time, Rome's overseas expansion brought it into conflict with eastern Mediterranean powers, paving the way for further conquests. During the Second Punic War, Philip V of Macedonia had entered an alliance with Carthage; soon afterward, he moved aggressively into Greece and was rumored to have designs on Egypt. Rome sent an army to stop him, and later foiled the plans of the Achaean League (see Chapter 4). This was when Polybius was sent to Rome as a hostage, and became a guest-friend in the family descended from Scipio Africanus, and later

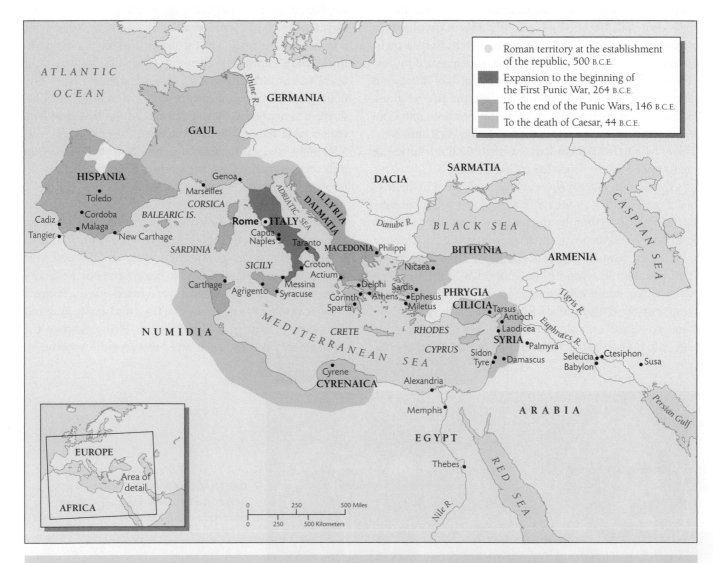

THE FURTHER EXPANSION OF ROME, 264–44 B.C.E. The rapid increase of Rome's territories opened up new opportunities and challenges. ▪ *Looking at the phases of expansion on this map, in what directions did Roman dominion move?* ▪ *Why was this the case?* ▪ *What particular problems might have been created by the eventual extension of Roman rule into Gaul, well beyond the "Roman lake" of the Mediterranean?*

witnessed the destruction of Carthage. Rome also thwarted similar efforts by the Seleucid monarch Antiochus III. In neither of these cases did Rome set out to conquer the eastern Mediterranean on purpose. By 146 B.C.E., however, both Greece and Macedonia had become Roman provinces, Seleucid Asia had lost most of its territories, and Ptolemaic Egypt had largely become a pawn of Roman commercial and political interests.

THE CONSEQUENCES OF IMPERIALISM

Rome's seemingly inadvertent conquest of Greece and Asia Minor transformed the economic, social, and cultural life of the republic. New wealth poured in, increasing the inequalities within Roman society and challenging traditional values of frugality and self-sacrifice. Small farmers left the land and swelled the impoverished urban population, unable to compete with the huge new plantations owned by aristocrats and worked by gangs of slaves. Slaves also played an increasing role in Roman cities as artisans, merchants, and household servants. Roman rule over the Hellenistic world had a particularly pervasive impact on cultural life—so much so that many Romans considered themselves to have been intellectually "conquered" by Greece. Hitherto self-assured and self-satisfied, they now felt their own language, history, and customs to be uncouth and barbaric compared to those of their cultivated colonial subjects.

Economic Change and Social Upheaval

Like all peoples of the ancient world, Romans took slavery for granted. But nothing in Rome's earlier experience prepared it for the huge increase in the number of slaves that resulted from its western and eastern conquests. In 146 B.C.E., 55,000 Carthaginians were enslaved after the destruction of their city; not long before, 150,000 Greek prisoners of war had met the same fate. By the end of the second century B.C.E., there were a million slaves in Italy alone. Rome's became one of the most slave-based economies in history, rivaling ancient Egypt or the antebellum American South.

The majority of Roman slaves worked as agricultural laborers on the vast (and growing) estates of the Roman aristocracy. Some of these estates were the result of earlier Roman conquests within Italy itself. But others were consolidated by aristocrats buying up the holdings of peasant farmers. Soldiers in particular, who might be required to

serve for years at a time on foreign campaigns, often found it impossible to maintain their farms. Instead, they moved to the city—where there was no way for free men to sustain themselves except through trade or violence. With abundant, cheap slaves to do all the rough work, moreover, there was no impetus for technological innovation. Meanwhile, expensive slaves did the specialized jobs: they were secretaries, bookkeepers, personal assistants, playwrights, musicians, sculptors, artists. There was almost no incentive to employ paid labor at all or even to train oneself in these arts, as the Greeks had. By the first century B.C.E., as a result, a third of Rome's 1 million inhabitants were receiving free grain from the state, partly to keep them alive and partly to keep them quiet. The poet Juvenal (see page 171) would later satirize the plebs as needing only "bread and circuses" to stay satisfied and docile.

As we have seen, the Roman economy had remained fundamentally agrarian until the mid-third century B.C.E. During the following century, however, Rome's eastern conquests brought it fully into the sophisticated commercial hub of the Hellenistic world. The principal beneficiaries of this were the equestrian class. As overseas merchants, they profited handsomely from Rome's voracious appetite for foreign luxury goods. And as representatives of the Roman government in the provinces, they operated mines, built roads, and collected taxes, always with an eye toward their own profits. They were also the principal moneylenders to the Roman state and to distressed individuals. Interest rates were high, and when the state could not pay its bills, it would often allow the moneylenders to repay themselves by exploiting the populations of the provinces.

Commoners who lost their lands suffered from these economic changes, but the principal victims of Rome's transformation were its slaves. Even though some were cultivated foreigners—mainly Greek-speaking—taken as prisoners of war, the standard policy of their owners was to get as much work out of them as possible until they died of exhaustion or were "freed" in old age to fend for themselves. The same irascible Cato the Censor who had demanded the destruction of Carthage even wrote a "how-to" book on this subject. The ready availability of slaves also made Roman slavery a far more impersonal and brutal institution than it had been in many other ancient civilizations. Of course, there were exceptions. Some domestic slaves were treated as trusted family members, and slave secretaries vital to the business of Roman governance and literature could even win fame or earn enough to buy their freedoms. Some slave artisans were permitted to run their own businesses, keeping some of the profits.

But the general lot of slaves was horrendous. Some businessmen owned slaves whom they trained as gladiators, to be mauled by wild animals or by other gladiators

Past and Present

Spectator Sports

Like the Romans' love for gladiatorial combat, Americans' love of football is inextricably tied to a sense of shared identity and fascination with violence and warfare. Although American football is not a bloodsport in a technical sense, part of its allure stems from the very great physical risks taken by its players, whose careers are often cut short by injury. Both pastimes form the core of far-reaching entertainment economies that would be dismantled by any attempts at reform: concessions, advertising, merchandising, and an array of other money-making activities.

 Watch related author interview on StudySpace
wwnorton.com/web/westernciv18

for the amusement of a paying public. The luxurious life-styles of the wealthy meant that dozens of slaves in every household were trapped in a cycle of menial tasks, as door-keepers, litter-bearers, couriers, valets, wet-nurses, and child-minders. In some great households, designated slaves had no other duties than to rub down the master after his bath or to keep track of the mistress's social engagements. It was a life that debased both slave and owner, according to many Roman critics, and thereby undermined the values of the republic.

New Money, New Values

In the early republic, as we have seen, Roman men had nearly absolute powers over their individual households. During the second century B.C.E., however, two innovations greatly altered this pattern of patriarchal control. One was the introduction of new laws that allowed married women to manage their own property instead of handing that wealth over to their husbands; if a married woman died, her possessions would then revert to her father or her father's heirs if she had no children of her own. Alongside this new law came more liberal laws that allowed women to initiate divorce proceedings.

These changes were intended to safeguard family wealth, but they eventually resulted in greater independence for women. A woman now had much more authority within the household because she contributed to its upkeep. If her husband did not show respect, she could leave him and deprive him of income. Ironically, the growth of Rome's slave system also gave women greater freedom, for slaves took over the traditional work of child rearing, household maintenance, and the endless tasks of spinning and weaving. Women from well-to-do families now spent more time away from the home and began to engage in a range of social, intellectual, and artistic activities. Indeed, women were among the chief consumers of the new Hellenistic fashions, commodities, and ideas available in Rome.

In earlier centuries, Romans had taken pride in the simplicity of their lives, their language, and their moral code. Now, however, elite Romans began to indulge in creature comforts and to cultivate Hellenistic habits as proof of their refinement. Bilingualism became increasingly common, and Greek literature became the standard against which Roman authors measured themselves. For Latin was not yet a literary language. It was fine for business or politics or farming, but if one wanted to express lofty or beautiful thoughts one did so in Greek, which was far more flexible and sophisticated.

Well-educated Greek slaves were therefore at a premium: to lend social cachet, to act as secretaries and personal assistants, and to tutor Roman children. The popularity of Greek plays, mostly comedies, was such that they quickly spawned Latin imitations, like those of Plautus (257?–184 B.C.E.) and Terence (195/185–159 B.C.E.). Terence's career path is suggestive of a larger pattern: a Greek-speaker of Libyan descent, he was sold as a slave-boy in Carthage and bought by a wealthy Roman called Terentius, who took him back to Rome and cultivated his talents, which he marketed under his own name. Six of Terence's Latin adaptations of Greek comedies survive, and they enjoyed enormous popularity well into the Middle Ages, eventually influencing the plays of Shakespeare.

In short, many Romans nursed an inferiority complex with respect to Greek culture. But others (including Cato) regarded these foreign influences with disgust. For them, the good old ways of paternal authority and stern military discipline were giving way to effeminacy and the decadence of soft living. Accordingly, conservative politicians deplored these new trends and passed laws that would restore "family values" and regulate the conspicuous consumption of luxuries, especially by women. These measures were ineffectual. Rome was being irreversibly transformed from a republic of self-reliant farmers into a complex metropolitan empire reliant on foreign slaves, foreign grain, and foreign luxuries, in which the gap between rich and poor was widening and where traditional behavioral constraints were giving way to new morals and ideas.

Philosophy and Spirituality in the Late Republic

The late republic was deeply influenced by Hellenistic philosophy, and both Epicureanism and Stoicism found strong adherents in Rome. The former was popularized by Lucretius (98–55 B.C.E.), author of a book-length philosophical poem, *On the Nature of Things*. But more congenial to Roman values was Stoicism, which soon numbered among its converts many powerful public figures. The most influential of these was Cicero (106–43 B.C.E.), famous in his day as an orator, statesman, and staunch defender of republican values. Cicero based his ethical teachings on the Stoic

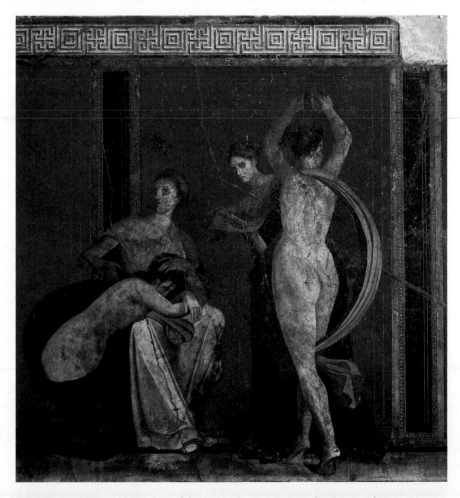

ROMAN MYSTERY RITES. One of the Roman houses preserved at Pompeii features an astonishing cycle of wall paintings, executed around 50 B.C.E., which give the house its name: Villa of the Mysteries. The exact meaning of these images is still debated, but some scholars have argued that they depict a succession of ritual practices. Here a young woman is being whipped, perhaps as part of an initiation ceremony, while another woman performs a dance.

premises that virtue is happiness and tranquillity of mind the highest good. The ideal man is therefore rational and indifferent to sorrow and pain. Yet Cicero diverged from the Stoics in his approval of the active, political life. He became an advocate for the revival of Roman tradition through service to the state. His elegant prose style also advanced the use of Latin as a language of eloquence and became the standard model for Latin composition: students learning Latin today still learn to read with Cicero.

The religious practices of Rome also changed markedly in this era. The most pronounced innovation was the spread of exotic mystery cults, which satisfied a need for more emotionally intense spiritual experiences than did traditional forms of Roman worship—again, especially for women, who were largely excluded from the rites of the patriarchal state religion. From Egypt came the cults of Isis and Osiris, while from Asia came the worship of the Great Mother, all emphasizing the power of female sexuality and reproduction. Despite the attractions of these new cults, Romans continued to honor their traditional gods alongside these new deities. Roman polytheism could absorb them all, so long as the ancestor gods of the household and of the city were paid due reverence.

"RESTORING THE REPUBLIC": THE STRUGGLE FOR POWER

In Rome itself, the period from the end of the Third Punic War in 146 to about 30 B.C.E. was one of turbulence. Politically motivated murders, bloody competition among rival dictators, wars, and insurrections were common occurrences. Slave uprisings also added to the general disorder. In 134 B.C.E., some 70,000 slaves defeated a Roman army in Sicily before being put down by emergency reinforcements. Slaves ravaged Sicily again in 104 B.C.E. But the most threatening revolt of all was led by Spartacus, a Thracian captive who was being trained as a gladiator. Along with a band of 200 fellow slaves from a gladiatorial training camp— they had all been bought by a wealthy entrepreneur—they escaped from Capua (near Naples; see the map on page 149), heavily armed, to the slopes of Mount Vesuvius, where their cause attracted a huge host of other fugitives.

From 73 to 71 B.C.E., this desperate army defeated trained Roman forces of as many as 10,000 men, and they overran much of southern Italy before Spartacus himself was killed. The Senate, terrified of the precedent set by the near victory of the rebels, ordered 6,000 of the captured slaves to be crucified along the length of the road from Capua to Rome (about 150 miles) as a warning to future insurgents. Crucifixion was a form of punishment reserved for slaves and non-Roman rebels, and it meant a slow, terrible, and public death from gradual suffocation and exposure.

The Reforming Efforts of the Gracchi

Meanwhile, these waves of rural rebellion were being mirrored by urban unrest in various forms, and the poorer classes were finding new champions among some progressive aristocrats. In 133 B.C.E., a grandson of Scipio Africanus, Tiberius Gracchus, was elected a tribune of the people. He took his office seriously and proposed to alleviate social and economic stress by instituting major reforms, chiefly the redistribution of property. As we have noted, small farmers had been losing their lands to patricians and equestrians whose new wealth allowed them to amass giant estates. To counter this, Tiberius Gracchus invoked old laws that had, under the early republic, limited the amount of land that could be held by a single person.

His motives were not entirely populist. There was a grave manpower shortage in the Roman army, which had been forced to expand its presence in the far reaches of the world and had left Rome itself prey to uprisings like that of Spartacus. Since a man had to meet certain property qualifications to serve in the Roman army, the available pool of citizen soldiers was contracting. So Tiberius Gracchus also aimed to refresh the reserves by creating new citizens.

With the support of his brother Gaius, Tiberius Gracchus proposed a law that would restrict estates to a maximum of 300 acres per citizen, plus 150 acres for each child in his family, with the excess land to be divided among poor settlers. Not surprisingly, most senators stood to lose from this legislation and so engineered its veto by Gracchus's fellow tribunes. But Gracchus retaliated, arguing that tribunes who opposed the people's interests were betraying their offices, and he announced plans to stand for reelection when his term expired. A conservative faction in the Senate then alleged that Gracchus had his sights set on a dictatorship, and with this excuse they attacked and murdered him and his supporters on the day of the elections.

Ten years later, Gaius Gracchus renewed his older brother's struggle after being elected to the same office. Although a version of Tiberius's land reforms had finally been enacted by the Senate, Gaius believed that the campaign had to go further. In 123 B.C.E., he enacted several laws for the benefit of the poor, stabilizing the price of grain in Rome by building public granaries along the Tiber and checking the administrative abuses of the senatorial class by giving the equestrians greater powers. He also imposed controls on provincial governors suspected of exploiting their subjects for personal gain. Most controversially, Gaius proposed to extend full Roman citizenship to all the allied states of Italy, a move that would have kept the army well supplied with new soldiers but which would also alter the political landscape of Rome to the detriment of the existing elite. Accordingly, the Senate proclaimed Gaius Gracchus an outlaw and authorized its consuls to deal ruthlessly with his supporters. In the ensuing conflict, Gaius and about 3,000 of his followers became the victims of a violent political purge.

Rivalry among Rome's Generals

Although the reforms of the Gracchi were ultimately unsuccessful, they exposed the weakness of the Senate and increased the power of the plebs, whose favor was now courted by a succession of ambitious men. Most of these were professional soldiers who controlled one or more legions of the Roman army and who traded on military victories abroad to win the confidence of the people and access to power.

The first of these was Gaius Marius, a man from an obscure provincial family who fought a successful campaign against Jugurtha of Numidia, whose small kingdom threatened Rome's hard-won supremacy in North Africa. In 107 B.C.E., Marius's popularity catapulted him to the consulship, despite the protests of the Senate's aristocracy, and he would be elected to that office six more times in the course of his life.

Marius was no statesman. But he set a powerful precedent by demonstrating how easily a general with an army behind him could override opposition—and that an army command could be an alternative path to political power. He also influenced the future of Rome by reorganizing and expanding the army. Desperate for more men to fight in Africa and in Gaul, which Rome was slowly infiltrating, Marius abolished the property qualification that had hitherto limited military service; the potential pool of soldiers now included the urban poor and landless peasants. As a result, a career as a Roman legionnaire became an end in itself, and a soldier's loyalty was directed toward his commander (whose success would win rewards for his men) rather than to an abstract ideal of patriotism or service to the state. Moreover, this change meant that factional fighting could lead to full-blown civil war, as legions loyal to one general were pitted against those of another.

This happened in Marius's own lifetime. The aristocratic general Lucius Cornelius Sulla had fought with distinction in the so-called Social War of 91–88 B.C.E., a conflict between Rome and her Italian allies that resulted in the extension of Roman citizenship throughout the peninsula. Thereafter, Sulla seemed the likely person to lead Rome's army to war in Asia Minor. Marius, however, did not agree; he forced the Senate to deny Sulla's claim. Sulla's response was to rally the five victorious legions that had just fought under his command and, with a Roman army at his back, to march on Rome.

This was a disturbing move, since strong taboos had long prevented any armed force from entering the city limits. But Sulla argued that his actions were in keeping with the *mos maiorum*, which Marius and the Senate had betrayed. He was then given the coveted army command in Asia Minor, after which Marius again seized control of the city. When Marius died soon afterward, a conservative backlash led the aristocracy to appoint Sulla to the office of dictator—but not for the traditional six months. Instead, Sulla's term had no limits, and he used this time to exterminate his opponents. He extended the powers of the Senate (whose ranks, depleted by civil war, he packed with men loyal to himself) and curtailed the authority of the peoples' tribunes. Then, after three years of rule, he decided that his job was done and retired to a life of luxury on his country estate.

Caesar's Triumph—and His Downfall

The purpose and effect of Sulla's dictatorship was to empower the aristocracy and terminally weaken the power of the plebs. Soon, however, new leaders emerged to espouse the people's cause, once again using the army as their tool of influence. The most prominent of these were Gnaeus Pompeius Magnus (106–48 B.C.E.) and Gaius Julius Caesar (100–44 B.C.E.). Initially, they cooperated in a plot to gain control of the government and to "restore the republic" by forming an alliance with a third general, Marcus Junius Crassus, the man credited with finally defeating Spartacus. This alliance was known as a *triumvirate* (tri-UM-vir-et), meaning "rule of three men," but it soon dissolved into open rivalry. Pompey (as generations of English-speaking historians have called him) had won fame as the conqueror of Syria and Palestine, while Caesar devoted his energies to a series of campaigns in Gaul. It was under his authority that the territories encompassing modern France, Belgium, and western Germany were added to the Roman Empire, extending its northern border along the length of the Rhine.

Caesar himself advertised these conquests in a series of self-congratulatory dispatches published in book form—*On the War in Gaul*—which secured his reputation at home and cemented the loyalty of his army. These victories also put him in a strong political position. It had become accepted that the best general should be the leader of Rome, and the example of Sulla had made it possible for that leader to be a dictator for life, a king in all but name. But it was Pompey, not Caesar, who was actually in Rome and in a position to influence the Senate directly. Indeed, in the face of tremendous popular protest and even some opposition from the aristocracy, Pompey had managed to get himself elected sole consul. Essentially, this meant that he could act as dictator. Using this authority, he declared that Caesar, who was still stationed in Gaul, was an enemy of the republic and that his ambition was to make himself king.

The result was a pervasive and deadly civil war. In 49 B.C.E. Caesar took up Pompey's challenge and crossed the Rubicon River, the northern boundary of Rome's Italian territories, thereby signaling his intention to take Rome by force. Pompey fled to the east in the hope of gathering an army large enough to confront Ceasar's legions. Caesar pursued him, and in 48 B.C.E. the two Roman armies

BUST OF JULIUS CAESAR. Caesar's nickname meant "Hairy," but it has come to be synonymous with imperial rule. It was the title preferred by modern German rulers, who called themselves *kaisers*, and by the tsars of Russia. In classical Latin, the "C" sound is hard, which means that the pronunciations of *caesar*, *kaiser*, and *tsar* are very similar.

met at Pharsalus in Greece. Pompey was defeated and fled to Alexandria, where he was murdered by a Roman officer attached to the court of Ptolemy XIII (62/61–47? B.C.E.).

This young pharaoh, a descendant of Alexander's general Ptolemy, was then about fourteen years old and engaged in a civil war of his own—against his elder sister and co-ruler, Cleopatra VII (69–30 B.C.E.). He must have thought that he could curry favor with Caesar by encouraging the murder of Pompey; but instead Caesar threw his support on the side of the twenty-one-year-old queen. The two must have become lovers soon after their first meeting, since their son Caesarion ("Little Caesar") was born just nine months later. After a brief struggle, Ptolemy was defeated and mysteriously drowned in the Nile. Cleopatra then took as consort her even younger brother, known as Ptolemy XIV, but she ruled as pharaoh of Egypt in her own right, much as Hatshepsut had done nearly a millennium and a half before (see Chapter 2).

After that, Caesar returned to Rome in triumph—literally. A *triumph* was a spectacular honor awarded to a victorious Roman general by the Senate and was the only legal occasion on which (unarmed) soldiers were allowed to parade in the streets of Rome. Triumphs had been celebrated since the earliest days of the republic, and they featured columns of prisoners and spoils of war, chained captives (often enemy kings) led in humiliation to their public executions, floats featuring live tableaux commemorating the achievements of the triumphant man, and thousands upon thousands of cheering Romans, who received extra rations of grain and gathered up coins thrown by the handful. Through it all, Caesar would have ridden in a chariot with a golden wreath held above his head while a slave stood behind him, murmuring in his ear the words *Memento mori*, "Remember: you will die." A triumph was so glorious and—under the republic—so rarely granted that those thus honored might forget their own mortality.

Caesar may well have done so. His power seemed absolute. In 46 B.C.E. he was named dictator for ten years; two years later, this was changed to a lifetime appointment. In addition, he assumed nearly every other title that could augment his power. He obtained from the Senate full authority to make war and peace and to control the revenues of the state. He even governed the reckoning of time, something that was regarded as controversial. In imitation of the Egyptian calendar (slightly modified by a Greek astronomer) he revised the Roman calendar so as to make a 365-day year with an extra day added every fourth year. This Julian calendar (as adjusted by Pope Gregory XIII in 1582) is still observed, and the seventh month is still named after Julius.

Caesar also took important steps toward eliminating the distinction between Italians and provincials within the empire by conferring citizenship on residents of Hispania

CLEOPATRA VII AS EGYPTIAN PHARAOH AND HELLENISTIC RULER. Like her ancestor, Ptolemy I, Cleopatra represented herself as both enlightened Greek monarch and as pharaoh. It was perhaps owing to her example that Julius Caesar was the first Roman leader to issue coins impressed with his own image. ■ *How does Cleopatra's self-representation compare to that of Hatshepsut (see page 44) or Ptolemy (see page 129)?*

(Spain) and the newly annexed provinces in Gaul. By settling many of his army veterans and some of the urban poor in these lands, moreover, he relieved economic inequities and furthered colonization. Even more important was Caesar's farsighted resolve to focus his efforts in northwestern Europe. Whereas Pompey, and before him Alexander, went East to gain fame and fortune, Caesar followed only the Phoenicians in recognizing the potential of the wild West. By incorporating Gaul into the Roman world he brought in a much-needed source of food and natural resources and created a new outlet for the spread of Roman settlement and culture.

In the eyes of many contemporaries, however, Caesar's achievements were signs that he actually did intend to make himself king: a hateful thought to those who still cherished the *mos maiorum* and glorified the early days of the republic. Indeed, it was around a descendant of Lucretia's avenger, Lucius Junius Brutus, that a faction of the Senate crystallized into an assassination conspiracy. On the Ides of March in 44 B.C.E.—the midpoint of the month, according to his own calendar—Caesar was attacked on the floor of the Senate's chamber and stabbed to death by a group of men. His body would later be autopsied, the first such examination in recorded history. It was found that he had sustained twenty-three wounds.

IDES OF MARCH COIN. This coin celebrates the assassination of Julius Caesar by Marcus Junius Brutus. Brutus is shown on the face; on the reverse, a cap of liberty (customarily worn by freed slaves) is flanked by two daggers. Below is the legend *EID-MAR*, the Latin abbreviation for "the Ides of March." ■ *Given that Caesar drew criticism for depicting himself on Roman coinage, what do you think is the significance of using Brutus's image in this way?*

THE PRINCIPATE AND THE *PAX ROMANA*, 27 B.C.E.–180 C.E.

In his will, Caesar had adopted his grandnephew Gaius Octavius (or Octavian, 63 B.C.E.–14 C.E.), then a young man of eighteen serving in Illyria, across the Adriatic Sea. On learning of Caesar's death, Octavian hastened home to claim his inheritance and to avenge his slain "father," whose name he took: he now called himself Gaius Julius Caesar the younger. He soon found that he had rivals among those supporters of Caesar who had not been implicated in the plot to kill him, most notably Marcus Antonius (or Mark Antony, 83–30 B.C.E.), who had served under Caesar's command in Gaul and who was ambitious to make himself governor of that whole province.

Octavian engineered his own election to the office of consul (though he was far too young for this honor) and used his powers to have Caesar's assassins declared outlaws. He then pursued Antony to Gaul, at the head of an army. Antony's forces were overwhelmed, and in 43 B.C.E. he and Octavian reconciled and formed an alliance, bringing in a third man, a senator called Marcus Aemilius Lepidus, to make up a second triumvirate. They then set about crushing the political faction responsible for Caesar's murder.

The methods they employed were brutal: prominent members of the opposition were hunted down and their property confiscated. The most notable of these victims was Cicero, who was murdered by Mark Antony's hired thugs. (This was a revenge killing: Cicero had actively sought to undermine Antony and had branded him a public enemy.) Meanwhile, the masterminds behind Caesar's assassination, Brutus and Gaius Cassius, left Rome and raised an army of legions from Greece and Asia Minor. But they were defeated by the united forces of Antony and Octavian on a battlefield near the Macedonian town of Philippi (founded by Alexander's father, Philip II) in 42 B.C.E. There, both Brutus and Cassius committed suicide.

With their mutual enemies effectively destroyed, tensions mounted between Antony and Octavian, whose friendship had never been firm. Antony went to Egypt and made an alliance with Cleopatra, plotting to use the resources of her realm against Octavian. Octavian, meanwhile, reestablished himself in Rome, where he skillfully portrayed Antony as having been seduced and emasculated by his foreign lover, reminding people that the Egyptian queen's son, Caesarion, threatened Octavian's position as Caesar's rightful heir.

For ten years, Antony played the king in Egypt, fathering three of Cleopatra's children and making big plans for annexing Rome's eastern provinces. Eventually, Octavian had him declared a traitor while the Senate declared war on Cleopatra—not on Antony, lest Octavian be accused of starting another civil war. In 31 B.C.E., Octavian's superior forces defeated those of Antony and Cleopatra in the naval battle of Actium, off the coast of Greece. Soon afterward, both Antony and Cleopatra committed suicide. Their children were taken back to Rome—Caesarion promptly disappeared—and although their lives were spared, they were paraded through the streets as captives. This marked the end of Egypt's long independence: Cleopatra had been its last pharaoh. After more than 3,000 years of self-rule, Egypt was now another province in Rome's empire.

The Government of Augustus

The victory at Actium ushered in a new period of Roman history. The new Gaius Julius Caesar was the only claimant to power left standing, and with no rivals left he had no further need for political purges. For the first time in nearly a century, Rome was not embroiled in civil war.

But it was no longer a republic, even though Octavian maintained the fiction that he was governing as a mere citizen. For four years, he ruled as sole consul, until he accepted the titles of *imperator* (emperor) and *augustus*. Although these honorifics had been in use under the republic—*imperator* meant "victorious general" and *augustus* meant "worthy of honor"—they now became attached to the person of the sole ruler. So although Rome had been an empire for centuries, it was only now that it had a single emperor. To avoid confusion, historians therefore refer to this phase of Rome's history as the Principate, from the title Augustus himself preferred: *princeps*, "prince" or "first man."

Because Augustus was determined not to be regarded as a tyrant or (worse) a king, he left most of Rome's republican institutions in place—but gradually emptied them of their power. In theory, the emperor served at the will of "the Senate and People of Rome," *SPQR*. In practice, though, he controlled the army, which meant that he also controlled the workings of government. Fortunately, Augustus was an able ruler. He introduced a range of public services, including a police force and fire brigade; he reorganized the army; and he allowed cities and provinces more substantial rights of self-government than they had enjoyed before. He instituted a new system of coinage throughout the empire, and he abolished the old, corrupt system of taxation, whereby tax collectors were compensated by being allowed to keep a portion of the monies they collected, which inevitably encouraged them to collect more than were legally due. Instead, Augustus appointed his own representatives as tax collectors, paid them regular salaries, and kept them under

Antony and Cleopatra

In his Parallel Lives, *the Greek intellectual Plutarch (c. 46–120 c.e.) paired the biographies of famous Greeks with those of famous Romans, always to the disadvantage of the latter; for example, Julius Caesar suffers in comparison to Alexander the Great, as Romulus does when set up against Theseus. The following excerpt is from Plutarch's* Life of Mark Antony, *in which the Hellenistic ruler of Egypt, Cleopatra, plays a starring role.*

Caesar and Pompey knew Cleopatra when she was still a girl, and ignorant of the world, but it was a different matter in the case of Antony, because she was ready to meet him when she had reached the time of life when women are most beautiful and have full understanding. So she prepared for him many gifts and money and adornment, of a magnitude appropriate to her great wealth and prosperous kingdom, but she put most of her hopes in her own magical arts and charms. . . . For (as they say), it was not because her beauty in itself was so striking that it stunned the onlooker, but the inescapable impression produced by daily contact with her: the attractiveness in the persuasiveness of her talk, and the character that surrounded her conversation was stimulating. It was a pleasure to hear the sound of her voice, and she tuned her tongue like a many-stringed instrument expertly to whatever language she chose, and only used interpreters to talk to a few foreigners. . . . She is said to have learned the languages of many peoples, although her predecessors on the throne did not bother to learn Egyptian, and some had even forgotten how to speak the Macedonian dialect.

She took such a hold over Antony that, while his wife Fulvia was carrying on the war in Rome against Octavian on his behalf, and the Parthian army . . . was about to invade Syria, Antony was carried off by Cleopatra to Alexandria, and amused himself there with the pastimes of a boy . . . and whether Antony was in a serious or a playful mood she could always produce some new pleasure or charm, and she kept watch on him by night and day and never let him out of her sight. She played dice with him and hunted with him and watched him exercising with his weapons and she roamed around and wandered about with him at night when he stood at people's doors and windows and made fun of people inside, dressed in a slave-woman's outfit; for he also attempted to dress up like a slave. He returned from these expeditions having been mocked in return, and often beaten, although most people suspected who he was. But the Alexandrians got pleasure from his irreverence . . . enjoying his humor and saying that he showed his tragic face to the Romans and his comic one to them.

Source: Plutarch, *Life of Marcus Antonius,* cc. 25–29, excerpted in *Women's Life in Greece and Rome: A Sourcebook in Translation,* eds. Mary R. Lefkowitz and Maureen B. Fant (Baltimore, MD: 1992), pp. 147–49.

Questions for Analysis

1. How do Cleopatra's behavior and accomplishments, in Plutarch's description of her, compare to those of Roman women?

2. Given what you have learned about the values of the Roman Republic, how would a Roman reader respond to this description of Antony's behavior under the influence of the Egyptian queen? What do you think were Plutarch's motives in portraying him in this light?

strict supervision. He simultaneously conducted a census of the empire's population for this purpose, and it was during one of these "enrollments" that the birth of Jesus is said to have taken place, according to the gospel of Luke (see Chapter 6). Augustus also established new colonies in the provinces, encouraging the emigration of Rome's urban and rural poor, thereby removing a major source of social tension and promoting the integration of the Roman heartland and its far-flung hinterland.

Although his rule had definitively ended the republic, Augustus represented himself as a stern defender of the *mos maiorum* and traditional Roman virtues. He rebuilt many of the city's ancient temples and prohibited the worship of foreign gods. In an attempt to increase the birthrate of

Rome's citizens, he penalized men who failed to marry, required widows to remarry within two years of their husbands' deaths, and rewarded women who gave birth to more than two children. He also introduced laws punishing adultery and making divorces more difficult to obtain. To hammer the message home, Augustan propaganda portrayed the imperial family as a model of domestic virtue and propriety. Yet these portrayals were only moderately successful because the emperor's own extramarital affairs were notorious, while the sexual promiscuity of his daughter Julia finally forced Augustus to have her exiled.

Meanwhile, more land was gained for Rome in the lifetime of Augustus than ever before. His generals advanced into central Europe, conquering the territories that are now Switzerland, Austria, and Bulgaria. Only in Germania did Roman troops meet defeat, when three legions were slaughtered in the Teutoburg Forest in 9 C.E., a devastating setback that convinced Augustus to hold the Roman borders at the Rhine and Danube Rivers.

Subsequently, though, the emperor Claudius would begin the conquest of Britain in 43 C.E., while the emperor Trajan (91–117 C.E.) would push beyond the Danube to add Dacia (now Romania) to the empire. Trajan also conquered territories in the heartland of Mesopotamia, but in so doing aroused the enmity of the Parthians, who now ruled in Persia. His successor, Hadrian (117–138 C.E.), accordingly halted Rome's expansion and embarked on a defensive policy epitomized by the construction of Hadrian's Wall in northern Britain. The empire had now reached its greatest extent (see the map on page 173); in the third century, as we shall see (see Chapter 6), the tide would turn and these limits would recede.

When Octavian died in 14 C.E., he was not only Caesar, Imperator, and Augustus; he was *pontifex maximus* (high priest) and "father of the country" (*pater patriae*). He was even deified by the Senate, which had also deified Julius Caesar at Augustus's urging. These titles would be passed on to his successors, as would the system of government he had devised. And even those who mourned the passing of the republic and loathed these displays of imperial hubris had to admit that the system worked. Rome enjoyed nearly two centuries of peace, prosperity, and stability because of it.

The true test of any political institution is its capacity to survive incompetent officeholders. Aside from one brief period of civil war in 68 C.E., the transition of power between emperors was generally peaceful and the growing imperial bureaucracy could manage affairs competently even when individual emperors proved vicious or ineffectual, as did Caligula (37–41 C.E.). Nevertheless, the fact that Rome had become an autocratic state became harder and harder to conceal. Many of Augustus's successors were heavy-handed and had difficult relationships with the Sen-

OCTAVIAN. Caesar's adopted heir was later granted the title "Augustus" by the Senate, and was also known as *princeps*, "first man." He would come to be worshiped as a god in Rome's provinces, and idealized statues like this one would be erected in temples and public places throughout the empire.

ate; and because the historians of this era were invariably members of the senatorial elite, they had a vested interest in sullying the reputations of these emperors. Hence the skilled administrators Tiberius (14–37 C.E.) and Claudius (41–54 C.E.) were accused by their biographers of sexual perversion on the one hand and idiocy on the other. Nero (54–68 C.E.) and Domitian (81–96 C.E.) were also reviled by the aristocracy but popular among the Roman people

HADRIAN'S WALL. Stretching 73.5 miles across northern England, this fortification (begun in 122 C.E.) marked the frontier of the Roman province of Britannia as established by the emperor Hadrian. (A later wall, built further north by Antoninus Pius in 142, was quickly abandoned.) Long stretches of the wall still exist, as do many of the forts built along it. The tree in this photograph stands on the site of a "mile castle," one of the smaller watchtowers built at intervals of a Roman mile and garrisoned by sentries.

Occasionally, the Roman Peace was broken. In Britannia, Roman legions had to put down a rebellion led by the Celtic warrior queen Boudica (d. 60/61 C.E.), which ended in a massacre of indigenous tribes; thousands of Britons lost their lives. Another rebellion was violently quashed in Judea, the most restive of all Roman provinces, leading to the destruction of the Temple at Jerusalem in 70 C.E. In 135 C.E., a second rebellion completed the destruction of the city. Although it was refounded by Hadrian as Aelia Capitolina, a colony for veterans of Rome's army, Jews were forbidden to settle there (see Chapter 6).

Such rebellions were not the norm, however. Although the Roman Empire had been gradually achieved by conquest, it was not maintained by force. Instead, Rome controlled its territories by offering incentives to assimilation. Local elites were encouraged to adopt Roman modes of behavior and dress in order to gain entrance to political office. Local gods became Roman gods and were adopted into the Roman pantheon of divinities. Cities were constructed on a Roman model of urban planning, and the amenities of urban life were introduced: baths, temples, amphitheaters, aqueducts, and paved roads (see *Interpreting Visual Evidence* on pages 174–75). Rights of citizenship were extended, and able provincials could rise far in the imperial government. Some, like the emperors Trajan and Hadrian—both raised in Hispania—came to control it.

Meanwhile, tens of thousands of army veterans were settled in the provinces, marrying local women and putting down local roots. It was common for soldiers born in Syria or North Africa to end their days peacefully in northern Gaul or Germania. In Camulodunum (now Colchester, England), the gravestone of a legionnaire called Longinus sketches a typical career: born in Serdica (modern Sofia, in Bulgaria) to a local man named Szdapezematygus, he rose through the ranks to become sergeant of the First Thracian Cavalry under Claudius and one of the first Roman colonists of Britannia.

Even the outer fringes of the empire need to be understood as part of Rome's orbit. Although historians speak of the empire's "borders" for the sake of convenience, these were in fact frontiers: highly fluid and permeable zones of intensive interaction. Roman influence reached far beyond these zones,

and in the provinces; indeed, Domitian's needed reforms of provincial government and his blatant disregard for senatorial privilege account for both the Senate's hostility and his subjects' approval.

The height of the Augustan system is generally considered to be the era between 96 and 180 C.E., often known as the reign of the "Five Good Emperors": Nerva (96–98 C.E.), Trajan (98–117 C.E.), Hadrian (117–138 C.E.), Antoninus Pius (138–161 C.E.), and Marcus Aurelius (161–180 C.E.). All were capable politicians, and since none but the last had a son that survived him, each adopted a worthy successor—a wise practice that allowed this generation of rulers to avoid the messy family dysfunctions that absorbed Augustus and his immediate heirs. They also benefited from the fact that Rome had few external enemies left. The Mediterranean was under the control of a single power for the first (and only) time in history. On land, Roman officials ruled from Britain to Persia. A contemporary orator justly boasted that "the whole civilized world lays down the arms which were its ancient burden, as if on holiday. . . . [A]ll places are full of gymnasia, fountains, monumental approaches, temples, workshops, schools." The continual bloodshed of civil wars and of Augustus's reign of terror had abated. Now was the time of the *Pax Romana*, the Roman Peace.

Competing Viewpoints

Two Views of Augustus's Rule

Augustus Speaks for Himself

The emperor Augustus was a master propagandist with an unrivaled capacity for presenting his own actions in the best possible light. This list of his own deeds was written by Augustus himself and was displayed on two bronze pillars set up in the Roman forum.

Below is a copy of the accomplishments of the deified Augustus by which he brought the whole world under the empire of the Roman people, and of the moneys expended by him on the state and the Roman people. . . .

1. At the age of nineteen, on my own initiative and at my own expense, I raised an army by means of which I liberated the Republic, which was oppressed by the tyranny of a faction.

2. Those who assassinated my father I drove into exile, avenging their crime by due process of law.

3. I waged many wars throughout the whole world by land and by sea, both civil and foreign. . . .

5. The dictatorship offered to me . . . by the people and by the Senate . . . I refused to accept. . . . The consulship, too, which was offered to me . . . as an annual office for life, I refused to accept.

6. [T]hough the Roman Senate and people together agreed that I should be elected sole guardian of the laws and morals with supreme authority, I refused to accept any office offered me which was contrary to the traditions of our ancestors.

7. I have been ranking senator for forty years. . . . I have been *pontifex maximus*, augur, member of the college of fifteen for performing sacrifices, member of the college of seven for conducting religious banquets, member of the Arval Brotherhood, one of the *Titii sodales*, and a *fetial* [all priestly offices].

9. The Senate decreed that vows for my health should be offered up every fifth year by the consuls and priests. . . . [T]he whole citizen body, with one accord, . . . prayed continuously for my health at all the shrines.

17. Four times I came to the assistance of the treasury with my own money . . . providing bonuses for soldiers who had completed twenty or more years of service.

20. I repaired the Capitol and the theater of Pompey with enormous expenditures on both works, without having my name inscribed on them. I repaired . . . the aqueducts which were falling into ruin in many places . . . I repaired eighty-two temples . . . I reconstructed the Flaminian Way. . . .

34. [H]aving attained supreme power by universal consent, I transferred the state from my own power to the control of the Roman Senate and people. . . . After that time I excelled all in authority, but I possessed no more power than the others who were my colleagues in each magistracy.

35. At the time I wrote this document I was in my seventy-sixth year.

Source: "Res Gestae Divi Augusti," in *Roman Civilization, Sourcebook II: The Empire,* eds. Naphtali Lewis and Meyer Reinhold (New York: 1966), pp. 9–19.

into the heartland of Germania and lands far to the East. By the middle of the third century C.E., when some frontier garrisons were withdrawn to take part in civil wars within the empire itself, many of these peoples moved into the empire's settled provinces, sometimes as plunderers but more often as aspiring Romans (see Chapter 6).

The Entertainments of Empire

The cultural and intellectual developments that began in Rome during the late republic came to fruition during the Principate, and are richly reflected in its literature. For the first time in its already long history, Latin began to replace

The Historian Tacitus Evaluates Augustus's Reign

Writing in the first decades of the second century C.E., the senatorial historian Tacitus (c. 56–117) began his chronicle of imperial rule, the Annals, *with the death of Augustus a century earlier.*

Intelligent people praised or criticized Augustus in varying terms. One opinion was as follows. Filial duty and a national emergency, in which there was no place for law-abiding conduct, had driven him to civil war—and this can be neither initiated nor maintained by decent methods. He had made many concessions to Antony and to Lepidus for the sake of vengeance on his father's murderers. When Lepidus grew old and lazy, and Antony's self-indulgence got the better of him, the only possible cure for the distracted country had been government by one man. However, Augustus had put the State in order not by making himself king or dictator but by creating the Principate. The empire's frontiers were on the ocean, or on distant rivers. Armies, provinces, fleets, the whole system was interrelated. Roman citizens were protected by the law. Provincials were decently treated. Rome itself had been lavishly beautified. Force had been sparingly used—merely to preserve peace for the majority.

The opposite view went like this. Filial duty and national crisis had been merely pretexts. In actual fact, the motive of Octavian, the future Augustus, was lust for power. Inspired by that, he had mobilized ex-army settlers by gifts of money, raised an army—while he was only a half-grown boy without any official status—won over a consul's brigade by bribery, pretended to support Sextus Pompeius [the son of Pompey], and by senatorial decree usurped the status and rank of a praetor. Soon both consuls . . . had met their deaths—by enemy action; or perhaps in the one case by the deliberate poisoning of his wound, and in the other at the hand of his own troops, instigated by Octavian. In any case, it was he who took over both their armies. Then he had forced the reluctant Senate to make him consul. But the forces given him to deal with Antony he used against the State. His judicial murders and land distributions were distasteful even to those who carried them out. True, Cassius and Brutus died because he had inherited a feud against them; nevertheless, personal enmities ought to be sacrificed to the public interest. Next he had cheated Sextus Pompeius by a spurious peace treaty, Lepidus by spurious friendship. Then Antony, enticed by treaties and his marriage with Octavian's sister, had paid the penalty of that delusive relationship with his life. After that, there had certainly been peace, but it was a bloodstained peace. . . . And gossip did not spare his personal affairs—how he had abducted [Livia] the wife of Tiberius Claudius Nero, and asked the priests the farcical question whether it was in order for her to marry while pregnant. Then there was the debauchery of his friend Publius Vedius Pollio. But Livia was a real catastrophe, to the nation, as a mother and to the house of the Caesars as a stepmother.

Source: Tacitus, *Annals* i.9–10. Based on *Tacitus: The Annals of Imperial Rome*, trans. Michael Grant (New York: 1989), pp. 37–39.

Questions for Analysis

1. How does Augustus organize his list, and why? What does he leave out and what does he choose to emphasize?

2. Tacitus presents two contrasting views of Augustus's motives. Which does he himself seem to believe? How does his account complement or undermine that of Augustus himself?

3. Could you write a new account of Augustus's life making use of both sources? How would you strike a balance between them? What would your own conclusion be?

Greek as a language of learning and poetry. Roman literature of this era is conventionally divided into two periods, the Golden Age of writings produced under the more or less direct influence of Augustus, and the Silver Age of the first and early second centuries C.E. Most Golden Age literature is, not surprisingly, propagandistic: its purpose was to advertise and justify Augustus's achievements. The poetry of Publius Virgilius Maro (Virgil, 70–19 B.C.E.) is typical, and we have already noted his strategic use of "prophecy" to link the reign of Augustus to the story of Aeneas (see page 146). Other major poets of this age were Quintus Horatius Flaccus (Horace, 65–8 B.C.E.) and Publius Ovidius Naso

SPOILS FROM JERUSALEM. A bas-relief inside the triumphal Arch of Titus in the Roman Forum shows plundered treasures of the Temple at Jerusalem, including the menorah, being carried in triumph through Rome after the quashing of a Jewish rebellion in 70 C.E.
- *What message(s) would this image convey to viewers?*

(Ovid, 43 B.C.E.–17 C.E.): the former a master of the lovely, short lyric and the latter our major source for Greek mythology, which he retold in a long poem called the *Metamorphoses* ("Transformations"). Ovid was also a satirist, and his frank advice to his readers on the best way to attract women at the race course and his own (probably fictional) strategy for conducting an adulterous affair with the wife of a senator are exemplary of the writings that resulted in his banishment.

After Augustus's death, Roman authors had more license and became incisive cultural critics. The tales of Petronius and Apuleius describe the more bizarre and sometimes sordid aspects of Roman life, and the satirist Juvenal (60?–140 C.E.) wrote with savage wit about the moral degeneracy he saw in his contemporaries. A similar attitude toward Roman society characterizes the writings of Tacitus (55?–117? C.E.), an aristocratic historian who describes the events and people of his age largely for the purpose of passing judgment on them. His *Annals* offer a subtle but devastating portrait of the political system constructed by Augustus and ruled by his heirs; his *Germania* contrasts the manly virtues of northern barbarians with the effeminate vices of decadent fellow Romans. Like Juvenal, Tacitus was a master of ironic wit. Referring to Rome's conquests, he has a barbarian chieftain say, "They create a wilderness and call it peace."

To many people today, the most repellant—or most fascinating and familiar—aspect of Roman culture during the Principate was its spectacular cruelty, exhibited (literally) in the public arenas erected in every Roman town. Gladiatorial contests were not new, but they were now presented in ampitheaters built to hold thousands. Everyone, even emperors, attended these events, and they became increasingly bloody and brutal as people demanded more and more innovative violence. Individual gladiators fought to the death with swords or the exotic weapons of their homelands. Teams of gladiators fought pitched battles, often simulating historic Roman victories. Occasionally, a wealthy entrepreneur would fill an arena with water and stage a naval battle. Hundreds of men and women would die in these organized slaughters. On other occasions, hundreds of half-starved animals imported from Africa, India, or the forests of Germania would tear one another (or their human victims) apart. When a fighter went down with a disabling wound, the crowd would be asked to decide whether to spare his life or to kill him. If the arena floor became too slippery with blood, the action would stop—but only so that a fresh layer of sand could be spread over the gore for the performance to continue.

Roman Art, Architecture, and Engineering

Like Latin literature, Roman art assumed a distinctive character during the Principate. Before this time, most artworks

Analyzing Primary Sources

Rome's Party Girls

The Satires *of the poet Juvenal circulated around the year 100 C.E. and attacked everything from the general erosion of public morality to the effete tastes of the elite. Some of his most pointed criticism was directed at contemporary women.*

 hat conscience has Venus, when she is drunk? Our inebriated beauties can't tell head from tail at those midnight oyster suppers when the best wine's laced with perfume, and tossed down neat from a foaming conch-shell, while the dizzy ceiling spins round, and the tables dance, and each light shows double. Why, you may ask yourself, does the notorious Maura sniff at the air in that knowing, derisive way as she and her dear friend Tullia pass by the ancient altar of Chastity? And what is Tullia whispering to her? Here, at night, they stagger out of their litters and relieve themselves, pissing in long hard bursts all over the goddess's statue. Then, while the Moon looks down on their motions, they take turns to ride each other, and finally go home. So you, next morning, on your way to some great house, will splash through your wife's piddle. Notorious, too, are the ritual mysteries of the Good Goddess, when flute-music stirs the loins, and frenzied women, devotees of Priapus, sweep along in procession, howling, tossing their hair, wine-flown, horn-crazy, burning with the desire to get themselves laid. . . . So the ladies, with a display of talent to match their birth, win all the prizes. No make-believe here, no pretense, each act is performed in earnest, and guaranteed to warm the age-chilled balls of a Nestor or a Priam.

Source: Juvenal, *Sixth Satire* 301–26; based on *Juvenal: The Sixteen Satires*, trans. Peter Green (New York: 1974), pp. 138–39 (modified).

Questions for Analysis

1. Compare Juvenal's account of female behavior to the legend of Lucretia, on the one hand, and Plutarch's description of Cleopatra, on the other. What can you conclude about attitudes to women and to sexual morality? Why and on what grounds would men living under the Principate hold women responsible for society's ills?

2. In your view, what are the benefits and the drawbacks of the *Satires* as a historical source?

---

displayed in Roman homes and public places were imported from Hellenistic capitals. Conquering armies also brought back wagonloads of statues, reliefs, and marble columns as plunder from Greece and Asia Minor. These became the property of the wealthy, and as demand for such works increased, hundreds of copies were made by Roman artisans. In many cases, these copies proved more durable than their originals: in Chapter 4, we were able to examine the lost Aphrodite of Knidos, courtesy of Roman sculptors.

Encouraged by the patronage of Augustus and his successors, artists began to experiment with more distinctively Roman styles and subjects. The relief sculpture of this period is particularly notable for its delicacy and naturalism, and sculptors also became adept at portraiture. On their coins, emperors were portrayed very much as they looked in real life; and since the matrices for coins were recut annually, we can trace on successive issues a ruler's receding hairline or his advancing double chin.

Painting and mosaic, however, were the Romans' most original and most intimate arts. Romans loved intense colors, and those who could afford it surrounded themselves with brilliant wall paintings and mosaics made of tiny fragments of glass and stone, which were often set into the floors of houses and public baths or which formed the centerpieces of gardens. Lavish mosaics have been found in the remains of Roman villas in all the territories of the empire, and similar design features indicate that many were mosaic "kits" that could be ordered from a manufacturer, who would ship out all the necessary components along with a team of workmen to assemble them.

Augustus liked to boast that he had found Rome a city of clay and left it a city of marble. It is certainly true that ambitious public works projects were initiated under the Principate, but in reality marble was too precious to be used in common construction. Instead, marble panels or ornaments were added to the facings of buildings that were otherwise built of concrete. For the Romans had discovered how to make a hard and reliable building material from a mixture of quicklime, volcanic ash, and pumice, and it was this—along with superior engineering skills—that allowed them

THE COLOSSEUM. Constructed between 75 and 80 C.E., this was the first ampitheater in Rome purposely built to showcase gladiatorial combats. Prior to this, gladiators would often fight in improvised arenas in the Forum or in other public places. ▪ *How does this fact change your perception of Roman history?*

banquet hall revolved day and night like the heavens. "At last," said Nero on moving day, "I can live like a human being."

The Reach of Roman Law

As impressive and ingenious as Roman architecture and engineering are, the most durable and useful of this civilization's legacies was its system of law. Over the course of several centuries, the primitive legal code of the Twelve Tables was largely replaced by a series of new precedents and principles. These reflect the changing political climate of Rome and the needs of its diverse and ever-growing population. They also reveal the influence of new philosophies, especially Stoicism; the decisions of specific judges; and the edicts of magistrates called *praetors*, who had the authority to define and interpret law in particular cases, and to issue instructions to judges.

to build massive structures like the Colosseum, which could accommodate 50,000 spectators at gladiatorial combats.

Roman engineers also excelled in the building of roads and bridges, many of which were constructed by Rome's armies as they moved into new territories. Like the Persian Royal Road of the sixth century B.C.E.—or the German Autobahn of the 1930s and the interstate highways of the United States begun in the 1950s—roads have always been, first and foremost, a device for moving armies and then, secondarily, for moving goods and people. Many of these Roman roads still survive or form the basis for modern European highways. In Britain, for example, the only major thoroughfares before the building of the high-speed motorways were Roman roads, to which the motorways now run parallel.

The inhabitants of Roman cities also enjoyed the benefits of a public water supply. By the early decades of the second century C.E., eleven aqueducts brought water into Rome from the nearby hills and provided the city with 300 million gallons per day, for drinking and bathing and for flushing a well-designed sewage system. These amenities were common in cities throughout the empire, and the homes of the wealthy even had indoor plumbing and central heating. Water was also funneled into the homes of the rich for private gardens, fountains, and pools. The emperor Nero built a famous Golden House with special pipes that sprinkled his guests with perfume, baths supplied with medicinal waters, and a pond "like a sea." In addition, a spherical ceiling in the

The most sweeping legal changes occurred during the Principate. This was partly because the reach of Roman law had to match the reach of the empire, which now extended over a much wider field of jurisdiction. But the major reason for the rapid development of Roman legal thinking during these years was the fact that Augustus and his successors

FEMALE GLADIATORS. Like men, enslaved women also fought as gladiators. This marble relief commemorates the freeing of two such fighters, "Amazon" and "Achillia," presumably as a reward for their successes in the arena.

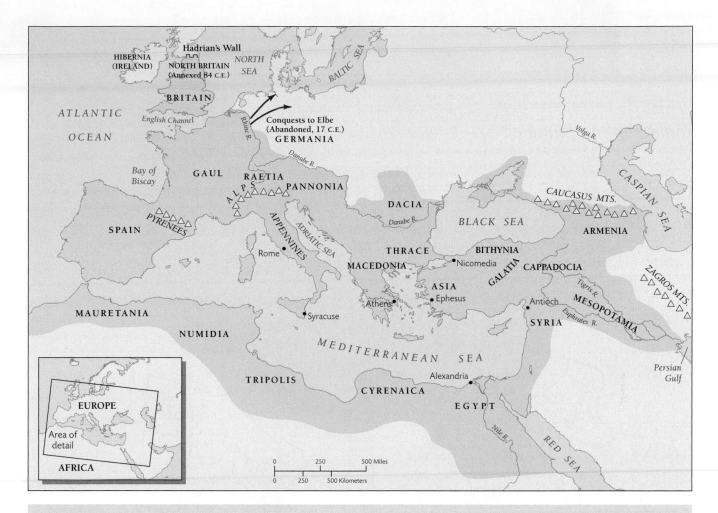

THE ROMAN EMPIRE AT ITS GREATEST EXTENT, 97–117 C.E. ▪ *How much farther north and west does the empire now reach compared to its earlier extent (see map on page 156)?* ▪ *How did geography influence the process of expansion?* ▪ *How did it dictate its limits?* ▪ *For example, what role do major river systems seem to play?*

appointed a small number of eminent jurists to deliver opinions on the issues raised by cases under trial in the courts. The five most prominent of these jurists flourished in the second century C.E.: Gaius (only this most common of his names is known), Domitius Ulpianus (Ulpian), Modestinus, Aemelianus Papinianus (Papinian), and Paulus. Although most of them came to hold high offices, they gained their reputations primarily as lawyers and commentators. Taken together, their legal opinions constitute the first philosophy of law and the foundation for all subsequent jurisprudence, a word derived from the Latin phrase meaning "legal wisdom."

As it was developed by the jurists, Roman law comprised three great branches or divisions: civil law, the law of nations, and natural law. Civil law was the law of Rome and its citizens, both written and unwritten. It included the statutes of the Senate, the decrees of the emperor, the edicts of magistrates, and ancient customs that had the force of law (like the *mos maiorum*). The law of nations was not specific to Rome but extended to all people of the world regardless of their origins and ethnicity: it is the precursor of international law. This law authorized and regulated slavery; protected the private ownership of property; and defined the mechanisms of purchase and sale, partnership, and contract. It was not superior to civil law but supplemented it, and it applied especially to those inhabitants of the empire who were not citizens, as well as to all foreigners.

The most interesting (and in many ways the most important) branch of Roman law was natural law, a product not of judicial practice but of legal philosophy. Roman Stoics, following in the footsteps of Cicero, posited that nature itself is rationally ordered and that careful study will reveal the laws by which the natural world operates, including the nature of justice. They affirmed that all men are by nature equal and that they are entitled to certain basic rights that governments have no authority to transgress. "True law," Cicero had said, "is right reason consonant with nature, diffused among all men, constant, eternal." Accordingly, no person or institution has the authority to infringe on this

Roman Urban Planning

Prior to Roman imperial expansion, most cities in the ancient world were not planned cities—with the exception of the new settlements established by Alexander the Great, notably Alexandria in Egypt. Rome itself was not carefully planned, but grew up over many centuries, expanding outward and up the slopes of its seven hills from the nucleus of the Forum. By the time of Augustus, it was a haphazard jumble of buildings and narrow streets. Outside of Rome, however, the efficiency of Roman government was in large part due to the uniformity of imperial urban planning. As their colonial reach expanded, Romans sought to ensure that travelers moving within their vast domain would encounter the same amenities in every major city. They also wanted to convey, through the organization of the urban landscape, the ubiquity of Roman authority and majesty.

A. Imperial Rome

B. Roman settlement in Aelia Capitolina (Jerusalem) after 135 C.E.

law, repeal it, or ignore it. This law supersedes any state or ruler; a ruler who transgresses it is a tyrant.

Although the jurists did not regard the philosophical concept of natural law as an automatic limitation on the workings of civil law, they did uphold it as an ideal. The practical law applied in local Roman courts often bore little resemblance to the law of nature, yet the development of a concept of abstract justice as a fundamental principle was one of the noblest achievements of Roman civilization. It has given us the doctrine of human rights—even if it has not ended abuses of those rights.

CONCLUSION

The resemblances between Rome's history and that of Great Britain and the United States have often been noted. Like the British Empire, the Roman Empire was founded on conquest and overseas colonization intended to benefit both the homeland and Britain's colonial subjects, who were seen as beneficiaries of the metropolis' "civilizing mission." Like America's, the Roman economy evolved from agrarianism to a complex system of domestic and foreign

Questions for Analysis

1. Looking closely at the map of Rome (map A), how have topographical features—like the river Tiber and the seven hills—determined the shape and layout of the city? What are the major buildings and public areas? What were the functions of these spaces, and what do they reveal about Roman society and values?

2. Compare the plan of Rome to those of Roman London (map C) and Roman Jerusalem (map B). What features do all three have in common, and why? What features are unique to each place, and what might this reveal about the different regions of the empire and the needs of the different cities' inhabitants?

3. Given that all Roman cities share certain features, what message(s) were Roman authorities trying to convey to inhabitants and travelers through urban planning? Why, for example, would they have insisted on rebuilding Jerusalem as a Roman city after the rebellion of 135 C.E.?

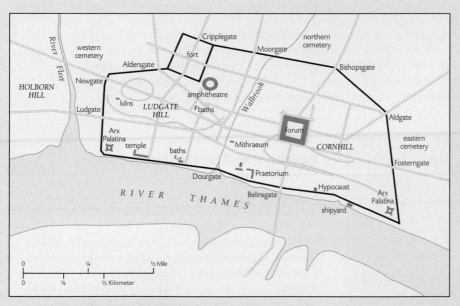

C. London under the Romans, c. 200 C.E.

markets, problems of unemployment, gross disparities of wealth, and vulnerability to financial crisis. And like both the British and the American empires, the Roman Empire justified itself by celebrating the peace its conquests allegedly brought to the world.

Ultimately, however, such parallels break down when we remember that Rome's civilization differed profoundly from any society of the modern world. It was not an industrialized society. Its government never pretended to be representative of all its citizens. Roman class divisions are not directly comparable to ours. The Roman economy rested on slavery to a degree unmatched in any modern state. As a result, technological advances were not encouraged, social stratification was extreme, and gender relations were profoundly unequal. Religious practice and political life were inseparable.

Nevertheless, the civilization of ancient Rome continues to structure our everyday lives in ways so profound that they can go unnoticed. Our days are mapped onto the Roman calendar. The Constitution of the United States is largely modeled on that of the republic, and Roman architecture survives in the design of our public buildings. Roman law forms the basis of most European legal codes and American judges still

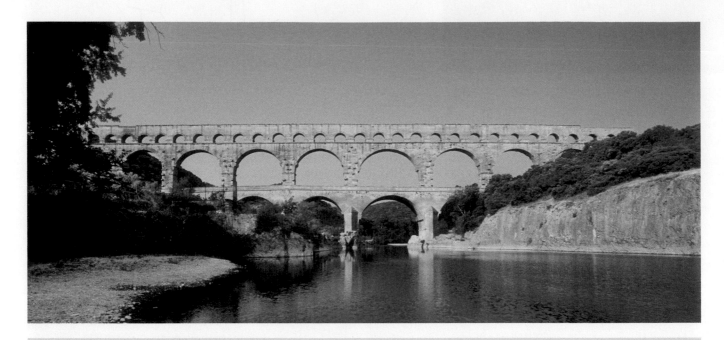

ROMAN AQUEDUCT IN SOUTHERN GAUL (PROVENCE). Aqueducts conveyed water from mountains and lakes to the larger cities of the Roman Empire. The massive arches shown here span the river Gardon (in southern France) and were originally part of a thirty-one-mile-long complex that supplied water to the city of Nemausus (Nîmes). It is now known as the Pont du Gard (Bridge of the Gardon), reflecting the use to which it was put after the aqueduct ceased to function, some eight centuries after its construction in the first century C.E. Some Roman aqueducts remained operational into the modern era: the one at Segovia, Spain, was still in use at the end of the twentieth century. ▪ *What does the magnitude and longevity of such projects tell us about Roman power and technology?*

After You Read This Chapter

Visit StudySpace for quizzes, additional review materials, and multimedia documents. **wwnorton.com/web/westernciv18**

REVIEWING THE OBJECTIVES

- The founding of the Roman Republic was both a cherished myth and a series of events. What factors contributed to this unique system of government?
- The shared identity and values of the Roman people differed in many ways from those of other ancient civilizations. What were some of these major differences?
- Rome's population was divided among classes of people who often struggled with one another for power. Identify these classes and their points of contention.
- The expansion of Rome's empire had a profound impact on Roman society. Why?
- The establishment of the Principate ushered in a new era in the history of Rome. What events led to this?

A ROMAN FLOOR MOSAIC. This fine mosaic from the Roman city of Londinium (London) shows Bacchus (Dionysus), the god of wine and revelry, mounted on a tiger. Tigers, native to India, were prized by animal collectors and were also imported for gladiatorial shows.

cite Gaius and Ulpian. Virtually all modern commemorative sculpture is inspired by Roman sculpture, and Roman authors continue to set the standards for prose composition in many Western countries. Indeed, most European languages are either derived from Latin—Romance languages are so called because they are "Roman-like"—or have borrowed Latin grammatical structures or vocabulary (German, for example). As we shall see in the following chapters, the organization of the modern Roman Catholic Church can be traced back to the structure of the Roman state: even today, the pope bears the title of Rome's high priest, *pontifex maximus*.

Perhaps the most significant of all Rome's contributions was its role as mediator between Europe and the civilizations of the ancient Near East and Mediterranean. Had Rome's empire not come to encompass much of Europe, there would be no such thing as the concept of Western civilization and no shared ideas and heritage to link us to those distant places and times. Although we shall pursue the history of Rome's fragmentation and witness the emergence of three different civilizations in the territories once united by its empire, we shall see that they all shared a common cultural inheritance. In that sense, at least, the Roman Empire did not collapse. But it was transformed, and the factors driving that transformation will be the subject of Chapter 6.

PEOPLE, IDEAS, AND EVENTS IN CONTEXT

- In what ways were the early Romans influenced by their **ETRUSCAN** neighbors and by their location in central Italy?
- What were the components of the **ROMAN REPUBLIC**'s constitution? What was the relationship between **ROMAN CITIZENSHIP** and the **ROMAN ARMY** in this era?
- How do the stories of **AENEAS**, **LUCRETIA**, and **CINCINNATUS** reflect core Roman values? How did those values, summarized in the phrase *MOS MAIORUM*, set the Romans apart from the other civilizations we have studied?
- Why did the Romans come into conflict with **CARTHAGE**? How did the **PUNIC WARS** and Rome's other conquests change the balance of power in the Mediterranean?
- How did imperialism and contact with **HELLENISTIC CULTURE** affect the core values of Roman society, its economy, and its political system? What role did **SLAVERY** play in this civilization?
- What were the major crises of the late republic, and what were the means by which ambitious men achieved power? How did **JULIUS CAESAR** emerge triumphant, and why was he assassinated?
- In what ways did the **PRINCIPATE** differ from the **ROMAN REPUBLIC**? What were the new powers of the **EMPEROR**, and how did **AUGUSTUS** exemplify these?
- How did the Romans consolidate their **EMPIRE** during the *PAX ROMANA*? By what means did they spread Roman culture?

THINKING ABOUT CONNECTIONS

- Polybius believed that the Roman Republic would last forever, because it fused together aspects of monarchy, aristocracy, and polity. What were the chief factors that led to its demise in the first century B.C.E.? Could these have been avoided—and if so, how?
- In what ways does the Roman Empire share the characteristics of earlier empires, especially that of Alexander? In what ways does it differ from them?
- The Roman Empire could be said to resemble our own civilization in different ways. What features does today's United States share with the republic? With the Principate? What lessons can we draw from this?

CONSTANTINVS MAIOR IMPERATOR
HERACLII ET TIBERII IMPERATOR

AR
COP
VS

PRIVILEGIA

STORY LINES

■ In a little over three centuries, Christianity grew from obscure beginnings in a small Roman province to become the official religion of the empire.

■ Meanwhile, the Roman Empire was becoming too large and diverse to be governed by a single centralized authority. Significant political, military, and economic changes occurred during the third century in response to these challenges.

■ In the fourth century, the founding of a new capital at Constantinople shifted the focus of imperial administration to the East. At the same time, mass migrations of frontier peoples created new settlements within the western half of Rome's empire.

■ Christianity's eventual association with political power changed the religion in profound ways. At the same time, Christian intellectuals adapted Rome's traditional culture to meet Christian needs.

CHRONOLOGY

c. 4 B.C.E.– c. 30 C.E.	Lifetime of Jesus
46–67 C.E.	Paul's missionary career
66–70	Jewish rebellion
132–135	Expulsion of Jews from Jerusalem
203	Death of Perpetua at Carthage
235–284	Rule of the "barracks emperors"
284–305	Diocletian divides the empire
312	Constantine's victory
313	Edict of Milan
325	Council of Nicaea convened
c. 370–430	Careers of Jerome, Ambrose, and Augustine
c. 376	Frontier migrations begin
391	Pagan religion outlawed
410	Visigoths sack Rome
476	Odovacar deposes Romulus Augustulus
493–526	Rule of Theodoric the Ostrogoth
c. 500–583	Careers of Boethius, Benedict, and Cassiodorus

Before
You
Read
This
Chapter

The Transformation of Rome

CORE OBJECTIVES

- **IDENTIFY** the historical factors that shaped early Christianity.

- **DESCRIBE** the pressures on Roman imperial administration during the third century.

- **TRACE** the ways that Christianity changed after it became a legal religion.

- **EXPLAIN** how barbarian migrations affected the empire.

- **UNDERSTAND** the difference between traditional Roman and Christian worldviews.

n the year 203 C.E., a young woman called Vivia Perpetua was brought before the Roman governor at Carthage. She was twenty-two years old, well educated, from a respectable family. At the time of her arrest she had an infant child who was still nursing. She also had two brothers (one of whom was arrested with her) and a father who doted on her. She must, one presumes, have had a husband, but he is conspicuously absent from the firsthand account of her experiences. Perpetua herself says nothing about him, though she says a great deal about her father's grief and the efforts he made to intercede on her behalf. Not only did he beg the judge for mercy, he begged his daughter to confess so that her life could be spared. He admitted to having loved her more than her brothers and blamed himself for the liberal education he had given her. Clearly, he had failed as a father: a Roman *paterfamilias* should never suffer humiliation through the conduct of a daughter; he should kill her with his own hands if she disgraced the family. For Perpetua's crime was terrible. It was not only treason against the Roman state but an act of gross impiety toward her father, her family, and her ancestors. Worse, it was punishable by a death so debasing that it was reserved for slaves, barbarian prisoners, and hardened criminals. It was inconceivable that a respectable Roman matron would be stripped naked before a holiday crowd and mauled by wild beasts in the arena of her own city. But that was the death Perpetua died. Perpetua was a Christian.

Early Christianity posed a challenge to the Roman Empire and its core values at almost every level, a challenge exemplified by Vivia Perpetua. To be a Christian was to be, by definition, an enemy of Rome, because Christians refused to venerate the emperor as the embodiment of Rome's gods; denying his association with divinity meant denying his authority. Moreover, the Christ whom Christians worshiped had himself been declared a criminal, a political insurgent,

and had been duly tried and put to death by the Roman state. Also disturbing was the way that Christians flouted the conventions of Roman society. Perpetua was young, yet she was disobedient to her father and ancestors. She was well born, yet she chose to endure the filth of a common jail. She was a woman, yet she denied the authority of men and renounced her femininity, dying in the dust like a gladiator. If this was what it meant to be a Christian, then being a Christian was incompatible with being a Roman.

How, then, did a Roman emperor become a Christian just a few centuries after Christ's death—and just a century or so after Perpetua's? What changes did both Rome and Christianity have to undergo in order for this to happen? And what other forces were at work, within the empire and beyond its borders, that helped bring this about?

The Rome in which Perpetua was raised stretched from central Asia to the British Isles, from the Rhine to her own province of North Africa. But as we shall see, the governance of this enormous state and its diverse population was straining the bureaucracy that had been built on the foundations of the old republic. By the end of the third century, it was increasingly obvious that Rome's western and eastern provinces could not be controlled by a single centralized authority. In the fourth century, Rome itself ceased to be the capital and hub of the empire; it now shared prestige with the new city of Constantinople, named by the Christian emperor who founded it. At the same time, Rome's settled provinces were coming under increased pressure from groups of people who had long lived along its borders but who were now moving from the periphery to the center. These peoples, too, would challenge what it meant to be Roman and would contribute to the transformation of the Roman world.

THE CHALLENGE OF CHRISTIANITY

Even faiths have histories. Like the Hebrew monotheism that undergirds Judaism or the central tenets of Zoroastrianism (see Chapter 2), Christianity was (and is) the product of historical processes. It began with the teachings of Jesus, who lived and worked among his fellow Jews in rural Judea and Galilee around the year 30 C.E. It took root, however, in the Hellenistic world we studied in Chapter 4: the cosmopolitan, Greek-speaking cities around the eastern Mediterranean, which had now been absorbed into the Roman Empire.

The Career of Jesus

Yeshua bar Yosef (Joshua, son of Joseph), known to the Greeks as Jesus, is one of the few figures of the ancient world—certainly one of the few commoners—about whose life we know a great deal. The earliest writings that mention Jesus specifically are the letters of his follower Paul of Tarsus, a Hellenized Jew who was active during the 50s and 60s C.E. These epistles are closely followed by many different narratives of Jesus's life and teachings, most written between c. 70 and 100 C.E. Four such accounts were eventually included in the New Testament, a collection of Christian scriptures appended to the Greek text of the Hebrew Bible around the third century C.E. In their original Greek, these accounts were called *evangelia* ("good messages"); we know them as *Gospels*, an Old English word that means the same thing.

Jesus was born around the year 4 B.C.E., a generation or so after Augustus came to power in Rome. (He was not born precisely in the first year of the Common Era as we now reckon it. When the monk Dionysius Exiguus first calculated time "in the year of Our Lord" during the sixth century, he made some mistakes.) When Jesus was around thirty years old, he was endorsed by a Jewish preacher of moral reform, John the Baptist, whom some considered to be a prophet. Thereafter, Jesus traveled widely around the rural areas of Galilee and Judea, preaching and displaying unusual healing powers. He accumulated a number of disciples, some of whom had political ambitions.

Around the year 30 C.E., Jesus staged an entry into Jerusalem during Passover, a major religious holiday that brought large and excitable crowds to the city. This move was interpreted as a bid for political power by both the Roman colonial government and the high-ranking Jews of the Temple. Three of the Gospel accounts say that Jesus also drew attention to himself by attacking merchants and moneychangers associated with the Temple. The city's religious leaders therefore arrested him and turned him over to the Roman governor, Pontius Pilatus (Pilate), for sentencing.

Pilate's main concern was to preserve peace during a volatile religious festival. He knew that his authority depended on maintaining good relations with local Jewish elites and with Herod, a recent convert to Judaism who ruled the province of Galilee in collaboration with Rome, as a client king of the empire. Because Jesus was a resident of Galilee, not a citizen of Roman Judea, Pilate sent Jesus to Herod for sentencing. But Herod sent him back to Pilate, politely indicating that dealing with Jesus fell under Roman jursidiction. So Pilate chose to make an example of Jesus by condemning him to death by crucifixion, the standard criminal penalty for those judged guilty of sedition. It had been rumored that Jesus planned to lead a rebellion, and something similar had happened in the second century B.C.E., when the Maccabbees overthrew Seleucid rule. Indeed, the Roman occupation of the region had only begun in 67 B.C.E. and was still resented by many Jews. Pilate would have been mindful of all this.

That might have been the end of the story. But soon after Jesus's execution, his followers began to assert that he had risen from the dead before being taken up into heaven. Moreover, they said that Jesus had promised to return again at the end of time. Meanwhile, he had promised spiritual support to his followers in their own preaching missions. His entire career now had to be rethought and reinterpreted by his followers: in life, he had been a teacher and healer; in death, he had been revealed as something more. The evidence of this reinterpretation has come down to us in the letters of Paul and in the Gospel narratives.

Jesus and Judaism

In 1947, an extraordinary cache of parchment and papyrus scrolls was discovered in a cave near Qumran on the shores of the Dead Sea. Over the course of the next decade, eleven more caves were found to house similar texts dating from the first century C.E. Only since the mid-1980s, however,

JESUS. This depiction of Jesus is from a third-century C.E. stone inlay.

have the texts of these Dead Sea Scrolls been widely available to scholars. Written in Hebrew, Greek, and Aramaic at various times between 100 B.C.E and 70 C.E., they have revolutionized our understanding of Judaism in the lifetime of Jesus, a period known as "Second Temple" Judaism. What these documents show, overwhelmingly, is the diversity of religious practice in this period, and the intense competition among groups of Jewish believers.

When Jesus was born, Roman rule in this region was still inspiring extreme responses. While many Jews were content to live under Rome's protection—especially the urban elite, who reaped the rewards of participation in the Roman economy and administration—there was talk of rebellion among rural communities and the urban poor. Many of those disadvantaged by Roman rule hoped for a messiah, an inspired leader who would establish Jewish autonomy and a new Jewish kingdom. The most extreme of these were the Zealots, whose activities eventually led to two disastrous revolts. The first, between 66 and 70 C.E., ended in the Romans' destruction of the Temple that had been rebuilt when Cyrus the Great released the Jews from captivity in Babylon, 600 years earlier (see Chapter 2). The second, in 132–35 C.E., caused the destruction of Jerusalem itself and prompted the Romans to expel the entire Jewish population.

Whereas the first exile of the Jews had ended after fifty years, this new diaspora would not be reversed until the controversial establishment of the modern state of Israel in 1948. For over 500 years, Jerusalem even ceased to exist; on its ruins the Romans built the colony of Aelia Capitolina (see Chapter 5). It was only in 638, when the Islamic Caliphate established Arab rule in the region and restored Jerusalem as a holy site, that Jews were allowed to settle there (see Chapter 7).

This political and religious context is essential to understanding the circumstances of Jesus's death and the different messages conveyed by his words and actions. The Dead Sea Scrolls reveal that significant divisions had arisen among Jewish communities, and that Jesus participated in several key debates. In his lifetime, the hereditary Temple priesthood was controlled by a group known as the Sadducees, elite Jews who collaborated closely with Rome; the high priest of the Temple was even appointed by the Roman Senate. As a result of their overt political agenda, the Sadducees were regarded with suspicion by many. Their chief rivals were the Pharisees, preachers of religious doctrine who were heirs to the prophetic tradition of the "First Temple" period of the sixth century B.C.E. In contrast to the Sadducees, who claimed the right to control the interpretation of the Torah, the five books attributed to Moses, the Pharisees argued that Yahweh had given Moses an oral Torah as well as a written one, which explained how these books should be

PAUL OF TARSUS. Many ancient images of Paul survive, and all depict him with the same features: a gaunt face, balding head, pointed black beard, and intense dark gaze. In the summer of 2009, archaeologists working in the catacombs of Thekla (named after a holy woman and follower of Paul) discovered this faded fresco. It has been identified as the oldest known portrait of this formative Christian figure and can be dated to the fourth century C.E.

applied to daily life. This oral tradition had been handed down from teachers to students and was now claimed as the special inheritance of the Pharisees.

The Pharisees were accordingly quite flexible in the practical application of religious law. For example, in order to allow neighbors to dine together on the Sabbath (when Jews were forbidden to work and could not even carry food outside their homes), the Pharisees ruled that an entire neighborhood could constitute a single household. They also believed in a life after death, a day of judgment, and the damnation or reward of individual souls. They actively sought out converts through preaching and looked forward to the imminent arrival of the Messiah whom God (through the prophets) had long promised. In all these respects they differed significantly from the Sadducees, who interpreted the Torah more strictly, who considered Judaism closed to anyone who had not been born a Jew and who had a vested interest in maintaining the political status quo. Even more radical than the Pharisees was a faction known as the Essenes, a quasi-monastic group that hoped for spiritual deliverance through repentance, asceticism, and sectarian separation from their fellow Jews.

Although some scholars see Essene influence behind the career of Jesus, his Jewish contemporaries probably saw him as some sort of Pharisee: Jesus's emphasis on the ethical requirements of the law rather than its literal interpretation is reflected in many of his teachings. Jesus's apparent belief in life after death and the imminent coming of "the kingdom of God" also fits within a Pharisaic framework, as does his willingness to reach out to people beyond the Jewish community. Nevertheless, he seems to have carried these principles considerably further than did the Pharisees.

For most Jews at this time, Judaism consisted of going up to the Temple on holy days; paying the annual Temple tax; reciting the morning and evening prayers; and observing certain fundamental laws, such as circumcision (for men), ritual purity (especially for women), and prohibitions on the consumption of certain foods. Jesus deemphasized such observances, and it may have seemed to some that he

wished to abolish them. But what made him most controversial was his followers' claim that he was the Messiah sent to deliver Israel from its enemies.

After Jesus's death, such claims grew more assertive, yet they never persuaded more than a small minority of Jews. But when Jesus's followers began to preach to non-Jewish audiences, they found many willing listeners. They began to represent Jesus in terms that made sense to the Greek-speaking communities of the Hellenistic world. Jesus, his followers now proclaimed, was not merely a messiah for the Jews. He was the "anointed one" (in Greek, *Christos*), the divine representative of God who had suffered and died for the sins of all humanity. He had now risen from the dead and ascended into heaven, and he would return to judge all the world's inhabitants at the end of time.

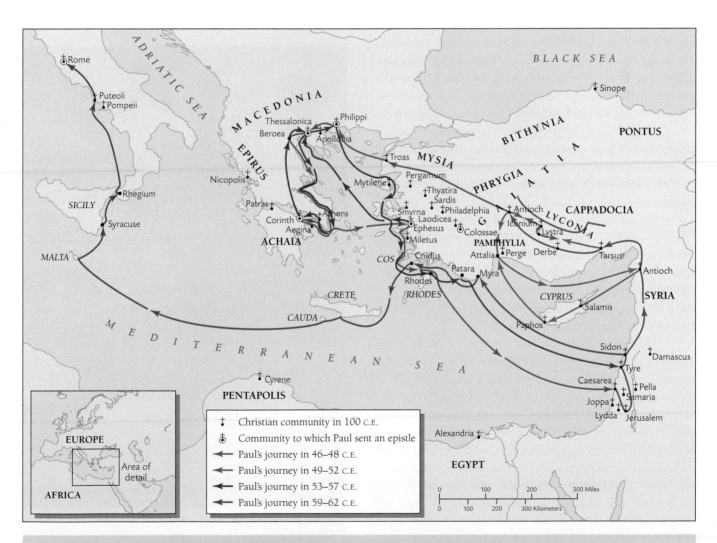

PAUL'S MISSIONARY JOURNEYS. Quite apart from its theological importance, Paul's career offers fascinating glimpses into the life of a Hellenized Roman citizen from one of the empire's eastern provinces. ▪ *What were the main phases of Paul's travels in the eastern Mediterranean?* ▪ *How were his itineraries shaped by geography and by various modes of transport?* ▪ *What conclusions about his mission can you draw from the extent of his travels and his major destinations?*

Christianity in the Hellenistic World

The key figure to develop this new understanding of Jesus's divinity was his younger contemporary, Paul of Tarsus (c. 10–c. 67 C.E.). Named Saul when he was born in the capital city of the Roman province of Cilicia (now south-central Turkey), he was the son of a Pharisee and staunchly sympathetic to that cause. The Acts of the Apostles, the continuation of Luke's Gospel and a major source for Saul's early life, says that he was dedicated to stamping out the cult that had grown up around the crucified Jesus. But at some point in his mid-twenties—a few years after Jesus's death—he underwent a dramatic conversion experience, changed his name to Paul, and devoted the rest of his life to spreading the new faith to Greek-speaking, mainly non-Jewish communities.

Unlike Peter and some other early apostles (from the Greek word meaning "one who is sent forth"), Paul had never met Jesus. Instead, he claimed to have received a direct revelation of his teachings. This led to a number of major disputes. For example, Peter and his companions believed that followers of Jesus had to be Jews or converts to Judaism. Paul declared that Jewish religious law was now irrelevant; Jesus had made a new covenant possible between God and humanity, and the old covenant between God and the Jews no longer applied. This position was vehemently opposed by the Jewish Christians of Jerusalem, a group led by Jesus's brother, James. But after a series of difficult debates that took place around 49 C.E., Paul's position triumphed. Although some early Christians would continue to obey Jewish law, most of the converts who swelled the movement were Gentiles. Paul began to call this new community of believers an ekklesia, the Greek word for a legislative assembly (see Chapter 3). The Latinized form of this word is translated as "church."

The earliest converts to Christianity were attracted for a variety of reasons. Some were Hellenized Jews like Paul himself. Jewish communities existed in most major cities of the eastern Mediterranean, including Rome, and had already begun to adapt their lifestyles and beliefs through contact with other cultures. Christianity also appealed to groups of non-Jews known as "God-fearers," who gathered around these Greek-speaking Jewish communities. God-fearers did not follow all the precepts of Jewish law, but they admired the Jews for their loyalty to ancestral tradition and their high ethical standards. Christianity was also attractive to ordinary cosmopolitan Greeks. Some saw Jesus as living by Stoic principles (Chapter 4) or as the embodiment of Ahura-Mazda, the good god of Zoroastrianism (Chapter 2). Others were already devotees of mystery religions, like the very old cult of the Egyptian goddess Isis (Chapter 1) or the newer worship of the warrior-god Mithras, popular among Rome's professional

soldiers. Both of these religions also revolved around stories of sacrifice, death, and regeneration and would have prepared their adherents to embrace the worship of Jesus. It was largely for the benefit of these converts that Christians began to practice elaborate initiation ceremonies such as baptism, a ritual purification common to many ancient religions and exemplified among Jews in the ministry of John the Baptist.

At the same time, there were significant differences between Christianity and these other religions. Most mystery cults stressed the rebirth of the individual through spiritual transformation, but Christianity emphasized the importance of community. By the middle of the second century, the Christian church at Rome had a recognizable structure, headed by a bishop (in Greek, *episcopos* or "overseer") and lesser officeholders, including priests, deacons, confessors, and exorcists. Women were extremely prominent in these churches, not only as patrons and benefactors

A FRECSO FROM THE CATACOMBS OF ROME. This image shows a catachumen (Greek for "instructed one") being baptized by the Holy Spirit in the form of an eagle. It is one of many paintings to be found in the ancient catacombs around Rome: subterranean burial and meeting places where Christians also hid during times of persecution. ■ *Why would such images have been important?*

A CHRISTIAN LOVE FEAST. This fresco, another image from the catacombs, shows Christians celebrating a feast. The inscription above it reads, "I join with you in love." ▪ *How would a Roman viewer interpret this scene?* ▪ *How might this interpretation differ from that of a Christian?*

More Christians could have responded as did Marcion, a second-century Christian scholar who declared that Jewish religious practices and the entire Hebrew Bible could be ignored. Most Christians, however, refused to abandon their religion's Jewish foundation. For them, the heroes of Jewish scripture prefigured Jesus, while the major events of Hebrew history could be read, allegorically, as Christian paradigms. Christ was the new Adam, reversing man's original sin: wood from the fateful Tree in Eden became the wood of the Cross on which he died. Christ, like Abel, had been slain at the hands of a brother and his blood continued to cry out from the ground. Christ was the new Noah, saving creation from its sins. Christ was prefigured in Isaac, in Joseph, in Moses. Furthermore, according to Christians, all the words of the Hebrew prophets point to Jesus, as do the Psalms and the Proverbs.

In short, Christian theologians argued that the Christian church is the true Israel and that when the Jews rejected Jesus, God rejected the Jews and made Christians his new chosen people. The Hebrew Bible was henceforth the Old Testament, vital to understanding Christianity but superseded by the New Testament. At the end of time, the Jews would see the error of their ways and convert. Until then, their only reason for existing was to testify to the truth of Christianity. From a Christian perspective, the Jews' own impiety had caused their exile from the Holy Land and would continue to bring suffering down on their descendants.

(a role Roman women often played in religious cults) but also as officeholders.

This high status accorded to women was unusual: in other ancient religions, women could be priests and officeholders—but only in cults open solely to women; they never took precedence over men. Many cults, like Mithraism, denied them access entirely. The fact that Christianity drew its adherents from a broad range of social classes also distinguished it from other cults, which were accessible mainly to those with money and leisure. In time, these unusual features were distorted by Christianity's detractors, who alleged that Christians were political insurgents like the Jesus they worshiped, that they engaged in illicit acts during "love feasts," or that they practiced human sacrifice and cannibalism.

As both Christianity and Judaism redefined themselves during the second and third centuries, they grew further apart. Judaism was adapting to the Romans' destruction of the Temple and the mass exile of Jews from Jerusalem and surrounding provinces. By and large, the scholars who reshaped it during these difficult years ignored Christianity. It simply did not matter to them, any more than did the cults of Mithras or Isis. Christians, however, could not ignore Judaism. Their religion rested on the belief that Jesus was the savior promised by God to Israel in the Hebrew Bible. The fact that so few Jews accepted this claim was a standing rebuke to their faith, one that threatened to undermine the credibility of the Christian message.

Christianity and the Roman State

As long as Christianity remained a minority religion within the Roman Empire, such attitudes had no effect on the position of Jews under Roman rule. Judaism remained a legally recognized religion and many Jews were further protected by their Roman citizenship. Indeed, the biblical book known as the Acts of the Apostles represents Paul as a Roman citizen who could not be summarily put to death (as the noncitizen Jesus had been) when brought up on charges of treason. Instead, Acts follows his progress through the Roman judicial system, until he is finally brought to trial at Rome and executed (by beheading) under Nero. Even after their rebellion, the Jews of the diaspora were allowed to maintain the special status they had always had under Roman rule and were not required, as other subject peoples were, to offer sacrifices to the emperor.

The Prosecution of a Roman Citizen

The Acts of the Apostles *was written by the same author as Luke's Gospel and was intended as a continuation of that book. It recounts the adventures and ministry of Jesus's original disciples and also follows the career of Paul, a Hellenized Jew who became a missionary to Gentiles throughout the Roman world. It offers fascinating glimpses into the workings of the Roman legal system because Paul, depicted here as a Roman citizen, would have had special rights under Roman law (as Jesus had not). In this passage, Paul has been accused of treason against the emperor by a group of Pharisees and has been sent to Felix, the governor of Judea. These events took place between 57 and 59 C.E.*

So the soldiers, according to their instructions, took Paul and brought him by night to [the city of] Antipatris. The next day, they let the horsemen go on with him, while they returned to the barracks. When they came to Caesarea and delivered the letter to the governor, they presented Paul also before him. On reading the letter, he asked what province he belonged to, and when he learned that he was from Cilicia he said, "I will give you a hearing when your accusers arrive." Then he ordered that he be kept under guard in Herod's headquarters.

Five days later, the high priest Ananias came down with some elders and an attorney, a certain Tertullus, and they reported their case against Paul to the governor. When Paul had been summoned, Tertullus began to accuse him, saying: "Your Excellency, because of you we have long enjoyed peace, and reforms have been made for this people because of your foresight. We welcome this in every way and everywhere with utmost gratitude. But, to detain you no further, I beg you to hear us briefly with your customary graciousness. We have, in fact, found this man a pestilent fellow, an agitator among all the Jews throughout the world, and a ringleader of the sect of the Nazarenes. He even tried to profane the temple, and so we seized him. By examining him yourself you will be able to learn from him concerning everything of which we accuse him." The Jews also joined in the charge by asserting that all this was true.

When the governor motioned to him to speak, Paul replied: "I cheerfully make my defense, knowing that for many years you have been a judge over this nation. As you can find out, it is not more than twelve days since I went up to worship in Jerusalem. They did not find me disputing with anyone in the temple or stirring up a crowd either in synagogues or throughout the city. Neither can they prove to you the charge that they now bring against me. But this I admit to you, that according to the Way, which they call a sect, I worship the God of our ancestors, believing everything laid down according to the law or written in the prophets. I have hope in God—a hope that they themselves also accept—that there will be a resurrection of both the righteous and the unrighteous. Therefore I do my best always to have a clear conscience toward God and all people. . . ."

But Felix, who was rather well informed about the Way, adjourned the hearing with the comment, "When Lysias the tribune comes down, I will decide your case." Then he ordered the centurion to keep him in custody, but to let him have some liberty and not to prevent any of his friends from taking care of his needs.

When some days later Felix came with his wife Drusilla, who was Jewish, he sent for Paul and heard him speak concerning faith in Christ Jesus. And as he discussed justice and self-control and future judgment, Felix was alarmed and said, "Go away for the present; when I have an opportunity I will summon you." At the same time he hoped that money would be given him by Paul. So he sent for him often and conversed with him. But when two years had elapsed, Felix was succeeded by Porcius Festus; and desiring to do the Jews a favor, Felix left Paul in prison.

Source: Acts of the Apostles 23:31–24:27, in *The New Oxford Annotated Bible*, New Revised Standard Version, eds. Bruce M. Metzger and Roland E. Murphy (New York: 1994).

Questions for Analysis

1. Based on this account, what legal procedures are in place for dealing with any Roman citizen accused of a crime?

2. What seems to be the relationship between the Jewish elite of Judea and the Roman governor? What is the role of their spokesman, Tertullus?

3. What is the nature of the accusation against Paul, and how does he defend himself?

As we have seen, nothing was more important to the Romans than *pietas* and respect for one's ancestors, and the Romans understood the Jews' traditions as a form of ancestor worship.

Christianity, by contrast, was a novelty religion. It carried neither the patina of antiquity nor the sanction of tradition— quite the contrary. It raised suspicions on many levels: it encouraged women and slaves to hold office and therefore to rise above their proper stations; it revolved around the worship of a criminal condemned by the Roman state; its secret meetings could be breeding grounds for rebellion. Nevertheless, the official attitude of the Roman state toward Christians was largely one of indifference. There were not enough of them to matter, and few of them had any political power. During the first and second centuries C.E., therefore, Christians were tolerated by Roman officials, except when local magistrates chose to make an example of someone who flagrantly flouted authority.

THE CHALLENGE OF IMPERIAL EXPANSION

The emergence of Christianity within the Roman Empire coincided with the empire's most dramatic period of growth and, as a result, with a growing variety of challenges. For a long time, Rome's emperors and administrators clung to the methods of governance that had been put in place under Augustus, methods which were based on a single centralized authority. The reality, however, was that Rome's empire was no longer centered on Rome, or even on Italy. It embraced ecosystems, linguistic groupings, ethnicities, cultures, economies, and political systems of vastly different kinds. More and more people could claim to be Roman citizens, and more and more people wanted a share of Rome's power. This placed enormous stress on the imperial administration, as the centrifugal forces of Rome's own making constantly pulled resources into her far-flung provinces, where cities had to be built, people governed, and communications maintained. The fact that the empire had few defensible borders was another problem. Hadrian had attempted to establish one after 122, by building a wall between Roman settlements in southern Britannia and the badlands of northern tribes (see Chapter 5); but this act was more symbolic than effective.

For much of the second century, such stresses were masked by the peaceful transfer of power among the so-called "Five Good Emperors": Nerva, Trajan, Hadrian, Antoninus Pius, and Marcus Aurelius. This harmonious state of affairs was partly accidental. None of these first four rulers had a surviving male heir, and so a custom developed whereby each adopted a young man of a good family and trained his successor in the craft of government. This sensible practice changed with the death of Marcus Aurelius in 180 C.E. Although he was the closest Roman equivalent to Plato's ideal of the philosopher-king, Marcus was not wise enough to recognize that his own son, Commodus, lacked the capacity to rule effectively. After his father's death, Commodus alienated the army by withdrawing from costly wars along the Danube. This move was also unpopular with the Senate, as were Commodus's violent tendencies and his scorn for the traditional norms of aristocratic conduct, including an alleged appearance as a gladiator in the Colosseum. In 192, a conspiracy was hatched inside his own palace, where he was strangled by his wrestling coach.

The Empire of the Severan Dynasty

Because Commodus had no obvious successor, the armies stationed in various provinces of the empire raised their own candidates. Civil war ensued, as it had during the crises of the late republic and in 68 C.E., when three men had struggled for imperial power. In this case, there were five major contenders. The eventual victor was a North African general called Septimius Severus (r. 193–211 C.E.).

Under Severus (*SEH-ver-uhs*) and his successors, the administration of Rome's empire changed to a greater extent than it had since the time of Augustus. In many respects, these changes were long overdue. Even the "Five Good Emperors" had been somewhat insulated from the realities of colonial rule. Many of them were able commanders, but they were not professional soldiers as Severus was. Another major difference was the fact that Severus had been born and raised in the North African town of Leptis Magna (now in Libya) and identified strongly with his father's Punic ancestors, seemingly more so than with his mother's patrician family. Unlike Trajan and Hadrian, who had also grown up in the provinces, Severus did not regard Rome as the center of the universe, and the time he spent in the imperial capital as a young man seems to have convinced him that little could be accomplished there.

In fact, Severus represents the degree to which the Roman Empire had succeeded in making the world Roman—succeeded so well that Rome itself was becoming practically irrelevant. One could be as much a Roman in Britannia or Africa as in central Italy. Severus's second wife, Julia Domna, exemplifies this trend in a different way. Descended from the Aramaic aristocracy who ruled the Roman client kingdom of Emesa (Syria), her father was the high priest of its sun-god, Ba'al. She was highly educated and proved an effective governer during her husband's almost perpetual absence from Rome.

Competing Viewpoints

The Development of an Imperial Policy toward Christians

> It was not until the third century that the Roman imperial government began to initiate full-scale investigations into the activities of Christians. Instead, the official position was akin to a policy of "don't ask, don't tell." Local administrators handled only occasional cases, and they were often unsure as to whether the behavior of Christians was illegal or criminal. The following letter was sent to the emperor Trajan by Gaius Plinius Caecilius Secundus (Pliny the Younger), the governor of Bithynia-Pontus (Asia Minor), around 112 C.E. Pliny was anxious to follow proper procedures in dealing with the new sect and wanted advice about this. His letter indicates what Romans did and didn't know about early Christian beliefs and practices.

From Pliny to Trajan

It is my regular custom, my lord, to refer to you all questions which cause me doubt, for who can better guide my hesitant steps or instruct my ignorance? I have never attended hearings concerning Christians, so I am unaware what is usually punished or investigated, and to what extent.... In the meantime, this is the procedure I have followed in the cases of those brought before me as Christians. I asked them whether they were Christians. If they admitted it, I asked them a second and a third time, threatening them with execution. Those who remained obdurate I ordered to be executed, for I was in no doubt ... that their obstinacy and inflexible stubbornness should at any rate be punished. Others similarly lunatic were Roman citizens, so I registered them to be sent back to Rome.

Later in the course of the hearings, as usually happens, the charge rippled outwards, and more examples appeared. An anonymous document was published containing the names of many. Those who denied that they were or had been Christians and called upon the gods after me, and with incense and wine made obeisance to your statue ... and who moreover cursed Christ ... I ordered to be acquitted.

Others, who were named by an informer, stated that they were Christians and then denied it. They said that they had been, but had abandoned their

Severus largely ignored the politics of the Senate and slighted what remained of its powers. He preferred to rule through the army, which he reorganized and expanded. Two of his reforms had long-term consequences. The first was a drastic raise in army pay, probably as much as 100 percent, which had the effect of securing the soldiers' absolute loyalty and diminishing their need to augment their wages through plunder. The other was a relaxation of the long-standing rule forbidding soldiers to marry while still in service. This dispensation encouraged men to put down roots in local communities, but it also made them reluctant to move when their legion was called up. On the one hand, this domesticated the army (hitherto a highly mobile fighting machine) and may have made it less effective. On the other, it gave the army a stake in the peaceful governance of Rome's colonies and further contributed to the decentralization of power.

Severus spent most of his imperial career with his army. He died at Eboracum (York) in 211, after conducting a series of successful negotiations with Pictish tribes north of Hadrian's Wall. On his deathbed, he is reported to have said to his sons, "Get along together, keep the soldiers rich, and don't bother about anyone else." His elder son, Caracalla, didn't heed the first of these injunctions for long: by the end of the year, he had assassinated his brother, Geta. He then attempted to erase his brother from the historical record by declaring a *damnatio memoriae* (literally, "a condemnation of memory") that banned the mention of Geta's name and defaced his image on public monuments. The second of his father's orders he obeyed in a certain sense, by extending the rights of Roman citizenship to everyone in the empire. This not only included the entire army in the franchise but increased the tax base. This was beneficial in some respects, allegiance some years previously.... They maintained, however, that all that their guilt or error involved was that they were accustomed to assemble at dawn on a fixed day, to sing a hymn antiphonally to Christ as God, and to bind themselves by an oath ... to avoid acts of theft, brigandage, and adultery.... When these rites were completed, it was their custom to depart, and then reassemble again to take food, which was, however, common and harmless. They had ceased, they said, to do this following my edict, by which in accordance with your instructions I had outlawed the existence of secret brotherhoods. So I thought it all the more necessary to ascertain the truth from two maidservants [i.e., slaves], who were called deaconnesses, even by employing torture. I found nothing other than a debased and boundless superstition....

From Trajan to Pliny

You have followed the appropriate procedures, my Secundus.... [N]o general rule can be laid down which would establish a definite routine. Christians are not to be sought out. If brought before you and found guilty, they must be punished, but in such a way that a person who denies that he is a Christian, and demonstrates this by his action ... may obtain pardon for his repentance, even if his previous record is suspect. Documents published anonymously must play no role in any accusation, for they give the worst example, and are foreign to our age.

Source: Excerpted from *Pliny the Younger: The Complete Letters*, trans. P. G. Walsh (Oxford: 2006), pp. 278–79 (X.96–97).

Questions for Analysis

1. How does Pliny's treatment of Christians differ according to their social class? How does it differ from Felix's treatment of Paul (p. 186)?

2. Why would Trajan insist that anonymous accusations, like those discussed by Pliny, should not be used as evidence? Why is this "foreign to our age"?

3. What do you conclude from this exchange about the relationship between religion and politics under the Roman Empire?

but it may also have cheapened Roman citizenship, which was no longer a prize to be won through service or the adoption of Roman values and manners. Another indication of his populism was Caracalla's sponsorship of the largest public baths ever constructed in Rome, an enormous complex that would rival St. Peter's Basilica had it survived (the sprawling remains can still be seen). His father's final piece of advice helped to shorten Caracalla's reign significantly, since it exacerbated his already pronounced tendency to alienate everyone who disagreed with him. He was assassinated in 217.

Caracalla's true successor was his mother's sister, Julia Maesa, who ruled through his nominal heir and cousin, her adolescent grandson. This youth was known as Heliogabalus (or Elagabalus, r. 218–22) because of his devotion to Ba'al. But when Heliogabalus caused controversy by attempting to replace Jupiter, Rome's patron god, with a Latinized

THE EMPRESS JULIA DOMNA. This Roman coin, dating from about 200 C.E., is one of several issued in the name of Severus's powerful wife. As the coin's legend shows, she ruled as "Julia Augusta," names associated with the imperial family since the time of Augustus Caesar.

version of this eastern deity, Sol Invictus ("Invincible Sun"), his own grandmother engineered his assassination. Another of her grandsons, Alexander Severus (r. 222–35 C.E.), took his place. Alexander, in turn, was ruled by his mother Julia Mamea, the third in a succession of strong women behind the Severan dynasty, who even traveled with her son on military campaigns. This eventually proved fatal. The new prominence of the army made Rome's legions engines of political advancement even more so than under the dictators of the late republic. Many aspiring generals could harness this power, and with it the support of their legions' provincial bases. In 235, in consequence, Alexander and his

THE EMPEROR SEPTIMIUS SEVERUS. This statue, carved during the emperor's lifetime, emphasizes his career as a military commander, showing him in the standard-issue uniform of a Roman legionnaire. How does this image of Severus compare to that of Augustus (see Chapter 5, page 166)? ■ *What do these differences suggest about the emperor's new role in the third century?*

mother were murdered at Moguntiacum (Mainz) in Upper Germania, when the army of the region turned against them. Nearly fifty years of civil unrest ensued.

The Test of Rome's Strength

From 235 to 284 C.E. there were no fewer than twenty-six "barracks emperors" in Rome: military commanders who, backed by a few loyal legions, struggled with one another and an array of problems. This period is sometimes called the "Third-Century Crisis" and interpreted as a time when the Roman Empire was nearly destroyed. It is more accurately interpreted as a time when the consequences of Roman imperialism made themselves acutely felt. Those aspects of the empire that were strong survived. Those that had always been fragile were further strained.

For example, the disruptions of the mid-third century exposed weaknesses in economic and administrative infrastructures. Inflation, caused by the devaluation of currency under Severus, nearly drained Roman coinage of its value. Meanwhile, aspiring emperors levied exorbitant taxes on civilians in their provinces, as warfare among rival claimants and their armies destroyed crops and interrupted trade, causing food shortages. Because Rome itself was almost entirely dependent on Egyptian grain and other goods shipped in from the East, its inhabitants suffered accordingly. Poverty and famine even led to a new form of slavery in Italy, as free artisans, local businessmen, and small farmers were forced to labor on the estates of large landholders in exchange for protection and food.

In 251, a terrible plague, probably smallpox, swept through the empire's territories and recurred in some areas for almost two decades. A similar plague had ravaged Rome a century earlier, but its effects had been mitigated by sound governance. Now, with an estimated 5,000 people dying every day in the crowded city, people sought local scapegoats. Christians were among those targeted. Beginning in the short reign of Decius (r. 249–51), all Roman citizens were required to swear a public oath affirming their loyalty to Rome, which meant worshiping Rome's gods. Those who did so received a certificate testifying to this fact, which they had to produce on demand. Large numbers of Christians were implicated when this edict was put into effect. The enlightened policies of earlier emperors were abandoned.

The Reorganized Empire of Diocletian

As it happens, the most zealous persecutor of Christians was also responsible for reining in these destructive forces. Diocletian (*die-oh-KLEE-shan*, r. 284–305) was a cavalry officer from the Roman province of Dalmatia (modern Croatia) who had risen through the ranks. He could have been another "barracks emperor," but he was determined not to be a victim of the cycle. Instead, he embraced the reality of Rome as a multicultural entity that could not be governed from one place by one person with one centralized bureaucracy. He appointed a fellow officer, Maximian, as co-emperor, putting him in charge of the western half of the empire and retaining the wealthier eastern half for himself. In 293, he delegated new authority to two junior emperors or "caesars," Galerius and Constantius. The result was a tetrarchy, a "rule of four," with each man governing a quarter of the empire, further subdivided into administrative units called *dioceses*. This system not only responded to the challenges of imperial administration, it was designed to secure a peaceful transfer of power, since the two young "caesars" were being groomed to take the place of the two senior "augusti."

Diocletian apparently recognized that disputes over succession had been a fatal flaw of the Augustan system. Also unlike Augustus, who had cloaked the reality of his personal power in the trappings of the republic, Diocletian presented himself as an undisguised autocrat. His title was not *princeps* ("first man"), but *dominus* ("lord"). In fact, his style of imperial rule borrowed more from the Persian model than it did from the Roman. Gone were the days of republican simplicity and the scorn of kingly pomp. Diocletian wore a diadem and a purple gown of silk interwoven with gold, and he introduced Persian-style ceremonies at his court. Under the Principate, the emperor's palace had been run like the household of any well-to-do Roman, only on a large scale. Diocletian, however, remained physically removed behind a maze of doorways, rooms, and curtains. Those lucky enough to gain an audience with him had to prostrate themselves, while a privileged few could kiss his robe. Too much familiarity with their soldiers had bred contempt for the "barracks emperors." As a soldier-turned-emperor himself, Diocletian was able to avoid this mistake.

Although Diocletian retained close personal control over the army, he took steps to separate military from civilian chains of command; never again would Roman armies make and unmake emperors. To control the devastatingly high rates of inflation that were undermining the economy, Diocletian stabilized the currency and attempted to fix prices and wages. He reformed the tax system. He even moved the administrative center of the empire from Italy to Nicomedia in the Roman province of Bithynia (modern Turkey). Rome remained the symbolic capital of the empire, not least because the Senate continued to meet there. But Diocletian had little need for the Senate's advice. The real power lay elsewhere.

THE CONVERSION OF CHRISTIANITY

By the beginning of the fourth century, the number of Christians living within the jurisdiction of Rome was statistically insignificant, probably no more than 5 percent of the total population in the West and possibly 10 percent of the Greek-speaking East. Still, it was making an impact, and one of Diocletian's methods for promoting unity within the empire was to take a proactive stance against any group perceived as subversive. This meant reviving the policies of Decius and Valerian, but taking an even harder line. Those who could not show proof of their loyalty to Rome's gods were stripped

THE TETRARCHY: DIOCLETIAN AND HIS COLLEAGUES. This grouping, carved from a valuable purple stone called porphyry, shows the two augusti, Diocletian and Maximian, embracing their younger caesars, Galerius and Constantius. ▪ *Why do you think that these rulers are portrayed with identical facial features and military regalia?* ▪ *What message does this convey?*

of their rights as citizens. Christians who had been serving in the army or in government offices were dismissed. So were Manicheans, followers of the Persian prophet Mani (c. 216–276), whose teachings paralleled Zoroastrianism by positing an eternal struggle between the forces of good and evil. Indeed, Christianity and Manichaeism must have seemed very similar to outsiders, and both were implicated in a full-scale purge of religious dissidents in 303. This was the Great Persecution, a time when many Christians became martyrs—a Greek word meaning "witnesses"—to their faith.

Christianity and Neoplatonism

Ironically, the very crises that prompted Diocletian's Great Persecution were contributing to a growing interest in Christianity. Its message of social justice and equality before God was attractive to those suffering from the breakdown of political, economic, and social structures. It also appealed to followers of a new and influential philosophical system called Neoplatonism ("New Platonism"), which drew upon the more mystical aspects of Plato's thought (Chapter 4). Its founder was Plotinus (204–270 C.E.), a Hellenistic philosopher from Egypt who had many followers among the Roman upper classes.

Plotinus taught that everything has its source in a single supreme being. The material world, too, is part of this creation, but it is merely the residue of the divine, from which all spirituality has been drained. Human beings are thus composed of matter (bodies) and emanations of the divine (souls). This means that the individual soul, originally a part of God, is now separated from its divine source by the fact of its embodiment. The highest goal of life is therefore to attain spiritual reunion with the divine, through contemplation and acts of self-denial that will help to liberate the soul from its earthly bondage. Asceticism (from the Greek word meaning "exercise" or "training") was therefore a major focus. Plotinus and his followers believed that the body could be tamed by

DIOCLETIAN'S DIVISION OF THE EMPIRE, C. 304 C.E. ▪ *What areas did each of the four divisions of the empire cover?* ▪ *What seems to be the strategy behind the location of the four major capitals, both within their respective quarters and in relation to one another?* ▪ *What is the status of Rome itself, according to this map?*

fasting and other forms of self-denial and thus made a more fitting vessel for the soul.

Neoplatonism became so popular in Rome that it almost supplanted Stoicism. (Although the two philosophies shared some fundamental characteristics, Stoicism did not hold out the hope of union with the divine.) Neoplatonism also struck a blow at traditional Roman precepts, including the worship of ancestors and the devotion to the empire's gods. It was thus a natural ally of Christianity, and many important Christian theologians would be influenced by it, while many educated Romans found their way to Christianity because of it. This was not, however, the path by which Christianity's first imperial convert reached the new faith.

Constantine's Vision

In 305, Diocletian built a palace near his hometown of Split on the Adriatic coast and retired there to raise cabbages—the first time a Roman ruler had voluntarily removed himself from power since Sulla had resigned his dictatorship, nearly four hundred years earlier (see Chapter 5). Diocletian obliged Maximian to retire at the same time, and the two caesars Galerius and Constantius moved up the ladder of succession, becoming augusti of the East and West, respectively. But the transfer of power was not as orderly as Diocletian had intended. One of the candidates to fill the vacant post of caesar was Constantius's son, Constantine, who was being trained at Galerius's court. But he was passed over, perhaps so that Galerius could pursue his own imperial agenda. So Constantine left the court at Nicomedia and joined his father in Gaul. From there, father and son went to Britannia and campaigned on the northern borders until 306, when Constantius died and named Constantine as his successor. This infuriated Galerius, but with Constantine in control of a large army (the legions of Gaul and the Rhineland, as well as Britannia) he was forced to concede.

Meanwhile, war broke out among several other claimants to imperial authority, reducing Diocletian's tetrarchy to rivalry. Constantine remained aloof from this struggle, waged mostly in Italy, and concentrated on securing his quarter of the empire. Beginning around 310, he also began to promote himself as a favored devotee of the sun-god Sol Invictus, whose cult had been revived by the emperor Aurelian (r. 270–75). This was a smart move. Increasingly, the "Invincible Sun" was associated not only with the Roman gods of light and war, Apollo and Mars, but also with Mithras, whose cult was popular with soldiers. It was increasingly popular in Rome as well, where the feast long dedicated to the sky-god Saturn, the Saturnalia, was now being celebrated as the rebirth of the sun after the winter solstice, on December 25.

From the worship of Sol Invictus to the worship of Christ was, at least for Constantine, a small step (see **Interpreting**

Visual Evidence on page 194). In 312, Constantine decided to march on Italy, which was now in the hands of a man called Maxentius, who had declared himself emperor in the West and was trying to build up a coalition of supporters. Among them was the Christian community of Rome. It may have been this that gave Constantine the idea of currying favor in the same way, or it may have been another kind of inspiration that led him to emblazon Christian symbols on his banners and the shields of his soldiers the night before a major battle north of Rome, at the Milvian Bridge over the Tiber. According to later legend, Constantine had seen a vision of two intertwined Greek letters inscribed on the sky, the first two letters in the name of Christ, and was told that "In this sign, you will conquer." He did.

In gratitude for his victory, Constantine showered benefits on the Christian clergy of Rome and patronized the construction of churches throughout the empire. He also forced Licinius, the augustus of the East, to join him in promoting religious tolerance when they met at Milan in 313. Their Edict of Milan guaranteed freedom of worship to all Rome's citizens, Christian and non-Christian. But it was apparent that Christianity was the favored faith of the imperial family and thus the pathway for anyone with political ambitions. Almost overnight, then, Christians ceased to be members of an illegal and often despised cult and became affiliates of a prestigious and profitable religion, one that was suddenly attractive to the ruling classes. The entire basis of Christianity's appeal had changed.

From Illegal Sect to Imperial Institution

In his letters, Paul of Tarsus had addressed small Christian assemblies that he called churches (ekklesiae). Sometimes he had even spoken of the whole Christian community as a church. But it is doubtful that Paul could have imagined a day when representatives of an official Church could meet openly, or a time when his letters to separate churches in Corinth, Ephesus, Rome, and elsewhere would be gathered together in a single book.

Early Christianity had grown organically; it had not been designed as a religious system. It had no absolute teachings, apart from the words of Jesus reported in the Gospels, which do not always agree on those teachings. And not all Christian communities had access to the same scriptures. Some churches had a few of Paul's letters; others had none. Some had bishops, priests, deacons, and other officeholders; others had only a handful of believers. Some counted women as their leaders; others disapproved of women in authority. Some had come under the influence of

Interpreting Visual Evidence

The Power of the Invincible Sun

Roman emperors often linked their power with those of Rome's traditional gods, and they were also worshiped as gods in their own right. Look carefully at the following images and consider the visual language of power that came to be associated with Sol Invictus, "the Invincible Sun," and eventually with Jesus Christ.

Questions for Analysis

1. How did Constantine invoke the iconography of Sol Invictus (image A)? What messages does this image convey?

2. How might Constantine's use of this imagery—after his initial conversion to Christianity—have been interpreted by Christians? How might it have been interpreted by followers of Rome's other religions? Do you think it was designed to be ambiguous?

3. Scholars dispute both the dating and the significance of this mosaic found beneath St. Peter's Basilica in Rome (image B). Is it likely that this is a representation of Jesus as Sol Invictus? If not, how would you explain the later association of this pagan deity with the Christian God?

A. This gold medallion was issued by Constantine in 313, a year after his victory at the Battle of the Milvian Bridge. The legend calls him "Invincible Constantine."

B. This mosaic comes from a necropolis (cemetery) found beneath St. Peter's Basilica in Rome. Its precise dating is in dispute, but it was made sometime between the mid-third and mid-fourth century.

Neoplatonism or Manichaeism; others considered Neoplatonism and Manichaeism to be perversions.

In every respect, then, the Christianity that emerged after Constantine's conversion had to reinvent itself. Rituals and doctrines that had been formulated to suit the needs of small, scattered communities now had to be reconciled. Members of this new Church needed to agree on a shared set of beliefs. They needed a shared set of scriptures. They needed a chain of command. All of these fundamental structures had to be hammered out in a painful process that never quite managed to forge a common understanding. Historically speaking, this is hardly surprising. The varieties of Christianity had been too separate for too long, and they were the products of the same diversity that made the Roman Empire hard to govern. Indeed, the degree to which the Christians of the fourth century were able to agree on so many things is remarkable, given these challenges.

The Hierarchy of the Church

When it came to organization, Rome's imperial administration provided practical models. Because the empire's basic unit of governance was the city, the city became the basic

CONSTANTINE'S CHRISTIAN SYMBOL. This fourth-century fresco shows the chi-rho symbol that Constantine claimed to have seen in the sky before his victory at the Milvian Bridge. Chi and rho are the first two letters in the Greek word *Christos*. Flanking this monogram are the first and last letters of the Greek alphabet, alpha and omega, which also refer to Jesus, "the beginning" and "the end."

unit of ecclesiastical administration, too. Each major city now had a bishop who oversaw all the churches and also the rural areas of his diocese, a term borrowed from Diocletian's reorganization of the empire. Bishops of the largest cities were called *metropolitans*, and those who ruled over the oldest and most prestigious Christian communities were called *patriarchs*. These patriarchal cities also jockeyed for preeminence: among the main contenders were Rome, whose inhabitants longed to be at the center of the world again; Alexandria, the capital of the Hellenistic world; and Constantinople, a new city founded by Constantine on the Hellespont between Europe and Asia.

Which of these Roman cities should be the capital of the Roman Church? The patriarch of Rome's claim rested on several foundations. Rome had long been venerated as the place where both Peter and Paul were martyred. And according to one of the Gospels (Matthew 16:18–19), Jesus had designated Peter as his representative on earth. Peter's successors, the subsequent bishops of Rome, thus claimed to exercise the same powers. Rome's bishop also enjoyed some political advantages over other patriarchs. Unlike the bishop of the new imperial capital at Constantinople, he could act with more freedom because he didn't have to deal directly with the emperor. But as far as eastern bishops were concerned, the patriarch of Constantinople should be the one to exercise control over the entire Church. This division of opinion—the product of cultural differences and contemporary politics—would continue to affect the development of Christian institutions. In time, it would lead to a very real division within Christianity, one that has never been resolved.

Orthodoxy, Heresy, and Imperial Authority

Christianity's new prominence also raised the stakes of disputes over its basic teachings. While followers of Jesus had disagreed about such matters almost since the time of his death, these disagreements were of little political consequence so long as Christianity remained an illegal movement. Under Constantine, however, doctrinal disputes had the potential to ignite riots and to undermine the credibility of the emperor. It was imperative, therefore, that these disputes be resolved through active imperial intervention.

The most divisive theological issue of the early Church concerned the nature of God. Jesus had taught his followers that he was the Son of God and that after his death he would leave behind him a comforting spirit that would also be an emanation of God. Accordingly, many Christians believed that God encompassed a Trinity of equal persons: Father, Son, and Holy Spirit. But other Christians, influenced by Neoplatonism, rejected the idea that Jesus could be equal with God. Instead, they maintained that Jesus was part of God's creation and shared in his divine essence; but he was not equal to God, or eternal. This latter school of thought was called Arianism, after the Christian teacher Arius who espoused it. (It should not be confused with Aryanism, a modern racial concept.) After protracted struggles, Arianism was condemned as a heresy, a word that comes from the Greek verb meaning "to choose for oneself" and which became the Church's term for false beliefs punished with damnation. Yet many Christians continued to adhere to the Arian view.

This new emphasis on orthodoxy (Greek for "correct teaching") was another major consequence of Christianity's conversion. The beliefs of early Christians had been fairly simple: there is one God; Jesus is the anointed one who suffered and died for the sins of mankind and who was raised from the dead; in order to be saved, his followers must renounce sin. But beginning in the fourth century, Christian theology would become ever more complex. Christian intellectuals had to demonstrate that their beliefs could withstand intense philosophical scrutiny and that Christianity was superior to Hellenistic philosophy. Just as there were many different schools of Greek and Roman thought, so there arose many different interpretations of Christian doctrine. Before Christianity became a legal religion, any doctrinal disputes could only be addressed informally, by small groups of bishops meeting at local councils that had no power to enforce their decisions. In the fourth century, doctrinal disputes had real political consequences.

As a result, the Roman state became increasingly enmeshed in the governance of the Church. Constantine began this process in 325 C.E., when he summoned Christian representatives to the first ecumenical ("worldwide") meeting of the Christian community, the Council of Nicea, where Arianism was condemned and discrepancies over the canon of the Christian Bible were resolved. Constantine's successors carried this intervention much further. Gradually, they claimed to preside over Church councils as Christ's representatives on earth, which entitled them to decide what Christian doctrine should be. Some even violently suppressed Christian groups who refused to accept imperial mandates, labeled them heretical, and subjected them to ecclesiastical penalties—condemnation and excommunication from the Church—and to criminal penalties, too. Essentially, these imperial interventions were an extension of Augustan policies, which had made the emperor *pontifex maximus*, Rome's high priest. In the fourth century, it began to look as though this trend would continue, and that secular and spiritual authority would be combined in the person of the emperor. But this would change in later centuries, as we shall see.

New Attitudes toward Women and the Body

Women were conspicuously absent from the new hierarchy of the Church and were also barred from the decision-making process at Nicea. Even though they had long been deacons and may even have performed priestly duties, women were now firmly and completely excluded from any position of power.

This was an enormous change, more fundamentally so than any other aspect of Christianity's conversion. Jesus had included many women among his close followers, yet one of the early gospels now rejected from the biblical canon was ascribed to Mary Magdalene. Paul had relied on women to organize and preside over churches and to finance his missionary journeys; he had declared in one letter (Galatians 3:28) that there should be no distinctions of gender, rank, or ethnicity among Christians. Women had been leaders of many early churches. Women like Perpetua were prominent among the martyrs and were often regarded as prophets. These strong roles had always been

controversial because they set Christianity apart from the traditional values of Roman society. But that had also been one of Christianity's main attractions.

What accounts for this drastic change? Three factors can be clearly identified. When Christianity was absorbed into the staunch patriarchy of Rome, it could no longer promote the authority of women effectively. As the Church came to mirror the imperial administration, it replicated the structures of governance that had been the province of men since the founding of the republic. The Church now had the capacity to exclude or censor writings that represented women as the companions of Jesus and founders of the religion based on his teachings. These efforts were so successful that it was not until the very end of the nineteenth century that a gospel attributed to Mary Magdalene (among other writings) was known to exist.

The second factor leading to the marginalization of women was the growing identification of Christianity with Roman cults that emphasized masculinity, particularly the worship of Sol Invictus and the soldier-god Mithras. This was a deliberate strategy on the part of the Church. It is easier to convert people to a new religion if that religion is not wholly new, and embraces elements of other religions. In common with these two cults, as well as with many of the other religions we have studied (like the worship of Osiris in Egypt), Christianity emphasized the heroic suffering and death of a male god and his eventual victory over death itself. Christ was increasingly identified with Sol Invictus and his birthday came to be celebrated on December 25, which marked the passing of the winter solstice and the return of lengthening days.

The third factor contributing to women's exclusion from power was the Christian emphasis on asceticism ("self-denial"), which changed attitudes toward the body. As we noted above, Neoplatonism taught that the goal of life was to liberate the soul from the tyranny of bodily desires, a teaching that it shared with Stoicism. None of this was emphasized in the teachings of Christ. Quite the contrary: the body was celebrated as God's creation, and Christ himself had encouraged feasting, touching, bathing, and marriage. His followers insisted that he had been bodily resurrected, and that the bodies of all the faithful would be resurrected, too. Although early Christians had to be willing to sacrifice their lives for their faith, if need be, they were not required to renounce pleasures.

After Christianity became legal, however, there were few opportunities to "bear witness" to the faith through martyrdom. Instead, some Christians began to practice asceticism as an alternative path to sanctity. This meant renunciation of the flesh, especially sex and eating, activities both associated with women, who were in charge of

Past and Present

Resisting Imperialism

 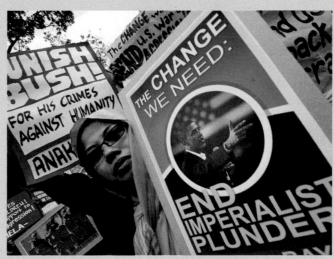

Attempts at conquest are always met with resistance. In the Roman province of Britannia, a Celtic warrior queen named Boadicea led an armed uprising against the imperial army that is still celebrated as a proud example of British independence—as this modern statue in London indicates. A more peaceful uprising against American imperialism took place in Manila on the eve of President Barack Obama's first inauguration in 2008.

 Watch related author interview on StudySpace
wwnorton.com/web/westernciv18

any household's food supply and who were (obviously) sexual partners. A new spiritual movement called monasticism also took hold, providing an alternative lifestyle for men who wanted to reject the world entirely; the word for this movement comes from the Greek word *monos*, "alone." Early monks lived as hermits and practiced extraordinary feats of self-abasement. Some grazed in the fields like cows; others penned themselves into small cages; still others hung heavy weights around their necks. A monk named Cyriacus would stand for hours on one leg, like a crane. Another, Simeon "the Stylite," lived on top of a high pillar for thirty-seven years, punishing his lice-infested flesh while crowds gathered below to marvel.

This extreme denial of the body was a departure not only from most previous Christian practices but from the practices of many civilizations up to this point—not to mention the realities of human existence. Ancient religions often celebrated sexuality as a delight, as well as a necessity.

Even Roman religion had a place for priestesses and female prophets. Moreover, marriage was so important a marker of social respectability that unmarried men were objects of deep suspicion. Furthermore, Romans had regarded citizens' bodies as being at the service of the state: men as soldiers and fathers, women as mothers and wives. Now, however, some Christians were asserting that their bodies belonged not to the state but to God, and that to serve God fully meant no longer serving the state—or posterity—by bearing children.

Virginity for both men and women was accordingly preached as the highest spiritual standard, with celibacy for those who had once been married valued almost as highly. Marriage remained acceptable for average people, the laity, but was often represented as a second-best option whose purpose was to prevent weak-minded people from being consumed by desire. Moreover, because pseudo-scientific theories stemming back to Aristotle posited that women were inherently more lustful than men, the denigration of sexuality had a disproportionately negative effect on attitudes toward women.

Christians and Pagans

The urban focus of Christianity is reflected in the Latin word referring to a non-Christian: *paganus*, meaning someone who lives in the countryside. The implication is that only someone with a hopelessly rustic outlook would cling to the old Roman religion and so spoil his chances of advancement in society. As Christians came to occupy positions of power within the empire, men with political ambitions were increasingly forced to convert—or at least conform—to Christian norms.

Constantine had retained both pagan and Christian officials in his court, and was careful to speak in terms that embraced a non-Christian audience. But his successors were less inclined to tolerate competing faiths. An interesting exception was Julian "the Apostate" (r. 360–63), Constantine's nephew, who abandoned Christianity and attempted to revive traditional Roman piety. But when Julian was killed in a battle with the Persians, his pro-pagan edicts were allowed to lapse. By 391, the emperor Theodosius (r. 379–95 C.E.) had prohibited pagan worship of any sort within the empire. This meant that within three generations, Christianity had gone from being a persecuted faith to a persecuting religion. Theodosius even removed the sacred altar of the goddess Victory from the Senate chamber in Rome, prompting pagan loyalists to prophesy the end of the empire. Fifteen years later, Rome fell to a barbarian army.

SHIFTING CENTERS AND MOVING FRONTIERS

In 324, Constantine broke ground for the capital city he named after himself. It was built on the site of a settlement called Byzantium, chosen for its strategic location at the mouth of the Black Sea and at the crossroads between Europe and Asia: the Hellespont (literally "the bridge to Greece"). This site gave Constantinople commanding advantages as a center for communications and trade. It also made the city readily defensible, because it was surrounded on three sides by water and protected on land by walls. It would remain the political and economic center of the Roman Empire until 1453, when the city was conquered by the Ottoman Turks (see Chapter 11).

East or West?

The founding of Constantinople epitomizes the shift in Rome's center of gravity from Italy and western Europe to the eastern Mediterranean. It also signaled Constantine's intention to abandon the political precedents set by Diocletian, including the institution of the tetrarchy. Instead, the imperial succession became hereditary. Constantine thus embraced a principle of dynastic monarchy that Romans had rejected 800 years earlier. Even more ominously, he divided

SAINT SIMEON THE STYLITE. This gold plaque dating from the sixth century depicts the exertions of the ascetic saint who defied the devil (shown as a huge snake) by abusing his own body. Admirers wishing to speak to the saint could climb the ladder shown on the left. ▪ *What do you make of the relationship between the luxurious medium of this image (gold) and the message it conveys?*

the empire among his three sons. Civil war ensued, made more bitter because each of these men represented a different faction within the Christian Church. In the meantime, the empire became more and more fragmented. The last ruler who could claim to govern a united Rome was the same Theodosius who outlawed its venerable religion. Then he, too, divided the empire between his sons.

As we have seen, there had always been linguistic and cultural differences between the Greek- and Latin-speaking peoples under Roman rule. Now, however, these differences became heightened. The eastern empire was becoming more populous, more prosperous, and more central to imperial policy; the western provinces were becoming poorer and more peripheral. Many western cities now relied on transfers of funds from their eastern counterparts, and they suffered when these funds dried up, when trade or communication failed, or when Roman legions were transferred elsewhere. Rome itself, which had been demoted to provincial status under Diocletian, now lost even that nominal position: the Italian city of Ravenna on the Adriatic coast became the new capital of the region and a more convenient stopping place for emperors and ambassadors traveling from Constantinople to the administrative centers of Milan and Trier. Only two of Constantine's successors ever visited Rome itself, and none of them lived there.

Internal and External Pressures

The shifting center of the empire and the widening gap between the eastern and western provinces were not the only fault lines emerging in this period. There were secessionist movements among many residents of Britannia, Gaul, Hispania, and Germania. The residents of Egypt were particularly affected by high levels of taxation, which targeted their rich agricultural lands. Meanwhile, North Africans and other citizens living in the empire's interior regions were increasingly ignored by authorities. Italians resented their new status as provincial subjects of Constantinople. Beneath the surface of imperial autocracy, the fourth-century empire was slowly dissolving into its constituent parts.

The empire was also coming under renewed pressure from its borders. Since the third century, the growing power of a new Persian dynasty, the Sassanids, had prompted a shift of Roman military weight to the eastern frontier, reducing the number of troops stationed elsewhere. Partly as a result of this, the northwestern territories suffered a devastating series of raids along the porous frontier of Germania. During the fourth century, relations between assimilated Romans and their barbarian neighbors were generally peaceful. But starting in the early fifth century, a new wave of settlers moved into the empire's oldest provinces, permanently altering their histories and cultures.

From the Periphery to the Center

In the eyes of many Romans, the tribes that lived along the empire's northern frontiers were barbarians in the pure sense of that (Greek) term: they did not speak either of the empire's civilized languages and they did not live in cities. But in no sense were they savage peoples. They were sophisticated agriculturalists and metalworkers who had enjoyed trading relationships with the Roman world for centuries. Many had been settled within Roman provinces for generations as farmers and craftsmen. Legionnaires from the hinterlands of Germania were core components in Roman armies. In some frontier areas, entire tribes had become Roman *foederati*: allied troops who reinforced Roman garrisons or took their places when legions were withdrawn. By the end of the fourth century, many of these tribes had even adopted the form of Christianity preached by disciples of Arius. Although this made them heretics from the perspective of the institutional Church, it also tied them more closely to Roman civilization. One general of mixed descent, Flavius Stilicho (359–408), was the military leader of the western empire under Theodosius.

What altered this relatively peaceful coexistence? Our study of many previous civilizations has prepared us to answer this question: the arrival of new peoples and the subsequent struggle for land and resources. During the mid-fourth century, a group of nomadic herdsmen known as the Huns began to migrate westward from central Asia, into the region north and east of the Black Sea. Around 370, their arrival forced a number of other groups, notably the Goths, to migrate south and west—and in a hurry. Within a few years, they had reached the Roman frontier along the Danube River. The Goths had been clients of the Roman state for several centuries. But now they were refugees and too numerous and too desperate to repel by force. The Romans therefore permitted them to cross the Danube and settle within the empire. In return for food and other supplies, they were to guard the region against other migrant groups.

Local officials, however, failed to uphold their end of the bargain. Instead, they forced the starving Goths to sell themselves and their children into slavery in return for food. In 378, the Goths revolted and the Roman army sent to suppress them was defeated at the battle of Adrianople. Peace was restored by accommodating the Goths' demands for goods and farmland and by enrolling them in the Roman army under their own military leaders. But when Theodosius divided the

A Senator Defends the Traditional Religion of Rome

In 382, the Emperor Theodosius ordered the removal of the ancient altar dedicated to the goddess of Victory (Nike) from the Senate chamber in Rome, as part of his efforts to make Christianity the dominant religion in the empire. This controversial move sparked heated debate and elicited strong protests from Rome's senatorial elites. The following statement of their case was made by Quintus Aurelius Symmachus (c. 345–402), who was at that time prefect of the city of Rome. It is principally addressed to the young western emperor, Valentinian.

o what is it more suitable that we defend the institutions of our ancestors, and the rights and destiny of our country . . . than to the glory of these times, which is all the greater when you understand that you may not do anything contrary to the custom of your ancestors? We demand then the restoration of that condition of religious affairs which was so long advantageous to the state. . . . Who is so friendly with the barbarians as not to require an Altar of Victory? . . . But even if the avoidance of such an omen were not sufficient, it would at least have been seemly to abstain from injuring the ornaments of the Senate House. Allow us, we beseech you, as old men to leave to posterity what we received as boys. The love of custom is great. . . . Where shall we swear to obey your laws and commands? By what religious sanction shall the false mind be terrified, so as not to lie in bearing witness? All things are indeed filled with God, and no place is safe for the perjured, but to be urged in the very presence of religious forms has great power in producing a fear of sinning. That altar preserves the concord of all, that altar appeals to the good faith of each, and nothing gives more authority to our decrees than that the whole of our order issues every decree as it were under the sanction of an oath. . . .

Let us now suppose that Rome is present and addresses you in these words: "Excellent princes, fathers of your country, respect my years to which pious rites have brought me. Let me use the ancestral ceremonies, for I do not repent of them. Let me live after my own fashion, for I am free. This worship subdued the world to my laws, these sacred rites repelled Hannibal from the walls, and the Senones [Gauls] from the capitol. Have I been reserved for this, that in my old age I should be blamed? I will consider what it is thought should be set in order, but tardy and discreditable is the reformation of old age." We ask, then, for peace for the gods of our fathers and of our country. It is just that all worship should be considered as one. We look on the same stars, the sky is common, the same world surrounds us. What difference does it make by what pains each seeks the truth? We cannot attain to so great a secret by one road; but this discussion is rather for persons at ease, we offer now prayers, not conflict.

Source: Excerpted from *A Select Library of the Nicene and Post-Nicene Fathers,* 2nd Series, Vol. X, (New York: 1896), pp. 411–14.

Questions for Analysis

1. How does Symmachus's defense exemplify the traditional values of the Roman Republic?

2. How does Symmachus justify the coexistence of Christianity and Rome's state religion? How would a Christian refute his position?

3. Less than a decade after the altar's removal, Theodosius outlawed all religions but Christianity. Based on your reading of this letter, how would that edict have affected Romans like Symmachus?

empire between his two young sons, their military advisers—including Stilicho, father-in-law of the emperor Honorius, the de facto ruler—constantly undermined one another. This provided an opening for Alaric, a young leader of the Goths, to advance his own agenda. Targeting the wealthier eastern provinces, he led his army into Greece, looting or capturing many ancient cities, including Athens.

In a desperate attempt to halt these incursions, Alaric was offered a Roman military command and encouraged to move into Italy: meaning that the price of peace in the eastern empire was Rome itself. Meanwhile, the Huns had arrived in the region corresponding to modern-day Hungary, forcing several other peoples westward toward the Rhine. On New Year's Eve in the year 406, a people known as the Vandals crossed the frozen Rhine and invaded Gaul. To repulse them, Stilicho (whose own father had been a Vandal) made an alliance with Alaric and his Goths. But Stilicho fell from imperial favor just a few months later, and the imperial government could no longer exercise any restraint on Alaric's actions.

Like Stilicho, Alaric seems to have wanted to win a permanent place for himself in the imperial hierarchy. But unlike Stilicho—and many Roman generals before him—he did not understand how to use violence as a means toward that end. His assault on Rome did not make him Rome's conqueror, it made him its destroyer. In 410, after a protracted period of siege, Alaric's army captured and sacked the city. But by now, Rome had little to offer in the way of either food or spoils. So many of the Goths moved on, eventually settling in southern Gaul and Hispania, where they established what came to be known as the Visigothic kingdom. Others, later labeled as the Ostrogoths, remained in Italy. The Vandals set out for the Iberian Peninsula, too, but ultimately crossed the Strait of Gibraltar to settle in North Africa. Other tribes, including the Franks and the Burgundians, followed the Vandals across the Rhine into Gaul and established kingdoms of their own.

A generation later the Huns—whose migrations had set all of these gears in motion—themselves invaded Roman territory under the leadership of their warlord, Attila. Britannia, meanwhile, had been abandoned by its remaining legions which were hastily withdrawn in 410. There, a mixed population of Romans and Celts eventually intermingled with invaders from northwestern Germania and Scandinavia: Angles, Saxons, and Jutes. These tribes were so efficient that they dominated all but the westernmost and northern portions of the island within a few generations. Many Celts retreated to the regions where Celtic languages are still spoken today, including Wales and Scotland. The rest of Britain would become Angle-land: England.

The last western Roman emperor was an ineffectual usurper derisively known as Romulus Augustulus ("Little Romulus Augustus"). In 476, he was deposed by Odovacar, a chieftain who headed a mixed band of barbarians, Huns, and disgruntled Romans. Viewed from the perspective of Constantinople, this event was decisive: now it was not only "New Rome," it was the only viable capital. And the best way for its imperial agenda to be carried forward in the western provinces was through a strong barbarian ruler. Luckily, the emperor Zeno (r. 474–91) knew just the man: Theodoric, the son of a Gothic king, who had been sent to Constantinople as a hostage and raised in the civilized surroundings of the imperial court. After a decade of fierce fighting, Theodoric and his imperially equipped Gothic army managed to drive the Huns from Italy and establish a kingdom based in Ravenna, which he ruled (with imperial support) until his death in 526.

The Impact of the Fifth-Century Migrations

The events of the fifth century widened the porousness of the empire's northern frontiers and penetrated to its core provinces: Italy, Gaul, Hispania, North Africa. Yet the groups that moved through these territories were small. They were joined by refugees and desperados, but they were never more than war bands. So why couldn't long-established imperial cities sustain themselves?

By the beginning of the fifth century, many Roman armies were already weakened. The best legions had been withdrawn from frontier provinces to protect richer eastern ones. Those that remained tended to be integrated into local civilian populations, staffed by married men who grew their own food and lived with their families, making it difficult to move troops even in an emergency. Furthermore, there was no mechanism for increasing the revenues needed to support the army. And even if the citizens of Rome's western provinces had been able to maintain a crack fighting force on the frontier, there would have been little reason for them to think that such expenditure was necessary. Their "barbarian" neighbors hadn't seemed threatening for generations. Many were so Romanized that differences between the groups are difficult to detect in surviving archaeological evidence.

In the eastern Roman Empire, by contrast, a thriving economy made it easier to equip and maintain a strong fighting force. Cities remained centers of commerce and industry,

THEODORIC THE OSTROGOTH. This coin shows the king in Roman dress but with the long hair characteristic of a barbarian nobleman. The inscription reads *Rex Theodericvs pivs princis*, "King Theodoric, pious prince." ▪ *How does this image compare to that of Constantine (see page 194)?*

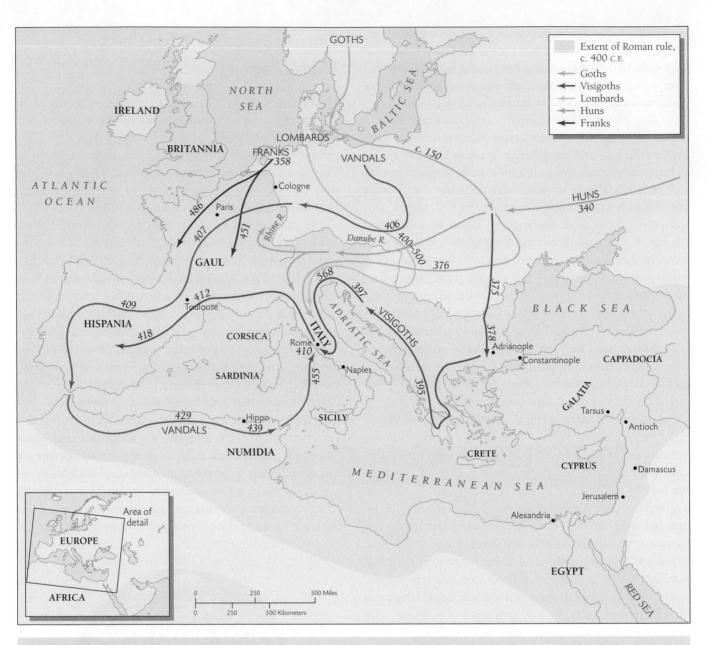

THE MIGRATIONS OF ROME'S FRONTIER PEOPLES. ▪ *What do the routes followed by these different peoples suggest about their destinations and motives?* ▪ *Why did so many converge on Rome, even though the city was no longer the capital even of the western Roman Empire?* ▪ *Why did the Romans refer to them as "barbarians"?*

which meant that citizens possessed greater taxable wealth and could sustain the burdens of the imperial bureaucracy more easily. Moreover, potential invaders could be bought off or bribed to direct their attention elsewhere—as Alaric had been. For all these reasons, the eastern empire prospered during the fifth century, while the western empire floundered. After the fifth-century migrations, these differences were exacerbated. Every territory that was plundered or occupied represented tax revenues lost, and the scale of these losses was enormous. Ten years after the Goths sacked Rome, the area was capable of producing only 15 percent of

the revenues it had generated in 407. Similar reductions in revenues resulted from attacks on Gaul and Hispania. After 420 or so, as the newcomers began to set up their own kingdoms, these areas ceased to pay any taxes at all to imperial authorities. When the Vandals captured North Africa in 439, the richest of all Rome's western provinces was lost.

The consequences of these structural changes were far-reaching. In the year 400, the economy of the western Roman Empire was characterized by the mass production of low-cost, high-quality consumer goods that circulated in massive quantities. Although regional and local systems of exchange continued after 500, long-distance trade in bulk goods could be sustained only in the Mediterranean. As markets disappeared in northwestern provinces, skilled artisans had to find other ways to make a living, or had to emigrate. Standards of living gradually declined, and so did the overall population. Indeed, it is likely that the population of western Europe did not return to its fourth-century levels for a thousand years, until just before the Black Death (see Chapter 10).

Other aspects of Roman life in these regions changed, too, but almost imperceptibly. Roman bureaucracies often survived, although the proceeds from taxes now went into the purses of the new barbarian rulers or Christian bishops. Roman agricultural patterns continued in most areas, frequently under the same landlords. Local Roman elites continued to dominate civic life, and Roman cities continued to dominate their surrounding regions, especially in southern Gaul and Hispania. Nor did the invasions bring an end to Roman culture or to the influence of Roman values. As King Theodoric the Goth was fond of remarking: "An able Goth wishes to be like a Roman; but only a poor Roman would want to be like a Goth."

THE SHAPING OF A NEW WORLDVIEW

Throughout this time of change, Christian intellectuals were formulating a new outlook on the world that would remain dominant for over a thousand years. As the empire sustained attack from external forces and began to fragment along old fault lines, it seemed clearer than ever that a new age was beginning. Christ had promised to come again at the end of time, when all human souls would be judged. How, then, should Christians live in this new world and prepare for that imminent event? The men who forged answers to this question were contemporaries who knew and influenced one another, though they did not always agree. They are now regarded as saints and "fathers" of the Church: Jerome (c. 340–420), who came from the northeastern edge of Italy, near the port of Aquilea; Ambrose (c. 340–397), who grew up in Trier and was eventually named bishop of Milan; and Augustine (354–430), born and raised in North Africa, where he became a bishop in later life.

Jerome: Translating the Christian Message

Jerome's signal contribution to the culture of the Roman West was his translation of the Bible from Hebrew and Greek into Latin. Known as the Vulgate or "common" version, it was not the first attempt to produce a Latin Bible—but it quickly became the standard, and remained so until the sixteenth century (see Chapter 13). Jerome's translation is vigorous, colloquial, and clear; its powerful prose and poetry would influence Latin authors for centuries. Jerome was also an influential commentator on the Bible's interpretation, encouraging readings that emphasized a passage's symbolic or allegorical significance, as well as its literal or historical meaning.

Jerome was not a notably original thinker, but he was an eloquent and effective translator of others' ideas as well as of others' words. He was among the first to argue that pagan learning could and should be studied by Christians as long as it was thoroughly adapted to Christian aims. The perennial problem, of course, was that one was always tempted to appreciate classical literature for its own sake, and not for the light it shed on Christian truths. Jerome himself never succeeded in subordinating his love for classical authors, especially Cicero, to his love for God. He liked to tell a story about a dream he'd experienced, in which he arrived at the gates of heaven and was asked by God if he was a Christian. When he replied that he was, God retorted, "You're not a Christian; you're a Ciceronian." Perhaps in an effort to compensate for this, Jerome became a rigorous ascetic and a fervent promoter of monasticism. He also held a narrow view of women's roles that exercised a strong influence on some later Christian teachers.

Ambrose and the Authority of the Church

Jerome was primarily a scholar. Ambrose, by contrast, was an aristocrat and man of the world who helped to define the relationship between the sacred authority of the Church and the secular authority of worldly rulers. As patriarch of the imperial administrative capital at Milan, he fearlessly rebuked the pious emperor Theodosius for a mismanaged massacre of innocent civilians in the Greek city of Thessalonian. Theodosius may have been the emperor, but until he did penance for his sins Ambrose refused to admit him into his church. On matters of faith, he declared, "The emperor is within the Church, not above the Church." Eventually, Theodosius capitulated and begged forgiveness of God's representative, Ambrose, in his cathedral at Milan.

Ambrose was also an admirer of Cicero—but because of his Stoicism, not his prose. He wrote an ethics handbook, *On the Duties of Ministers*, which drew heavily on Cicero's treatise *On Duties*, written nearly four centuries earlier for the senatorial elite of the Roman republic. Unlike Cicero, however, Ambrose argued that the motive and goal of human conduct should be reverence for God, not social or political advancement. Even more fundamentally, Ambrose argued that God assists all Christians by sharing with them the power of divine grace, but extends more grace to some Christians than to others. Ambrose's emphasis on the necessity and mystery of grace (Why does God give more grace to some than to others?) would be refined and amplified by his disciple, Augustine.

The Salvation of Saint Augustine

Apart from Jesus, Augustine is often considered the greatest of all Christianity's founders. He may be the most important Christian thinker of all time. His theology is essential to the doctrine of the medieval Church and thus to modern Catholicism, and it also had a profound effect on Martin Luther and on the development of Protestant Christianities (see Chapter 13). In our own twenty-first century, many Christian philosophers of various denominations describe themselves as neo-Augustinians.

Augustine's understanding of Christianity was the result of a long process of self-discovery, which he described in a remarkable book, the *Confessions*, a series of autobiographical reflections addressed to God. Augustine was not, as Jerome and Ambrose were, a confident Christian from the cradle. His father was not a Christian, and although his mother was, he scorned her influence and refused baptism. Full of ambition and eager to make his mark, he left North Africa for Italy as a young man, winning early fame as a teacher and charismatic orator. All the while, he gravitated from one philosophical system to another without finding intellectual or spiritual satisfaction. He regarded Christianity as a religion for fools, and only his increasing doubts about the alternatives (notably Manichaeism) and the appeal of Ambrose's teachings drove him to enquire further. After a spiritual epiphany described in his *Confessions*, Augustine decided to embrace Christianity at the significant age of thirty-three (the age when Jesus died). Yet his struggle to grasp and explain its paradoxes occupied him for the rest of his life. His skills as a preacher and commentator led to his rapid advancement in the Church hierarchy, and he returned to North Africa as the bishop of Hippo Regis in 395.

Although he led an extremely active life—when he died in 430, he was defending Hippo against the Vandals—Augustine still found time to write more than a hundred profound, complex, and powerful treatises analyzing the problems of Christian belief. All of these grapple with a basic question: if humanity is the creation of an omnipotent God whose nature is entirely good, why are human beings so profoundly sinful? Augustine was convinced of humans' innate capacity for evil, and he believed this tendency was evident even in babies. He adduced himself as a supreme example. In the *Confessions*, he remembers that he and a few other boys once stole some pears from a neighbor's garden, not because they were hungry or even because the pears were beautiful, but simply for the sake of doing something bad. He also recounted his many sexual adventures as a young man and recalled that rather than asking God's help in suppressing his desires he prayed, "O God, give me chastity—but not just now!" In short, he argued that the human inclination toward evil is innate. But how, if we are the creatures of a good God?

Augustine traced the origin of evil back to the Garden of Eden, where God had given Adam and Eve, the first human couple, the freedom either to follow his will or their own. Thereafter, God simply left Adam and Eve's descendants to do the same, by withdrawing from human beings the divine power (grace) by which they might overcome their own wills in order to follow his. All the evils that plague the world are thus the result of the human propensity to place one's own desires ahead of God's. This fact alone would justify God's condemnation of all mankind. But because God is merciful, he chose instead to save some human beings through the sacrifice of his son, Jesus.

Why only some? Because human beings are inherently sinful, Augustine reasoned, they cannot achieve salvation on their own; they need to be led to accept Jesus by an act of God's grace—hence the power of Augustine's own transformative experience, which led him to embrace Christianity *against his own will* but in accordance with God's. God alone makes this choice, and by granting grace to some and not to others he predestines a portion of the human race to salvation and sentences the rest to be damned. If this seems unfair, Augustine would answer that strict fairness would condemn everyone to hell. Moreover, he would say that the basis for God's choice is a mystery shrouded in his omnipotence—far beyond the realm of human comprehension.

Defending the City of God

Augustine's audience consisted of converted Christians and intelligent skeptics like himself. And after the sack of Rome in 410, he knew that some staunchly traditional Romans blamed Christianity for it. According to them, the attack on their city was the consequence of gross impiety, exemplified by the removal of the altar of Victory from the Senate chamber. In response, Augustine wrote one of his most famous works, *On the City of God*, a new interpretation of human history. He argued that mankind has always been divided into two opposing societies: those who live for the world and those who seek eternal life. The former belong to the City of Man, and their rewards are the riches, fame, and power they may win on earth, all of which are tainted by sin. Only those predestined to salvation, members of the City of God, will be saved on Judgment Day.

Although Augustine is the architect of much Christian theology, he believed that he was doing no more than drawing out truths from the Bible. But he also knew that many biblical texts are obscure and that a certain amount of education is needed to understand them. In consequence, he approved of some Christians' acquiring a classical education, as he himself had done, as long as they directed their learning toward its proper end: the study of the Bible. Along with Jerome, Augustine thus formulated the rationale for Christianity's preservation of the pagan past.

CLASSICAL LEARNING AND THE CHRISTIAN LIFE

Jerome, Ambrose, and Augustine were members of the first generation to grow up in a world where Christianity was legal, even normal. For three centuries there had been no such thing as a Roman Christian: this was a contradiction in terms. Now, however, many Romans *were* Christians. How could these identities be reconciled? As we have seen, none of these influential teachers wanted to discard the heritage of the past. But for all of them it posed serious challenges. Many new converts thought they could embrace both Christian and pagan beliefs simultaneously—and why not? Since the time of Socrates, philosophy had been characterized by its capacity to absorb and blend many competing ideas. Christian intellectuals wanted to be regarded as philosophers, but they also wanted to replace the doctrines of pagan philosophy with the doctrine of Christ. To do this, they needed to make classical learning applicable to a Christian way of life.

Preserving and Recycling the Classics

Reinterpreting classical culture for a Christian audience involved careful selection, something made easier by the fact that a gradual winnowing of Greek texts had already occurred in Alexandria and continued in Rome. Roman readers had little interest in the scientific works of an earlier age, and by the third century many extraordinary advances made by Hellenistic scientists (see Chapter 4) were ignored, simplified, or suppressed by popular authors like Galen and

THE CITY OF MAN. This image illustrating a late-medieval manuscript of Augustine's *City of God* displays the violence that characterizes the City of Man by showcasing one example from the Old Testament and another from Roman mythology: Cain kills his brother, Abel, while Romulus murders his brother, Remus. Its message is that all human forms of government are the product of human sin.

Ptolemy. Nor did the Romans have much interest in Greek philosophy, drama, or epic. Later Roman tastes ran toward comedies, novels, and pastiches of Latin classics. One favorite pastime consisted of rearranging the verses of Virgil's *Aeneid* so that they described sexual exploits. Christians, too, could play at this game. In the fourth century, Faltonia Betitia Proba (c. 322–c. 370), the wife of a Roman senator, used Virgil's poetry to replace Aeneas with Christ.

Those pagan authors whose works were most immediately useful to Christians, like Cicero and Virgil, therefore enjoyed continued celebrity. Those texts that had long educated students in the liberal arts were also preserved, alongside major classics of Latin poetry as well as histories that recorded the errors of Rome's pagan past. But texts that could not be readily adapted to Christian purposes were subjected to careful editing. One of the men who undertook this task was Anicius Manlius Severinus Boethius (*boh-EE-thee-uhs*, c. 480–524), an aristocrat attached to the court of Theodoric. He is often described as the "last of the Romans," and his goal was to preserve the best aspects of ancient learning by compiling a series of handbooks and anthologies which packaged and explained classical texts in ways appropriate for Christian readers.

Roman or Barbarian?

These two letters from Sidonius Apollinaris (c. 430–c. 480) illustrate the ways in which cultural assimilation was rapidly blurring the distinctions between "Roman" and "barbarian" in the West. Sidonius was himself the descendant of an illustrious Roman provincial family in Gaul. He was one of the most admired Latin stylists of his day, and although he eventually became a bishop and was regarded as a saint, his letter collection (from which these extracts are taken) tells us much more about the literary culture of Romano-Visigothic Gaul than it does about his Christianity. His two correspondents also exemplify this new hybrid culture. Arbogastes (ahr-go-BAHS-tees) was the Frankish governor of the Roman city of Trier (in what is now Germany). Syagrius (sigh-AG-ree-uhs) was from an ancient Roman family and became, effectively, the king of a large region now corresponding to northern France and Belgium.

Letter 4:17: Sidonius to his Friend Arbogastes

y honored Lord, your friend Eminentius has handed me a letter written by your own hand, a really literary letter, replete with the grace of a three-fold charm. The first of its merits is certainly the affection which prompted such condescension to my lowly condition, for if not a stranger I am in these days a man who courts obscurity; the second virtue is your modesty. . . . In the third place comes your urbanity, which leads you to make a most amusing profession of clumsiness, when as a matter of fact you have drunk deep from the spring of Roman eloquence and, dwelling by the Moselle, you speak the true Latin of the Tiber: you are intimate with the barbarians but are innocent of barbarisms, and are equal in tongue, as also in strength of arm, to the leaders of old, I mean those who were wont to handle the pen no less than the sword. Thus the splendor of the Roman speech, if it still exists anywhere, has survived in you, though it has long been wiped out from the Belgian and Rhenic lands: with you and your eloquence surviving, even though Roman law has ceased at our border, the Roman speech does not falter. For this reason . . . I rejoice greatly that at any rate in your illustrious breast there have remained traces of our vanishing culture. If you extend these by constant reading you will discover for yourself as each day passes that the educated are no less superior to the unlettered than men are to beasts.

Boethius devoted special attention to logic, translating several of Aristotle's treatises from Greek into Latin. Because Roman philosophers had never been much interested in logic, Boethius thus forged a crucial link between classical Greek thought and the new intellectual culture of Christianity. This is most evident in *The Consolation of Philosophy*, which he wrote in prison after Theodoric condemned him to death for treason. (The justice of the charge is unclear.) In this treatise, Boethius concludes that happiness is not found in earthly rewards such as riches or fame but in the "highest good," which is God. Yet he comes to this realization not through any reference to Christian revelation but through a series of imaginary conversations with "Lady Philosophy," the embodiment of wisdom. For the next millennium, Boethius's *Consolation* was one of the most read and imitated books in the West: the ultimate example of classical philosophy's absorption into the Christian worldview.

Monastic Education

The vital work of preserving selected classics and interpreting their meaning was increasingly done by monks, whose way of life had undergone some significant changes during the fourth century. Leaders of the monastic movement recognized that few men were capable of ascetic feats, and some disapproved of such showmanship. Rather, they advocated a more moderate approach and emphasized the benefits of communal life. In the Roman East, the most important figure in this new monasticism was Basil of Caesarea (c. 330–379). Basil's guidelines prohibited monks from engaging in prolonged fasts or extreme discipline of the flesh. Instead, he encouraged useful work and silent meditation.

In the Roman West, the most influential proponent of the monastic movement was a contemporary of Boethius,

Letter 5:5: Sidonius to his Friend Syagrius

ou are the great-grandson of a consul, and in the male line too—although that has little to do with the case before us; I say, then, you are descended from a poet, to whom his literary glory would have brought status had not his magisterial glories done so . . . and the culture of his successors has not declined one whit from his standard, particularly in this respect. I am therefore inexpressibly amazed that you have quickly acquired a knowledge of the German tongue with such ease.

And yet I remember that your boyhood had a good schooling in liberal studies and I know for certain that you often declaimed with spirit and eloquence before your professor of oratory. This being so, I should like you to tell me how you managed to absorb so swiftly into your inner being the exact sounds of an alien race, so that now after reading Virgil under the schoolmaster's cane and toiling and working the rich fluency of [Cicero] . . . you burst forth before my eyes like a young falcon from an old nest.

You have no idea what amusement it gives me, and others too, when I hear that in your presence the barbarian is afraid to perpetrate a barbarism in his own language. The bent elders of the Germans are astounded at you when you translate letters, and they adopt you as umpire and arbitrator in their mutual dealings. . . . And although these people are stiff and uncouth in body and mind alike, they welcome in you, and learn from you, their native speech combined with Roman wisdom.

Only one thing remains, most clever of men: continue with undiminished zeal, even in your hours of ease, to devote some attention to reading; and, like the man of refinement that you are, observe a just balance between the two languages: retain your grasp of Latin, lest you be laughed at, and practice the other, in order to have the laugh of them. Farewell.

Source: Reprinted by permission of the publishers and the Trustees of the Loeb Classical Library from *Sidonius: Volume II–Letters,* Loeb Classical Library, Volume 420, prepared by W. H. Semple and E. H. Warmington from material left by W. B. Anderson, pp. 127–29, 181–83, Cambridge, MA: Harvard University Press, copyright © 1965 by the President and Fellows of Harvard College. Loeb Classical Library® is a registered trademark of the President and Fellows of Harvard College.

Questions for Analysis

1. For what qualities does Sidonius praise Arbogastes? What might have been the motive behind his extravagant compliments?

2. For what different qualities does Sidonius praise Syagrius? Given that Syagrius controlled much of the former Roman province of northern Gaul, what would have been his reasons for learning the local language?

Benedict of Nursia (c. 480–c. 547), the son of a Roman aristocrat. Benedict founded a monastery at Monte Cassino, southeast of Rome, where he urged his followers to adopt "a simple rule for beginners." Adapted from a much harsher set of precepts called *The Rule of the Master*, Benedict's *Rule* is notable for its brevity, flexibility, and practicality. It established a carefully defined cycle of daily prayers, lessons, and communal worship. It laid down guidelines for what monks should eat (a sufficiency of simple food, a small amount of wine, meat only for the sick or on special occasions), and how the work of the monastery should be performed. Physical labor was encouraged—idleness, Benedict declared, was "an enemy of the soul"—but there was also time for private study and contemplation. In all such matters, Benedict left much to the discretion of the leader of the monastery, whom all the monks were expected to obey without hesitation. This man was the abbot, from the Syriac word *abba*, "father."

Cassiodorus and the Classical Canon

Benedict was no admirer of classical pagan culture, but he did believe that monks must study the Bible in order to perform their daily cycle of prayers properly and to participate fully in a life of worship. This meant that they had to be educated along the lines prescribed by Augustine. And because many monks entered religious life as children, the monastery would need to provide schooling. Through this somewhat roundabout path, classical learning entered the monastic curriculum.

The man largely responsible for this was Flavius Magnus Aurelius Cassiodorus Senator (c. 490–c. 583), a younger contemporary of Benedict. Like Boethius, Cassiodorus (*cass-ee-oh-DOHR-uhs*) was attached to Theodoric's court and was for many years the secretary in charge of the king's correspondence. He also wrote a *History of the*

CASSIODORUS. This frontispiece from a Bible, produced in a monastery in Britain around the year 700, depicts Cassiodorus as a copyist and keeper of books. Monasteries were instrumental in changing the form of the book from the ancient scroll to the modern codex. Because their parchment pages were heavy, codices were customarily stored in cupboards, lying flat, as we see them here.

Goths, which depicted Theodoric's people as part of Rome's history. After Theodoric's death, Cassiodorus founded an important monastery at Vivarium in southern Italy. There, he composed commentaries on the Psalms as well as his most influential work, the *Institutes*.

Inspired by Augustine and his own classical education, Cassiodorus believed that study of classical literature was an essential preliminary to a proper understanding of the Bible. The *Institutes* is essentially a syllabus, a list of readings arranged so that a monk would begin with simpler, straightforward works of pagan literature before moving on to more difficult works and finally to the demanding study of theology. Cassiodorus thereby defined a classical canon that formed the basis of Christian education in the Roman West.

In order to ensure that his monks had access to the necessary readings, Cassiodorus encouraged the copying of books. He argued that this was precisely the sort of manual labor that Benedict had advocated. Under his influence, monasteries thus became engines for the collection, preservation, and transmission of knowledge. It is worth noting that nearly all the Greek and Latin texts on which we rely for our study of western civilizations survive because they were copied in monasteries.

Monasteries also developed and disseminated an important new information technology: the codex. For millennia, the book had been a scroll, a clumsy format that made searching for a particular passage difficult and con-

After You Read This Chapter

Visit StudySpace for quizzes, additional review materials, and multimedia documents. **wwnorton.com/web/westernciv18**

REVIEWING THE OBJECTIVES

- A number of historical factors shaped the way that Jesus's teachings were received. Describe the most important of these.
- The expansion of Rome and the strain on its central government posed significant challenges in the third century. How did Roman emperors respond?
- Christianity's acceptance as a legal religion changed it in profound ways. Why was this?
- In the fourth and fifth centuries, a new wave of migrations penetrated to the very heart of the empire. What made this possible?
- The differences between traditional Roman and Christian cultures were gradually reconciled through the efforts of Christian intellectuals. Why was this considered necessary?

fined the reader to one passage at a time. The codex facilitates indexing (from the Latin word for "finger") because a reader can flip back and forth among various pages and keep a finger in one place while looking at another. Codices also store information more safely and efficiently, because they compress many hundreds of pages within protective bindings. They are less wasteful, too, because texts can be copied on both sides of a page. They even make finding a given book easier, since titles can be written on the codex's spine. It's arguable, in fact, that the invention of the codex was more revolutionary than the invention of printing a thousand years later. Unless you are scrolling through a digital version, your copy of *Western Civilizations* is a codex.

CONCLUSION

Since the English historian Edward Gibbon published the first volume of *The Decline and Fall of the Roman Empire* in 1776 (a year when Britain's own empire suffered a setback), more has been written about "the fall of Rome" than on the passing of any other civilization. Gibbon himself blamed Christianity, depicting it as a debilitating disease that sapped the empire's strength. Others have accused the barbarians whose movements put pressure on Rome's frontiers. But even in the time of Julius Caesar, Roman moralists had already declared that Rome was in decline. Indeed, any self-respecting Roman republicans would say that Rome fell when Augustus came to power.

More recent scholarship has influenced the narrative offered in this chapter, which views transformation as a more accurate way of understanding this period. No civilization is static and unchanging; civilizations, like human beings, are living organisms. Indeed, any evidence of Rome's decline can also be read as evidence of its adaptability. The imperial policies of Septimius Severus and Diocletian responded to the realities of Rome's size and diversity. The settlement of frontier peoples in Rome's western provinces gave rise to hybrid polities that found new uses for Roman buildings, political offices, and laws. Through Christianity, the language, administrative structures, and culture of ancient Rome were preserved and extended. The flexibility of the Roman political system made this possible, because it was inclusive to a degree no modern empire has ever matched.

Still, this transformation changed what it meant to be Roman, to the extent that historians now call this period "late antiquity" to distinguish it from the classical world that preceded it. By the seventh century, indeed, so much had changed that the contours of three distinctive civilizations can be discerned, each one exhibiting different aspects of Roman influence and crystallizing around different regions of the former empire. We will explore each of these civilizations in Chapter 7.

PEOPLE, IDEAS, AND EVENTS IN CONTEXT

- What were the main differences between **JESUS** and other Jewish leaders of his day?
- How did **PAUL OF TARSUS** reach out to the peoples of the Hellenistic world? How did his teachings influence the development of early Christianity?
- In what ways did **DIOCLETIAN**'s division of the empire and his institution of the **TETRARCHY** respond to longstanding problems?
- How and why was Christianity changed under **CONSTANTINE**? What effects did this have on attitudes toward women and their role in the church?
- How did the relocation of the imperial capital to **CONSTANTINOPLE** contribute to the growing divide between the **GREEK EAST** and the **LATIN WEST**? How did the mass migrations of frontier peoples then transform the Latin West?
- What were the key contributions of **JEROME**, **AMBROSE**, and **AUGUSTINE** to the development of a specifically Christian outlook by the end of the fourth century?
- How did **BOETHIUS**, **BENEDICT**, and **CASSODORUS** reshape classical culture in the fifth century?

THINKING ABOUT CONNECTIONS

- In your opinion, which phenomenon had a more profound impact on Rome: the overextension of imperial power or the mass migration of peoples from Rome's frontier? Why?
- Few historians would now agree with the judgment of Edward Gibbon, who posited that Christianity destroyed the Roman Empire. But to what extent did Christianity alter the traditional values and infrastructure of the Roman state? Were these alterations inevitable?

Before You Read This Chapter

Rome's Three Heirs, 500–950

CORE OBJECTIVES

- **EXPLAIN** why Justinian's efforts to reunite the Roman Empire proved destructive.

- **DEFINE** the distinctive features of Byzantine culture.

- **IDENTIFY** the reasons for Islam's rapid expansion.

- **DESCRIBE** the relationship between monasticism and secular power in early medieval Europe.

- **UNDERSTAND** the importance of the Carolingian Empire.

A round the year 600, Anglo-Saxon tribes settled on the island of Britain were approached by missionaries sent from Rome. These Latin-speaking evangelists faced an enormous challenge: they had to find a way to convert tribal leaders and also to translate the central ideas of their faith into languages and concepts that made sense in a new cultural context. They also needed to look for ways to meld Roman practices with Anglo-Saxon ones, building churches on sacred sites and gradually turning the worship of pagan gods into the rituals of Christianity. An account of these negotiations comes down to us in a remarkable book written several generations later. In *The History of the English Church and People*, a monk named Bede (c. 672–735) described how Celtic and Anglo-Saxon peoples were uneasily united under the Roman Church and came to adopt Latin as a language of learning and worship. But he also shows how Roman Christian ideals were changed and adapted in the process, in order to meet new needs and express a new worldview.

This is but one example of the ways in which Rome's legacy was transmitted and transformed during the pivotal period known as the Middle Ages. This term is a vague one,

211

and it doesn't begin to express the diverse realities—or perceptions—of the generations of people who lived during this thousand-year period. For the idea of "the Middle Ages" is really a modern invention: in the seventeenth century, intellectuals began to argue that an intermediate, "medieval period" (*medium ævum*) separated their own "modern age" from the glorious accomplishments of classical Greece and the empire of ancient Rome, which many European states were trying to emulate by establishing empires of their own. But in fact, it is arguable that the period between 500 and 1500 was the beginning of that "modern age." In this era, the foundations of modern political institutions were laid. In this era, the relationships among Judaism, Christianity, and Islam were first articulated—relationships that continue to affect our daily lives. In this era, three new civilizations became heirs of the Western civilizations formerly encompassed by the Roman Empire: the New Rome of Byzantium, the new empire of Islam, and

the western European territories that looked increasingly to the Roman Church for leadership. Each of these interlocking civilizations preserved and modified different aspects of their shared Roman inheritance. Our world is still being shaped by the interactions among them.

JUSTINIAN'S IMPERIAL AMBITIONS

As we observed in Chapter 6, the eastern and western territories of Rome's empire were becoming divided along linguistic, cultural, and economic lines. By the end of the fourth century, this division also became political. The Ostrogothic conquest of Italy under Theodoric (r. 493–526)—which was supported by the imperial government—briefly placed Constantinople in a position to influence affairs in the old Roman

THE MEDITERRANEAN WORLD UNDER JUSTINIAN, 527–565. Compare this map with the one on page 192. Here, the green shading represents those regions controlled by Justinian. ▪ *What was the geographical extent of Justinian's empire?* ▪ *Which areas of the former Roman Empire did Justinian not attempt to reconquer?* ▪ *What may have been the strategy behind these campaigns?*

heartland. But none of Theodoric's short-lived successors was able to rule this territory effectively, and in 535 the Ostrogothic kingdom was overthrown in an attempt to reunify the Roman Empire.

The man responsible for this was Justinian (r. 527–65), the most ambitious emperor since Constantine. Although the empire that he ruled was largely Greek-speaking, Justinian himself came from the Latin-speaking province of Dardania (now Serbia). A student of history, he saw himself as the heir to the Principate established by Augustus, and like Augustus he was aided by an astute and determined wife, Theodora, who played an influential role in his reign. Although his efforts ultimately failed, they had a lasting influence on the entire Mediterranean world.

Justinian's Attempted Reconquest

Justinian's initial efforts to strengthen and reunite the Roman Empire seemed successful. In 533, his general Belisarius conquered the Vandal kingdom of northwest Africa, thereby facilitating campaigns in Ostrogothic Italy and Visigothic Spain. By 536, Belisarius appeared poised to occupy Rome's old homeland, where he was welcomed as a savior by some former subjects of the Ostrogoths. But these early victories were illusory. Although the Mediterranean was under Roman control, the human and financial costs of these campaigns drastically strained imperial resources. Belisarius's army in Italy was overextended, and Justinian's need to levy soldiers led to oppressive taxes on vitally important regions like Egypt and Syria, which undermined support for his imperial project. The Romans of Italy and North Africa, meanwhile, resented the costs their own "liberation" imposed on them.

Justinian's campaigns also distracted attention from dangers closer to Constantinople: in particular, the developing strength of Persia under the Sassanid dynasty. To respond to the Persians' advances, Justinian's successors were eventually forced to withdraw their troops from Italy and North Africa. This left both regions dangerously exposed to further invasions and yet still failed to guarantee the safety of the eastern frontier. Only a heroic reorganization of the empire's resources after 610 (see below) saved Constantinople, but it put an end to Justinian's dream of reunification.

The pressure and perils of warfare during this period were further exacerbated by a pandemic known as the Justinianic Plague, which broke out in 541–42 and which even afflicted Justinian himself (though he recovered). It was probably caused by the same bacteria that spawned the terrible Black Death of the fourteenth century (see Chapter 10), and it may have been just as deadly. Although the plague appears to have devastated the urban region around Constantinople

with particular ferocity, it has recently been confirmed to be a global phenomenon, affecting regions from China (where it appears to have originated) to Scandinavia and reaching down into Africa and the Indian Ocean. It is estimated to have killed a large percentage of the world's population at that time, some 25 million people; and it would recur in some places every generation or so for the next 200 years. It certainly assisted in weakening Justinian's bid for extended imperial power, while at the same time strengthening the disruptive force of barbarian and Arab war-bands on the empire's frontiers. And ironically, it spread so rapidly and so far because of the very efficient infrastructures (roads, bridges, trading networks) that bound the Roman Empire together and linked it to its neighbors.

Justinian's Impact on the West

Justinian's wars proved more devastating to Italy than the previous incursions of barbarian peoples, almost as devastating as the plague named for him. Around Rome, the vital supply lines of the aqueducts were cut and the elaborate system of conduits, drainage ditches, and reservoirs was destroyed. Parts of the Italian countryside returned to marshland, and some areas would not be drained again until the twentieth century. In 568, a new people, the Lombards, took advantage of the chaos to conquer the northern third of the peninsula. Thereafter, Italy would be divided between Lombard territories in the north and imperial territories in the southeast, with Rome and its region precariously sandwiched between them. The controlling forces within these territories would change greatly over time, but this tripartite division remained the essential political configuration of Italy until the nineteenth century. In fact, it still divides Italian politics to this day.

Constantinople's control over North Africa lasted only a few generations longer. Weakened by religious conflict and heavy taxation, this area fell easily to invading Muslims in the seventh century, along with Egypt and the rest of Roman Africa (see below). When it did, Christianity in North Africa largely disappeared, although a vibrant Christian community continued to flourish in Ethiopia. Meanwhile, tensions between Arian Visigoths and their Latin subjects continued even after the Visigothic king officially converted in 587. This mutual hostility would subsist until the Visigothic kingdom, too, was largely absorbed by Islam. By the end of the eighth century, Christian rulers controlled only the northernmost parts of the Iberian Peninsula, and Al-Andalus (Muslim Spain) became part of a wider Islamic world.

The Codification of Roman Law

Justinian's most positive and lasting accomplishment was his codification of Roman law. This was a necessary project, and long overdue: since the time of the third-century jurists (see Chapter 5), the number of imperial statutes and legal decisions had multiplied, and the resulting body of law was both massive and self-contradictory. Moreover, conditions had changed so radically within the empire that many legal principles could no longer be applied. When Justinian came to power in 527, one of his first initiatives was to bring existing precedents into harmony with actual historical conditions and thereby to restore the prestige and power of the imperial office.

To carry out this work, Justinian appointed a team of lawyers under the supervision of a jurist called Tribonian. Within two years, this commission published the first result of its labors: the Code, a systematic compilation of imperial statutes which was later supplemented by another book, the Novels (*Novellae*, "new laws"), containing the legislation of Justinian and his immediate successors. By 532, the commission had also completed the Digest, a summary of the writings of Rome's great legal authorities, including the jurists of the Principate. Its final product was the *Institutes,* a textbook of legal principles. Together, these four volumes constitute the *Corpus Juris Civilis*, the "body of civil law."

Justinian's *Corpus* was a brilliant achievement. In the eastern Roman Empire, it immediately became the foundation on which all subsequent legal developments would rest. Although little known in western Europe for centuries, it eventually influenced the legal systems of many nations. The nineteenth-century Napoleonic Code—still the basis of law in France, Spain, much of Latin America, and the state of Louisiana—is essentially based on the *Corpus* of Justinian.

The *Corpus* also had a profound impact on political philosophy. Starting from the maxim that "what pleases the prince has the force of law," it granted unlimited powers to the emperor and was therefore adopted by early modern rulers as a foundation for absolutism (see Chapter 15). But the *Corpus* also provided some support for constitutional forms of government, because it maintained that a sovereign's powers are delegated to him by the people and that what

JUSTINIAN AND THEODORA. These sixth-century mosaics from the Church of San Vitale in the imperial capital of Ravenna (Italy) show the emperor and empress processing toward the main altar of the church carrying the holy vessels used for the consecration of bread and wine. ▪ *What do these images convey about the sacred and secular powers of both figures?*

is mandated by the people can also be taken away by them. Equally important is the fundamental principle that the state is a corporate body, not the extension of an individual's private property. The modern conception of the state as a public entity derives from the legal maxims of the *Corpus*.

THE ROMAN EMPIRE OF BYZANTIUM

With the failure of Justinian's project of imperial reunification, the history of the eastern Roman Empire can be said to enter a new phase. Indeed, many historians regard it as essentially a new entity, the Byzantine Empire, a name derived from the ancient port where Constantinople was situated. Byzantium thus became *one* of Rome's three heirs—not the sole heir of Roman authority, as Justinian had hoped. But according to the citizens of this empire, it never ceased to be Rome, and they were never anything but Romans. They saw themselves as carrying forward Roman traditions, values, and institutions under new circumstances.

As a result of Justinian's policies, however, this new Rome was struggling for survival. By 610, the Greek-speaking imperial dynasty that began with Heraclius (r. 610–41) was unable to extend its influence farther west than the Adriatic. Meanwhile, the Persians had conquered almost all of the empire's eastern and southern territories in Syria and Palestine. They had even plundered Jerusalem and carried off a precious relic believed to be part of the original cross on which Jesus had been crucified. With an enormous effort, Heraclius rallied his remaining military powers and routed the Persians, recapturing Jerusalem and retrieving the relic in 627.

But these gains were short-lived. Arab armies, inspired by the new religion of Islam, were able to profit from the empire's exhaustion. They soon occupied the recently reconquered Byzantine territories and claimed Jerusalem as a holy site for Muslims, too. They also absorbed the entire Persian Empire and rapidly made their way westward to North Africa. They then took to the sea, and in 677 attempted a naval conquest of Constantinople. Repulsed, they made another attempt in 717 by means of a concerted land and sea operation. This new threat was countered by the emperor Leo III (r. 717–41). Deploying keen strategy and a secret incendiary mixture known as "Greek fire" (of course, the Byzantines called it "Roman fire"), Leo's forces were able to defeat the Arabs. Over the next few decades, moreover, Byzantium reconquered most of Asia Minor, which remained the imperial heartland for the next 300 years.

Sources of Stability

In many ways, the internal politics of the Byzantine Empire were as tumultuous as the history of its changing neighborhood. Because all power was concentrated in the imperial court at Constantinople and because emperors followed their predecessors in claiming autonomous rule, opposition usually took the form of intrigue, treason, and violence. Indeed, Byzantine politics is now so famous for its cloak-and-dagger complexity that the word *byzantine* has come to denote devious machinations or elaborate systems of courtship and bureaucracy. In reality, though, many able rulers wielded their powers very effectively in Constantinople, where a centralized government continued to function even in times of upheaval. No polity in western Europe had anything resembling such effective mechanisms of government until a much later period.

Strong, self-perpetuating political institutions thus constituted a major source of stability in Byzantium and offer an explanation for the extraordinary longevity of the empire's core provinces: nearly a thousand years. The imperial bureaucracy in Constantinople regulated prices and wages, maintained systems of licensing, and controlled exports and trade. Its highly educated officials also supervised many aspects of social and cultural life, overseeing schools, the organization of the Orthodox Church, and the observance of religious rites and holidays. Even the popular sport of chariot racing—New Rome's exciting answer to gladiatorial combat—fell under strict supervision, as did the regulation of the various teams' fiercely competitive fans. Established bureaucracies also regulated the army and navy, the courts, and the diplomatic service, endowing these agencies with organizational strengths incomparable for their time.

Another source of stability was Byzantium's sound and well-managed economy, which was far superior to that of western Europe. Commerce and cities continued to flourish as they had done in late antiquity. Constantinople became a central emporium for Far Eastern luxury goods and western raw materials. The empire also nurtured and protected its own industries, most notably the manufacture and weaving of silk, and it was renowned for its stable gold and silver coinage. Nor was Constantinople the only great urban center. The Hellenistic capital Antioch and the bustling cities of Thessalonica and Trebizond were very large and prosperous. Any one of them would have dwarfed any western European city; Constantinople may have had a population of close to a million. In the West at this time, Paris was a village and Rome may have had a few thousand people living among the ruins.

THE SECRET WEAPON OF BYZANTIUM: "GREEK FIRE." This depiction of Greek fire in action illustrates a chronicle by John Skylitzes, a Byzantine historian who flourished in the eleventh century. This manuscript was copied in Sicily during the twelfth century and is now preserved in the Biblioteca Nacional de España in Madrid.

This emphasis on Byzantine trade and industry is justified because both were advanced and both provided most of the surplus wealth that sustained the state. But agriculture lay at the heart of the Byzantine economy, so much so that peasant farmers struggled to maintain their independence from large estates owned by wealthy aristocrats and monasteries. And as in the final centuries of the Roman republic, they were only able to do so with the help of legislation. When the aristocracy eventually gained control during the eleventh century, however, free peasants were transformed into impoverished tenant-farmers, as had been the case in Italy during the third century C.E. This was one of the less fortunate ways in which Byzantium resembled its ancient predecessor.

Orthodoxy, Iconoclasm, and Identity

Law, strong governance, and a thriving economy: viewed from our perspective, these seem to be the basis of Byzantine civilization. Yet the inhabitants of New Rome seem to have cared more about religious orthodoxy. On the one hand, their intense preoccupation with questions of doctrine could be a catalyst for political and social dissension; on the other hand, it endowed the empire's inhabitants with a sense of shared purpose and a shared identity. In old Rome, the *mos maiorum* had undergirded Roman pride and superiority (Chapter 5); in New Rome, Orthodox Christianity occupied the same fundamental place. The stakes of Byzantine doctrinal disputes were further heightened by the fact that emperors took an active role in them.

The most contentious issue, and one that came to a head in the eighth century, was a violent clash over the meaning and use of religious images, known as the Iconoclast ("image-breaking") Controversy. As we saw in Chapter 6, Christians had long been accustomed to expressing their devotion to Christ and the saints through the making and veneration of images. There was even a legend that the author of Luke's Gospel had been a painter, the maker of the first icon. At the same time, however, there was always an awareness that any representation of a holy person came close to being a form of idolatry, something that Jewish tradition strongly condemned and something that made Christians look like idol-worshipers in the eyes of their religious rivals, especially Muslims. Although both Latin and Orthodox Christians insisted that images were only *aids* to worship, not *objects* of worship, the line between the two was very fine.

In Byzantium, where the veneration of icons was an especially potent part of daily devotion, any suggestion that such images should be suppressed or destroyed was bound to be contentious. But that is precisely what the Iconoclasts advocated. They argued that honoring images was blasphemous because nothing made by human beings should be worshiped, an injunction expressed in the Ten Commandments given to Moses (Exodus 20:4). Moreover, they contended that Christ's divinity could not be represented artistically; it was beyond the power of even the most skilled craftsman. For their part, traditionalists retorted that the images themselves were never objects of worship; rather, icons were windows through which a glimpse of Heaven might be granted to human beings on earth.

The Iconoclast movement was initiated by the same Emperor Leo III who had saved Constantinople from invasion by Muslims, and it is even possible that the icono-clasm so central to Islamic belief (Qur'an, V. 92) played an influential role in his thinking. In other words, cracking down on icons may have been his attempt to answer one of Islam's greatest criticisms of Christianity. There may also have been political and financial considerations behind the campaign: by proclaiming a radical new religious movement, the emperor may have intended to strengthen his control over the Orthodox Church and thus to combat the growing power of monasteries. And indeed, the great monasteries of Byzantium were major producers of icons as well as books: the manufacture of both was considered a labor especially suited to the monastic life. So when the monasteries rallied to the cause of images, they were bitterly suppressed by Leo's successors, who took this opportunity to confiscate much of their wealth.

The Iconoclast Controversy was resolved toward the end of the eighth century in favor of the promoters of religious imagery, the Iconodules ("image servants"). But it had some long-lasting effects. One was the destruction of many artworks produced or preserved in Byzantium, by previous imperial edict. This means that examples of Christian artistry from the first eight centuries after Jesus's death are very rare and can be found mainly in Italy, Palestine, or Egypt, which were beyond the reach of the Iconoclast emperors. A second consequence was the widening of a religious and political breach between the Greek East and the Latin West. Prior to Emperor Leo's iconoclastic initiatives, the patriarch of Rome—known familiarly as "papa" in Latin slang—had often been a close ally of Byzantium's rulers. But iconoclasm called into question not only the veneration of images but the cult of the saints, and by extension the claims of papal primacy that were based on the Roman patriarch's claim to be Saint Peter's successor (see Chapter 6).

The ultimate defeat of iconoclasm crystallized some aspects of belief and practice that came to be characteristic of Byzantine identity. One was a renewed emphasis on the Orthodox faith of the empire as the key to its political unity and military success. Defense of religious tradition became the touchstone of political legitimacy, and vice versa. This emphasis on tradition helped Greek orthodoxy gain new adherents in the ninth and tenth centuries, but it subsequently enforced the hegemony of Constantinople's own Christian traditions, marginalizing those of Syria and Armenia. Fear of heresy also tended to inhibit freedom of thought and not just in religious matters. Although the Byzantine emperors eventually founded a university in Constantinople, its students and faculty were discouraged from expressing dissenting opinions or engaging in any significant degree of intellectual speculation—in marked contrast to the freewheeling intellectual atmosphere cultivated by the universities of western Europe (see Chapters 8 and 9).

DEVOTIONAL IMAGE—OR DANGEROUS IDOL? This icon of *Christos Pantokrator* ("Christ the Almighty") was painted in the sixth century and is one of the oldest such images in existence. It is preserved at the Orthodox monastery of St. Catherine on Mount Sinai (Egypt). ▪ *According to the proponents of iconoclasm, why would such an image be considered blasphemous?*

Debating the Power of Icons

> The Iconoclast Controversy of the eighth century divided Byzantine society and was a factor in the growing division between the Latin Church of Rome and the Greek Orthodox Church. The excerpts below are representative of the two main arguments voiced at the time. The first is from a treatise by John of Damascus (c. 675–749), a Christian in the service of the Muslim Umayyad caliphs. The second is an official report issuing from the synod convened by the emperor Constantine V (r. 741–75) in 754. Constantine was carrying forward the iconoclastic policies of his father, Leo III.

John of Damascus, *On Holy Images*

Now adversaries say: God's commands to Moses the law-giver were, "Thou shalt adore the Lord thy God, and thou shalt worship him alone, and thou shalt not make to thyself a graven thing that is in heaven above, or in the earth beneath." . . .

These injunctions were given to the Jews on account of their proneness to idolatry. Now we, on the contrary, are no longer in leading strings . . . We have passed the stage of infancy, and reached the perfection of manhood . . . and know what may be imaged and what may not. . . . An image is a likeness of the original with a certain difference, for it is not an exact reproduction of the original. Thus, the Son is the living, substantial, unchangeable Image of the invisible God, bearing in Himself the whole Father, being in all things equal to Him, differing only in being begotten by the Father. . . . That which is divine is immutable; there is no change in Him, nor shadow of change. . . . God has noted and settled all that He would do, the unchanging future events before they came to pass. In the same way, a man who wished to build a house, would first make and think out a plan. Again, visible things are images of invisible and intangible things, on which they throw a faint light. Holy Scripture clothes in figure God and the angels. . . . If, therefore, Holy Scripture, providing for our need, ever putting before us what is intangible, clothes it in flesh, does it not make an image of what is thus invested with our nature, and brought to the level of our desires, yet invisible? . . . For the invisible things of God since the creation of the world are made visible through images. We see images in creation which remind us faintly of God, as when, for instance, we speak of the holy and adorable Trinity, imaged by the sun, or light, or burning rays, or by a running fountain, or a full river, or by the mind, speech, or the spirit within us, or by a rose tree, or a sprouting flower, or a sweet fragrance. . . .

Source: Excerpted from *St. John Damascene on Holy Images*, trans. Mary H. Allies (London: 1898), pp. 6–12.

Tradition and Innovation

Although Orthodox religion was central to the identity of Romans in Byzantium, so was their direct link with the Hellenistic past and the heritage of ancient Greece. Byzantine schools based their instruction on classical Greek literature to a degree that might seem surprising given the more tentative attitude toward classical learning in western Europe (see Chapter 6). Educated people around the Byzantine court who quoted only a single line of Homer could expect their listeners to recognize the entire passage from which it came. In the English-speaking world, only the King James Bible has ever achieved the same degree of cultural saturation. For the Romans of Byzantium, indeed, Homeric epics were a kind of sacred text: a literary model, an instructional textbook, and a guide to personal morality and wisdom.

Byzantine scholars also studied the philosophy of Plato and the historical prose of Thucydides intensively. By contrast, Aristotle's works were less well known, while many other philosophical traditions of antiquity were deemed

Canons of the Synod of 754

It is the unanimous doctrine of all the holy Fathers and of the six Ecumenical Synods, that no one may imagine any kind of separation or mingling in opposition to the unsearchable, unspeakable, and incomprehensible union of the two natures in the one *hypostasis* or person. What avails, then, the folly of the painter, who from sinful love of gain depicts that which should not be depicted— that is, with his polluted hands he tries to fashion that which should only be believed in the heart and confessed with the mouth? He makes an image and calls it Christ. The name *Christ* signifies *God and man.* Consequently it is an image of God and man, and consequently he has in his foolish mind, in his representation of the created flesh, depicted the Godhead which cannot be represented, and thus mingled what should not be mingled. Thus he is guilty of a double blasphemy—the one in making an image of the Godhead, and the other by mingling the Godhead and manhood . . . like the Monophysites, or he represents the body of Christ as not made divine and separate and as a person apart, like the Nestorians.

The only admissible figure of the humanity of Christ, however, is bread and wine in the holy Supper. This and no other form, this and no other type, has he chosen to represent his incarnation. Bread he ordered to be brought, but not a representation of the human form, so that idolatry might not arise. And as the body of Christ is made divine, so also this figure of the body of Christ, the bread, is made divine by the descent of the Holy Spirit; it becomes the divine body of Christ by the mediation of the priest who, separating the oblation from that which is common, sanctifies it. . . .

Source: Excerpted from *The Seven Ecumenical Councils of the Undivided Church*, trans. H. R. Percival, in *Nicene and Post-Nicene Fathers*, 2d Series, eds. P. Schaff and H. Wace (repr. Grand Rapids, MI: 1955), pp. 543–44.

Questions for Analysis

1. To what other phenomena does John of Damascus compare the making of images? How do these comparisons help him to make his argument in favor of them?

2. To what phenomena do the theologians of the synod compare the making of images? Why do they declare the bread and wine of the Eucharist to be the only legitimate representations of Christ?

3. What is the significance of the fact that John of Damascus did not fall under the jurisdiction of the emperor of Byzantium but that of the Muslim Umayyad caliph? What conclusions can you draw about the relative freedoms in these two realms?

---

dangerous to orthodox belief. Paradoxically, Justinian, who had presided over the codification of ancient Roman (and thus pagan) law, registered his distrust of philosophy by shutting down the Athenian academies that had existed since Plato's day. Eventually, the emperor Alexius Comnenus (d. 1118) would ban the teaching of Aristotelian logic. The traditions of Greek scientific inquiry and the advances of Hellenistic science were also neglected. Tradition was more highly prized than originality, as was preservation over innovation. The benefit of this, for posterity, is that Byzantium rescued Greek and Hellenistic writings for later ages. The vast majority of ancient Greek texts known today survive only because they were copied by Byzantine scribes.

In further contrast to western Europe, as we shall see, Byzantine classicism and learning were the products of an educational system that extended to the laity and was open to women as well as to men. Byzantine commitment to the formal education of women was especially unusual. Although most girls from aristocratic or prosperous families were educated at home by private tutors, they nevertheless mingled freely with their male counterparts at court or on social occasions, and many female intellectuals were praised for being able to discourse like Plato or Pythagoras. There were even female physicians in the Byzantine Empire, another extraordinary departure both from ancient tradition and from the practices of western Europe until the latter part of the nineteenth century.

Byzantine achievements in the realms of architecture and art are also remarkable. The finest example of both may be the church of Hagia Sophia (Greek for "Holy Wisdom") in Constantinople, constructed at enormous cost under the patronage of Justinian. It quickly came to define an architectural style unique to Byzantium. Its purpose was not to express pride in human accomplishment but rather to symbolize the mysteries of the Christian religion and the holy knowledge imparted by Christ to the soul of the believer. For this reason, the architects paid little attention to the external appearance of the building. The interior, however, was decorated with richly colored mosaics, gold leaf, colored marble columns, and bits of tinted glass set on edge to refract rays of sunlight like sparkling gems. Light appeared to be generated from within. The magnificent dome over its central square represented an unprecedented engineering feat and was upheld by four great arches springing from pillars at the four corners of the square. The result was an architectural framework that is marvelously strong but delicate. Its effect is heightened by the many windows placed around the dome's rim, which convey the impression that it floats in mid-air.

Many aspects of Byzantine arts and learning exerted strong influence on the craftsmen and scholars of western Europe through its continued economic and cultural contact with New Rome. The basilica of San Marco in Venice (c. 1063) reflects this influence distinctly, as do medieval mosaics in such cities as Ravenna and Palermo. Greek-speaking monasteries in southeastern Italy maintained especially close ties with their counterparts in the eastern empire, and many were allowed to practice the rituals of the Orthodox Church. Greek books—including the comedies of Aristophanes (Chapter 4)—were copied and preserved there. But much of the heritage of Western civilizations that was cultivated in Byzantium was largely inaccessible elsewhere in Europe, because the knowledge of Greek became increasingly rare.

HAGIA SOPHIA. This great monument to the artistry, engineering skill, and spirituality of Byzantium was built during the reign of Justinian. The four minarets at its corners were added in 1453, after Constantinople was absorbed into the empire of the Ottoman Turks. Hagia Sophia is now a mosque and a museum.

MUHAMMAD AND THE TEACHINGS OF ISLAM

In many ways, the civilization that formed around the religion of Islam mirrors the Roman Empire in its global reach and longevity; in this, it is truly one of Rome's heirs. Islam (Arabic for "submission") also resembles the early republic of Rome in that it demands from its followers not just adherence to common forms of worship but also to certain social and cultural norms. But whereas the Roman Empire came to undergird Christianity, and elevated it to the status of a major faith by legalizing it, the Islamic faith was itself the engine of imperial expansion. Indeed, Islam is unique among the major religions in the way it has *created* political empires rather than depending on them.

The Revelations of Muhammad

Islam had its beginnings in Arabia, a desert land considered so forbidding that neither the Romans nor the Persians sought to conquer it. Arabian society was tribal and did not revolve around urban settlements. Many Arabs were herdsmen, living off the milk of their camels and the produce

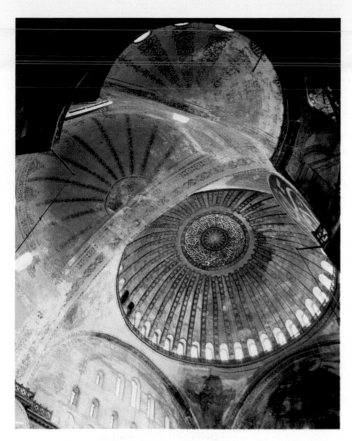

INTERIOR OF HAGIA SOPHIA. The revolutionary structure of the church, shown here, made it appear as if the enormous dome floated on light and air.

of desert oases. But like the Hittites in the second millennium B.C.E. (Chapter 1), their very mobility, ingenuity, and pioneering spirit made them excellent explorers and long-distance traders. In the second half of the sixth century, when protracted wars between Byzantium and Persia made travel dangerous for merchants, the Arabs quickly established themselves as guides, couriers, and guardians of transit routes between Africa and Asia.

As part of this process, towns began to emerge. The most prominent of these was Mecca, an ancient sacred site that lay at the crossroads of major caravan routes. Mecca was home to the Kaaba (*KAH-ah-bah*), a shrine housing the Black Stone worshiped by many Arabian tribes. (It may be a meteorite, and hence of celestial origin.) The tribe that controlled this shrine, the Quraish (*kur-AYSH*), thus came to dominate the economic and religious life of the whole region, forming an aristocracy of traders and entrepreneurs.

Muhammad, the founder of Islam, was a member of this tribe. He was born in Mecca about 570. Orphaned early in life, he entered the service of a rich widow whom he later married, thereby attaining financial security.

Until middle age he lived as a prosperous trader, little different from his fellow townsmen. But around 610, he experienced a spiritual epiphany. At this time, the Arab tribes worshiped many gods. Yet like the ancient Hebrews, they also acknowledged one god as more powerful. For the Hebrews, God was Yahweh; for the Arabs, Allah. But whereas the Hebrews' embrace of monotheism was a long and gradual process, Muhammad's conversion was sudden, the immediate consequence of revelation. Thereafter, Muhammad received further revelations that became the basis for his teachings, and by which he was persuaded to accept the calling of a prophet and to proclaim the new faith to his tribe.

At first, he was not very successful in gaining converts. In Mecca, tribal leaders probably feared that his teachings would diminish the importance of the Kaaba. The town of Yathrib to the north, however, had no such concerns. Its representatives invited Muhammad to live among them and to serve as judge and arbiter in local rivalries. Muhammad and a few loyal friends accepted this invitation in 622. Because this migration—in Arabic, the Hijrah (*HIJ-ruh*)—marks the beginning of Muhammad's wider influence, Muslims regard it as the beginning of time. Just as Christians date all events according to the birth of Jesus (see Chapter 6), so Muslims begin their dating system with the Hijrah.

Muhammad changed the name of Yathrib to Medina ("City of the Prophet") and established himself as the town's ruler. In so doing, he consciously organized his followers into a political community held together by shared economic ambitions as well as by a shared set of beliefs and rituals. Yet he did not abandon his desire to exercise political and prophetic authority among his own people, the Quraish. Accordingly, he and his followers began raiding Quraish caravans traveling beyond Mecca. The Quraish defended themselves, but they could not continue to operate an extensive commercial enterprise in the face of such violent threats. By 630, Muhammad had worn down the opposition and was invited back to Mecca. His kinsmen submitted themselves to his authority and accepted his teachings. Muhammad, for his part, ensured that the Kaaba's shrine was revered as Islam's holiest place, a status it maintains today. And because Mecca had long been a pilgrimage site and gathering place for tribes throughout Arabia, many people were exposed to Muhammad's teachings. At the time of his death in 632, Islam had become an established faith.

Muhammad and the Qur'an

As its name indicates, the faith of Islam calls for absolute submission to Allah, the same God worshiped by Jews and

A Sura from the Qur'an

The Qur'an preserves the teachings of Muhammad in a series of suras, *or chapters. Composed in verse forms that draw on much older traditions of Arabic poetry, they are meant to be sung or chanted. Indeed, the word* Qur'an *means "recitations," referring both to Muhammad's method of revealing divine truths and to the Muslim practice of memorizing and repeating portions of this sacred scripture.*

Sura 81: The Overturning

In the Name of God the Compassionate
the Caring

When the sun is overturned
When the stars fall away
When the mountains are moved
When the ten-month pregnant
    camels are abandoned
When the beasts of the wild
    are herded together   5
When the seas are boiled over
When the souls are coupled
When the girl-child buried alive
is asked what she did to deserve
    murder
When the pages are folded out   10
When the sky is flayed open
When Jahím [the Day of Reckoning]
    is set ablaze

When the garden is brought near
Then a soul will know what it
    has prepared
I swear by the stars that slide,   15
stars streaming, stars that sweep
    along the sky
By the night as it slips away
By the morning when the fragrant
    air breathes
This is the word of a messenger
    ennobled,
empowered, ordained before
    the lord of the throne,   20
holding sway there, keeping trust
Your friend [Muhammad] has
    not gone mad
He saw him on the horizon clear
He does not hoard for himself
    the unseen
This is not the word of a satan
    struck with stones   25

Where are you going?
This is a reminder to all beings
For those who wish to walk straight
Your only will is the will of God lord
    of all beings

Source: From *Approaching the Qur'an: The Early Revelations*, trans. Michael Sells (Ashland, OR: 1999), pp. 48–50.

Questions for Analysis

1. What impressions of Arab culture emerge from this sura? What does the litany of unlikely or mystical events reveal about the values of Muhammad's contemporaries?

2. How does Muhammad speak of himself and his role in society?

Christians. Hence, the Muslim saying "there is no god but Allah" is more accurately translated as "there is no divinity but God." For Muslims, the history and prophecies of the Hebrews are important components of their religion, as are the teachings of Jesus, who is venerated as a great prophet. But they consider Muhammad to be the last and greatest prophet, and the closest to God.

Muhammad's teachings are so essential because they established the rituals and practices that help to ensure salvation of all Muslims. These teachings are preserved in the sacred scripture of Islam, the Qur'an (kuhr-AHN), an Arabic word meaning "recitations." This is because Muhammad recited his revelations to his listeners, and these were eventu-

ally gathered together and transcribed, a process that continued after Muhammad's death. Unlike the Christian Gospels, which offer different perspectives on Jesus's ministry and which were recorded a generation or two after his death, the Qur'an is considered a direct link with Muhammad. It is also unlike most books of the Bible because it takes the form of poetry, drawing on ancient genres of Arabic song.

Like Christianity, Islam teaches that a day of judgment is coming—and soon. On this day, the righteous will be granted eternal life in a paradise of delights, but wrongdoers will be damned to a realm of eternal fire. Every person is therefore offered a fundamental choice: to begin a new life of divine service or to follow their own

THE KAABA. This holy shrine remains the focus of worship for all Muslims, especially during the annual pilgrimage to Mecca. According to legend, Muhammad resolved a dispute among several tribes as to which should have the honor of lifting the Black Stone into place when the Kaaba was rebuilt. Muhammad's solution was to invite representatives of the tribes to hold the four corners of a carpet and to lift the stone together while he himself directed its placement. ■ *What is the significance of this story?* ■ *What message does it convey about the Prophet's important role in his own society?*

scholar qualified to comment on matters of faith, who may also act as a judge in disputes (as Muhammad had done in Medina). Although Muslims value the opportunity to come together for prayer, there is no prescribed liturgy as in the Roman and Orthodox Churches. Like Judaism, Islam emphasizes the inextricable connection between religious observance and daily life, between spirituality and politics. There is no opposition of sacred and secular authority, as in Christianity. But in marked contrast to Judaism, Islam is a religion that aspires to unite the world in a shared faith. This means that Muslims, like Christians, consider it their duty to engage in the work of conversion. This further means that there will inevitably be competition between the followers of these faiths, as both try carry out this mission.

THE WIDENING ISLAMIC WORLD

As we have frequently noted, the death of any charismatic leader precipitates a series of crises. Muhammad and Alexander the Great represent very different types of leadership, but both created communities whose very survival seemed to depend on that leadership. Neither designated his own successor, and both left behind a number of close followers who disagreed as to the proper uses of the power they had inherited. Although the very survival of Islam seemed unlikely after Muhammad's death, within a generation it had come to encompass much of the ancient Near East.

The Arabic Conquest of the West

Muhammad's closest followers were his father-in-law, Abu-Bakr (*ah-boo-BAHK-uhr*), and an early convert named Umar. After Muhammad's death, these two men took the initiative by naming Abu-Bakr *caliph*, a word meaning "deputy" or "representative." In this capacity, Abu-Bakr began a campaign to subdue various tribes that had been loyal to Muhammad but were not willing to accept his own authority as Muhammad's successor. In the course of this, Abu-Bakr's forces began to move northward beyond the borders of Arabia, where they met only minimal resistance from Byzantine and Persian armies.

When Abu-Bakr died two years later, he was succeeded as caliph by Umar, who continued to direct his growing warrior bands against Byzantium and Persia. In the following years, Arab victories were virtually continuous. In 636, the Arabs routed a Byzantine army in Syria and then

path. If they choose to follow God, they will be blessed; if they do not, God will turn away from them. Thus the only sure means of achieving salvation is observance of the Five Pillars of the faith: submission to God's will as described in the teachings of Muhammad, frequent prayer, ritual fasting, the giving of alms, and an annual pilgrimage to Mecca (*Hajj*).

Unlike Christianity, Islam is a religion without sacraments or priests. It more closely resembles Judaism as it developed after the Diaspora, when Jews no longer had access to the Temple and no need for a Temple priesthood but instead gathered around a master teacher (*rabbi*). Similarly, Muslims often rely on a community leader (*imam*) or quickly swept over the entire area, occupying the leading cities of Antioch, Damascus, and Jerusalem. In 637, they destroyed the main army of the Persians and took the Persian capital of Ctesiphon. The rest of the realm offered little resistance. By 651, the Arabian conquest of the entire Persian Empire was virtually complete.

Islamic forces now turned westward toward North Africa, capturing Byzantine Egypt by 646 and extending their control throughout the rest of North Africa during the following decades. Attempts to capture Constantinople in 677 and 717 were not successful, as we noted earlier, but in 711 the Arabs crossed from North Africa into Visigothic Spain and quickly absorbed most of that territory, too. Within less than a century, followers of Islam had conquered the ancient Near East and much of the Roman Mediterranean; in the process, the desert-dwelling Arabs had transformed themselves into the world's most daring seafarers.

How can we explain this prodigious achievement? On a basic level, what motivated the Arabs had motivated the Sumerians, the Neo-Assyrians, the Greeks, the Macedonians, and the Romans: the search for richer territory and new wealth. There is little evidence that Arab Muslims attempted to convert subject peoples to the faith of Islam at this time. Instead, they aimed to establish themselves as a superior ruling class. Yet religious enthusiasm certainly played a crucial role in forging a shared identity among tribes hitherto at war with one another. This identity and sense of superiority must have been further strengthened by the absence of any serious opposition. Indeed, many of the local populations living within the Persian and Byzantine empires were restive and exhausted by the demands of these far-reaching imperial bureaucracies. To them, conquest brought deliverance. The Arabs did not demand that Jews or Christians convert to Islam, and because they exacted fewer taxes than the Byzantines and the Persians, they were often

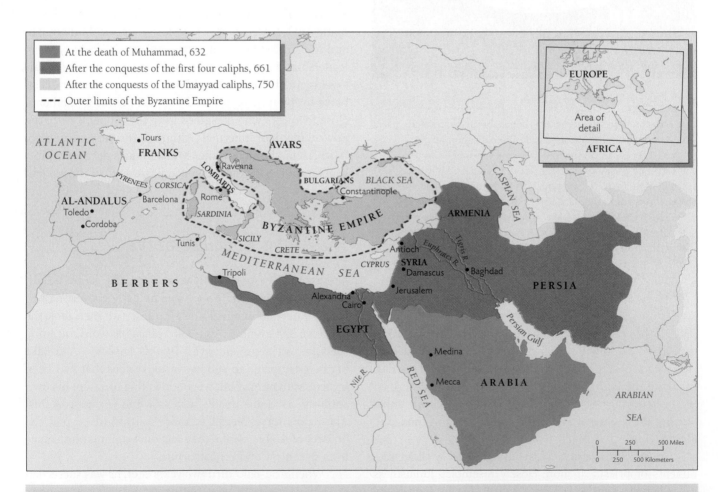

THE EXPANSION OF ISLAM TO 750. This map shows the steady advance of Islam, through Arab conquests, from the time of Muhammad to the middle of the eighth century. ▪ *What was the geographical extent of Islam in 750?* ▪ *What role did the Byzantine Empire play in the expansion of Islam?* ▪ *What conclusions can you draw regarding the period of especially rapid expansion in the generation after Muhammad's death?*

preferred to the old rulers. For all these reasons, Islam quickly spread over the territory between Egypt and Iran, and has been rooted there ever since.

The Shi'ite–Sunni Schism

As these Arab conquests widened the world of Islam, disputes continued to divide the Muslims of Mecca. When the caliph Umar died in 644, he was replaced by a member of the Umayyad (oo-MY-yad) family, a wealthy clan that had resisted Muhammad's authority. Opponents of this new caliph, Uthman, rallied instead around Muhammad's cousin and son-in-law, Ali, whose family ties to Muhammad made him seem a more appropriate choice. When Uthman was murdered in 656, Ali's supporters declared him the new caliph. But Uthman's powerful family refused to accept this. Ali was murdered and another member of the Umayyad family replaced him. From 661 to 750, this Umayyad dynasty ruled the Islamic world, establishing its capital at Damascus in Syria.

THE GREAT UMAYYAD MOSQUE AT DAMASCUS. This mosque was built by Caliph al-Walid between 705 and 715. Byzantine influence is apparent in its arched colonnades, its mosaics, and its series of domes, all of which were replicated in much subsequent Islamic architecture. The mosaic over the central doorway, shown here, indicates that the visitor is entering paradise. The mosque was constructed on the foundations of a Roman temple and also incorporates a later Christian shrine dedicated to Saint John the Baptist.
■ *Why would the caliph have chosen this site for his mosque?*

Ali's followers, however, did not accept defeat. They formed a separate group known as the Shi'ites (from *shi'a*, the Arabic word for "faction"). The Shi'ites insisted that only descendants of Ali and his wife, Muhammad's daughter Fatimah, could legitimately rule the Muslim community. Moreover, the Shi'ites did not accept the customary religious practices (*sunna*) that had developed under the first two caliphs who succeeded Muhammad— his father-in-law Abu-Bakr and his disciple Umar. Hence those Muslims who supported the Umayyad family and who *did* regard these customs as binding were called Sunnis. This division between Shi'ites and Sunnis has lasted until the present day. Often persecuted by the Sunni majority as heretics, Shi'ites consider themselves the only true exponents of Islam. Today, Shi'ites predominate in Iran and are the largest single Muslim group in Iraq, yet they constitute only one-tenth of the world's Muslims.

The Umayyad and Abbasid Dynasties

The political triumph of the Umayyads in 661 and the military conquests of their supporters created a strong state cen-tered on Damascus, formerly an administrative capital of the Roman Empire. And in many ways, the Umayyad Caliphate functioned as a Roman successor state; it even continued to employ Greek-speaking bureaucrats trained in the techniques of Byzantine governance. Through these means, the Umayyads dominated the Mediterranean for several generations.

But the failure of their two massive attacks on Constantinople checked their power, which was also being challenged by a rival dynasty, the Abbasids, who claimed descent from one of Muhammad's uncles and who regarded the Umayyads as usurpers. In 750, the Abbasids led a successful rebellion with the help of the Persians, forcing the Umayyads to retreat to their territories in Al-Andalus (Spain). In contrast with the Umayyads, the Abbasid Caliphate stressed Persian elements over Roman ones. Symbolic of this change was the shift in capitals from Damascus to Baghdad, where the second Abbasid caliph, al-Mansur (r. 754–75), built a new city near the ruins of the old Persian capital. The Abbasid caliphs also modeled their behavior on that of Persian princes and their administration on the autocratic rule of the former Persian Empire, imposing heavy taxation to support a large professional army and presiding over an extravagantly luxurious court. This is the world described in the *Arabian*

Nights, a collection of stories written in Baghdad under the Abbasids. The dominating presence in these stories is Harun al-Rashid, who ruled from 786 to 809. His reign marked the height of Abbasid power.

Meanwhile, the Umayyad dynasty continued to rule in Spain and continued to claim that it was the only legitimate successor of Muhammad. Relations between the Umayyads of Al-Andalus and Abbasids of Persia were therefore very cold; but because their realms were far apart, the hostility between them rarely erupted into war. Instead, the two courts competed for preeminence through literary and cultural patronage, much as the Hellenistic kingdoms had done. Philosophers, artists, and especially poets flocked to both. The *Arabian Nights* was one product of this rivalry in Baghdad. Not to be outdone, the caliphs at the Spanish capital of Córdoba amassed a library of more than 400,000 volumes—at a time when a monastery in western Europe that possessed 100 books qualified as a major center of learning. Nothing remotely comparable had been seen in the Mediterranean since the time of the Ptolemies in Alexandria.

ARABIC CALLIGRAPHY. Muslim artists experimented with the art of calligraphy to make complex designs, sometimes abstract but often representing natural forms. This ink drawing on paper actually incorporates Arabic words. It dates from the seventh century, and also represents the Muslim mastery of papermaking.

Islamic Commerce and Industry

Alongside its political and military triumphs, the transformation of tiny settlements into thriving metropolitan commercial centers is one of Islam's most remarkable achievements. So is the Arabs' capacity to adapt themselves to life in highly urbanized regions and to build on the long-established commercial infrastructures of Egypt, Syria, and Persia. Conversion to Islam further increased the economic reach of this infrastructure as trading contacts grew in tandem with the growth of the Islamic world. By the tenth century, Arab merchants had penetrated into southern Russia and equatorial Africa and had become masters of the caravan routes that led eastward to India and China. Ships from the Muslim world established new trade routes across the Indian Ocean, the Persian Gulf, and the Caspian Sea, and for a time dominated the Mediterranean as well.

The growth of Muslim commerce in this period was driven and sustained by a number of important new industries. Mosul, in Iraq, was a center for the manufacture of cotton cloth; Baghdad specialized in glassware, jewelry, pottery, and silks; Damascus was famous for its fine steel and for its woven-figured silk known as "damask"; Morocco and portions of Al-Andalus were both noted for leatherworking; Toledo also produced excellent swords. Drugs, perfumes, carpets, tapestries, brocades, woolens, satins, metal goods, and a host of other products turned out by skilled artisans were carried throughout the Mediterranean world. They were also carried into central Asia, along the network of roads to China that came to be known as the Silk Road, after the most prized commodity for which these goods were traded. With them went the Islamic faith, which took root among some peoples of modern India, Pakistan, and Afghanistan.

One commodity in particular deserves special mention: paper. Muslim Arabs and Persians learned papermaking from the Chinese and became masters of the art in their own right. By the end of the eighth century, Baghdad alone had more than a hundred shops where blank paper or books written on paper were sold. Paper was cheaper to produce, easier to store, and far easier to use than papyrus or parchment. As a result, paper replaced papyrus in the Muslim world by the early eleventh century—even in Egypt, the heartland of papyrus production for almost 4,000 years.

The ready availability of paper brought about a revolution. Many of the characteristic features of Islamic civilization—bureaucratic record keeping, high levels of literacy and book production (especially copies of the Qur'an), even the standard form of cursive Arabic script known as Kufic—would have been impossible without the widespread availability of paper. Only in the thirteenth century would western Europeans master papermaking, but they would still continue to rely on the more durable parchment made from animal hides for the copying of most books and documents. It was not until the advent of print that paper began to replace parchment as the reading and writing material of western Europe (see Chapter 12).

Mobility, Opportunity, and Status

As the reach of Islam extended through conquest and commerce, so Muslim culture became highly cosmopolitan, blending Arab customs with the civilizations of Byzantium and Persia, which were themselves the heirs of ancient empires stretching back to the time of Hammurabi's Babylon. The preeminence of trade and ease of travel also increased geographical mobility, and therefore social mobility. Muhammad's teachings further encouraged social mobility because the Qur'an stressed the equality of all Muslim men. At the courts of Baghdad and Córdoba, therefore, careers were open to men of talent, regardless of birth or wealth. Because literacy was remarkably widespread, many could rise through education and achieve top offices through enterprise and skill.

For those men wishing instead to embrace the religious life alone, Islam offered two main alternatives. One was that of the ulama, a learned man whose studies qualified him to offer advice on aspects of religious law and practice. These men often exerted great influence on the conduct of public life. Complementary to them were the Sufis, mystics who might be equated with Christian monks were it not for the fact that they seldom withdrew from the life of the community. While the ulama stressed adherence to religious law, the Sufis stressed individual contemplation and the cultivation of spiritual ecstasy. Some Sufis were "whirling dervishes," so known in the West because of their mystical dances; others were faqirs, associated in the West with snake charming; still others were quiet, meditative men. Sufis were usually organized into brotherhoods and eventually made many successful efforts to convert the peoples of Africa and India to Islam. Sufism also provided a channel for the most intense religious impulses. The ability of the ulama and the Sufis to coexist is testimony to the cultural pluralism of the Islamic world.

The absence of comparable careers for religious women, even comparable to those available to Christian nuns, is a reminder of the limits often imposed by gender. There are significant exceptions, of course. For example, Muhammad's favored wife, Aisha (ah-EE-sha, d. 678), was revered as a scholar and played an important role in the creation and circulation of hadith (Arabic for "narrative"): stories and sayings that shed light on the Prophet's life and teachings. But in general, women did not benefit from Muslim egalitarianism and opportunity. They were considered valuable but mostly as indicators of a man's wealth and status. The Qur'an allowed any Muslim man to marry as many as four wives, which often meant that the number of women available for marriage was far smaller than the number of men who desired to marry. This made for intense competition, and those men who had wives and daughters needed to ensure that their prized assets were safeguarded. So women were usually kept from the sight of men who were not members of the family, or trusted friends. Along with female servants and the concubines also owned by a wealthy man, they were housed in a segregated part of the residence called the haram ("forbidden place"), guarded by eunuchs (men, usually sold as slaves, who had been castrated prior to adolescence). Within these enclaves, women vied with one another for precedence and worked to advance the fortunes of their children. But this was often the only form of power they could exercise.

Islam's Neighbors

For the inhabitants of Byzantium, the triumph of the Abbasid Caliphate in the eighth century released the Mediterranean from the pressures of Umayyad expansion. Farther west, the Franks of Gaul also benefited from the advent of the Abbasids. Because an Umayyad dynasty still controlled Al-Andalus, the great Frankish ruler Charlemagne (SHAHR-leh-mayn, r. 768–814) could counter these neighboring Muslims' power by maintaining strong diplomatic and commercial relations with the more distant Abbasid Caliphate. The most famous symbol of this connection was an elephant called Abul Abbas, a gift from Harun al-Rashid to Charlemagne. More important, however, was the flow of silver that found its way from the Abbasid Empire north through Russia and the Baltic into the Rhineland, where it was exchanged for Frankish exports of furs, wax, honey, leather, and especially slaves—Europeans, often Slavic peoples, who were captured and sold for profit by other Europeans. Through these channels, jewels, silks, spices, and other luxury goods from India and the Far East also flowed north and west into Frankish territory. These trading links with the Abbasid world helped fund the extraordinary achievements of Charlemagne's own empire, which had a lasting effect on the culture and politics of Europe.

Past and Present

The Meanings of Medievalism

The people who lived during the thousand-year period that we call the Middle Ages didn't think of themselves as "medieval." And indeed, this modern term tends to be used to describe modern phenomena—whether things that we seek to condemn (terrorism, persecution) or that we wish to glorify. The romantic image of Joan of Arc, on the left, was used to rally Americans to the cause of France and its allies during World War I. The image on the right shows warfare as imagined by the game called *Arthur II*.

 Watch related author interview on StudySpace
wwnorton.com/web/westernciv18

THE CONVERSION OF NORTHWESTERN EUROPE

At the end of the sixth century, the Frankish chronicler Gregory of Tours (c. 538–594) considered himself to be a Roman, living in a Roman world of towns, trade, and local administration. Gregory was proud of his family's senatorial status and took it for granted that he and his male relatives should be bishops who ruled, by right of birth and status, over their cities and the surrounding countryside. Like others of his class, Gregory still spoke and wrote Latin—a rather different Latin from the polished prose of Cicero but a Latin that would certainly have been comprehensible to the Romans of the republic. Although Gregory was aware that the western territories of the Roman Empire were now ruled by Frankish, Visigothic, and Lombard kings, he regarded at least some of these kings as Roman succes-

sors because they ruled in accordance with Roman models. In the case of the Franks, the king even ruled with the approval of the Roman emperor in Constantinople. It was also a source of satisfaction to Gregory that all these barbarian kings had converted to Roman Christianity and no longer embraced the heresy of Arianism. This, too, reinforced their *romanitas* and lent legitimacy to their rule.

Two hundred years later, the greatest of all Frankish kings, Charlemagne (742–814), was crowned as a new kind of Roman emperor in the West. By this time, there was no longer a sense of direct continuity with the earlier Roman world or a sense of obligation to the Roman emperor in Byzantium. When intellectuals at Charlemagne's court set out to reform the political, religious, and cultural life of their time, their goal was to revive a Roman Empire from which they considered themselves estranged. They sought a *renovatio Romanorum imperii*, "a renewal of the empire of the Romans." This awareness of a break with the Roman past developed during the seventh century, and was the consequence of profound economic, religious, and cultural changes.

Economic and Political Instability

Even though the economy of the Roman Empire had become increasingly regionalized from the third century C.E. onward (see Chapter 6), the Mediterranean remained a crucial nexus of trade and communication. Gold coinage continued to circulate in both the eastern and the western provinces; a luxury trade in silks, spices, swords, and jewelry continued to move west; and slaves, wine, grain, and leatherwork still moved east from Gaul, Hispania, and North Africa toward Constantinople, Egypt, and Syria. By about 650, however, this Mediterranean world became more disintegrated. This was partly a result of Justinian's failed efforts to reconquer the empire's western territories, but imperial overtaxation of agricultural land, especially in Egypt and North Africa, also played a role. So did the temporary disruptions to traditional trade routes caused by Arab raiders—temporary, because Muslim merchants and rulers would soon do much to reconstruct and encourage patterns of commerce.

But the most significant causes of economic instability in northwestern Europe were internal, not external. The cities of Italy, Gaul, and Hispania could no longer maintain their walls, their public buildings, and their urban infrastructures as they had done under the Roman Empire. Although Christian bishops and their aristocratic kinsmen still governed from these cities and continued to provide a market for certain kinds of luxury goods, barbarian kings and their nobles were moving to the countryside during the seventh century, living as much as possible from the produce of their own estates rather than purchasing their supplies in the marketplace. At the same time, much agricultural land was passing out of cultivation. The slaves or servile peasants who had farmed the large plantations for hundreds of years had no efficient Roman state to enforce their obedience. They were able to become more independent—yet they were also less effective, working just a few acres by themselves. Productivity declined, as did revenues from tolls and taxes.

The systems of coinage that circulated in western Europe were also breaking down, which meant that wealth ceased to be readily portable, hindering long-distance exchange. The Arab conquests may have further reduced the supply of gold available in western Europe, because it was now being channeled eastward. But in any case, gold coins were too valuable to be useful in a local market economy. When we find evidence of such coins in western Europe at this time, they are more likely to have been plundered, hoarded, or given as gifts rather than used to facilitate commerce. By the 660s, those rulers who were still in a position to mint coins and guarantee their value had shifted from a gold to a silver coinage. Indeed, Europe would remain a silver-based economy for the next thousand years, until the supply of gold from European conquests in Africa and America once again made a gold standard viable (see Chapter 12).

As a result of these processes, western Europe came to rely on a two-tier economy of a kind that had not been necessary in any Western civilization since the Lydians introduced a standardized currency in the sixth century B.C.E. (see Chapter 2). Gold, silver, and luxury goods circulated among the very wealthy, but most people relied on barter and various substitute currencies to facilitate transactions. Lords collected rents from their peasants in food or labor, but then found it difficult to convert these in-kind payments into the weapons, jewelry, and silks that brought prestige in aristocratic society. This was problematic not only for social reasons but for political ones: the power of lords depended on their ability to bestow rich gifts on their followers (see **Interpreting Visual Evidence** on pages 230–31). When they could not acquire these items through trade, they had to win them through plunder and extortion. Either way, the process led to violence.

The successful chieftains of this era therefore tended to be those whose areas of influence adjoined wealthy but poorly defended territories that could be easily attacked or blackmailed. Such "soft frontiers" provided warlords and kings with land and booty which they could then distribute to their followers. Successes of this sort would bring more followers to a lord's service, allowing him to further extend his influence; and as long as more conquests were made, the process of amassing power and wealth would continue. But power acquired through plunder and conquest was inherently unreliable. A few defeats might speedily reverse the fortunes of the lords reliant on it, leaving their followers to seek plunder elsewhere.

Another factor contributing to the instability of power in this world was the difficulty of ensuring its peaceful transfer. The barbarian rulers who established themselves during the mass migrations of the fifth and sixth centuries did not come from the traditional royal families of their peoples, and thus they faced opposition from many of their own warriors. Moreover, the groups who took possession of territories within the western Roman Empire during these years were rarely (if ever) composed of a single affinity group; they were usually made up of many different tribes, including a sizable number of displaced Romans. Such unity as they possessed was largely the creation of the charismatic chieftain who led them, and this charisma was not easily passed on by inheritance.

The Ship Burial of Sutton Hoo

The two most impressive finds in the history of British archaeology have been made by amateurs. The most recent, in the summer of 2009, was the largest hoard of worked gold and silver ever found in one place (more than 5 kilograms of gold and 2.5 kilograms of silver; image A), discovered by a man in Staffordshire walking over a neighbor's farm with a metal detector.

The hoard's extraordinary value and range of artifacts—and their historical implications—can only be guessed at now; even the dating is inconclusive.

The other find, made in 1939, was a royal gravesite dating from the seventh century (image B), which many scholars believe to be the tomb of King Redwald of East Anglia, described by Bede as a baptized Christian who refused to give up the worship of his ancestral gods. The king's body was placed in a wooden

structure in the middle of a ninety-foot-long ship that had been dragged to the top of a bluff (a hoo), eleven miles from the English Channel. The ladder in the photograph of the original excavation reaches into the burial chamber.

The contents of the grave included:

• a lamp and a bronze bucket that had been suspended from a chain

• a ceremonial helmet (image C) modeled on those worn by Roman cavalry officers

A. The Staffordshire hoard, found in 2009.

B. The original excavation of the burial chamber at Sutton Hoo, 1939.

The Prosperous Kingdom of the Franks

Of all the groups that set up kingdoms in western Europe during the fifth and sixth centuries, only the Franks succeeded in establishing a single dynasty from which leaders would be drawn for the next 250 years.

This dynasty reached back to Clovis (r. c. 481–511), a warrior-king who established an alliance between his family and the powerful bishops of Gaul by converting to Roman Christianity—emulating the example of Constantine on many levels. Clovis's family came to be known as the Merovingians, after his legendary grandfather just before the withdrawal of the legions from Britain in 410—but decorated like helmets found in eastern Sweden

- a sword and a large, circular shield, resembling those found in Swedish burial sites

- exquisitely crafted belt buckles and shoulder clasps (image D), made of gold and garnet, and worked with designs

- a pair of silver spoons with long handles, possibly crafted in Byzantium, and inscribed in Greek with the names PAULOS and SAULOS (Paul and Saul)

- a large silver dish (72 cm in diameter) made in Byzantium between 491 and 518

- a bronze bowl from the eastern Mediterranean

- a six-stringed lyre in a bag made of beaver skin, similar to lyres found in Germany

- a purse containing thirty-seven gold coins, each from a different Merovin-

gian mint, the most recent datable to the 620s

- heaps of armor, blankets, cloaks, and other gear

Questions for Analysis

1. What do these artifacts, and the context in which they were found, reveal about the extent of Anglo-Saxon contact with the rest of the world? Which regions are represented, and why?

2. Based on this evidence, what conclusions can you draw about Anglo-Saxon culture and values?

3. Do any of these graves' goods indicate that the occupant was a Christian king? Why or why not?

C. A Sutton Hoo helmet.

D. Sutton Hoo buckles.

Merovech, who was said to have been fathered by a sea monster (meaning, in effect, that no one really knew who Clovis's grandfather was). Clovis's own name proved even more long-lasting than the dynasty he founded. As the language of the Franks merged with the Latin of Gaul to become French, the name "Clovis" lost its hard *C* while the pronunciation of the *V* was softened. Thus "Clovis" became "Louis," the name borne by French kings up to the time of the French Revolution over a millennium later (see Chapter 18).

The Merovingians were not the only noble family in Gaul with a claim to kingship, but they were more successful

ABBEY CHURCH, ISLAND OF IONA. This tiny island off Scotland's west coast is the site of many Iron Age forts and has been home to a monastic community since the sixth century. Missionaries from Iona were instrumental in converting the Celtic tribes of northern Britain to Christianity.

in defending it than their counterparts in Visigothic Spain, Lombard Italy, and both the Anglo-Saxon and Celtic territories of Britain. In part, this was due to their capacity to transfer power from one generation to another. In medieval Europe, as at other times and places, the right of inheritance was not limited to the eldest male claimant of each competing royal family. When it came to property or power, all the sons of a king—and frequently all his male cousins and nephews, and even his daughters—could consider themselves rightful heirs. So even when the rule of any family was not threatened by outsiders, the transfer of power was almost always bloody.

In Gaul, however, the often brutal conflicts between rival Merovingian kings did not materially disrupt the strength and sophistication of their governance. Many elements of late Roman local administration survived throughout this period. Latin literacy, fostered by a network of monasteries linked to the Frankish court, remained an important element in this administration, providing a foundation on which Charlemagne would later build. Even the cultural revival associated with the reign of Charlemagne (see below) really began in the late seventh century at the monastic foundations fostered by members of the Merovingian family and other powerful lords.

Such monasteries grew remarkably during the seventh century and became the engines that made Merovingian Gaul wealthier and more stable than other regions of northwestern Europe. Approximately 550 monasteries were thriving by the year 700, more than 300 of which had been established in the preceding century alone. Frankish bishops also prospered along with their cities, amassing most of

their landed possessions by the end of the seventh century, possessions from which their successors would continue to profit until the time of the French Revolution.

This massive redistribution of wealth reflected a fundamental shift in the economic gravity of the Frankish kingdom. In the year 600, the wealth of Gaul was still concentrated in the south, where it had been throughout the late Roman period. By the year 750, however, the economic center of the kingdom lay north of the Loire, in the territories that extended from the Rhineland westward to the North Sea. It was here that most of the new monastic foundations of the seventh century were established.

Behind this shift in prosperity lay a long and successful effort to bring under cultivation the rich, heavy soils of northern Europe. This effort was largely engineered by the new monasteries, which harnessed the peasant workforce and pioneered agricultural technologies adapted to the climate and terrain. The most important invention was a heavy, wheeled plow capable of cutting and turning grassland sod and clay, soils very different from those of the Mediterranean. This innovation in turn necessitated the development of more efficient devices for harnessing animals (particularly oxen) to these plows. Gradually warming weather also improved the fertility of the wet northern soils, lengthening the growing season and so making possible more efficient crop-rotation systems. As food became more plentiful, the population began to expand. Although much of Frankish Gaul remained a land of scattered settlements separated by dense forests, it was far more populous by 750 than it had been in the time of Clovis. All these developments would continue during the reign of Charlemagne, and beyond.

Analyzing Primary Sources

From Anglo-Saxon Slave Girl to Frankish Queen

The Anglo-Saxon Saint Balthild rose to prominence as the wife of the Merovingian king Clovis II (r. 639–57), but she began life as a slave. After the king's death, she was left in a precarious position at the Frankish court as regent for her son, Clothar III, and was eventually forced to enter the convent she had founded at Chelles, near Paris. The following excerpt from her Latin vita *("life") describes her speedy ascent to a position of power. It was probably written by a nun of Chelles.*

raise should first be sung of Him Who made the humble great and raised the pauper from the dunghill and seated him among the princes of his people. Such a one is the woman present to our minds, the venerable and great lady Balthild the queen. Divine Providence called her from across the seas. She, who came here as God's most precious and lofty pearl, was sold at a cheap price. Erchinoald, a Frankish magnate and most illustrious man, acquired her and in his service the girl behaved most honorably.... For she was kind-hearted and sober and prudent in all her ways, careful and plotting evil for none.... And since she was of the Saxon race, she was graceful in form with refined features, a most seemly woman with a smiling face and serious gait. And she so showed herself just as she ought in all things, that she pleased her master and found favor in his eyes. So he determined that she should set out the drinking cup for him in his chamber and, honored above all others as his housekeeper, stand at his side always ready to serve him.... She gained such happy fame that, when the said lord Erchinoald's wife died, he hoped to unite himself to Balthild, that faultless virgin, in a matrimonial bed....

[But] when she was called to the master's chamber she hid herself secretly in a corner and threw some vile rags over herself so that no one could guess that anyone might be concealed there.... She hoped that she might avoid a human marriage bed and thus merit a spiritual and heavenly spouse.... Thereafter it happened, with God's approval, that Balthild, the maid who escaped marriage with a lord, came to be espoused to Clovis, son of the former king Dagobert. Thus by virtue of her humility she was raised to a higher rank....

Source: Excerpted from *Sainted Women of the Dark Ages*, ed. and trans. John E. Halborg, Jo Ann McNamara, and E. Gordon Whatley (Chapel Hill, NC: 1992), pp. 268–70.

Questions for Analysis

1. Based on what you have learned about the prevalence of the slave trade in ancient and early medieval civilizations, what might you speculate about Balthild's actual role in Erchinoald's household?

2. Balthild would have been a contemporary of the king buried at Sutton Hoo. Is it likely that she would have been a Christian when she was sold into slavery in England? Why or why not?

3. In light of Balthild's later status as a queen and regent for her son, why would her biographer stress that she was "careful and plotting evil for none"? To what allegations or incidents might the author of this life be responding?

The Power of Monasticism

As we just noted, the seventh century witnessed a rapid increase in the foundation of monastic houses all over northwestern Europe. Although monasteries had existed in Gaul, Italy, and Hispania since the fourth century, most were located in highly Romanized areas. In the fifth century, a powerful monastic movement began in Ireland as well, and eventually spread to the Celtic regions of Britain and from there to the Continent. The Irish missionary Columbanus (540–615), for example, was the founder of Merovingian monasteries at Luxeuil and Fontaine. Important monasteries were also established on the island of Iona, off the western coast of what is now Scotland, and at Lindisfarne, off Britain's northeastern coast. In all of these cases, close ties were forged between monks and local tribal leaders or powerful families, much to the political and economic gain of all parties.

Most monastic foundations of the seventh century were deliberately located in rural areas but at strategic trading crossroads, where they played a crucial role. Indeed, the material advantages of monastic innovation were a powerful incentive toward Christian conversion in the communities directly affected by the improved living conditions they fostered. Prosperity was also a powerful advertisement for authority: a lord or chieftain who had the support of a monastery and the beneficent Christian God was obviously worthy of loyalty. Because monasteries played such a key role in economic development and political order, lords often granted them special privileges, helping to free them from the control of local bishops and giving them jurisdiction over their own lands. Thus, monasteries became politically powerful not only because they had been founded by powerful men, but because they were lordships in their own right.

Frequently, these new foundations were double monasteries that accommodated women as well as men. Often they were established for women only. In either case, they were often ruled by abbesses drawn from noble or royal families. Monasticism thus became a road to political power for women. It also gave women—commoners as well as queens—freedoms they did not have elsewhere, or at any other time in history up to this point. Within the monastery, women had more control over their own minds and bodies. They could also wield enormous influence, promoting their families' diplomatic and dynastic interests but without the dangers and uncertainties of pregnancy. And they were guaranteed salvation, at a time when salvation outside the cloister seemed a perilously uncertain prospect. Moreover, the prayers of holy women were regarded as particularly effective in securing divine support or retribution. This further enriched convents through donations of land and wealth, although it could not always safeguard them from violence, or their inhabitants from abduction and rape.

Monasteries for women also served the interests of men, which is why kings and lords supported them. They were dynamic repositories of prayer, regarded as essential to furthering the ambitions of their male benefactors and protecting them from harm. They provided a dignified place of retirement for inconvenient but politically powerful women, such as the sisters and daughters of rivals or the widow of a previous ruler. And by limiting the number of powerful women who could reproduce, female monasteries also reduced the number of male claimants to power. Establishing aristocratic and royal women in such convents was thus an important way of controlling successions and managing political disputes.

Monasticism played an important role in missionary activity, too. As noted above, the work of Irish monks was crucial to the spread of Christianity in northern parts of Britain and in other areas of northern Europe virtually untouched by the Roman Empire. Missionaries were also sponsored by the fledgling papacy in Rome and by the Merovingian royal family—especially its women. The best example of this is the conversion of Britain's Anglo-Saxon tribes, which we glimpsed in the opening paragraph of this chapter. In 597, a group of forty Benedictine monks were sent by Pope Gregory I (r. 590–604) to the southeastern kingdom of Kent, where their efforts were assisted by Frankish translators—and by the fact that the local king, Æthelbehrt (*EH-thel-behrt*), had married a Frankish princess who was already a Christian. This pattern of influence repeated itself all over southern and eastern Britain. Writing a hundred years later in the monastery of Monkwearmouth in Northumbria, the historian Bede could claim that the tribes of England were now united in their shared allegiance to the Roman Church and its English archbishop, whose seat was the cathedral in Æthelbert's capital at Canterbury. Bede credited the Roman pope for initiating this remarkable feat, and the monastic rule under which he himself lived for bringing it to fruition.

The Papacy of Gregory the Great

Pope Gregory I, also known as Gregory the Great, was the first bishop of Rome to envision a new role for the papacy in northwestern Europe. We have seen that the Roman *papa* had begun to assert his superiority over other patriarchs throughout the Christian world; but in reality, he was subordinate to the emperors in Constantinople and to the greater prestige of its patriarch. As Byzantine power in Italy declined, however, Gregory sought to create a more autonomous Latin Church by focusing attention on the untapped resources of the wild West. An influential theologian, he is considered the intellectual successor of Jerome, Ambrose, and Augustine (see Chapter 6) because he greatly extended the applicability of their teachings to the world outside the Romanized Mediterranean.

Among Gregory's doctrinal contributions were an emphasis on the necessity of penance for the forgiveness of sins and the concept of Purgatory as a place where the soul could be purified before it was admitted into heaven—instead of being sent immediately to perpetual damnation. Alongside this emphasis on penance, Gregory emphasized the importance of pastoral care: the proper instruction, encouragement, and control of the laity. He also sought to

THE LINDISFARNE GOSPELS. This page from one of the astonishing illuminated ("light-filled") books produced by the monastery at Lindisfarne shows the opening of the Gospel of John. ▪ *Why would monastic scribes have devoted so much time, energy, and skill to the decoration of a text? How do these artistic motifs compare to those featured on the metalwork found at Sutton Hoo (pages 230 and 231)?* ▪ *What conclusions can you draw from these similarities?*

THE COVER OF THE LINDAU GOSPELS. This book, bound in gilded silver and encrusted with jewels and ivory cameos, was presented by Pope Gregory the Great to a Lombard queen around the year 600. ▪ *Given what you have learned about the economic and cultural circumstances of northern Europe, what is the significance of this rich gift?* ▪ *What would Gregory have been attempting to achieve by giving it?*

increase the affective power of Christian worship by promoting the performance of music. Song has always been essential to religious ritual, but Gregory encouraged it to such a degree that the very style of singing that emerged in this period is known as "Gregorian chant."

Gregory was also a statesman and leader in the model of his Roman forebears. Within Italy, he ensured the survival of the papacy against Lombard invaders by clever diplomacy and expert management of papal estates and revenues. He maintained good relations with Byzantium while asserting his authority over the other bishops of the Latin Church. His support of communities living under the *Rule* of Saint Benedict (see Chapter 6) helped make Benedictine monasticism the predominant monastic force in the West. Yet Gregory's influence was not always benign. He was the first

prominent theologian to articulate the Church's official policy toward Jews, which became increasingly negative. Building on Gregory's example, later popes would insist that the Jews' alleged role in Christ's crucifixion and their denial of his divinity had deprived them of their rights in a Christian world.

THE EMPIRE OF CHARLEMAGNE

Toward the end of the seventh century, tensions among noble families in the Merovingian heartland of Neustria and those in the Frankish border region of Austrasia were increasing. The Austrasian nobles had profited from their steady push into the "soft frontier" east of the Rhine,

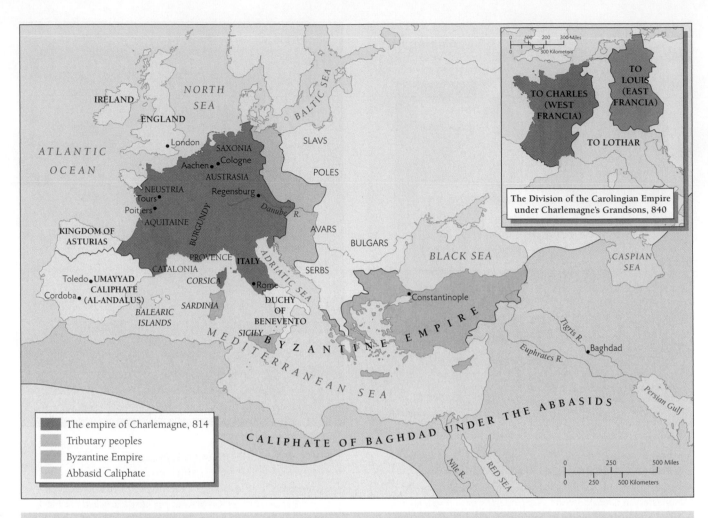

The empire of Charlemagne, 814
Tributary peoples
Byzantine Empire
Abbasid Caliphate

The Division of the Carolingian Empire under Charlemagne's Grandsons, 840

THE EMPIRE OF CHARLEMAGNE IN 814. When Charlemagne died in 814, he had created an empire that embraced a large portion of the lands formerly united under the western Roman Empire. ▪ *What were the geographical limits of his power?* ▪ *How were these limits dictated by the historical forces we have been studying?* ▪ *Along what lines was Charlemagne's empire divided after his death?*

acquiring wealth and military power in the process. The Merovingians, settled in Neustria, had no such easy conquests at their disposal. Moreover, a considerable portion of their land had been given to monasteries in the course of the seventh century, which decreased their wealth and their capacity to attract followers. A succession of short-lived kings then opened the door to a series of civil wars, and finally to a decisive challenge to the dynasty.

Kings and Kingmakers

In 687, an Austrasian nobleman called Pepin (635/45–714) succeeded in forcing his way into power by making himself the Frankish king's right-hand man. He took the title *maior domus*, "great man of the house," and began to exercise royal authority while maintaining the fiction that he

was merely a royal servant. He did this effectively for more than twenty-five years. After his death, his illegitimate son Charles Martel ("the Hammer," 688–741) further consolidated control over both the Merovingian homeland and the Frankish royal administration. For two generations, the Merovingian kings were largely figureheads in a realm ruled by Charles Martel and his sons.

Charles Martel is sometimes considered the second founder (after Clovis) of the Frankish kingdom. His claim to this title is twofold. First, in 733 or 734 he repelled a Muslim force that had ventured into Frankish territory, meeting them in battle at Tours, some 150 miles from the Merovingian stronghold at Paris. Although the Arab-led contingent was a raiding party rather than a full-scale army, this incursion may have been regarded as an attempted conquest on the part of the Umayyad dynasty of Al-Andalus; in any case, Charles's victory won him great prestige. More important, Charles had developed an alliance with Benedictine missionaries from England, who were attempting to convert the Low Countries and central Germany to Christianity. Charles's family had long been active in the drive to conquer and settle these areas, and he understood clearly how missionary work and Frankish expansion could go hand in hand. Charles assisted these conversion efforts. In return, the leader of the English Benedictines, Boniface (c. 672–754), brought him into contact with the papacy and assisted his efforts to control Frankish churches.

Although Charles never sought to become king himself, he was so clearly the effective ruler of Gaul that the Franks did not bother to choose a new king when the reigning Merovingian died in 737. But then Charles himself died in 741, and his sons Carloman and Pepin were forced to allow the election of a new king while they continued to exercise power behind the scenes. This compromise did not last long, however; in 750, Carloman withdrew from public life by entering a monastery, and Pepin decided to seize the throne for himself. This turned out to be harder than he may have expected. Even though the reigning king was ineffectual, Frankish identity was bound up with loyalty to Clovis's descendants; although tribal leaders had the power to elect a new king, they were reluctant to do so. Pepin therefore turned to the Frankish bishops, who were unwilling to support him without backing from the pope. To gain this, Pepin was able to trade on his family's support of the Benedictines. The pope, for his part, saw that a powerful leader of the Franks could be a potential ally in his political struggle with the Byzantine emperors over iconoclasm (which the papacy opposed) and in his military struggle against the Lombard kings for control of central Italy.

So Boniface, acting as papal emissary, anointed Pepin king of the Franks in 751. This was a new ritual, but it had a powerful biblical precedent: the ceremony by which the prophet Samuel had made Saul the first king of Israel, by anointing him with holy oil (see Chapter 2). Indeed, the significance of the Old Testament association would grow under Pepin's son Charlemagne (associated with David) and his grandson Louis the Pious (associated with Solomon). To contemporary observers, however, the novelty of these proceedings underscored the uncertainty of the process by which a legitimate king had been deposed and a new king created. And as we will see, this king-making process was the first step on a long road that would ultimately limit the power of later medieval kings and modern constitutional monarchs alike: the principle that kingship is an office and can be occupied, at least theoretically, by anyone—and that if a ruler is ineffectual or tyrannical, he can be deposed and replaced by a new officeholder.

The Reign of Charlemagne

Pepin's position as king was a tenuous one, and when he died it seemed likely that the Frankish kingdom would break up into mutually hostile regions: Austrasia, Neustria, and (to the southwest) Aquitaine. That it did not was the work of Pepin's son, Charles, known to the French as Charlemagne and to the Germans as Karl der Grosse—"Charles the Great." It is from him, as well as from his grandfather Charles Martel, that this new Frankish dynasty takes the name "Carolingian" (from *Carolus*, the Latin form of "Charles").

When Charlemagne came to power in 768, he managed to unite the Franks by the tried and true method of attacking a common, outside enemy. In a series of conquests, the Franks succeeded in annexing the Lombard kingdom of northern Italy, most of what is now Germany, portions of central Europe, and Catalonia (in southeastern Spain). These conquests seemed to set a seal of divine approval on the new Carolingian dynasty. More important, they provided the victorious Franks with spoils of war and vast new lands that enabled Charlemagne to reward his closest followers.

Many of the peoples whom Charlemagne conquered were already Christians. In pagan Saxony, however, Charlemagne's armies campaigned for twenty years before subduing the inhabitants and forcing their conversion. This created a precedent with momentous consequences, because it linked military conquest with conformity of belief. In time, the assumption that the subjugation of a vanquished people should be accompanied by their religious conversion would become ingrained in the philosophy and practice of most Western civilizations.

To rule his new empire, Charlemagne enlisted the help of the Frankish warrior class he had enriched and elevated to positions of prominence. These counts (in Latin, *comites*, "followers") supervised local governance within their territories. Among their many duties was the administration of justice and the raising of armies. Charlemagne also established a network of other local officials who convened courts, established tolls, administered royal lands, and collected taxes. To facilitate transactions and trade, he created a new coinage system based on a division of the silver pound into units of twenty shillings, each worth twelve pennies—a system that would last in parts of continental Europe and in Britain into the 1970s (when it was replaced by a decimal-based currency). As we noted

The Capitularies of Charlemagne

Charlemagne's careful governance of his domains would set a high standard for other rulers far into the future. One of the means by which this governance was carried out was through capitularies (from a Latin word denoting a document divided into chapters), which contained instructions issued by the central administration of the court to local counts and other authorities. The following are directives addressed in 785 to the administrators of Saxony, a region recently conquered by Charlemagne, whose inhabitants were forcibly converted to Christianity.

Capitulary Concerning the Parts of Saxony

1. Decisions were taken first on the more important items. All were agreed that the churches of Christ which are now being built in Saxony and are consecrated to God should have no less honor than the temples of idols had, but rather a greater and more surpassing honor.

2. If anyone takes refuge in a church, let no one presume to drive him out of that church by force; rather let him be in peace until he is brought to plead his case, . . . and after this let him be brought to the presence of our lord the king. . . .

3. If anyone makes forcible entry to a church, and steals anything from it by violence or stealth, or if he sets fire to the church, let him die.

4. If anyone in contempt of the Christian faith should spurn the holy Lenten fast and eat meat, let him die; but let the priest enquire into the matter, lest it should happen that someone is compelled by necessity to eat meat.

* * *

6. If anyone is deceived by the devil, and believes after the manner of pagans that some man or some woman is a witch and eats people, . . . let him pay the penalty of death.

7. If anyone follows pagan rites and causes the body of a dead man to be consumed by fire, . . . let him pay with his life.

8. If there is anyone of the Saxon people lurking among them unbaptized, and if he scorns to come to baptism, . . . let him die.

9. If anyone sacrifices a man to the devil, . . . let him die.

* * *

12. If anyone rapes the daughter of his lord, he shall die.

13. If anyone kills his lord or his lady, he shall be punished in the same way.

* * *

18. On Sundays there are to be no assemblies or public gatherings, except in cases of great need or when an enemy is pressing; rather let all attend church to hear the word of God. . . .

* * *

33. With regard to perjury, the law of the Saxons is to apply.

34. We forbid the Saxons to come together as a body in public gatherings, except on those occasions when our *missus* [messenger] assembles them on our instructions; rather,

let each and every count hold court and administer justice in his own area. And the clergy are to see to it that this order is obeyed.

Source: From *The Reign of Charlemagne: Documents on Carolingian Government*, ed. and trans. H. R. Loyn and John Percival (New York: 1975), pp. 31–34.

Questions for Analysis

1. What types of behavior does this capitulary attempt to regulate? What seem to be the major challenges faced by Charlemagne's administrators in this new territory?

2. In only one case does this capitulary mention the law of the Saxon people themselves, in the clause relating to perjury (number 12). Why would Charlemagne's administrators consider it advisable to punish this particular crime in accordance with Saxon custom?

3. How would you characterize Charlemagne's method of dealing with a conquered people? In your estimation, is this policy likely to be effective?

above, much of the silver for this new coinage originated in the Abbasid Caliphate and was payment for furs, cloth, and especially slaves captured in Charlemagne's wars, who were now being transported to Baghdad. The silver, in turn, circulated as far north as Scandinavia, Russia, and the Baltic Sea.

Like Carolingian administration generally, this new monetary system depended on the regular use of written records, which means that the sources supporting historical research on Charlemagne's empire are numerous. But Charlemagne did not rely on the written word alone to make his will felt. Periodically, his court sent special messengers, known as *missi*, on tours through the countryside to relay his instructions and report back on the conduct of local administrators. This was the most thorough system of governance known in Europe since the height of the Roman Empire, reaching many parts of the Continent that the Romans had never occupied. It set a standard for royal administration that would be emulated and envied for centuries.

Christianity and Kingship

In keeping with the traditions established by his father and grandfather, Charlemagne took his responsibilities as a Christian king seriously. As his empire expanded, moreover, he came to see himself as the leader of a unified Christian society, Christendom, which he was obliged to defend. Like his contemporaries in Byzantium and the Muslim world—as well as his Roman predecessors—he recognized no distinction between religion and politics. Indeed, he conceived kingship as a sacred office created by God to protect the Church and promote the salvation of his Christian people. Religious reforms were therefore no less central to proper kingship than were justice and defense. In some ways, indeed, a king's responsibilities for his kingdom's spiritual welfare were more important than his other, secular responsibilities.

These ideas were not new in the late eighth century, but they took on a new importance because of the extraordinary power Charlemagne wielded. Like other rulers of this period, Charlemagne was able to appoint and depose bishops and abbots, just as he did his counts and other officials. He extended his authority by changing the liturgy of Frankish churches, reforming the rules of worship in Frankish monasteries, declaring the tenents of Christian belief, ruthlessly prohibiting pagan practices, and forcibly imposing basic Christian observances on the conquered peoples of Saxony. As the dominant political power in central Italy, Charlemagne was also the protector of the papacy. Although he acknowledged the pope as spiritual leader of Christendom, Charlemagne dealt with the bishop of Rome much as he did with other bishops in his empire. He supervised and approved papal elections, and he also protected the pope from his many enemies. To Charlemagne, such measures were clearly required if God's new chosen people, the Franks, were to avoid the fate that befell biblical Israel whenever Hebrews turned away from obedience to God.

The Carolingian Renaissance

Similar political motivations lay behind the phenomenon known as the Carolingian Renaissance, a cultural and intellectual flowering that took place around the Carolingian court. Like their biblical exemplars David and Solomon, Charlemagne and his son Louis the Pious considered it a crucial part of their role to be patrons of learning and the arts. In doing so, they created an ideal of the court as an intellectual and cultural center that would profoundly influence western European cultural life until the First World War (see Chapter 24).

Behind the Carolingians' support for scholarship was the conviction that learning was the foundation on which Christian wisdom rested and that such wisdom was essential to the salvation of God's people. Charlemagne therefore recruited intellectuals from all over Europe to further the cause of scholarship. Foremost among these was the

CHARLEMAGNE'S IMAGE OF AUTHORITY. A silver penny struck between 804 and 814 in Mainz (as indicated by the letter *M* at the bottom) represents Charlemagne in a highly stylized fashion, as a Roman emperor with a military cloak and laurel wreath. The inscription reads *Karolus Imp Avg* (Charles, Emperor, Augustus). Charlemagne's portrait is closely modeled on both Hellenistic and Roman coins.

ROMAN HISTORY IN CAROLINGIAN MINISCULE. The very survival of Livy's history of the Roman Republic, originally written during the reign of Augustus Caesar, is a product of the Carolingian Renaissance. Furthermore, the clear layout and beautifully formed script of this manuscript copy helped readers without detailed knowledge of Latin to make out the words. For example, the first two words of the heading near the bottom are *Incipit Liber* ("[Here] begins the book") and the sentence following it begins with a reference to the Carthaginian general Hannibal.

Anglo-Saxon monk Alcuin, whose command of classical Latin established him as the intellectual leader of Charlemagne's court. Under Alcuin's direction, Carolingian scholars produced much original Latin poetry and an impressive number of theological and pastoral tracts. But their primary efforts were devoted to collating, correcting, and recopying ancient Latin texts, including, most importantly, the text of the Latin Bible, which had accumulated many generations of copyists' mistakes in the 400 years since Jerome's translation (see Chapter 6).

To detect and correct these errors, Alcuin and his associates gathered as many different versions of the biblical text as they could find and compared them, word by word. After determining the correct version among all the variants, they made a new, corrected copy and destroyed the other versions. They also developed a new style of handwriting, with simplified letter forms and spaces inserted between words, reduce so as to the likelihood that subsequent copyists would misread the corrected texts. Reading was further facilitated by the addition of punctuation. This new style of handwriting, known as Carolingian miniscule, is the foundation for the typefaces of most modern books—including this one.

The Revival of the Western Roman Empire

On Christmas Day in the year 800, Charlemagne was crowned emperor by Pope Leo III. Centuries later, popes would cite this epochal event as precedent for the political superiority they claimed over the ruler of the "Holy Roman Empire," as it came to be called (see Chapter 9). In the year 800, however, Pope Leo was entirely under Charlemagne's thumb. Yet Charlemagne's biographer, Einhard, would later claim that the coronation was planned without the emperor's knowledge. For one thing, it was certain to anger the imperial government in Byzantium, with which Charlemagne had strained relations. Nor did the imperial title add much to Charlemagne's position; he was already a de facto emperor in his own right. Why, then, did he accept the title and, in 813, transfer it to his son Louis?

Historians are still debating this question. What is clear, in any case, is the symbolic significance of the action. Although the Romans of Byzantium no longer influenced western Europe directly, they continued to regard it (somewhat vaguely) as an outlying province of their empire. Moreover, the emperor in Constantinople claimed to be the political successor of Caesar Augustus. Charlemagne's assumption of the title was therefore a clear slight to the reigning empress Irene (r. 797–802), whose occupation of the imperial throne was controversial because she was a woman; and it deepened Byzantine suspicion of his cordial relationship with Byzantium's enemy, Harun al-Rashid, the Abbasid caliph in Baghdad. But for Charlemagne's followers—and for all the medieval rulers who came after him—the assumption of the imperial title was a declaration of independence and superiority. With only occasional interruptions, western Europeans would continue to crown Roman emperors until the nineteenth century, while territorial claims and concepts of national sovereignty continued to rest on Carolingian precedent. Whatever his own motives may have been, Charlemagne's revival of the western Roman Empire was crucial to the developing self-consciousness of western Europe.

DISPUTED LEGACIES AND NEW ALLIANCES

When Charlemagne died in 814, his empire descended intact to his only surviving son, Louis the Pious. Under Louis, however, the empire disintegrated, and it was divided among his three sons in 840. Western Francia (the core of modern France) went to Charles the Bald; eastern Francia (which became key principalities of Germany) went to Louis the German; and a third kingdom (stretching from the Rhineland to Rome) went to Lothair, along with the imperial title. But when Lothair's line died out in 856, this fragile compromise dissolved into open warfare, as the East and West Franks fought over Lothair's former territories and the imperial power that went with them. The heartland of this disputed domain, known to the Germans as Lotharingia and to the French as Alsace-Lorraine, would continue to be a site of bitter contention until the end of the Second World War (see Chapter 26).

The Collapse of the Carolingian Empire

Louis faced an impossible situation of a kind we have studied many times before: the task of holding together an artificial constellation of territories united by someone else. Charlemagne's empire had been built on successful conquest. By 814, however, Charlemagne had pushed the borders of his empire beyond the practical limits of his administration. To the southwest, he now faced the Umayyad rulers of Al-Andalus; to the north, the pagan inhabitants of Scandinavia; and in the east, his armies were too preoccupied with settling the territories they had already conquered to secure the Slavic lands that lay beyond. At the same time, the pressures that had driven these conquests—the need for land and plunder to cement the allegiance of followers—had become ever more pronounced as a result of their very success. The number of counts had tripled, from approximately 100 to 300, and each of them wanted more wealth and power.

Frustrated by their new emperor's inability to reward them, the Frankish aristocracy turned against him and on each other. Smoldering hostilities among Austrasians, Neustrians, and Aquitanians—which Charlemagne had stifled by directing their energies elsewhere—flared up again. As centralized authority broke down, the vast majority of the empire's free inhabitants found themselves increasingly dominated by local lords who treated them as if they were serfs. At the same time, internal troubles in the Abbasid Empire caused a breakdown in the commercial system through which Scandinavian traders brought Abbasid silver into Carolingian domains. Deprived of their livelihood, these traders turned to raiding, which is what the Norse word *viking* means. Under these combined pressures, the Carolingian Empire fell apart, and a new political map of Europe began to emerge.

The Impact of the Viking Invasions

Scandinavian traders were already familiar figures in the North Sea and Baltic ports of Europe when Charlemagne came to power. They had begun to establish strategic settlements from which they navigated down the rivers to Byzantium (through the Black Sea) and the Abbasid Caliphate (through the Caspian Sea). But when the power of the Abbasids declined, Viking raiders turned to plunder, ransom, tribute collection, and slaving. At first, these were small-scale operations. But soon, some Viking attacks involved organized armies numbering in the thousands. The small tribal kingdoms of the Anglo-Saxons and Celts made the British Isles easy targets, as were the divided kingdoms of the Franks.

By the tenth century, the Vikings controlled independent principalities in eastern England, Ireland, the islands of Scotland, and the region of France that is still called "Norseman-land," Normandy. A Viking people known as the Rus' established the beginnings of a kingdom that would become Russia. At the end of the tenth century, Vikings ventured farther west and colonized Iceland, Greenland, and a distant territory they called Vinland (Newfoundland, Canada). In 1016, a Viking army placed a Danish king on the English throne.

The threat of Viking attacks began to lessen with Scandinavia's conversion to Christianity, which proceeded rapidly from the late tenth century onward. But it was more effectively mitigated by the fact that Viking populations quickly assimilated into the cultural and political world of northwestern Europe. By 1066, when the "Norsemen" of Normandy conquered England, the English—many of whom were descended from Vikings themselves—perceived them to be French. Driving this rapid assimilation may have been the raids of the Magyars,

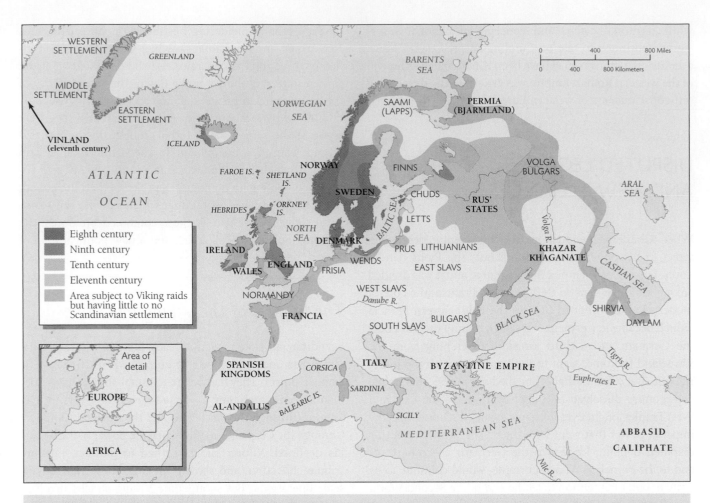

PATTERNS OF VIKING ACTIVITY AND SETTLEMENT, c. 800–1100. The Vikings were instrumental in maintaining commercial contacts among northern Europe, Byzantium, and Islam until the eighth century, when changing historical forces turned them into raiders and colonists. ■ *What area was the original homeland of the Vikings?* ■ *What geographic region did the Vikings first conquer, and why?* ■ *The areas marked in green show territories that were later targeted by pillagers. Why would the Vikings have avoided settlement in these areas?*

a non-Indo-European people who crossed the Carpathian Mountains around 895 and carried out a number of devastating campaigns throughout continental Europe before settling in what is now Hungary. The disparate inhabitants of the new Viking colonies may have been forced to unite against this common enemy and thus have come to share a sense of common identity.

The overall effect of the Vikings on Europe continues to be a matter of scholarly controversy. The destruction they caused is undeniable, and many of the monasteries of Frankish, Anglo-Saxon, and Celtic lands were destroyed—along with countless precious books and historical artifacts. Yet the Vikings were not the only source of disorder in the ninth and tenth centuries. The civil wars and local political rivalries that had replaced the centralized states of Charlemagne

and the Islamic caliphates contributed mightily to the chaos of the post-Carolingian world and made the Vikings' successes easily won. Nor were the Vikings a source of disorder alone. In Ireland and eastern England, Vikings founded a series of new towns. As long-distance traders, Vikings transported large quantities of silver into western Europe, fueling the European economy.

In those few regions where people did succeed in fending off Viking attacks, the unifying force of victory was strong. The best example of this phenomenon is England, which had never been part of Charlemagne's empire and which had remained divided into small kingdoms at war with one other—despite Bede's wishful history of "an English church and people." Yet in a direct response to the Viking threat, a loosely unified kingdom emerged for the

A DRAGON-PROWED VIKING LONGBOAT. This manuscript illumination—from a book copied in Anglo-Saxon England—depicts one of the vessels terrifyingly well known to the shore-dwelling peoples of northwestern Europe. Concerted efforts to ward off Viking invasions led to the establishment of the first unified English kingdom.

first time under Alfred the Great (r. 871–99). His success in defending his own small kingdom from Viking attacks, combined with the destruction of every other competing royal dynasty, allowed Alfred and his heirs to assemble effective armed forces, institute mechanisms of local government, found new towns, and codify English laws. In addition, Alfred established a court school and fostered a distinctive Anglo-Saxon literary culture. While the Anglo-Saxon vernacular had been a written language since the time of the Roman missions, it now came to rival Latin as a language of administration, history, scholarship, and spirituality. Moreover, oral traditions of poetic composition and storytelling were preserved and extended, as exemplified by the epic *Beowulf*. Until the eleventh century, Anglo-Saxon was the only European vernacular used for regular written communication.

The Disintegration of the Islamic World

As we noted above, the declining power of the Abbasid dynasty in Persia was one of the forces that contributed to the escalation of Viking raids. A major cause of this decline was the gradual impoverishment of the Abbasids' economic base, the agricultural wealth of the ancient Tigris-Euphrates basin, which resulted from ecological crises and a devastating revolt by the enslaved African workforce there. Tax revenues from the Abbasid Caliphate were also declining, as provincial rulers in North Africa, Egypt, and Syria retained larger and larger portions of those revenues for themselves. As their sources of income became depleted, the Abbasids were unable to support either their large civil service or the mercenary army on which they relied for defense. This army was manned largely by slaves and hired troops whose loyalties lay with the individual rulers who employed them, not with the caliphs. Massively expensive building projects, including the construction of the new Abbasid capital at Baghdad, further exacerbated the fiscal, military, and political crisis.

Behind the Abbasid collapse lay two fundamental developments of great significance for the future of the Islamic world: the growing power of regional rulers and the sharpening religious divisions between Sunnis and Shi'ites, and among the Shi'ites themselves. In 909, regional and religious hostilities came together when a local Shi'ite dynasty known as the Fatimids seized control of the Abbasid province of North Africa. In 969, the Fatimids succeeded in conquering Egypt also. Meanwhile, another Shi'ite group, rivals of both the Fatimids and the Abbasids, attacked Baghdad in 927 and Mecca in 930, seizing the Kaaba. Although an Abbasid Caliphate would continue to exist in Baghdad until 1258, when invading Mongol armies dispatched it (see Chapter 10), its empire had effectively disappeared by the 930s. In its place a new order began to emerge in the eastern Mediterranean, centered around an independent Egyptian kingdom and a new Muslim state based in Persia.

In Al-Andalus, disputes over succession within the Umayyad dynasty were matched by new external pressures. Beginning in the mid-ninth century, the small Christian kingdoms of northern and eastern Iberia began to encroach on Muslim territory, increasing the internal difficulties of the Umayyad caliphate. By the opening years of the eleventh century, the caliphate had dissolved, to be replaced by a host of smaller kingdoms, some of which paid tribute to the Christian rulers of the north.

The fractured political unity of the Islamic world deepened the divisions that had always existed among Muslim groups. While Islamic rulers were extremely tolerant of religious and cultural differences when dealing with Jews and Christians, dissent within Islam itself was another mat-ter. Under the strong rule of the caliphates, some different groups had learned to coexist; but with the disappearance of these centralized states it would be difficult to reconcile the ideal of universality with the realities of regional and ethnic differences.

CONCLUSION

The three civilizations that emerged as Rome's heirs each exhibit aspects of Roman civilization, which was itself a product of older civilizations. Which was Rome's true successor? It depends on the criteria used to make this evaluation. If imperial Rome's most fundamental characteristics were the maintenance of legal and political institutions, the answer is Byzantium. If one is looking for a

After You Read This Chapter

Visit StudySpace for quizzes, additional review materials, and multimedia documents. **wwnorton.com/web/westernciv18**

REVIEWING THE OBJECTIVES

- Justinian's attempted reunification of the Roman Empire proved destructive. What were its effects in the East? In the West?
- Byzantine culture was distinctive in many ways. What are some of its important features?
- The rapid expansion of Islam can be explained with reference to several historical factors. What were they?
- What accounts for the close relationship between monasticism and secular power in early medieval Europe?
- What was the Carolingian Empire, and why is it important?

civilization that combines the rich legacies of the ancient Near East, Egypt, and the Hellenistic world, the answer is Islam, which also emulated Rome in promoting commerce and cultural exchange. If one associates Rome chiefly with the city itself and the Latin language of the first Romans, or with the Christian patriarch of Rome, the answer is northwestern Europe.

There are also many connections to be drawn among these three successors. All took on their defining characteristics in the sixth and seventh centuries and, by the eighth century, had developed unique strengths and weaknesses. Moreover, they had fruitful—if uneasy—relationships with one another, and many mutual dependencies. Italian traders were active in Constantinople, and Muslim traders were common in the ports of southern Italy and Gaul. Anglo-Saxon merchants were regular visitors to the Mediterranean. Jewish merchants in the Rhineland were carrying on an active trade with the communities of Muslim Egypt, while Viking traders had opened trade routes from the Baltic through Russia to the Black Sea and were busily founding cities from Novgorod to Dublin.

But developments of the ninth and tenth centuries would disrupt these networks and created new centers of power. Western Europeans began to share a sense of common Christian identity: within the vast territory that extended from the Baltic to the Mediterranean, and from the Pyrenees to Poland, every ruler was (or would soon be) looking to the Roman Church for spiritual guidance and to his fellow rulers for aid and alliance. At the same time, western Europe became a society mobilized for war to a degree unmatched in either Byzantium or the Islamic world. In the centuries to come, this militarization was to prove a decisive factor in the shifting relationship among Rome's heirs.

PEOPLE, IDEAS, AND EVENTS IN CONTEXT

- In what ways do **JUSTINIAN'S CODE OF ROMAN LAW** and the building of **HAGIA SOPHIA** reflect his desire to revive the glories of ancient Rome?

- What were **BYZANTIUM**'s sources of stability, and of dissent? What effect did the **ICONOCLAST CONTROVERSY** have on Byzantine society?

- What factors contributed to **MUHAMMAD**'s rise to power? What are the **FIVE PILLARS OF ISLAM**, and what is the role of the **QUR'AN**?

- To what extent were the **UMAYYAD** and **ABBASID CALIPHATES** heirs of Rome? What made Islamic culture of this period distinctive?

- How did the **MEROVINGIAN** kings of the Franks acquire and hold power? How did **BENEDICTINE MONASTICISM** contribute to the economy of western Europe, and how was it linked to politics?

- How did **CHARLEMAGNE** build an empire, and how did the **CAROLINGIAN RENAISSANCE** revive and extend **CLASSICAL LEARNING**?

- How did the **VIKINGS** contribute to the developments of the ninth and tenth centuries?

THINKING ABOUT CONNECTIONS

- Arguably, each of these three civilizations could claim the mantle of the Roman Empire. In your view, which one has the strongest claim to carrying forward the legacies of the classical past?

- How do the historical circumstances in which Islam emerged compare to those that shaped early Christianity? What are some key similarities and differences?

STORY LINES

- Around the year 1000, new agricultural technologies and new social groupings transformed the economy and landscape of Europe.

- The rejuvenation of towns and trade created new opportunities for advancement. But at the same time, the decentralization of political power led to the violent rule of lords who could harness human and material resources to their own advantage.

- Meanwhile, a reforming movement within the Church increased the authority of the papacy, which attempted to assert its supremacy over secular rulers and to control violence by directing it against Europe's neighbors.

- One manifestation of this Church-sanctioned violence was the First Crusade, which began when a Muslim attack on Byzantium became the pretext for a holy war.

- Crusading broadened cultural and economic contacts with the East, but it also led to increased intolerance of "others," both outside Europe and within it.

Before You Read This Chapter

The Expansion of Europe, 950–1100

CORE OBJECTIVES

- **EXPLAIN** the reasons for the fragmentation of political power throughout most of Europe in this period.

- **IDENTIFY** the most important outcomes of the medieval agricultural revolution.

- **DESCRIBE** the effects of the reforming movement with the Church.

- **UNDERSTAND** the motives behind the Crusades.

- **TRACE** the political, economic, social, religious, and cultural effects of the Crusades.

In the version of history popularized by medieval minstrels, Charlemagne and his knights are able to defeat an Islamic army on enemy soil, in the mountainous borderlands of Spain. They then face only one remaining obstacle: the castle of a Muslim king whose stalwart courage commands the Christians' respect. So when ambassadors from the king promise his conversion in exchange for the safety of his people, Charlemagne readily agrees. One of his men must now negotiate the terms of surrender. Roland, Charlemagne's noblest knight, suggests that his stepfather Ganelon be the chosen messenger. But Ganelon is furious, certain that the mission will end in his death. Secretly, he resolves to betray both his stepson and his liege lord: he convinces the Muslim king that Charlemagne intends to trick him, and thus incites the king to attack the Christian warriors as they travel homeward through the mountain passes of the Pyrenees. Because Roland is the bravest knight, Ganelon knows that he will volunteer to command the rear guard.

And so it happens. Roland's men are ambushed and his sworn companion, Olivier, urges him to call for help. But Roland refuses: he will never endanger his lord by any such dishonorable deed. Instead, he will fight to the death and,

247

with his last ounce of strength, break his sword, Durandal. For it would never do to have this sacred gift of Charlemagne—made holier still by the relic in its pommel—fall into the hands of heathens. As Roland reminds Olivier, "We must not be the theme of mocking songs." The worst thing imaginable is shame; the best, to become the hero of just such an epic.

Like Homer's *Iliad*, the *Song of Roland* is the product of an oral storytelling tradition that took shape over hundreds of years. Written down around the year 1100, it reflects the many ways in which the world had changed since the time of Charlemagne. Its very language exemplifies one such change: the language we call French, no longer the Frankish tongue of Charlemagne. In Charlemagne's time, moreover, there was no such thing as knighthood or chivalry, there were no major castles, there was no holy war against Muslims. All of these features were added to the story over time, to mirror a new reality and, most immediately, the ethos of the First Crusade (1095–99).

In this chapter, we will begin to trace the processes that transformed western Europe from an economic backwater and political patchwork into the premier power among the three successor civilizations of the Roman Empire. With the increased authority and prestige of the Roman Church, European Christendom came to embrace the formerly outlying provinces of Scandinavia, Hungary, Poland, and Bohemia. Christian colonists and missionaries would also push eastward into Prussia, Lithuania, Livonia, and the Balkans. Allied Christian armies would come to dominate Muslim Spain and Constantinople. They would also establish (and eventually lose) a Latin kingdom centered on Jerusalem and come to control commerce in the Mediterranean as well as trade routes to Central Asia and China. This expansion would be accompanied by a revolution in agricultural production, significant urbanization, a rising standard of living, and a growing population. It would foster the growth of territorial monarchies, create a wealthy but highly stratified new social order, and spur remarkable intellectual and cultural achievements.

A TOUR OF EUROPE AROUND THE YEAR 1000

The mapmakers of antiquity (see Chapter 4) had used the term Europe to refer to one of three known continents, and they divided it from Asia by the river Don and from Africa by the Straits of Gibraltar. We have seen that many of Europe's territories were gradually brought into the

orbit of Western civilizations through trade, imperial conquest, the Jewish diaspora, and the spread of Christianity and Islam. Meanwhile, waves of immigration from the steppes of Asia increased the already rich ethnic and cultural diversity of Europe, as did the movements of the Vikings and their interactions with both newer and more established groups. So while Charlemagne (see Chapter 7) had tried to promote an idea of a Europe as unified and coterminous with Christendom, Europe was not (and could never be) wholly Christian; and it was certainly not unified. So what was it?

This chapter is entitled "The Expansion of Europe" for two main reasons: because the very idea of Europe gains increasing coherence during this pivotal period and because Europeans' forceful annexation of territories along the Continent's eastern frontiers and throughout the Mediterranean is a crucial development. Indeed, some influential historians argue that Europe was really invented in this era, through an ongoing process of internal and external colonization. That is, new kingdoms and communities were being created by conquest and settlement within Europe— complicating ethnic identities, kinship networks, and tribal loyalties—but also well beyond it. Europeans were becoming the agents of imperialism, not its targets. This is a striking change. The West's center of gravity had always been the Mediterranean and its adjacent lands in Anatolia, the Near East, and North Africa; it was from there that influences flowed to the less civilized lands of the farther West. The movements of peoples, too, had usually been westward. But now that trajectory was being reversed.

Viking Initiatives

In the aftermath of the Viking invasions, new political entities began to emerge in Europe. Some, on the far-flung fringes of the known world, were formed when the Vikings themselves became colonists: Iceland, Greenland, and (briefly) Newfoundland. Indeed, Iceland can claim to be Europe's oldest state and the world's first parliamentary democracy. Its political institutions date back to the year 930, when settlers formed a legislative assembly called the Althing, a Norse word with the same meaning as the Latin *res publica*. Icelanders would build one of the most culturally distinctive polities of the Middle Ages and would produce a fascinating and influential body of poetic forms and literary entertainments, notably the *sagas*: sprawling family histories that unfold over generations, feature diverse casts of characters, and range from the hilarious to the ruthless (often both at once). Modern action films and epics are heavily indebted to the sagas and their historical contexts.

In regions where Vikings settled among more established groups—throughout the British Isles, Scandinavia, and the Low Countries—they both absorbed and affected these cultures. In Normandy, for example, the descendants of Vikings maintained marriage alliances and ties of kinship with the rest of the Norse world while at the same time intermarrying with the Franks and adopting their language.

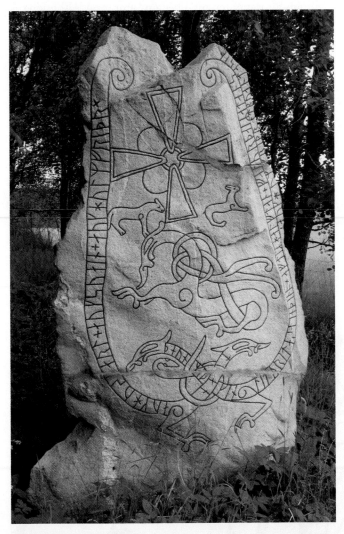

LINGSBERG RUNESTONE. This is one of two commemorative runestones erected at Lingsberg, Sweden, at the beginning of the eleventh century. The runic inscription records that a woman named Holmfríðr had it placed here in memory of her husband, Halfdan, whose father had been a Viking raider in England. Runic alphabets were in use among Germanic-speaking peoples of the North prior to the adoption of the Latin alphabet. Some runic letters survive in Anglo-Saxon and Old Norse, including the *edh*, the letter ð in the name of Holmfríðr, which is pronounced *th* as in *the*.

The Rise of Rus' and the Kingdoms of Eastern Europe

One group of Vikings would establish an important kingdom on the broad steppes of Eurasia, at the heart of a region that still bears their name: Russia. Originally from Sweden, the Rus' were active raiders and traders in the Baltic region, where they came to dominate the Finns and Slavic peoples who lived along the seaboard. According to their earliest chronicle, they were invited to rule over these warring tribes and so extended their reach through the navigation of Eurasian waterways while also moving further inland, to Novgorod. By the year 1000, they had conquered the fortress of Kiev.

This was a key outpost of the frontier region controlled by the Khazars, a Turkic people who had established an empire along the Silk Road to China and whose effective practices of assimilation extended their influence still further (many had embraced a form of Judaism centuries before). From Kiev, on the shores of the river Dneiper, the Rus' had easy access to the Black Sea and thence to Constantinople and Baghdad. They were thus in a position to trade directly with the eastern Roman Empire in Byzantium, and with Arabic, Persian, and Turkic peoples who also had access to China. Through a series of strategic intermarriages, moreover, they forged further connections with many of the royal and aristocratic dynasties of western Europe. This placed Kievan Rus' at the heart of economic and political activity in the medieval world.

Meanwhile, the dominion of the Rus' over northern Slavic peoples was countered by the crystallization of Slavic kingdoms farther to the south: Serbia and Croatia on the Adriatic, which grew up within long-settled provinces of the old Roman Empire, and Poland. The ruling families of Croatia embraced the Latin Christianity of Rome in this period; so did those of Poland. The Serbians, however, were drawn more into the orbit of Byzantium, and with it Greek Orthodoxy. Sandwiched between them, and on the borders of Rus', was Hungary, comprising the old Roman province of Pannonia and stretching eastward toward the Carpathian mountains. It had been conquered by the Huns in the late fourth century and had since attracted numerous other immigrants. The most recent arrivals were the Magyars, a nomadic people from the region of the Urals whose language, like that of the Finns, was non-Indo-European (Chapter 7). The Magyars were expert herdsmen and horsemen. They also served as mercenaries fighting for various warring kings in western Europe and for the emperor in Byzantium. Around 895, they united under a leader called Arpád and took control of the fertile land of the Danube river basin, where they became farmers and cattle ranchers. Arpád's descendants would later embrace Latin Christianity and would work to integrate the kingdom of Hungary into western Europe through dynastic marriage and diplomacy.

New Scandinavian Kingdoms and the Empire of Cnut the Great

While Rus' was on the rise, other groups of Vikings were establishing territorial control over parts of their Scandinavian homeland—by borrowing forms of governance that drew on Carolingian and Byzantine models and by embracing Latin Christianity as a way of legitimizing their rule. Around the year 1000, three strong kingdoms had emerged: Norway, Sweden, and Denmark. Each built on the legacy of powerful Viking forebears who had already established strong Norse settlements in the lands of the Franks, the Anglo-Saxons, and the Irish: their kings' reputation for fearlessness in battle and generosity afterward, their capacity to dominate seas and riverways and thereby to supply the lifeblood (silver and gold currency) of the medieval economy, and their canny practices of adaptation and intermarriage.

What made these new states special was their rulers' very deliberate manipulation of this heritage, blended with the strategic decision to convert their followers to Christianity and to the political conventions of the Continent. They simultaneously glorified their own distinctive culture and economic achievements while tying them to newer models of government. For these reasons, scholars have often spoken of this as Europe's "Viking Age," and it exemplifies the cross-currents of colonial enterprise mentioned above. For on the one hand, older western civilizations can be said to have colonized Scandinavia; on the other hand, it was really Scandinavians who were doing the colonizing.

The empire forged by King Cnut (*kuh-NOOT*) of Denmark is a good example of this. At the time of his death in 1035, Cnut the Great ruled over Norway, much of Sweden, and England as well as his native Denmark; he had a controlling interest in large parts of Ireland and portions of the Low Countries, too. He also had diplomatic and family ties to the independent principalities of Flanders and Normandy, the new kingdom of Poland (through his mother, a Polish princess), and to the imperial family of Germany (through his daughter, who became empress). Although his was, in many ways, a personal empire and (like that of Alexander) came apart after his death, it had long-term effects on the political organization of northwestern Europe. Most notably, it set the stage for the Norman Conquest of England (see **Interpreting Visual Evidence** on page 262). Cnut's empire could only have been brought together as a result of the initiatives that had made raiding Vikings into settled kings who were still able to exploit the far-flung networks of trade, influence, and kinship that had allowed their forebears to flourish in earlier times.

Mediterranean Microcosms

The dynamism of the new states of eastern Europe, Rus', and Scandinavia stands in contrast to the very different

MAGYAR HORSEMAN. This tenth-century wall painting from Aquileia (on the Adriatic coast of northern Italy) illustrates the superior horsemanship and dexterity that made Hungarian warriors sought-after mercenaries.

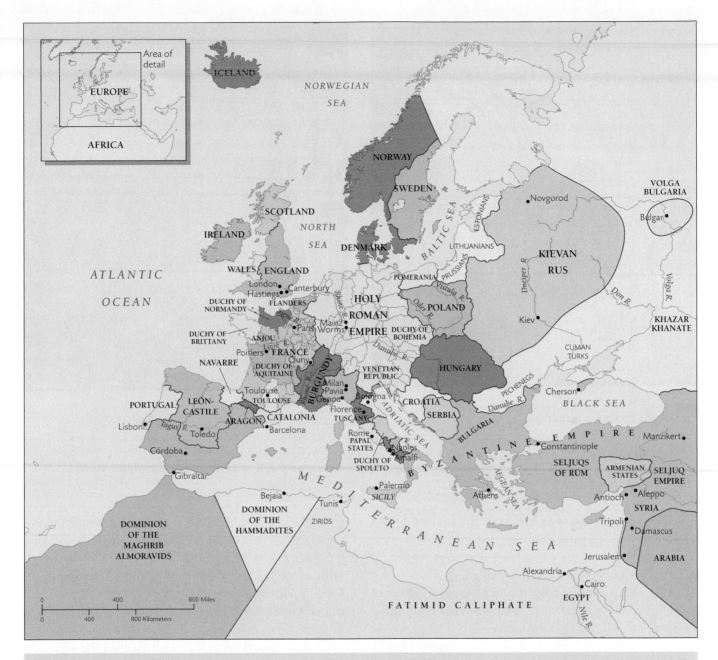

EUROPE , c. 1000. This map shows the patchwork of political power in western Europe after the millennium, although it cannot accurately illustrate the degree of fragmentation within these major territories, especially those of the Holy Roman Empire. ▪ *What factors account for the close relationship between Italy and the German principalities?* ▪ *How are they related to the northwestern regions of the Continent and the British Isles?* ▪ *Which geopolitical entities would you expect to emerge as dominant in the following centuries?*

dynamics that governed relations in an older part of western civilizations: the Mediterranean. If the map above struggles to capture the patchwork of principalities and polities of Europe's mainland, it fails utterly to convey the contours of political, religious, cultural, and economic interactions in this maritime world. It is useful, in fact, to imagine the Mediterranean coastal regions and islands as interlocking components of a different zone entirely, and to further imagine that a community on the shores

of North Africa—say, Muslim Tunis—would have more in common, and more contact, with Christian Barcelona than with another African Muslim community farther inland.

Indeed, it is extremely tricky (and probably futile) to pin down the identity and allegiances of any one group or individual in this zone. The medieval Mediterranean was a complex organism made up of diverse microcosms whose contours and interrelationships were more determined by geography,

EMPEROR OTTO THE GREAT. In this opening from a deluxe set of Gospels he commissioned for himself, Otto is shown seated on a throne and vested with the regalia of imperial and royal authority, surrounded by clerical and secular counselors, and receiving tribute from a procession of deferential women representing the four regions of his domain: Slavinia, Germania, Gallia, and Roma. Compare this image to that of Emperor Justinian on page 214 (Chapter 7). ▪ *In what ways is Otto making use of similar iconography?* ▪ *What claims to power does he make thereby?*

prevailing winds, trading patterns, and climate than by the vaunted control of a particular ruler. In many places, it made little difference who the ostensible rulers were, especially since the persons and forms of rule changed so often.

Take Sicily, for example: the first overseas colony of Rome (Chapter 5), it had been part of the Phoenician maritime empire of Carthage and, before that, a major Greek settlement (Chapters 2 and 3). All of those elements would still have been part of Sicily's historical DNA when it was invaded by the Vandals in the fifth century and afterward by the Goths. It was then reconquered by Justinian and became part of Byzantium—so important a part, in fact, that one Byzantine emperor tried to move the capital from Constantinople to Palermo. In the course of the tenth century, it became an emirate of the Fatimid Caliphate based in Egypt. In the eleventh, it was progressively infiltrated by Norman mercenaries who eventually succeeded in establishing a Norman (but only nominally Christian) kingdom there in 1072. So who were the Sicilians? More important, who did they think they were—and how stable was that identity over this long period of continual change? These are not easy questions to answer.

In any such case, it is better to think in terms of influences, connections, and orbits of exchange than about stable borders or identities; this holds true of many areas of Europe in this period but is especially true when speaking of regions joined by water. Gaining "control" of any constellation of Mediterranean communities—constantly in flux—meant harnessing its inherent complexity and commercial power, something not best done through violent conquest or military occupation. Indeed, an exemplary light-handed interference was what enabled the Venetians to build a successful and long-lived trading empire in the Adriatic and then in the eastern Mediterranean and Aegean Seas. The Venetians opened up the sea lanes and ports that would be crucial to the implementation of a more military form of European expansion: the Crusades.

The Heirs of Charlemagne

What of Europe's heartland, which had become the empire of Charlemagne (Chapter 7)? The most powerful monarchs on the Continent were the Saxon kings of eastern Francia (in what is now Germany). Like the Anglo-Saxon kings of England, they modeled themselves on Charlemagne, but they drew on different aspects of his rule. While England was becoming an effective administrative monarchy, with centralized financial and judicial systems, royal power on the Continent rested on the profits of continual expansion. So just as the Carolingians had built their power on the conquest of Saxony in the eighth century, the Saxon kings now built theirs on the conquests of Slavic lands to the east. They also nurtured their image as guardians of Christendom: in 955, King Otto I of Saxony defeated the then-pagan Magyars while carrying a sacred lance that had belonged to Charlemagne.

This victory established Otto as a dominant power and, by extension, as Charlemagne's worthy successor. In 962, accordingly, he went to Rome to be crowned emperor by Pope John XII, who hoped Otto would help him defeat his own enemies. But Otto turned the tables on the pope, deposing him and selecting a new pope to replace him. Otto thereby laid the foundation for his successors' claims to imperial autonomy, in imitation of the Byzantine emperors. He also advertised his inheritance of Carolingian and Roman power through his patronage of arts and learning. Under Otto's influence, the Saxon court became a refuge for men and women of talent. The first known female playwright, Hrotsvitha of Gandersheim (c. 935–c. 1002), was raised there, and grew up hearing the works of classical authors read aloud. When she entered a royal convent, she wrote plays blending Roman comedy with the stories of early Christian martyrs for the entertainment and instruction of her fellow nuns. Otto also presided over the establishment of cathedral schools and helped the bishops of his domain turn their own courts into cultural centers.

However, Otto could not control either the papacy or the independent towns of northern Italy unless he maintained a permanent presence there. And if he remained in Italy too long, his authority in Saxony broke down. Balancing local realities with imperial ambitions thus presented a dilemma that neither he nor his successors were able to solve. The result was a gradually increasing rift between local elites and the king in his guise as Holy Roman Emperor. This alienation would accelerate in the eleventh century, when the imperial crown passed to a new dynasty, the Salians, centered not in Saxony but in neighboring Franconia. By the 1070s, when the Salian emperor Henry IV attempted to assert control over Saxony, he touched off a war that was to have momentous repercussions (see below).

Aspects of Charlemagne's legacy also survived in the Mediterranean world. In Catalonia, counts descended from Carolingian appointees continued to administer justice in public courts of law throughout the tenth century, and to draw revenues from tolls and trade. The city of Barcelona grew rapidly as both a long-distance and a regional market under the protection of these counts. In Aquitaine also,

the counts of Poitiers and Toulouse continued to rest their authority on Carolingian foundations.

In Charlemagne's own Frankish kingdom, however, Carolingian rule collapsed under the combined weight of Viking raids, economic disintegration, and the growing power of local lords. A few Carolingian institutions—such as public courts and a centrally minted coinage—survived in some regions, but they were used to build up new, autonomous principalities such as Anjou and Flanders. The Norse-Frankish rulers of Normandy also used these techniques effectively. But in the Franks' traditional heartland, however, even this modicum of Carolingian authority disappeared. The Franks still had a king, but this king was no longer a descendant of Charlemagne. Moreover, his domain had been reduced to the tiny region around Paris: the only territorial remnant that the local count, Hugh Capet, had managed to defend against the Vikings. In 987, this modest feat earned him the title King of the Franks. Marooned on this Ile de France (literally, "island of France"), the Capetian kings clung to the fiction that they were the heirs of Charlemagne's greatness. It would be another 200 years before one of them made this fiction a political reality (see Chapter 9).

AN AGRICULTURAL REVOLUTION

Like all economies prior to the nineteenth century, the medieval economy rested largely on agriculture. Although agricultural innovation tends to occur slowly, it is still appropriate to call the profound changes that took place in this period revolutionary. Indeed, it is arguable that this medieval agricultural revolution was more important than that of the modern era.

New Technologies

As we noted in Chapter 7, the driving force behind this agricultural boom was technological. The new heavy-wheeled plow, fitted with an iron-tipped coulter and dragged by a team of oxen or horses, could cut and turn the rich soil of northern Europe far more effectively than traditional Mediterranean plows. Related improvements in collars and harnesses enhanced the efficiency of plow animals and made it possible for them to pull heavy loads without choking themselves. The development of iron horseshoes (around 900) and the tandem harnessing of paired teams (around 1050) also made the use of horses more effective, not only in the field but for the transport of agricultural surpluses to new markets.

LIGHT PLOW AND HEAVY PLOW. Compare these two contemporary depictions of plowing: the one at left is taken from a Greek manuscript copied in Byzantium and shows the light plow in use throughout the Mediterranean and Near East since antiquity; the other shows the heavy wheeled plow adapted to northern Europe. Note that the peasant using the light plow has to press his foot on it to give it added weight. Another major innovation of the heavy European plow was the long moldboard, which turned over the ground after the plowshare cut into it. The padded horse collar allowed horses to throw their full weight into pulling.

Labor-saving devices further increased productivity. Since most work was done by individuals using hand tools, the more widespread use of iron for hoes, forks, shovels, and scythes made work faster and easier. The wheelbarrow was a crucial invention, as was the harrow, a tool drawn over the field after plowing to level the earth and mix in the seed. Watermills represented another major innovation. The Romans had relied mainly on human- and animal-powered wheels to grind grain into flour, even though they had known about the use of running water as a power source. But the need for greater efficiency and the lack of slave labor led medieval engineers—usually monks—to experiment with various ways of harnessing water power. Secular landowners followed suit, recognizing the mill as a source of economic and political power to which they could control access through the imposition of tolls.

Mills were also adapted to a variety of purposes beyond the grinding of grain: they drove saws for lumber, processed cloth, pressed olive oil, provided power for iron forges, and crushed pulp for manufacturing paper. The importance of mills cannot be overstated: they would remain the world's only source of mechanical power for manufacturing until the invention of the steam engine powered the Industrial Revolution (see Chapter 19).

New Conditions for Growth

Although many of these technologies had been invented in the eighth century, it was only in the eleventh that they became sufficiently widespread as to have a decisive impact.

Climate change certainly played a role in this. Starting in the eighth or ninth century, average temperatures in Europe gradually rose by about 1° or 2°C (3.6°F)—the same increment that has led to global warming today. Eventually, these higher temperatures made it possible to raise crops as far north as Greenland and to produce wine in southern England. Moreover, the warming climate benefited northern Europe by drying the soil and lengthening the growing season, while hotter summers and diminishing rainfall hurt Mediterranean agriculture in equal measure.

These new technologies also became more widespread after the settlement of Viking and Magyar peoples decreased the threat of invasion and the consequent disruption of planting cycles and damage to crops. Left in relative peace, monasteries could develop and implement the tools described above, which were then copied by local lords who saw the benefits of managing their own lands more efficiently, rather than raiding others'. It became clear to entrepreneurial peasants, too, that investment in agricultural improvements would yield surpluses and result in profits. Productivity was also linked to increased population, fundamental changes in patterns of settlement, and the organization of the peasant workforce.

Harnessing People

In the centuries after the fragmentation of Roman imperial power, most farmers in northern Europe lived on individual plots of land worked by themselves and their families. Starting in the ninth century, however, many of these individual holdings merged into large, common fields that could be farmed collectively by the inhabitants of entire villages. The resulting complex is sometimes called a *manor* (from the Latin verb *manere,* meaning "to dwell").

In many cases, the impetus for the consolidation of manors came from the peasants themselves. Large fields could be farmed more efficiently than small fields. Investment costs were lower and could be shared equally: a single plow and a dozen oxen might suffice for an entire village, obviating the need for every farmer to maintain his own plow and team. Common fields were potentially more productive, too, allowing villagers to experiment with new crops and to support larger numbers of animals on common pastures. In time, prosperous peasants might be able to establish a parish church, a communal oven, a blacksmith, a mill, and a tavern. They could also converse, socialize, and assist their neighbors. In a difficult and demanding natural environment, these were important considerations.

In other cases, a manor could be created or co-opted by a local lord or a monastery acting as a lord. Manors were attractive because their greater productivity meant that lords could take a larger share of the peasants' surplus; it was also easier to control and exploit peasants who lived together in villages and who were bound to one another by ties of kinship and dependence. Over time, some lords were therefore able to reduce formerly free peasants to the status of serfs who could not leave the land without permission. Like slaves, serfs inherited their servile status; but unlike slaves, they were not supposed to be sold apart from the lands they worked. Practically speaking, there may have been little difference between a serf and and a free peasant—indeed, some serfs may have been better off. But as we have seen, social mobility is often tied to geographical mobility; and the inability of serfs to move freely would prevent them from achieving the liberties of those workers who could (see below).

The Conquest of the Land

The manor's organization of labor opened up more land for cultivation and made that cultivation more efficient. For centuries, farmers had known that if they sowed the same crop in the same field year after year, they would eventually exhaust the soil. The traditional solution was to divide one's land, planting half in the fall to harvest in the spring, and leaving the other half to lie fallow. In the dry, thin soils of the Mediterranean, this remained the most common cropping pattern throughout the Middle Ages. In the more fertile soils of northern Europe, however, farmers slowly discovered that a three-field crop-rotation system could produce a sustainable increase in overall production. One-third of the land would lie fallow or be used as pasture, so that manure would fertilize the soil; one-third would be planted with winter wheat or rye, sown in the fall and harvested in the early summer; and one-third would be planted in the spring with another crop to be harvested in the fall. These fields were then rotated over a three-year cycle.

This system increased the amount of land under cultivation from 50 to 67 percent, while the two separate growing seasons provided some insurance against loss due to natural disasters or inclement weather. The system also produced higher yields per acre, particularly if legumes or fodder crops like oats were a regular part of the crop-rotation pattern and replaced the nitrogen that wheat and rye leach out of the soil. Both humans and animals could eat oats, and legumes provided a source of protein to balance the intake of carbohydrates from bread and beer, the two main staples of the peasant diet in northern and central Europe. Additional fodder supported more and healthier animals, increasing the efficiency of plow beasts, diversifying the economy of the manor, and providing an additional source of protein through meat and milk. The new crop-rotation system also helped spread labor more evenly over the course of the year.

THE GROWTH OF TOWNS AND TRADE

As we observed in Chapter 7, the urban infrastructure of the western Roman Empire was weakened in the course of the fifth and sixth centuries. A few Roman cities continued to thrive under the lordship of bishops, but many—including Rome itself—began to crumble as their depleted populations could no longer maintain public buildings, services, and defensive walls. In most areas, monasteries replaced cities as the nuclei of civilization in northwestern Europe. Then, under Charlemagne and his imitators, towns came to be planted by royal initiative, as centers for markets and administration. In Anglo-Saxon England, too, King Alfred and his successors established new towns in strategic locations while at the same time reviving older Roman cities. They also issued a reliable and well-regulated currency that encouraged commerce.

Fostering Commerce

Although many towns were devastated by the Viking raids of the tenth century, the agricultural revolution helped to revitalize them—as did the influx of silver and gold set in circulation by the Vikings themselves. The rapid urbanization of

1. Cathedral
2. Alt St. Thomas
3. Alt St. Peter
4. Jung St. Peter
5. St. Nikolaus
6. St. Johann
7. St. Wilhelm
8. St. Stephen

0 50 100   200   300m

▢ Roman fortification, the 'city'

▦ Frankish settlement, called 'New City', walled at end of ninth century

▢ Extension of Frankish settlement before 1200 to include Alt St. Peter's parish

▥ Jung St. Peter's parish, walled 1202–1220

▨ St. Nikolaus parish, walled thirteenth and fourteenth centuries

▦ St. Johann Parish, walled 1374–1390

- - - St. Wilhelm parish, walled 1387–1441

THE METAMORPHOSIS OF A MEDIEVAL CITY. The city of Strasbourg, on the long-disputed border between modern Germany and France, exemplifies the multilayered dynamics of urban change throughout the Middle Ages. It began as a Roman settlement, which became the nucleus for an episcopal see—hence the cathedral (1) located in the ancient precinct. It was fortified with new walls at the end of the ninth century, as the Carolingian Empire was collapsing and the Vikings were on the move. It then responded to the renewed prosperity of the eleventh and twelfth centuries, far outgrowing its original bounds, and continued to expand for several centuries thereafter. ▪ *Note the scale of the map. What can you conclude from this about the density of settlement in a medieval city?*

Europe in the eleventh and twelfth centuries was also fostered by the initiatives of monasteries and secular lords who saw the economic advantages to be gained from providing safe havens for travelers and trade. This was especially true in the principalities of the Rhineland, the Low Countries, and the independent counties of Flanders and Champagne. Many towns grew up around monasteries, which provided protection and encouraged innovation. In southwestern Europe, existing towns prospered from their status as ports or their location along the overland routes connecting the Mediterranean with the Atlantic. In Italy, which had been decimated by five centuries of warfare and invasion, the growth of towns gave rise to especially dramatic changes.

Initially, the renewed prosperity of Italy depended on the Byzantine emperors' suppression of piracy in the eastern Mediterranean. Hence, the most successful cities around the turn of the millennium were situated in the Byzantine-controlled areas of the peninsula: Venice in the north and Amalfi, Naples, and Palermo in the south. These were the trading posts that brought silks, spices, and other luxuries from the East into western Europe. In the eleventh century, however, the Norman invasions of southern Italy frequently disrupted this trade, while Turkish invasions of Asia Minor turned Byzantium's attention to the empire's eastern frontier. This opened new opportunities to the northern ports of Genoa and Pisa, whose merchant navies took over the task of policing the eastern Mediterranean.

From Italy and other Mediterranean ports, exotic goods flowed northward to the towns of Flanders and to the organized system of fairs—international markets convened at certain times of the year—that enriched the county of Champagne. Flemish towns, in turn, kept up a brisk trade with England, processing English wool

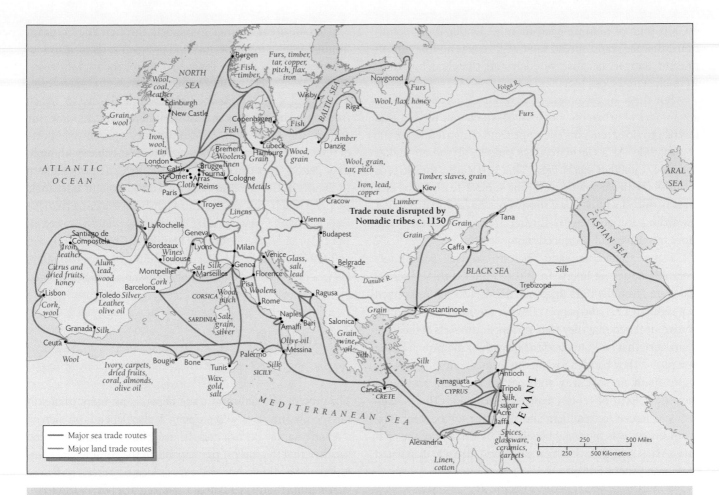

Map labels:

Bergen — Furs, timber, tar, copper, pitch, flax, iron
Fish, timber
NORTH SEA
Wool, coal, leather
Edinburgh
New Castle
Novgorod
Furs
Volga R.
Wisby
BALTIC SEA
Riga
Wool, flax, honey
Copenhagen
Fish
Fish
Amber
Danzig
ATLANTIC OCEAN
Iron, wool, tin
London
Bremen
Woolens
Hamburg
Lübeck
Wood, grain
Grain
ARAL SEA
Grain, wool
Calais
St.-Omer
Arras
Brugge
Tournai
linen
Cologne
Wool, grain, tar, pitch
Timber, slaves, grain
Cloth
Reims
Metals
Paris
Iron, lead, copper
Kiev
Lumber
Troyes
Cracow
Trade route disrupted by Nomadic tribes c. 1150
Grain
Tana
CASPIAN SEA
Linens
Vienna
La Rochelle
Santiago de Compostela
Iron, leather
Geneva
Budapest
Grain
Caffa
Bordeaux
Wines
Lyons
Milan
Toulouse
Belgrade
BLACK SEA
Silk
Citrus and dried fruits, honey
Alum, lead, wood
Salt Silk
Venice
Glass, salt, lead
Montpellier
Genoa
Florence
Danube R.
Trebizond
Lisbon
Cork
Marseilles
Pisa
Woolens
Ragusa
Barcelona
CORSICA
Wood, pitch
Rome
Cork, wool
Toledo Silver
Leather, olive oil
SARDINIA
Salt, grain, silver
Naples
Bari
Grain
Constantinople
Granada
Silk
Amalfi
Salonica
Grain, wine, oil
Ceuta
Palermo
Messina
Olive oil
Silk
Famagusta
CYPRUS
Antioch
Tripoli
LEVANT
Wool
Bougie
Bone
Tunis
SICILY
Silk
Silk
Silk, sugar
Acre
Jaffa
Ivory, carpets, dried fruits, coral, almonds, olive oil
Wax, gold, salt
Candia
CRETE
Spices, glassware, ceramics, carpets
MEDITERRANEAN SEA
Alexandria
Linen, cotton

— Major sea trade routes
— Major land trade routes

0   250   500 Miles
0   250   500 Kilometers

MEDIEVAL TRADE ROUTES. ▪ *What does this map reveal about the relationship between waterways and overland routes during the eleventh and twelfth centuries?* ▪ *Which regions appear to be most extensively interconnected, and why?* ▪ *How does the trade in certain specialized goods create certain commercial patterns?*

into the cloth which, alongside wheat and wine, was the staple commodity of medieval Europe. Eventually, merchants would succeed in opening up a direct route by sea between Italy and the Atlantic ports of northern Europe, after which it became practical to import raw wool directly from England to towns like Florence, which began producing its cloth.

It would be misleading, however, to overemphasize the role of long-distance trade in the urbanization of medieval Europe. Some towns that were dependent on such commerce, like Venice and Genoa, attracted populations approaching 100,000 by 1300. But others that grew to be as large, including Paris and London, drew primarily on the wealth of their surrounding hinterlands for food, raw materials, and the bulk of their population. Furthermore, towns large and small existed in a symbiotic relationship with the countryside, providing

markets for the food surplus of outlying farms and transforming raw materials into marketable goods through manufacturing.

"Town Air Makes You Free"

To modern eyes, most medieval towns would still have seemed half rural. (Indeed, New York City would have seemed so until the end of the nineteenth century.) Streets were often unpaved, houses had gardens for raising vegetables, and animals were everywhere: in the early twelfth century, the heir to the throne of France was killed when his horse tripped over a pig running loose in the streets of Paris. Sanitary conditions were poor, and the air reeked of excrement, both animal and human. (Even in 1900, this was also true of New York, where 150,000 horses produced

45,000 tons of manure each month.) Under these conditions, disease could spread rapidly. Fire was another omnipresent danger, because wooden and thatched buildings were clustered close together.

But these inconveniences were far outweighed by the advantages of urban life, not least of which was the fact that towns provided a means of escape from the strictures of the countryside. As a German adage puts it, "Town air makes you free" (*Stadtluft macht Frei*). This is because the citizens of most medieval towns were not subject to the arbitrary jurisdiction of a lord—or if they were, the lord realized that rewarding initiative with further freedoms fostered still more initiative and produced more wealth.

Many Catalonian and Flemish towns accordingly received charters of liberty from the counts of these regions, and were given the right to govern themselves. Others seized that right: in 1127, the people of Arras, on the Franco-Flemish border, declared that they were no longer the serfs of the local monastery that had nurtured the growth of their town in the first place. They banded together to form a commune, swearing to maintain solidarity with one another and setting up their own form of representative government. The monastery was forced to free them and then free to tax them. The arrangement was mutually beneficial: by the end of the century, Arras was the wealthiest and most densely populated town in northern Europe.

CHRISTIAN BANKERS AND THEIR CLIENTS. As long-distance trade expanded in the Middle Ages, merchants developed new methods of financing their ventures. Many of these practices conflicted with the official policy of the medieval Church, which decried these new investments as usury. This Italian manuscript depicts the seven vices associated with moneylending, but also makes it clear that the people involved in this practice are Christians. (Compare their attire to that of the Jews pictured on page 298 in Chapter 9.)

Urban areas further expanded through the constant immigration of free peasants and escaped serfs in search of a better life. For once a town had established its independence, newcomers could claim the status of citizens after a year and a day; thereafter, the only authority to which they were subject was that of the town's officials. For this reason, some powerful lords and rulers resisted the efforts of towns to claim independence. Almost inevitably, though, they paid a high price for this. In Rome, the pope's claim to secular authority over the city led to frequent uprisings. In the French city of Laon, the bishop who asserted his lordship over a newly formed commune was murdered in 1112. In 1127, the count of Flanders, Charles the Good (r. 1119–27), was assassinated by a family of powerful officials who resented his claims that they were, in fact, his serfs.

Portable Wealth: Money and Credit

The growth of towns and trade depends on more than surplus goods, initiative, and mobility. It also depends on money: a reliable supply of cash and the availability of credit. It is no accident that the earliest participants in the commercial revolution of the Middle Ages were cities located in regions whose rulers minted and regulated a strong currency: Byzantium, Al-Andalus, and the Christian kingdoms of Spain, the old Roman region of Provence (southern France), Anglo-Saxon England, and Flanders. Yet precisely because there were so many currencies in circulation, the economy also depended on moneychangers and bankers who could extend credit to merchants, thus obviating the need to travel roads and waterways with bags full of cash.

Most of the sophisticated financial mechanisms for extending credit and making investments had long been in place throughout the Islamic world and Byzantium, but in western Europe much of this crucial activity was carried forward by Jewish bankers situated within the network of close-knit Jewish communities that connected cities like Constantinople, Baghdad, and Córdoba to the burgeoning cities of the north. In many regions, Jews had a virtual monopoly on these activities, because Christians were technically forbidden to lend money at interest or to make a profit from investments. This practice was called *usury* (from the Latin word for "interest"), and Christian theologians cited various passages from the Old and New Testaments that seemed to condemn it. But in practice, the Roman Church turned a blind eye to such practices. Indeed, many prominent churchmen, including bishops, made fortunes lending money, as did many laymen—especially in towns like Arras and Florence.

Still, the moral stigma attaching to this necessary practice meant that Jews were often the ones targeted at times of crisis, just as they were the people to whom rulers would turn most readily when they needed funds—helping to explain why many kings, princes, and bishops protected the Jewish communities in their realms and often extended special privileges to them in exchange for money. The unfortunate result of this Christian hypocrisy was the circulation of conspiracy theories harmful to Jews, who were perceived as exercising control over Christians through secret channels of communication and a stranglehold on finance. Jewish communities' reliance on the protection of powerful men also made them vulnerable when those men withdrew their support or were incapable of controlling the violence unleashed by their own policies.

VIOLENCE, LORDSHIP, AND MONARCHY

The new wealth of western Europe fostered social mobility, yet it also created a more stratified society. In the Carolingian period, the nobility had comprised a relatively small number of ancient families who counted one another as equals and married among themselves. During the tenth and eleventh centuries, however, new families began to emerge as territorial lords and princes, rivaling and sometimes surpassing the old aristocracy in power and wealth. Some of these new families were descended from lesser officeholders in the Carolingian administration, men who had established independent powers after the empire collapsed and who used their public offices for private gain. Others were successful interlopers who seized control of undefended manors and sustained warbands of treasure-hungry young men.

Tools of Power: Castles and Knights

The predatory lords who emerged in this period protected their territories, their families, and their followers by building strongholds: castles, from the Latin word *castellum*, "little fortress." These structures, seldom known in Europe before the Viking invasions, came to dominate the landscape in the eleventh and twelfth centuries. The castle was both defensive and offensive. It rendered its owner more secure from arson and attack—though it was vulnerable to siege—and it enabled him to dominate the surround-

ing countryside. Indeed, castles often formed the nucleus of a new town by providing protection for the peasants and merchants who clustered their dwellings close to its walls. In case of attack, these outliers could move inside.

Although most early castles were modest structures built of wood, situated on earthwork mounds surrounded by a ditch or moat, stone walls and keeps (fortified towers) soon replaced wooded palisades as the level of competitive violence increased. In Italy, rival families even built castles and towers in the middle of towns. Eventually, some castellans ("castle-holders") acquired enough power and booty to challenge more established lords, laying claim not only to property and influence but to rank. These new lords didn't descend from Roman senators or Carolingian counts; instead, they boasted of lineages reaching back to successful warlords like Rollo the Viking, whom the Normans claimed to be their first duke (from the Latin word *dux*, "leader").

In addition to castle-holding, both the older aristocracy and these self-made lords needed the help of warriors to enforce their claims to power. Accordingly, each lord maintained a private army of men heavily equipped with the new weaponry and armor that the widespread availability of iron—and new techniques for smelting it—made possible. These men fought on horseback, and were therefore called "horsemen": in French, *chevaliers*, and in English, *knights*.

Knighthood was a career that embraced men of widely varying status. Some eleventh-century knights were the younger sons of lords who sought to increase their chances of winning wealth by attaching themselves to the households of greater lords. Others were youths recruited from the peasantry, mounted and armed. All that bound them together was their function, which was the violent prosecution of their lord's interests. Gradually, though, knights also came to regard themselves as belonging to a special military caste with its own rules of conduct. The beginnings of this process are discernible in the *Song of Roland*, and further developments would transform the meaning of chivalry from "horsemanship" to something very different (see below).

Kings, Lords, and Vassals

Despite the emergence of self-governing cities and predatory lordships, the idea of kingship was still a powerful one in continental Europe. For example, the weak Capetian rulers of Paris kept alive the pretense that everyone dwelling in the lands once ruled by more powerful Frankish kings still owed allegiance to them, while the Ottonians claimed

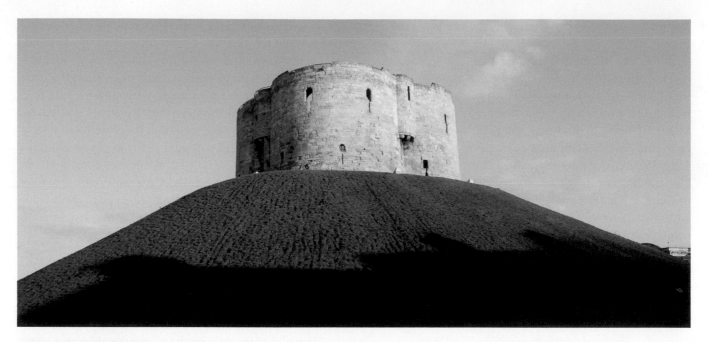

YORK CASTLE (ENGLAND). This fortification exemplifies some of the major phases of medieval castle-building. The large mound is the remains of an earthwork erected on the orders of William the Conqueror in 1068, when it would have been crowned by a wooden palisade: this most basic type of construction is called a motte-and-bailey castle. York's castle remained a wooden tower until it was destroyed by fire and rebuilt in stone after 1245. It is now known as Clifford's Tower, after a rebel leader called Sir Roger Clifford, who was held prisoner there prior to his execution in 1322.

to be kings in northern Italy as well as in their own Saxon domain. In practice, however, neither was able to control the territories they claimed to rule. Effective political and military power lay in the hands of dukes, counts, castellans, and knights, all of whom channeled the increasing wealth of the countryside into their own hands. From their castles, these lords (*domini*) constructed dominions: lordships within which they exercised not only property rights but also the rights to mint money, judge legal cases, raise troops, wage war, collect taxes, and impose tolls.

The Problem of "Feudalism"

This highly diffused distribution of power is conventionally known as "feudalism." But this vague term is unsatisfactory, for several reasons. First and foremost, it is a modern concept not used in the period of history we are discussing. Moreover, it has been used by different people to mean many different things. For example, scholars influenced by the work of Karl Marx (1818–1883, see Chapter 20) use the term *feudalism* to describe an economic system in which wealth is entirely agricultural and cities have not yet formed; as we have seen, this does not reflect the histori-

cal reality of the eleventh and twelfth centuries. For other scholars, feudalism has been construed as an aristocratic social order in which propertied men are bound together by kinship and shared interests; again, this does not explain the varieties of power wielded in this period. Still others have spoken of feudalism as a system of landholding in which lesser men hold land from greater men in return for services of various kinds; but it was not always the greater men who held the most land. Meanwhile, the term has also been used to refer to a system whereby great lords and kings grant land in order to raise troops.

Because all of these definitions of "feudalism" are anachronistic, most recent historians of the Middle Ages have abandoned the use of the term altogether. If, however, we look for a common denominator, we can say that "feudalism" denotes the abuse of official privileges for personal gain: making use of public resources or institutions for private purposes. In this case, there is general agreement that such practices took shape in Frankish lands after the Carolingian Empire had disintegrated and later spread to other areas of Europe, changing as they were adapted to different circumstances. In some regions, these customs fed a developing ideology that justified new kinds of dominion by which kings were supposed to be able to subordinate other powerful men. In this sense, "feudalism" legitimated royal power and helped to lay the groundwork for the emergence of European nation-states.

Although the people living at this time would never have heard the term "feudalism," they would have understood the word at its root: *feudum*, usually translated as "fief" (FEEF). A fief is a gift or grant that creates a kind of contractual relationship between the giver and receiver. This gift could be land, but it could also be the revenues from a toll or a mill, or an annual sum of money. In return, the recipient owed the giver loyalty or services of some kind. In many cases, the gift implied that the recipient was subordinate to the giver and had in fact become the giver's *vassal*, from a Celtic word meaning "boy." This relationship was dramatized in an act of *homage*, a powerful ceremony that made the vassal "the man" (in French, *homme*) of his lord. Typically, the vassal would kneel and place his hands together in a position of prayer, and the lord would cover the clasped hands with his own. He would then raise up his new "man" and exchange a kiss with him. The symbolic importance of these gestures is clear: the lord (*dominus*) was literally the dominating figure. He could protect and raise up his man—but could also discipline him. The role of the vassal, meanwhile, was to support the lord and do nothing to incur his displeasure.

In regions where no centralized authority existed, such personal relationships were essential to creating and maintaining order. However, these relationships were not understood in the same ways all over Europe. Many castellans and knights held their lands freely, owing no service whatsoever to the count or duke within whose territories their lands lay. Nor were these relationships neatly hierarchical. "Feudalism" created no "feudal pyramids," in which knights held fiefs from counts, and counts held fiefs from kings, all in an orderly fashion. Sometimes, kings would insist that the world *should* be structured this way, but they were seldom able to ensure or enforce this.

A New Type of Monarchy: England

The first place where we can begin to observe the efforts of a particular line of kings to establish a monarchy that dominated other powerful lordships is England. In 1066, Duke William of Normandy claimed that he was the rightful successor of the English king, Edward, who had just died. But the English elected a new king, Harold, ignoring William's claim. So William crossed the English Channel to take the kingdom by force, defeating Harold at the Battle of Hastings (see **Interpreting Visual Evidence** on page 262). Now, however, William had to subjugate all of the other chieftains who held power in England, many of whom also aspired to be king.

William accomplished this, first, by asserting that he was king by imperial conquest as well as by succession, and that all the land of England thereby belonged to him. Then William rewarded his Norman followers with fiefs: extensive grants of land taken from their English holders, which the Norman lords were allowed to exploit and subdue. In return, William received their loyalty and a share of their revenues.

The Norman conquerors of England were already accustomed to holding land in return for service to their duke, back in Normandy. But in England, their subordination to the king was further enforced by the effective machinery of the Anglo-Saxon state and by longstanding customs that had the force of law. As king of England, therefore, William was able to exercise a variety of public powers that he could not have enjoyed in Normandy. In England, only the king could coin money and only the king's money was allowed to circulate. As kings of England, William and his successors also inherited the right to collect a national land tax, the right to supervise justice in royal courts, and the right to raise an army. They also retained the Anglo-Saxon officers of local government, known as sheriffs, to help them administer and enforce their rights.

William was thereby able to insist that all the people of England owed ultimate loyalty to the king, even if they did not hold a scrap of land directly from him. William's kingship thus represented a powerful fusion of Carolingian-style traditions of public power with the new forms of lordship that had grown up in the tenth and eleventh centuries, bolstered by indigenous Anglo-Saxon forms of governance. It was a new type of monarchy.

The Struggle for Imperial Power

We can contrast the wide-ranging powers of the new Anglo-Norman kings of England with those of Germany. No German king could claim to rule more than a single principality, and his imperial authority over a host of other rulers was only maintained through a close alliance with the Church. For this reason, the emperor relied heavily on ecclesiastical leaders: his chief administrators were archbishops and bishops whom the emperor himself had appointed and installed in their sacred offices, just as Charlemagne had done. Even the pope was frequently an imperial appointee. The fact that leading churchmen were often members of the imperial family also helped to counter the power of regional rulers.

But in the latter half of the eleventh century, this close cooperation between sacred and secular authority was fractured, and so was the ultimate power of the German monarch.

The Graphic History of the Bayeux Tapestry

One of the most famous historical documents of all time is not a document at all: it is an embroidered strip of linen 231 feet long (originally much longer) and 20 inches wide. It is also not an actual tapestry, as its name misleadingly implies, but an elaborate exercise in needlepoint. It tells the story of the Norman Conquest of England and the events leading up to it. The circumstances of its making remain mysterious, but it was certainly commissioned by someone close to William the Conqueror (1027–1087), the Norman duke who claimed the throne of England in 1066. Indeed, its purpose was to demonstrate the truth of William's claim and to justify his invasion of England when Harold Godwinson (c. 1022–1066), was crowned king of England in his place (image B). One likely patron is Queen Edith of England, the widow of the late King Edward (r. 1042–66) and sister of Harold, who became a friend and adviser to William. Edith was noted for her skill in embroidery as well as for her political acumen, and she would have been able to oversee the making of this visual history by the women of her household. Two of its evocative scenes, with translations of accompanying Latin texts, are reproduced here.

A. Here Harold Sails the Sea. In this scene from the first portion of the Tapestry, Harold has been sent on an embassy by King Edward. He feasts with friends in a hall on the English coast before crossing the Channel.

B. Here is Seated Harold, King of the English. Although Harold may have promised to relinquish his claim to the English throne in William's favor, the central scene of the tapestry is his coronation. Stigant, the archbishop of Canterbury, stands on his right. Outside the cathedral, the people of London look on curiously. Some appear to be surprised or alarmed.

Questions for Analysis

1. Like a graphic novel or a comic strip, the Bayeux Tapestry tells its story through images; words (in very simple Latin) play a minor role. What do the Tapestry's artists choose to express exclusively through visualization? When do they choose to state something verbally? What might be the motivation behind these choices? What is left out of the story, or left ambiguous? What might be the reason(s) for this?

2. In addition to being a source for political and military historians, the Bayeux Tapestry provides us with fascinating glimpses into the daily life and material culture of the Middle Ages. What, for example, can you conclude about the necessary preparations for a voyage by sea? About the history of clothing, or weaponry, or animals?

3. If Queen Edith is responsible for making the Tapestry, it would constitute one of the few surviving historical accounts by a woman prior to the twentieth century. Would the fact of the creator's gender change your perception of this artifact or of these particular scenes? Why or why not?

R exrogat Abbatem; Mathildim supplicatatq;

MATILDA OF TUSCANY MEDIATES BETWEEN EMPEROR AND POPE. Matilda was one of the most powerful rulers in eleventh-century Europe, controlling many strategic territories in northern Italy. Fluent in German as well as Latin and Italian, she was a key mediator in the struggle between the emperor and the pope and a supporter of the reforming movement within the Church. The Latin inscription accompanying this manuscript miniature reads: "The King entreats the Abbot [i.e., the pope] and even humbles himself before Matilda." • *How does this image represent the relationships among these figures?* • *Which appears to be the most powerful, and why?*

In 1056, the six-year-old Henry IV (1050–1106) succeeded his father as king and emperor; and as we will frequently note, political competition among the advisers of underage rulers often escalates into larger conflicts. In this case, the German princes of various regions—led by the disenfranchised Saxon nobility—tried to gain control of the royal government at the expense of Henry's regents. When Henry began to rule in his own right, in 1073, these hostilities escalated into a civil war. At the same time, the newly elected pope, Gregory VII (r. 1073–85), began to insist that no laymen—not even royal ones—should have any influence within the Church. (This would become a core contention in a movement toward increased papal power, to be discussed in the next section.)

King Henry, of course, resisted any initiative that would prohibit him from selecting his own bishops and abbots: for these were the key players in the administration of his realm. So Pope Gregory allied himself with the rebellious Saxon nobility and together they moved to depose Henry. In order to save his crown, Henry was therefore forced to acknowledge the pope's superiority by begging forgiveness. Crossing the Alps into Italy in 1077, in the depths of winter, he found Gregory installed at the castle of Canossa under the protection of one of Europe's most powerful rulers, Matilda of Tuscany. Encouraged by Matilda, who interceded on his behalf, Henry performed an elaborate ritual of penance, standing for three successive days outside the gates of the castle, barefoot, stripped of his imperial trappings, clad in the sackcloth of a supplicant.

This performance of subjection and servitude forestalled Henry's deposition, but it did not resolve his dispute with the nobility of German lands. And it also symbolically reversed the relationship between secular power and religious power. Since the time of Constantine, popes had been dependent on the rulers who protected them. Now an emperor had been bested by the pope. For the other kings and lords of Europe, Henry's humiliation was a chilling example of what could happen when a king let himself be made a vassal.

RELIGIOUS REFORM AND PAPAL POWER

The increased power of the papacy in the eleventh century was a result of the processes we have been surveying in this chapter, but it was also a development that would have been hard to foresee at the time of Charlemagne's death. In the wake of the Viking invasions and the redistribution of power within the former Carolingian Empire, no ruler could maintain Charlemagne's hold on the Church. Many parish churches had been abandoned or destroyed, while those that survived were often regarded as the personal property of some local family, whose responsibility for protecting parishioners could become an excuse to oppress them. Bishoprics, too, were co-opted by families who regarded Church lands and offices as their private property. Monasteries underwent a further process of privatization, becoming safe havens for aristocratic younger sons and daughters with little inclination for religious life. Meanwhile, the holders of papal office were its worst abusers. Most were incompetent or corrupt, the sons or tools of powerful Roman families. Many fathered sons who themselves succeeded to high ecclesiastical office, including that of pope. As the guardian of the tombs of Peter and Paul, the bishop of Rome had long occupied a privileged position. Now, however, the papacy's credibility had been severely compromised.

The Monastic Reform Movement

The first successful attempts to restore the spiritual authority of the Roman Church can be traced to the founding of a new kind of monastery in Burgundy (now southeastern France). In 910, a Benedictine abbey called Cluny freed itself from any obligation to local families by placing itself under the direct protection of the papacy. And although it had a wealthy benefactor, that benefactor relinquished control over Cluny's property; instead, Duke William of Aquitaine and his family gained the spiritual support and prayers of the monks, whose intercessions might help to save warlike men from eternal damnation.

This arrangement would set a new precedent for the relationship between monasteries and powerful families for centuries to come, as Cluny began to sponsor other monasteries on the same model. Indeed, the foundation of these daughter houses was another innovation: prior to this, all Benedictine monasteries had been independent of one another, united only by their observance of Benedict's *Rule*. Now Cluny established a network of Cluniac clones across Europe, all of which remained subordinate to the mother house. By 1049, there were sixty-seven such Cluniac priories (as the daughter monasteries were called), each one performing the same elaborate round of prayer and worship for which Cluny became famous, and each one entirely free from the control of local lords who hoped to reap spiritual rewards from their support of the pious monks.

Cluniac influence was strongest in the former Frankish territories and in Italy, where the virtual absence of effective kingship allowed monastic reforms to thrive unchecked. In Germany and England, by contrast, fostering monastic reform emerged as an essential responsibility of Christian rulers whose role model was the pious Charlemagne. These rulers, too, followed Cluniac example by insisting on the strict observance of poverty, chastity, and obedience within the monastery, and on the performance of liturgical prayer. Yet because they were the guarantors of the monasteries' freedom from outside interference, it was they who appointed the abbots, just as they also appointed the bishops of their kingdoms. As a result of this trend, and the concurrent Norman conquest of England, future kings of England would have more direct control over Church lands than other European rulers. In Germany, a prince's right to appoint spiritual leaders would be the central cause of strife with the papacy (see below).

Despite the differences in sponsorship, these parallel reforming movements made monasticism the dominant spiritual model for Latin Christianity. The peaceful, orderly round of daily worship in monasteries and convents was regarded as mirroring a perfect celestial harmony, and monastic prayers were considered uniquely effective because of nuns' and monks' holy way of life. Monasteries also had an important influence on the piety of ordinary people, because many monastic communities maintained parishes that ministered directly to the laity. The spiritual practices that had been unique to monks and nuns in earlier centuries therefore came to influence daily life outside the cloister.

THE ABBEY CHURCH AT CLUNY. Its extraordinary wealth and power made Cluny a major target during the French Wars of Religion and again during the French Revolution, when locals who had been subjected to its lordship for centuries razed most of the buildings to the ground (see Chapters 14 and 18). This artist's reconstruction shows the vast abbey church as it might have looked by the twelfth century, after several extensive building campaigns. In its day, Cluny was one of the largest structures in Europe and a quintessential example of the architectural style known as Romanesque.

2. CLUNY (NO).

A Miraculous Reliquary

Although pilgrimages had been a part of Christian religious practice for centuries, they became much more central elements of popular piety from the tenth century on. Pilgrims brought money and spiritual prestige to the monasteries and cathedrals that housed miracle-working relics, and competition among monastic houses sometimes led one house to steal the relics of another. But some critics worried that these newly popular shrines were encouraging idolatry. Bernard of Angers (c. 960–1028) was one such critic. His account of a visit to the shrines of several saints, including that of Sainte Foy ("Saint Faith") at Conques, reveals the negative impression that ornate reliquaries made on him—and the power of wonder-working relics to correct that impression.

t is an ancient custom in all of Auvergne, Rodez, Toulouse, and the neighboring regions that the local saint has a statue of gold, silver, or some other metal . . . [that] serves as a reliquary for the head of the saint or for a part of his body. The learned might see in this a superstition and a vestige of the cult of demons, and I myself . . . had the same impression the first time I saw the statue of Saint Gerard . . . resplendent with gold and stones, with an expression so human that the simple people . . . pretend that it winks at pilgrims whose prayers it answers. I admit to my shame that turning to my friend Bernerius and laughing, I whispered to him in Latin, "What do you think of the idol? Wouldn't Jupiter or Mars be happy with it?" . . .

Three days later we arrived at [the shrine of] St. Faith. . . . We approached [the reliquary] but the crowd was such that we could not prostrate ourselves like so many others already lying on the floor. Unhappy, I remained standing, fixing my view on the image and murmuring this prayer, "St. Faith, you whose relics rest in this sham, come to my assistance on the day of judgment." And this time I looked at my companion . . . because I found it outrageous that all of these rational beings should be praying to a mute and inanimate object. . . .

Later I greatly regretted to have acted so stupidly toward the saint of God.

This was because among other miracles [that] Don Adalgerius, at that time dean and later . . . abbot [of Conques], told me [was] a remarkable account of a cleric named Oldaric. One day when the venerable image had to be taken to another place, . . . he restrained the crowd from bringing offerings and he

The Reliquary of Saint Faith, Early Tenth Century.

insulted and belittled the image of the saint. . . . The next night, a lady of imposing severity appeared to him: "You," she said, "how dare you insult my image?" Having said this, she flogged her enemy with a staff. . . . He survived only long enough to tell the vision in the morning.

Thus there is no place left for arguing whether the effigy of St. Faith ought to be venerated since it is clear that he who reproached the holy martyr nevertheless retracted his reproach. Nor is it a spurious idol where nefarious rites of sacrifice or of divination are conducted, but rather a pious memorial of a holy virgin, before which great numbers of faithful people decently and eloquently implore her efficacious intercession for their sins.

Source: Bernard of Angers, "The Book of the Miracles of St. Faith," in *Readings in Medieval History*, 3rd ed., ed. and trans. Patrick J. Geary (Peterborough, Ont., Canada: 2003), pp. 333–34 (slightly modified).

Questions for Analysis

1. Why does Bernard initially object to the display of relics in ornate reliquaries? Why would he consider this practice blasphemous? How does he become reconciled to it?

2. Can you think of present-day practices that resemble the medieval fascination with collecting, displaying, and venerating relics? What do such practices reveal about any society?

Relics and Pilgrims

One potent example of this new popular spirituality is the growing devotion to relics. Monasteries were often the repositories of cherished objects associated with saints, such as fragments of bone or pieces of cloth cut from the garments of some holy person. These souvenirs were believed to possess special protective and curative powers. Hence, a relic was usually buried beneath the altar of a church during the ceremony of its consecration, in order to render the church building sacrosanct. Relics were also collected and displayed in elaborate reliquaries made of precious metals and studded with jewels, casings that reflected and augmented the value of the holy objects contained within them.

Indeed, relics were so valuable that monasteries and cathedrals competed with one another for their acquisition and even plotted the "holy theft" of a particularly prized treasure. For instance, the relics of Nicholas, a fourth-century bishop of Myra (in Turkey), were stolen from the saint's tomb during the eleventh century. These were brought to Bari in southeastern Italy, where Benedictine monks built a magnificent church to house them. It became a major—and lucrative—attraction for pilgrims.

The possession and display of relics thus became a way for monasteries to attract attention and generate revenue, since those who sought cures or favors at the shrine of a saint would often make a donation to the monastery in the saint's honor. If a saint was especially famous for a particular type of miracle, pilgrims might travel thousands of miles to visit a shrine. Saint Nicholas was famous for increasing the wealth of his suppliants, and for bestowing gifts—hence his later incarnation as Santa Claus. The relics of Sainte Foy ("Saint Faith") of Conques (southern France) were renowned for their power to rectify injustices, restore order, and heal the maladies that afflicted the poor. Those of the apostle James at Compostela (northern Spain) became the chief destination on a major pilgrimage route, rivaling even the holy sites of Rome and Jerusalem in its popularity. Pilgrimage was another of the important ways in which the new patterns of Christian piety that developed in monasteries began to spread to the laity.

The Reform of the Secular Clergy

By the eleventh century, the movement toward spiritual renewal in the monasteries of Europe began to embrace the sees of bishops. This was a major change: bishops and the priests who served in their dioceses were secular clergy, living in the world (*saeculum* in Latin); it had long been expected that they would share some of the worldly preoccupations and lifestyles of their parishioners. But as the values and priorities of monasticism began to spread outward, abbots were more often appointed to episcopal office. Meanwhile, even nonmonastic bishops were forced to adopt stricter standards of personal conduct. Bishops also began to rebuild and expand their cathedral churches to make them more suitable reflections of divine majesty, in accordance with Cluniac example.

As their influence grew, the monasteries under the sway of Cluny began to lobby for even larger reforms, amounting to a fundamental dismantling of customs that reached back to the organization of the Church under Constantine, seven centuries earlier. They centered their attacks on the practice of simony (*SIGH-mony*), a term describing any use of ecclesiastical office for personal gain, including the purchase or sale of a bishopric or a priest's living (i.e., house, goods, and annual salary). In other words, the reform movement targeted the very structure of the Church as a network of independent lordships held by powerful men in trust for their families.

Even more radical was the reformers' demand that secular clergy share the lifestyles of monks, taking vows not only of personal poverty but of celibacy. Although some early councils of the Church had attempted to regulate the marriage of bishops and priests, none had been successful. And for good reason: the task of ministering to the laity was very different from the monk's task of perpetual prayer and communal life. For a thousand years, it had been conceded that the demands of priestly celibacy were unreasonable, and would deprive a priest's parishioners of an additional resource and ministry— that of his wife. In the year 1000, therefore, the vast majority of parish priests all across Europe were married, and in the eastern Orthodox Church they would remain so. Married bishops were rarer, but not unknown. In Brittany, the archbishop of Dol and his wife publicly celebrated the marriages of their daughters, endowing them with lands belonging to the bishopric; in Milan, the archbishops flatly rejected reformers' calls for celibacy, declaring that their patron saint, Ambrose (see Chapter 6), had been married, too.

The Reform of the Papacy

In Rome, the most powerful bishopric of all remained resolutely unreformed until 1046, when the German emperor Henry III deposed three rival Roman nobles who claimed to be pope and appointed in their place his own relative, a monk who adopted the name Leo IX (r. 1049–54). Leo and his supporters took control of the papal court and began to promulgate decrees against simony and clerical marriage. They then took steps to enforce these decrees by traveling throughout the Continent, disciplining and removing from office clerics deemed guilty of simony or obstinately

Past and Present

Ideas of Crusade

The launching of the First Crusade was the beginning of a trend that decisively shaped the relations between western Europeans and their neighbors, and that continues today. The very use of the word "crusade" is apt to cause trouble—as when President George W. Bush spoke of "this crusade, this war on terrorism" to which he pledged the United States after September 11, 2001.

 Watch related author interview on StudySpace
wwnorton.com/web/westernciv18

determined not to "put away" their wives—whom the reformers insisted on calling "concubines" as a way of discrediting these respectable relationships.

Implicit in Leo's reforming efforts was a new vision of the Church as a type of monarchy, with the pope at the apex of a spiritual pyramid: an ideal difficult for any secular ruler to realize and one that would severely limit the power of other ecclesiastical officeholders. Not surprisingly, therefore, Leo and his successors met with considerable opposition from powerful leaders within the Church itself, and they could only enforce their claims in regions where they had the support of secular rulers. Chief among these was the pious emperor Henry III, whose protection insulated papal reformers from the Roman nobility, who would otherwise have deposed or assassinated them.

But when Henry III died in 1056, the regents of his child heir Henry IV (whose reign we discussed above) were neither able nor willing to stand behind the reform-

ing movement. In 1058, the Roman aristocracy seized this opportunity to install one of their own number on the papal throne. By this time, however, the reform movement had gathered momentum; a year later, a new pope had been installed and was determined to counter any interference from either the German or Italian nobility. To this end, Nicholas II (r. 1059–61) created a new legislative body, the College of Cardinals (from the Latin for "collection" of "hinges"). Hitherto, local bishops around Rome had served the papacy as advisers and assistants, but now the College became the nexus for the creation of papal policy. It also ensured the continuity of the papal office by overseeing the selection of new popes, a role it still plays today.

Needless to say, this novel arrangement infuriated the advisers of the young Henry IV, since it removed the emperor's prerogative to oversee the process of papal elections himself. And it set the stage for the confrontations that were to follow.

The Investiture Conflict

A few years after Henry IV began to rule in his own right, the new College of Cardinals selected as pope a zealous reformer called Hildebrand, a Cluniac monk of Tuscan origins who had been a protégé of Leo IX. He took the name Gregory VII. Initially, pope and emperor treated one another with deference. Henry IV's position in Germany had been weakened by his wars with the Saxon nobility, and he needed papal backing to restore his authority. In his letters to the new pope, he therefore blamed the advisers of his youth for the troubles that had arisen between his own court and that of Rome, and he promised to make amends. Gregory, in turn, spoke of pope and emperor as the two eyes of a single, Christian body. On the surface, it appeared that harmonious relations might be restored.

Two year later, however, relations between papacy and empire were riven by a conflict that would permanently alter the relationship between spiritual and temporal leaders in western Europe. Superficially, the issue that divided Gregory and Henry was that of investiture, the right to appoint bishops and to equip them with the trappings of office. Since the time of the Carolingians, this had been the prerogative of the emperor—as it was in Byzantium. But to Gregory, this practice smacked of simony, since a lay lord would obviously choose bishops who would be politically useful to him, regardless of their spiritual qualifications.

The issue, however, was not the political power of bishops; it was the control of that power. For paradoxically, the papal reform movement as it developed under Gregory was predicated on liberating the Church from powerful worldly influences in order that the Church itself might become more worldly and powerful. This was the principle that lay behind the discouraging of clerical marriage, too: Church offices and Church property had to be protected by the Church for the Church. Allowing priests to marry might encourage the handing down of offices to sons, just as allowing rulers to appoint bishops encouraged these bishops to act as the rulers' agents. These practices tainted the austere authority that the pope was trying to cultivate, and it also threatened to alienate property and power that the papacy wanted to harness for its own purposes.

Gregory therefore took the reform movement to a new level, insisting that adherence to these principles was not just a matter of policy but a matter of religious dogma, a term defined as "a truth necessary for salvation." When Henry IV refused to accept this and proceeded to invest the new archbishop of Milan, Gregory reminded him that, as the successor of Saint Peter and the representative of Christ on earth, he himself had the power to save or damn all souls. To drive the point home, Gregory excommunicated a number of Henry's advisers, including several of the bishops who had participated in the investiture at Milan. Henry thereupon renounced his obedience to Gregory, calling on him to resign. Gregory responded by excommunicating Henry, along with his supporters.

In itself, the excommunication of a king was not terribly unusual. Gregory, however, went much further by equating excommunication with deposition, declaring that since Henry was no longer a faithful son of the Church, he was no longer the king of Germany and his subjects had a sacred duty to rebel against him. It was this that occasioned Henry's humiliating stand before the castle at Canossa in January of 1077. But the story does not end there, because Henry used his restored powers to crush his Saxon opponents and eventually to drive Gregory himself from Rome. In 1085, the aged pope died in exile in southern Italy. By then, however, he had established the principles on which papal governance would be based for the remainder of the Middle Ages.

In 1122, the conflict over investiture was provisionally resolved through compromise at the Concordat of Worms (*VOHRMS*) in Germany. Its terms declared that the emperor was forbidden to invest prelates with the *religious* symbols of their office but was allowed to invest them with the symbols of their rights as *temporal* rulers, in his capacity as their overlord. In practice, then, the rulers of Europe retained a great deal of influence over ecclesiastical appointments. But they also had to acknowledge that bishops were now part of a clerical hierarchy headed by the pope, and that they were supposed to be loyal to the Church in Rome and not to the ruler of the region in which they lived.

CRUSADING CAUSES AND OUTCOMES

Gregory VII's equation of excommunication with deposition had given the pope a powerful new weapon to use against wayward rulers. Indeed, according to a series of pronouncements issued in his name, Gregory insisted that the pope has the power to judge all men but cannot himself be judged by any earthly authority. Moreover, he has the power to free any man from his obligations to his lord because every Christian owes ultimate loyalty to the pope, the arbiter of eternal life or death. These were big claims. How could they be realized? Gregory's immediate successors would soon be driven to great lengths in their efforts to establish the credibility of the newly reformed and powerful papacy. In the end, it took the appeal of a Byzantine emperor and the preaching of a crusade against Islam to unite western Christendom under the papal banner.

THE BYZANTINE EMPIRE, c. 1025. ■ *According to the map, what political challenges faced the Byzantine Empire in the eleventh century?* ■ *How was the long-standing influence of Muslims in the Near East likely to affect the character of Byzantine culture?* ■ *How did the domain of Kievan Rus' potentially create additional economic and military pressure on Byzantium, directly as well as indirectly?*

The Expansion and Limitations of Byzantium

As Europe expanded and changed, the eastern Roman Empire was undergoing its own series of transformations. The decline of the Abbasid Caliphate in Baghdad had relieved some of the pressures on its borders in the course of the ninth century. But at the same time, Byzantium was facing some new threats. In the mid-ninth century, Muslims from North Africa captured the Byzantine islands of Sicily and Crete. Meanwhile, the migration of pagan Slavs into the Balkans was rapidly undermining Byzantine control of that region; and a formidable power had emerged in the north, as the Viking Rus' established themselves along the river systems that fed into the Black and Caspian Seas. The Rus's most important trading partner was the Abbasid Caliphate, with which they exchanged slaves, honey, wax, and furs for silver, Indian spices, and Chinese silks. But the Rus' knew their way to Constantinople, too. In 860, while the Byzantine emperor and his army were busy on the eastern frontier, a fleet of them sailed into the Black Sea and sacked the capital.

The best that the emperor in Byzantium could do was to make these newer enemies their allies. Greek-speaking missionaries began the process by converting some of the Balkan Slavs to Orthodox Christianity, devising for them a written language known as Old Church Slavonic and creating the Cyrillic alphabet still used today in Bulgaria, Serbia, and Russia. As we have often seen, domination went hand in glove with conversion: the Byzantines also established a military and commercial alliance with the kingdom centered around Kiev, and in 911 hundreds of Rus' served with the Byzantine navy in an attack on Muslim Crete. Diplomatic relations were also established: in 957, a Kievan princess named Olga was lavishly entertained on a state visit to Constantinople. And in 989, the emperor Basil II turned to

Vladimir, prince of Kiev, for the troops he needed to win a civil war against an imperial rival. In return for Vladimir's help, Basil married him to his sister Anna; and Vladimir, along with his people, accepted baptism into the Orthodox Church. (Russia has remained strongly Orthodox to this day, despite Soviet efforts to dismantle the Russian Orthodox Church in the twentieth century.)

In the tenth century, the eastern Roman Empire further strengthened its position by launching a series of successful campaigns against the Abbasids, reconquering territories that had been lost since the seventh century. But although most of the peoples of this region had remained Christian through three centuries of Islamic rule, the Armenians and the Syrians in particular had their own distinctive Christian traditions that were at odds, both doctrinally and linguistically, with the Greek-speaking church at Constantinople. Reincorporating these "heretics" into the empire strained the limits of Orthodoxy to a considerable degree, and these efforts also created a center of power that lay outside the imperial capital at Constantinople. Accordingly, rivalries divided the eastern nobility and the imperial court, eventually erupting into warfare after one aristocratic family attempted a coup.

Meanwhile, projects of reconquest and expansion were overextending the Byzantine military and its treasury. In an effort to raise cash, some emperors in the mid-eleventh century began to debase the gold coinage that had kept the empire competitive with the Islamic Caliphate, thus undermining Byzantine commerce at the very moment when Venice, Genoa, and Pisa were consolidating their control in the eastern Mediterranean and taking over the lucrative trade between Muslim North Africa (including Egypt) and western Europe.

A failing economy, ongoing dynastic civil war, the weakened condition of the army, and uneasy relations with the new kingdoms of the Balkans (especially Hungary) proved nearly fatal to Byzantine sovereignty. And then the empire was confronted with yet another threat. The Seljuq Turks, a powerful dynasty of Sunni Muslims who were building their own empire based in Persia, began to move westward in the latter part of the eleventh century. In 1071, they captured Armenia and moved swiftly into the Byzantine heartland of Anatolia (Turkey), where they destroyed a Byzantine army sent to deflect them.

At a blow, the wealthiest and most productive part of the empire fell into Muslim hands—and not those of the Abbasids with whom the Byzantines had contended for centuries. In the same year, the Seljuqs captured Jerusalem, which had been part of a Shi'ite caliphate based in Egypt, ruled by the Fatimids. By 1081, when the eastern nobility of Byzantium finally emerged triumphant in their ongoing bid for the imperial throne, the new emperor Alexius Comnenus (r. 1081–1118) found himself at the head of a crippled state.

The Call for a Crusade

Alexius was an able emperor. In the first decade of his rule, he managed to shore up the failing economy and secure his hold over Bulgarian territory in the Balkans. He then began to plan a campaign against the Seljuqs. But with what forces? The Byzantine army had been decimated in Greece by a far superior cavalry of Norman knights in 1085. For by this time, the Normans had established independent principalities in southern Italy and Sicily and were moving farther east, taking advantage of the perpetual power vacuum in the Mediterranean and showcasing the effective tactics of chivalry. As it happened, this encounter between the Byzantine emperor and western

ROLAND AS A CRUSADING KNIGHT. The association between knighthood and crusading helped to raise the social status of knights and contributed to the refinement of a chivalric ethos. Here, a crusading knight, dressed head to foot in expensive chain mail, is shown kneeling in homage to his lord, God.

Europe's most formidable warriors was historically significant. It convinced Alexius that such heavily armed horsemen would be successful if pitted against the lightly armored Seljuqs.

It was in the hopes of recruiting a mercenary force, therefore, that Alexius approached Pope Urban II (r. 1088–99). This was a move that played into the hands of the reformed papacy. Urban was trying hard to realize some of the powerful claims that his recent predecessors had made on behalf of papal authority, and this seemed like a golden opportunity. By coming to the aid of the eastern Roman Empire, he would show the restive princes of western Europe that the papacy was a force to be reckoned with. At the same time, he hoped to show that Latin military and spiritual might was greater than that of the weakened Greeks, thereby healing the schism between Orthodox and

Latin Christianities and realizing the centuries-old dream of a universal Christian Church based in Rome, with the pope at its head. In addition, Urban would thereby show support for another reforming effort that had gained momentum in recent years: a peace movement that was attempting to quell the endemic violence unleashed by competitive bands of knights and their rapacious lords. What better way to defuse the situation than to ship those violent energies overseas, deploying them against a common enemy?

So Alexius received a favorable reply, but he got far more than he had asked for—or wanted. He had needed a modest contingent of a few thousand troops, to help him reconquer Anatolia. What he got was a vast army of 100,000 men, charged by Urban II to retake the holy city of Jerusalem for Christendom. For Urban decided to interpret Alexius's

THE ROUTES OF THE CRUSADERS, 1096–1204. Compare the routes followed by participants in the first three Crusades. ▪ *What were the three main routes followed by crusaders?* ▪ *What geographical and political factors appear to be determining these trajectories?* ▪ *Why was the Fourth Crusade so different?*

Competing Viewpoints

Preaching the First Crusade: Two Accounts

> We owe the following account of Urban II's call for a crusade to Fulcher of Chartres, a priest who was present at the Council of Clermont in 1095 and who later served as a chaplain to the first Norman king of Jerusalem, Baldwin. It forms part of Fulcher's contemporary chronicle of the First Crusade. The second account of the motives behind the crusade comes from a biography of the Byzantine emperor Alexius Comnenus, written by his daughter Anna (1083–1153), who also lived through these events.

Pope Urban II's Call at Clermont, November 1195

Most beloved brethren: Urged by necessity, I, Urban, by the permission of God chief bishop and prelate over the whole world, have come into these parts as an ambassador with a divine admonition to you, the servants of God. . . .

Although, O sons of God, you have promised more firmly than ever to keep the peace among yourselves and to preserve the rights of the Church, there remains still an important work for you to do. Freshly quickened by the divine correction, you must apply the strength of your righteousness to another matter which concerns you as well as God. For your brethren who live in the east are in urgent need of your help, and you must hasten to give them the aid which has often been promised them. For, as most of you have heard, the Turks and Arabs have attacked them and have conquered the territory of Romania [the Byzantine Empire] as far west as the shore of the Mediterranean and the Hellespont. . . . They have occupied more and more of the lands of those Christians, and have overcome them in seven battles. They have killed and captured many, and have destroyed the churches and devastated the empire.

If you permit them to continue thus for a while with impunity, the faithful of God will be much more widely attacked by them. On this account I, or rather the Lord, beseech you as Christ's heralds to publish this everywhere and to persuade all people of whatever rank, footsoldiers and knights, poor and rich, to carry aid promptly to those Christians and to destroy that vile race from the lands of our friends. I say this to those who are present, but it is meant also for those who are absent. Moreover, Christ commands it.

All who die by the way, whether by land or by sea, or in battle against the pagans, shall have immediate remission of sins. This I grant them through the power of God with which I am invested. O what a disgrace, if such a despised and base race, which worships demons, should conquer a people which has the faith of omnipotent God and is made glorious with the name of Christ! With what reproaches will the Lord overwhelm us if you do not aid those who, with us, profess the Christian religion!

Let those who have been accustomed to wage unjust private warfare against the faithful now go against the infidels and end with victory this war which should have been begun long ago. Let those who for a long time have been robbers now become knights. Let those who have been fighting against their brothers and relatives now fight in a proper way against the barbarians. Let those who have been serving as mercenaries for small pay now obtain the eternal reward. Let those who have been wearing themselves out in both body

request very loosely. Speaking before an assembled crowd at an ecclesiastical council at Clermont (central France) in 1095, he announced that he fully supported the peace movement. He said, furthermore, that any knights who wished to fight, pillage, and wreak havoc could do so for a just and Christian cause by liberating the Holy Land from its Muslim captors. At home, said Urban, most knights were riffraff and marauders, destined for hellfire and damnation; abroad, they would be crusaders, which meant that anyone fighting or dying in the service of Christ would win absolution for his sins. By taking up the cross (*crux*, hence "crusade"), a warrior stood to win glory, booty, and salvation.

This was an irresistible trifecta for many pious, ambitious, or opportunistic men. Consequently, the ultimate and soul now work for a double honor. Behold! On this side will be the sorrowful and poor, on that, the rich; on this side, the enemies of the Lord, on that, his friends. Let those who go not put off the journey, but rent their lands and collect money for their expenses; and as soon as winter is over and spring comes, let them eagerly set out on the way with God as their guide.

Source: S. J. Allen and Emilie Amt, eds., *The Crusades: A Reader* (Peterborough, ON, Canada: 2003), pp. 39–40.

Anna Comnena Describes the Beginnings of the First Crusade

[Alexius] had no time to relax before he heard a rumour that countless Frankish armies were approaching. He dreaded their arrival, knowing as he did their uncontrollable passion, their erratic character and their irresolution, not to mention . . . their greed for money. . . . So far from despairing, however, he made every effort to prepare for war if need arose. What actually happened was more far-reaching and terrible than rumour suggested, for the whole of the West and all the barbarians who lived between the Adriatic and the Straits of Gibraltar migrated in a body to Asia, marching across Europe country by country with all their households. The reason for this mass-movement is to be found more or less in the following events. A certain Kelt, called Peter [the Hermit] . . . left to worship at the Holy Sepulchre and after suffering much ill-treatment at the hands of the Turks and Saracens who were plundering the whole of Asia, he

returned home with difficulty. Unable to admit defeat, . . . he worked out a clever scheme. He decided to preach in all the Latin countries. A divine voice, he said, commanded him to proclaim to all the counts in France that all should depart from their homes, set out to worship at the Holy Shrine, and . . . strive to liberate Jerusalem. . . . Surprisingly, he was successful. . . . Full of enthusiasm and ardour they thronged every highway, and with these warriors came a host of civilians, outnumbering the sand of the sea shore or the stars of heaven, carrying palms and bearing crosses on their shoulders. There were women and children, too, who had left their own countries. . . .

The upheaval that ensued as men *and* women took to the road was unprecedented within living memory. The simpler folk were in very truth led on by a desire to worship at Our Lord's tomb and visit the holy places, but the more villainous characters . . . had an ulterior purpose, for they hoped on their

journey to seize the capital [Jerusalem] itself, looking upon its capture as a natural consequence of the expedition. . . .

Source: Excerpted from Anna Comnena, *The Alexiad*, trans. E. R. A. Sewter (New York: 1969), pp. 308–11.

Questions for Analysis

1. Given Urban II's explanation of the problems confronting the Byzantine Empire, how do you account for the fact that the Crusades were directed toward the Holy Land and not to the relief of Byzantium?

2. How does Anna Comnena represent the motives of Peter the Hermit and the crusaders? What distinctions does she make among the participants?

3. Are there points of comparison between these two accounts? On what do they agree? How would you explain the differences between them?

response to Urban's call exceeded all expectations. Indeed, his message was amplified by other preachers, including a zealous priest called Peter the Hermit, who claimed (falsely) that he had been prevented by the Seljuqs from visiting the Holy Land. Within a year, tens of thousands of warriors and a large number of women and children from all over western Europe were on the march toward Constantinople,

where they intended to gather before departing for Jerusalem. As with any large enterprise, the participants' motives must have varied. A few might have hoped to win principalities for themselves. Others were drawn by the prospect of adventure. Many were the dependents of greater men, who had no choice but to accompany their lords; some hoped to free themselves from dependence by fighting. Most probably had no idea how long the journey would be or knew anything about the places for which they were destined.

But the dominant motive for joining this First Crusade was religious. Except for a few of the greatest lords—mostly Normans from Sicily and southern Italy—the prospect of winning new lands was both unlikely and undesired. Indeed, one of the greatest challenges facing the Christian kingdom that was established in Jerusalem after 1099 was the fact that crusaders so rarely wanted to stay. After fulfilling their vows, the vast majority went home. So why did they go in the first place? The risks of dying on such a journey were high; the costs of embarking were enormous. Crusading knights needed a minimum of two years' revenues in hand to finance the journey. To raise such sums, most were forced to mortgage lands and borrow heavily from family, friends, monasteries, and merchants. They then had to find some way to pay back these loans if and when they returned home. By any rational assessment, the Crusade was a fool's errand.

The seeming irrationality of this endeavor underscores the importance of reckoning with the crusaders' piety, and even their desire to emulate legendary heroes like Roland. Crusading was the ultimate pilgrimage, the holy places of Jerusalem the ultimate Christian shrines. If anyone could receive special blessings by traveling to Compostela, Conques, or Bari, how much more blessed would be those who fought through to the Holy Land! Urban II made this point explicit at Clermont, promising that crusaders would be freed from all penances imposed by the Church. Some zealots went even further, promising that crusaders would be entirely freed from otherworldly punishments for all sins committed up to that point in their lives, and that the souls of those who died on crusade would go straight to heaven.

Crusade preaching also emphasized the vengeance that Christ's soldiers should exact on his pagan enemies. So to some crusaders, it seemed absurd to wait until they arrived in the Holy Land to undertake this aspect of their mission. Muslims might hold Jesus's property at Jerusalem, but Christian theology held Jews responsible for the death of Jesus himself. Assaults against Jewish communities therefore began in the spring of 1096 and quickly spread eastward with the crusaders. Hundreds of Jews were killed in the German towns of Mainz, Worms, Speyer, and Cologne, and hundreds more were forcibly baptized as the price for escaping death at the hands of crusading knights. Many individual churchmen attempted to prevent these attacks, among them the bishops in whose dioceses Jews lived. But the Church's own negative propaganda thwarted these efforts, and pogroms against Europe's Jews would remain a regular and predictable feature of Christian crusading and its modern manifestations.

The Christian Conquest of Jerusalem

Surprised by the nature and scale of the response to his appeal, Emperor Alexius did his best to move the crusaders quickly through Constantinople and into Asia Minor. But differences in outlook between the crusaders and the Byzantine emperor quickly became apparent. Alexius had little interest in an expedition to Jerusalem, and insisted that the crusaders promise to restore any territory they captured to him; from his standpoint, the crusader army was a threat, not least because it was headed by several of the Norman knights who had attempted to infiltrate his empire only ten years earlier. To the crusaders—whose mission had been shaped by Pope Urban's policies (not those of Alexius)—this seemed like treachery. The crusaders, furthermore, did not understand the Byzantine emperor's willingness to make alliances with some Muslim rulers (the Shi'ite Fatimids of Egypt and the Abassids of Baghdad) against other Muslim rulers (the Sunni Seljuqs). They ignorantly concluded that the Byzantines were working to undermine the crusading effort, perhaps even supporting the Muslims against them. Such suspicions contributed to their growing conviction that the eastern Roman Empire was itself an obstacle to the successful recovery of Jerusalem.

Viewed from the perspective of Alexius, the Crusade was a disaster. But from that of the papacy and the crusaders themselves, it was a triumph. In 1098, crusaders captured the old Hellenistic city of Antioch and with it most of the Syrian coast. At the end of 1099, they took Jerusalem, indiscriminately slaughtering its Muslim, Jewish, and Christian inhabitants. Their quick success stemmed mainly from the fact that their Muslim opponents were at that moment divided among themselves: the Fatimids had in fact recaptured Jerusalem just months before the crusaders arrived, and the defeated Seljuqs were at war with one another. Western military tactics, in particular the dominance of heavily armored knights, also played an important role in the crusaders' success. Equally critical was the naval support offered by Genoa and Pisa, whose merchant adventurers hoped to control the Indian spice trade that passed through the Red Sea and on to Alexandria in Egypt if the papacy's cause was successful. The Crusade thereby contributed to the further decline of Byzantine commerce and decisively altered the balance of power between Byzantium and western Europe.

The Consequences of Crusade

For Byzantium, the consequences of the crusading movement were clearly tragic. On the Muslim world, however, the impact was more modest. The crusader kingdoms

Analyzing Primary Sources

An Arab Aristocrat Encounters the Crusaders

Usama ibn Munqidh (1095–1188) was an Arab Muslim from Syria, whose family maintained a prominent place in the local administration even after the conquests of the Seljuqs and the Christian crusaders. He traveled widely and worked in various Islamic cities as a diplomat and scholar. He ended his life in the service of Salah ad-Din (Saladin), the great Muslim leader who reconquered Jerusalem the year before Usama's death. The following excerpt is from Usama's memoir, which he called The Book of Contemplation. *The Templars mentioned in the account are the Christian military order of the Knights of the Temple, who dedicated themselves to protecting pilgrims in Jerusalem and guarding the holy sites. Their headquarters were in the main mosque of the city, which stood on the Temple Mount.*

 nyone who is recently arrived from the Frankish lands is rougher in character than those who have become acclimated and have frequented the company of Muslims. Here is an instance of their rough character (may God abominate them!):

Whenever I went to visit the holy sites in Jerusalem, I would go in and make my way up to the al-Aqsa Mosque, beside which stood a small mosque that the Franks had converted into a church. When I went into the al-Aqsa Mosque—where the Templars, who are my friends, were—they would clear out that little mosque so that I could pray in it. One day, I went into the little mosque, recited the opening formula 'God is great!' and

stood up in prayer. At this, one of the Franks rushed at me and grabbed me and turned my face towards the east, saying, 'Pray like *this*!'

A group of Templars hurried towards him, took hold of the Frank and took him away from me. I then returned to my prayers. The Frank, that very same one, took advantage of their inattention and returned, rushing upon me and turning my face to the east, saying, 'Pray like *this*!'

So the Templars came in again, grabbed him and threw him out. They apologized to me, saying, 'This man is a stranger, just arrived from the Frankish lands sometime in the past few days. He has never before seen anyone who did not pray towards the east.'

'I think I've prayed quite enough,' I said and left. I used to marvel at that

devil, the change of his expression, the way he trembled and what he must have made of seeing someone praying towards Mecca.

Source: Usama ibn Munqidh, *The Book of Contemplation: Islam and the Crusades,* trans. Paul M. Cobb (New York: 2008), p. 147.

Questions for Analysis

1. What does Usama's account reveal about the variety of relationships among Christians and Muslims in the crusader kingdom of Jerusalem?

2. Who is the true outsider in this scenario? What does Usama's treatment by the Templars suggest about the policy of Christian leaders toward the city's Muslim residents?

established by victorious Norman and Frankish warlords were never more than a sparsely settled cluster of colonies along the coastline of Syria and Palestine. Because the crusaders did not control the Red Sea, the main routes of Islamic commerce with India and the Far East were unaffected by the change in Jerusalem's religious allegiance.

In any case, those crusaders who remained to settle in the region did not *want* to interfere with the overland caravan routes that wound through their new territories. Trade brokered by Arab, Persian, and Jewish merchants therefore

continued despite periodic interruptions. The greatest economic gains for western Europeans therefore went to the Italian maritime republics of Venice and Genoa, and to the western markets now open to Muslim merchants for their goods. Both sides also gained in military terms: western Europeans learned new techniques of fortification, and Muslims learned new methods of siege warfare and new respect for the uses of heavy cavalry.

The larger impact of the Crusades on western Europe is more difficult to assess. From one standpoint, the establishment of the short-lived crusader states represents the limits of Europe's expansion during this otherwise extraordinary period of growth. Trade with the Islamic world, and beyond it with India and the Far East, brought enormous prosperity to some, but these trading links had existed before the Crusades and continued long after they ended.

Of course, the most long-lasting consequence of the First Crusade has also proved the most deadly in the long run. Both Christian and Islamic doctrines of holy war—which had been developed in earlier centuries—continue to be so destructive in the twenty-first century. Almost immediately, crusading rhetoric would dictate the terms of western Europeans' attitudes toward the wider world and even toward one another, as we shall see in the following chapters. It fostered a new political and religious ethos that would inform the "reconquest" of the Iberian Peninsula by the Christian rulers of Spain and lead to the massacre or forced conversion of Muslims and Jews. Crusading rhetoric underlay English wars against the Welsh and the Scots, and its language justified the massacre and dispossession of "heretics" in southern France by northern French imperialists. It justified the conquest of the Baltic region and, later, the subsequent conquest of the Americas and the colonization of Asia, Africa, and Australia. And it has continued to exacerbate global animosities to this day.

Even Christian theology was transformed by contact with Islam. For one thing, Muslim scholars were the ones who had inherited, preserved, and developed not only Hellenistic medicine and science but the philosophy of Aristotle, which would form the basis of a new Christian philosophy in the twelfth and thirteenth centuries (see Chapter 9). For another, Europeans had been almost entirely ignorant of Muslim beliefs prior to the Crusades, assuming that Muslims were pagans who worshiped a god called Mahomet or Mahoun. But by 1143, a scholar called Robert of Ketton (c. 1100–c. 1160), originally from a small town in England, had completed a Latin translation of the Qur'an, working in Spain with the encouragement of the abbot of Cluny. In the 1130s, he and a friend, Hermann of Carinthia (in Slovenia), had traveled to Byzantium and the crusader kingdoms, where they became students of Arabic. They exemplify the world of possibilities that had been opened up to northwestern Europeans as a result of the processes we have been studying in this chapter.

Muslim Philosophy and Christian Theology

The scholars of Byzantium took a conservative approach to Greek philosophy, in every sense of the word (see Chapter 7).

THE CULTURE OF THE MUSLIM WEST

It would be misleading to assert that all the consequences of the Crusades were negative. The positive outcomes were hugely important, too. Increased intellectual and cultural contact between the Latin West and the Islamic world had an enormous impact on western European learning, literature, music, and art. Perhaps most importantly, the study and practical applications of mathematics were revolutionized when Europeans adopted Arabic numerals and the concept of zero—first promoted beyond the Islamic world, not surprisingly, by the son of a Pisan merchant who grew up in Algeria, Leonardo Fibonacci (c. 1170–c. 1250).

ARISTOTLE TEACHING ARAB ASTRONOMERS. In this Arabic manuscript from the thirteenth century, Aristotle is represented as a contemporary of the astronomers he is instructing. ■ *What does this suggest about Muslims' attitude toward Greek philosophy?*

The dialogues of Plato and some works of Aristotle were copied and studied, but the latter's ideas were so hard to reconcile with Orthodox theology that Emperor Alexius Comnenus eventually banned the teaching of Aristotelian logic altogether. Ironically, then, the cultures that provided the most direct access to Greek learning were Arabic-speaking, and it was through Arabic translations that western European intellectuals became acquainted with these ideas—thanks to the labor of Arabists like Robert and Hermann.

Even before the rise of Islam, a number of Greek philosophical texts had been translated into Syriac, a Semitic language closely related to Arabic. Arabic translations soon followed, many sponsored by the Abbasid court at Baghdad, which established a special school for this purpose known as the House of Wisdom. By the end of the tenth century, Arabic translations of Plato, Aristotle, Plotinus, and other Greek authors were widely available and intensively studied throughout the Muslim world. Even in the remote Persian city of Bukhara, the great Muslim philosopher and physician Avicenna (Ibn Sīnā, 980–1037) was able to read all of Aristotle's works before he reached the age of eighteen.

Like their counterparts in Byzantium, Muslim philosophers strove to reconcile Greek and Hellenistic philosophical traditions with each other and with the tenets of Islamic theology. Reconciling Aristotelianism and Neoplatonism was the easier task. Many of the translations and commentaries of Aristotle from which Muslim philosophers worked had already been filtered through the philosophical traditions of Alexandria and Rome. Moreover, Aristotle and the Neoplatonists shared a number of common assumptions, including the eternity of the world and the capacity of the human mind to understand the rational principles that govern the world's workings. Both traditions also stressed the freedom of individual humans to choose between good and evil.

Combining Greek philosophy with Islamic theology was more difficult. Like Judaism and Christianity, Islam holds that a single omnipotent God created the world as an act of pure will and that the world will continue to exist only so long as God wills it. This runs counter to the classical Greek view of the world as eternal. Moreover, both Christian and Islamic theology rest on the immortality of the individual human soul, another doctrine flatly in conflict with Aristotelian and Neoplatonic thought. There were also conflicts over the concept of free will; and again, Muslims and Christians had more in common with one another on this head than with ancient Greek tradition. Although medieval theologians strongly emphasized the individual responsibility of believers to choose between good and evil, virtually all Muslims—like most Christians—believed that nothing good could occur unless God actively

willed it. Islamic philosophers adopted an array of different intellectual tactics to deal with these challenges and, in doing so, laid the groundwork for the Christian theologians who relied on them (see Chapter 9).

Muslim Science, Medicine, and Mathematics

Many Muslim philosophers were also distinguished physicians and scientists. The study of philosophy could bring a man renown (or censure) but few tangible rewards, whereas successful physicians and astrologers might rise to positions of wealth and power. Both astrology and medicine were applied sciences that relied on careful, accurate observation of natural phenomena. Muslim observations of the heavens were so accurate, indeed, that some astronomers corroborated the findings of Hellenistic scientists (see Chapter 4) that the earth must rotate on its axis and revolve around the sun. But

IVORY PYXIS FROM AL-ANDALUS. Fashioned in the tenth century, this little round box is made from a segment of elephant tusk and would have had a matching lid (now lost). Such boxes usually held spices or incense. Its decorative motifs are echoed in Islamic architecture on a larger scale, reminding us that medieval Islam did not prohibit the representation of natural and fanciful figures, as is often supposed.

because these theories conflicted with the (mistaken) assumptions of Aristotle—that the earth remained stationary with the sun and planets revolving around it—they were not generally accepted in the Islamic world or in Europe. Yet they may have influenced Nicolaus Copernicus (1473–1543), who is usually credited as the first to suggest that the earth orbited the sun (see Chapter 16).

Muslim accomplishments in medicine were equally remarkable. Avicenna discovered the contagious nature of tuberculosis, described pleurisy and several varieties of nervous ailments, and noted that diseases could spread through contaminated water and soil. His *Canon of Medicine* would remain an authoritative textbook in the Islamic world and in western Europe until the seventeenth century. Later Islamic physicians would learn the value of cauterization and of styptic agents, diagnose cancer of the stomach, prescribe antidotes in cases of poisoning, and make notable progress in treating eye diseases. They recognized the infectious character of bubonic plague, pointing out that it could be transmitted by clothing.

Muslim physicians were also pioneers in organizing hospitals and licensing medical practitioners. At least thirty-four great hospitals were located in the principal cities of Persia, Syria, and Egypt, each with separate wards for particular illnesses, a dispensary for giving out medicine, and a library. Chief physicians and surgeons lectured to students and graduates, examined them, and issued licenses to practice medicine. Even the owners of leeches (used for bloodletting, a standard medical practice of the day) had to submit their medicinal worms for inspection at regular intervals.

Islamic scientists made important advances in optics and chemistry, as well as mathematics. Using Arabic numerals—which Muslim scholars actually adopted from the Hindus—mathematicians developed a decimal arithmetic based on place values and hinged on the concept of the zero. Their work enabled fundamental advances in entirely new areas, both of which bear Arabic names: algebra and algorithms. Building on Greek geometry and their own astronomical observations, they also made great progress in spherical trigonometry.

Muslim mathematicians thus brought together and pushed forward all the areas of mathematical knowledge that would later be adopted and developed in western Europe from the sixteenth century on. And they made an indispensible contribution to the burgeoning European economy, since the sophisticated accounting systems that supported commerce would have been impossible if merchants and bankers had continued to use the clumsy numbers adopted by the Romans. (Try balancing your checking account in Roman numerals!) Thanks to Arabic mathematics, western Europeans could now add, subtract, divide, and multiply quickly and accurately, with or without the help of another Muslim invention, the abacus.

Muslim Literature and Art

Poetry was integral to Muslim culture. It had been a highly developed art form long before the emergence of Islam, and then it became even more important to the development and dissemination of Muslim identity because it was the form in which Muhammad framed the Qur'an (see Chapter 7).

Like medicine and astronomy, poetry was also a route to advancement. Not all poetry was composed in Arabic; particularly around the Abbasid court, poets writing in Persian enjoyed great renown. The best known of these is Umar Khayyam (d. 1123), whose *Rubaiyat* was turned into a popular English verse cycle by the Victorian poet Edward Fitzgerald (1809–1883). Although Fitzgerald's translation

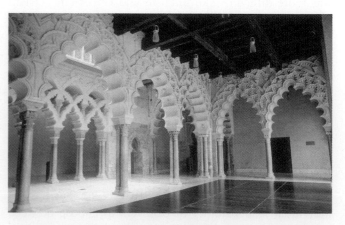

MUSLIM ARCHITECTURE AND GARDEN DESIGN Both images display how Muslim architects and designers borrowed features from many cultures but combined them in distinctively graceful ways.

Analyzing Primary Sources

A Hebrew Poem from Muslim Spain

In the courts of tenth- and eleventh-century Muslim Spain, Jewish poets began to write a new style of Hebrew verse closely modeled on contemporary Arabic examples. Samuel the Nagid was perhaps the most remarkable of this group of poets. He became the military leader of the Muslim kingdom of Granada as well as the head of the Jewish community there. In addition to his three volumes of poetry, he also wrote treatises on Hebrew grammar and religious law.

 our debt to God is righteously to live,

And His to you, your recompense to give.

Do not wear out your days in serving God;

Some time devote to Him, some to yourself.

To Him give half your day, to work the rest;

But give the jug no rest throughout the night.

Put out your lamps! Use crystal cups for light.

Away with singers! Bottles are better than lutes.

No song, nor wine, nor friend beneath the sward—

These three, O fools, are all of life's reward.

Source: Raymond P. Scheindlin, ed. and trans., *Wine, Women, and Death: Medieval Hebrew Poems on the Good Life* (Philadelphia, PA: 1986), p. 47.

Questions for Analysis

1. What values does this poem express? What is its perspective on the relationship among devotion to God, duty, and pleasure?

2. What does the career of Samuel the Nagid—poet, general, scholar—suggest about Jewish identity in this place and time? What does it suggest about the relations between Jewish and Muslim communities in medieval Spain?

---

distorts much, the lush sensuality of Umar's poetic imagery ("a jug of wine, a loaf of bread—and thou") faithfully reflects themes that were common to much Muslim poetry. Much of this poetry was addressed by men to other men, a fact that occasioned no concern within the elite circles in which it was composed and performed. Jews also participated in this elite literary world, especially in Al-Andalus, where they wrote similarly sensuous, playful lyrics in both Hebrew and Arabic, praising wine, sexual intimacy, and their own songs. Muslim Spain also saw a great flowering of Jewish intellectual life, which paralleled and intersected with that of the Muslim society around them.

Perhaps the most distinctive of Islamic arts are architectural and decorative, the arts that created the spaces in which poets and scientists interacted with their patrons. Many characteristic elements of Muslim architecture (the dome, the column, and the arch) were adapted from Byzantine models, but were then combined with the intricate tracery and ambitious scale of Persian buildings to form a new architectural vocabulary. Building styles were further inflected by the many different cultures that embraced Islam, from Spain to Egypt to

India and beyond. Muslim artistry was also expressed in the magnificent gardens and fountains that adorned palaces and in the more portable magnificence of gorgeous carpets, tooled leather, brocaded silks and tapestries, inlaid metalwork, enameled glassware, and painted pottery—all decorated with Arabic script, interlacing geometric designs, plants, fruits, flowers, and fantastic animal figures (another Persian influence). These complex designs can often seem strikingly modern, precisely because they anticipate the abstract forms that were considered new in the twentieth century. Indeed, they were the product of a culture that increasingly frowned upon the realistic depiction of natural forms.

The Islamic Influence on Western Europe

Prior to the contacts facilitated by the Crusades, the cultural, economic, intellectual, and political achievements of Islamic civilization had completely overshadowed those of Latin Christian Europe. Even thereafter, the new Europe that emerged in the twelfth century would rely heavily on what it had learned from the Islamic world. This is reflected in the large number of Arabic and Persian words that passed into European languages. Essential words for commerce and trade include *traffic, tariff, alcohol, muslin, orange, lemon, alfalfa, saffron, sugar, syrup,* and *musk,* to name just a few. The word *admiral* also comes from Arabic (from the title *emir*), as do words that tell the story of Europe's reliance on Muslim science and technology: *alchemy, algebra, algorithm, alkali, almanac, amalgam, cipher, soda, magazine,* and *zero*—not to mention the names of stars, such as Aldebaran and Betelgeuse.

The Muslim world also had an enormous influence on the imagination and the self-perception of Christian Europe. Byzantine civilization was at once too closely linked to Latin Christendom and, from the eleventh century on, too weak to compel western Europeans to take much account of it. Western Christians tended to look down on the Byzantine Greeks, but they respected and feared Muslims. And they were right to do so, for Islamic civilization at its zenith (to use another Arabic word) was one of the world's greatest. It brought Arabs, Persians, Turks, Egyptians, Africans, Indians, and Asians together in a common cultural and religious system, creating a diverse society and a splendid legacy of original discoveries and accomplishments that continue to shape the world today. The expanding Europe of the Middle Ages reaped the benefits of its interactions with this rich culture.

CONCLUSION

Before the year 1000, western Europe was the least powerful, least prosperous, and least sophisticated of the three civilizations that had emerged out of the Roman world. A hundred

After You Read This Chapter

 Visit StudySpace for quizzes, additional review materials, and multimedia documents.
wwnorton.com/web/westernciv18

REVIEWING THE OBJECTIVES

- The fragmentation of power in the ninth and tenth centuries created a world very different from that of Charlemagne. Describe some of the key changes. What were their causes?
- The agricultural revolution of the Middle Ages had far-reaching economic, social, and political consequences. What were they?
- The reforming movement with the Church changed the relationship between the papacy and the secular rulers of Christendom. Explain why.
- The motives behind the Crusades were political as well as religious. Why was this the case?
- The Crusades had profound effects on western Europe, Byzantium, and Islam, as well as on the relationships among different groups within these societies. In what ways were these three civilizations transformed?

years later, it was a force to be reckoned with. This metamorphosis rested on economic foundations: increasingly efficient agriculture, a growing population, and expanding trade. These changes produced a dynamic, expansionist, self-confident, and mobile society in which individuals cast off old roles and took on new ones with bewildering speed. No less important, however, were the political and military changes that began to alter the map of Europe in these centuries. By 1100, the heavily armored, mounted knight had emerged as the most formidable military weapon of the day, and new conceptions of power—both spiritual and temporal—were being articulated and contested within Europe, and on crusade.

But it was not yet possible either for Europe's rulers to control the energies of the workers, town-dwellers, merchants, knights, and scholars whose endeavors were transforming their world. A new approach to political organization was needed. Up to this point, the civilizations of the West had rested on two basic types of government: city-states and empires. City-states were more capable of mobilizing the loyalty of their citizens; as a result, they could sometimes win extraordinary victories against more-powerful imperial rivals, as the Greeks did against the Persians. But city-states were frequently divided by internal economic and social rivalries; and in the long run, they were not strong enough to defend themselves against foreign conquerors. Empires, by contrast, could win battles and maintain powerful administrative bureaucracies, but they were generally too far-flung to inspire deep loyalties among their subjects.

Where, then, do the emerging kingdoms of medieval Europe fit into this picture? How would the struggle for the control of western Europe's expanding resources be carried forward in the wake of the Crusades? And what cultural, spiritual, social, and intellectual innovations would result? These are the questions we address in Chapter 9.

PEOPLE, IDEAS, AND EVENTS IN CONTEXT

- How was Europe affected by **VIKING** raids and settlements? Which territorial rulers imitated **CAROLINGIAN** models in the wake of these initiatives?
- What new technologies drove the **AGRICULTURAL REVOLUTION** of the Middle Ages? Why did the organization of labor on **MANORS** sometimes lead to **SERFDOM**?
- What conditions led to the growth of medieval **TOWNS** and why did the formation of urban **COMMUNES** foster new types of liberty? How were money and credit essential to medieval commerce?
- Why is **FEUDALISM** a problematic concept? How did the ceremony of **HOMAGE** symbolize the relationship between a **VASSAL** and his lord?
- What were the causes of the **INVESTITURE CONFLICT**?
- Why did **ALEXIUS COMNENUS** ask **POPE URBAN II** for assistance? Why did the pope use this as a pretext for urging the **FIRST CRUSADE**?
- How and why did **MUSLIM LEARNING AND CULTURE** exercise a profound influence on western Europeans?

THINKING ABOUT CONNECTIONS

- In what ways does the Investiture Conflict reflect the unique historical circumstances of the late eleventh century, and in what ways can it be viewed as an extension of longer-term phenomena?
- Based on what we have learned about the relationship between political power and religious power in previous chapters, would you say that the clash between the papacy and the Holy Roman Empire was inevitable?
- Given the many negative aspects of the crusading movement—and its eventual failure—how might you explain the continuing appeal of crusading rhetoric down to the present day?

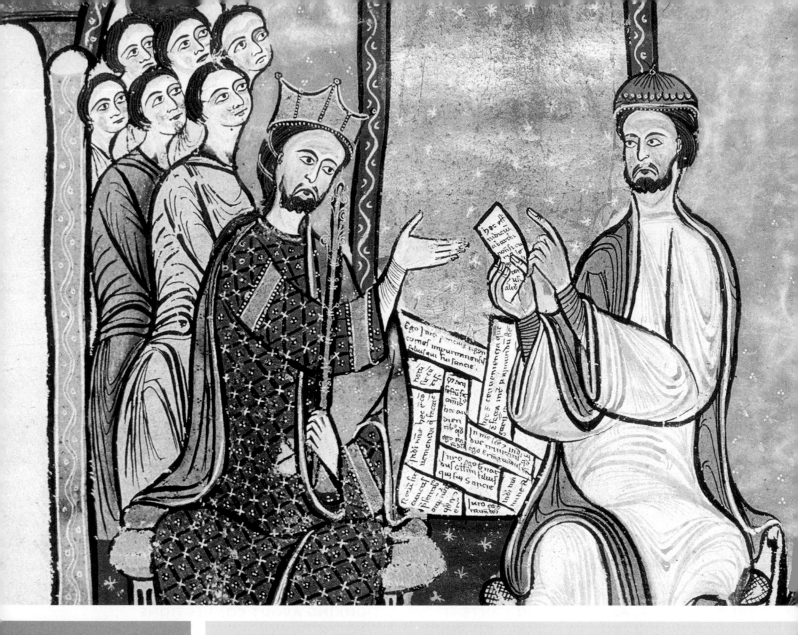

STORY LINES

- The power of Europe's new monarchies and of the papacy depended on new methods of oversight, administration, and documentation.

- Schools and universities were therefore crucial to the development of these institutions, and they also provided ambitious men with unprecedented intellectual, social, and political opportunities.

- Continued crusading movements in the twelfth and thirteenth centuries intensified contacts between Latin Christendom and the Muslim world while posing a threat to many minority groups within Europe, and to the Byzantine Empire.

- The Church's presence in the daily lives of the laity produced vibrant forms of spirituality yet placed strict limitations on women, religious dissidents, and non-Christians.

- Meanwhile, Europe's princely courts, wealthy towns, universities, and cathedrals fostered new forms of entertainment, art, and architecture.

Before
You
Read
This
Chapter

CHRONOLOGY

1079–1142	Lifetime of Peter Abelard
c. 1090–c. 1164	Lifetime of Heloise
1098–1179	Lifetime of Hildegard of Bingen
1099	First Crusade ends
1122–1204	Lifetime of Eleanor of Aquitaine
c. 1140	Gratian's *Concordance of Discordant Canons*
1152–1190	Reign of Frederick II Barbarossa
1180–1223	Reign of Philip II Augustus
1187	Muslim reconquest of Jerusalem
1192–1194	Alfonso II of Aragon compiles the *Liber feudorum maior*
1194–1250	Lifetime of Frederick II the Great
1198–1216	Reign of Pope Innocent III
1204	Capture and sack of Constantinople
1209	Franciscan order established Beginning of the Albigensian Crusade
1215	Magna Carta and the canons of the Fourth Lateran Council are both formulated
1216	Dominican order established

The Consolidation of Europe, 1100–1250

9

CORE OBJECTIVES

- **IDENTIFY** the differences among Europe's emerging monarchies.

- **DESCRIBE** the ongoing effects of crusading.

- **UNDERSTAND** the connections between new religious movements and the power of the papacy.

- **DEFINE** scholasticism and trace its development.

- **EXPLAIN** the changing meaning of *chivalry*.

A t the turn of the twelfth century, the eldest son of a nobleman did something unusual: he traded lordship for scholarship. His name was Peter Abelard. In his own estimation, he was the smartest man in the world, and the most attractive. He was certainly one of the most ambitious. After leaving his father's lands in Brittany and besting all the established teachers in Paris, he was appointed to the position of master in the cathedral school, one of the highest academic posts then available. There he met Heloise, the niece of a priest called Fulbert.

Heloise had received an excellent education in a nearby convent, but the normal path of intellectual advancement—Abelard's school—was closed to her. So Fulbert arranged for her to become Abelard's private pupil. She soon became more than that: his intellectual partner, his lover, and his wife. This last step was particularly problematic, because marriage was no longer an option for clerics and would therefore ruin Abelard's chances of a brilliant career in the Church. So it remained a secret, as did Heloise's subsequent pregnancy and the birth of their son. But her uncle eventually found out and took revenge on Abelard, sending some local thugs to castrate him.

Heloise and Abelard lived out the remainder of their lives in isolation from one another, and most of what we know about their relationship comes from letters they exchanged years later, when Heloise was the leader of a new religious community and Abelard was laying the intellectual foundations of the first university.

The developments of the twelfth and thirteenth centuries altered Europe in profound and lasting ways, affecting individuals, communities, and entire regions. This period witnessed the emergence of large-scale territorial monarchies and the papacy as dominant forces, while cathedral schools and universities turned out larger and larger cohorts of the professional men needed to run the bureaucracies that supported secular and religious authority. New opportunities for social advancement and new spiritual practices transformed daily life, many of these the direct and indirect consequences of the Crusades. Also as a result of the Crusades, both ancient

ABELARD AND HELOISE. This image from a thirteenth century manuscript shows Abelard in a scholar's gown and cap and Heloise wearing a nun's habit; their gestures indicate that they are engaged in heated debate. The story of their fervent attraction and doomed marriage was already famous during their lifetimes, and by the time this manuscript was copied, theirs had become the ultimate example of star-crossed love.

texts and novel ideas generated the intellectual revolution in which Abelard and Heloise participated. Artistic and technological influences were galvanizing forces, too, financed by prelates and kings, princely courts and wealthy towns engaged in an integrated and far-reaching economy. Moreover, new literary forms took shape as the spoken vernaculars of Europe came to challenge Latin, becoming languages of learning, devotion, and entertainment. By the middle of the thirteenth century, the political institutions and cultural identities that still define Europe had been formed.

THE MAKING OF MEDIEVAL MONARCHIES

As we learned in Chapter 8, traditional forms of power were challenged by significant trends in the tenth and eleventh centuries. Independent towns and lords often refused to acknowledge royal authority, and kings could no longer rely on close-knit kin groups or the broad imperial powers wielded by a ruler like Charlemagne. How, then, did some European rulers build the foundations of states that continue to exist today? For crucially, the *idea* of a national state—a state that consolidates its people's sense of a shared identity and destiny—was an idea forged in the twelfth and thirteenth centuries. It would endure to become the basis on which the political system of the modern world is still constructed.

But not all attempts at state transformation were equally successful. For example, the France that emerged in the twelfth century would almost collapse 200 years later (see Chapter 10). Other monarchies would not be consolidated until the nineteenth century (Germany is the best example) and, even then, *political* unification could not hide the continued fact of cultural and linguistic disintegration (as evident in Italy, Belgium, and Switzerland to this day). Yet it became so vital for modern European states to trace their origins to the medieval past that those states without a medieval pedigree would eventually be obliged to invent one.

England: From Conquest to Consolidation

The conquest of England in 1066 allowed the first Norman king, William, to experiment with a new type of kingship. In theory, he commanded the allegiance of every person dwelling in his kingdom, over and above the allegiance owed to kin, a local lord, or even the Church. In practice, however, William needed to impose his will on his new subjects, and this often took the form of violence. It was also expressed through the highly effective administrative structures of his Anglo-Saxon predecessors, which he adapted to his own needs.

This process was carried forward by his son Henry I (r. 1100–35), whose approach to kingship was unusual in its focus on effective governance rather than warfare. Henry strengthened the Anglo-Norman system of local administration and instituted a system of traveling judges to administer royal justice in the countryside. His biggest innovation was the introduction of a method of financial accounting carried out by an office known as the Exchequer, so called because clerks moved counters around on a checkered cloth to calculate receipts and expenditures.

Henry's hands-on approach to royal lordship was both new and unpopular. Then, as now, those opposed to "big government" could react violently against it, and after Henry's death those reactions provoked a civil war that lasted throughout the reign of his cousin and successor, Stephen (r. 1135–54)—until the people of England began to long for a king who would bring back the good old days of centralized rule.

The Reign of Henry II

They found such a king in Henry's grandson Henry of Anjou (b. 1133, r. 1154–89), who at the age of twenty-one was already the duke of Normandy and the lord of two other independent French counties, Anjou and Maine. He also controlled the Aquitaine, thanks to his recent alliance with its powerful and brilliant ruler, Eleanor (1122–1204), who had annulled her first marriage to the French king Louis VII in order to marry Henry. As a result, England found itself integrated into the political and cultural world of the Continent in unprecedented ways.

Henry II restored his grandfather's administration and began, steadily, to extend its reach. He ordered juries (from the Latin *jus*, meaning both "law" and "oath") of reliable local men to report every major crime that occurred in their districts, and also empowered them to investigate civil cases. These innovations stand at the origin of our modern legal system. Henry II also made it easier for common people to seek justice in the royal courts. All of these measures brought an unprecedented number of average people into the exercise of government and thus increased their sense of loyalty to the king and their personal investment in his rulership.

But these innovations also brought Henry into conflict with the Church, because the extension of royal justice impinged on that of ecclesiastical courts: tribunals overseen by bishops that claimed the exclusive right to try and sentence clergy accused of committing crimes—even capital crimes like murder. Henry, by contrast, declared that clerics convicted of serious crimes in church courts should lose their clerical status and be handed over to the royal court for sentencing. The principle underlying this was one that aimed to promote a sense of shared identity and accountability: clients should be English subjects before they were servants of the Roman Church.

Opposition to this policy came from an unexpected quarter: Thomas Becket, a longtime friend and supporter of Henry's, who was now the archbishop of Canterbury. Thomas was a self-made man, the son of immigrants who had benefited from the social mobility of town life (he grew up in London) to obtain an education and thereby rise through the ranks of the Church. He saw the advantages to be gained from maintaining the independence of ecclesiastical procedures, and feared that Henry's goal was to undermine the power of the clergy.

THE MURDER OF THOMAS BECKET. In this illumination from a thirteenth-century prayer book, one of the knights has struck the archbishop so violently that he has broken his sword. ▪ *How might a contemporary viewer have interpreted this symbolism?*

Map legend:

- Angevin Empire under Henry II, c. 1180
- French Royal domain, 1180
- Disputed frontier, 1180
- Holy Roman Empire, 1180

**Main map labels:**

Edinburgh

SCOTLAND

NORTH SEA

Carlisle

Durham

IRELAND

Stamford Bridge

Dublin

York

WALES

ENGLAND

Hereford

Ely

Gloucester

Cambridge

Oxford

London

Runnymede

Canterbury

Southampton · Winchester

Calais

Bruges · Antwerp

Ypres · Lille · Brussels

FLANDERS

English Channel

Arras

HOLY

Amiens

Bayeux · Rouen

VERMANDOIS

Caen · Beauvais

Rheims · Verdun

ROMAN

Mont-St.-Michel · NORMANDY

St. Denis

LORRAINE

ATLANTIC OCEAN

BRITTANY

MAINE

Chartres

Paris

CHAMPAGNE

Brétigny

ILE DE FRANCE

Troyes

EMPIRE

ANJOU

BURGUNDY

Nantes

TOURAINE

Poitiers

Bourges

Dijon

POITOU

Autun

Bay of Biscay

AQUITAINE

Geneva

Lyon

Bordeaux · Angoulême

Perigueux

PROVENCE

GASCONY

Albi

Avignon

TOULOUSE · Montpellier

NAVARRE

Aigues-Mortes

Marseilles

LANGUEDOC · Narbonne

MEDITERRANEAN SEA

CORSICA

ARAGON

CATALUNYA

Inset map (top right):

France at the Death of Philip Augustus 1223

ENGLAND

ATLANTIC OCEAN

- Royal domain
- Under English rule

Paris

FRANCE

Compostela

Bay of Biscay

AQUITAINE

LÉON

Inset map (bottom left):

EUROPE

Area of detail

AFRICA

HENRY II'S ANGEVIN EMPIRE AND THE KINGDOM OF FRANCE, 1180–1223. ▪ *What areas did Henry II's empire control in 1180?* ▪ *What advantages would the king of France have when challenging English control over continental territories—even though his own power was confined to the "island" (Ile) of France around Paris?*

Henry responded by exiling Thomas from England for several years. When Thomas returned in 1170, he was assassinated in his own cathedral by four of Henry's knights. Thomas was quickly proclaimed a martyr and a saint, and his tomb at Canterbury became one of the most important pilgrimage sites of the Middle Ages. Henry, for his part, was compelled to appear as a barefoot pentitent at this tomb and ask the saint's forgiveness for his sins.

In the long run, Henry II did not win the right to sentence clerics in royal courts, but he did retain the right to nominate clerics to high office and thereby to exercise a large measure of control over those courts' personnel. The most concrete proof of Henry II's success is that his government continued to work efficiently even after his death, to the extent that his crusading son Richard "the Lionheart" (r. 1189–99) could rule his father's empire for ten years *in absentia*, spending only about six months in England during all that time.

The Meaning of Magna Carta

When Richard was killed by a crossbow bolt while besieging a castle, he was succeeded by his brother John (r. 1199–1216), an efficient administrator but a far less enthusiastic warrior. By 1204, military and legal losses forced John to cede nearly all of his father's Continental possessions to the powerful young king of France, Philip II; only the Aquitaine, the inheritance of his mother Eleanor, remained. This was politically disastrous for John. Not only did it deplete his resources, it angered the most powerful lords of England, nearly all of whom were of Norman descent and who thus lost their ancestral lands when John lost Normandy. John's response was to attempt a recovery of lost territories by raising taxes to equip an army, thereby angering the nobility further. In 1215, they forced John to set his seal to Magna Carta, a "great charter" that defined the barons' rights while limiting those of the king.

Magna Carta established some important general principles that would continue to shape the laws of England and, eventually, her North American and Australian colonies. It stipulated that the king could levy no taxes without the consent of the kingdom at large, that no free man could be punished until he had been judged guilty by a jury of his peers in accordance with the law, that no one could be arrested and imprisoned without a warrant, and that no unqualified or ignorant person should hold public office. The charter also provided for the establishment of a representative body of barons: Parliament (a word derived from the French "talking together"). Above all, Magna Carta expressed the extraordinary idea that a king is bound by the law.

We have frequently noted the achievements of the various powerful lawgivers whose contributions have been essential to Western civilizations, starting with Hammurabi (see Chapter 1). But for the most part, those lawgivers held themselves to be above the law. Although medieval monarchs—in England and elsewhere—attempted to behave as though this were true for them as well, they would ultimately be forced to concede the rule of law itself.

Magna Carta thus contributed to the slow process that transformed the inhabitants of England into people with a common national identity and shared values. It also normalized the idea that strong, centralized government was a good thing: when the barons of England revolted again in the reign of John's son, Henry III (r. 1216–72), they did so because Henry's rule was not effective enough.

In time, Parliament became a legislative body that could help run the kingdom and authorize new expenditures. Since Magna Carta had demanded that no taxation be imposed without the common consent of the realm, kings had to convene Parliament to explain why such taxation was necessary and to secure such consent. Meetings of Parliament were also used to take advice about pressing concerns, to hear judicial cases, to review local administration, to hear complaints from the countryside, and to promulgate new laws. Gradually, England was changing from a conquered territory within a larger Norman empire into a constitutional monarchy grounded in representative government and ruled by law.

The Emergence of France

Compared to the Anglo-Saxon and Anglo-Norman kings of England, the king of the Franks presided over a miniscule kingdom over which he exercised little control. After the dissolution of Carolingian royal authority, the kings who succeeded Hugh Capet (987–96) had trouble making good on any claim to lordship beyond the immediate hinterland of Paris. Most of Charlemagne's institutions of governance had collapsed and been further weakened by Viking raids or by ongoing pressure from the Viking state of Normandy. When the Angevin Empire of Henry II was at its height, therefore, the kingdom of Louis VII (r. 1137–80)—who had lost both his wife Eleanor and her lands to that same Henry—was tiny and insignificant.

But in many ways the Capetian dynasty was fortunate. Against all biological odds, they managed to produce an unbroken line of able male heirs for over 300 years (from 987 to 1328), without interruption—men who were also long lived. On average, each Capetian king ruled for 30 years, which contributed greatly to political stability. And this kingdom, though small, was a rich center of agriculture and trade, which provided a steadily increasing source of income. The prestige of the Capetians was also enhanced by their patronage of the new University of Paris founded by Abelard, which made the royal capital the intellectual capital of Europe (see below). Beyond all this, the Capetians proved to be shrewd politicians, carefully husbanding their strengths while more powerful enemies overreached themselves.

The epitome of these strengths was Philip II (r. 1180–1223), a man who styled himself "Augustus" and who was the first to use the title "king of France": king of a sovereign state (rather than "king of the Franks," a loose agglomeration of people). Philip came to the throne at the age of eighteen, having witnessed the struggles of his father Louis VII against the superior strength of Henry II. He understood that he could not win a direct confrontation with either Henry or his son Richard. John, however—known to his detractors as "Soft Sword"—was another matter. Philip declared that John owed him homage and allegiance in return for Normandy and its adjacent territories, and then took advantage of his position as John's overlord to undermine John's control over these lands. When John objected, Philip declared all John's lands to be forfeit to the French crown and backed this declaration with armies that won decisive victories in 1204 and 1214.

With Normandy and the other Angevin territories of northern France added to his domain, Philip now had the resources to build an effective system of local administration. He wisely chose to maintain the bureaucratic structures put in place there by generations of Anglo-Norman rule, but he also appointed royal overseers, known as bailiffs, who had full judicial, administrative, and military authority. Philip drew these men from among the needy knights and lesser nobility of his own domain and rotated them frequently from region to region. This ensured their loyalty to Philip and also prevented them from developing personal ties to the regions they governed.

Philip's administrative pattern, which recognized regional diversity while promoting centralized royal control, would continue to characterize French government down to the time of the French Revolution (see Chapter 18). Philip's son, Louis VIII (r. 1223–26), would extend this strategy to newly conquered territories in the southeast. His son, Louis IX (r. 1226–70), would deepen and legitimize it by his devotion to justice at home and crusading abroad. Even in his lifetime, Louis IX would be celebrated as the paragon of good kingship, and soon after his death he would be canonized as Saint Louis. His successors would draw on that legacy for centuries to come. (See Chapter 10.)

But the French Parlement (later known as the Estates General) never played the crucial role in French government that Parliament did in England. There are many reasons for this, but the most fundamental was the French nobility's successful claim to exemption from taxation, something that would remain a political problem until the French Revolution. Other significant points of comparison between England and France continue to mark the intertwined history of these two states. England, a far smaller country, was much more tightly unified at a much earlier date. English nobles could and did rebel against their kings, but could rarely draw sustained support from regional resentments. In France, however, regional separatism remained (and still remains) a significant force, to the extent that ambitious insurgents have long capitalized on regional animosity toward the French government when making bids for power.

England and France were also governed in different ways. English kings could rely on local men to do much of the work of local government without pay. This made English administration inexpensive, and it also meant that royal policies had to be popular in order to be implemented. French kings, by contrast, ruled through salaried officers who had little connection to local communities. They had less need to summon representative assemblies and, as a result, lacked effective mechanisms for mobilizing public support. In the eigtheenth century, these features would be the undoing of the French monarchy.

German Kingship and the Holy Roman Empire

We have seen (in Chapter 8) that the struggles between the German emperor Henry IV and the papacy ultimately led to the weakening of imperial authority. But in the middle of the twelfth century, a newly elected emperor made an ambitious attempt to restore the power of the German monarchy and to free it from papal control. This was Frederick, later known as Barbarossa ("Red Beard," r. 1152–90), who coined the term "Holy Roman Empire" to describe his realm—thereby asserting that its holiness derived from the blessing of God and did not necessarily depend on the intervention of the pope.

Frederick forged a close alliance with other German princes by supporting their efforts to control their own territories. In exchange, he exacted their support of his efforts to reassert imperial control over the wealthy cities of northern Italy. This strategy worked, but it sparked a series of destructive wars. Led by Milan and sanctioned by the pope, the cities of northern Italy formed an alliance, the Lombard League, which put up a staunch resistance to Frederick's rule and finally forced him to guarantee their political independence in return for large cash payments. Meanwhile, Frederick attempted to bypass the power of the papacy by supporting a series of papal pretenders, or "antipopes." This move was successfully countered by the reigning pope, Alexander III (r. 1159–81), who drove a shrewd bargain with Frederick:

THE HOLY ROMAN EMPIRE AND ITS NEIGHBORS, c. 1200. ▪ *How would the borders of the Holy Roman Empire have been defined during the Middle Ages?* ▪ *Why were the German states not able to unify during this period?* ▪ *Why would the prospect of a single heir to the Holy Roman Empire and to the kingdom of the Two Sicilies have been a threat to the papacy?*

if Frederick would concede the sovereignty of the pope's rule within Rome and its adjacent territories—lands that came to be known as the Papal States—then Alexander would concede the emperor's sovereignty within his domains and even his overlordship of the Church within those domains. Frederick eventually agreed, thereby gaining the pope's support for his rule in northern Italy.

When Frederick left for the Holy Land in 1189—joining Richard the Lionheart of England and Philip Augustus of France on a (failed) crusade to reconquer Jerusalem—he left his realm in a powerful position. Although he died on that venture, his careful planning bore fruit in the reign of his son, Henry VI, who succeeded to his father's throne without opposition and enjoyed a huge income from the north Italian towns; he ultimately became the king of Sicily, too. This strengthened the empire's position even further, for now the Papal States were surrounded by the lands of a single powerful ruler. However, Henry VI died in 1197 at the age of thirty-two, leaving only a three-year-old son, the future Frederick II, as his heir apparent.

ON THE ART OF HUNTING WITH BIRDS. This beautifully illuminated manuscript of Frederick II's famous treatise on falconry was commissioned by his son, Manfred, shortly after his father's death in 1250. It is now in the Vatican Library, Rome.

Frederick II, often called "the Great," is one of the most fascinating of all medieval rulers. Having grown up in Sicily, at the heart of the multicultural Mediterranean, he spoke Arabic and Italian as well as Latin, German, and French. He was both a patron of learning and a scholar in his own right, the author of an important treatise on falconry that is still considered a model of scientific investigation. He maintained a menagerie of exotic animals, a troop of Muslim archers, and a harem of veiled and secluded women, all of whom traveled with him on his journeys. But despite this appearance of exoticism, he was devoted to pursuing his grandfather's policies, supporting the territorial princes in Germany while enforcing imperial rights in Italy.

Much had changed, however, as a result of the two decades' civil war that followed his own father's death. In Germany, the princes had become so entirely autonomous that there was little Frederick could do except to recognize their privileges in exchange for their loyalty. In Italy, the cities of the Lombard League had ceased to pay their taxes and were striving for independence; meanwhile, the powerful administrative structure of Sicily had fallen into chaos.

Frederick tackled all these problems and eventually restored control over the disparate territories of his empire. In 1237, though, he made the mistake of asserting a right to rule the northern Italian cities directly, bypassing their own independent governments. The result was another Lombard League and another lengthy war, which continued until Frederick's death in 1250. The papacy took every advantage of this situation, even excommunicating Frederick and, after his death, denying the rights of his heirs. When Frederick's last legitimate son died in 1254, the prospect of effective imperial rule died with him. For the next 500 years, until the founding of the modern German and Italian states, political power in the lands of the Holy Roman Empire would be divided among several hundred territorial princes.

The "Reconquest" of Spain

Although the Christian kingdoms clustered to the north and east of the Iberian Peninsula were even more distinct from one another than were the principalities of Germany, a unified kingdom of Spain would emerge as the most powerful monarchy in Europe and the wider Atlantic world by the end of the Middle Ages (a process we will continue to trace in future chapters). The key to this extraordinary development lay in the successful alliances forged among the peninsula's Christian rulers and their eventual defeat of neighboring Muslim kingdoms. This process is somewhat misleadingly termed "the Reconquista," the "reconquest" of Christian lands. In reality, the Roman province of Hispania had been only nominally Christian when the Visigoths settled there in the fifth century (see Chapter 6), and the Visigoths themselves had barely converted to Latin Christianity before the Muslims arrived in 711 (see Chapter 7). But conceptualizing this struggle as a holy war to "reconquer" Christian territory allowed Christian propagandists to cast it as another Crusade and, on those grounds, to earn support for their efforts.

By the middle of the twelfth century, there were four major Christian kingdoms in Iberia. In the far north and west were the states of Navarre, which straddled the Pyrenees, and León-Castile, governed as a united kingdom after 1037. Beyond these kingdoms' southern frontier lay a broad swathe of Muslim territory. Farther to the east was the Crown of Aragon, formed in 1137 when the count of Barcelona, who ruled the independent principality of Catalonia, married the queen of Aragon. Farthest west was the new kingdom of Portugal, which had been the first territory gained by Christian conquests in the ninth century and which won independence from León-Castile in 1139.

Like their counterparts elsewhere in Europe, the kings of Spain struggled to control the power of great lords. Centuries of warfare between Muslims and Christians and among competing Christian clans had left the landscape sown with enormous castles, and even those that were nominally

THE "RECONQUEST" OF SPAIN, 900–1250. ■ *Where were the frontiers of the Christian kingdoms in 900? 1150? 1250?* ■ *What geographical factors might have helped to sustain these small kingdoms?* ■ *Why might Castile have become the largest of the Christian kingdoms over time?* ■ *How could Aragon and Catalonia have maintained important positions as wealthy and significant powers?*

LOARRE CASTLE, ARAGON. No single photograph can capture the size or setting of this massive castle complex in the foothills of the Pyrenees. Initially fortified in the eleventh century as a base for Christian expansion into Muslim territory, it was further enlarged in the twelfth century. The encircling wall and towers were added in the thirteenth and fourteenth centuries.

keep either kingdom from achieving supremacy for the next 200 years, until the marriage of Ferdinand of Aragon and Isabella of Castile joined the two in a unified Spanish monarchy which also included Navarre. In 1492, their united army captured Granada while an Italian adventurer named Christopher Columbus set sail under their flag. The first event completed the "reconquest," while the second began Spain's successful conquest of a new and hitherto undreamed-of world (see Chapter 12).

Papal Dominion and Canon Law

Like their secular counterparts, the popes of this era were attempting to establish greater authority by building up bureaucratic structures that increased the visibility of papal power. Specially commissioned papal legates ("legal representatives") began to be sent out from Rome to convey and enforce papal commands, many of which arose from the hundreds (and eventually thousands) of legal cases that poured into Rome as the pope sought to establish a reputation for justice. This extension of the papacy's jurisdiction required the development of a systematic body of law by which such cases could be judged. A crucial step in this development was the codification of papal decrees and decisions of Church councils reaching back to the second century: a thousand years. These formed a body of legal precedents known as canons, from the Greek word meaning "rules" or "supports." The problem, though, was that these precedents often contradicted one another, and so any usable compilation had to determine which was most authoritative.

controlled by kings were in fact the property of castellans who used them as power bases. A ruler seeking to establish sovereignty thus had to use a combination of force and cunning to bring these rival powers to heel. Indeed, the kings of this region came to deploy a combination of tactics that we have already seen at work in England: a mixture of violent conquest and the development of effective administrative structures that made royal power a fact of everyday life.

This is best exemplified by King Alfonso II of Aragon (r. 1162–96), who was also the count of Barcelona and the first to rule the united Crown of Aragon. Alfonso used documentation as the ultimate tool of power, presiding over the compilation of a richly illuminated "big book of fiefs" (*Liber feudorum maior*) between 1192 and 1194 (see **Interpreting Visual Evidence** on page 293). This book recounted property transactions and family lineages dating back centuries, citing documents in the royal archives. Alfonso thereby grounded his authority on his command of history and written records.

Throughout the remainder of the twelfth century and into the thirteenth, Christian influence in Spain continued to spread southward until all that remained of Muslim dominion was the small kingdom centered on Granada in the extreme southwest. Castile became by far the largest kingdom in area, but it was rivaled in wealth and consequence by the more urbanized and commercially connected Aragon. Indeed, wars between Castile and Aragon would

The resulting *Concordance of Discordant Canons*, first redacted around 1139 and later known as the *Decretum*, is attributed to a jurist known only as Gratian, who was active in the study and teaching of law in Bologna. Significantly, Gratian's codification was influenced by the *Corpus Juris Civilis* codified under Justinian (Chapter 7). This is because another outcome of the Crusades, and of western Europe's increased contact with Byzantium, was the revitalized study of Roman law and the tradition of legal commentary associated with the great jurists of the

Picturing Legal Transactions

Between the years 1192 and 1194, King Alfonso II of Aragon (r. 1162–96) and his court scribes compiled a remarkable book. The codex known today as "the big book of fiefs" (*Liber feudorum maior*) may have been made to assist Alfonso and his descendants in legitimizing their authority over the many areas they controlled. But it was also a way of expressing that authority: its very existence represented a new claim to royal power. In its original form, it consisted of 888 parchment folios (1,776 pages) on which 903 separate documents were copied.

This "big book" represents a new trend in Europe. In most places, claims to property were made on the basis of custom and memory, not on documentation. When property changed hands, the chief witnesses were people, and when questions arose it was these people (or their heirs) whose testimony proved ownership. In Catalonia, the habit of documenting things had a long history, and it was not unusual for individual families to keep archives of documents. At the same time, however, documentation was never sufficient on its own: verbal exchanges of agreement and the public performance of transactions constituted legally binding ceremonies meaningful to the entire community, and the validity of these actions was not dependent on the making of a written record.

With all this in mind, it is striking that seventy-nine of the documents copied into the book are accompanied by images that convey important messages about documentation and its limitations.

On the book's opening frontispiece (image A), King Alfonso consults with his chief archivist, Ramón de Caldes. Ramón discusses one of the charters taken from a large pile at his elbow, while a scribe makes copies behind him—perhaps to aid in the compilation of the "big book." The king is backed by men who look on approvingly.

One of the charters copied into the "big book" is accompanied by the second image (B). It records that the viscount of Nîmes betrothed his daughter, Ermengarde of Carcassone, to the count of Roussillon. Ermengarde, her flowing hair uncovered as a sign of her maidenhood, stands between her bearded father and her seated mother, Cecilia of Provence.

Questions for Analysis

1. Why would a book designed to document property transactions contain images, too? What functions could they have served?

2. Why would the artist of the "big book" have depicted the king consulting his archivist in the very first image? How does he depict the relationship between them? Why does he include a group of men as witnesses to their discussion?

3. Women figure prominently in many of the book's images, including the one below. On what basis could you argue that their active presence is crucial to the transactions being described?

A. King Alfonso and Ramón de Caldes.

B. Betrothal of Ermengarde to the Count of Roussillon.

later Roman Empire (Chapter 5). The *Decretum* was also made possible by the new intellectual trends that were simultaneously giving rise to the universities of Europe (see below).

The *Decretum* claimed ecclesiastical jurisdiction for all sorts of cases, including such matters as marriage, inheritance, and bequests. Although these cases were supposed to be heard in local ecclesiastical courts overseen by bishops, popes increasingly insisted that they alone could issue dispensations exempting certain petitioners from established precedents—such as the annulment of Eleanor's marriage to Louis VII—and moreover that the papal court should function as a final court of appeals in all cases touching the Church.

Thinking back to the dispute between Henry II of England and Archbishop Thomas Becket, we can better understand what was at stake: both secular and ecclesiastical rulers now defined their power in terms of law, and they had to defend their rights against encroachment by others. And just as kings had to become more skillful administrators, so the popes of this era were almost invariably trained as canon lawyers, which was a real departure from the monastic origins of the reforming movement discussed in Chapter 8.

One example of this new breed of popes was Alexander III, who dealt so skillfully with Frederick Barbarossa. Another was Innocent III (r. 1198–1216), who combined an expertise in canon law with a zeal for continuing the work of the Crusades, even within Europe.

CONTINUING THE CRUSADES

When Pope Urban II urged the quarrelsome knights of northwestern Europe to take up the cross against the enemies of Christ in 1095, he was responding to the Byzantine emperor's request for reinforcements in his war with the Seljuq Turks, with the aim of recapturing imperial territories in Anatolia. But the pope's own conception of the crusaders' mission was broader and extended beyond the frontiers of Byzantium to the great cities of Antioch and Jerusalem, which had been in the hands of Muslims after centuries. And as we saw in Chapter 8, many crusaders acted on a still broader interpretation of their mission by attacking "enemies of Christ" in the Rhineland: the Jewish communities of Mainz, Speyer, and Worms.

So from the first, both the reason for crusading and the target of Christian aggression were apt to change. Like a weapon forged for a specific purpose whose uses could not be controlled, the crusading ethos could be copied and

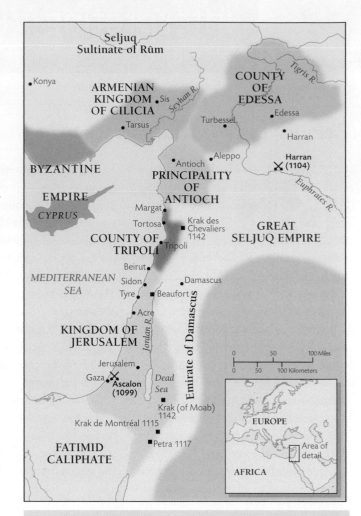

THE CRUSADER STATES. This map shows the fragile colonies known as the Crusader States at their greatest extent, around 1100. ▪ *What geographical, political, and military factors would make these states vulnerable?*

disseminated more widely, directed at other targets and for other motives. In the eyes of the Byzantine emperor, some Muslims were valued allies; for the crusaders themselves, who did not understand the politics of the eastern Mediterranean, this was a distinction that made no sense. And even though the papacy never officially sanctioned violence against Jews, individual popes would, in the centuries following the First Crusade, authorize the use of force against many different kinds of people who could be construed as "enemies of Christ" because they stood in opposition to the Roman Church. While historians, for convenience, often speak of the Crusades as divided into seven or more distinct phases (the Second Crusade, the Third Crusade, etc.), the people of the time—both aggressors and victims—experienced crusading as a continuous, snowballing movement. It was (and is still) a powerful and deadly force.

Crusader States and Crusading Orders

The military successes of the First Crusade were due not only to the might of the crusaders but to the diversity of (and divisions among) the many peoples who inhabited the coastline of the eastern Mediterranean. This is an area we have been studying since Chapter 1, and that had been formed by successive waves of colonization over the course of many millennia. The fragile principalities known as "the Crusader States" should therefore be understood as laying a thin veneer of western European influence on top of a deep, complex culture that would withstand any superficial changes.

Those Europeans who stayed and flourished here were those who were able to adapt themselves, and their expectations. Most probably retained some aspects of their former identities—as Normans or Franks, as loyal to the Roman Church—but they and their descendants became intertwined with the local populations, intermarrying and adopting their fashions, food, and outlook. In time, they had more in common with their immediate neighbors (Syrian and Armenian Christians, adherents of Greek Orthodoxy, Shi'ite and Sunni Muslims) than with their distant families "back home." Second- and third-generation settlers might never visit western Christendom in the course of their lives.

Because of all these factors, the four main Crusader States were very different from the territorial monarchies that were being consolidated in parts of Europe at this time. They were more like the loosely configured and combative lordships of the tenth and eleventh centuries than like burgeoning bureaucratic kingdoms. As such, they were mostly short-lived. The largest, the inland county of Edessa founded in 1098, stretched as far east as the Tigris River and had to be heavily fortified against constant internal uprisings and external threats. Its Latin Christian population was always a tiny minority, and by 1150 it had been mostly subsumed into the Seljuq Empire, with some portions reverting to Byzantium.

Edessa's position was made even more precarious because its Frankish rulers had friendlier relations with their Armenian subjects (with whom they largely intermarried) than with the crusader principality of Antioch to the west, which comprised parts of what is now Syria and Turkey. Although Antioch was named a patriarchate of the Roman Church, it also had a tiny Latin Christian population. And, after the fall of Edessa, it was largely dependent on Constantinople, and later Armenia, for protection from the Seljuq Turks. It ceased to exist in 1268, when its lands became part of a vast new empire, that of the Mongols (see Chapter 10).

The third major state, the county of Tripoli, was founded in 1109 and linked these two northern states with the kingdom of Jerusalem. Its strategic commercial position exposed it to constant raids and threats of invasion, which led its rulers to entrust most of the frontier to one of the military orders dedicated to perpetual pursuit of the crusading effort: the Knights Hospitaller. Originally charged with care of pilgrims in the Hospital of St. John at Jerusalem, founded in 1023, members of this religious order became militarized after 1099 and came to control the islands of Rhodes and Malta as well as many strategic fortifications in the eastern Mediterranean. Their massive *Krak des Chevaliers* ("Knights' Castle," in a mixture of Arabic and French) survives as a monument to their might. In fact, the Hospitallers long outlived the Crusader States, maintaining a sovereign presence in the region into the early nineteenth century; the order is now headquartered in Rome.

The Kingdom of Jerusalem and the Conquest of Saladin

The kingdom of Jerusalem, the fourth and most symbolically important of the Crusader States, was really a network of cities and fortresses that constantly changed hands, as much the target of rival crusaders as of any Muslim raiders. Its cosmopolitan population was a testament to the number of peoples who claimed the Holy Land for their own, with major concentrations of Muslims (both Sunni and Shi'a) and Orthodox Christians (Greek and Syrian) alongside smaller communities (Jews, Samaritans)—all of whom dwarfed the Latin Christian population of the region. As a result, those

KRAK DES CHEVALIERS. The necessity of securing hand-won territory in the Holy Land led to the construction of enormous castles like this one, built by the Knights Hospitaller in the early twelfth century when crusading movements were launched in Europe itself. Similar castles would be built to subjugate peoples deemed rebellious or heretical.

who claimed kingship in Jerusalem were heavily dependent on support from other Crusader States as well as from various European princes; yet the cachet of Jerusalem was such that any contingent of reinforcements sent by an ambitious ally could be attempting to seize power there. Defense of the kingdom therefore came to rest heavily on another of the new crusading orders, the Knights Templar. Founded during the reign of King Baldwin II (r. 1118–31), the Templars were based in a wing of the captured Al-Aqsa Mosque, which was now the royal palace and thought to be part of King Solomon's original Temple complex: hence the order's name.

Although the kingdom of Jerusalem persisted in theory until 1291, it ceased to have any purchase on Jerusalem itself after 1187. In this year, a remarkable Kurdish chieftain called Salāh ad-Dīn (c. 1138–1193), who had become the Sunni sultan of both Egypt and Syria, rallied Muslim opposition to the occupying crusader forces and succeeded in recapturing the Holy City. He became the target of a renewed crusading effort (the Third Crusade, 1189–92), which spurred three kings to take the cross: England's Richard the Lionheart, France's Philip Augustus, and the Holy Roman Empire's Frederick Barbarossa. But Frederick was killed, Philip left early, and Richard was captured on the way home. Meanwhile, the victorious Saladin (as he was known in Europe) became celebrated not only among Muslims but also among crusaders, who considered him a paragon of chivalry. Richard even considered arranging a marriage between his sister, Joan of Sicily, and Saladin's brother, thereby establishing allied rule in Jerusalem. But this never happened, and Jerusalem remained in Muslim hands. The city of Acre (Akko, in northern Israel) then became the new capital of the Christian kingdom, until its fall in 1291 marked the end of any viable western European presence in the region—until the short-lived conquests of Napoleon at the end of the eighteenth century (see Chapter 18).

The Extension of Crusading Ideas into European Colonial Projects

Once unleashed, the crusading ethos could not be contained by efforts to liberate the Holy Land. The promise that those who killed "the enemies of Christ" with papal approval would be absolved of their sins and win eternal salvation, while potentially winning lands and riches in the process, was soon applied to a host of other initiatives—especially those that could open new lands for settlement and bring more peoples into the orbit of the Roman Church. Beginning in the 1160s, accordingly, the rulers of Denmark and the German duchy of Saxony began to colonize the Baltic coast and lands between the Elbe and Oder Rivers.

This was represented as a missionary movement, but it was also an attempt to control trading and raiding activities in that region. And it was not carried forward peacefully; the missionary monks who spearheaded it (literally) were members of the military crusading order of the Teutonic Knights. In 1204, they managed to carve out a new bishopric around Riga (present-day Latvia), where they set about converting the indigenous inhabitants. But when they mounted a biblical drama featuring some battle scenes from the Old Testament, the new "converts" fled in terror at the sight of armed actors: it was all too real.

Meanwhile, the English were launching crusades against the "infidel" Irish and Welsh (who were actually Christian), justifying this on the grounds that the Celts were barbarians who would benefit from the civilizing influence of their superior overlords. It had been a short step from the calling of crusades against foreigners to those aimed at fellow Europeans.

The Crusade against Constantinople and the Revenge of Venice

The First Crusade had begun as an attempt to aid Constantinople. The Fourth Crusade (1202–4) ended in its destruction. The object of this expedition, which had been called by Pope Innocent III at the time of his election in 1198, was Egypt, where Saladin's successors continued to rally Muslim opposition to European colonial efforts. This meant launching an attack by sea, since the remaining crusader outposts had become too weak and scattered to enable the movement of armies by land. The natural embarkation point was Venice.

A major player in maritime trade since the ninth century, Venice had already benefited enormously from the Crusades, supplying the ships and supplies that transported and sustained the waves of aspiring conquerors while reaping the benefits of closer ties with Byzantium, with which the Italian city shared many interests. But relations with Constantinople worsened throughout the twelfth century, as the Crusades increasingly damaged Byzantine trade and threatened its security. In 1182, popular anticrusading sentiment had led enraged citizens of Constantinople to massacre enclaves of Italian merchants and seamen; those who were not killed were banished, the Venetians among them.

The Venetians therefore had a reason to resent the Byzantines. And they were now overrun by an army of eager and impoverished crusaders who could not pay for the passage to Cairo; it would cost the Venetians enormously in time, money, and men to ship them there. So in the end, the crusaders paid the Venetians with the services they could render. Rather than sailing for Egypt, the crusading expedition

Past and Present

Medieval Plots and Modern Movies

From westerns to science fiction to action movies to romantic comedies, most of the films that draw big audiences today are based loosely or closely on literary genres that were popularized during the Middle Ages: tales of chivalry and heroism, forbidden love, supernatural events, and magical adventures.

 Watch related author interview on StudySpace
wwnorton.com/web/westerncivi18

was diverted to Zara on the Dalmatian coast of the Adriatic, a former Venetian port that had rebelled and sought the protection of the king of Hungary. Despite the fact that Hungary was loyal to Rome, the city was attacked and taken.

From there, the crusaders moved on to Constantinople. After a terrible siege, the city was savagely overrun and sacked in 1204, its people killed or left homeless, its churches and public buildings severely damaged, and its books and artworks consigned to flames or seized as loot (like the porphyry statue of the Roman tetrarchs shown in Chapter 6 on page 191, which is still in Venice). In the aftermath, the Venetians were able to colonize the city itself, controlling the shipping in and around Constantinople as well as the island of Crete and many cities on the Greek mainland. Only in 1261 was Byzantine rule reestablished in the capital; but by that time, the empire had shrunk to a fraction of its former size. Meanwhile, crusading efforts continued within western Christendom.

Innocent III's Crusade for a Unified Christendom

Although Pope Innocent III expressed alarm at the turn taken by the Crusade he had called, he accepted the spoils of war that were offered to him and set his seal of approval on the Latin occupation of Greek territory. He was an ambitious man. Elected to the papal dignity at the age of thirty-seven (probably the youngest holder of the office in history), his goal was to unify all Christendom—and the wider world—under papal hegemony. Unlike Gregory VII (Chapter 8), Innocent never questioned the right of kings and princes to rule in their own secular spheres. Instead, he saw the pope's role as regulatory and disciplinary, which meant that when rulers sinned they should be reprimanded or excommunicated by the pope—who could thereby call into question the legitimacy of their rule. And Innocent

THE JEWISH BADGE. The distinctive apparel that marked Jews as different from their Christian neighbors varied from region to region. In some places it was a pointed hat like the one worn by the Old Testament Jews in this manuscript illumination from a fourteenth-century French vernacular Bible. This hat would later become associated with witchcraft or idiocy, as in the dunce's cap or the witch's peak. In other regions, Jews wore a distinctive patch on their clothing, often colored yellow to make it more visible.

was even more insistent than his predecessors on the obligation of every Christian to obey the pope as Jesus Christ's representative on earth.

Innocent sought to achieve this goal in many different ways. He made the papacy financially and politically independent by expanding and consolidating papal territories in central Italy. (Vatican City is now the last surviving remnant of these territories, and it continues to function as an independent state within Rome and Italy.) He loudly proclaimed his power as kingmaker and king-breaker by brokering the selection of the Holy Roman Emperor, and he also disciplined both Philip Augustus of France (for marital misconduct) and John of England, who was at one point compelled to grant England itself to the papacy, as a fief. Innocent further claimed, with varying degrees of success, a comparable lordship over Aragon, Sicily, and Hungary. He even levied the first income tax on the clergy, in order to support the Crusade that brought Orthodox Christians to heel.

The crowning achievement of Innocent's pontificate was the ratification of his agenda at a representative assembly of the western Church, the Fourth Lateran Council of 1215 (so called because it was held in the Roman palace of St. John Lateran). This council defined the central dogmas of Latin Christianity and made one of them the acknowledgment of papal supremacy. Since a dogma is defined as "a truth necessary for salvation," this meant that all Christians had to acknowledge the pope's ultimate power; those unwilling to do so (including the Christians of Byzantium) were, by definition, heretics—and as heretics, they could be prosecuted and punished.

In a further effort to achieve unity and uniformity within Christendom, the Fourth Lateran Council took an unprecedented interest in the religious education and habits of every Christian. It responded to the urbanization of Europe by establishing free primary schools (for boys) in all the major cities, requiring bishops to recruit effective preachers, and outlawing all kinds of misbehavior on the part of the clergy. It also sought to increase the distance between Christians and their Muslim and Jewish neighbors by discouraging social relationships, economic exchanges, and intermarriage. Most disturbingly, Innocent's council mandated that "infidels" be visibly distinguished from Christians by the wearing of distinctive clothing, the origins of the infamous "Jewish badge" (see Chapter 26).

The Crusade against Heresy

Innocent's reign achieved the height of papal power, but it also fomented violence and sowed seeds of dissent. Future popes continued to centralize the government of the Church, but they also became involved in protracted political and military struggles that compromised the papacy's credibility. Because the Papal States bordered on the kingdom of Sicily, Innocent's successors quickly came into conflict with Emperor Frederick II, who became an inveterate opponent of papal monarchy. But instead of excommunicating him and calling for his deposition, as Innocent might have done, they called a crusade against him. Yet Innocent himself had paved the way for this by launching a series of Crusades against heretics, now defined as any group or individual who did not fall into line with the papacy's policies—and who were, by association, "enemies of Christ." The most notorious of these campaigns was the Albigensian Crusade, launched in 1209 and ostensibly directed against a heretical sect called the Cathars, but which really justified the colonization of what is now southern France by land-hungry knights from northern France. Although the Albigensian Crusade can be said to have ended by 1255, it created lasting tensions within the forcibly enlarged French kingdom that would lead the inhabitants of this devastated region to ally with the English during the Hundred Years' War (see Chapter 10) and make southern France particularly susceptible to violent religious warfare during and after the Reformation (see Chapter 13). Indeed, the language, culture, and political orientation of southern France are still very different from that of Paris and its environs. In order to understand how this happened, we must turn to some larger religious developments within Europe.

UNITY AND DISSENT IN THE WESTERN CHURCH

The Investiture Conflict (Chapter 8) engaged both clergy and laity in debates over the essential meaning of Jesus Christ's life and teachings. In many regions of western Europe, the papacy's claim to supremacy was supported, but in others there was marked resistance to its encroachment on centuries-old practices and social networks. After all, bishops had been members of the aristocracy since the time of Constantine, and it was customary for bishoprics to be controlled by certain families. Meanwhile, priests had been married men since the establishment of the first Christian churches; and the wives of priests were not only their husbands' partners, they were also ministers to the communities in which they lived. When the papacy preached against "fornicating priests" and their "concubines," it was delegitimizing relationships that had been essential to local communities for generations. No wonder, then, that nothing else was talked about "even in the women's spinning rooms and the artisans' workshops," as one contemporary reported.

On the one hand, then, the reforms of Pope Gregory VII and his successors gave the common people an important role to play, by urging them to reject certain practices and urging retaliation against offenders. Combined with the fervor that had been whipped up by the Crusades, the result was more-widespread interest in spiritual matters and increased participation in religious life—as well as increased violence. On the other hand, however, the reforming movement severely limited the ways in which the laity were allowed to express their spirituality or to participate meaningfully in the life of the Church.

The New Monasticism

One of the first manifestations of the new popular piety was the growth and diversification of monastic move-

ments. The abbey of Cluny had revived the observance of Benedict's *Rule* in the course of the tenth century and, at the same time, had kept Cluny and its daughter houses independent of local lords. As a result, these monasteries became lordships in their own right, acquiring extensive lands and enormous wealth. Those seeking to reject worldliness, therefore, had to look elsewhere. The result, beginning in the late eleventh century, was the founding of new monastic orders.

The one that became most widespread was founded at the monastery of Cîteaux in 1098. Cistercian monks followed Benedict's *Rule*, but in the purest and most austere way possible, and they founded new monasteries in wildernesses and remote areas, far from worldly temptations. They also shunned all unnecessary decoration and elaborate liturgical rites. Instead, they practiced contemplation and private prayer, and they committed themselves to hard manual labor. Under the charismatic leadership of Bernard of Clairvaux (1090–1153), a spellbinding preacher and one of the most influential personalities of his age, the Cistercian order grew exponentially, from 5 houses in 1115 to 343 by 1153. This astonishing increase meant that many more men and women were becoming professional religious. It also meant that still more pious people were donating funds and lands to support monasteries and thereby participating indirectly in their life of devotion.

Another manifestation of popular piety was a new focus on the sacrament of the Mass, the liturgical reenactment of Christ's last meal with his disciples. This celebration, the Eucharist, had always been an important part of Christian religious and social practice (see Chapter 6), but only in the twelfth century did it become the central act of worship in the western Church. Bernard of Clairvaux was instrumental in making it so, by developing and preaching the doctrine of transubstantiation. According to this doctrine, every Mass is a miraculous event, because the priest's blessing transforms the bread and wine on the altar into the body and blood of Christ: hence the term *transubstantiation*, since earthly substances thereby become the substance of Christ's divine body.

Popular reverence for the Eucharist became so great that the Church initiated the practice of elevating the consecrated bread, known as the Host, so that the whole congregation could see it. Not incidentally, this new theology of the Eucharist further enhanced the prestige of the priesthood by seeming to endow it with wonder-working powers. In later centuries, the Latin words spoken at the consecration of the Host, *Hoc est corpus meum* ("This is my body"), were understood as a magical formula: *hocus pocus*.

The Canons of the Fourth Lateran Council

In 1215, Innocent III presided over an ecumenical assembly of Church leaders in the papal palace and church of Saint John Lateran in Rome. The resulting canons both reaffirmed older legislation and introduced a number of new laws that responded to widespread social, economic, and cultural changes. Published in the same year as Magna Carta, they too became a standard set of principles and continued to be applied within the Church until they were modified by the Council of Trent in the sixteenth century.

Canon 1

. . . There is one Universal Church of the faithful, outside of which there is absolutely no salvation. In which there is the same priest and sacrifice, Jesus Christ, whose body and blood are truly contained in the sacrament of the altar under the forms of bread and wine; the bread being changed (*transsubstantiatio*) by divine power into the body, and the wine into the blood, so that to realize the mystery of unity we may receive of Him what He has received of us. And this sacrament no one can effect except the priest who has been duly ordained in accordance with the keys of the Church, which Jesus Christ Himself gave to the Apostles and their successors. . . .

. . .

Canon 3

We excommunicate and anathematize every heresy that rises against the holy, orthodox, and Catholic faith . . . condemning all heretics under whatever names they may be known, for while they have different faces they are nevertheless bound to each other by their tails, since in all of them vanity is a common element. Those condemned, being handed over to the secular rulers of their bailiffs, let them be abandoned, to be punished with due justice, clerics being first degraded from their orders.

. . .

Canon 9

Since in many places within the same city and diocese there are people of different languages having one faith but various rites and customs, we strictly command that the bishops of these cities and dioceses provide suitable men who will, according to the different rites and languages, celebrate the divine offices for them, administer the sacraments of the Church and instruct them by word and example.

Canon 10

. . . It often happens that bishops, on account of their manifold duties or bodily infirmities, or because of hostile invasions or other reasons, to say nothing of lack of learning, which must be absolutely condemned in them and is not to be tolerated in the future, are themselves unable to minister the word of God to the people, especially in large and widespread dioceses. Wherefore we decree that bishops provide suitable men, powerful in work and word, to exercise with fruitful result the office of preaching; who in place of the bishops, since these cannot do it, diligently visiting the people committed to them, may instruct them by word and example. . . .

Canon 11

Since there are some who, on account of the lack of necessary means, are unable to acquire an education or to meet opportunities for perfecting themselves, the Third Lateran Council in a salutary decree provided that in every cathedral church a suitable benefice be assigned to a master who shall instruct *gratis* the clerics of that church and other poor students, . . . we, confirming the aforesaid decree, add that, not only in every cathedral church but also in other churches where means are sufficient, a competent master be appointed . . . who shall instruct *gratis* and to the best of his ability the clerics of those and other churches in the art of grammar and in other branches of knowledge.

. . .

Canons 14–16

That the morals and general conduct of clerics may be better, let all strive to live chastely and virtuously, particularly those in sacred orders, guarding against every vice of desire . . .

. . . All clerics shall carefully abstain from drunkenness. . . .

We forbid hunting and fowling to all clerics; wherefore, let them not presume to keep dogs and birds for these purposes. . . .

Clerics shall not hold secular offices or engage in secular and, above all, dishonest pursuits. They shall not attend the performances of mimics and buffoons, or theatrical representations. They shall not visit taverns except in case of necessity, namely, when on a journey.

They are forbidden to play games of chance or be present at them. They must have a becoming crown and tonsure and apply themselves diligently to the study of the divine offices and other useful subjects. Their garments must be worn clasped at the top and neither too short nor too long. They are not to use red or green garments or curiously sewed-together gloves, or beak-shaped shoes . . .

• • •

Canon 68

In some provinces a difference in dress distinguishes the Jews or Saracens from the Christians, but in certain others such a confusion has grown up that they cannot be distinguished by any difference. Thus it happens at times that through error Christians have relations with the women of Jews or Saracens, and Jews and Saracens with Christian women. Therefore, that they may not, under pretext of error of this sort, excuse themselves in the future for the excesses of such prohibited intercourse, we decree that such Jews and Saracens of both sexes in every Christian province and at all times shall be marked off in the eyes of the public from other peoples through the character of their dress. . . .

Moreover, during the last three days before Easter and especially on Good Friday, they shall not go forth in public at all, for the reason that some of them on these very days, as we hear, do not blush to go forth better dressed and are not afraid to mock the Christians who maintain the memory of the most holy Passion by wearing signs of mourning. . . .

Source: Excerpted from H. J. Schroeder, *Disciplinary Decrees of the General Councils: Text, Translation and Commentary* (St. Louis, MO: 1937), pp. 236–96.

Questions for Analysis

1. Based on this selection of canons, how would you characterize the main concerns of the Fourth Lateran Council? What is it attempting to regulate, and why? What changing historical circumstances do the canons reflect?

2. In what ways do the canons distinguish between clergy and laity? How does legislation work to maintain those distinctions?

3. Why do the canons place so much emphasis on clothing and appearance? Why would it be important for both clerics and "infidels" (Jews and Muslims) to dress in distinctive ways?

Holy Women, Human and Divine

Popular devotion to the Eucharist was matched by another new and hugely influential religious practice: the veneration of Jesus's mother, Mary. In this development, too, Bernard of Clairvaux played an important role, traveling around Europe to promote a theology that made Mary central to Christianity, the very embodiment of the Church. Eventually, Catholic teaching would hold that Mary had not only given birth to Jesus while still a virgin but that she remained a virgin even after Jesus's birth—and, more radically, that she herself had been conceived without sin. This made Mary the exact opposite of Eve, the woman whose disobedience had (according to Judeo-Christian tradition) brought sin into the world for the first time; for through God's grace, Mary had given birth to Christ, a second Adam, whose obedient sacrifice of himself atoned for that original sin.

New doctrines also raised Mary from the position of God's humble handmaid to that of heaven's queen, with the power to intercede on behalf of all, even the worst sinners. Her soaring reputation as a miracle worker and advocate is amply testified by the thousands of devotional images created during this period, the many stories and hymns celebrating her virtues and miracles, and the fact that practically all the magnificent new cathedrals of the age were dedicated to "Our Lady." This explains the many churches of Notre Dame in France, the Frauenkirchen of Germany, and so on.

The burgeoning cult of the Blessed Virgin had two contradictory effects. On the one hand, it elevated a female figure to a prominent place in the official Church for the first time, and it thereby celebrated virtues associated with femininity: motherhood, healing, nourishment, mercy, kindness. On the other hand, it made Mary an unobtainable, paradoxical model of female perfection: she alone could be both virgin and parent, Christ's mother and bride, God's maidservant and queenly consort. No real woman could begin to emulate her, and thus real women were increasingly compared to Eve and perceived as weak, deceitful, and disobedient. Moreover, the veneration of a

THE MYSTERY OF THE MASS. In this manuscript illumination, the visionary Hildegard of Bingen (see below) illustrates the doctrine of transubstantiation. In the lower register, the bread and wine of the Mass have been placed on the altar and are being transformed into the body and blood of the crucified Christ, depicted in the upper register. Paired scenes from Christ's life (his birth and death, his ministry and resurrection) emphasize the fact that earthly substances—bread and wine—participate in a divine cycle of regeneration. Note that Hildegard does not imagine the mediating figure as a priest, but as the (female) Church, represented as a crowned queen and associated with the Virgin Mary. ■ *What might be the significance of this choice?*

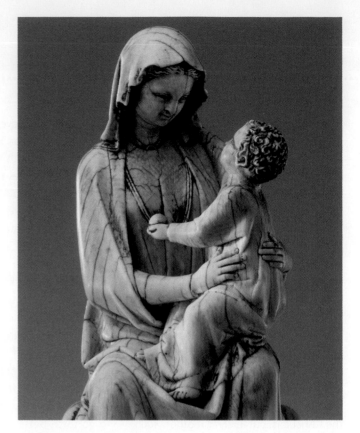

VIRGIN AND CHILD. This exquisite ivory sculpture (just over seven inches high) was carved in Paris in the mid to late thirteenth century, as an aid to private devotion and prayer. The mother of Jesus, Mary, was also regarded as the mother of all humanity, the *alma mater* ("nourishing mother") who could be relied on to protect and heal those who asked for her help.

single, idealized woman coincided exactly with the suppression of most real women's access to positions of power within the Church; as the cult of the Blessed Virgin grew, so the opportunities for aspiring holy women shrank.

This did not go unremarked at the time. As we noted above, the career of Heloise (c. 1090–1164) exemplifies both the avenues of advancement for women and also the successful blocking of those avenues by new constraints on women's activities. Heloise's exact contemporary, Hildegard of Bingen (1098–1179), was even more creative in her efforts to make a place for herself and her female followers, and more outspoken than Heloise in her criticism of attempts to thwart them. Like Heloise, she was an abbess and a highly original thinker. But she was not, like Heloise, a scholar; she was a mystic who claimed to receive regular revelations from God.

Hildegard expressed these visions in her own version of Latin, writings that were later transcribed and illustrated under her close supervision. She also composed hymns and ambitious musical dramas for her nuns—music now widely available on CD, MP3, and the Internet—and prepared treatises on subjects as diverse as cosmology and medicine. Her advice was frequently sought by religious and secular authorities, including Bernard of Clairvaux and Frederick Barbarossa, and she even received a special papal dispensation that allowed her to preach publicly.

Despite all this, Hildegard had to fight constantly for her rights and those of her nuns during her lifetime, and after her death efforts to have her recognized as a saint were thwarted by the papacy. Indeed, she was one of the first candidates for whom a new canonization process was instituted in the papal curia, as a way of controlling the popular veneration of charismatic figures whom the Church considered threatening. So while many high-ranking clergy of her own day recognized her holiness, the papal courts of subsequent centuries would not acknowledge it. The standards of acceptable female behavior had become too narrow to contain her. It would take 800 years for Hildegard to be officially canonized as a saint, in 2012.

Heresy or Piety?

Christianity has been successfully transmitted to many different civilizations because it is relatively open-ended and absorbent of new influences. In this era, however, the medieval Church began to lose its capacity to respond inclusively to new challenges, preferring instead to crack down on "heresies" that undermined its power. This trend would eventually lead to a reforming movement so intense that it could not be contained within the Church: the Protestant Reformation (see Chapter 13). For the more the Church claimed the right to control every aspect of belief and practice, the more it made itself vulnerable to those who challenged its enforcement. This resulted in large-scale movements of popular opposition to centralized authority, and also to more Crusades aimed at harnessing popular piety to that same authority.

The best way to understand this is through Innocent III's very different responses to rather similar popular movements. On the one hand, the pope resolved to crush all disobedience; on the other, he wanted to support idealistic groups that could be made to acknowledge papal authority, so as not to frustrate all dynamic spirituality. Thus, Innocent labeled as heretical a religious movement that began in southern France, that of the Cathars (from the Greek word for "purity"). He accused Cathars of beliefs that resemble Zoroastrianism (see Chapter 2) and Manichaeism (see Chapter 6), alleging that they held all material creation to be evil, and even that they believed the power of God to be opposed by that of a malevolent deity associated with Satan or the fallen angel Lucifer. The fact that many Cathar leaders were women made the movement heretical by definition.

More typical of twelfth-century religious dissent was Waldensianism, so called because it is said to have originated with the teachings of a merchant called Waldes. Waldensians were laypeople who wished to imitate the life of Christ to the fullest. They were active in the vernacular translation and study of the Gospels and dedicated to lives of poverty and preaching. None of this contradicted any contemporary doctrines, and for a while the Church did not interfere with Waldensians' ministry. But when

Two Conversion Experiences

> Both Peter Waldo (or Waldes), later branded as a heretic, and Francis of Assisi, later canonized as a saint, were moved to take up a life of preaching and poverty after undergoing a process of conversion. These experiences exhibit some striking similarities, despite the different fates of these two men. The first account is that of an anonymous chronicler in Peter's home town of Lyons; the second is by Francis's contemporary and hagiographer, Thomas of Celano (c. 1200–c. 1260/70).

The Conversion of Peter Waldo

At about this time, in 1173, there was a citizen of Lyons named Peter Waldo, who had made a great deal of money by the evil means of usury. One Sunday he lingered by a crowd that had gathered round a traveling storyteller, and was much struck by his words. He took him home with him, and listened carefully to his story of how St. Alexis had died a holy death in his father's house. Next morning Waldo hastened to the schools of theology to seek advice about his soul. When he had been told of the many ways of coming to God he asked the master whether any of them was more sure and reliable than the rest. The master quoted to him the words of the Lord, "If thou wilt be perfect go sell what thou hast and give it to the poor and thou shalt have treasure in heaven. And come follow me."

Waldo returned to his wife and gave her the choice between having all his movable wealth or his property in land. . . . She was very upset at having to do this and chose the property. From his movable wealth he returned what he had acquired wrongly, conferred a large portion on his two daughters, whom he placed in the order of Fontevrault without his wife's knowledge, and gave a still larger amount to the poor.

At this time a terrible famine was raging through Gaul and Germany. . . . Waldo generously distributed bread, soup and meat to anyone who came to him. On the [Feast of the] Assumption of the Virgin [August 15] he scattered money among the poor in the streets saying, "You cannot serve two masters, God and Mammon." The people around thought he had gone out of his senses. Then he stood up on a piece of high ground and said, "Friends and fellow-citizens, I am not mad as you think. . . . I know that many of you disapprove of my having acted so publicly. I have done so both for my own sake and for yours: for my sake, because anybody who sees me with money in future will be able to say that I am mad; for your sake, so that you may learn to place your hopes in God and not in wealth." . . .

1177 Waldo, the citizen of Lyons whom we have already mentioned, who had vowed to God that he would possess neither gold nor silver, and take no thought for the morrow, began to make converts to his opinions. Following his example they gave all they had to the poor, and willingly devoted themselves to poverty. Gradually, both in public and in private they began to inveigh against both their own sins and those of others. . . .

1178 Pope Alexander III held a council at the Lateran palace. . . . The council condemned heresy and all those who fostered and defended heretics. The pope embraced Waldo, and applauded the vows of voluntary poverty which he had taken, but forbade him and his companion to assume the office of preaching except at the request of the priests. They obeyed this instruction for a time, but later they disobeyed, and affronted many, bringing ruin on themselves.

Source: Excerpted from *Chronicon universale anonymi Laudunensis*, ed. and trans. Robert I. Moore in *The Birth of Popular Heresy* (London: 1975), pp. 111–13 (slightly modified).

The Conversion of Francis of Assisi

There was a man by the name of Francis, who from his earliest years was brought up by his parents proud of spirit, in accordance with the vanity of the world. . . . These are the wretched circumstances among which the man whom we venerate today as a saint, for he is truly a saint, lived in his youth; and almost up to the twenty-fifth year of his age, . . . he outdid all his contemporaries in vanities and he came to be a promoter of evil and was more abundantly zealous for all kinds of foolishness. . . . And while, not knowing how to restrain himself, he was . . . worn down by a long illness, [he] began to think of things other than he was used to thinking upon. When he had recovered somewhat and had begun to walk about the house with the support of a cane to speed the recovery of his health, he went outside one day and began to look about at the surrounding landscape with great interest. But the beauty of the fields, the pleasantness of the vineyards, and whatever else was beautiful to look upon, could stir in him no delight. He wondered therefore at the sudden change that had come over him. . . . From that day on, therefore, he began to despise himself. . . .

Now since there was a certain man in the city of Assisi whom he loved more than any other because he was of the same age as the other, and since the great familiarity of their mutual affection led him to share his secrets with him; he often took him to remote places, places well-suited for counsel, telling him that he had found a certain precious and great treasure. This one rejoiced and, concerned about what he heard, he willingly accompanied Francis whenever he was asked. There was a certain grotto near the city where they frequently went and talked about this treasure. The man of God, who was already holy by reason of his holy purpose, would enter the grotto, while his companion would wait for him outside; and filled with a new and singular spirit, he would pray to his Father in secret. . . .

One day, however, when he had begged for the mercy of God most earnestly, it was shown to him by God what he was to do. . . . He rose up, therefore, fortified himself with the sign of the cross, got his horse ready and mounted it, and taking with him some fine cloth to sell, he hastened to the city called Foligno. There, as usual, he sold everything he had with him . . . and, free of all luggage, he started back, wondering with a religious mind what he should do with the money. . . . When, therefore, he neared the city of Assisi, he discovered a certain church . . . built of old in honor of St. Damian but which was now threatening to collapse because it was so old. . . . And when he found there a certain poor priest, he kissed his sacred hands with great faith, and offered him the money he had with him, . . . begging the priest to suffer him to remain with him for the sake of the Lord. . . .

When those who knew him . . . compared what he was now with what he had been . . . they began to revile him miserably. Shouting out that he was mad and demented, they threw the mud of the streets and stones at him. . . . Now . . . the report of these things finally came to his father . . . [who] shut him up mercilessly in a dark place for several days . . . It happened, however, when Francis' father had left home for a while on business and the man of God remained bound in the basement of the house, his mother, who was alone with him and did not approve of what her husband had done, spoke kindly to her son. . . . and loosening his chains, she let him go free. . . .

He [the father] then brought his son before the bishop of the city, so that, renouncing all his possessions into his hands, he might give up everything he had. . . . Indeed, he [Francis] did not wait for any words nor did he speak any, but immediately putting off his clothes and casting them aside, he gave them back to his father. Moreover, not even retaining his trousers, he stripped himself completely naked before all. The bishop, however, sensing his disposition and admiring greatly his fervor and constancy, arose and drew him within his arms and covered him with the mantle he was wearing. . . .

Source: Excerpted from Thomas of Celano, "The First Life of Saint Francis" in *Saint Francis of Assisi: Writings and Biographies*, ed. Marion A. Habiq (Chicago: 1973), pp. 229–41.

Questions for Analysis

1. How do the conversions of Peter and Francis reflect the social and economic changes of the twelfth century? What new sources of tension and temptation are evident?

2. How do these two accounts describe these new converts' relationship(s) with their families, communities, and Church authorities? What are the similarities and differences, and why would these be important factors in determining the sanctity of either?

3. The story of Peter's conversion is written by an anonymous chronicler of Lyons, that of Francis by his follower and official biographer. How do these different perspectives shape these two accounts? Which is the more reliable, and why?

they began to preach without authorization they were condemned as heretics. In response, they began to articulate a more radical opposition to the established hierarchy. Many of their leaders, too, were women.

At the same time, however, Innocent embraced two other popular movements and turned them into two new religious orders, the Dominicans and the Franciscans. Like the Waldensians, the friars ("brothers") of these orders imitated the life of Jesus and his apostles by wandering through the countryside and establishing missions in Europe's growing towns, preaching and offering spiritual and material assistance to the poor. They also embraced poverty and begged for a living, hence their categorization as *mendicants*, from the Latin verb *mendicare*, "to beg." In the end, the only thing that separated them from the Waldensians was their willingness to subject themselves to papal authority.

The Dominican order, formally known as the Order of Preachers, was founded by the zealous Dominic of Osma (1170–1221), a Castilian theologian. Approved in 1216, it was particularly dedicated to the prosecution of heretics and to the conversion of Jews and Muslims. At first, the Dominicans hoped to achieve these ends by preaching and public debate; and to further these goals, many of its members pursued academic careers in the nascent universities and thus contributed to the development of philosophy and theology (see below). The most influential intellectual of the Middle Ages, Thomas Aquinas (1225–1274), was a Dominican. But the Dominicans soon became associated with the use of other persuasive techniques through the administration of the Inquisition, which became formalized in the thirteenth century. (It is now called the Congregation for the Doctrine of the Faith and is still staffed by members of the order.)

The Franciscans, formally known as the Order of the Friars Minor ("Little Brothers"), were committed less to doctrine and discipline than to the welfare of the poor and the cultivation of personal spirituality. Whereas Dominic and his earliest followers were ordained priests, the founder of the Franciscans was the ne'er-do-well son of an Italian merchant, Francis of Assisi (1182–1226), who eventually rebelled against the materialistic values of his father. Stripping himself (literally) of all his worldly possessions, he put on the tattered garb of a beggar and began to preach salvation in town squares. Unlike Dominic, Francis did this without official approval, thereby risking papal censure. Indeed, the pope might well have rejected Francis as a heretic. But when he showed himself willing to profess obedience in 1209, Innocent granted Francis and his followers permission to preach.

Although the rapid growth of the Franciscan order would eventually necessitate more administrative stability and doctrinal training for all its members, many Franciscans continued to engage in revivalistic outdoor preaching and to offer a model for apostolic living. This was not, however, an approved religious lifestyle for women. Francis's most important female follower, Clare of Assisi (1194–1253), wanted to found an order along the same lines, but members of the Order of Poor Ladies (also known as the Poor Clares) were not allowed to work directly among the people, as men did, but instead lived in cloistered convents supported by charitable donations. Their counterparts in northern Europe were the Beguines, communities of laywomen who lived in loosely organized communal quarters and ministered directly to the poor. Their relationship with Church officials was strained, because the Beguines embraced many of the precepts and practices associated with the Waldensians, including the unauthorized translation and study of the Bible. The fact that they were women made them even more suspect.

Christians against Jews

Although violence and exploitation continued to prey on Europe's Jewish communities, the Church's official position never explicitly endorsed the views that Jews posed a threat to Christians, yet it did little to combat such attitudes, either. As a result, many ordinary people came to believe that their Jewish neighbors were agents of evil who routinely crucified Christian children, consumed Christian blood, profaned the body of Christ in the Eucharist, and spread disease in Christian communities by poisoning wells. Fanciful stories of Jewish wealth added an economic element to the development of anti-Semitism, as did the fact that the Jews' social and cultural networks were the engine of the medieval economy. From this fact, conspiracy theorists inferred the existence of organized Jewish plots to undermine Christian society, which were regularly cited as justifications for mass executions and other atrocities.

The precarious position of Europe's Jews worsened throughout the twelfth and thirteenth centuries as both secular and ecclesiastical authorities devised more systematic mechanisms for policing undesirable segments of society: not only heretics but the indigent poor, prostitutes, "sodomites," and lepers. The canons of the Fourth Lateran Council had mandated that Jews be exposed through the wearing of the Jewish badge, and this made them easier targets in times of unrest. At the same time, the protections which Europe's rulers had once extended

THE BURNING OF JEWS. This manuscript account, written in the German vernacular, records an incident in which Jews were accused of poisoning the wells in a Christian town—and shows the punishment meted out to them. The wooden enclosure may represent the walls of the Jewish ghetto. As in the image on page 298, the Jews are identified by their distinctive conical hats.

to their Jewish subjects were gradually withdrawn. In Spain, the "Reconquista" had absorbed many of the Muslim kingdoms in which Jews had enjoyed a measure of tolerance, and they were not easily accommodated within the emerging monarchies of Christian Spain. Starting in the 1280s, rulers elsewhere in Europe began to expel their Jewish subjects from their kingdoms altogether, in most cases because they could no longer pretend to repay the enormous sums they had extorted from Jewish money-lenders: this was the case in the kingdoms of Sicily (1288), England (1290), and France (1306). Further expulsions followed during the fourteenth century in the Rhineland, and in 1492 from Spain. By 1500, only northern Italy and various eastern European regions (encompassed today by Poland, Belarus, and Ukraine) were home to sizable Jewish communities. They would survive there until the more efficient persecutions of the Nazi Holocaust eradicated them (see Chapter 26).

AN INTELLECTUAL REVOLUTION

The Fourth Lateran Council responded to the growing urbanization of Europe by mandating the education of the laity and insisting on more rigorous training for all clergy. These measures responded to a number of factors that were working to transform the cultural landscape of Europe and to open up new opportunities for advancement through education. The growth of towns had led to the growth of schools in those towns, for the most part founded by local bishops or monasteries. Meanwhile, the Crusades became conduits for the transmission of Muslim learning and, through Muslim mediation, the precepts of ancient Greek philosophy. The infusion of these new ideas created an extraordinary new forum for intellectual endeavor: the university. In much the same way that ease of travel and communication had fostered a scientific revolution in the cities of the Hellenistic world (see Chaper 4), so the conditions that gave rise to the university mark the beginning of a revolution in the intellectual history of Europe.

Access to Education

Around 800, Charlemagne had ordered that primary schools be established in every city and monastery of his realm. But it was not until the economic revival of the late eleventh century that educational opportunities were more widely available. By 1179, Pope Alexander III decreed that all cathedrals should set aside income for at least one schoolteacher, whose task would be to accept all comers, rich or poor, without fee. He predicted, correctly, that this measure would increase the number of well-trained clerics and administrators, supplying the growing bureaucracy of the Church. The recently martyred Thomas Becket had been an early beneficiary of such schooling.

At first, cathedral schools existed almost exclusively for the training of parish priests, but their curriculum was soon broadened as the growth of both ecclesiastical and

TWO CONCEPTIONS OF ELEMENTARY EDUCATION. In the lefthand illumination from a fourteenth-century manuscript, a master of grammar points to the day's lesson in a book while simultaneously keeping order with a cudgel. On the right, a later woodcut represents education as more benign: Lady Wisdom shows an eager schoolboy how to learn his letters while unlocking the door of knowledge, a multi-tiered tower where scholarly men representing the different branches of learning smile out at him.

secular governments escalated demand for trained men with more sophisticated skills. The most fundamental elements of this curriculum were known as the *trivium*, "the three ways": grammar, logic, and rhetoric. This meant a thorough grounding in Latin through the study of classical Roman authors, such as Cicero and Virgil, and training in the formulation and expression of sound arguments. Students who mastered the trivium were fit to perform basic clerical tasks, but those who wanted to achieve the reputation and advantages of scholars had to master the remaining branches of learning. These were arithmetic, geometry, astronomy, and music: the *quadrivium* or "four ways." Together, these seven liberal arts—so called because they liberated those who acquired them from menial labor—were the prerequisites for advanced study in philosophy, theology, law, and medicine.

Until about 1200, most students in urban schools would have belonged to the minor orders of the clergy. This means that they took vows of obedience and were immune from prosecution by secular authorities, but they were not required to remain celibate—unlike priests

and bishops, who were in major orders. Even those who hoped to become lawyers or bureaucrats usually found it advantageous to "take orders" in case powerful ecclesiastical offices became open to them: Heloise tried to discourage Abelard from marrying her for this very reason, because it would destroy his chances of being appointed a bishop or papal legate. Abelard, a nobleman's son, is by no means typical of the men who rose to prominence in this era through education. His contemporary and rival, Suger, is more representative. An orphan of obscure origins, he became abbot of the royal monastery of Saint-Denis and *de facto* chancellor of France.

By the thirteenth century, most boys who entered schools were not members of the clergy and never intended to be. Some were children of wealthy families, who regarded Latin literacy as a badge of status and a practical necessity. Others were future notaries, estate managers, and merchants who needed to be literate and numerate in order to succeed in these careers. Many alternative schools were eventually established to cater to these vocational students, and would become largely independent of ecclesiastical control. In many cases, Latin ceased to be the language of instruction in these schools and was replaced by the vernacular language of the region.

Formal schooling remained restricted to males. Yet many girls and women became highly educated, especially those reared in convents or princely courts. Heloise had an unusual degree of access to the educational milieu of Paris, but the fact remains that she had clearly received excellent preparatory training in the convent before she began her studies with Abelard. Most laywomen were taught at home, sometimes by private tutors but more often by other women. In fact, laywomen were more likely to be literate than laymen, and it is for this reason that women were often the patrons of poets and the primary readers and owners of books. Significantly, the effigy that Eleanor of Aquitaine commissioned for her own tomb shows her lying awake till Judgment Day, reading, flanked by her sleeping husband and son.

The Development of Scholasticism

The educational revolution that began in the eleventh century led to the development of new critical methods for framing and resolving complex theological and

THE TOMB OF ELEANOR OF AQUITAINE. Eleanor probably commissioned the effigies for the tombs representing herself, her husband Henry II, and her son Richard the Lionheart—both of whom died years before she did. She was eventually buried alongside them in the vault of the convent of Fontevrault in Anjou, where she spent the last years of her life. ■ *Notice that Eleanor's effigy shows her reading a book. How does this reinforce or challenge what we have learned about women's access to education?*

philosophical problems. These methods are collectively known as *scholasticism*, because they had their origins in the pedagogy of medieval schools. Scholastic methods are highly systematic and highly respectful of authority, but they also rely on rigorous questioning and argumentation. They therefore place great emphasis on evidence derived from reason. Indeed, scholasticism can be defined as a way of reconciling various forms of knowledge through logical debate, often called *dialectic*.

The earliest practitioner of the scholastic method is often considered to be Anselm of Canterbury (1033–1109), a Benedictine monk from northern Italy who became archbishop of Canterbury. The central premise of Anselm's teaching was that the human mind can combine knowledge gained through education and experience with divine revelation—as long as one has faith in God and careful scholastic training. As he put it, "I believe in order to understand," so that belief can be enriched and strengthened by understanding.

Building on the writings of Augustine and Boethius (see Chapter 6), and so (indirectly) on the teachings of Plato (see Chapter 4), Anselm developed various rational proofs for the underlying truths of Christian doctrine. The most famous of these is his proof for the existence of God, known as the ontological proof ("proof from the fact of existence") because it reasons that human beings could not have ideas of goodness or truth or justice unless some higher being had instilled these ideas in us. He further reasoned that God, as the essence of all ideals, must be "that than which nothing greater can be conceived" and as such must exist, or else God could not be the greatest thing conceivable.

Anselm's writings were influential, but the philosopher who popularized the scholastic method was Abelard. It was largely thanks to him that Paris became the intellectual capital of Europe. As a cathedral town and seat of the French monarchy, it already boasted a number of schools, but it was only after Abelard was appointed to the schoolmaster's chair at Notre-Dame that Paris became a magnet for ambitious young men, many of whom were attracted to Abelard's unorthodox teaching style. We can glimpse it through the audacious treatise called the *Sic et Non* ("Yes and No" or "So and Not So"). In this book, Abelard

Peter Abelard Critiques Theological Contradictions

In 1120, Abelard published the Sic et Non, *"So and Not So," a pioneering work of dialectic theology and a model for the development of later scholastic methods. In it, he arranged passages from Scripture as well as writings of the Church Fathers that had bearing on important doctrinal issues and that appeared to offer contradictory views. His eventual aim, as the prologue to this work indicates, was to reconcile these differences through the use of critical analysis.*

There are many seeming contradictions and even obscurities in the innumerable writings of the church fathers. Our respect for their authority should not stand in the way of an effort on our part to come at the truth. The obscurity and contradictions in ancient writings may be explained upon many grounds, and may be discussed without impugning the good faith and insight of the fathers. A writer may use different terms to mean the same thing, in order to avoid a monotonous repetition of the same word. Common, vague words may be employed in order that the common people may understand; and sometimes a writer sacrifices perfect accuracy in the interest of a clear general statement. Poetical, figurative language is often obscure and vague. . . .

Doubtless the fathers might err; even Peter, the prince of the apostles, fell into error; what wonder that the saints do not always show themselves inspired? The fathers did not themselves believe that they, or their companions, were always right. Augustine found himself mistaken in some cases and did not hesitate to retract his errors. He warns his admirers not to look upon his letters as they would upon the Scriptures, but to accept only those things which, upon examination, they find to be true.

All writings belonging to this class are to be read with full freedom to criticise, and with no obligation to accept unquestioningly; otherwise the way would be blocked to all discussion, and posterity be deprived of the excellent intellectual exercise of debating difficult questions of language and presentation. But an explicit exception must be made in the case of the Old and New Testaments. In the Scriptures, when anything strikes us as absurd, we may not say that the writer erred, but that the scribe made a blunder in copying the manuscripts, or that there is an error in interpretation, or that the passage is not understood. The fathers make a very careful distinction between the Scriptures and later works. They advocate a discriminating, not to say suspicious, use of the writings of their own contemporaries.

In view of these considerations, I have ventured to bring together various dicta of the holy fathers, as they came to mind, and to formulate certain questions which were suggested by the seeming contradictions in the statements. These questions ought to serve to excite tender readers to a zealous inquiry into truth and so sharpen their wits. The master key of knowledge is, indeed, a persistent and frequent questioning. Aristotle, the most clear-sighted of all the philosophers, was desirous above all things else to arouse this questioning spirit, for in his *Categories* he exhorts a student as follows: "It may well be difficult to reach a positive conclusion in these matters unless they be frequently discussed. It is by no means fruitless to be doubtful on particular points." By doubting we come to examine, and by examining we reach the truth.

Source: Peter Abelard, prologue to the *Sic et Non*, trans. James Harvey Robinson in *Readings in European History*, 2 vols. (Boston, MA: 1904), vol. 1, pp. 450–51.

Questions for Analysis

1. On what grounds can religious authorities be challenged, according to Abelard? What distinctions does he make between criticism of the Scriptures and of other authorities, and why?

2. Abelard did not attempt, in this work, to resolve the contradictions among his sources. Based on what you have learned, why would his project have seemed threatening to the authority of the Church?

gathered a collection of seemingly contradictory statements from the Church Fathers, organized around 150 key theological problems. Like his contemporary Gratian, the codifier of canon law, his ultimate ambition was to show that these divergent authorities could be reconciled—in this case, through the skillful use of dialectic.

Yet Abelard did not propose any solutions in the *Sic et Non*, and the work therefore caused grave concern. More inflammatory still were Abelard's meditations on the doctrine of the Trinity, which circulated in a book of lectures that was denounced and burned in 1121. Twenty years later, Bernard of Clairvaux had Abelard brought up on another charge of heresy at the Council of Soissons, where he was condemned a second time. Bernard's own mystic spirituality stood in direct opposition to Abelard's tireless quest for reasoned understanding. Abelard, for his part, found no solace in the monastic life beloved of Bernard: teaching was the activity that nurtured his faith. Luckily, teaching also expanded his fame and allowed him to train many pupils who eventually vindicated his teachings. After Abelard's death, his student Peter Lombard would ask the same fundamental questions that his master had done, but he took care to resolve the tensions which the *Sic et Non* had left open-ended. His great work, known as the *Sentences*, became the standard theological textbook of the medieval university, on which all aspirants to the doctorate were required to comment.

The Nature of the University

The emergence of the university—a unique public forum for advanced study, the questioning of received ideas, and the resolution of critical problems—was the natural extension of Abelard's teachings. His reputation and that of his students attracted many other intellectuals to Paris, and together they began to offer more varied and advanced instruction than anything obtainable in the average cathedral school. By 1200, this loose association of teachers had formed themselves into a *universitas* ("corporation" in Latin), and the resulting faculty began to collaborate in the higher academic study of the liberal arts, with a special emphasis on theology. At about the same time, the students of law based in Bologna came together in a *universitas* whose speciality was law.

Paris and Bologna provided the two basic models on which all medieval universities were based. In southern Europe, such universities as Montpellier, Salamanca, and Naples were patterned after Bologna, where the students themselves constituted the corporation: they hired the teachers, paid their salaries, and fined or discharged them for poor instruction. The universities of northern Europe, were like that of Paris: guilds of teachers who governed themselves and established fees for tuition and rules of conduct. They eventually embraced four faculties—liberal arts, theology, law, and medicine—each headed by a dean. By the end of the thirteenth century, the northern universities also expanded to include separate, semi-autonomous colleges, which usually provided housing for poorer students and were often endowed by a private benefactor. Over time, these colleges became centers of instruction as well as residences. The universities of Oxford and Cambridge still retain this pattern of organization: the colleges of which they are composed are semi-independent educational units.

Most of the academic degrees granted in our modern universities derive from those awarded in the Middle Ages, even though the actual courses of study are very different. No university curriculum included history or vernacular languages or anything like the social sciences prior to the nineteenth century. The medieval student was assumed to know Latin grammar thoroughly before entrance into a university; he had learned it in the primary (or "grammar") schools discussed above. On admission, he was required to spend about four years studying the basic liberal arts, which meant doing advanced work in Latin rhetoric and mastering the rules of logic. If he passed his examinations, he received the preliminary degree of bachelor of arts (the prototype of our BA). But to ensure himself a place in professional life he had to devote additional years to the pursuit of an advanced degree, the master of arts (MA) or the doctor of laws, medicine, or theology. This was accomplished by reading and commenting on standard texts such as Peter Lombard's *Sentences* (theology), Gratian's *Decretum* (law), or Aristotle's *Physics* (medicine). The requirements for the degree of doctor of philosophy (PhD) included even more specialized training, and those for the doctorate in theology were particularly arduous: by the end of the Middle Ages, it took twelve or thirteen years to earn this degree, over and above the eight years required to earn the MA. University degrees of all grades were recognized as standards of attainment and became pathways to a variety of careers.

Student life in medieval universities was rowdy. Because many students began their studies between the ages of twelve and fifteen, they were working through all the challenges of adolescence and early adulthood as they worked toward their degrees; this helps to explain the many injunctions against drunkenness, gambling, and other pursuits

THE SPREAD OF UNIVERSITIES. This map shows the geographical distribution of Europe's major universities and indicates the dates of their foundation. ▪ *Where were the first universities founded, and why?* ▪ Notice the number and location of the universities founded in the fourteenth and fifteenth centuries. ▪ *What pattern do you see in these later foundations?* ▪ *What might explain this?*

included among the canons of the Fourth Lateran Council. Moreover, university students generally believed that they constituted an independent and privileged community, apart from the local communities in which they lived. This often led to riots or even pitched battles between "town" and "gown."

That said, the time devoted to actual study was very intensive. Because books were prohibitively expensive, the primary mode of instruction was the lecture (Latin for "reading") in which a master would read an authoritative work aloud to his students and comment on it while the students took notes. As students advanced in their disciplines, they were expected to develop their own skills of analysis and interpretation in formal, public disputations. Advanced disputations could become extremely complex and abstract; sometimes they might last for days. Often they sparked public debates of great magnitude. The Ninety-five

Theses posted by Martin Luther in 1517 were actually a set of debating points organized along these lines (see Chapter 13).

Classical Thought, Arabic Learning and Scholastic Theology

The intellectual revolution of the Middle Ages was hugely indebted to the intellectual legacy of Islam, which was filtering into Europe via the Crusades. As we saw in Chapter 8, Muslim philosophers had been honing an array of different techniques to deal with the challenge of reconciling classical thought with Islamic belief, and these techniques contributed fundamentally to the development of Christian theology.

The most influential of these Muslim philosophers was Ibn Rushd, known to his Christian disciples as Averroès (*ah-VER-oh-ayz*, 1126–1198). Born in the Andalusian capital of Córdoba, in Muslim Spain, Averroès single-handedly advanced the study of Aristotelian logic by publishing a series of careful commentaries that sought to purge the Greek philosopher's works of all later (and confusing) influences and thus to allow for their proper analysis and interpretation. Soon translated from Arabic into Latin, these commentaries were received in western Christendom alongside new translations of Aristotle's texts (conveyed to Latin readers via Arabic) and so fundamentally influenced the way all subsequent European scholars understood Aristotle. The prestige of Averroès was so great that Christian intellectuals called him simply "the Commentator," just as they called Aristotle, "the Philosopher"—as if there were no others.

Ultimately, Averroès's learning was suppressed by the new Muslim dynasty that came to power in his lifetime, the Almohads, who demanded that all philosophical inquiry be subordinated to orthodox Muslim belief. After burning several of Averroès's works, they exiled him to Morocco. Thereafter, Islamic philosophy may have had more impact on Europe than in some Islamic kingdoms.

The greatest Jewish scholar of this period, Moses Maimonides (*my-MAHN-eh-dees*, c. 1137–1204), was also driven into exile by the Almohads; he traveled first to North Africa and then to Egypt, where he became famous as a teacher, jurist, and physician. Also like Averroès, he exercised great influence on Christian theologians through his systematic exposition of Jewish law in the *Mishneh Torah*, which earned him the nickname "the second Moses."

Because many aspects of the rabbinic tradition, Greek philosophy, and Arabic learning were not readily compatible with Christian faith, they therefore had to be filtered through

THE INFLUENCE OF AVERROÈS. This portrait of the Muslim polymath Averroès is featured in a fourteenth-century fresco celebrating the achievements of the Christian theologian Thomas Aquinas (c. 1225–1274). ■ *What does his inclusion in this context indicate about the relationship between Muslim and Christian intellectual traditions?*

the dialectical methods pioneered by Abelard and his pupils. By far the greatest accomplishments in this endeavor were made by Thomas Aquinas (1225–1274), who became the leading theologian at the University of Paris. As a member of the Dominican order, Thomas was committed to the defense of Catholic Christianity. But he also believed that the study of the physical world was a legitimate way of gaining knowledge of the divine, because God had created both the world and the many ways of knowing it. Imbued with a deep confidence in the value of both human reason and human experience, Thomas worked quietly and steadily on his two great summaries of theology, the *Summa contra Gentiles* (a compendium of the arguments for refuting non-Christian religions) and the comprehensive *Summa Theologiae*. The theology of the modern Roman Catholic Church still rests on Thomistic methods, doctrines, and principles.

COURTS, CITIES, AND CATHEDRALS

In the eleventh century, it was still possible to describe European society as divided among "those who worked, those who prayed, and those who fought." By 1200, such a description no longer bore much relationship to reality. New elites had emerged in the burgeoning cities of Europe. The wealthiest members of society were merchants and bankers, and aristocrats either had to best them (by engaging in trade themselves) or join them through strategic intermarriage. The aristocracy still fought, but so did upwardly mobile knights, urban crossbowmen, longbowmen, citizen militias, and peasant levies. Meanwhile, such lines as existed between town and countryside were easily crossed. And the pupils of the new schools made up a growing professional class that further defied neat categorization. We have noted that careers in the Church or royal bureaucracies were particularly open to self-made, educated men. But medieval courts and cities also provided opportunities for advancement.

From Chevalerie *to* Chivalry

The ennoblement of chivalry and the emergence of medieval court culture were connected to the growing wealth of Europe, the competition among monarchies, and contemporary developments in military technology exhibited

by the Crusades. In 1100, a knight could get by with a woolen tunic and leather corselet, a couple of horses, a groom, and a sword. A hundred years later, a knight needed full-body armor made of iron, a visored helmet, a broadsword, a spear, a shield, and several warhorses capable of carrying all this gear. By 1250, a knight also had to keep up appearances at tournaments, which meant maintaining a string of horses, sumptuous silk clothing for himself and caparisons for his steeds, and a retinue of liveried squires and servants. As the costs of a warrior's equipment rose, the number of men who could personally afford it declined dramatically, which made knightly display something increasingly prized by the nobility and upstart merchants alike. Knights who did not inherit or

MAKING A KNIGHTLY APPEARANCE. The costs of maintaining a chivalric lifestyle mounted steeply in the twelfth and thirteenth centuries, not only because a knight needed the most up-to-date equipment but because he was expected to cut a gallant figure at tournaments and to dazzle female spectators. This image is one of many sumptuous full-page illuminations in the Manesse Codex, made in Zurich in the early fourteenth century and preserving the compositions of earlier courtly poets.

gain sufficient property to support themsleves had to seek wealthy brides or the protection of a lord who could afford to equip them.

There were still other factors contributing to the prestige of knighthood. As part of a larger effort to control the violent competition for land and wealth, both secular and ecclesiastical rulers had begun to promote a new set of values that would come to redefine chivalry: bravery, loyalty, generosity, and civility. This new chivalry appealed to knights because it distinguished them from all the other "new men" who were emerging as powerful in this period, especially merchants and clerics. It also appealed to the nobility, whose status in this socially mobile world no longer depended on descent from high-born ancestors; families who *did* have such ancestors did not necessarily have the wealth to maintain a noble lifestyle, while many families who lived as "nobility" did not have prestigious ancestors.

What, then, was "nobility"? Was high status a matter of birth or was it the result of individual achievement? The amalgamation between knighthood and nobility offered something to those on both sides of the question. To the older aristocracy, it was a visible sign of good breeding. To professional warriors like many crusaders, and to the merchants and bureaucrats who later adopted its language and customs, chivalry offered a way of legitimizing social positions attained through bravery or skill. As a result, mounted combat—whether on the battlefield, in tournaments, or in the hunt—would remain the defining pastime of European gentlemen until the end of the First World War (see Chapter 24).

The Culture of the Court

Closely linked to this new ideology of chivalry was a new emphasis on *courtoisie*, "courtliness," the refined behavior appropriate to a court. This stemmed in part from practical necessity. Those great lords who could support a knightly retinue would have households full of energetic, lusty young men whose appetites had to be controlled. Hence, the emerging code of chivalry encouraged its adherents to view noble women as objects of veneration who could only be wooed and won by politesse, poetry, and valiant deeds; they had to be courted. Non-noblewomen, though, were fair game and could be taken by force if they did not yield willingly to the desires of a knight.

Whole new genres of poetry, song, and storytelling emerged in the twelfth century to celebrate the allied cultures of chivalry and courtliness. These genres stand in marked contrast to the older entertainments of Europe's warrior class, the heroic epics that are often the earliest literary artifacts of various vernacular languages: the Anglo-Saxon *Beowulf*, the *Song of Roland*, the Norse sagas, the German *Song of the Nibelungs*, and the Spanish *Poem of the Cid*. These epics portray a virile, violent society. Gore flows freely; skulls are cleaved; manly valor, honor, and loyalty are the major themes. If women are mentioned, it is often as prizes to be won in battle.

The courtly entertainments introduced in the twelfth century are very different in style, subject matter, and authorship. Many of them were addressed to, and commissioned by, women. In some cases, they were even composed by women or were composed in close collaboration with a female patron. An example of the former is the collections of *lais* (versified stories) of Marie de France, who was active during the reigns of Henry II and Eleanor of Aquitaine, and who may have been an abbess as well as a member of the Anglo-Norman aristocracy. An example of the latter is one of the Arthurian tales composed by Marie's contemporary, Chrétien de Troyes (KRAY-tyan duh TWAH, fl. 1165–90), who spent some time working under the patronage of Eleanor's daughter (by her first husband, Louis VII), Marie of Champagne.

Romances were engaging tales of love and adventure, often focusing on the exploits of King Arthur and his knights or some other heroic figure of the past, like Alexander the Great. But they were also attuned to the interests and concerns of women: threats to women's independence, enforced or unhappy marriages, disputed inheritances, fashion, fantasies of power. The heroine of one anonymous romance is a woman who dresses as a knight and travels the world performing valiant deeds. Other heroines accompany their husbands on Crusades or quests, or defend their castles against attack, or have supernatural powers. Following in Chrétien's footsteps, the German poets Wolfram von Eschenbach and Gottfried von Strassburg vied to produce romances that retained the scope and complexity of heroic epics while featuring women in strong, central roles: Wolfram's *Parzival*, the story of the search for the Holy Grail, and Gottfried's *Tristan*, which retold the Celtic story of the adulterous love between Tristan and Isolde. Both inspired the operatic reconceptions of Richard Wagner (1813–1883).

The poetic tradition initiated by the southern French troubadours and northern French trouvères (terms deriving from the verbs *trobar/trouver*: "to discover, to invent") also contributed to the culture of chivalry and inspired the work of German *minnesänger* ("love singers"). Much troubadour poetry displays sensitivity to feminine beauty and the natural world, and pays eloquent tribute to the political and sexual power of women. Take, for example, a lyric of Bernart de Ventadorn (c. 1135–1195), one of Eleanor's protégés:

> When leaves and grass are lush with renewed growth
> The beauty of my Lady blossoms forth . . .
> I am her slave, her vassal, she my lord;
> I pay her homage, hope to have a word
> Of kindness, or of love, exchanged for mine
> But she is cruel: she will not make a sign.

Other troubadour songs celebrated old-fashioned warlike virtues, as in the verses of Bernart's contemporary, Bertran de Born (c. 1140–1214), a friend of Eleanor's son Richard the Lionheart:

> It pleases me to hear the mirth and song
> Of birds, filling the wood the whole day long.
> But more it pleases me to see the fields
> All planted thick with tents, to see the shields
> And swords of my companions ranged for war,
> To hear the screams, to see the blood and gore.

To what extent do the entertainments of the court reflect the reality of noblewomen's status? Certainly, there were women throughout this period who wielded tremendous power, particularly in Scandinavia and parts of southern Europe, where women could inherit property, rule in their own right, and were treated as lords in fact and in name (as in Bernart's song). Queen Urraca ruled the combined kingdom of León-Castile from 1109 until 1126. Ermengarde of Narbonne (c. 1127–1197) ruled her strategically placed county from early adolescence to the time of her death. Eleanor remained sole ruler of Aquitaine throughout her long life, and she played a crucial role in the government of England at various times. The strong-willed Blanche of Castile (1188–1252), Eleanor's granddaughter, ruled France during the minority of her son Louis IX and again when he went on crusade.

Queens are not, of course, typical, but their activities in this period reflect some of the opportunities open to other well-born women—and the freedoms that set most western European women apart from their counterparts in the Byzantine and Muslim worlds. A striking symbol of this is the figure of the queen in the game of chess. In the Muslim courts where the game originated, the equivalent of the queen was a male figure, the king's chief minister, who could move only diagonally, and only one square at a time. In twelfth-century Europe, however, this piece became the queen. Eventually, she was the only figure powerful enough to move all over the board.

Urban Opportunities and Inequalities

In 1174, a cleric called William FitzStephen wrote a biography of his former employer, Thomas Becket, who had recently been canonized. In it, William went out of his way to extoll the urban culture of London that had produced this saintly man and other "men of superior quality," as well as all the splendid sights and pastimes to be had there: feasting, churchgoing, ice skating, bear baiting, plays, sports—and of course the pleasures of moneymaking. Towns were crucibles of activity, and as such became cultural powerhouses as well as economic ones. They were launching pads for the careers of ambitious men.

As we noted in Chapter 8, many of the towns that emerged in the eleventh century were governed by associations of citizens who undertook a wide variety of civic responsibilities. But urban governance was also apt to fall into the hands of oligarchs, a trend that became increasingly marked during the thirteenth century when the enormous wealth generated by some forms of commerce led to marked social inequalities, much as in the Greek poleis (see Chapter 3). In Italy, some cities even sought to control the resulting violence by turning to an outsider who would rule as a dictator for a (supposedly) limited term. Other cities adopted the model of Venice and became formal oligarchies, casting off all pretense to democracy. Some cities remained republics in principle, like Florence, but became increasingly oligarchical in practice. Aristocratic families lived in fortified towers surrounded by the houses of their supporters, and their rivalries often produced a violent culture of vendetta.

But even in places where town governance was controlled by a powerful few, there were many meaningful opportunities for collective activity. Urban manufacturing was regulated by professional associations known as guilds or (in some regions) confraternities. Guilds promoted the interests of their members by trying to preserve monopolies and limit competition. To these ends, terms of employment and membership were strictly regulated. If an apprentice or a journeyman worker (from the French *journée*, meaning "day" and, by extension, "day's work") wished to become a master, he had to produce a "masterpiece" to be judged by the masters of the guild. If the market was considered too weak to support additional master craftsmen, even a masterpiece would not secure a craftsman the coveted right to set up his own shop and thus earn enough to marry.

Illicit Love and the Code of Chivalry

Little is known about Marie de France, author of a series of popular verse tales that are among the earliest chivalric romances, but she may have been a nun or abbess living in the Anglo-Norman realm of Henry II and Eleanor of Aquitaine. The following excerpt is from her Lais, *adapted from stories told in the Franco-Celtic county of Brittany (Abelard's home).*

he Bretons, who lived in Brittany, were fine and noble people. In days gone by these valiant, courtly and noble men composed lays for posterity and thus preserved them from oblivion. . . . One of them, which I have heard recited, should not be forgotten. It concerns Equitan, a most courtly man, lord of Nantes, justiciary and king.

Equitan enjoyed a fine reputation and was greatly loved in his land. He adored pleasure and amorous dalliance: for this reason he upheld the principles of chivalry. Those who lack a full comprehension and understanding of love show no thought for their lives. Such is the nature of love that no one under its sway can retain command over reason. Equitan had a seneschal, a good knight, brave and loyal, who took care of his entire territory, governing it and administering its justice. Never, except in time of war, would the king have forsaken his hunting, his pleasures or his river sports, whatever the need might have been.

As his wedded wife the seneschal had a woman who was to bring great misfortune to the land. She was a lady of fine breeding and extremely beautiful with a noble body and good bearing. Nature had spared no pains when fashioning her: her eyes sparkled, her face and mouth were beautiful and her nose was well set. She had no equal in the kingdom, and the king, having often heard her praised, frequently sent her greetings and gifts. . . . He went hunting in her region on his own and on returning from his sport took lodging for the night in the place where the seneschal dwelt, in the very castle where the lady was to be found. He had ample occasion to speak with her, to express his feelings and display his fine qualities. He found her most courtly and wise, beautiful in body and countenance. . . .

That night he neither slept nor rested, but spent his time reproaching and reprimanding himself. "Alas," he said, "what destiny brought me to this region? Because of this lady I have seen, my heart has been overwhelmed by a pain so great that my whole body trembles. I think I have no option but to love her. Yet, if I did love her, I should be acting wrongly, as she is the seneschal's wife. I ought to keep faith with him and love him, just as I want him to do with me. . . ."

Source: From "Equitan," in *The Lais of Marie de France*, trans. Glyn S. Burgess and Keith Busby (Harmondsworth, UK: 1985), pp. 56–57.

Questions for Analysis

1. Despite the king's initial misgivings, he and the seneschal's wife eventually have an affair and plot to murder her husband, only to be caught in their own trap. Given this outcome, how would you interpret Marie's remarks about courtliness and "the code of chivalry"? What are the tenets of this code, according to the king?

2. What social tensions does this story reflect, and how might it shed light on historical realities? What moral might contemporary readers draw from it?

Most guilds were closed to Jews and Muslims and they also restricted the opportunities available to women, who had little influence over the terms and conditions under which they worked.

Guilds and confraternities were therefore instruments of economic control, but they were also important social, political, and cultural institutions. Most combined the functions of religious association, drinking club, and benevolent society, looking after members and their families in hard times, supporting the dependents of members who died, and helping to finance funerals. Guilds also empowered their members in much the same way that unions do today, providing them with political representation and raising their social status. In the wealthy town of Arras, there was even a guild of professional entertainers, the confraternity of jongleurs, which became the most powerful organization in the town by 1250.

The Varieties of Vernacular Entertainment

Like courts, towns fostered new kinds of vernacular entertainment in the twelfth and thirteenth centuries. Even the genres of Latin poetry, song, and drama produced in this period can be considered "vernacular" because they made use of vernacular elements (like rhyme, not a feature of classical Latin poetry), dealt with current events, and were popular with a wide audience. In one of Heloise's letters to Abelard, she recalls that he was so renowned for the beauty of his love songs that "every street and tavern resounded with my name." It's possible that some of Abelard's songs were sung in French but more probable that they used the edgy, colloquial Latin popular among the student singer-songwriters known as "goliards," which means something like "daredevils." Their lyrics celebrated the carefree life of the open road, the pleasures of drinking and dice, the joys of love, and the agonies of poverty.

Perhaps the genre most representative of urban culture is the fabliau, a "fable" or short story with a salacious, irreverent, or satirical twist. Fabliaux drew attention to the absurdities of urban life and lampooned the different types of people who were striving to reinvent themselves in the permissive world of the town: the oafish peasant, the effete aristocrat, the corrupt priest, the sex-starved housewife, the wily student, the greedy merchant, the con man. Gender-bending and reversals of fortune are common themes. In one fabliau, a young noble woman is forced by her impoverished father to marry a buffoonish

ROMANESQUE AND GOTHIC. Some distinguishing features of the Romanesque and Gothic styles are exhibited in these two churches, both dedicated to the Virgin Mary and built within a century of one another. On the left is the west front of the Church of Notre-Dame-la-Grande in Poitiers, the ancestral domain of Eleanor of Aquitaine. Constructed between 1135 and 1145, it featured rounded arches, strong stone walls, massive supporting pillars, and small windows. On the right is the cathedral of Notre-Dame at Reims in Champagne, built between 1220 and 1299. The emphasis on stolid, horizontal registers is here replaced by soaring, vertical lines. The gabled portals, pointed arches, and bristling pinnacles all accentuate the height of this structure, while the multitude of stained-glass windows—chiefly the enormous rose window—flood the vast interior with colored light.

shopkeeper who thereby gains a knighthood. To shame him, she dresses herself as a knight and beats her husband in a jousting match. In another, a priest tricks a poor peasant out of his cow by promising that God will reward him by doubling his "investment" in the work of the Church. When the cow breaks out of the priest's pasture and runs for home, she brings the priest's cow, too, and the peasant is delighted by the fulfillment of the promised miracle.

The Medieval Cathedral

The cathedrals constructed in Europe's major cities during this period exemplify the ways in which the cultural communities of the court, the schools, and the town came together. For although any cathedral-building campaign would have been spearheaded by a bishop looking to glorify his episcopal see, it could not be completed without the support of the nobility, the resources of the wealthy, the learning of trained theologians, and the talents of urban craftsmen. And cathedrals were not merely edifices: they were theaters for the performance of liturgy, music, drama, and preaching.

Cathedrals were not, in themselves, new: the seat of a bishop had long been known as his *cathedra*, his throne, and the church that housed it was the principal church of the diocese. But the size, splendor, and importance of cathedrals increased exponentially in the twelfth and thirteenth centuries alongside the growing power of the Church, the population of cities, and the wealth and knowledge necessary for their construction. Indeed, the cathedrals of this period are readily distinguishable from their predecessors by their architectural style, which came to be called "Gothic," while the style of earlier buildings is known as "Romanesque."

As the term suggests, Romanesque buildings use the basic elements of public architecture under the Roman Empire: the rounded arch, massive stone walls, and sturdy supporting columns. These features convey regularity and stability, and they also made churches places of refuge that could be fortified and defended in troubled times. By contrast, the structural elements of Gothic architecture are the pointed arch, groined and ribbed vaulting, and the flying buttress, an external support that strengthened the much thinner stone walls and enormous stained-glass windows whose light illuminated elaborate decorative programs that made the cathedral a microcosm of the medieval world and an encyclopedia of medieval knowledge.

These new Gothic cathedrals were not buildings that could be defended in wartime and, it was thought, would never have to be: they were manifestations of urban pride, expressions of practical and intellectual genius, and symbols of a triumphant and confident Church. Their builders would have been dismayed to learn that the modern term *Gothic* was actually intended to be derogatory, the name for art forms that Renaissance artists—who favored Roman models—considered barbaric (see Chapter 12). They would have been still more shocked to learn that cathedrals were among the first monuments targeted for destruction during the Reformation, the revolutions of the eighteenth and nineteenth centuries, and the wars of the twentieth. One of the prime examples of Gothic architecture, the cathedral dedicated to the Virgin Mary at Reims (shown on page 318), was largely destroyed during World War I; what the visitor sees today is a reconstruction.

CONCLUSION

A century ago, the American medievalist Charles Homer Haskins described the intellectual, religious, and cultural changes of this era as "the Renaissance of the twelfth century" and the beginning of northwestern Europe's enduring cultural prestige. A generation later, his student Joseph Strayer located "the medieval origins of the modern state" in this same period and, with them, the modern ideas of national sovereignty and national identity. In recent decades, the British medievalists R. I. Moore and Robert Bartlett have also argued that this era marks the beginning of the modern world, but not in positive ways. Moore sees the growth of strong institutions like the Church and the state as leading to "the formation of a persecuting society" in which governmental bureaucracies are used to identify, control, and punish groups of people deemed threatening to those in power through a never-ending "war on heresy." Bartlett views this era as the key phase in a brutal process of "conquest and colonization" visible in the eastern expansion of the Holy Roman Empire, the Norman conquest of England, the growth of papal power, the Crusades, and other movements.

Common to all of these paradigms is a recognition that the expansion of European power and influence that began around the year 1000 continued into the twelfth century and was consolidated in the thirteenth. By 1250, Europe had taken on the geographic, political, linguistic, and cultural characteristics that continue to define it today.

Whether or not a direct line runs between the developments of this period and the world in which we live, many European nations look to these centuries for their origins and for the monuments of their cultural heritage. Magna Carta is still cited as a foundational document of English law and the English constitutional monarchy, while the territories united under the rule of the French kings still form the nation of France. The doctrines crystallized in medieval canon law and scholastic theology have become the core doctrines of the Roman Catholic Church, and devotion to the Virgin Mary is still central to the piety of millions. The religious orders that emerged to educate and

After You Read This Chapter

Visit StudySpace for quizzes, additional review materials, and multimedia documents. wwnorton.com/web/westernciv18

REVIEWING THE OBJECTIVES

- The emerging monarchies of Europe shared certain features but differed from one another in significant ways. What were the major similarities and differences of kingship in England, France, and Iberia?

- How did the meaning and purposes of crusading change in the twelfth and thirteenth centuries?

- The growth of papal power made religion an important part of daily life for all Christians in unprecedented ways, but it also limited lay spirituality and the rights of non-Christians. How?

- Scholasticism was the method of teaching and learning fostered by medieval schools but it was also a method of debating and resolving problems. How did scholasticism assist in the reconciliation of classical and Christian thought?

- Why did the meaning of chivalry change in the twelfth century? What new literary genres and art forms of the High Middle Ages were fostered by courts, universities, and towns?

curb a burgeoning medieval population continue their ministries. The daughter houses of medieval monastic orders continue to proliferate in lands unknown to medieval people: Japan, Australia, New Zealand, the Americas. Students still pursue the degrees first granted in medieval universities, and those who earn them wear the caps and gowns of medieval scholars. Meanwhile, poets still aspire to the eloquence of troubadours, singers record the music of Hildegard, and Hollywood films are based on chivalric romances and the tragic love of Abelard and Heloise. It is difficult to tell where the Middle Ages end and the modern world begins.

PEOPLE, IDEAS, AND EVENTS IN CONTEXT

- What was at stake in the clash between **HENRY II** of England and **THOMAS BECKET**?
- What was **MAGNA CARTA** and why was it made? How did **PHILIP AUGUSTUS** consolidate royal authority in France, and why were the German emperors unable to do so?
- Why were the **CRUSADER STATES** short-lived and fragile? How did the **RECONQUESTA** continue the Crusades?
- What were the main goals of **INNOCENT III**? How did the **FRANCISCANS** and **DOMINICANS** advance his agend?
- How do the **CULT OF THE VIRGIN** and the careers of **HILDEGARD OF BINGEN** and **HELOISE** exemplify the ideals and realities of women's roles in the Church?
- What is **SCHOLASTICISM**? How did **THOMAS AQUINUS** respond to the influence of Classical and Muslim philosophies?
- Why were **PETER ABELARD**'s teachings condemned by the Church? In what sense can he be considered the founder of the **UNIVERSITY OF PARIS**?
- How did noblewomen like **ELEANOR OF AQUITAINE** contribute to the emergence of a new vernacular culture? What types of entertainment are characteristic of medieval cities?

THINKING ABOUT CONNECTIONS

- The growth of towns, monarchies, and the Church increased the degree of control that those in power could exercise; but this growth also increased access to education and new forms of social mobility. Is this a paradox, or are these two phenomena related?
- The U.S. Constitution is based on the legal principles and institutions that emerged in medieval England, but it also drew on Roman models. Which do you consider to be more influential, and why?
- Some historians have argued that the extent and methods of persecution discernible in the Middle Ages are unprecedented in the history of Western civilizations. How would you support or refute this thesis? For example, does the persecution of Jews in medieval Europe differ from their treatment under the neo-Assyrians and Chaldeans, or under the Roman Empire? Why or why not?

Before
You
Read
This
Chapter

The Medieval World, 1250–1350

CORE OBJECTIVES

- **DESCRIBE** the effects of the Mongol conquests.

- **IDENTIFY** the key characteristics of the medieval world system and the responses to it.

- **DEFINE** the concept of sovereignty and its importance in this era.

- **UNDERSTAND** the reasons for the papacy's loss of prestige.

- **EXPLAIN** the rapid spread of the Black Death in this historical context.

When Christopher Columbus set out to find a new trade route to the East, he carried with him two influential travel narratives written centuries before his voyage. One was *The Book of Marvels*, composed around 1350 and attributed to John de Mandeville, an English adventurer (writing in French) who claimed to have reached the far horizons of the globe. The other was Marco Polo's *Description of the World*, an account of that Venetian merchant's journey through the vast Eurasian realm of the Mongol Empire to the court of the Great Khan in China. He had dictated it to an author of popular romances around 1298, when both men (Marco Polo and his ghostwriter) were in prison—in Columbus's own city of Genoa, coincidentally. Both of these books were the product of an extraordinary era of unprecedented interactions among the peoples of Europe, Asia, and the interconnected Mediterranean world. And both became extraordinarily influential, inspiring generations of mercantile adventurers, ambitious pilgrims, and armchair travelers. Eventually, they would fuel the imaginations of those future mariners who launched a further age of discovery (see Chapter 12).

In many ways, these narratives were as fantastical as they were factual. That makes them problematic sources for historians to use, but it also makes them representative of an era that seemed wide open to every sort of influence. This was a time when ease of communication and commercial exchange made Western civilizations part of an interlocking network that potentially spanned the globe. Although this network would prove fragile in the face of a large-scale demographic crisis, the Black Death, it created a lasting impression of infinite possibilities. Indeed, it was only *because* of this network's connective channels that the Black Death was able to wreak such devastation in the years around 1350. Looking back, we can see the century leading up to this near-global crisis as the beginning of a new global age.

Europeans' integration with this widening world not only put them into contact with unfamiliar cultures and commodities, it opened up new ways of looking at the world they already knew. New artistic and intellectual responses are discernible in this era, as are a host of new inventions and technologies. At the same time, involvement in this wider world placed new pressures on long-term developments within Europe: notably the growing tensions among large territorial monarchies, and between these secular powers and the authority of the papacy. By the early fourteenth century, the papal court would literally be held hostage by the king of France. A few decades later, the king of England would openly declare his own claim to the French throne. The ensuing struggles for sovereignty would have a profound impact on the balance of power in Europe, and further complicate Europeans' relationships with one another and with their far-flung neighbors.

THE MONGOL EMPIRE AND THE REORIENTATION OF THE WEST

In our long-term survey of Western civilizations, we have frequently noted the existence of strong links between the Mediterranean world and the Far East. Trade along the network of trails known as the Silk Road can be traced far back into antiquity, and we have seen that such overland networks were extended by Europe's waterways and by the sea. But it was not until the late thirteenth century that Europeans were able to establish direct connections with India, China, and the so-called Spice Islands of the Indonesian archipelago. For Europeans, these connections would prove profoundly important, as much for their impact on the European imagination as for their economic significance. For the peoples of Asia, however, the more frequent appearance of Europeans was less consequential than the events that made these journeys possible: the rise of a new empire that encompassed the entire continent.

The Expansion of the Mongol Empire

The Mongols were one of many nomadic peoples inhabiting the vast steppes of Central Asia. Although closely connected with the Turkish populations with whom they frequently intermarried, the Mongols spoke their own distinctive language and had their own homeland, located to the north of the Gobi Desert in what is now known as Mongolia. Essentially, the Mongols were herdsmen whose daily lives and wealth depended on the sheep that provided shelter (sheepskin tents), woolen clothing, milk, and meat. But the Mongols were also highly accomplished horsemen and raiders. Indeed, it was to curtail their raiding ventures that the Chinese had fortified their Great Wall, many centuries before. Primarily, though, China defended itself from the Mongols by attempting to ensure that they remained internally divided, with their energies turned against each other.

In the late twelfth century, however, a Mongol chief named Temujin (c. 1162–1227) began to unite the various tribes under his rule. He did so by incorporating the warriors of each defeated tribe into his own army, gradually building up a large and terrifyingly effective military force. In 1206, his supremacy over all these tribes was reflected in his new title: Genghis Khan, from the Mongol words meaning "universal ruler." This new name also revealed wider ambitions, and in 1209 Genghis Khan began to direct his enormous army against the Mongols' neighbors. Taking advantage of the fact that China was then divided into three warring states, he launched an attack on the Chin Empire of the north, managing to penetrate deep into its interior by 1211. These initial attacks were probably looting expeditions rather than deliberate attempts at conquest, but the Mongols' aims were soon sharpened under Genghis Khan's successors. Shortly after his death in 1227, a full-scale invasion of both northern and western China was under way. In 1234, these regions also fell to the Mongols. By 1279, one of Genghis Khan's numerous grandsons, Kublai Khan, would complete the conquest by adding southern China to this empire.

For the first time in centuries, China was reunited, and under Mongol rule. It was also connected to western and central Asia in ways unprecedented in its long history, since Genghis Khan had brought crucial commercial cities and Silk Road trading posts (Tashkent, Samarkand, and Bukhara) into his empire. One of his sons, Ögedei (*EHRG-*

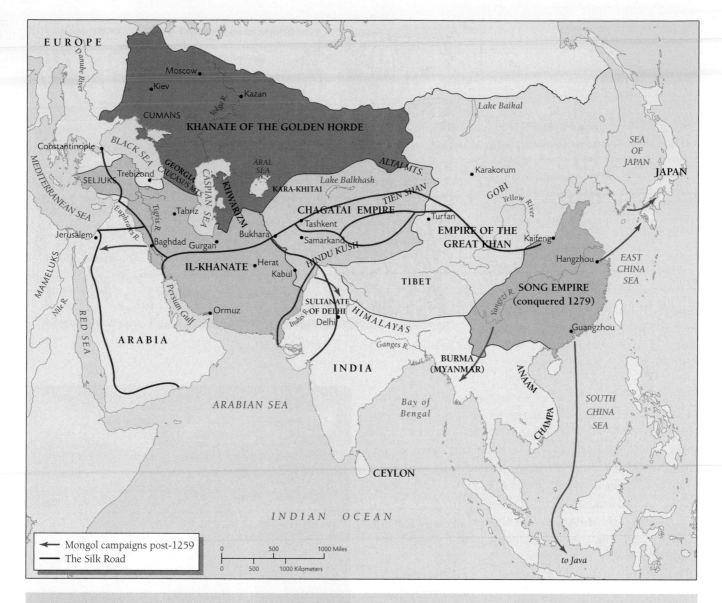

EUROPE · Danube River · Moscow · Kiev · Kazan · CUMANS · **KHANATE OF THE GOLDEN HORDE** · Lake Baikal · Constantinople · BLACK SEA · GEORGIA · CAUCASUS MTS. · ARAL SEA · ALTAI MTS. · Karakorum · SEA OF JAPAN · **JAPAN** · Trebizond · SELJUKS · CASPIAN SEA · KHWARIZM · Lake Balkhash · **KARA-KHITAI** · TIEN SHAN · GOBI · Yellow River · MEDITERRANEAN SEA · Euphrates R. · Tigris R. · Tabriz · **CHAGATAI EMPIRE** · Tashkent · Turfan · **EMPIRE OF THE GREAT KHAN** · Kaifeng · EAST CHINA SEA · Jerusalem · Baghdad · Gurgan · Bukhara · Samarkand · HINDU KUSH · Hangzhou · MAMELUKS · Nile R. · Persian Gulf · **IL-KHANATE** · Herat · Kabul · **TIBET** · **SONG EMPIRE** (conquered 1279) · Ormuz · **SULTANATE OF DELHI** · Delhi · Indus R. · HIMALAYAS · Guangzhou · RED SEA · ARABIA · Ganges R. · **INDIA** · **BURMA (MYANMAR)** · ANAM · CHAMPA · SOUTH CHINA SEA · ARABIAN SEA · Bay of Bengal · CEYLON · INDIAN OCEAN · to Java

Mongol campaigns post-1259
The Silk Road

0   500   1000 Miles
0   500   1000 Kilometers

THE STATES OF THE MONGOL EMPIRE. Like Alexander's, Genghis Khan's empire was swiftly assembled and encompassed vast portions of Europe and Asia. ▪ *How many different Mongol khanates were there after 1260, when Kublai Khan came to power, and were these domains mapped onto older divisions within Western civilizations?* ▪ *How might the Mongol occupation of the Muslim world have aided the expansion of European trade?* ▪ *At the same time, why would it have complicated the efforts of crusader armies in the Holy Land?*

uh-day), building on these achievements, laid plans for an even more far-reaching expansion of Mongol influence. Between 1237 and 1240, the Mongols under his command conquered the Russian capital at Kiev and then launched a two-pronged assault directed at the rich lands of the eastern European frontier. The smaller of the two Mongol armies swept through Poland toward Germany; the larger army went southwest toward Hungary. In April of 1241, the smaller Mongol force met a hastily assembled army of Germans and Poles at the battle of Liegnitz, where the two sides fought to a bloody standstill. Two days later, the larger Mongol army annihilated the Hungarian army at the river

Sajo. It could have moved even deeper into Europe after this important victory, but it withdrew when Ögedei Khan died in December of that same year.

Muscovy and the Mongol Khanate

As we have seen in previous chapters, the Russian capital at Kiev had fostered crucial diplomatic and trading relations with both western Europe and Byzantium, and with the Islamic Caliphate at Baghdad. That dynamic changed with the arrival of the Mongols, who shifted the locus of

THE BATTLE OF LIEGNITZ, 1241. This image from a fourteenth-century chronicle shows heavily armored knights from Poland and Germany (at right) confronting the swift-moving mounted archers of the Mongol cavalry. Mongol warriors often had the advantage over Europeans because their smaller, faster horses carried lighter loads and because the warriors themselves could shoot down their opponents at long range. ▪ *Which army appears to be gaining the upper hand here?*

power from Kiev to their own camp on the lower Volga River. This became known as the Khanate of the Golden Horde, an integral part of the larger Mongol Empire for 150 years. Its magnificent name evokes the impression made by tents that shone with wealth, some literally hung with cloth of gold. It derives from the Mongol word meaning "encampment" and the related Turkish word *ordu* ("army").

Initially, the Mongols ruled their Russian territories directly, installing their own administrative officials and requiring Russian princes to show their obedience to the Great Khan by traveling in person to the Mongol court in China. But after Kublai Khan's death in 1294, the Mongols began to tolerate the existence of several semi-independent principalities from which they demanded regular tribute. Kiev never recovered its dominant position, but one of these newer principalities would eventually form the core of a Russian state called Muscovy, centered on the duchy of Moscow. As the tribute-collecting center for the Mongol Khanate, Moscow received some protection against attack. Its dukes were even encouraged to absorb neighboring territories in this region, in order to increase Moscow's security. But this also meant that the Muscovite dukes could extend their powers even further without attracting too much attention from their Mongol overlords, whose power base was far away.

Compared to Kiev, Moscow's location was less advantageous for forging commercial contacts with the Baltic and Black Sea regions. Its direct ties with western Europe were also less developed, but this had little to do with geography. The Moscovites were staunchly loyal to the Orthodox

A MONGOL ROBE IN CLOTH OF GOLD. The majestic term *Khanate of the Golden Horde* captures both the power and the splendor of the Mongol warriors who conquered Rus' and many other lands. The robe depicted here dates from the late thirteenth or early fourteenth century and was made from cloth of gold: silk woven with gold (and sometimes silver) thread, a precious but surprisingly durable material that was also used for banners and even tents. A robe similar to this one was sold at auction in 2011, for nearly a quarter of a million dollars.

Church of Byzantium and had watched relations between the Latin West and the Greek East deteriorate drastically during the Crusades. They became openly hostile to western Europeans after Constantinople was captured and sacked by crusaders in 1204 (see Chapter 9), an event that led Moscovites to see themselves as the last remaining protectors of the Orthodox Roman Church. Eventually, as we shall see in Chapter 12, they would claim to be the rightful heirs of Roman imperial power.

The Making of the Mongol Ilkhanate

As Ögedei Khan moved into the lands of Rus' and eastern Europe, Mongol armies were also sent to subdue the vast territory that had been encompassed by the former Persian Empire, then by the empires of Alexander and Rome. Indeed, the strongest state in this region was known as the sultanate of Rûm, the Arabic word for "Rome." This was a Sunni Muslim sultanate that had been founded by the Seljuq Turks in 1077, just prior to the launching of the First Crusade, and which consisted of Anatolian provinces formerly belonging to the eastern Roman Empire. It had

successfully withstood waves of crusading aggression from Latin Christendom while capitalizing on the further misfortunes of Byzantium, taking over several key ports on the Mediterranean and the Black Sea while cultivating a flourishing overland trade as well. But in 1243, the Seljuqs of Rûm were forced to surrender to the Mongols, who had already succeeded in occupying what is now Iraq, Iran, portions of Pakistan and Afghanistan, and the Christian kingdoms of Georgia and Armenia.

Thereafter, the Mongols easily found their way into regions weakened by centuries of Muslim infighting and Christian crusading movements. Byzantium, as we noted in Chapter 9, had been fatally weakened by the Fourth Crusade: Constantinople was now controlled by the Venetians, and Byzantine successor states centered on Nicaea (in Anatolia) and Epirus (in northern Greece) were hanging on by their fingertips. The capitulation of Rûm left

THE MONGOL RULER OF MUSLIM PERSIA, HIS CHRISTIAN QUEEN, AND HIS JEWISH HISTORIAN. The *Compendium of Chronicles* by the Jewish-born Muslim polymath Rashid al-Din (1247–1318) exemplifies the pluralistic culture encouraged by Mongol rule: written in Persian (and often translated into Arabic), it celebrates the achievements of Hulagu Khan (1217–1265), a grandson of Genghis and brother of Kublai, who consolidated Persia and its neighboring regions into the Ilkhanate. But it also embeds those achievements within the long history of Islam. This image depicts Hulagu with his wife, Dokuz Khatun, who was a Turkic princess and a Christian. ■ *Why would Rashid al-Din have wanted to place the new Mongol dynasty in this historical context?*

remaining Byzantine possessions in Anatolia without a buffer, and most of these were absorbed by the Mongols. In 1261, the emperor Michael VIII Peleologus (r. 1259–82) managed to regain control of Constantinople and its immediate hinterland, but the depleted empire he ruled was ringed about by hostile neighbors. The crusader principality of Antioch, which had been founded in 1098, finally succumbed to the Mongols in 1268. The Mongols themselves were only halted in their drive toward Palestine by the Mamluk Sultanate of Egypt, established in 1250 and ruled by a powerful military caste of non-Arab Muslims.

All of these disparate territories came to be called the Ilkhanate, the "subordinate khanate," meaning that its Mongol rulers paid deference to the Great Khan. The first Ilkhan was Hulagu, brother of China's Kublai Khan. His descendants would rule this realm for another eighty years, eventually converting to Islam but remaining hostile toward the Mamluk Muslims, who remained their chief rivals.

The Pax Mongolica *and Its Price*

Although the Mongols' expansion of power into Europe had been checked in 1241, their combined conquests made them masters of territories that stretched from the Black Sea to the Pacific Ocean: one-fifth of the earth's surface, the largest land empire in history. Within this domain, no single Mongol ruler's power was absolute. Kublai Khan (1260–1294), who took the additional title *khagan*, or "Great Khan," never claimed to rule all Mongol khanates directly. In his own domain of China and Mongolia, his power was highly centralized and built on the intricate (and ancient) imperial bureaucracy of China; but elsewhere, Mongol governance was directed at securing a steady payment of tribute from subject peoples, which meant that local rulers could retain much of their power.

This distribution of authority made Mongol rule flexible and adaptable to local conditions—in this, it resembled the Persian Empire (see Chapter 3) and could also be regarded as building on Hellenistic and Roman examples. But if their empire resembled those of antiquity in some respects, the Mongol khans differed from most contemporary Western rulers in being highly tolerant of all religious beliefs. This was an advantage in governing peoples who observed an array of Buddhist, Christian, and Muslim practices, not to mention Hindus, Jews, and the many itinerant groups and individuals whose languages and beliefs reflect a melding of many cultures.

This acceptance of cultural and religious difference, alongside the Mongols' encouragement of trade and love of rich things, created ideal conditions for some merchants and artists. Hence, the term *Pax Mongolica* ("Mongol Peace") is often used to describe the century from 1250 to 1350, a period in many ways analogous to that fostered by the Roman Empire at its greatest extent (see Chapter 5). No such term should be taken at face value, however: this peace was bought at a great price. Indeed, the artists whose varied talents created the gorgeous textiles, utensils, and illuminated books prized by the Mongols were not all willing participants in a peaceful process. Many were captives or slaves subject to ruthless relocation. During more settled years, the Mongols would often transfer entire families and communities of craftsmen from one part of the empire to another, encouraging a fantastic blend of artistic techniques, materials, and motifs. The result was an intensive period of cultural exchange that might combine Chinese, Persian, Venetian, and Russian influences (among many others) in a single work of art. These objects encapsulate the many conflicting legacies of the Mongols' empire.

The Mongol Peace was also achieved at the expense of many flourishing Muslim cities that had preserved the heritage of even older civilizations and that were devastated or crippled during the bloody process of Mongol expansion. The city of Heràt, situated in one of Afghanistan's few fertile valleys and described by the Persian poet Rumi as "the pearl in the oyster," was entirely destroyed by Genghis Khan in 1221 and did not fully recover for centuries. Baghdad, the splendid capital of the Abbasid Caliphate and a haven for artists and intellectuals since the eighth century (Chapter 8), was savagely besieged and sacked by the Mongols in 1258. Amid many other atrocities, the capture of the city resulted in the destruction of the House of Wisdom, a library and research center where Muslim scientists, philosophers, and translators preserved classical knowledge (including the works of Plato and Aristotle) and advanced cutting-edge scholarship in such fields as mathematics, engineering, and medicine. Baghdad's destruction is held to mark the end of Islam's golden age, since the establishment of the Mongol Ilkhanate in Persia eradicated a continuous zone of Muslim influence that had blended cultures stretching from southern Spain and North Africa to India.

Bridging East and West

To facilitate the movement of people and goods within their empire, the Mongols began to control the caravan routes that led from the Mediterranean and the Black Sea through Central Asia and into China, policing bandits and making conditions safer for travelers. They also encouraged and streamlined trade by funneling many exchanges through the Persian city of Tabriz, on which both land and sea routes from China converged. These measures accelerated and intensified the contacts possible between the Far East and the West. Prior to Mongol control, such commercial networks had been inaccessible to most European merchants. The Silk Road was not so much a highway as a tangle of trails and trading posts, and there were few outsiders who understood its workings. Now travelers at both ends of the route found their way smoothed.

Among the first travelers from the West were Franciscan missionaries whose journeys were bankrolled by European rulers. In 1253, William of Rubruck was sent by King Louis IX of France as his ambassador to the Mongol court, with letters of introduction and instructions to make a full report of his findings. Merchants quickly followed. The most famous of these are three Venetians: the brothers Niccolò and Matteo Polo, and Niccolò's son, Marco (1254–1324). Marco Polo's account of his travels (which began when he was sev-

enteen) includes a report of his twenty-year sojourn in the service of Kublai Khan and the story of his journey home through the Spice Islands, India, and Persia. As we noted above, this book had an enormous effect on the European imagination; Christopher Columbus's copy still survives.

Even more impressive in scope than Marco's travels are those of the Muslim adventurer Ibn Battuta (1304–1368), who left his native Morocco in 1326 to go on the sacred pilgrimage to Mecca—but then kept going. By the time he returned home in 1354, he had been to China and sub-Saharan Africa as well as to the ends of both the Muslim and Mongolian worlds: a journey of over 75,000 miles.

Yet the window of opportunity that made such journeys possible was relatively narrow. By the middle of the fourteenth century, hostilities among and within various components of the Mongol Empire were making travel along the Silk Road perilous. The Mongols of the Ilkhanate, who dominated the ancient trade routes that ran through

THE MEDIEVAL WORLD SYSTEM, c. 1300. At the turn of the fourteenth century, Western civilizations were more closely connected to one another and to the rest of the world than ever before: waterways and overland routes stretched from Greenland to the Pacific coast of Southeast Asia. ▪ *How has Europe's relationship with its neighbors changed as a result of its integration into this wider world?* ▪ *How might we need to see seemingly marginal territories (like Rus' or Hungary, Scotland or Norway) as central to one or more interlocking components of this system?*

VENETIAN AMBASSADORS TO THE GREAT KHAN. Around 1270, the Venetian merchants Niccolò and Matteo Polo returned to Europe after their first prolonged journey through the empire of the Great Khan, bearing with them an official letter to the Roman pope. This image, from a manuscript of Marco Polo's *Description of the World*, shows his father and uncle at the moment of their arrival in the Great Khan's court, to which they have seemingly brought a Christian cross and a Bible. ▪ *Based on what you've learned about the Mongols and the medieval world, is it plausible that the Polo brothers would have carried these items with them?*

Persia, came into conflict with merchants from Genoa who controlled trade at the western ends of the Silk Road, especially in the transport depot of Tabriz. Mounting pressures finally forced the Genoese to abandon Tabriz, thereby breaking one of the major links in the commercial chain forged by the Mongol Peace. Then, in 1346, the Mongols of the Golden Horde besieged the Genoese colony at Caffa on the Black Sea. This event simultaneously disrupted trade while serving as a conduit for the Black Death, which passed from the Mongol army to the Genoese defenders, who returned with it to Italy (see below).

Over the next few decades, the European economy would struggle to overcome the devastating effects of the massive depopulation caused by plague, which made recovery from these setbacks slower and harder. In the meantime, in 1368, the last Mongol rulers of China were overthrown. Most Westerners were now denied access to its borders, while the remaining Mongol warriors were restricted to cavalry service in the imperial armies of the new Ming dynasty. The conditions that had fostered an integrated trans-Eurasian cultural and commercial network were

no longer sustainable. Yet the view of the world that had been fostered by Mongol rule continued to exercise a lasting influence. European memories of the Far East would be preserved and embroidered, and the dream of reestablishing close connections between Europe and China would survive to influence a new round of commercial and imperial expansion in the centuries to come.

THE EXTENSION OF EUROPEAN COMMERCE AND SETTLEMENT

Western civilizations' increased access to the riches of the Far East during the period of the Pax Mongolica ran parallel to a number of ventures that were extending Europeans' presence in the Mediterranean and beyond it. These endeavors were both mercantile and colonial, and in many cases resulted in the control of strategic trade routes or islands by representatives of a single adventurous state.

The language of crusading, with which we have become familiar, now came to be applied to these economic and political initiatives, whose often violent methods could be justified on the grounds that they were supporting papally sanctioned Christian causes. To take one prominent example, the strategic goal of the Crusades that targeted North Africa in this era was to cut the economic lifelines that supported Muslim settlements in the Holy Land. Yet the only people who stood to gain from this were the merchants who dreamed of controlling the commercial routes that ran through Egypt, not only those that connected North Africa to the Silk Road but the conduits of the sub-Saharan gold trade.

The Quest for African Gold

The European trade in African gold was not new. It had been going on for centuries, facilitated by Muslim middlemen whose caravans brought a steady supply from the Niger River to the North African ports of Algiers and Tunis. In the early thirteenth century, rival bands of merchants from Catalonia and Genoa had established trading colonies in Tunis to expedite this process, exchanging woolen cloth from northern Europe for both North African grain and sub-Saharan gold.

But the medieval demand for gold accelerated during the late thirteenth and fourteenth centuries and could not be satisfied by these established trading relationships. The luxuries coveted by Europeans were now too costly to be bought solely with bulk goods, which were in any case a cumbersome medium of exchange. Although precious textiles (usually silk) were a form of wealth valued by the Mongols, the burgeoning economy of the medieval world demanded a reliable and abundant supply of more portable currency. Silver production, which had enabled the circulation of coinage in Europe, fell markedly during the 1340s as Europeans reached the limits of their technological capacity to extract silver ore from deep mines. This shortfall would lead to a serious cash-flow problem, since more European silver was moving east than could now be replenished from extant sources.

Gold therefore represented an obvious alternative currency for large transactions, and in the thirteenth century some European rulers began minting gold coins. But Europe itself had few natural gold reserves. To maintain and expand these currencies, new sources of gold were needed. The most obvious source was Africa, especially Mali and Ghana—which was called "the Land of Gold" by Muslim geographers.

Models of Mediterranean Colonization: Catalonia, Genoa, and Venice

The heightened European interest in the African gold trade, which engaged the seafaring merchants of Genoa and Catalonia in particular, coincided with these merchants' creation of entrepreneurial empires in the western Mediterranean. During the thirteenth century, Catalan adventurers conquered and colonized a series of western Mediterranean islands, including Majorca, Ibiza, Minorca, Sardinia, and Sicily. Except in Sicily, which already had a large and diverse population that included many Christians (see Chapter 8), the pattern of Catalan conquest was largely the same on all these islands: expulsion or extermination of the existing population, usually Muslim; the extension of economic concessions to attract new settlers; and a heavy reliance on slave labor to produce foodstuffs and raw materials for export.

These Catalan colonial efforts were mainly carried out by private individuals or companies operating under royal charters; they were not actively sponsored by the state. They therefore contrast strongly with the established colonial practices of the Venetian maritime empire, whose strategic ventures were focused mainly on the eastern Mediterranean, where the Venetians dominated the trade in spices and silks. Venetian colonies were administered directly by the city's rulers or their appointed colonial governors. These colonies included long-settled civilizations like Greece, Cyprus, and the cities of the Dalmatian coast, meaning that Venetian administration laid just another layer on top of many other economic, cultural, and political structures.

The Genoese, to take yet another case, also had extensive interests in the western Mediterranean, where they traded bulk goods such as cloth, hides, grain, timber, and sugar. They too established trading colonies, but these tended to consist of family networks that were closely integrated with the peoples among whom they lived, whether in North Africa, Spain, or the shores of the Black Sea.

From the Mediterranean to the Atlantic

For centuries, European maritime commerce had been divided between this Mediterranean world and a very different northeastern Atlantic world, which encompassed northern France, the Low Countries, the British Isles, and Scandinavia. Starting around 1270, however, Italian merchants began to sail through the Straits of Gibraltar and

Two Travel Accounts

Two of the books that influenced Columbus and his contemporaries were travel narratives describing the exotic worlds that lay beyond Europe: worlds that may or may not have existed as they are described. The first excerpt below is taken from the account dictated by Marco Polo of Venice in 1298. The young Marco had traveled overland from Constantinople to the court of Kublai Khan in the early 1270s, together with his father and uncle. He became a gifted linguist, and remained at the Mongol court until the early 1290s, when he returned to Europe after a journey through Southeast Asia, Indonesia, and the Indian Ocean. The second excerpt is from the Book of Marvels attributed to John de Mandeville. This is an almost entirely fictional account of wonders that also became a source for European ideas about Southeast Asia. This particular passage concerns a legendary Christian figure called Prester ("Priest") John, who is alleged to have traveled to the East and become a great ruler.

Marco Polo's Description of Java

Departing from Ziamba, and steering between south and south-east, fifteen hundred miles, you reach an island of very great size, named Java. According to the reports of some well-informed navigators, it is the greatest in the world, and has a compass above three thousand miles. It is under the dominion of one king only, nor do the inhabitants pay tribute to any other power. They are worshipers of idols.

The country abounds with rich commodities. Pepper, nutmegs, spikenard, galangal, cubebs, cloves and all the other valuable spices and drugs, are the produce of the island; which occasion it to be visited by many ships laden with merchandise, that yields to the owners considerable profit.

The quantity of gold collected there exceeds all calculation and belief. From thence it is that . . . merchants . . . have imported, and to this day import, that metal to a great amount, and from thence also is obtained the greatest part of the spices that are distributed throughout the world. That the Great Khan [Kublai] has not brought the island under subjection to him, must be attributed to the length of the voyage and the dangers of the navigation.

Source: *The Travels of Marco Polo*, trans. William Marsden, rev. and ed. Manuel Komroff (New York: 1926), pp. 267–68.

John de Mandeville's Description of Prester John

This emperor Prester John has great lands and has many noble cities and good towns in his realm and many great, large islands. For all the country of India is separated into islands by the great floods that come from Paradise, that divide the land into many parts. And also in the sea he has many islands. . . .

on up to the wool-producing regions of England and the Low Countries. This was a step toward the extension of Mediterranean patterns of commerce and colonization into the Atlantic Ocean. Another step was the discovery (or possibly the rediscovery) of the Atlantic island chains known as the Canaries and the Azores, which Genoese sailors reached in the fourteenth century.

Efforts to colonize the Canary Islands, and to convert and enslave their inhabitants, began almost immediately. Eventually, the Canaries would become the focus of a new wave of colonial settlement sponsored by the Portuguese, and the base for Portuguese voyages down the west coast of Africa. They would also be the jumping-off point from which Christopher Columbus would sail

This Prester John has under him many kings and many islands and many varied people of various conditions. And this land is full good and rich, but not so rich as is the land of the Great Khan. For the merchants do not come there so commonly to buy merchandise as they do in the land of the Great Khan, for it is too far to travel to. . . .

[Mandeville then goes on to describe the difficulties of reaching Prester John's lands by sea.]

This emperor Prester John always takes as his wife the daughter of the Great Khan, and the Great Khan in the same way takes to wife the daughter of Prester John. For these two are the greatest lords under the heavens.

In the land of Prester John there are many diverse things, and many precious stones so great and so large that men make them into vessels such as platters, dishes, and cups. And there are many other marvels there that it would be too cumbersome and too long to put into the writing of books. But of the principal islands and of his estate and of his law I shall tell you some part.

This emperor Prester John is Christian and a great part of his country is Christian also, although they do not hold to all the articles of our faith as we do. . . .

And he has under him 72 provinces, and in every province there is a king. And these kings have kings under them, and all are tributaries to Prester John.

And he has in his lordships many great marvels. For in his country is the sea that men call the Gravelly Sea, that is all gravel and sand without any drop of water. And it ebbs and flows in great waves as other seas do, and it is never still. . . . And a three-day journey from that sea there are great mountains out of which flows a great flood that comes out of Paradise. And it is full of precious stones without any drop of water. . . .

He dwells usually in the city of Susa [in Persia]. And there is his principal palace, which is so rich and so noble that no one will believe the report unless he has seen it. And above the chief tower of the palace there are two round pommels of gold and in each of them are two great, large rubies that shine full brightly upon the night. And the principal gates of his palace are of a precious stone that men call sardonyxes [a type of onyx], and the frames and the bars are made of ivory.

And the windows of the halls and chambers are of crystal. And the tables upon which men eat, some are made of emeralds, some of amethyst, and some of gold full of precious stones. And the legs that hold up the tables are made of the same precious stones. . . .

Source: *Mandeville's Travels*, ed. M. C. Seymour (Oxford: 1967), pp. 195–99 (language modernized from Middle English by R. C. Stacey).

Questions for Analysis

1. What does Marco Polo want his readers to know about Java, and why? What does this suggest about the interests of these intended readers?

2. What does Mandeville want his readers to know about Prester John and his domains? Why are these details so important?

3. Which of these accounts seems more trustworthy, and why? Even if we cannot accept one or both at face value, what insight do they give us into the expectations of Columbus and the other European adventurers who relied on these accounts?

westward across the Atlantic Ocean in the hope of reaching Asia (see Chapter 12).

There was also a significant European colonial presence in the northern Atlantic, and had been for centuries. Viking settlers had begun to colonize Greenland in the late tenth century, and around 1000 had established a settlement in a place they called Vinland: the coast of Newfoundland in present-day Canada. According to the sagas that tell the story of these explorations, written down in the late twelfth and thirteenth centuries, a band of adventurers led by Leif Eiriksson had intended to set up a permanent colony there. Numerous expeditions resulted in the construction of houses, a fortification, and even attempts to domesticate livestock transported from Scandinavia. Yet North America

THE CHURCH AT HVALSEY, GREENLAND. Located on the southern tip of Greenland, Hvalsey was originally a farmstead established in the late tenth century by the uncle of Eirik the Red, father of the explorer Leif. The church at Hvalsey, pictured here, was built in the twelfth century and would have been roofed with turf. It was the site of the last documented event in the history of Norse settlement on the island, a wedding that took place in 1408. By that time, the population had largely died out due to starvation and disease.

did not become home to a permanent European population at this time; the sagas report that relations with indigenous peoples were fraught, and there may have been other factors hindering settlement.

However, Norse settlers did build a viable community on Greenland, which eventually formed part of the kingdom of Norway. This was facilitated by the warming of the earth's climate between 800 and 1300—the same phenomenon that partly enabled the agricultural revolution discussed in Chapter 8. For several centuries, these favorable climatic conditions made it possible to sustain some farming activities on the southern coastline of that huge island, supplemented by fishing, hunting, and foraging. But with the gradual cooling of the climate in the fourteenth century, which caused famines even in the rich farmlands of Europe, this fragile ecosystem was gradually eroded and the Greenlanders died out.

WAYS OF KNOWING AND DESCRIBING THE WORLD

The success of European commercial and colonial expansion in this era both drove and depended on significant innovations in measuring and mapping. It also coincided with intellectual, literary, and artistic initiatives that aimed to capture and describe the workings of this wider world, and to imagine its celestial (or infernal) counterparts.

Economic Tools: Balance Sheets, Banks, Charts, and Clocks

The economic boom that resulted from the integration of European and Asian commerce called for the refinement of existing business models and accounting techniques. New forms of partnership and the development of insurance contracts helped to minimize the risks associated with long-distance trading. Double-entry bookkeeping, widely used in Italy by the mid-fourteenth century, gave merchants a much clearer picture of their profits and losses by ensuring that both credits and debits were clearly laid out in parallel columns, a practice that facilitated the balancing of accounts. The Medici family of Florence established branches of their bank in each of the major cities of Europe and were careful that the failure of one would not bankrupt the entire firm, as earlier branch-banking arrangements had done. Banks also experimented with advanced credit techniques borrowed from Muslim and Jewish financiers,

DEVIL WITH EYEGLASSES. Spectacles were most commonly worn by those who made a living by reading and writing, notably bureaucrats and lawyers. In this conceptualization of hell, the devil charged with keeping track of human sin wears eyeglasses.
■ *What might this image reveal about popular attitudes toward record-keeping and the growing legal and administrative bureaucracies of the later Middle Ages?*

allowing their clients to transfer funds without any real money changing hands—and without endangering their capital by carrying it with them. Such transfers were carried out by written receipts: the direct ancestors of the check, the money order, and the currency transfer.

Other late medieval technologies kept pace in different ways with the demands for increased efficiency and accuracy. Eyeglasses, first invented in the 1280s, were perfected in the fourteenth century, extending the careers of those who made a living by reading, writing, and accounting. The use of the magnetic compass helped ships sail farther away from land, making longer-distance Atlantic voyages possible for the first time. And as more and more mariners began to sail waters less familiar to them, pilots began to make and use special charts that mapped the locations of ports. Called *portolani*, these charts also took note of prevailing winds, potential routes, good harbors, and known perils.

Among the many implements of modern daily life invented in this era, the most familiar are clocks. Mechanical clocks came into use shortly before 1300 and proliferated immediately thereafter. They were too large and expensive for private purchase, but towns vied with one another to install them in prominent public buildings, thus advertising municipal wealth and good governance. Mechanical timekeeping had two profound effects. One was the further stimulation of interest in complex machinery of all sorts, an interest already awakened by the widespread use of mills in the eleventh and twelfth centuries (see Chapter 8).

More significant was the way that clocks regulated daily life. Until the advent of clocks, time was flexible. Although days had been *theoretically* divided into hours, minutes, and seconds since the time of the Sumerians (see Chapter 1),

PORTOLAN CHART. Accurate mapping was essential to the success of maritime colonial ventures in the thirteenth and fourteenth centuries. The chart shown here is the oldest surviving example of a map used by mariners to navigate between Mediterranean ports. (The word *portolan* is used to describe such charts.) It dates from the end of the thirteenth century, and its shape clearly indicates that it was made from an animal hide. Although parchment was extremely durable, it would have slowly worn away owing to prolonged exposure to salt water and other elements—hence the rarity of this early example.

there had never been a way of mapping these temporal measurements onto an actual day. Now, clocks relentlessly divided time into exact units, giving rise to new expectations about labor and productivity. People were expected to start and end work "on time," to make the most of the time spent at work, and even to equate time with money. Like the improvements in bookkeeping, timekeeping made some kinds of work more efficient, but it also created new tensions and obsessions.

Knowledge of the World and of God

In the mid-thirteenth century, Thomas Aquinas had constructed a theological view of the world as rational, organized, and comprehensible to the inquiring human mind (see Chapter 9). Confidence in this picture began to wane in the fourteenth century, even before the Black Death posed a new challenge to it. Philosophers such as William of Ockham (d.c. 1348), an English member of the Franciscan order, denied that human reason could prove fundamental theological truths such as the existence of God. He argued that human knowledge of God, and hence salvation, depends entirely on what God himself has chosen to reveal through scripture. Instead, Ockham urged humans to investigate the natural world and to better understand its laws—without positing any necessary connection between the observable properties of nature and the unknowable essence of divinity.

This philosophical position, known as nominalism, had its roots in the philosophy of Plato (see Chapter 4) and has had an enormous impact on modern thought. The nominalists' distinction between the rational comprehensibility of the real world and the spiritual incomprehensibility of God encourages investigation of nature without reference to supernatural explanations: one of the most important foundations of the modern scientific method (see Chapter 16). Nominalism also encourages empirical observation, since it posits that knowledge of the world should rest on sensory experience rather than abstract theories. The philosophical principles laid down by these observers of the medieval world are thus fundamental to modern science.

Creating God's World in Art

Just as a fascination with the natural world informed developments in medieval science, the artists of this era were paying close attention to the way plants, animals, and human beings really looked. Carvings of leaves and flowers were increasingly made from direct observation and are clearly recognizable to modern botanists as distinct

Vikings Encounter the Natives of North America

Although Norse voyagers had explored and settled the coast of Newfoundland around the year 1000, written accounts of these exploits were not made or widely circulated until the thirteenth century. The excerpt below comes from one of these narrative histories, the Grænlendinga Saga *("Greenlanders' Saga"). Its hero is Thorfinn Karlsefni, a Norwegian adventurer who arrives in Greenland and marries Gudrid, the twice-widowed sister-in-law of the explorer Leif Eiriksson. Leif had established the original colony of Vinland, but had since returned to Greenland.*

here was still the same talk about Vinland voyages as before, and everyone, including [his wife] Gudrid, kept urging Karlsefni to make the voyage. In the end he decided to sail and gathered a company of sixty men and five women. He made an agreement with his crew that everyone should share equally in whatever profits the expedition might yield. The took livestock of all kinds, for they intended to make a permanent settlement there if possible.

Karlsefni asked Leif if he could have the houses in Vinland; Leif said that he was willing to lend them, but not to give them away.

They put to sea and arrived safe and sound at Leif's Houses and carried their hammocks ashore. Soon they had plenty of good supplies, for a fine big rorqual* was driven ashore; they went down and cut it up, and so there was no shortage of food.

The livestock were put out to grass, and soon the male beasts became very frisky and difficult to manage. They had brought a bull with them.

Karlsefni ordered timber to be felled and cut into lengths for a cargo for the ship, and it was left out on a rock to season. They made use of all the natural resources of the country that were available, grapes and game of all kinds and other produce.

The first winter passed into summer, and then they had their first encounter with Skrælings,[†] when a great number of them came out of the wood one day. The cattle were grazing near by and the bull began to bellow and roar with great vehemence. This terrified the Skrælings and they fled, carrying their packs which contained furs and sables and pelts of all kinds. They made for Karlsefni's houses and tried to get inside, but Karlsefni had the doors barred against them. Neither side could understand the other's language.

Then the Skrælings put down their packs and opened them up and offered their contents, preferably in exchange for weapons; but Karlsefni forbade his men to sell arms. Then he hit on the idea of telling the women to carry milk out to the Skrælings, and when the Skrælings saw the milk they wanted to buy nothing else. And so the outcome of their trading expedition was that the Skrælings carried their purchases away in their bellies, and left their packs and furs with Karlsefni and his men.

After that, Karlsefni ordered a strong wooden palisade to be erected round the houses, and they settled in.

---

species. Statues of humans also became more realistic in their portrayals of facial expressions and bodily proportions. According to a story in circulation around 1290, a sculptor working on a likeness of the German emperor allegedly made a hurried return trip to study his subject's face a second time, because he'd heard that a new wrinkle had appeared on the emperor's brow.

This trend toward naturalism extended to manuscript illumination and painting. The latter was, to a large extent, a new art. As we saw in Chapter 1, wall paintings are among the oldest forms of artistic expression in human history, and throughout antiquity and the Middle Ages artists had decorated the walls of public and private buildings with frescoes (paintings executed on "fresh"—wet—plaster). But in addition to frescoes, Italian artists in the thirteenth century began to adapt the techniques used by icon painters in Byzantium, making freestanding pictures on pieces of wood or canvas using tempera (pigments mixed with water and natural gums). Because these altarpieces, devotional images, and portraits were portable, they were also more commercial. As long as artists could afford the necessary materials, they did not have to wait for specific commissions. This meant that they had more freedom to choose their subject matter and to put an individual stamp on their

About this time Karlsefni's wife, Gudrid, gave birth to a son, and he was named Snorri.

Early next winter the Skrælings returned, in much greater numbers this time, bringing with them the same kind of wares as before. Karlsefni told the women, 'You must carry out to them the same produce that was most in demand last time, and nothing else.' . . .

[B]ut a Skræling was killed by one of Karlsefni's men for trying to steal some weapons. The Skrælings fled as fast as they could, leaving their clothing and wares behind . . .

'Now we must devise a plan,' said Karlsefni, 'for I expect they will pay us a third visit, and this time with hostility and in greater numbers. This is what we must do: ten men are to go out on the headland here and make themselves conspicuous, and the rest of us are to go into the wood and make a clearing there, where we can keep our cattle when the Skrælings come out of the forest. We shall take our bull and keep him to the fore.'

The place where they intended to have their encounter with the Skrælings had the lake on one side and the woods on the other.

Karlsefni's plan was put into effect, and the Skrælings came right to the place that Karlsefni had chosen for the battle. The fighting began, and many of the Skrælings were killed. There was one tall and handsome man among the Skrælings and Karlsefni reckoned that he must be their leader. One of the Skrælings had picked up an axe, and after examining it for a moment he swung it at a man standing beside him, who fell dead at once. The tall man then took hold of the axe, looked at it for a moment, and then threw it as far as he could out into the water. Then the Skrælings fled into the forest as fast as they could, and that was the end of the encounter.

Karlsefni and his men spent the whole winter there, but in the spring he announced that he had no wish to stay there any longer and wanted to return to Greenland. They made ready for the voyage and took with them much valuable produce, vines and grapes and pelts. They put to sea and reached Eiriksfjord safely and spent the winter there.

*A kind of whale, the largest species of which is a blue whale.

†A Norse word meaning "savages," applied to the different indigenous peoples of Greenland and of North America.

Questions for Analysis

1. What policies do the Norse settlers adopt toward the native peoples they encounter on the coast of New-foundland? How effective are they?

2. Given their extensive preparations for colonization and the success of their early efforts, why do you think that Karlsefni and his companions abandoned their settlement in North America? Are there clues discernible in the text?

3. Compare this encounter to the sources describing other interactions between Europeans and the indigenous inhabitants of the New World after 1492 (see Chapters 12 and 14). How do you account for any similarities? What are some key differences?

work—one of the reasons why we know the names of many more artists from this era.

One of these, Giotto di Bondone of Florence (c. 1267–1337), painted both walls and portable wooden panels. Like some of his contemporaries, Giotto (*gee-OHT-toh*) was pre-eminently an imitator of nature. Not only do his human beings and animals look lifelike, they seem to do natural things. When Christ enters Jerusalem on Palm Sunday, boys climb trees to get a better view; when Saint Francis is laid out in death, someone checks to see whether he has really received the *stigmata*, the marks of Christ's wounds; and when the Virgin's parents, Joachim and Anna, meet after a long separation, they embrace and kiss one another tenderly. Although many of the artists who came after Giotto moved away from naturalism, this style would become the norm by 1400. It is for this reason that Giotto is often regarded as the first painter of the Renaissance (see Chapter 11).

A Vision of the World We Cannot See

One of Giotto's exact contemporaries had a different way of capturing the spiritual world in a naturalistic way, and he worked in a different medium. Dante Alighieri (1265–1321)

Seals: Signs of Identity and Authority

For much of human history, applying a seal to a document was the way to certify its legality and to identify the people who had ratified it. During antiquity and the early Middle Ages, this meant only powerful men—kings, bishops, heads of monasteries—and occasionally powerful women. But as participation in documentary practices became more and more common, corporations (like universities and crusading orders), towns, and many individual people also came to use seals. The devices (images) and legends (writing) on these seals were carefully chosen to capture central attributes of their owners' personality or status. Seals were made by pressing a deeply incised lead matrix onto hot wax or resin, which would quickly dry to form a durable impression. The images reproduced here are later engravings that make the features of the original seals easier to see.

A. Seal of the town of Dover, 1281. Dover has long been one of the busiest and most important port cities of England because of its strategic proximity to France; indeed, the Dover Strait that separates this town from Calais, just across the English Channel, is only twenty-one miles wide. In 1281, when this seal was used, ferries and other ships like the one depicted here (in a later engraving) would have made this crossing several times a day. The legend around the edges of the seal reads (in Latin): "Seal of the commune of barons of Dover." It reflects the extraordinary status accorded to the freemen of Dover by the English crown: because of their crucial role in the economy and defense of the kingdom, they were considered a corporate body and entitled to representation in Parliament alongside individual barons.

B. Personal seal of Charles II, king of Naples and Sicily, 1289. Charles II (b. 1254, r. 1285–1309) was the son and heir of Charles of Anjou, who became King Charles I of Sicily in 1266 and died in 1285. This means that Charles II had succeeded his father and had reigned as king for four years before he used this seal to ratify an agreement to his own daughter's marriage in 1289. Yet the seal in image B was clearly made for him when he was a young man—probably when he was first knighted. It depicts him as count of Anjou (see the heraldic fleur-de-lys) and gives him his other princely titles, including "Son of King Charles of Sicily." Although he was thirty-five-years old, a king in his own right, and a father, he was still using this older seal!

Questions for Analysis

1. Medieval towns represented themselves in a variety of ways on their seals: sometimes showing a group portrait of town councilors, sometimes a local saint, sometimes a heraldic beast, sometimes distinctive architectural features. Why would Dover choose this image? What messages does this seal convey?

2. Think carefully about the mystery of Charles II's seal. Usually, an important agreement like a marriage contract (with the son of the French king, no less!) would have carried a king's official, royal seal. What are all the possible reasons why Charles would still have been using this outdated seal? What are the possible ramifications of this choice? In your role as historian-detective, how would you go about solving this mystery?

3. The seals of medieval women were almost always shaped like almonds (pointed ovals— the technical term is *vesica-shaped*). Yet Ingeborg's seal is round, like the seals of men and corporations. Why might that be the case?

4. In general, what are the value of seals for the study of history? What are the various ways in which they function as sources?

C. Seal of Ingeborg Håkansdotter, duchess of Sweden, 1321. Ingeborg (1301–1361) was the daughter of King Håkon V of Norway and was betrothed to a Swedish duke, Erick Magnusson, when she was only eleven years old. After a dramatic series of events that left her a young widow, she became the regent for her son, Magnus was elected king of both Norway and Sweden in 1319. Ingeborg herself was barely eighteen at the time. The legend on her seal (image C) reads "Ingeborg by the Grace of God Duchess of Norway"—her official title.

THE MEETING OF JOACHIM AND ANNA BY GIOTTO.
According to legend, Anna and Joachim were an aged and infertile couple who were able to conceive their only child, Mary, through divine intervention. Hence, this painting may portray the moment of her conception—but it also portrays the affection of husband and wife. ■ *What human characteristics and values does it convey to the viewer?*

of Florence pioneered what he called a "sweet new style" of poetry in his native tongue, which was now so different from the Latin of Roman Italy that it had become a language in its own right. Yet as a scholar and devotee of classical Latin verse, Dante also strove to make this Italian vernacular an instrument for serious political and social critique. His great work, known in his own day as the *Comedy* (called by later admirers the *Divine Comedy*) was composed during the years he spent in exile from his beloved city, after the political party he supported was ousted from power in 1301.

The *Comedy* describes the poet's imaginary journey through hell, purgatory, and paradise, a journey beginning in a "dark wood": a metaphor for the personal and political crises that threatened Dante's faith and livelihood. In the poem, the narrator is led out of this forest and through the first two realms (hell and purgatory) by the Roman poet Virgil (see Chapter 5), who represents the best of classical culture. But he can only be guided toward knowledge of the divine in paradise by his deceased beloved, Beatrice, who symbolizes Christian wisdom. In the course of this visionary pilgrimage, Dante's narrator meets the souls of many historical personages and contemporaries, questioning them closely and inviting them to explain why they met their sev-

eral fates: this is his ingenious way of commenting on current events and passing judgment on his enemies. In many ways, this monumental poem represents the fusion of classical and Christian cultures, Latin learning and vernacular artistry.

PAPAL POWER AND POPULAR PIETY

Dante's *Comedy* responded creatively to the political turmoil that engulfed Italy during his lifetime, a situation that was transforming the papacy in ways that he condemned. Indeed, many of the men whom Dante imaginatively placed in Hell were popes or men who had held high office in the Church, or foreign rulers who sought to subjugate Italian territories (like the Holy Roman Emperor), or rapacious Italian princes and factional leaders who fought among themselves, creating a state of permanent warfare among and within cities (like Dante's native Florence). But despite the weakening authority of the papal office, which caused violent divisions within the Church, popular piety arguably achieved its strongest expressions during this era.

The Legacy of Innocent III

As we saw in Chapter 9, Innocent III's reign marked the height of papal power, but it also sowed seeds of disaster. The popes of the thirteenth century continued to centralize the government of the Church, as Innocent had done, but they simultaneously became involved in protracted political struggles that compromised the papacy's credibility.

For example, because the Papal States bordered on the kingdom of Sicily—which comprised the important city of Naples and southern Italy, too—subsequent popes came into conflict with its ruler, the emperor Frederick II, who proved a fierce opponent. And instead of excommunicating him and calling for his deposition, as Innocent might have done, the reigning pope called a crusade against him—a cynical admission of crusading's overtly political motives. To implement this crusade, the papacy became preoccupied with finding a military champion to advance their cause. They found him in Charles of Anjou, the youngest brother of the French king Louis IX (see below). But Charles made matters worse by antagonizing his own subjects, who offered their allegiance to the king of Aragon. The pope then made Aragon the target of another crusade, which resulted in the death of the new French king, Philip III (r. 1270–85). In the wake of this debacle, Philip's son, Philip IV, resolved to punish the papacy for misusing its powers.

The Limits of Papal Propaganda

In 1300, Pope Boniface VIII (r. 1294–1303) celebrated a papal jubilee in Rome and offered a full crusader's indulgence to every pilgrim: the promise of absolution from all sins. It was a tacit recognition that Rome, not Jerusalem, was now the center of the Christian world—and also a tacit admission that the Crusades of the past two centuries had failed.

But just nine years after this confident assertion of Rome's unassailable status, Rome had become obsolete. The new capital of Christendom was in France, because King Philip IV had challenged Boniface to a political duel and won. The pretext was unimpressive: Boniface had protested against Philip's plan to bring a French bishop to trial on a charge of treason—thus violating the bishop's ecclesiastical immunity. Philip, who had probably anticipated this objection, accused Boniface of heresy and sent a troop of knights to arrest him. At the papal residence of Anagni in 1303, Boniface (then in his seventies) was so mistreated by Philip's thugs that he died a month later. Philip then pressed his advantage. He forced the new pope, Clement V, to thank him publically for his zealous defense of the faith and then, in 1309, moved the entire papal court from Rome to Avignon (*AH-vee-nyon*), a city near the southeastern border of his own realm.

THE PAPAL PALACE AT AVIGNON. This great fortified palace was begun in 1339 and symbolizes the apparent permanence of the papal residence in Avignon. ▪ *Why would it have been constructed as a fortress as well as a palace?*

The papacy's capitulation to French royal power illustrates the enormous gap that had opened up between rhetoric and reality in the centuries since the Investiture Conflict (see Chapter 8). Although Boniface was merely repeating an old claim, that kings ruled only by divine approval as recognized by the Church, the fact was that the Church now exercised its authority only by bowing to the superior power of a particular king.

The Babylonian Captivity of the Papacy

The papacy would remain in Avignon for nearly seventy years, until 1378 (see Chapter 11). This period is often called the "Babylonian Captivity" of the papacy, recalling the Jews' exile in Babylon during the sixth century B.C.E. (see Chapter 2). Even though the move was probably supposed to be temporary, it was not reversed after Philip IV's death in 1314, perhaps because many found that doing business in Avignon was easier than doing business in Rome. Not only was it closer to the major centers of power in northwestern Europe, it was now far removed from the tumultuous politics of Italy and was safe from the aggressive attentions of the German emperors.

All of these considerations were important for a succession of popes closely allied with the aims of the French monarchy. In time, Avignon began to feel like home; in fact it *was* home for all of the popes elected there, who were natives of the region, as were nearly all the cardinals whom they appointed. This further cemented their loyalty to the French king. And the longer the papacy stayed, the larger its bureaucracy grew and the harder it was to contemplate moving it.

Although the papacy never abandoned its claims to the overlordship of Rome and the Papal States, making good on these claims required decades of diplomacy and a great deal of money. The Avignon popes accordingly imposed new taxes and obligations on the wealthy dioceses of France, England, Germany, and Spain. Judicial cases from ecclesiastical courts also brought large revenues into the papal coffers. Most controversially, the Avignon popes claimed the right to appoint bishops and priests to vacant offices anywhere in Christendom, directly, therefore bypassing the rights of individual dioceses and allowing the papacy to collect huge fees from successful appointees.

By these and other measures, the Avignon popes further strengthened administrative control over the Church. But they also further weakened the papacy's moral authority. Stories of the court's unseemly luxury circulated widely, especially during the reign of the notoriously corrupt Clement VI (r. 1342–52), who openly sold spiritual benefits for money (boasting that he would appoint a jackass to a bishopric if he thought it would turn a profit) and insisted that his sexual transgressions were therapeutic. His reign coincided with the Black Death, whose terrifying and demoralizing effects were not alleviated by the quality of his leadership.

Uniting the Faithful: The Power of Sacraments

Despite the centralizing power of the papacy, which came to fruition under Innocent III, most medieval Christians accessed the Church at a local level, within their communities. Somewhat paradoxically, this was another of Innocent III's legacies: because he had insisted that all people should have direct access to religious instruction, nearly all of Europe was covered by a network of parish churches by the end of the thirteenth century. In these churches, parish priests not only taught the elements of Christian doctrine, they administered the sacraments ("holy rites") that conveyed the grace of God to individual Christians, marking significant moments in the life cycle of every person and significant times in the Christian calendar.

Medieval piety came to revolve around these seven sacraments: baptism, confirmation, confession (or penance), communion, marriage, extreme unction (last rites for the dying), and ordination (of priests). Baptism, a ceremony of initiation administered in the early centuries of Christianity to adults (see Chapter 6), had become a sacrament administered to infants as soon as possible after birth, to safeguard their souls in case of an early death. The confirmation of adolescents reaffirmed the promises made on a child's behalf at baptism by parents and godparents. Periodic confession of sins to a priest guaranteed forgiveness by God; for if a sinner did not perform appropriate acts of penance, atonement for sins would have to be completed in purgatory—that netherworld between heaven and hell explored by Dante, whose existence was made a matter of Church doctrine

for the first time in 1274 (though its existence had been posited by Pope Gregory the Great centuries earlier—see Chapter 7).

Marriage was a relatively new sacrament, increasingly emphasized but very seldom practiced as a ceremony; in reality, marriage in this period required only the exchange of solemn promises and was often formed simply by an act of sexual intercourse or the fact of cohabitation. Extreme unction refers to the holy oil with which the priest anointed the forehead of a dying person, signifying the final absolution of all sins and thus offering a final assurance of salvation. Like baptism, this rite could, in an emergency, be administered by any Christian believer. The other sacraments, however, could be administered only by a properly ordained priest— or, in the case of confirmation and ordination, by a bishop. Ordination was therefore the only sacrament reserved for the small percentage of Christians who became priests, and it conveyed to the priest the special authority to share God's grace through the sacraments: a power that could never be lost, even by a priest who led an immoral life.

This sacramental system was the foundation on which the practices of medieval popular piety rested. Pilgrimages, for example, were a form of penance and could lessen one's time in purgatory. Crusading was a kind of extreme pilgrimage that promised the complete fulfillment of all penances the crusader might owe for all the sins of his (or her) life. Many other pious acts—saying the prayers of the rosary, for example, or giving alms to the poor—could also serve as penance for one's sins while constituting good works that would help the believer in his or her journey toward salvation.

The Miracle of the Eucharist

Of these sacraments, the one was most central to the religious lives of medieval Christians was the communion ceremony of the Mass, also known as the Eucharist. As we noted in Chapter 9, the ritual power of the Mass was greatly enhanced in the twelfth century, when the Church began promoting the doctrine of transubstantiation. Christians attending Mass were taught that when the priest spoke the ritual words "This is my body" and "This is my blood," the substances of bread and wine on the altar were miraculously transformed into the body and blood of Jesus Christ. To consume one or both of these substances was to ingest holiness; and so powerful was this idea that most Christians received the sacramental bread just once a year, at Easter. Some holy women, however, attempted to sustain themselves by consuming only the single morsel of bread consecrated at daily Mass.

"THIS IS MY BODY": THE ELEVATION OF THE HOST.
This fresco from a chapel in Assisi was painted by Simone Martini in the 1320s. It shows the moment in the Mass when the priest raises the eucharistic host so that it can be seen by the faithful. The Latin phrase spoken at this moment, *Hoc est corpus meum* ("This is my body"), came to be regarded as a magical formula because it could transform one substance into another: *hocus pocus.* ▪ *Since medieval Christians believed that the sight of the host was just as powerful as ingesting it, how would they have responded to this life-size image of the elevation?* ▪ *What does the appearance of angels (above the altar) signify?*

The fundamental theme of preachers in this era, that salvation lay open to any Christian who strove for it, helps to explain the central place of the Mass and other sacraments in daily life. It also led many to seek out new paths that could lead to God. As we noted in Chapter 9, some believers who sought to achieve a mystical union with God (through rigorous prayer, penance, and personal sacrifice) were ultimately condemned for heresy because they did not subordinate themselves to the authority of the Church. But even less radical figures might find themselves treading on dangerous ground, especially if they published their ideas. For example, the German preacher Master Eckhart (c. 1260–1327), a Dominican friar, taught that there is a "spark" deep within every human soul and that God lives in this spark. Through prayer and self-renunciation, any person could therefore retreat into the inner recesses of her being and access divinity. This conveyed the message that a layperson might attain salvation through her own efforts, without the intervention of a priest or any of the sacraments he alone could perform. As a result, many of Eckhart's teachings were condemned. But views like these would find support in the teachings of popular preachers after the Black Death, when close-knit communities revolving around the parish church were broken up or weakened (see Chapter 11).

STRUGGLES FOR SOVEREIGNTY

When the French king Philip IV transplanted the papal court from Rome to Avignon, he was not just responding to previous popes' abuse of power: he was bolstering his own. By the middle of the thirteenth century, the growth of strong territorial monarchies, combined with the increasing sophistication of royal justice, taxation, and propaganda, had given some secular rulers a higher degree of power than any western European ruler had wielded since the time of Charlemagne (see Chapter 7).

Meanwhile, monarchs' willingness to support the Church's crusading efforts not only yielded distinct economic and political advantages, it also allowed them to assert their commitment to the moral and spiritual improvement of their realms. Although a king still needed to be anointed with holy oil at the time of his coronation in order to claim that he ruled "by the grace of God"—a rite that required a bishop and, by extension, papal support—a king's authority in his own realm rested on the acquiescence of the aristocracy and on popular perceptions of his reputation for justice, piety, and regard for his subjects' prosperity. On the wider stage of the

Yet, to share in the miracle of the Eucharist, one did not have to consume it. One had only to witness the elevation of the host, the wafer of bread raised up by the priest, which "hosted" the real presence of Jesus Christ. Daily attendance at Mass simply to view the consecration of the host was therefore a common form of devotion, and this was facilitated by the practice of displaying a consecrated wafer in a special reliquary called a monstrance ("showcase"), which could be set up on an altar or carried through the streets. Believers sometimes attributed astonishing properties to the eucharistic host, feeding it to sick animals or rushing from church to church to see the consecrated bread as many times as possible in a day. Some of these practices were criticized as superstitious. But, by and large, these expressions of popular piety were encouraged and fervently practiced by many.

medieval world, it also rested on his successful assertion of his kingdom's sovereignty.

The Problem of Sovereignty

Sovereignty can be defined as inviolable authority over a defined territory. In Chapter 9, we noted that Philip Augustus was the first monarch to call himself "king of France" and not "king of the French." In other words, he was defining his kingship in geographical terms, claiming that there was an entity called France and that he was king within that area.

But what was France? Was it the tiny "island" (Île-de-France) around Paris, which had been his father's domain? If so, then France was very small—and very vulnerable, which would make it hard to maintain a claim to sovereignty. Was it, rather, any region whose lord was willing to do homage to the French king, like Champagne or Normandy? In that case, the king would need to enforce these rights of lordship constantly and, if necessary, exert his rule directly—as Philip did when he took Normandy away from England's King John in 1214.

But what if some of France's neighboring lords ruled in their own right, as did the independent counts of Flanders, thus threatening the security of France's borders? In that case, the king would either need to forge an alliance with these borderlands or negate their independence. He would need to assert his sovereignty by absorbing these regions into an ever-growing kingdom.

This is the problem: a claim to sovereignty is only credible if it can be backed up with real power, and a state's or ruler's power must never seem stagnant or passive. The problem of sovereignty, then, is a zero-sum game: one state's sovereignty is won and maintained by diminishing that of other states. Although many French citizens today would assert that France has, in some mystical way, always existed in its present form, the fact is that France and every other modern European state was being cobbled together in the medieval period through a process of annexation and colonization—just as the United States was assembled at the expense of the empires that had colonized North America (the British, French, and Spanish), not to mention the killing or displacement of autonomous native peoples.

The process of achieving sovereignty is thus an aggressive and often violent one, affecting not only the rulers of territories but their peoples, too. In Spain, the "Reconquest" of Muslim lands, which had accelerated in the twelfth century, continued apace in the thirteenth and fourteenth, to the detriment of these regions' Muslim and Jewish inhabitants. German princes continued to push northward into the Baltic, where native peoples'

resistance to colonizing efforts was met with brutal force. Meanwhile, the Scandinavian kingdoms that had been forming in the eleventh and twelfth centuries were warring among themselves and their neighbors for the control of contested regions and resources. Italy and the Mediterranean became a constant battleground, as we have observed. Among all these emerging states, the two most strident and successful in their assertion of sovereignty were France and England.

The Prestige of France: The Saintly Kingship of Louis IX

After the death of Philip Augustus in 1223, the heirs to the French throne continued to pursue an expansionist policy, pushing the boundaries of their influence out to the east and south. There were significant pockets of resistance, though, notably from the southwestern lands that the kings of England had inherited from Eleanor of Aquitaine (see Chapter 9) and from the independent towns of Flanders that had escaped conquest under Philip Augustus. In 1302, citizen militias from several of these towns, fighting on foot with farming implements and other unconventional weapons, even managed to defeat a heavily armed French cavalry. This victory at the Battle of Courtrai (Kortrijk) is still celebrated as a national holiday in Belgium (although, ironically, its ultimate meaning is currently at the center of a divisive controversy between French- and Flemish-speaking Belgians).

This defeat was a setback for Philip IV of France, but we have already observed that Philip had other ways of asserting the power of French sovereignty. Much of that power derived from his grandfather, Louis IX (r. 1226–70), who would probably have been horrified by the ways his grandson used it. Louis was famous for his piety and for his conscientious exercise of his kingly duties. Unlike most of his fellow princes, he not only pledged to go on crusade—he actually went. And while both of his campaigns were notorious failures (he died on the second, in 1270) they cemented Louis's saintly reputation and political clout.

First, Louis's willingness to risk his life (and that of his brothers) in the service of the Church would give him tremendous influence in papal affairs—a key factor in making his youngest brother, Charles of Anjou, the king of Naples and Sicily. Second, the necessity of ensuring the good governance of his kingdom during his years of absence prompted Louis to reform or invent many key aspects of royal governance, which made France the bureaucratic rival of England for the first time. Third, Louis's first crusading venture was

A CONTAINER FOR THE CROWN OF THORNS. The Sainte-Chapelle, built by Louis IX, was a giant reliquary for the display of this potent artifact and symbol that Christ's divine majesty, which increased the prestige of king of France.

seen as confirmation that the king of France had inherited the mantle of Charlemagne as the protector of the Church and the representative of Christ on earth. Although it was a military fiasco, this crusade found lasting artistic expression in the Sainte-Chapelle (Holy Chapel), a gorgeous jewel box of a church that Louis built in Paris for his collection of Passion relics—that is, artifacts thought to have been used for the torture and crucifixion of Christ. The most important of these was the Crown of Thorns, intended by Pilate as a mocking reference to "the king of the Jews" (see Chapter 6). Now that this holy crown belonged to Louis and was housed in Paris, it could be taken as a sign that Paris was the new Jerusalem.

Widely regarded as a saint in his lifetime, Louis was formally canonized in 1297—by the same Pope Boniface VIII brought down by Philip IV. Indeed, Boniface partly intended this gesture as a rebuke to the saint's grandson. Philip himself, however, turned it to his advantage. He even used his grandfather's pious reputation as a cloak for his frankly rapacious treatment of the Knights Templar, whose military order he suppressed in 1314 so that he could confiscate its extensive property and dissolve his own debts to the order. He had expelled the Jews from his realm in 1306 for similar reasons.

Castles and Control: Edward I and the Expansion of English Rule

The expulsion of Jews who depended on a king's personal protection had actually been a precedent set by Philip's contemporary and kinsman, Edward I of England (r. 1272–1307). Unlike Philip, Edward had to build up the sovereignty of his state almost from scratch. His father, Henry III (1216–1272), had a long but troubled reign. Inheriting the throne as a young boy, shortly after his father John's loss of Normandy and capitulation to Magna Carta (see Chapter 9), Henry had to contend with factions among his regents and, later, the restive barons of his realm who rose against him on several occasions. His son Edward even sided with the rebels at one point, but later worked alongside his father to suppress them. When Edward himself became king in 1272, he took steps toward ensuring that there would be no further revolts on his watch, tightening his control on the aristocracy and their lands, diffusing their power by strengthening that of Parliament, reforming the administration of the realm, and clarifying its laws.

Having seen to the internal affairs of England, Edward looked to its borders. Since Welsh chieftains had been major backers of the barons who had rebelled against his father, Edward was determined to clean up the border region and bring "wild Wales" within the orbit of English sovereignty. He initially attempted to do this by making treaties with various Welsh princes, but none of these arrangements were stable or gave Edward the type of control he wanted. He accordingly embarked on an ambitious and ruthless campaign of castle-building, ringing the hilly country with enormous fortifications on a scale not seen in most of Europe; they were more

CAERNARVON CASTLE. One of many massive fortifications built by Edward I, this castle was the birthplace of the first English "Prince of Wales" and the site where the current Prince of Wales, Charles, was formally invested with that title in 1969. ▪ *Castles of this size and strength had been constructed in the Crusader States and on the disputed frontiers of Muslim and Christian Spain but never before in Britain (see the photos on pages 292 and 295 of Chapter 9).* ▪ *What does their construction reveal about Edward's attitude toward the Welsh?*

A Declaration of Scottish Independence

In April of 1320, a group of powerful Scottish lords gathered at the abbey of Arbroath to draft a letter to Pope John XII in Avignon. The resulting "Declaration of Arbroath" petitioned the exiled pope (a Frenchman loyal to the French king) to recognize the Scots as a sovereign nation and to support their right to an independent kingdom that would be free from encroachment by the English. The Scots' elected king, Robert the Bruce, had been excommunicated by a previous pope, who had also upheld English claims to lordship in Scotland. The letter therefore makes a number of different arguments for the recognition of the Scots' right to self-governance.

 e know, most holy father and lord, and have gathered from the deeds and books about men in the past, that . . . the nation of the Scots has been outstanding for its many distinctions. It journeyed from the lands of Greece and Egypt by the Tyrrhenian Sea and the Pillars of Hercules, . . . but could not be subdued anywhere by any peoples however barbaric. . . . It took possession of the settlements in the west which it now desires, after first driving out the Britons and totally destroying the Picts, and although often attacked by the Norwegians, Danes and English. Many were its victories and innumerable its efforts. It has held these places always free of all servitude, as the old histories testify.

One hundred and thirteen kings of their royal lineage have reigned in their kingdom, with no intrusion by a foreigner.

If the noble qualities and merits of these men were not obvious for other reasons, they shine forth clearly enough in that they were almost the first to be called to his most holy faith by the King of Kings and Lord of Lords, our Lord Jesus Christ, after his Passion and Resurrection, even though they were settled on the most distant boundaries of the earth. . . .

Thus our people lived until now in freedom and peace . . . , until that mighty prince Edward [I] king of England (the father of the present king) in the guise of a friend and ally attacked our kingdom in hostile fashion, when it had no head and the people were not harbouring any evil treachery, nor were they accustomed to

wars or attacks. His unjust acts, killings, acts of violence, pillagings, burnings, imprisonments of prelates, burnings of monasteries, robbings and killings of regular clergy, and also innumerable other outrages, which he committed against the said people, sparing none on account of age or sex, religion or order—no one could write about them or fully comprehend them who had not been instructed by experience.

From these countless ills we have been set free, with the help of Him who follows up wounds with healing and cures, by our most energetic prince, king and lord Sir Robert [the Bruce, r. 1306–29]. . . . By divine providence his succession to his right according to our laws and customs which we intend to maintain to the death, together with the due consent

like crusader castles, and Edward certainly treated the Welsh (who were actually his fellow Christians) as infidels. Indeed, he treated conquered Wales like a crusader state, making it a settler colony and subjecting the Welsh to the overlordship of his own men. When his son, the future Edward II, was born in 1284 at the great castle he had built at Caernarvon, he gave the infant the title "Prince of Wales," a title usually borne by a Welsh chieftain.

Edward then turned to Scotland, England's final frontier. Until now, control of Scotland had not been an English concern: the Scottish border had been peaceful for many years, and the Scottish kings did homage to the English king for some of their lands. In 1290, however, the succession to the Scottish throne was disputed among many rival

claimants, none of whom had enough backing to secure election. Edward intervened, pressing his own claim to the kingdom and seemingly prepared to take Scotland by conquest. To avoid this, the Scots forged an alliance with the French, but this did not prevent Edward's army from fighting its way through to Scone Abbey in 1296.

Scone was a symbolic target: the site of the Stone of Destiny on which Scottish kings were traditionally enthroned. So Edward seized this potent symbol, brought it back to Westminster Abbey in London, and embedded it in the coronation chair of his namesake, Edward the Confessor, the last Anglo-Saxon king of England (see Chapter 8). Save for a brief hiatus in 1950 (when the stone was stolen from the abbey by Scottish nationalists, students and assent of us all, have made him our prince and king. . . . But if he should give up what he has begun, seeking to subject us or our kingdom to the king of the English, . . . we would immediately strive to expel him as our enemy and a subverter of his right and ours, and we would make someone else our king, who is capable of seeing to our defence. For as long as a hundred of us remain alive, we intend never to be subjected to the lordship of the English, in any way. For it is not for glory in war, riches or honours that we fight, but only for the laws of our fathers and for freedom, which no good man loses except along with his life.

Therefore, most holy father and lord, we implore your holiness with all vehemence in our prayers that you . . . look with paternal eyes on the troubles and difficulties brought upon us and the church of God by the English. And that you deign to admonish and exhort the king of the English, who ought to be satisfied with what he has (since England was formerly enough for seven kings or

more), to leave us Scots in peace, living as we do in the poor country of Scotland beyond which there is no dwelling place, and desiring nothing but our own. . . .

It is important for you, holy father, to do this, since you see the savagery of the heathen raging against Christians (as the sins of Christians require), and the frontiers of Christendom are being curtailed day by day, and you have seen how much it detracts from your holiness's reputation if (God forbid!) the church suffers eclipse or scandal in any part of it during your time. Let it then rouse the Christian princes who are covering up their true motivation when they pretend that they cannot go to the assistance of the Holy Land on account of wars with their neighbours. The real reason that holds them back is that in warring with their smaller neighbours they anticipate greater advantage to themselves and weaker resistance. . . .

But if your Holiness too credulously trusts the tales of the English fully, or does not leave off favouring the English

to our confusion, then we believe that the Most High will blame you for the slaughter of bodies. . . . Dated at our monastery at Arbroath in Scotland 6 April 1320 in the fifteenth year of our said king's reign.

Questions for Analysis

1. On what grounds does this letter justify the political independence of the Scots? What different arguments does it make? Which, in your view, is the most compelling one?

2. Why does this letter mention crusading? What are the Scottish lords implying about the relationship between Europe's internal conflicts and the ongoing wars with external adversaries?

3. Imagine that you are an adviser to the pope. Based on your knowledge of the papacy's situation at this time, would you advise him to do as this letter asks? Why or why not?

at the University of Glasgow) it would remain there until 1996, as a sign that the sovereignty of Scotland had yielded to that of England. (It will be temporarily returned to London when the next English monarch is crowned.)

Edward considered the subjugation of Scotland to be England's manifest destiny: he called himself "the Hammer of the Scots," and when he died he charged his son Edward II (r. 1307–1327) with the completion of his task. But Edward, unlike his father, was not a ruthless and efficient advocate of English expansion. And he had to contend with a rebellion led by his own queen, Isabella of France, who also engineered his abdication and murder. Their son, Edward III (r. 1327–1377), would eventually renew his grandfather's expansionist policies—but his main target would be France,

not Scotland. He would thus launch Europe's two strongest monarchies into a war that lasted over a hundred years.

The Outbreak of the Hundred Years' War

The Hundred Years' War was the largest, longest, and most wide-ranging military conflict since Rome's wars with Carthage in the third and second centuries B.C.E. (see Chapter 5). Although England and France were its principal antagonists, almost all of the major European powers became involved in it at some stage. Active hostilities began in 1337 and lasted until 1453, interrupted by truces of varying lengths.

The most fundamental source of conflict, and the most difficult to resolve, was the fact that the kings of England held the duchy of Gascony as vassals of the French king; this had been part of Eleanor of Aquitaine's domain, added to the Anglo-Norman Empire in 1154 (see Chapter 9). In the twelfth and thirteenth centuries, when the French kings had not yet absorbed this region into their domain, this fact had seemed less of an anomaly. But as Europe's territorial monarchies began to claim sovereignty based on the free exercise of power within the "natural" boundaries of their domains, the English presence in "French" Gascony became more and more problematic. That England also had close commercial links, through the wool trade, with Flanders—which consistently resisted French imperialism—added fuel to the fire. So did the French alliance with the Scots, who continued to resist English imperialism.

Complicating this volatile situation was the disputed succession of the French crown. In 1328, the last of Philip IV's three sons died without leaving a son to succeed him: the Capetian dynasty, founded by the Frankish warlord Hugh Capet in 987 (see Chapter 8), had finally exhausted itself. A new dynasty, the Valois, came to the throne—but only by insisting that women could neither inherit royal power nor pass it on. For otherwise, the heir to France was Edward III of England, whose ambitious mother, Isabella, was Philip IV's only daughter. When his claim was initially passed over, Edward was only fifteen and in no position to protest. In 1337, however, when the disputes over Gascony and

Scotland erupted into war, Edward raised the stakes by claiming to be the rightful king of France, a claim that subsequent English kings would maintain until the eighteenth century.

Although France was richer and more populous than England by a factor of at least three to one, the English crown was more effective in mobilizing the entire population, for reasons that we discussed in Chapter 9. Edward III was therefore able to levy and maintain a professional army of seasoned and well-disciplined soldiers, cavalry, and archers. The huge but virtually leaderless armies assembled by the French proved no match for the tactical superiority of these smaller English forces. English armies pillaged the French countryside at will, while civil wars broke out between embattled French lords. A decade after the declaration of war, French knights were defeated in two humiliating battles, at Crécy (1346) and Calais (1347). The English seemed invincible. Yet they were no match for an adversary approaching from the Far East.

FROM THE GREAT FAMINE TO THE BLACK DEATH

By 1300, Europe was connected to Asia and the lands in between by an intricate network that fostered commerce, communication, and connections of all kinds. Yet Europe was also reaching its own ecological limits. Between 1000 and 1300, the population had tripled, and a sea of grain

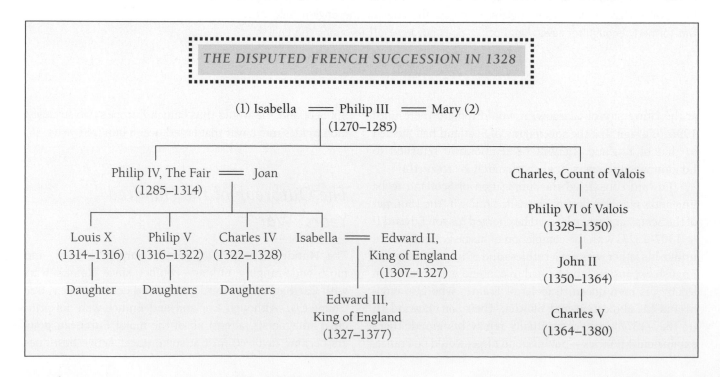

THE DISPUTED FRENCH SUCCESSION IN 1328

(1) Isabella ═══ Philip III ═══ Mary (2)
(1270–1285)

Philip IV, The Fair ═══ Joan
(1285–1314)

Charles, Count of Valois

Philip VI of Valois
(1328–1350)

Louis X (1314–1316)   Philip V (1316–1322)   Charles IV (1322–1328)   Isabella ═══ Edward II, King of England (1307–1327)

Daughter   Daughters   Daughters

Edward III, King of England (1327–1377)

John II
(1350–1364)

Charles V
(1364–1380)

Past and Present

Global Pandemics

The image on the left shows citizens from the town of Tournai (now in Belgium) marching in a procession to ward off the plague. They are praying and doing penance for their sins by beating their own bodies with whips, a practice called *flagellation*. On the right, citizens of Mumbai (India), wearing protective masks to ward off infection, stand in line to receive testing for the swine flu virus.

 Watch related author interview on StudySpace
wwnorton.com/web/westernciv18

fields stretched, almost unbroken, from Ireland to the Ukraine. Forests had been cleared, marshes drained, and pastureland reduced by generations of peasants performing lifetimes of backbreaking labor. But still, Europe was barely able to feed its people. At the same time, the warming trend that had begun in the late eighth century reversed itself. Even a reduction of one or two degrees centigrade is enough to cause substantial changes in rainfall patterns, shorten growing seasons, and lessen agricultural productivity. So it did in Europe, with disastrous consequences.

Evil Times: The Seven Years' Famine

Between the years 1315 to 1322, the cooling climate caused nearly continuous adverse weather conditions in northern Europe. Winters were extraordinarily severe: in 1316, the Baltic Sea froze over and ships were trapped in the ice. Rains prevented planting in spring or summer, and when a crop did manage to struggle through it would be dashed by rain and hail in autumn. In the midst of these natural calamities, dynastic warfare continued in the sodden wheatfields, as the princes of Scandinavia and the Holy Roman Empire fought for supremacy and succession. In the once-fertile fields of Flanders, French armies slogged through mud in continued efforts to subdue the Flemish population. On the Scottish and Welsh borders, uprisings were ruthlessly suppressed and the paltry storehouses of the natives were pillaged to feed the English raiders.

The result was human suffering more devastating than that caused by any famine affecting Europe since that time: hence the acceptance of the name "Great Famine" to describe this terrible crisis. Weakened by years of malnutrition and relentless efforts to counteract the climactic effects on the landscape, between 10 and 15 percent of the population of northern Europe perished. Many starved, and others

Analyzing Primary Sources

The Code of Chivalry: Putting Honor before Plunder

The Hundred Years' War between England and France pitted these two countries' warrior aristocracies against one another. Yet these knights had a great deal in common: they all spoke French, many were closely related, and they were supposed to share a common set of values. The following excerpt is taken from The Book of Chivalry *written in French by Geoffroi de Charny, a French nobleman and veteran of this war's first major battles who ultimately died in combat at Poitiers in 1356. Because the war was fought almost entirely on French soil, Geoffroi was keenly aware of the toll it took on the land and its people. In the following passage, he addresses the problem of how a knight can sustain his honor when he is driven to acquire booty for himself through the theft of others' property.*

Those Who Are Brave but Too Eager for Plunder

 now need to consider yet another category of men-at-arms, who deserve praise, who are strong and skillful, bold and sparing no effort, some of whom always want to be at the forefront, riding as foragers to win booty or prisoners or other profit from the enemies of those on whose side they fight. And they know well how to do it skillfully and cleverly; and because they are so intent on plunder, it often happens that on the entry into a town won by force, those who are so greedy for plunder dash hither and thither and find themselves separated from those of their companions who have no thought for gain but only for completing their military undertaking. And it often happens that such men, those who ride after and hunt for great booty, are killed in the process—frequently it is not

known how, sometimes by their enemies, sometimes through quarrels in which greed for plunder sets one man against another. It often occurs that through lack of those who chase after plunder before the battle is over, that which is thought to be already won can be lost again and lives or reputations as well. It can also happen in relation to such people who are very eager for booty that when there is action on the battlefield, there are a number of men who pay more attention to taking prisoners and other profit, and when they have seized them and other winnings, they are more anxious to safeguard their captives and their booty than to help to bring the battle to a good conclusion. And it may well be that a battle can be lost in this way. And one ought instead to be wary of the booty which results in the loss of honor, life, and possessions. In this vocation one should therefore set

one's heart and mind on winning honor, which endures for ever, rather than on winning profit and booty, which one can lose within one single hour. And yet one should praise and value those men-at-arms who are able to make war on, inflict damage on, and win profit from their enemies, for they cannot do it without strenuous effort and great courage. But again I shall repeat: he who does best is most worthy.

Questions for Analysis

1. How does Geoffroi justify the act of plundering? What insights into contemporary military tactics does this passage provide?

2. Given that Geoffroi would have seen Englishmen pillaging French lands, do you find his justification of this activity surprising? Why or why not?

---

fell victim to epidemic diseases that affected both animals and people. In southern Europe, around the shores of the Mediterranean, the effects of climate change were more muted, and there were also different channels through which food could be distributed. Nonetheless, the overall health of this region suffered from the disruption of trade and the shortage of some staple goods, as well as from the highly unstable political situation we have already discussed.

As food grew scarcer, prices climbed unpredictably. Plans for future crops, which kept hope alive, would be dashed when spring arrived and flooded fields prevented seeds from germinating. Cold summers and autumns were spent foraging for food. Hunting was restricted to the nobility, but even those who risked the death penalty for poaching found little game. Wages did not keep pace with rising costs, and so those who lived in towns

The map labels, reading across the map:

ATLANTIC OCEAN

NORTH SEA

BALTIC SEA

December 31, 1350

June 30, 1350

Bergen

Wisby

Moscow

December 31, 1349

June 30, 1349

December 31, 1348

Drogheda • Lancaster • Durham
Dublin • Preston • York
Kilkenny • Chester • Lincoln
Nottingham
Norwich • Yarmouth
Oxford • Cambridge
Bristol • London
Weymouth • Canterbury
Southampton • Calais
Bruges
Ghent
Liége
Amiens
Paris
Angers
Strasbourg
Colmar
Basel • Zurich
Lucerne • St. Gall

Lübeck • Rostock • Danzig
Bremen • Hamburg
Frankfurt an der Oder • Thorn
Osnabrück
Magdeburg
Cologne
Erfurt
Frankfurt • Würzburg
Nuremberg
Mühldorf • Vienna

December 31, 1348
June 30, 1348
Danube R.

BLACK SEA

Bordeaux
ALPS MTS.
Milan
PYRENEES MTS.
Toulouse • Montpellier • Genoa • Verona • Venice
Huesca • Narbonne • Marseilles • Pisa • Bologna • Florence • Ancona • Sebenico
Saragossa • Lérida • Siena • Perugia • Ragusa
Teruel • Barcelona • Rome
ADRIATIC SEA
Constantinople
Valencia
Seville
Naples
Almeria
MEDITERRANEAN SEA

June 30, 1347

Messina
Agrigento • Catania
Syracuse
December 31, 1347

EUROPE
Area of detail
AFRICA

- Plague-stricken towns and areas
— Progress of plague at certain dates
■ Towns and areas not stricken by the plague

0   100   200   300 Miles
0   100   200   300 Kilometers

THE PROGRESS OF THE BLACK DEATH, FOURTEENTH CENTURY. ▪ *What trajectories did the Black Death follow once it was introduced into Europe?* ▪ *How might the growth of towns, trade, and travel have contributed to the spread of the Black Death?* ▪ *Would such a rapid advance have been likely during the early Middle Ages or even in the ancient world?*

and depended on markets had less to spend on scarce provisions. Only a year after the famine began, townspeople were dying of ailments that would not have been fatal in good years.

The effects of the famine were especially devastating for children, since even those who survived would be highly susceptible to disease, owing to the severe impairment of their immune systems. It may have been the Great Famine, then, that paved the way for the more transient (if more horrific) destruction of the Black Death.

A Crisis of Connectivity: Tracking the Black Death

The Black Death is the name given to a deadly pandemic that spread from China to Mongolia, northern India, and the Middle East during the 1330s and 1340s. By 1346, the plague had reached the Black Sea, where it was transmitted to the Genoese colonists at Caffa (as we noted above). From there, in 1347, Genoese ships inadvertently

Responses to the Black Death

> *Many chroniclers, intellectuals, and private individuals have left accounts of the plague in which they attempt to understand why it had occurred, how it spread, and how communities should respond to it.*

The Spread of the Plague According to Gabriele de' Mussi (d. 1356), a Lawyer in Piacenza (Northern Italy)

Oh God! See how the heathen Tartar races, pouring together from all sides, suddenly infested the city of Caffa [on the Black Sea] and besieged the trapped Christians there for almost three years. . . . But behold, [in 1346] the whole army was affected by a disease which overran the Tartars and killed thousands upon thousands every day. It was as though arrows were raining down from heaven to strike and crush the Tartars' arrogance. All medical advice and attention was useless; the Tartars died as soon as the signs of disease appeared on their bodies: swellings in the armpit or groin caused by coagulating humours, followed by a putrid fever.

The dying Tartars, stunned and stupefied by the immensity of the disaster brought about by the disease, and realising that they had no hope of escape, lost interest in the siege. But they ordered corpses to be placed in catapults and lobbed into the city in the hope that the intolerable stench would kill everyone inside. What seemed like mountains of dead were thrown into the city, and the Christians could not hide or flee or escape from them, although they dumped as many of the bodies as they could in the sea. And soon the rotting corpses tainted the air and poisoned the water supply. . . . Moreover one infected man could carry the poison to others, and infect people and places with the disease by look alone. No one knew, or could discover, a means of defence.

Thus almost everyone who had been in the East . . . fell victim . . . through the bitter events of 1346 to 1348—the Chinese, Indians, Persians, Medes, Kurds, Armenians, Cilicians, Georgians, Mesopotamians, Nubians, Ethiopians, Turks, Egyptians, Arabs, Saracens and Greeks. . . .

* * *

As it happened, among those who escaped from Caffa by boat were a few sailors who had been infected with the poisonous disease. Some boats were bound for Genoa, others went to Venice and to other Christian areas. When the sailors reached these places and mixed with the people there, it was as if they had brought evil spirits with them. . . .

* * *

Scarcely one in seven of the Genoese survived. In Venice, where an inquiry was held into the mortality, it was found that more than 70 percent of the people had died. . . . The rest of Italy, Sicily and Apulia and the neighbouring regions maintain that they have been virtually emptied of inhabitants. . . . The Roman Curia at Avignon, the provinces on both sides of the Rhône, Spain, France, and the Empire cry up their griefs. . . .

* * *

Everyone has a responsibility to keep some record of the disease and the deaths, and because I am myself from Piacenza I have been urged to write more about what happened there in 1348. . . .

brought it to Sicily and northern Italy. From Italy, it spread westward along trade routes, first striking seaports, then turning inland with the travelers who carried it. It moved with astonishing rapidity, advancing about two miles per day, summer or winter. By 1350, it had reached Scandinavia and northern Russia, then spread southward again until it linked up with the original waves of infection that had brought it from Central Asia to the Black Sea. It continued to erupt in local epidemics for the next 300 years; some localities could expect a renewed outbreak every decade. The last Europe-wide instance occurred between 1661 and 1669, although there were

I don't know where to begin. Cries and laments arise on all sides. Day after day one sees the Cross and the Host being carried about the city, and countless dead being buried.... The living made preparations for their [own] burial, and because there was not enough room for individual graves, pits had to be dug in colonnades and piazzas, where nobody had ever been buried before. It often happened that man and wife, father and son, mother and daughter, and soon the whole household and many neighbours, were buried together in one place....

A Letter from the Town Council of Cologne to the Town Council of Strasbourg (Germany), 12 January 1349

Very dear friends, all sorts of rumours are now flying about against Judaism and the Jews prompted by this unexpected and unparalleled mortality of Christians.... Throughout our city, as in yours, many-winged Fame clamours that this mortality was initially caused, and is still being spread, by the poisoning of springs and wells, and that the Jews must have dropped poisonous substances into them. When it came to our knowledge that serious charges had been made against the Jews in several small towns and villages on the basis of this mortality, we sent numerous letters to you and to other cities and towns to uncover the truth behind these rumours, and set a thorough investigation in train....

If a massacre of the Jews were to be allowed in the major cities (something which we are determined to prevent in our city, if we can, as long as the Jews are found to be innocent of these or similar actions) it could lead to the sort of outrages and disturbances which would whip up a popular revolt among the common people—and such revolts have in the past brought cities to misery and desolation. In any case we are still of the opinion that this mortality and its attendant circumstances are caused by divine vengeance and nothing else. Accordingly we intend to forbid any harassment of the Jews in our city because of these flying rumours, but to defend them faithfully and keep them safe, as our predecessors did—and we are convinced that you ought to do the same....

Source: From Rosemary Horrox, ed. and trans., *The Black Death* (Manchester: 1994), pp. 16–21, 219–20.

Questions for Analysis

1. How does Gabriele de' Mussi initially explain the causes of the plague? How does his understanding of it change as he traces its movements from East to West—and closer to Italy?

2. Why does the Council of Cologne wish to quell violence against the Jews? How does this reasoning complement or challenge what we have learned so far about the treatment of Jews in medieval Europe?

3. In your view, do these two perspectives display a rational approach to the horrors of the Black Death? Why or why not?

sporadic outbreaks in Poland and Russia until the end of the eighteenth century.

What caused the Black Death? In 2011, scientists were able to confirm that it can be traced to the deadly microbe *Yersinia pestis*, and that it did indeed originate in China. *Y. pestis* actually causes three different kinds of contagion: bubonic plague and its even deadlier cousins, septicemic plague and pneumonic plague. In its bubonic form, this microbe is carried by fleas that travel on the backs of rats; humans catch it only if they are bitten by an infected flea or rat. Bubonic plague attacks the lymphatic system, producing enormous swellings (buboes) of the lymph nodes in the groin, neck, and armpits. Septicemic plague occurs when an infected flea introduces the microbe directly into the human bloodstream, causing death within hours, often before any symptoms of the disease can manifest themselves. Pneumonic plague, perhaps the most frightening variation, results when *Y. pestis* infects the lungs, allowing the contagion to spread silently and invisibly, in the same ways as the common cold.

One of the things that made the Black Death so terrifying, therefore, was that it manifested itself in several different ways. Those afflicted by the hideous bubonic plague might actually recover, while others—seemingly untouched—might die suddenly, mysteriously. Immediate reactions understandably ranged from panic to resignation. Observers quickly realized that the plague was contagious, but precisely how it spread remained enigmatic. Some believed that it was caused by breathing "bad air" and so urged people to flee from stricken areas, which caused the disease to spread even faster.

Others looked for scapegoats and revived old conspiracy theories that implicated Jews in the poisoning of wells. Scores of Jewish communities were attacked and thousands of their inhabitants massacred in the Rhineland, southern France, and Christian Spain. (No such attacks are known to have occurred in Muslim areas of Spain or elsewhere in the Muslim world.) The papacy and some local authorities tried to halt these attacks, but these admonitions came too late. Another response to the plague was the flagellant movement, so called because of the whips (*flagella*) with which traveling bands of penitents lashed themselves in order to appease the wrath of God. But the unruly and sometimes hysterical mobs that gathered around the flagellants aroused the concern of both ecclesiastical and secular authorities, and the movement was suppressed by papal order.

CONCLUSION

The century between 1250 and 1350 was a time of significant change within all Western civilizations. The growing power of some monarchies led to encroachments on territories and cities that had once been independent, and that fueled resistance to these internal acts of colonization. The papacy, whose power had seemed so secure at the turn

After You Read This Chapter

Visit StudySpace for quizzes, additional review materials, and multimedia documents. **wwnorton.com/web/westernciv18**

REVIEWING THE OBJECTIVES

- The conquests of the Mongols had a significant impact on Europe. How?
- The expansion of commerce and communication between Eastern and Western civilizations created a new world system. What were some key characteristics of this system? What kinds of exchange did it enable?
- What were the short- and longer-term causes for the papacy's loss of prestige? Why was the papal court moved to Avignon?
- What is sovereignty? What were the effects of competition for sovereign among European rulers?
- What caused the Black Death? In what sense can it be seen as a product of the new world system that began with the Mongol conquests?

of the thirteenth century, would itself become a pawn in the keeping of the French king by the beginning of the fourteenth. Rome thereby lost its last source of authority while the New Rome, Constantinople, struggled to rebuild its prestige in the face of Mongol expansion. Yet for the Mongol khans and the merchants they favored, for seafaring civilizations like Venice and Genoa, for ambitious students at the universities, and for men on the make, the opportunities for advancement and mobility were great.

And there were still other factors at play during this era. Even in good times, Europe's population had outgrown its capacity to produce food, and when the climate grew cooler, years of cold summers and heavy rainfall took an enormous toll. Those regions most closely tied to the new global networks were also densely settled and urban, which made the shortage of food and the spread of disease more acute there. In short, the benefits and drawbacks of increased globalization were already beginning to manifest themselves in the early fourteenth century—700 years ago. The Black Death can be understood as the ultimate example of medieval connectivity and also as a modern phenomenon.

The scale of mortality caused by this pandemic is almost unimaginable, to us as to those who survived it. At least a third, and probably half, of Europe's people died between 1347 and 1353. In the countryside, entire villages disappeared. Cities and towns, overcrowded and unsanitary, were particularly vulnerable to plague and, thereafter, to outbreaks of violence. The immediate social consequences were profound, and so were the economic ones. Crops rotted in the fields, manufacturing ceased, and trade came to a standstill in affected areas. Basic commodities became scarcer and prices rose, prompting ineffectual efforts to control prices and to force the remaining able-bodied laborers to work.

These were the short-term effects. How did the Black Death matter to those who survived it—including ourselves? According to Ibn Khaldun (1332–1406), a Muslim historian who is considered one of the founders of modern historical methods, it marked the end of the old world and the beginning of a new one, which would require new systems of government, bodies of knowledge, and forms of art. Was he right? We will begin to answer that question in Chapter 11.

PEOPLE, IDEAS, AND EVENTS IN CONTEXT

- What accounts for the success of **GENGHIS KHAN** and his successors? What circumstances enabled **MARCO POLO**'s travels to China? To what extent does the term *PAX MONGOLICA* describe this era in history?

- How did seafaring communities like that of **GENOA** rise to prominence in this era? Why were new navigational aids like **PORTOLAN CHARTS** necessary?

- How do the paintings of **GIOTTO** capture contemporary attitudes toward the world? How does **DANTE**'s artistry respond to the religious and political trends of his day?

- What was at stake in the controversy between **BONIFACE VIII** and **PHILIP IV**? Why is the papacy's residency at **AVIGNON** called the **BABYLONIAN CAPTIVITY**? What is a **SACRAMENT**, and why were these rites so important?

- In what different ways did **LOUIS IX** of France and **EDWARD I** of England contribute to the sovereignty of their respective kingdoms? What was the relationship between claims to sovereignty and the causes of the **HUNDRED YEARS' WAR**?

- How did climate change contribute to the outbreak of the **GREAT FAMINE**?

- What were the long-term and short-term causes of the **BLACK DEATH**?

THINKING ABOUT CONNECTIONS

- If the Mongol khan Ögedei had not died in 1241, the Mongols could conceivably have continued their westward movement into Europe. Given what you have learned about Mongol rule, how might this have changed the history of the world?

- How do the patterns of conquest and colonization discussed in this chapter compare to those of earlier periods, particularly those of antiquity? How many of these developments were new in 1250–1350?

- We live in a world in which the global circulation of people, information, goods, and bacteria is rapid. How does the medieval system compare to ours? What features seem familiar?

Rebirth and Unrest, 1350–1453

CORE OBJECTIVES

- **TRACE** the economic and social effects of the Black Death.

- **EXPLAIN** the relationship between the Middle Ages and the Renaissance.

- **DESCRIBE** the intellectual, cultural, and technological innovations of this era.

- **DEFINE** the concept of national monarchy and summarize its implications.

- **UNDERSTAND** the significance of the conciliar movement and its defeat by the papacy.

In June 1381, thousands of laborers from the English countryside rose up in rebellion against local authorities. Most were peasants or village craftsmen who were dismissed as ignorant by contemporary chroniclers. Yet the revolt was carefully coordinated: Plans were spread in coded messages circulated by word of mouth and by the followers of a renegade Oxford professor, John Wycliffe, who had called for the redistribution of Church property and taught that common people should be able to read the Bible in their own language. The rebellion's immediate catalyst had been a series of exorbitant taxes levied by Parliament for the support of the ongoing war with France. But its more fundamental cause was an epidemic that had occurred thirty years earlier. The Black Death had reduced the entire population of Europe by 30 to 50 percent and had drastically altered the world of those who survived it. In this new world, workers were valuable and could stand up to those who paid them poorly or treated them like slaves. In that fateful summer of 1381, the workers of England even vowed to kill representatives of both the Church and the government— to kill (as they put it) all the lawyers—and to destroy all the documents that had been used to keep them in subjection. It was a revolution, and it partly succeeded. Although the leaders were eventually captured and executed, the rebellion had made the strength of the common people known to all.

The fourteenth century is often seen as a time of crisis in the history of Western civilizations. Famine and plague cut fearful swaths through the population; war was a brutally recurrent fact of life; and the papacy spent seventy years in continuous exile from Italy, only to see its prestige decline further after its return to Rome. But this was also a time of extraordinary opportunity and achievement. The exhausted land of Europe recovered from centuries of overfarming, while workers gained the economic edge; eventually, some even gained social and political power. Meanwhile, popular and intellectual movements sought to reform the Church. A host of intellectual, artistic, and scientific innovations contributed to all of these phenomena.

This era of rebirth and unrest has been called by two different names: the later Middle Ages and the Renaissance. The latter refers to an intellectual and artistic movement that began in northern Italy, where the citizens of warring city-states desperately sought new models of governance and cultural cohesion by looking back to the older civilizations of Greece and Rome. But these are not two separate historical periods; rather they reflect two different ways of looking back at an era that is considered to be the immediate precursor of modernity. To understand it, we need to study it holistically. And we need to begin with a survey of Western civilizations after the Black Death.

THE PLAGUE CLAIMS A VICTIM. A priest gives last rites to a bedridden plague victim as a smiling devil pierces the dying man with a spear and as Christ looks mercifully down from heaven. ▪ *What are the possible meanings of this image?* ▪ *What does it reveal about contemporary attitudes toward death by plague?*

LIFE AFTER THE BLACK DEATH

By 1353, when the bubonic plague began to loosen its death grip on Europe, the Continent had lost nearly half of its population. This happened suddenly, within a half century, owing to a combination of famine and disease (see Chapter 10). In the following century, recurring outbreaks of the plague and frequent warfare in some regions would result in further drastic reductions. In Germany, some 400,000 villages disappeared. Around Paris, more than half of the farmland formerly under cultivation became pastureland. Elsewhere, abandoned fields returned to woodland, increasing the forested areas of Europe by about a third.

Life after the Black Death would therefore be radically different for those who survived it, because this massive depopulation would affect every aspect of existence, from nutrition to social mobility to spirituality.

First and foremost, it meant a relative abundance of food. The price of grain fell, which made it more affordable.

At the same time, the scarcity of workers made peasant labor more valuable: wages rose and work became easily obtainable. With wages high and food prices low, ordinary people could now afford more bread and could also spend their surplus cash on dairy products, meat, fish, fruits, and wine. As a result, the people of Europe were better nourished than they had ever been—better than many are today. A recent study of fifteenth-century rubbish dumps has concluded that the people of Glasgow (Scotland) ate a healthier diet in 1405 than they did in 2005.

The Rural Impact

In the countryside, a healthier ecological balance was almost immediately reestablished in the wake of the plague. And gradually, with the lessened demand for fuel and building materials, forests that had almost disappeared began to recover and expand. Meanwhile, the declining demand for grain allowed many farmers to expand their livestock herds. By turning arable land into pastureland, farmers reduced the need to hire so many workers and they also improved the fertility of the soil through manuring. Some farmers were even able to enlarge their holdings, because so much land had been abandoned.

Most of these innovations were made by small farmers because many great lords—individuals as well as monasteries—were slower to adjust to the changing circumstances. But some large landholders were quick to seize the advantage, responding to the shortage of workers and the rising cost of wages by forcing their tenants to perform additional unpaid labor. In parts of eastern Europe, many free peasants became serfs for the first time as a result. In Castile, Poland, and Germany, too, lords succeeded in imposing new forms of servitude.

In France and the Low Countries, by contrast, peasants remained relatively free, although many were forced to pay a variety of new fees and taxes to their lords or to the king. In England, where peasant bondage had been more common than in France, serfdom eventually disappeared altogether. Although the Peasants' Revolt of 1381 was ultimately unsuccessful, increased economic opportunity allowed English serfs to vote with their feet, either by moving to town or to the lands of a lord who offered more favorable terms: lower rents, more animals, fewer work requirements, and greater personal freedoms. Geographical mobility and social mobility are, as we have often noted, intertwined.

The Urban Impact

Mortality rates were high in the crowded cities and towns of Europe, but not all cities were equally affected by the plague and many recovered quickly. In London and Paris, for example, large-scale immigration from the countryside reversed the short-term declines caused by the plague. Many of these newcomers were women, whose economic opportunities (usually very limited) were greatly enhanced by urban labor shortages. Other urban areas suffered more from internal violence or warfare than from disease. In Florence, for example, the population rebounded quickly after the Black Death but was eventually depleted by civil unrest: by 1427, it had dropped from around 300,000 to about 100,000. In Toulouse (southwestern France), the population remained fairly stable until 1430, when it was reduced by a staggering 75 percent as a result of the ravages of the Hundred Years' War.

So while the overall population of Europe declined drastically because of the plague, it is noteworthy that a far larger percentage of all people were living in towns by 1500: approximately 20 percent as opposed to 10 or 15 percent prior to the Black Death. Fueling this urban growth was the increasing specialization of the late-medieval economy. With farmers under less pressure to produce grain in bulk, land could be devoted to livestock, dairy farming, and the production of a more diverse array of fruits and vegetables; and these could now be exchanged more efficiently on the open market.

Towns with links to extant trading networks benefited accordingly. In northern Germany, a group of entrepreneurial cities formed a coalition to build an entirely new mercantile corporation, the Hanseatic League, whose members came to control commerce from Britain and Scandinavia to the Baltic. In northern Italy, the increased demand for luxury goods—which even some peasants and urban laborers could now afford—brought renewed wealth to the spice- and silk-trading city of Venice and also to the fine-cloth manufacturers of Milan and the jewelers of Florence. Milan's armaments industry also prospered, supplying its warring neighbors and the armies of Europe.

Of course, not all urban areas flourished. The Franco-Flemish cities that had played such a large role in economic and cultural life since the eleventh century suffered a serious economic depression, exacerbated by incessant wars in the region. But, on the whole, surviving Europeans profited from the plague. A century afterward, they were poised to extend their commercial networks farther into Africa, Asia, and (ultimately) the Americas (see Chapter 12).

Popular Revolts and Rebellions

Although the consequences of the Black Death were ultimately beneficial for many, Europeans did not adjust easily to this new world; established elites, in particular, resisted the demands of newly powerful workers. When these demands were not met, violence erupted. Between 1350 and 1425, hundreds of popular rebellions challenged the status quo in many regions of Europe. In 1358, peasants in northeastern France rose up violently against their lords, destroying property, burning buildings and crops, and even murdering targeted individuals. This incident is known as the Jacquerie Rebellion, because all French peasants were caricatured by the aristocracy as "Jacques" ("Jack").

In England, as we have already noted, a very different uprising occurred in June of 1381, far more organized and involving a much wider segment of society. Thousands of people marched on London, targeting the bureaucracies of the royal government and the Church, capturing and killing the archbishop of Canterbury, and meeting personally with the fourteen-year-old king, Richard II, to demand an end to serfdom and taxation and to call for the redistribution of property. It ended with the arrest and execution of the ringleaders. In Florence, workers in the cloth industry—known as the Ciompi (*chee-OHM-pee*)—protested high unemployment and mistreatment by the manufacturers who also ran the Florentine government. They seized control of the city, demanding relief from taxes, full employment, and political representation. They maintained power for a remarkable six weeks before their reforms were revoked.

The local circumstances that lay behind each of these revolts were unique, but all of them exhibit certain common features. First of all, they were not bread riots spurred by destitution: those who took part in them were not protesting starvation wages, they were empowered by the new economic conditions and wanted to leverage their position in order to enact even larger changes. Some rebellions, like the English Peasants' Revolt, were touched off by resistance to new and higher taxes. Others, like the Jacquerie and the revolt of the Ciompi, took place at moments when unpopular governments were weakened by factionalism and military defeat. The English revolt was also fueled by the widespread perception of corruption within the Church and the royal administration.

Behind this social and political unrest, therefore, lies not poverty and hunger but the growing prosperity and self-confidence of village communities and urban laborers who were taking advantage of the changed economic circumstances that arose from the plague. For the most part, the rebels' hopes that they could fundamentally alter the conditions of their lives were frustrated. Kings, aristocrats, and urban oligarchs sometimes lost their nerve in the middle of an uprising, but they were almost always successful, after a time, in reasserting dominance. Yet this tradition of popular rebellion would remain an important feature of Western civilizations. It would eventually fuel the American War of Independence and the French Revolution (see Chapter 18), and it continues to this day.

Aristocratic Life in the Wake of the Plague

Although the urban elites and rural aristocracies of Europe did not adapt easily to "the world turned upside down" by the plague, this was hardly a period of crisis for those in power. Quite the contrary: many great families became far wealthier than their ancestors had ever been. Nor did the plague undermine the dominant position they had established. It did, however, make their situations substantially more complex and uncertain, at a time when the costs of maintaining a fashionable lifestyle were escalating rapidly.

Across Europe, most noble families continued to derive much of their revenue from vast land holdings. Many also tried to increase their sources of income through investment in trading ventures. In Catalonia, Italy, Germany, and England, this became common practice. In France and Castile, however, direct involvement in commerce was regarded as socially demeaning and was, therefore, avoided by established families. Commerce could still be a route to ennoblement in these kingdoms; but once aristocratic rank was achieved, one was expected to abandon these employments and adopt an appropriate way of life: living in a rural

A HUNTING PARTY. This fifteenth-century illustration shows an elaborately dressed group of noblemen and noblewomen setting out with falcons, accompanied by their servants and their dogs. Hunting, an activity restricted to the aristocracy, was an occasion for conspicuous consumption and display.

castle or urban palace surrounded by a lavish household, embracing the values and conventions of chivalry (engaging in the hunt, commissioning a family coat of arms), and serving the ruler at court and in war.

What it meant to be "noble" became, as a result, even more difficult to define than it had been during the twelfth and thirteenth centuries. In countries where noble rank entailed clearly defined legal privileges—such as the right to be tried only in special courts—proven descent from noble ancestors might be sufficient to qualify a family as noble in the eyes of the law. Legal nobility of this sort was, however, a somewhat less exclusive distinction than one might expect. In fifteenth-century Castile and Navarre, 10 to 15 percent of the total population had claims to be recognized as noble on these terms. In Poland, Hungary, and Scotland, the legally privileged nobility was closer to 5 percent, whereas in England and France fewer than 2 percent could plausibly claim the legal privileges of noble status.

Fundamentally, however, nobility was expressed and epitomized by an individual's lifestyle. Hereditary land ownership, political influence, deference from social inferiors, courtly manners, and the ostentatious display of wealth— these combined to constitute a family's honor and hence to mark it as noble. This means that, in practice, the social distinctions between noble and non-noble families were very hard to discern. And even on the battlefield, where the mark of nobility was to fight on horseback, the supremacy of the mounted knight was being threatened by the growing importance of professional soldiers, archers, crossbowmen, and artillery experts. There were even hints of a more radical critique of the aristocracy's claims to innate superiority. As the English rebels put it in 1381: "When Adam dug and Eve spun, Who then was a gentleman?" In other words, all social distinctions are entirely artificial.

Precisely because nobility was contested, those who claimed it took elaborate measures to assert their exclusive right to this status through conspicuous consumption. This accounts, in part, for the extraordinary number, variety, and richness of the artifacts and artworks that survive from this period. Aristocrats— or those who wanted to be classed as such—vied with one another in hosting lavish banquets, which required numerous costly utensils, specially decorated dining chambers, legions of servants, and the most exotic foods attainable. They dressed in rich and extravagant clothing: close-fitting doublets and hose with long pointed shoes for men, multilayered silk dresses with ornately festooned headdresses for women. They maintained enormous households: in France, around 1400, the Duke of Berry had 400 matched pairs of hunting dogs and 1,000 servants. They took part in elaborately ritualized tournaments and pageants, in which the participants pretended to be the heroes of chivalric romances. Aristocrats also emphasized their tastes and refinement by supporting authors and artists and some-

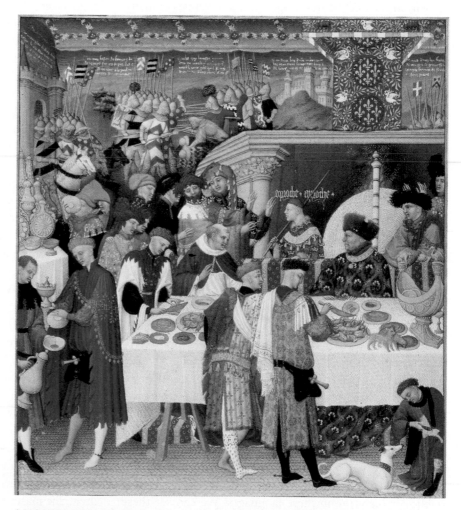

A NOBLE BANQUET. Uncle of the mad king Charles VI, the Duke of Berry left politics to his brothers, the Duke of Burgundy and the Duke of Anjou. In return, he received enormous subsidies from the royal government, which he spent on sumptuous buildings, festivals, and artworks, including the famous Book of Hours (prayer book), which includes this image. Here, the duke (seated at right, in blue) gives a New Year's Day banquet for his household, who exchange gifts while his hunting dogs dine on scraps from the table. In the background, knights confront one another in a tournament.

times by becoming accomplished artists themselves. Nobility existed only if it was recognized, and to be recognized noble status had to be constantly reasserted and displayed.

Rulers contributed to this process; indeed, they were among its principal supporters and patrons. Kings and princes across Europe competed in founding chivalric orders such as the Knights of the Garter in England and the Order of the Star in France. These orders honored men who had demonstrated the idealized virtues of knighthood, virtues celebrated as characteristic of the nobility as a whole. By exalting the nobility as a class, then, chivalric orders helped cement the links that bound the nobility to their kings and princes. These bonds were further strengthened by the gifts, pensions, offices, and marriage prospects that kings and princes could bestow on their noble followers.

Given the decline in the agricultural revenues of many noble estates, such rewards of princely service were critically important to maintaining noble fortunes. Indeed, the alliance that was forged in the fifteenth century between kings and their noble supporters would become one of the most characteristic features of Europe's ruling class. In France, this "Old Regime" (*ancien régime*) alliance lasted until the French Revolution of 1789. In Germany, Austria, and Russia, it would last until the outbreak of World War I. In England, it persisted in some respects until World War II.

Capturing Reality in Writing

The writings of literary artists who survived the Black Death, or who grew up in the decades immediately following it, are characterized by intense observations of the real world—and by appeals to a far larger and more diverse audience than their predecessors. We have noted that vernacular languages were becoming powerful vehicles for poetry and narrative in the twelfth century (see Chapter 9). Now they were being used to express some of the most innovative and critical perspectives on changing social mores, political developments, and philosophical outlooks. Behind this phenomenon lie three interrelated developments: the growing identification between vernacular language and the community of a realm, the still-increasing accessibility of education, and the emergence of a substantial reading public for literature in these languages. We can see these influences at work in three of the major authors who flourished during this period: Giovanni Boccaccio, Geoffrey Chaucer, and Christine de Pisan.

Boccaccio (*bohk-KAHT-chee-oh*, 1313–1375) is best known for *The Decameron*, a collection of prose tales about sex, adventure, and trickery. He presents these stories as being told over a period of ten days (hence the title of the book, which means "work of ten days"), by and for a sophisticated party of young women and men who have taken up residence in a country villa outside Florence in order to escape the ravages of the Black Death. Boccaccio borrowed the outlines of many of these tales from earlier sources, especially the fabliaux discussed in Chapter 9, but he couched them in a freely colloquial Italian. Whereas Dante had used the same Florentine dialect to evoke the awesome landscape of sacred history in the exquisite verse of his *Divine Comedy* (Chapter 10), Boccaccio used it to capture the foibles of human beings and their often graphic sexual exploits in plainspoken prose.

The English poet Geoffrey Chaucer (c. 1340–1400) is similar in many ways to Boccaccio, whose influence on him was profound. Chaucer was among the first generation of English authors whose compositions can be understood by modern readers of that language with relatively little effort. By the late fourteenth century, the Anglo-Saxon (Old English) tongue of England's preconquest inhabitants had mixed with the French dialect spoken by their Norman conquerors, to create the language which is the ancestor of our own: Middle English.

Chaucer's masterpiece is *The Canterbury Tales*. Like *The Decameron*, this is a collection of stories held together by a framing narrative. In this case, the stories are told by an array of people traveling together on a pilgrimage from London to the shrine of Saint Thomas Becket at Canterbury. But there are also significant differences between *The Decameron* and *The Canterbury Tales*. Chaucer's stories are in verse, for the most part, and they are recounted by people of all different classes—from a high-minded knight to a poor university student to a lusty widow. Each character tells a story that is particularly illustrative of his or her own occupation and outlook on the world, forming a kaleidoscopic human comedy.

This period, a generation or so after the Black Death, also saw the emergence of professional authors who made their living through the patronage of the aristocracy and the publication of their works. One of the first was a woman, Christine de Pisan (c. 1365–c. 1434). Although born in northern Italy, Christine spent her adult life in France, where her husband was a member of the king's household. When he died, the widowed Christine wrote to support herself and her children. She mastered a wide variety of literary genres, including treatises on chivalry and warfare, which she dedicated to King Charles VI of France. She also wrote for a larger and more popular audience. For example, her imaginative *Book of the City of Ladies* is an extended defense of the character, capacities, and history of women, designed to help female readers refute their male detractors. Christine also took part in a vigorous pamphlet campaign that condemned the misogynistic claims made by influential (male) authors like Boccaccio. This debate was ongoing for several hundred years and became so famous that it was given a name: the *querelle des femmes*, "the debate over women." Remarkably, Christine also wrote a song in praise of Joan of Arc. Sadly, she probably lived long enough to learn that this other extraordinary woman had been put to death for behaving in a way that was considered dangerously unwomanly (see below).

Visualizing Reality

Just as the desire to capture real experiences and convey real emotions was a dominant trait of the literature produced after the Black Death, so it was in the visual arts. This is evident both in the older arts of manuscript illumination and also in the new kinds of sculpture we discussed in Chapter 10.

CHRISTINE DE PISAN. One of the most prolific authors of the Middle Ages, Pisan used her influence to uphold the dignity of women and to celebrate their history and achievements. Here she is seen describing the prowess of an Amazon warrior who could defeat men effortlessly in armed combat.

A further innovation in the fifteenth century was the technique of painting in oils, a medium pioneered in Flanders, where artists found a ready market for their works among the nobility and wealthy merchants.

Oil paints were a revolutionary development: because they do not dry as quickly as water-based pigments, a painter can work more slowly and carefully, taking time with more difficult aspects of the work and making corrections as needed. Masterful practitioners of this technique include Rogier van der Weyden (c. 1400–1464), who excelled at communicating both deep spiritual messages and the minute details of everyday life (see **Interpreting Visual Evidence** on page 366). Just as contemporary saints saw divinity in material objects, so too an artist could portray the Virgin and Child against a background vista of ordinary life, with people going about their business or a man urinating against a wall. This was not blasphemous. To the contrary, it conveyed the message that the events of the Bible are constantly present, here and now: Christ is our companion, such artworks suggest, not some distant figure whose life and outlook are irrelevant to us.

The same immediacy is also evident in medieval drama. Plays were often devotional exercises that involved the efforts of an entire community, but they also celebrated that community. In the English city of York, for example, an annual series of pageants reenacted the entire history of human salvation from the Creation to the Last Judgment in a single summer day, beginning at dawn and ending late at night. Each pageant was produced by a particular craft guild and showcased that guild's special talents: "The Last Supper" was performed by the bakers, whose bread was a key element in their reenactment of the first Eucharist, while "The Crucifixion" was performed by the nail makers and painters, whose wares were thereby put on prominent display in the depiction of Christ's bloody death on the cross. In Italy, confraternities competed with one another to honor the saints with songs and processions. In Catalonia and many regions of Spain, there were elaborate dramas celebrating the life and miracles of the Virgin, one of which is still performed every year in the Basque town of Elche: it is the oldest European play in continuous production. In northern France, the Low Countries, and German-speaking lands, civic spectacles were performed over a period of several days, celebrating local history or the place of the community in the sacred history of the Bible. But not all plays were pious. Some honored visiting kings and princes. Others celebrated the flouting of social conventions, featuring cross-dressing and the reversal of hierarchies. They were further expressions of the topsyturvy world created by the Black Death.

Why a Woman Can Write about Warfare

Christine de Pisan (c. 1365–c. 1434) was one of the West's first professional writers, best known today for her Book of the City of Ladies *and* The Treasure of the City of Ladies, *works that aimed to provide women with an honorable and rich history and to combat generations of institutionalized misogyny. But in her own time, Christine was probably best known for the work excerpted here,* The Book of the Deeds of Arms and of Chivalry, *a manual of military strategy and conduct written at the height of the Hundred Years' War, in 1410.*

As boldness is essential for great undertakings, and without it nothing should be risked, I think it is proper in this present work to set forth my unworthiness to treat such exalted matter. I should not have dared even to think about it, but although boldness is blameworthy when it is foolhardy, I should state that I have not been inspired by arrogance or foolish presumption, but rather by true affection and a genuine desire for the welfare of noble men engaging in the profession of arms. I am encouraged, in the light of my other writings, to undertake to speak in this book of the most honorable office of arms and chivalry. . . . So to this end I have gathered together facts and subject matter from various books to produce this present volume. But inasmuch as it is fitting for this matter to be discussed factually, diligently, and sensibly . . . and also in consideration of the fact that military and lay experts in the aforesaid art of chivalry are not usually clerks or writers who are expert in language, I intend to treat the matter in the plainest possible language. . . .

As this is unusual for women, who generally are occupied in weaving, spinning, and household duties, I humbly invoke . . . the wise lady Minerva [Athena], born in the land of Greece, whom the ancients esteemed highly for her great wisdom. Likewise the poet Boccaccio praises her in his *Book of Famous Women*, as do other writers praise her art and manner of making trappings of iron and steel, so let it not be held against me if I, as a woman, take it upon myself to treat of military matters. . . .

O Minerva! goddess of arms and of chivalry, who, by understanding beyond that of other women, did find and initiate among the other noble arts and sciences the custom of forging iron and steel armaments and harness both proper and suitable for covering and protecting men's bodies against arrows slung in battle—helmets, shields, and protective covering having come first from you—you instituted and gave directions for drawing up a battle order, how to begin an assault and to engage in proper combat. . . . In the aforementioned country of Greece, you provided the usage of this office, and insofar as it may please you to be favorably disposed, and I in no way appear to be against the nation from which you came, the country beyond the Alps that is now called Apulia and Calabria in Italy, where you were born, let me say that like you I am an Italian woman.

Source: From *The Book of the Deeds of Arms and of Chivalry*, ed. Charity Cannon Willard and trans. Sumner Willard (University Park, PA: 1999), pp. 11–13.

Questions for Analysis

1. Christine very cleverly deflects potential criticism for her "boldness" in writing about warfare. What tactics does she use?

2. The Greco-Roman goddess Athena (Minerva) was the goddess of wisdom, weaving, and warfare. Why does Christine invoke her aid? What parallels does she draw between her own attributes and those of Minerva's?

THE BEGINNINGS OF THE RENAISSANCE IN ITALY

Rummaging through some old books in a cathedral library, an Italian bureaucrat attached to the papal court at Avignon was surprised to find a manuscript of Cicero's letters—letters that no living person had known to exist. They had probably been copied in the time of Charlemagne, but had then been forgotten for hundreds of years. How many other works of this great Roman orator had been lost to posterity? Clearly, thought Francesco Petrarca (1304–1374), he was living in an age of ignorance. A great gulf seemed to open up between his own time and have written to you long ago," he said in a Latin letter to the Greek poet Homer (dead for over 2,000 years), "had it not been for the fact that we lack a common language."

Petrarch was famous in his own day as an Italian poet, a Latin stylist, and a tireless advocate for the resuscitation of the classical past. The values that he and his followers began to espouse would give rise to a new intellectual and artistic movement in Italy, a movement strongly critical of the present and admiring of a past that had disappeared with the fragmentation of Rome's empire and the end of Italy's greatness. We know this movement as the Renaissance, from the French word for "rebirth" that was applied to it in the eighteenth century and popularized in the nineteenth, when the term *medieval* was also invented. It has since become shorthand for the epoch *following* the Middle Ages—but it was really part of that same era.

Renaissance Classicism

Talking about "the Renaissance," then, is a way of talking about some significant changes in education and artistic outlook that transformed the culture of northern Italy from the late fourteenth to the early sixteenth centuries and that eventually influenced the rest of Europe in important ways. The term has often been taken literally, as though the cultural accomplishments of antiquity had ceased to be appreciated and therefore needed to be "reborn." Yet we have been tracing the enduring influence of classical civilization for many chapters, and we have constantly noted the reverence accorded to the heritage of antiquity, not to mention the persistence of Roman law and Roman institutions.

That said, one can certainly find distinguishing traits that make the concept of "renaissance" newly meaningful in this era. For example, there was a significant quantitative difference between the ancient texts available to scholars in the first thousand years after Rome's fragmentation and those that became accessible in the fourteenth and fifteenth centuries. The discovery of "new" works by Livy, Tacitus, and Lucretius expanded the classical canon considerably, supplementing the well-studied works of Virgil, Ovid, and Cicero. More important was the expanded access to ancient Greek literature in western Europe. In the twelfth and thirteenth centuries, as we have seen in Chapters 8 and 9, Greek scientific and philosophical works became available to western Europeans thanks to increased contact with Islam, via Latin translations of Arabic translations of the original Greek.

Still, no Greek poems or plays were yet available in Latin translations, and neither were the major dialogues of Plato. Moreover, only a handful of western Europeans could

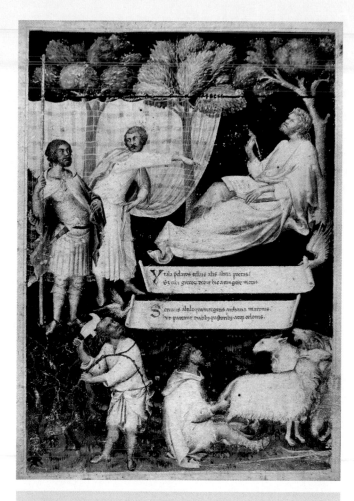

PETRARCH'S COPY OF VIRGIL. Petrarch's devotion to the classics of Roman literature prompted him to commission this new frontispiece for his treasured volume of Virgil's poetry. It was painted by the Sienese artist Simone Martini, who (like Petrarch) was attached to the papal court at Avignon. It is an allegorical depiction of Virgil (top right) and his poetic creations: the hero Aeneas (top left, wearing armor) and the farmer and shepherd whose humble labors are celebrated in Virgil's lesser-known works. The figure next to Aeneas is the fourth-century scholar Servius, who wrote a famous commentary on Virgil. He is shown drawing aside a curtain to reveal the poet in a creative trance. The two scrolls proclaim (in Latin) that Italy was the country that nourished famous poets and that Virgil helped it to achieve the glories of classical Greece. ▪ *How does this image encapsulate and express Petrarch's devotion to the classical past?*

that of the ancients: a middle age that separated him from those well-loved models.

For centuries, Christian intellectuals had regarded "the dark ages" as the time between Adam's expulsion from Eden and the birth of Christ. But now, Petrarch (the name by which English-speakers call Petrarca) redefined that concept and applied it to his own era. According to him, the Middle Ages was not the pagan past but the time that separated him from direct communion with the classics. Yet this did not stop him from trying to bridge the gap. "I would

Realizing Devotion

These two paintings by the Flemish artist Rogier van der Weyden (*FAN-der-VIE-den*, c. 1400–1464) capture some of the most compelling characteristics of late medieval art, particularly the trend toward realistic representations of holy figures and sacred stories. On the left (image A), the artist depicts himself as the evangelist Luke, regarded in Christian tradition as a painter of portraits; he sketches the Virgin nursing the infant Jesus in a town house overlooking a Flemish city. On the right (image B), van der Weyden imagines the entombment of the dead Christ by his followers, including the Virgin (left), Mary

Magdalene (kneeling), and the disciple John (right). Here, he makes use of a motif that became increasingly prominent in the later Middle Ages: Christ as the Man of Sorrows, displaying his wounds and inviting the viewer to share in his suffering. In both paintings, van der Weyden emphasizes the humanity of his subjects rather than their iconic status (see Chapter 7), and he places them in the urban and rural landscapes of his own world.

Questions for Analysis

1. How are these paintings different from the sacred images of the earlier Middle Ages (see, for example, pages 214 and 217)? What messages does the artist convey by setting these events in his own immediate present?

2. In what ways do these paintings reflect broad changes in popular piety and medieval devotional practices? Why, for example, would the artist display the dead and wounded body of Christ—rather than depicting him as resurrected and triumphant, or as an all-seeing creator and judge?

3. In general, how would you use these images as evidence of the worldview of the fifteenth century? What do they tell us about people's attitudes, emotions, and values?

A. Saint Luke drawing the portrait of the Virgin.

B. The Deposition.

read the language of classical Greece. But as the Mongols and, after them, the Ottoman Turks put increasing pressure on the shrinking borders of Byzantium (see below), more and more Greek-speaking intellectuals fled to Italy, bringing their books and their knowledge with them.

Thanks to these developments, some Italian intellectuals not only had increased access to more classical texts, they also used these texts in new ways. For centuries, Christian scholars had worked to bring ancient writings and values into line with their own beliefs (see Chapter 6). By contrast, the new reading methods pioneered by Petrarch and others fostered an increased awareness of the conceptual gap that separated the contemporary world from that of antiquity. This awakened a determination to recapture truly ancient worldviews and value systems, and it would eventually be expressed in visual terms, too. In the second half of the fifteenth century, especially, classical models contributed strikingly to the distinctive artistic style that is most strongly associated with the Renaissance (something we will address in Chapter 12).

Another distinguishing feature of this new perspective on the classical past was the way that it became overtly materialistic and commercialized. The competition among and within Italian city-states fostered a culture of display that used the symbols and artifacts of ancient Rome as pawns in an endless power game. Meanwhile, the relative weakness of the Church contributed to the growth of claims to power based on classical models—even by Italian bishops and Church-sponsored universities. When the papacy was eventually restored to Rome, it too had to compete in this Renaissance arena, by patronizing the artists and intellectuals who espoused these aesthetic and political ideals.

Renaissance Humanism

The most basic feature of this new intellectual and political agenda is summarized in the term *humanism*. This was a program of study that aimed to replace the scholastic emphasis on logic and theology—which would continue to be central to the curriculum of medieval universities like Paris and Oxford—with the study of ancient literature, rhetoric, history, and ethics. That is, the goal of a humanist education was the understanding of the human experience as viewed through the lenses of the classical past, and devoted to the fulfillment of human potential in the present. By contrast, a scholastic education filtered human experience through the teachings of scripture and the Church fathers, with human salvation as the ultimate goal.

Moreover, some intellectuals like Petrarch believed that the university curriculum concentrated too much on abstract speculation, rather than the achievement of virtue and ethical conduct in the here-and-now. He felt that the true Christian thinker must cultivate literary eloquence and so inspire others to do good through the pursuit of beauty and truth. And according to him, the best models of eloquence were to be found in the classics of Latin literature, which were also filled with ethical wisdom. Petrarch dedicated himself, therefore, to rediscovering such texts and to writing his own poems and moral treatises in a Latin style modeled on classical authors.

Humanists accordingly preferred ancient writings to those of more recent authors, including their own contemporaries. And although some humanists wrote in Italian as well as Latin, most regarded vernacular literature as a lesser diversion suitable only for the uneducated; serious scholarship and praiseworthy poetry could be written only in Latin or Greek. Proper Latin, moreover, had to be the classical Latin of Cicero and Virgil (Chapter 5), not the evolving language common to universities, international diplomacy, the law, and the Church. Renaissance humanists therefore condemned the living Latin of their day as a barbarous departure from classical (and therefore "correct") standards of Latin style. And ironically, their determination to revive this older language actually killed the lively Latin that had continued to flourish in Europe. By insisting on outmoded standards of grammar, syntax, and diction, they turned Latin into a fossilized discourse that ceased to have any direct relevance to daily life. They thus contributed, unwittingly, to the ultimate triumph of the various European vernaculars they despised, as well as to the demise of Latin as a common medium of communication.

Because humanism was an educational program designed to produce virtuous citizens and able public officials, it largely excluded women because women were largely excluded from Italian political life. Here again there is a paradox: as more and more Italian city-states fell into the hands of autocratic rulers, the humanist educational curriculum lost its immediate connection to the republican ideals of ancient Rome. Nevertheless, humanists never lost their conviction that the study of the "humanities" (as the humanist curriculum came to be known) was the best way to produce political leaders.

Why Italy?

These new attitudes toward education and the ancient past were fostered in a northern Italy for historically specific reasons. After the Black Death, this region was the most densely populated part of Europe; other urban areas, notably northeastern France and Flanders, had been decimated by the Great Famine as well as the plague. This region also differed from the rest of urbanized Europe because aristocratic families customarily lived in cities rather than in rural castles and consequently became more fully involved in public affairs than their counterparts north of the Alps. Moreover, many town-dwelling aristocrats were engaged in banking or mercantile enterprises, while many rich mercantile families imitated the manners of the aristocracy. The Florentine ruling family, the Medici, originally made their fortune in banking and commerce and yet were able to assimilate into the nobility.

These developments help to explain the emergence of the humanist ideals described above. Newly wealthy families were not content to have their sons learn only the skills necessary to becoming successful businessmen; they sought teachers who would impart the knowledge and finesse that would enable them to cut a figure in society, mix with their noble neighbors, and speak with authority on public affairs. Consequently, Italy produced and attracted a large number of independent intellectuals who were not affiliated with monasteries, cathedral schools, or universities—many of whom served as schoolmasters for wealthy young men while acting as cultural consultants and secretaries for their families. These intellectuals advertised their learning by producing political and ethical treatises and works of literature that would attract the attention of wealthy patrons or reflect well on the patrons they already had. As a result, Italian schools and private tutors turned out the best-educated laymen in all of Europe, men who constituted a new generation of wealthy, knowledgeable patrons ready to invest in the cultivation of new ideas and new forms of literary and artistic expression.

A second reason why late-medieval Italy was the birthplace of the Renaissance movement has to do with its vexed political situation. Unlike France and England, or the kingdoms of Spain, Scandinavia, and eastern Europe, Italy had no unifying political institutions. Italians therefore looked to the classical past for their time of glory, dreaming of a day when Rome would be, again, the center of the world. They boasted that ancient Roman monuments were omnipresent in their landscape and that classical Latin literature referred to cities and sites they recognized as their own.

Italians were particularly intent on reappropriating their classical heritage because they were seeking to establish an independent cultural identity that could help them oppose the intellectual and political supremacy of France. The removal of the papacy to Avignon had heightened antagonism between the city-states of Italy and the burgeoning nation-state beyond the Alps. This also explains the Italians' rejection of the scholasticism taught in northern Europe's universities and their embrace of intellectual alternatives. As Roman literature and learning took hold in the imaginations of Italy's intellectuals, so too did Roman art and architecture, for Roman models could help Italians create an artistic alternative to the dominant French school of Gothic architecture, just as Roman learning offered an intellectual alternative to the scholasticism of Paris.

Finally, this Italian Renaissance could not have occurred without the underpinning of Italian wealth gained through the commercial ventures described in Chapter 10. This wealth meant that talented men seeking employment and patronage were more likely to stay at home, fueling the artistic and intellectual competition that arose from the intensification of urban pride and the concentration of individual and family wealth in urban areas. Cities themselves became the primary patrons of art and learning in the fourteenth century.

The Renaissance of Civic Ideals

Petrarch's personal goal was a solitary life of contemplation and asceticism. But subsequent Italian intellectuals, especially those of Florence, developed a different vision of life's true purpose. For them, the goal of classical education was civic enrichment. Humanists such as Leonardo Bruni (c. 1370–1444) and Leon Battista Alberti (1404–1472) agreed with Petrarch on the importance of eloquence and the value of classical literature, but they also taught that man's nature equips him for action, for usefulness to his family and society, and for serving the state—ideally a city-state after the Florentine model. In their view, ambition and the quest for glory are noble impulses that ought to be encouraged and channeled toward these ends. They also refused to condemn the accumulation of material possessions, arguing that the history of human progress is inseparable from the human dominion of the earth and its resources.

Many of the humanists' civic ideals are expressed in Alberti's treatise *On the Family* (1443), in which the nuclear family is presented as the fundamental unit of the city-state and, as such, to be governed in such a way as to further the city-state's political and economic goals. Alberti accordingly argued that the family should mirror the city-state's organization. He therefore consigned women—who, in reality, governed the household—to childbearing, child rearing, and subservience to men even within this domestic realm. He asserted, furthermore, that women should play no role whatsoever in the public sphere. Although such dismissals of women's abilities were fiercely resisted by actual women, the humanism of the Renaissance was characterized by a pervasive denigration of them—a

A Renaissance Attitude toward Women

Italian society in the fourteenth and fifteenth centuries was characterized by marriage patterns in which men in their late twenties or thirties customarily married women in their mid- to late teens. This demographic fact probably contributed to the widely shared belief that wives were essentially children, who could not be trusted with important matters and who were best trained by being beaten. Renaissance humanism did little to change such attitudes. In some cases, it even reinforced them.

 fter my wife had been settled in my house a few days, and after her first pangs of longing for her mother and family had begun to fade, I took her by the hand and showed her around the whole house. I explained that the loft was the place for grain and that the stores of wine and wood were kept in the cellar. I showed her where things needed for the table were kept, and so on, through the whole house. At the end there were no household goods of which my wife had not learned both the place and the purpose. . . .

Only my books and records and those of my ancestors did I determine to keep well sealed. . . . These my wife not only could not read, she could not even lay hands on them. I kept my records at all times . . . locked up and arranged in order in my study, almost like sacred and religious objects. I never gave my wife permission to enter that place, with me or alone. . . .

[Husbands] who take counsel with their wives . . . are madmen if they think true prudence or good counsel lies in the female brain. . . . For this very reason I have always tried carefully not to let any secret of mine be known to a woman. I did not doubt that my wife was most loving, and more discreet and modest in her ways than any, but I still considered it safer to have her unable, and not merely unwilling, to harm me. . . . Furthermore, I made it a rule never to speak with her of anything but household matters or questions of conduct, or of the children.

Source: Leon Battista Alberti, "On the Family," in *The Family in Renaissance Florence*, ed. and trans. Renée N. Watkins (Columbia, SC: 1969), pp. 208–13, as abridged in Julie O'Faolain and Lauro Martines, eds., *Not in God's Image: Women in History from the Greeks to the Victorians* (New York: 1973), pp. 187–88.

Questions for Analysis

1. For what reasons did Alberti argue that a wife should have no access to books or records?

2. Would you have expected humanism to make attitudes to women more liberal and "modern"? How do views like Alberti's challenge such assumptions?

3. Compare Alberti's view of women to that of Christine de Pisan (page 364). How do you think Christine would have responded to this passage?

denigration often mirrored in the works of classical literature that these humanists so much admired.

The Emergence of Textual Criticism

The humanists of Florence eventually surpassed Petrarch in their knowledge of classical literature and philosophy, especially that of ancient Greece. In this, they were aided by a number of Byzantine scholars who had migrated to Italy in the first half of the fifteenth century and who gave instruction in the ancient form of their own native language. Wealthy, well-connected Florentines increasingly aspired to acquire Greek masterpieces for themselves, which often involved journeys back to Constantinople. In 1423, one adventurous bibliophile managed to bring back 238 manuscript books, among them rare works of Sophocles, Euripides, and Thucydides. These were quickly paraphrased in Latin and thus made accessible to western Europeans for the first time.

This influx of new classical texts spurred a new interest in textual criticism. A pioneer in this activity was Lorenzo Valla (1407–1457). Born in Rome and active primarily as a secretary to the king of Naples and Sicily, Valla had no allegiance to the republican ideals of the Florentine humanists. Instead, he turned his skills to the painstaking analysis of Greek and Latin writings in order to show how the historical study of language could discredit old assumptions and even unmask some texts as forgeries. For example, some papal propagandists argued that the papacy's claim to secular power in Europe derived from rights granted to the bishop of Rome by the emperor Constantine in the fourth century, enshrined in a document known as "The Donation of Constantine." By analyzing the language of this spurious text, Valla proved that it could not have been written in the time of Constantine because it contained more recent Latin usages and vocabulary.

This demonstration not only discredited more traditional scholarly methods, it made the concept of anachronism central to all subsequent textual study and historical thought. Indeed, Valla even applied his expert knowledge of Greek to elucidating the meaning of Saint Paul's letters, which he believed had been obscured by Jerome's Latin translation (see Chapter 6). This work was to prove an important link between Italian Renaissance scholarship and the subsequent Christian humanism of the north, which in turn fed into the Reformation (see Chapter 13).

THE END OF THE EASTERN ROMAN EMPIRE

The Greek-speaking refugees who arrived in Italy after the Black Death were self-appointed exiles. They were responding to the succession of calamities that had reduced the once-proud eastern Roman Empire to a scattering of embattled provinces. As we've noted, when Constantinople fell to western crusaders in 1204, the surrounding territories of Byzantium were severed from the capital that had held them together as constituent parts of that empire (see Chapter 9). When the Latin presence in Constantinople was finally expelled in 1261, imperial power had been so weakened that it extended only into the immediate hinterlands of the city and to parts of the Greek Peloponnese. The rest of the empire had become a collection of small principalities that existed in precarious alliance with the Mongols and indeed depended on the Pax Mongolica for survival (see Chapter 10). Then, with the coming of the Black Death, the imperial capital suffered the loss of half of its inhabitants and

shrunk still further. Meanwhile, the disintegration of the Mongol Empire laid the larger region of Anatolia open to a new set of invaders.

The Rise of the Ottoman Turks

Like the Mongols, the Turks were originally a nomadic people whose economy depended on raiding. When the Mongols arrived in northwestern Anatolia, the Turks were already established there and were being converted to Islam by the resident Muslim powers of the region: the Seljuq Sultanate of Rûm and the Abbasid Caliphate of Baghdad. But when the Mongols toppled these older powers, they eliminated the two traditional authorities that had kept Turkish border chieftains in check. Now they were free to raid, unhindered, along the soft frontiers of Byzantium. At the same time, they remained far enough from the centers of Mongol authority to avoid being destroyed themselves. One of their chieftains, Osman Gazi (1258–1326), established his own independent kingdom. Eventually, his name would characterize the Turkish dynasty that controlled the most ancient lands of Western civilizations for six centuries: the Ottomans.

By the mid-fourteenth century, Osman's successors had solidified their preeminence by capturing a number of important cities. These successes brought the Ottomans to the attention of the Byzantine emperor, who hired a contingent of them as mercenaries in 1345. They were extraordinarily successful—so much so that the eastern Roman Empire could not control their movements. They struck out on their own and began to extend their control westward. By 1370, their holdings stretched all the way to the Danube. In 1389, they defeated a powerful coalition of Serbian forces at the battle of Kosovo, which enabled them to begin subduing Bulgaria, the Balkans, and eventually Greece. In 1396, the Ottoman army even attacked Constantinople itself, although it withdrew to repel an ineffectual crusading force that had been hastily sent by the papacy.

In 1402, another attack on Constantinople was deflected—this time, by a more potent foe who had ambitions to match those of the Ottomans. Timur the Lame (Tamerlane, as he was called by European admirers) was born to a family of small landholders in the Mongol Khanate of Chagatai (named for its first ruler, the second son of Genghis Khan). Although Timur may have been a Turk himself, he acted as the spiritual heir of the Mongol Empire. While still a young man, he rose to prominence as a military leader and gained a reputation for tactical genius. He was no politician, though, and never officially assumed the title of khan in any of the territories he dominated. Instead, he moved ceaselessly from conquest to conquest, becoming the master of lands stretching

THE HEAD OF TIMUR THE LAME. This bust of the Mongol leader known in the West as Tamerlane is based on a forensic reconstruction of his exhumed skull.

from the Caspian Sea to the Volga River, as well as most of Persia. For a time, it looked briefly as if the Mongol Empire might be reunited under his reign. But Timur died in 1405, on his way to invade China, and his various conquests fell into the hands of local rulers. Mongol influence continued in the Mughal Empire of India, whose rulers claimed descent from the followers of Genghis Khan. But in Anatolia, the Ottoman Turks were once again on the rise.

The Fall of Constantinople

After the death of Timur, Ottoman pressure on Constantinople resumed and escalated. During the 1420s and 1430s, monasteries and schools that had been established since the fourth century found themselves in the path of an advancing army, and a steady stream of fleeing scholars strove to salvage a millennium's worth of Byzantine books—many of them preserving the heritage of ancient Greece and the Hellenistic

world. Then, in 1451, the Ottoman sultan Mehmet II turned his full attention to the conquest of the imperial city. In 1453, after a brilliantly executed siege, his army succeeded in breaching its walls. The Byzantine emperor was killed in the assault, the city itself was plundered, and its remaining population was sold into slavery. The Ottomans then settled down to rule their new capital in a style reminiscent of their Byzantine predecessors.

The Ottoman conquest of Constantinople administered an enormous shock to European rulers and intellectuals—and, indeed, the latter would profit mightily from this event. Yet its actual political and economic impact was minor. Ottoman control may have reduced European access to the Black Sea, but the bulk of the Far Eastern luxury trade with Europe had never passed through Black Sea ports in the first place. Europeans got most of their spices and silks through Venice, which imported them from Alexandria and Beirut, and these two cities did not fall to the Ottomans until the 1520s. Moreover, as we saw in Chapter 10, Europeans already had colonial ambitions and significant trading interests in Africa and the Atlantic that connected them to far-reaching networks.

But if the practical effects of the Ottoman conquest were modest where western Europe was concerned, the effects on the Turks themselves were transformative. Vast new wealth poured into Anatolia, which the Ottomans increased by carefully tending to the industrial and commercial interests of their new capital city, Constantinople, which they also called Istanbul—the Turkish pronunciation of the Greek phrase *eis tan polin* "in (or to) the city." Trade routes were redirected to feed the capital, and the Ottomans became a naval power in the eastern Mediterranean as well as in the Black Sea. As a result, Constantinople's population grew rapidly, from fewer than 100,000 in 1453 to more than 500,000. By 1600, it was the largest city in the world outside of China.

Slavery and Social Advancement in the Ottoman Empire

Despite the Ottomans' careful attention to commerce, their empire continued to rest on the spoils of conquest. To manage its continual expansion, the size of the Ottoman army and administration grew exponentially, drawing more and more manpower from conquered territories. And because both army and bureaucracy were largely composed of slaves, the demand for more soldiers and administrators could best be met through further conquests that would capture yet more slaves. Those conquests, however, required a still larger army and an even more extensive bureaucracy—and so the cycle continued. It mirrors, in many respects, the

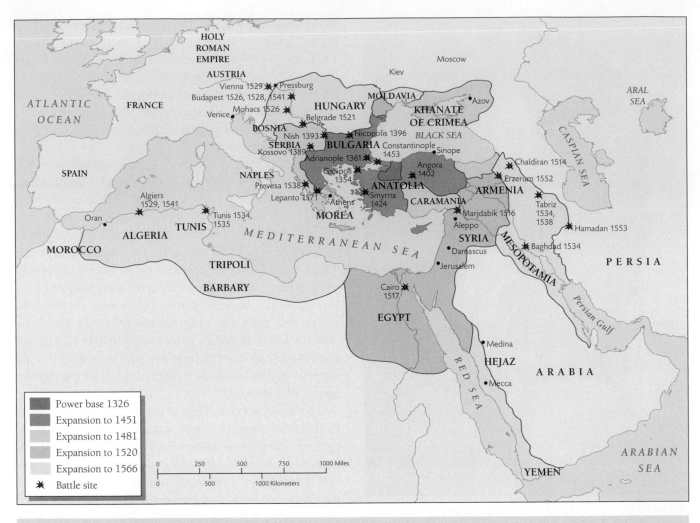

THE GROWTH OF THE OTTOMAN EMPIRE. Consider the patterns of Ottoman expansion revealed in this map. ▪ *Where is Constantinople, and how might the capture of Constantinople in 1453 have facilitated further conquests?* ▪ *Compare the extent of the Ottoman Empire in 1566 with that of the Byzantine Empire under Justinian (see the map on page 212). How would you account for their similarities?*

dilemma of the Roman Empire in the centuries of its rapid expansion beyond Italy (see Chapter 5), which created an insatiable demand for slaves.

Not only were slaves the backbone of Ottoman government, they were also critical to the lives of the Turkish upper class. One of the important measures of status in Ottoman society was the number of slaves in one's household. After the capture of Constantinople, new wealth would permit some elites to maintain households in the thousands. By the sixteenth century, the sultan alone possessed more than 20,000 slave attendants, not including his bodyguard and elite infantry units, both of which also comprised slaves.

Where did all of these slaves come from? Many were captured in war. Many others were taken on raiding forays into Poland and Ukraine and sold to Crimean slave merchants, who shipped their captives to the slave markets of Constantinople. But slaves were also recruited (some willingly, some by coercion) from rural areas of the Otto-

man Empire itself. Because the vast majority of slaves were household servants and administrators rather than laborers, some men willingly accepted enslavement, believing that they would be better off as slaves in Constantinople than as impoverished peasants in the countryside. In the Balkans especially, many people were enslaved as children, handed over by their families to pay the "child tax" the Ottomans imposed on rural areas too poor to pay a monetary tribute. Although an excruciating experience for families, this practice did open up opportunities for social advancement. Special academies were created at Constantinople to train the most able of the enslaved male children to act as administrators and soldiers, some of whom rose to become powerful figures in the Ottoman Empire.

For this reason, slavery carried relatively little social stigma. Even the sultan himself was most often the son of an enslaved woman. And because Muslims were not permitted to enslave other Muslims, the vast majority of Ottoman

SULTAN MEHMET II, "THE CONQUEROR" (r. 1451–81).
This portrait, executed by the Ottoman artist Siblizade Ahmed, exhibits features characteristic of both Central Asia and Europe. The sultan's pose—his aesthetic appreciation of the rose, his elegant handkerchief—are indicative of the former, as is the fact that he wears the white turban of a scholar and the thumb ring of an archer. But the subdued coloring and three-quarter profile may reflect the influence of Italian portraits. ■ *What did the artist achieve through this blending of styles and symbols?* ■ *What messages does this portrait convey?*

welcome refuge from the persecutions and expulsions that had characterized Jewish life in late-medieval Europe. After their expulsion from Spain in 1492 (see Chapter 12), more than 100,000 Spanish (Sephardic) Jews ultimately immigrated to the territories of the Ottoman Empire.

Because the Ottoman sultans were Sunni Muslims, they often dealt harshly with other Muslim sects. But they were extremely tolerant of non-Muslims. They organized the major religious groups of their empire into legally recognized units and permitted them considerable rights of self-government. They were especially careful to protect and promote the authority of the Greek Orthodox patriarch of Constantinople over the Orthodox Christians of their empire. As a result, the Ottomans enjoyed staunch support from their Orthodox Christian subjects during their wars with the Christians of western Europe.

Russia: "The Third Rome"

The Orthodox Church also received staunch support from the Russian people, whose own Church had been founded by Byzantine missionaries in the tenth century (see Chapter 8) and whose written language was based on the Greek alphabet and Greek grammar. Indeed, the emerging duchy of Muscovy (see Chapter 10) saw itself as the natural protector and ally of the eastern Roman Empire, and its alienation from western Europe increased as Byzantium grew weaker and the responsibility for defending Orthodox Christianity devolved onto the Russian Church.

But when the patriarch of Constantinople agreed to submit to the authority of Rome in 1438, in the desperate hope that the papacy would rally military support for the besieged city, Russian clergy refused to follow suit. After Constantinople fell to the Turks—predictably, without any help from Latin Christendom—the Russian Church emerged as the only surviving proponent of Orthodox Christianity.

Its sense of isolation was increased by developments on its western borders. In the thirteenth century, the small kingdom of Poland had struggled to defend itself from absorption by German princes. But when the Holy Roman Empire's strength waned after the death of Frederick the Great (see Chapter 9), Poland's situation grew more secure. In 1386, its reigning queen, Jadwiga, subsequently enabled its dramatic expansion when she married Jagiello, the duke of neighboring Lithuania, thus doubling the size of her kingdom. Lithuania had begun to carve out an extensive territory stretching from the Baltic to modern-day Belarus and Ukraine, and this expansionist momentum increased after its union with Poland. In 1410, a combined Polish and Lithuanian force defeated the Teutonic Knights at the Battle of Tannenberg,

slaves were Christian—although many eventually converted to Islam. And because so many of the elite positions within Ottoman government were held by these slaves, the paradoxical result was that Muslims, including the Turks themselves, were effectively excluded from the main avenues of social and political influence in the Ottoman Empire. Avenues to power were therefore remarkably open to men of ability and talent, most of them non-Muslim slaves.

Nor was this power limited to the government and the army. Commerce and business also remained largely in the hands of non-Muslims, most frequently Greeks, Syrians, and Jews. Jews in particular found in the Ottoman Empire a crushing the military order that controlled a crucial region lying between the allied kingdoms. Thereafter, Poland-Lithuania began to push eastward toward Muscovy.

Although many of Lithuania's aristocratic families were Orthodox Christians, the established church in Poland was loyal to Rome. Thus, when the inhabitants of Muscovy started to feel threatened by Poland-Lithuania, one way of constructing a shared Muscovite identity was to direct hostility toward Latin Christendom. Another was to take up the imperial mantle that had been abandoned when Constantinople fell, and to declare the Muscovite state the divinely appointed successor to Rome. To drive the point home, Muscovite dukes began to take the title of tsar, "caesar." "Two Romes have fallen," said a Muscovite chronicler, "the third is still standing, and a fourth there shall not be."

WARFARE AND NATION BUILDING IN EUROPE

War has always been an engine for the development of new technologies. This is something we have noted since Chapter 1, but in the era after the Black Death the pace and scale of warfare was escalated to an unprecedented degree—and so was the deployment of new weapons. Although explosives had been invented in China, and originally used in displays of fireworks, they were first put to devastating and destructive effect in Europe. In fact, the earliest cannons were as dangerous to those who fired them as to those who were targeted. But by the middle of the fifteenth century, they were reliable enough to revolutionize the nature of warfare. In 1453, heavy artillery played a leading role in the outcomes of two crucial conflicts: the Ottoman Turks breached the ancient defenses of Constantinople with cannon fire and the French captured the English-held city of Bordeaux, bringing an end to the attenuated conflict known as the Hundred Years' War.

Thereafter, cannons made it more difficult for rebellious aristocrats to hole up in their stone castles and so consequently aided in the consolidation of national monarchies. Cannons placed aboard ships made Europe's developing navies more effective. A handheld firearm, the pistol, was also invented in the fourteenth century, and around 1500 the musket ended forever the military dominance of heavily armored cavalry, giving the advantage to foot soldiers recruited from the ranks of average citizens.

This suggests that there is a symbiotic relationship between warfare and nation building as well as between warfare and technology. Because Europeans were almost constantly at war from the fourteenth century to the middle

of the twentieth, governments claimed new powers to tax their subjects and to control their subjects' lives. Armies became larger, military technology deadlier. Wars became more destructive, society more militarized. As a result of these developments, the most successful European states were aggressively expansionist and aggressively engaged in creating an idea of national identity that would bind people together against a common enemy.

The Hundred Years' War Resumes

The hostilities that make up the Hundred Years' War can be divided into three main phases (see the maps on page 000). The first phase dates from the initial declaration of war in 1337 (see Chapter 10), after which the English won a series of startling military victories before the Black Death put a temporary halt to the hostilities. The war then resumed in 1356, with another English victory at Poitiers. Four years later, in 1360, Edward III decided to leverage his strong position: he renounced his larger claim to the French throne, and in return he was to be guaranteed full sovereignty over a greatly enlarged duchy of Gascony and the promise of a huge ransom for the king of France, whom he held captive.

But the terms of the treaty were never honored, nor did it resolve the underlying issues that had led to the war itself, namely the problem of making good on any claim to sovereignty in contested territory and the question of the English king's place in the French royal succession. The French king continued to treat the English king as his vassal, while Edward and his heirs quickly renewed their claim to the throne of France.

Although there were no pitched battles in France itself for two decades after this, a destabilizing proxy war developed during the 1360s and 1370s, which spread violence to neighboring regions. Both the English troops (posted in Gascony) and the French troops (eager to avenge their losses) were reluctant to settle down. Many organized into "Free Companies" of mercenaries and hired themselves out in the service of hostile factions in Castile and competing city-states in northern Italy. By 1376, when the conflict between England and France was reignited, the Hundred Years' War had become a Europe-wide phenomenon.

England's Disputed Throne and the Brief Victory of Henry V

In this second phase of the war, the tide quickly shifted in favor of France. The new king, Charles V (r. 1364–80), imposed a series of taxes to fund the raising of an army,

A FIFTEENTH-CENTURY SIEGE WITH CANNONS. Cannons were an essential element in siege warfare during the Hundred Years' War.

restored order by disbanding the Free Companies, and hired the leader of one of these bands as the commander of his army. He thereby created a professional military that could match the English in discipline and tactics. By 1380, English territories in France had been reduced to a core area around the southwestern city of Bordeaux and the port of Calais in the extreme northeast.

Meanwhile, the aging Edward III has been succeeded by his nine-year-old grandson, Richard II (r. 1377–99), who was too young to prosecute a claim to the French crown. This was problematic, because the war had been extremely popular in England. Indeed, its mismanagement by Richard's advisers was one of the issues that triggered the Peasants' Revolt in 1381. And when Richard came of age and showed no signs of martial ambition, many of his own aristocratic relatives turned against him. Richard retaliated against the ringleader of this faction, his cousin Henry of Lancaster, by sending him into exile and confiscating his property. Henry's supporters used this as pretext for rebellion. In 1399, Richard was deposed by Henry and eventually murdered.

As a usurper whose legitimacy was always in doubt, Henry IV (r. 1399–1413) struggled to maintain his authority in the face of retaliatory rebellions and other challenges to his kingship. The best way to unite the country would have been to renew the war against France, but Henry was

frequently ill and in no position to lead an army into combat. But when his son Henry V succeeded him in 1413, the new king immediately began to prepare for an invasion. His timing was excellent: the French royal government was foundering owing to the insanity of the reigning king, Charles VI (r. 1380–1422). A brilliant diplomat as well as a capable soldier, Henry V sealed an alliance with the powerful Duke of Burgundy, who was allegedly loyal to France but stood to gain from its defeat at the hands of the English. Henry also made a treaty with the German emperor, who agreed not to come to France's aid.

When he crossed the Channel in the autumn of 1415, Henry V's troops thus faced a much-depleted French army that could not rely on reinforcements. Although it was still vastly larger and boasted hundreds of mounted knights, it was undisciplined. It was also severely hampered by bad weather and deep mud when the two armies clashed at Agincourt on October 25 of that year—conditions that favored the lighter English infantry. Henry's men managed to win a crushing victory.

Then, over the next five years, Henry conquered most of northern France. In 1420, the ailing Charles VI was forced to recognize him as heir to the throne of France, thereby disinheriting his own son. (This prince bore the ceremonial title of *dauphin*, "the dolphin," from the heraldic device of the borderland province he inherited.) Henry sealed the deal by marrying the French princess, Catherine, and fathering an heir to the joint kingdom of England and France.

Joan of Arc's Betrayal and Legacy

Unlike his great-grandfather Edward III, who used his claim to the French throne largely as a bargaining chip to secure sovereignty over Gascony (see Chapter 10), Henry V honestly believed himself to be the rightful king of France. And his astonishing success in capturing the kingdom seemed to put the stamp of divine approval on that claim. But Henry's successes in France also transformed the nature of the war, turning it from a profitable war of conquest and plunder into an extended and expensive military occupation. It might have been sustainable had Henry been as long-lived as many of his predecessors. But he died early in 1422, just short of his thirty-sixth birthday. King Charles VI died only a few months later.

The new king of England and France, Henry VI (r. 1422–61), was only an infant, and yet the English armies under the command of his regents continued to press southward into territories held by the dauphin. Although it seemed unlikely that English forces would ever succeed in dislodging him, confidence in the dauphin's right to the throne had been shattered by his own mother's declaration that he was illegitimate. It might have happened that England would once again rule an empire comprising much of northern France, as it had for a century and a half after the Norman conquest.

But this scenario fails to reckon with Joan of Arc. In 1429, a peasant girl from Lorraine (a territory only nominally part of France) made her way to the dauphin's court and announced that an angel had told her that he, Charles, was the rightful king, and that she, Joan, should drive the English out of France. The fact that she even got a hearing underscores the hopelessness of the dauphin's position, as does the extraordinary fact that he gave her a contingent of troops. With this force, Joan liberated the strategic city of Orléans, then under siege by the English, after which a series of victories culminated in Charles's coronation in the cathedral of Reims, the traditional site for the crowning of French kings.

But, despite her miraculous success, Joan was an embarrassment whose very charisma made her dangerous: a peasant leading aristocrats, a woman leading men, and a commoner who claimed to have been commissioned by God. When, a few months later, the Burgundians captured her in battle and handed her over to the English, the king she had helped to crown did nothing to save her. Accused of witchcraft, condemned by the theologians of Paris, and tried for heresy by an English ecclesiastical court, Joan was burned to death in the market square at Rouen in 1431. She was nineteen years old.

The French forces whom Joan had inspired, however, continued on the offensive. In 1435, the duke of Burgundy withdrew from his alliance with England, and when the young English king, Henry VI, proved first incompetent and then insane, a series of French military victories brought hostilities to an end with the capture of Bordeaux in 1453. English kings would threaten to renew the war for another century, and Anglo-French hostility would last until the defeat of Napoleon in 1815. But after 1453, English control over French territory would be limited to the port of Calais, which eventually fell in 1558.

The Long Shadow of the Hundred Years' War

The Hundred Years' War challenged the very existence of France. The disintegration of that kingdom, first during the 1350s and 1360s, and again between 1415 and 1435, glaringly revealed the fragility of the bonds that tied the king to the nobility, and the royal capital Paris to the kingdom's

JOAN OF ARC. A contemporary sketch of Joan was drawn in the margin of this register documenting official proceedings at the Parlement of Paris in 1429.

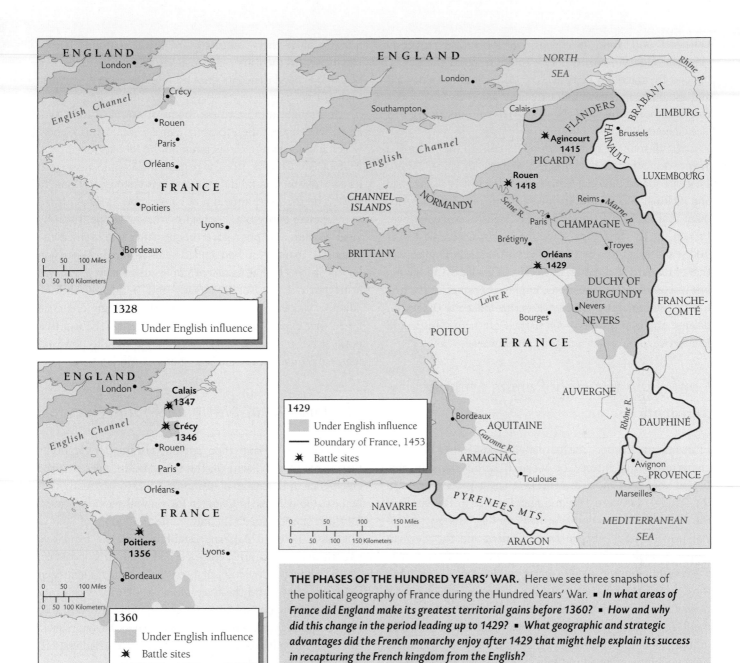

ENGLAND
London

Crécy
Rouen
Paris
Orléans

FRANCE

Poitiers

Lyons

Bordeaux

0 50 100 Miles
0 50 100 Kilometers

1328
Under English influence

ENGLAND
London

Calais
1347

Crécy
1346
Rouen

Paris

Orléans

FRANCE

Poitiers
1356

Lyons

Bordeaux

0 50 100 Miles
0 50 100 Kilometers

1360
Under English influence
✳ Battle sites

ENGLAND
London

NORTH SEA
Rhine R.

Southampton

Calais

FLANDERS
HAINAULT
BRABANT
LIMBURG
Brussels

✳ Agincourt 1415

PICARDY

LUXEMBOURG

CHANNEL ISLANDS

NORMANDY

Rouen 1418 ✳

Seine R.

Reims
Marne R.

Paris

CHAMPAGNE

BRITTANY

Brétigny

Troyes

Orléans 1429 ✳

DUCHY OF BURGUNDY

FRANCHE-COMTÉ

Bourges

Nevers

NEVERS

Loire R.

POITOU

FRANCE

AUVERGNE

Rhône R.

DAUPHINÉ

Bordeaux

AQUITAINE

Garonne R.

ARMAGNAC

Toulouse

Avignon

PROVENCE

Marseilles

NAVARRE

PYRENEES MTS.

MEDITERRANEAN SEA

ARAGON

1429
Under English influence
Boundary of France, 1453
✳ Battle sites

0 50 100 150 Miles
0 50 100 150 Kilometers

THE PHASES OF THE HUNDRED YEARS' WAR. Here we see three snapshots of the political geography of France during the Hundred Years' War. ▪ *In what areas of France did England make its greatest territorial gains before 1360?* ▪ *How and why did this change in the period leading up to 1429?* ▪ *What geographic and strategic advantages did the French monarchy enjoy after 1429 that might help explain its success in recapturing the French kingdom from the English?*

---

outlying regions. Nonetheless, the king's power was actually increased by the war's end, laying the foundations on which the power of early modern France would be built.

The Hundred Years' War also had dramatic effects on the English monarchy. When English armies in France were successful, the king rode a wave of popularity that fueled an emerging sense of English identity. When the war turned against the English, however, defeats abroad undermined support for the monarch at home. Of the nine English kings who ruled England between 1307 and 1485, five were deposed and murdered by factions.

This was a consequence of England's peculiar form of kingship, whose strength depended on the king's ability to

mobilize popular support through Parliament while maintaining the support of his nobility through successful wars. Failure to maintain this balance was even more destabilizing in England than it would have been elsewhere, precisely because royal power was so centralized. In France, the nobility could endure the insanity of Charles VI because his government was not powerful enough to threaten them. In England, neither the nobility nor the nation could afford the weak kingship of Henry VI. The result was an aristocratic rebellion against the king that led to a full-blown civil war: the Wars of the Roses, so called—by the novelist Sir Walter Scott (1771–1832)—because of the floral emblems, red and white, adopted by the two competing noble families

Lancaster and York. It ended only when a Lancastrian claimant, Henry Tudor (r. 1485–1509), resolved the dynastic feud by marrying Elizabeth of York, ruling as Henry VII and establishing a new Tudor dynasty whose symbol was a rose with both white and red petals. His son was Henry VIII (see Chapter 13).

So, despite England's ultimate defeat, the Hundred Years' War strengthened English identity in several ways. First, it equated national identity with the power of the state and its king. Second, it fomented a strong anti-French sentiment that led to the triumph of the English vernacular over French for the first time since the Norman conquest over 300 years earlier: the first English court to speak English was that of Richard II, a patron of Geoffrey Chaucer. And having lost its continental possessions, England became, for the first time, a self-contained island nation that looked to the sea for defense and opportunity—not to the Continent. This would later prove to be an advantage in many ways.

Conflict in the Holy Roman Empire and Italy

Elsewhere in Europe, the perpetual warfare that began to characterize the history of Western civilizations in this period was even more destructive than it proved to be in the struggle between England and France. In the lands of the Holy Roman Empire, armed conflict among territorial princes, and between these princes and the German emperor, weakened all combatants significantly. Periodically, a powerful emperor would emerge to play a major role, but the dominant trend was toward the continuing dissolution of power, with German princes dividing their territories among their heirs while free cities and local lords strove to shake off the princes' rule. Between 1350 and 1450, near anarchy prevailed in many regions. Only in the eastern regions of the empire were the rulers of Bavaria, Austria, and Brandenburg-Prussia able to strengthen their authority, mostly by supporting the efforts of the nobility to subject their peasants to serfdom and by conquering and colonizing new territories on their eastern frontiers.

In northern and central Italy, the last half of the fourteenth century was also marked by incessant conflict. With the papacy based in Avignon, the Papal States collapsed and Rome itself was riven by factional violence. Warfare among northern city-states added to the violence caused by urban rebellions in the wake of the plague. But around 1400, Venice, Milan, and Florence had succeeded in stabilizing their differing forms of government. Venice was now ruled by an oligarchy of merchants; Milan by a family of despots; and Florence was ruled as a republic but dominated by the influence of a few wealthy clans, especially the Medici banking family. Having settled their internal problems, these three cities then began to expand their influence by subordinating other cities to their rule.

Eventually, almost all the towns of northern Italy were allied with one of these powers. An exception was Genoa, which had its own trading empire in the Mediterranean and Atlantic (see Chapter 10). The papacy, meanwhile, reasserted its control over central Italy when it was restored to Rome in 1377. The southern kingdom of Naples and Sicily persisted as a separate entity but a constantly unstable one, riven by local warfare and poor government. After 1453, when the Hundred Years' War had ended and Ottoman expansion had been checked at Constantinople, an uneasy peace was achieved in Italy. But diplomacy and frequently shifting alliances did little to check the ambitions of any one state for further expansion, and it could not change the fact that none of these small-scale states could oppose the powerful national monarchies or empires that surrounded Italy.

The Growth of National Monarchies

In France and England, then, as well as in smaller kingdoms like Scotland and Portugal, the later Middle Ages saw the emergence of European states more cohesive than any that had existed before. (In Chapter 12, we will see how powerful this cohesion made the new united kingdom of Spain.) The basic political patterns established in the formative twelfth and thirteenth centuries had made this possible, yet the active construction of a sense of national identity in these territories, and the fusion of that identity with kingship, were new phenomena. Forged by war and fueled by the growing cultural importance of vernacular languages, this fusion produced a new type of political organization: the national monarchy.

The advantages of these national monarchies when compared to older forms of political organization—such as the empire, the principality, or the city-state—would become very evident. When the armies of France or Spain invaded the Italian peninsula at the end of the fifteenth century, neither the militias of the city-states nor the far-flung resources of Venice were a match for them. Germany and the Low Countries would suffer similar invasions only a few generations later and, along with Italy, would remain battlegrounds for competing armies until the middle of the nineteenth century. But the new national monarchies brought significant disadvantages, too. They guaranteed the prevalence of warfare in Europe as they continued their struggle for sovereignty and territory, and they would eventually transport their rivalry to every corner of the globe in the late nineteenth and early twentieth centuries.

Analyzing Primary Sources

The Condemnation of Joan of Arc by the University of Paris, 1431

After Joan's capture by the Burgundians, she was handed over to the English and tried for heresy at an ecclesiastical court set up in Rouen. It was on this occasion that the theology faculty of Paris pronounced the following verdict on her actions.

You, Joan, have said that, since the age of thirteen, you have experienced revelations and the appearance of angels, of St. Catherine and St. Margaret, and that you have very often seen them with your bodily eyes, and that they have spoken to you. As for the first point, the clerks of the University of Paris have considered the manner of the said revelations and appearances . . . Having considered all . . . they have declared that all the things mentioned above are lies, falsenesses, misleading and pernicious things and that such revelations are superstitions, proceeding from wicked and diabolical spirits.

Item: You have said that your king had a sign by which he knew that you were sent by God, for St. Michael, accompanied by several angels, some of which having wings, the others crowns, with St. Catherine and St. Margaret, came to you at the chateau of Chinon. All the company ascended through the floors of the castle until they came to the room of your king, before whom the angel bearing the crown bowed. . . .

As for this matter, the clerks say that it is not in the least probable, but it is rather a presumptuous lie, misleading and pernicious, a false statement, derogatory of the dignity of the Church and of the angels. . . .

Item: you have said that, at God's command, you have continually worn men's clothes, and that you have put on a short robe, doublet, shoes attached by points, also that you have had short hair, cut around above the ears, without retaining anything on your person which shows that you are a woman, and that several times you have received the body of Our Lord dressed in this fashion, despite having been admonished to give it up several times, the which you would not do. You have said that you would rather die than abandon the said clothing, if it were not at God's command, and that if you were wearing those clothes and were with the king, and those of your party, it would be one of the greatest benefits for the kingdom of France. You have also said that not for anything would you swear an oath not to wear the said clothing and carry arms any longer. And all these things you say you

have done for the good and at the command of God. As for these things, the clerics say that you blaspheme God and hold him in contempt in his sacraments; you transgress Divine Law, Holy Scripture, and canon law. You err in the faith. You boast in vanity. You are suspected of idolatry and you have condemned yourself in not wishing to wear clothing suitable to your sex, but you follow the custom of Gentiles and Saracens.

Source: Carolyne Larrington, ed. and trans., *Women and Writing in Medieval Europe* (New York: 1995), pp. 183–84.

Questions for Analysis

1. Paris was in the hands of the English when this condemnation was issued. Is there any evidence that its authors were coerced into making this pronouncement?

2. On what grounds was Joan condemned for heresy?

3. In what ways does Joan's behavior highlight larger trends in late medieval spirituality and popular piety?

THE TRIALS OF THE ROMAN CHURCH

Although the century after the Black Death would witness the papacy's return to Rome, it would also witness changes in the Church that would have far-reaching consequences in the centuries to come. Like other large landowners, the monasteries of Europe suffered from the economic changes brought about by the new world order, as did the Church's bishops, who confronted the same dilemmas as the secular nobility. But no ecclesiastical institution suffered more severe trials than the papacy, which endured almost seventy years of exile from Rome followed by a debilitating forty-year schism. It then faced a protracted battle with reformers who sought to reduce the pope's role in Church governance. Even though the papacy won this battle in the short term, the renewed abuse of papal power would, in the long run, bring about the permanent schism caused by the Reformation of the sixteenth century (see Chapter 13).

The Great Western Schism

In the decades that were transforming European society in so many other ways, calls for the papacy's return to Rome grew more insistent. It was eventually brought about by the letter-writing campaign of the nun and mystic Catherine of Siena (1347–1380), whose teasing but pious missives to Gregory XI (r. 1370–78) alternately shamed and coerced him. In 1377, he was persuaded to make the move.

But the papacy's restoration was short lived. A year after Gregory's return to Rome, he died. His cardinals—many of them Frenchmen—struggled to interpret the wishes of the volatile Romans, whose habit of expressing themselves through violence was unsettling to outsiders. Later, the cardinals would claim to have capitulated to the Roman mob when they elected an Italian candidate, Urban VI. When Urban fell out with them soon afterward, the cardinals fled the city and, from a safe distance, declared his selection invalid because it had been made under duress. They then elected a new pope, a Frenchman who took the name Clement VII. Urban retaliated by naming a new and entirely Italian College of Cardinals and by refusing Clement access to the city. The French pope and his cardinals withdrew ignominiously to the papal palace in Avignon, while the Italian pope remained in Rome.

The resulting rift is known as the Great Schism, or the Great Western Schism (to distinguish it from the Great East–West Schism between the Latin and Orthodox Churches). Between 1378 and 1417, the Roman Church was divided between two (and, ultimately, three) competing papacies, each claiming to be legitimate and each denouncing the heresy of the others.

Not surprisingly, Europe's religious allegiances fractured along the political lines drawn by the ongoing Hundred Years' War: France and her allies Scotland, Castile, Aragon, and Naples recognized the pope in Avignon; whereas England, Germany, northern Italy, Scandinavia, Bohemia, Poland, and Hungary recognized the Roman pope. Nor was there any obvious way to end this embarrassing state of affairs. The two rival Colleges of Cardinals continued to elect successors every time a pope died, perpetuating the problem. Finally, in 1409, some cardinals from both camps met at Pisa, where they ceremoniously declared the deposition of both popes and named a new one from among their number. But neither of the popes reigning in Rome and Avignon accepted that decision, so there were now three rival popes excommunicating one another instead of only two.

The Council of Constance and the Failure of the Conciliar Movement

This debacle was ultimately addressed between 1414 and 1418 at the Council of Constance, the largest and longest ecclesiastical gathering since the Council of Nicea, over a thousand years before (see Chapter 6). Its chief mission was to remove all rival claimants for papal office before agreeing on the election of a new pope: an Italian who took the name Martin V. But many of the council's delegates had even more far-reaching plans for the reform of the Church, ambitions that stemmed from the legal doctrine that gave the council power to depose and elect popes in the first place.

This doctrine, known as conciliarism, holds that supreme authority within the Church rests not with the pope but with a representative general council—and not just the council convened at Constance but any future council. The delegates at Constance thus decreed that general councils should meet regularly to oversee the governance of the Church, and to act as a check on the unbridled use of papal power.

Had conciliarism triumphed, the Reformation of the following century might not have occurred. But, predictably, Martin V and his successors did everything they could to undermine this doctrine, precisely because it limited their power. When the next general council met at Siena in 1423, Pope Martin duly sent representatives—who then turned around and went back to Rome. (The Council of Constance had specified that councils must meet frequently but had not specified how long those meetings should last.) The following year, the delegates to a general council at Basel took steps to ensure that the pope could not dismiss it, after which a lengthy struggle for power ensued between the advocates of papal monarchy and the conciliarists. Twenty-five years later, in 1449, the Council of Basel dissolved itself, bringing to an end a radical experiment in conciliar government—and dashing the hopes of those who thought it would lead to an internal reformation thorough enough to keep the Roman Church intact.

Spiritual Challenges

We have noted that the spiritual and social lives of medieval Christians were inextricably intertwined; indeed, any distinction between the two would have made little sense to

Past and Present

Replacing "Retired" Popes

When Benedict XVI decided to retire from papal office in February 2013, pundits and theologians alike struggled to find a precedent for this extraordinary decision. Most reached back to the year 1417, when Pope Martin V was elected at the Council of Constance (left) to replace the "retired" Gregory XII. But in this case, the retirement was not voluntary—and it was accompanied by the enforced resignation of an additional rival pope and the excommunication of yet another. The installation mass of Pope Francis in March 2013 (right) was much more universally celebrated and much more public than that of his medieval predecessor.

 Watch related author interview on StudySpace
wwnorton.com/web/westernciv18

the people of this era. The parish church stood literally at the center of their lives. Churchyards were communal meeting places, sometimes even the sites of markets, and church buildings were a refuge from attack and a gathering place for parish business. The church's holidays marked the passage of the year, and the church's bells marked the hours of the day. The church was holy, but it was also essential to daily life.

Yet, in the wake of the Black Death, when many parishes ceased to exist and many communities were decimated, an increasing number of medieval Christians were not satisfied with these conventional practices and developed forms of piety that were distinctly controversial. Many are regarded today as saints, but this was not necessarily the case in their lifetimes. Indeed, the distinction between the superhuman powers of a saint and those of a witch could be difficult to discern. As Joan of Arc's predicament reveals, medieval women found it particularly challenging to find outlets for their piety that would not earn

them the condemnation of the Church. (Executed as heretic, Joan would be officially exonerated a generation later, but she would not be canonized as a saint until 1920, when belief in her intercession during World War I gained wide support and was considered a decisive factor in the victory of France and its allies.)

Many women therefore internalized their devotional practices or confined them to the domestic sphere—sometimes to the inconvenience of their families and communities. For example, the young Catherine of Siena (who later convinced the papacy to return to Rome) refused to help with the housework or to support her working-class family; instead, she took over one of the house's two rooms for her own private prayers, confining her parents and a dozen siblings to the remaining room. Julianne of Norwich (1342–1416) withdrew from the world into a small cell built next to her local church, where she spent the rest of her life in prayer and contemplation. Her

Council or Pope?

> The Great Schism spurred a fundamental and far-reaching debate about the nature of authority within the Church. Arguments for papal supremacy rested on traditional claims that the popes were the successors of Saint Peter, to whom Jesus Christ had delegated his own authority. Arguments for the supremacy of a general council had been advanced by many intellectuals throughout the fourteenth century, but it was only in the circumstances of the schism that these arguments found a wide audience. The following documents trace the history of the controversy, from the declaration of conciliar supremacy at the Council of Constance (Haec Sancta), to the council's efforts to guarantee regular meetings of general councils thereafter (Frequens), to the papal condemnation of appeals to the authority of general councils issued in 1460 (Execrabilis).

Haec Sancta Synodus (1415)

This holy synod of Constance . . . declares that being lawfully assembled in the Holy Spirit, constituting a general council and representing the Catholic Church Militant, it has its power directly from Christ, and that all persons of whatever rank or dignity, even a Pope, are bound to obey it in matters relating to faith and the end of the Schism and the general reformation of the church of God in head and members.

Further, it declares that any person of whatever position, rank, or dignity, even a Pope, who contumaciously refuses to obey the mandates, statutes, ordinances, or regulations enacted or to be enacted by this holy synod, or by any other general council lawfully assembled, relating to the matters aforesaid or to other matters involved with them, shall, unless he repents, be . . . duly punished. . . .

Source: R. L. Loomis, ed. and trans., *The Council of Constance* (New York: 1961), p. 229.

Frequens (1417)

The frequent holding of general councils is the best method of cultivating the field of the Lord, for they root out the briars, thorns, and thistles of heresies, errors, and schisms, correct abuses, make crooked things straight, and prepare the Lord's vineyard for fruitfulness and rich fertility. Neglect of general councils sows the seeds of these evils and encourages their growth. This truth is borne in upon us as we recall times past and survey the present.

Therefore by perpetual edict we . . . ordain that henceforth general councils shall be held as follows: the first within the five years immediately following the end of the present council, the second within seven years from the end of the council next after this, and subsequently

younger contemporary, the housewife Margery Kempe (c. 1372–c. 1439), resented the fact that she had a husband, several children, and a household to support, and thus could not take such a step. In later life, she renounced her wifely duties and devoted her life to performing acts of histrionic piety, which alienated many of those who came into contact with her. For example, she was so moved by the contemplation of Jesus's sufferings on the cross that she would cry hysterically for hours, disrupting the Mass. When on pilgrimage in Rome, she cried at the sight of babies that reminded her of the infant Jesus, or young men whom she thought resembled him.

The extraordinary piety of such individuals could be inspiring, but it could also threaten the Church's control over religious life and the links that bound individuals to their communities. It could, therefore, be dangerous. More safely orthodox was the practical mysticism preached by Thomas à Kempis, whose *Imitation of Christ* (c. 1427) taught readers how to appreciate aspects of the divine in their everyday lives. Originally written in Latin, *The Imitation* was quickly every ten years forever. . . . Thus there will always be a certain continuity. Either a council will be in session or one will be expected at the end of a fixed period. . . .

Source: R. L. Loomis, ed. and trans., *The Council of Constance* (New York: 1961), pp. 246–47.

Execrabilis (1460)

An execrable abuse, unheard of in earlier times, has sprung up in our period. Some men, imbued with a spirit of rebellion and moved not by a desire for sound decisions but rather by a desire to escape the punishment for sin, suppose that they can appeal from the Pope, Vicar of Jesus Christ—from the Pope, to whom in the person of blessed Peter it was said, "Feed my sheep" and "whatever you bind on earth will be bound in heaven"—from this Pope to a future council. How harmful this is to the Christian republic, as well as how contrary to canon law, anyone who is not ignorant of the law can understand. For . . . who would not consider it ridiculous to appeal to something which does not now exist anywhere nor does anyone know when it will exist? The poor are heavily oppressed by the powerful, offenses remain unpunished, rebellion against the Holy See is encouraged, license for sin is granted, and all ecclesiastical discipline and hierarchical ranking of the Church are turned upside down.

Wishing therefore to expel this deadly poison from the Church of Christ, and concerned with the salvation of the sheep committed to us . . . with the counsel and assent of our venerable brothers, the Cardinals of the Holy Roman Church, together with the counsel and assent of all those prelates who have been trained in canon and civil law who follow our Court, and with our own certain knowledge, we condemn appeals of this kind, reject them as erroneous and abominable, and declare them to be completely null and void. And we lay down that from now on, no one should dare . . . to make such an appeal from our decisions, be they legal or theological, or from any commands at all from us or our successors. . . .

Source: Reprinted by permission of the publisher from Gabriel Biel, *Defensorium Obedientiae Apostolicae et Alia Documenta*, ed. and trans. Heiko A. Oberman, Daniel E. Zerfoss, and William J. Courtenay (Cambridge, MA: 1968), pp. 224–27. Copyright © 1968 by the President and Fellows of Harvard College.

Questions for Analysis

1. On what grounds does *Haec Sancta* establish the authority of a council? Why would this be considered a threat to papal power?

2. Why was it considered necessary for councils to meet regularly (*Frequens*)? What might have been the logical consequences of such regular meetings?

3. On what grounds does *Execrabilis* condemn the appeals to future councils that have no specified meeting date? Why would it not have condemned the conciliar movement altogether?

translated into many vernacular languages and is now more widely read than any other Christian book except the Bible.

Popular Reform Movements

For the most part, the threat of heretical movements was less dangerous to the Church than the corruption of the papacy. But in the kingdoms of England and Bohemia (the modern Czech Republic), some popular movements did pose serious challenges. The key figure in both cases was John Wycliffe (c. 1330–1384), an Oxford theologian and powerful critic of the Church. A survivor of the Black Death, Wycliffe lived at a time when the authority and integrity of the papacy were at a particularly low ebb. Indeed, he concluded that the empty sacraments of a corrupt Church could not save anyone. He therefore urged the English king to confiscate ecclesiastical wealth and to replace corrupt priests and bishops with men who would live according to apostolic standards of poverty and piety.

THE GREAT SCHISM, 1378–1417. During the Great Western Schism, the various territories of Europe were divided in their allegiances. ■ *According to the map key, who were they choosing between?* ■ *What common interests would have united the supporters of the Avignon pope or of the Roman pope?* ■ *Why would areas like Portugal and Austria waver in their support?*

Some of Wycliffe's followers, known to their detractors as Lollards (from a word meaning "mumblers" or "beggars"), went even further, dismissing the sacraments as fraudulent attempts to extort money from the faithful. Lollard preachers also advocated for direct access to the scriptures and promoted an English translation of the Bible sponsored by Wycliffe himself.

Wycliffe's teachings played an important role in the Peasants' Revolt of 1381, and Lollardy gained numerous adherents in the decades after his death. The movement was even supported by a number of aristocratic families; certainly the idea of dissolving the Church's wealth would have been attractive to many of those who stood to gain from it. But, after a failed Lollard uprising in 1414, both the movement and its supporters went underground in England.

In Bohemia and eastern Europe, however, Wycliffe's ideas lived on and struck even deeper roots. They were adopted by Jan Hus (c. 1373–1415), a charismatic teacher at the royal university in Prague. In contrast to the Lollards,

WYCLIFFE'S ENGLISH BIBLE. Although John Wycliffe was not directly responsible for this translation of the Bible, it was made in the later fourteenth century by his followers. Written in the same Middle English vernacular used by Geoffrey Chaucer for his popular works, it was designed to be accessible to lay readers who did not understand Latin. This page shows the beginning of the Gospel of John: "In ye bigynnyng was / ye word & ye word / was at god & god was the word. Yis was in ye bi / gynninge at god, all yingis weren maad bi him. . . ." ▪ *Compare this translation to a modern one. How different (or not) is this version of English?* ▪ *What might have been the impact of this language on readers and listeners in the late fifteenth century?* ▪ *How would translation have helped to further the reforming efforts of Wycliffe and his disciples?*

THE TEACHINGS OF JAN HUS. An eloquent religious reformer, Jan Hus was burned at the stake in 1415 after having been found guilty of heresy at the Council of Constance. This lavishly illustrated booklet of his teachings was published over a century later in his native Bohemia and includes texts in the Czech vernacular and in Latin. ▪ *What does its later publication suggest about the uses to which Hus's image and theology were put during the Protestant Reformation?*

who had scornfully dismissed the Mass and thereby lost much popular support, Hus emphasized the centrality of the Eucharist to Christian piety. Indeed, he demanded that the laity be allowed to receive not only the conse-crated bread but also the consecrated wine, which was usually reserved solely for priests. This demand became a rallying cry for the Hussite movement. Influential nobles also supported Hus, partly in the hope that the reforms he demanded might restore revenues they had lost to the Church over the previous century.

Accordingly, most of Bohemia was behind him when Hus traveled to the Council of Constance to publish his views and to urge the assembled delegates to undertake sweeping reforms. But rather than giving him a hearing, the other delegates to the council convicted Hus of heresy and had him burned at the stake. Back home, Hus's supporters raised the banner of open revolt, and the aristocracy took advantage of the situation to seize Church property. Between 1420 and 1424, armed bands of fervent Hussites resoundingly defeated several armies, as priests, artisans, and peasants rallied to pursue Hus's goals of religious reform and social justice.

These victories increased popular fervor, but they also made radical reformers increasingly volatile. In 1434, accordingly, a more conservative arm of the Hussite movement was able to negotiate a settlement with the Bohemian church. By the terms of this settlement, Bohemians could receive both the bread and wine of the Mass, which thus placed them beyond the pale of Latin orthodoxy and effectively separated the Bohemian national church from the Church of Rome.

Lollardy and Hussitism exhibit a number of striking similarities. Both began in the university and then spread to the countryside. Both called for the clergy to live in simplicity and poverty, and both attracted noble support, especially in their early days. Both movements were also strongly nationalistic, employing their own vernacular languages (English and Czech) and identifying themselves with the English or Czech people in opposition to a "foreign" Church. They also relied on vernacular preaching and social activism. In all these respects, they established patterns that would emerge again in the vastly larger currents of the Protestant Reformation (see Chapter 13).

CONCLUSION

The century after the Black Death was a period of tremendous creativity and revolutionary change. The effects of the plague were catastrophic, but the resulting food surpluses, opportunities for expansion, and labor shortages encouraged experimentation and opened up broad avenues for enrichment. Europe's economy diversified and expanded, and increasing wealth and access to education produced new forms of art and new ways of looking at the world. Hundreds and perhaps thousands of new schools were

After You Read This Chapter

Visit StudySpace for quizzes, additional review materials, and multimedia documents. **wwnorton.com/web/westernciv18**

REVIEWING THE OBJECTIVES

- The Black Death had short-term and long-term effects on the economy and societies of Europe. What were some of the most important changes?
- The later "Middle Ages" and "the Renaissance" are often perceived to be two different periods, but the latter was actually part of the former. Explain why.
- What were some of the intellectual, cultural, and artistic innovations of this era in Italy and elsewhere in Europe?
- How were some European kingdoms becoming stronger and more centralized during this period? What are some examples of national monarchies?
- The conciliar movement sought to limit the power of the papacy. How? Why was this movement unsuccessful?

established, and scores of new universities would emerge as a result. Women were still excluded from formal schooling but nevertheless became active—and in many cases dominant—participants in literary endeavors, cultural life, and religious movements. Average men and women not only became more active in cultivating their own worldly goals, they also took control of their spiritual destinies at a time when the institutional Church provided little inspiring leadership.

Meanwhile, some states were growing stronger and more competitive while other regions remained deeply divided. The rise of the Ottoman Empire eventually absorbed many of the oldest territories of Western civilizations, including the venerable Muslim caliphate at Baghdad, the Near Eastern portions of the former Mongolian Empire, the Christian Balkans and Greece, and—above all—the surviving core of the eastern Roman Empire at Constantinople. Greek-speaking refugees streamed into Italy, many bringing with them classics of Greek philosophy and literature hitherto unknown in Europe. Fueled by new ideas and a fervid nostalgia for the ancient past, Italians began to experiment with new ways of reading ancient texts, advocating a return to classical models while at the same time trying to counter the political and artistic authority of the more powerful kingdoms north of the Alps.

In contrast to Italy, these emerging national monarchies cultivated group identity through the promotion of a shared vernacular language and allegiance to a strong, more centralized state. These tactics would allow smaller kingdoms like Poland and Scotland to increase their territories and their influence and would lead France and England into an epic battle for sovereignty and hegemony. The result, in all cases, was the escalation of armed conflict as incessant warfare drove more powerful governments to harvest a larger percentage of their subjects' wealth through taxation, which they proceeded to invest in ships, guns, and the standing armies made possible by new technologies and more effective administration.

In short, the generations who survived the calamities of famine, plague, and warfare seized the opportunities their new world presented to them. In the latter half of the fifteenth century, they stood on the verge of an extraordinary period of expansion and conquest that enabled them to dominate the globe.

PEOPLE, IDEAS, AND EVENTS IN CONTEXT

- Compare and contrast the **BLACK DEATH**'s effects on rural and urban areas.
- In what ways do rebellions like the **ENGLISH PEASANTS' REVOLT** reflect the changes brought about by the plague? How do the works of **GIOVANNI BOCCACCIO, GEOFFREY CHAUCER,** and **CHRISTINE DE PISAN** exemplify the culture of this era?
- What was **HUMANISM**? How was it related to the artistic and intellectual movement known as the **RENAISSANCE**?
- How did the **OTTOMAN EMPIRE** come to power? What were some consequences of its rise?
- On what grounds did **MUSCOVY** claim to be "the third Rome"? What is the significance of the title **TSAR**?
- What new military technologies were in use during the **HUNDRED YEARS' WAR**? How did this conflict affect other parts of Europe, beyond England and France? What role did **JOAN OF ARC** play?
- How did the **COUNCIL OF CONSTANCE** respond to the crisis of the **GREAT SCHISM**?
- Why did **CONCILIARISM** fail? How did **JOHN WYCLIFFE** and **JAN HUS** seek to reform the Church?

THINKING ABOUT CONNECTIONS

- In the year 2000, a group of historians was asked to identify the most significant historical figure of the past millennium. Rather than selecting a person (e.g., Martin Luther, Shakespeare, Napoleon, Adolf Hitler), they chose the microbe *Yersinia pestis,* which had caused the Black Death. Do you agree with this assessment? Why or why not?
- In your view, which was more crucial to the formation of the modern state: the political and legal developments we surveyed in Chapter 9 or the emergence of national identities we discussed in this chapter? Why?
- Was the conciliar movement doomed to failure, given what we have learned about the history of the Roman Church? How far back does one need to go, in order to trace the development of disputes over ecclesiastical governance?

Before
You
Read
This
Chapter

Innovation and Exploration, 1453–1533

CORE OBJECTIVES

- **UNDERSTAND** the relationship between Renaissance ideals and the political and economic realities of Italy.

- **IDENTIFY** the key characteristics of Renaissance arts and learning during this period.

- **DEFINE** the term *Reconquista* and its meaning in Spain.

- **DESCRIBE** the methods and motives of European colonization during this period.

- **EXPLAIN** why Europeans were able to dominate the peoples of the New World.

W hat if exact copies of an idea could circulate quickly, all over the world? What if the same could be done for the latest news, the oldest beliefs, the most beautiful poems, the most exciting—and deadly—discoveries? It would be doing for knowledge what the invention of coinage did for wealth: making it portable, easier to use and disseminate. Indeed, it's no accident that the man who developed such a technology, Johannes Gutenberg of Mainz (c. 1398–1468), was the son of a goldsmith who made coins for the bishop of that German city. Both crafts were based on the same principle and used the same basic tools. Coins are metal disks that have each been stamped with identical words and images, impressed on them with a reusable matrix. The pages of the first printed books—and later newspapers, leaflets, and pamphlets—were stamped with ink spread on rows of movable type (lead or cast-iron letter forms and punctuation marks) slotted into frames to form lines of words. Once a set of pages was ready, a press could make hundreds of copies in a matter of hours, many hundreds of times faster than the same page could be copied by hand. Afterward, the type could be reused.

A major stimulus for this invention was the more widespread availability of paper, a trend that had begun in the late thirteenth century. Parchment, northern Europe's chief writing material since the advent of the codex (see Chapter 6), was extremely expensive to manufacture and required special training on the part of those who used it—one reason why writing remained a specialized skill for much of the Middle Ages, while the ability to read was common. Paper, made from rags turned into pulp by mills, was both cheaper and far easier to use; accordingly, books became cheaper and written communication became easier and more widespread. Growing levels of literacy led to a growing demand for books, which in turn led to experimentation with different methods of book production—and to Gutenberg's breakthrough of the 1450s. By 1455, his workshop had printed multiple copies of the Latin Bible, of which forty-eight complete or partial volumes survive. Although printing never entirely replaced traditional modes of publication via manuscript, it made the cost of books affordable and revolutionized the spread of information.

In fact, the printing press played a crucial role in many of the developments that we will study in this chapter. The artistic and intellectual experiments that contributed to an Italian Renaissance were rapidly exported to other parts of Europe, and specifications for innovative weapons would be printed on the same presses that churned out humanist biographies. News of Columbus's first voyage and the subsequent conquests of the Americas would spread via the same media as critiques of European imperialism there. Printing not only increased the volume and rapidity of communication, it made it more difficult for those in power to censor dissenting opinions.

But at the same time as it created new forms of agency, the printing press also become an indispensable tool of more traditional powers, making it possible for rulers to govern growing empires abroad and increasingly centralized states at home. The "reconquest" of Spain and the extension of Spanish imperialism to the New World were both facilitated by the circulation of printed propaganda. The widespread availability of reading materials even helped to standardize national languages, by enabling governments to promote one official printed dialect over others. Hence the "king's English," the variety of the language spoken around London, was imposed as the only acceptable literary and bureaucratic language throughout the English realm, contributing to the growth of a common linguistic identity among readers. For these reasons, among others, many historians consider the advent of print to be both the defining event and the driving engine of modernity, and

it coincided with another essentially modern development: the discovery of a "New World."

RENAISSANCE IDEALS—AND REALITIES

The intellectual and artistic movement that had begun in Italy during the fourteenth century was, as we noted in Chapter 11, characterized by an intense interest in the classical past and by a new type of educational program known as humanism. These Renaissance ideals—and the realities that both undergirded and complicated them—would be extended and diversified in the later fifteenth century through the medium of the printing press. By the time the Ottoman conquest of Constantinople was complete, just a year before Gutenberg's workshop began to produce pages of the Bible, decades of uncertainty and warfare had propelled hundreds of refugees from the eastern Roman Empire into Italy. Many carried with them precious manuscripts of Greek texts that had long been unavailable in western Europe: the epics of Homer, the major surviving works of Athenian dramatists, the dialogues of Plato. Prior to the invention of print, such manuscripts could be owned and studied by only a very few, very privileged men. Now printers in Venice and other European cities rushed to produce cheap editions of these texts as well as Greek grammars and glossaries that could facilitate reading them.

Within a few decades, so many men were engaged in the study of Plato that an informal "Platonic Academy" had formed in Florence. There, the work of intellectuals like Marsilio Ficino (1433–1499) and Giovanni Pico della Mirandola (1463–1494) was fostered by the patronage of the wealthy Cosimo de' Medici. Based on his reading of Plato, Ficino's philosophy moved away from the focus on ethics and civic life that had been such a feature of earlier humanist thought. He taught instead that the individual should look primarily to the salvation of his immortal soul, to free it from its "always miserable" mortal body: a very Platonic idea that was also compatible with much late-medieval Christian piety. His disciple Pico likewise rejected the everyday world of public affairs but took a more exalted view of man's intellectual and artistic capacities, arguing that man (but not woman) can aspire to union with God through the exercise of his unique talents. Ficino's great achievement was his translation of Plato's works into Latin, which made them widely accessible in Europe for the first time—again, thanks to the medium of print.

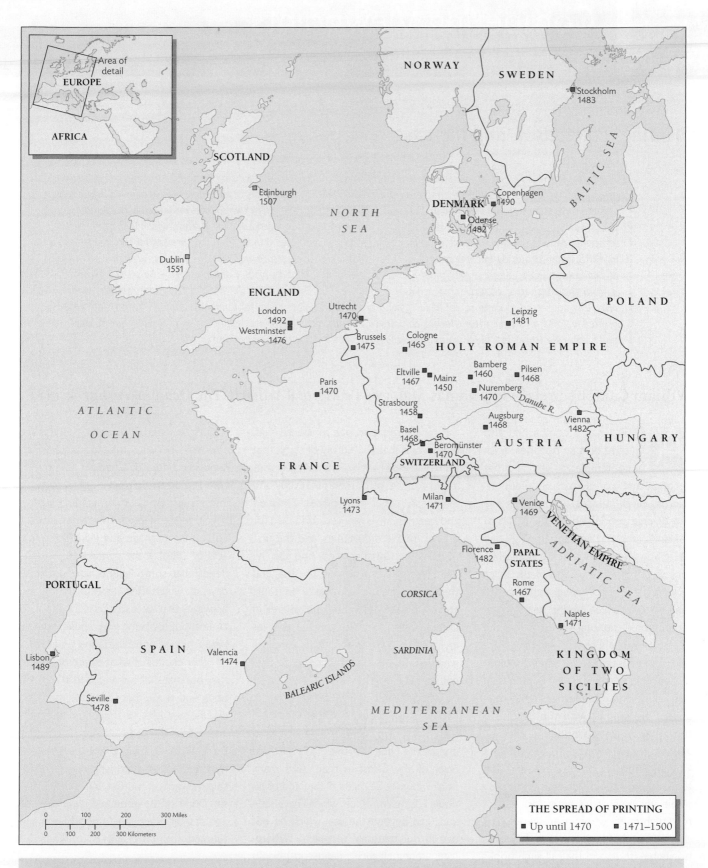

THE SPREAD OF PRINTING

- Up until 1470
- 1471–1500

THE SPREAD OF PRINTING. This map shows how quickly the technology of printing spread throughout Europe between 1470 and 1500. ■ *In what regions were printing presses most heavily concentrated?* ■ *What factors would have led to their proliferation in the Low Countries, northern Italy, and Germany—as compared to France, Spain, and England?* ■ *Why would so many have been located along waterways?*

Printing, Patriotism, and the Past

> The printing press helped to create new communities of readers by standardizing national languages and even promoting patriotism. And while it enabled authors of new works to reach larger audiences, it also allowed printers to popularize older writings that had previously circulated in manuscript. The two sources presented here exemplify two aspects of this trend. The first is the preface to a version of the legend of King Arthur, which was originally written by an English soldier called Sir Thomas Malory, who completed it in 1470. It was printed for the first time in 1485, when it quickly became a best seller. The author of this preface was also the printer, William Caxton of London, who specialized in publishing books that glorified England's history and heritage. The second excerpt is from the concluding chapter of Machiavelli's treatise The Prince. Like the book itself, these remarks were originally addressed to Lorenzo de' Medici, head of Florence's most powerful family. But when The Prince was printed in 1532, five years after Machiavelli's death, the author's passionate denunciation of foreign "barbarians" and lament for Italy's lost glory would have resonated with a wider Italian-speaking public.

William Caxton's preface to Thomas Malory's *Le Morte d'Arthur* ("The Death of Arthur"), 1485

AFTER I had accomplished and finished diverse histories, both of contemplation and of other historical and worldly acts of great conquerors and princes, ... many noble and diverse gentlemen of this realm of England came and demanded why I had not made and imprinted the noble history of the Holy Grail, and of the most renowned Christian king and worthy, King Arthur, which ought most to be remembered among us Englishmen before all other Christian kings.... The said noble gentlemen instantly required me to imprint the history of the said noble king and conqueror King Arthur, and of his knights, with the history of the Holy Grail ... considering that he was a man born within this realm, and king and emperor of the same: and that there be, in French, diverse and many noble volumes of his acts, and also of his knights. To whom I answered that diverse men hold opinion that there was no such Arthur, and that all such books as have been made of him be feigned and fables, because some chronicles make of him no mention.... Whereto

they answered, and one in special said, that in him that should say or think that there was never such a king called Arthur might well be accounted great folly and blindness.... For in all places, Christian and heathen, he is reputed and taken for one of the Nine Worthies, and the first of the three Christian men. And also, he is more spoken of beyond the sea, and there are more books made of his noble acts than there be in England, as well in Dutch, Italian, Spanish, and Greek, as in French.... Wherefore it is a marvel why he is no more renowned in his own country....

Then all these things aforesaid alleged, I could not well deny but that there was such a noble king named Arthur, reputed one of the Nine Worthies, and first and chief of the Christian men. And many noble volumes be made of him and of his noble knights in French, which I have seen and read beyond the sea, which be not had in our maternal tongue.... Wherefore, among all such [manuscript] books as have late been drawn out briefly into English I have ... undertaken to imprint a book of the noble histories of the said

King Arthur, and of certain of his knights, after a copy unto me delivered—which copy Sir Thomas Malory did take out of certain books of French, and reduced it into English. And I, according to my copy, have done set it in print, to the intent that noble men may see and learn the noble acts of chivalry, the gentle and virtuous deeds that some knights used in those days, by which they came to honor, and how they that were vicious were punished and oft put to shame and rebuke; humbly beseeching all noble lords and ladies (with all other estates of what estate or degree they be) that shall see and read in this said book and work, that they take the good and honest acts to their remembrance, and follow the same.... For herein may be seen noble chivalry, courtesy, humanity, friendliness, hardiness, love, friendship, cowardice, murder, hate, virtue, and sin. Do after the good and leave the evil, and it shall bring you to good fame and renown.

Source: Sir Thomas Malory, *Le Morte d'Arthur* (London: 1485), (text and spelling slightly modernized).

From the conclusion of Niccolò Machiavelli's *The Prince* (completed 1513, printed 1533)

Reflecting in the matters set forth above and considering within myself where the times were propitious in Italy at present to honor a new prince and whether there is at hand the matter suitable for a prudent and virtuous leader to mold in a new form, giving honor to himself and benefit to the citizens of the country, I have arrived at the opinion that all circumstances now favor such a prince, and I cannot think of a time more propitious for him than the present. If, as I said, it was necessary in order to make apparent the virtue of Moses, that the people of Israel should be enslaved in Egypt, and that the Persians should be oppressed by the Medes to provide an opportunity to illustrate the greatness and the spirit of Cyrus, and that the Athenians should be scattered in order to show the excellence of Theseus, thus at the present time, in order to reveal the valor of an Italian spirit, it was essential that Italy should fall to her present low estate, more enslaved than the Hebrews, more servile than the Persians, more disunited than the Athenians, leaderless and lawless, beaten, despoiled, lacerated, overrun and crushed under every kind of misfortune.... So Italy now, left almost lifeless, awaits the coming of one who will heal her wounds, putting an end to the sacking and looting in Lombardy and the spoliation and extortions in the Realm of Naples and Tuscany, and cleanse her sores that have been so long festering. Behold how she prays God to send her some one to redeem her from the cruelty and insolence of the barbarians. See how she is ready and willing to follow any banner so long as there be someone to take it up. Nor has she at present any hope of finding her redeemer save only in your illustrious house [the Medici] which has been so highly exalted both by its own merits and by fortune and which has been favored by God and the church, of which it is now ruler. . . .

This opportunity, therefore, should not be allowed to pass, and Italy, after such a long wait, must be allowed to behold her redeemer. I cannot describe the joy with which he will be received in all these provinces which have suffered so much from the foreign deluge, nor with what thirst for vengeance, nor with what firm devotion, what solemn delight, what tears! What gates could be closed to him, what people could deny him obedience, what envy could withstand him, what Italian could withhold allegiance from him? THIS BARBARIAN OCCUPATION STINKS IN THE NOSTRILS OF ALL OF US. Let your illustrious house then take up this cause with the spirit and the hope with which one undertakes a truly just enterprise. . . .

Source: Niccolò Machiavelli, *The Prince,* ed. and trans. Thomas G. Bergin (Arlington Heights, IL: 1947), pp. 75–76, 78.

Questions for Analysis

1. What do these two sources reveal about the relationship between patriotism and the awareness of a nation's past? Why do you think that Caxton looks back to a legendary medieval king, whereas Machiavelli's references are all to ancient examples? What do both excerpts reveal about the value placed on history in the popular imagination?

2. How does Caxton describe the process of printing a book? What larger conclusions can we draw from this about the market for printed books in general?

3. Why might Machiavelli's treatise have been made available in a printed version, nearly twenty years after its original appearance in manuscript? How might his new audience have responded to its message?

The Politics of Italy and the Philosophy of Machiavelli

But not all Florentines were galvanized by Platonic ideals. Indeed, the most influential philosopher of this era—and one of the most widely read authors of all time—was a thoroughgoing realist who spent more time studying Roman history than Greek philosophy: Niccolò Machiavelli (1469–1527). Machiavelli's political writings reflect the unstable political situation of his home city as well as his wider aspirations for a unified Italy that could revive the glory of ancient Rome. We have observed that Italy had been in political disarray for centuries, a situation exacerbated by the "Babylonian Captivity" of the papacy and the controversies raging after its return to Rome (see Chapters 10 and 11). Now Italy was becoming the arena in which bloody international struggles were being played out. The kings of France and Spain both had imperial ambitions, and both claimed to be the rightful champions of the papacy. Accordingly, both sent invading armies into the peninsula while they busily competed for the allegiance of the various city-states, which in turn were torn by internal dissension.

In 1498, Machiavelli became a prominent official in the government of a new Florentine republic, set up four years earlier when a French invasion of the region had led to the expulsion of the ruling Medici family. His duties largely involved diplomatic missions to other Italian city-states. While in Rome, he became fascinated with the attempt of Cesare Borgia, son of Pope Alexander VI, to create his own principality in central Italy. He noted with approval Cesare's ruthlessness and his complete subordination of personal ethics to political ends. He remembered this example in 1512, when the Medici returned to overthrow the Florentine republic and Machiavelli was deprived of his position, imprisoned, tortured, and exiled. He now devoted his energies to the articulation of a political philosophy suited to the times and to the tastes of the family that had ousted him from his job.

On the surface, Machiavelli's two great works of political analysis appear to contradict each other. In his *Discourses on Livy*, which drew on the works of that Roman historian (see Chapter 5), he praised the ancient Roman Republic as a model for his own contemporaries, lauding constitutional government, equality among citizens, and the subordination of religion to the service of the state. There is little doubt, in fact, that Machiavelli was a committed believer in the free city-state as the ideal form of human government. But Machiavelli also wrote *The Prince*, "a handbook for tyrants" in the eyes of his critics, and he dedicated this work to Lorenzo, son of Piero de' Medici, whose family had overthrown the Florentine republic that Machiavelli had served.

THE STATES OF ITALY, c. 1494. This map shows the divisions of Italy on the eve of the French invasion in 1494. Contemporary observers often described Italy as being divided among five great powers: Milan, Venice, Florence, the Papal States, and the united Kingdoms of Naples and Sicily. ▪ *Which of these powers would have been most capable of expanding their territories?* ▪ *Which neighboring states would have been most threatened by such attempts at expansion?* ▪ *Why would Florence and the Papal States so often find themselves in conflict with each other?*

Because *The Prince* has been so much more widely read than *Discourses*, it has often been interpreted as an endorsement of power for its own sake. Machiavelli's real position was quite different. In the political chaos of early-sixteenth-century Italy, he saw the likes of Cesare Borgia as the only hope for revitalizing the spirit of independence among his contemporaries, and so making Italy fit, eventually, for self-governance. However dark his vision of human nature, Machiavelli never ceased to hope that his contemporaries would rise up, expel French and Spanish occupying forces, and restore ancient traditions of liberty and equality. He regarded a period of despotism as a necessary step toward that end, not as a permanently desirable form of government.

Machiavelli continues to be a controversial figure. Some modern scholars, like many of his own contemporaries, represent him as disdainful of conventional morality, interested solely in the acquisition and exercise of power. Others see him as an Italian patriot. Still others see him as a realist influenced by Saint Augustine (see Chapter 6), who understood that, in a fallen world populated by sinful people, a ruler's good intentions do not guarantee that his policies will have good results. Accordingly, Machiavelli insisted that a prince's actions must be judged by their consequences and not by their intrinsic moral quality. He argued that "the necessity of preserving the state will often compel a prince to take actions which are opposed to loyalty, charity, humanity, and religion." As we shall see in later chapters, many subsequent political philosophers would go even further than Machiavelli in arguing that the preservation of the state—and the avoidance of political chaos—does indeed warrant the exercise of absolute power on the part of the ruler (see Chapters 14 and 15).

The Ideal of the Courtier

Machiavelli's political theories were informed by years of diplomatic service in the courts of Italy, and so was his engaging literary style. Indeed, he never abandoned his interest in the literary arts of the court and continued to write poems, plays, and adaptations of classical comedies. In this he resembled another poet-courtier, Ludovico Ariosto (1474–1533), who undertook diplomatic missions for the Duke of Ferrara and some of Rome's most powerful prelates. His lengthy verse narrative, *Orlando Furioso* (The Madness of Roland), was a retelling of the heroic exploits celebrated in the French *Song of Roland* (see Chapter 8)—but without the heroism. Although very different in form and tone from *The Prince*, it shared that work's skepticism of political or chivalric ideals. Instead, it emphasized the comedy of its lovers' passionate exploits and sought to charm an audience who sought consolation in pleasure and beauty.

Thus a new Renaissance ideal was born, one that promoted the arts of pleasing the powerful secular and ecclesiastical princes who were in a position to employ clever men like Machiavelli and Ariosto: the ideal of the courtier. The components of this ideal were embodied by their contemporary, the diplomat and nobleman Baldassare Castiglione (1478–1529), who would later write a manual for those who aspired to acquire these skills. If *The Prince* was a forerunner of modern self-help books, *The Book of the Courtier* was an early handbook of etiquette; and both stand in sharp contrast to the treatises on public virtue composed in the previous century. Whereas Bruni and Alberti (see Chapter 11) had taught the sober virtues of strenuous service on behalf of the city-state, Castiglione taught how to attain the elegant and seemingly effortless skills necessary for advancement in princely courts.

More than anyone else, Castiglione articulated and popularized the set of talents still associated with the "Renaissance man": one accomplished in many different pursuits, witty, cultured, and stylish. And in many ways, this new ideal actually represents a *rejection* of the older ideals associated with the Renaissance as a rebirth of classical education for public men. Castiglione even rejected the misogyny of the humanists by stressing the ways in which court ladies could rise to influence and prominence through the graceful exercise of their womanly powers. Widely read throughout Western civilizations, his *Courtier* set the standard for polite behavior until the First World War.

The Dilemma of the Artist

Without question, the most enduring legacy of the Italian Renaissance has been the contributions of its artists, particularly those who embraced new media and new attitudes toward the human body. We have already noted (see Chapter 11) the creative and economic opportunities afforded by painting on canvas or wood, which freed artists from having to work on site and entirely on commission: such paintings are portable—unlike wall paintings—and can be displayed in different settings, reach different markets, and be more widely distributed. We also saw that the use of oil paints, pioneered in Flanders, further revolutionized painting styles. To these benefits, the artists of Italy added an important technical ingredient: mastery of a vanishing (one-point) perspective that gave to painting an illusion of three-dimensional space. They also experimented with effects of light and shade, and studied intently the anatomy and proportions of the human body. These techniques also influenced the sculptors of this age.

New Illusions and the Career of Leonardo

THE IMPACT OF PERSPECTIVE. Masaccio's painting *The Trinity with the Virgin* illustrates the startling sense of depth made possible by observing the rules of one-point perspective.

Behind all of the beautiful artworks created in this era, which led to the glorification of the artist as a new type of hero, lie the harsh political and economic realities within which these artists worked. Increasing private wealth and the growth of lay patronage opened up new markets and created a huge demand for buildings and objects that could increase those grappling for prestige. Portraiture was a direct result of this trend, since princes and merchants alike sought to glorify themselves and their families and to compete with their neighbors and rivals. An artist therefore had to study the techniques of the courtier as well as the new artistic techniques in order to succeed in winning a patron. He also had to be ready to perform other services for which he had to cultivate other talents: overseeing the building and decoration of palaces; designing tableware, furniture, fanciful liveries for servants and soldiers; and even decorating guns. Some artists, like Leonardo da Vinci, were prized as much for their capacity to invent deadly weapons as for their paintings and sculptures.

For much of the fifteenth century, the majority of the great painters were Florentines who followed in the footsteps of the precocious Masaccio (1401–1428), who had died prematurely at the age of twenty-seven. His lasting legacy was the pioneering use of one-point perspective and dramatic lighting effects. Both are evident in his painting of the Trinity, where the body of the crucified Christ appears to be thrust forward by the impassive figure of God the Father, while the Virgin's gaze directly engages the viewer. Masaccio's most obvious successor was Sandro Botticelli (1445–1510), who excelled in depicting graceful motion and the sensuous pleasures of nature. He is most famous today for paintings that evoke classical mythology and that seem to be devoid of any Christian frame of reference.

The most adventurous and versatile artist of this period was Leonardo da Vinci (1452–1519). Leonardo personifies the Renaissance ideal: he was a painter, architect, musician, mathematician, engineer, and inventor. The illegitimate son of a notary, he set up an artist's shop in Florence by the time he was twenty-five and gained the patronage of the Medici ruler, Lorenzo the Magnificent. Yet Leonardo had a weakness: he worked slowly, and he had difficulty finishing anything. This naturally displeased Lorenzo and other Florentine patrons, who regarded artists as craftsmen who worked on specific projects, and on their patrons' time—not their own. Leonardo, however, strongly objected to this view; he considered himself to be an inspired, independent innovator. He therefore left Florence in 1482 and went to work for the of Sforza dictators Milan, whose favor he courted by emphasizing his skills as a maker of bombs, heavy ordinance, and siege engines. He remained there until the French invasion of 1499; he then wandered about, finally accepting the patronage of the French king, under whose auspices he lived and worked until his death.

Paradoxically, considering his skill in fashioning deadly weapons, Leonardo was convinced of the essential divinity of all living things. He was a vegetarian—unusual at the time—and when he went to the marketplace to buy caged birds he released them to their native habitat when he had finished observing them. His approach to painting was that it should be the most accurate possible imitation of nature. He made careful studies: blades of grass, cloud formations, a waterfall. He obtained human corpses for dissection and reconstructed in drawing the minutest features of anatomy, carrying this knowledge over to his paintings. *The Virgin of the Rocks* typifies not only his technical skill but also his passion for science and his belief in the universe as a well-ordered place.

THE BIRTH OF VENUS. This painting was executed by Sandro Botticelli in Florence, and represents the artist's imaginative treatment of stories from ancient mythology. Here, he depicts the moment when Aphrodite, goddess of love, was spontaneously engendered from the foam of the sea by Chronos, the god of time.

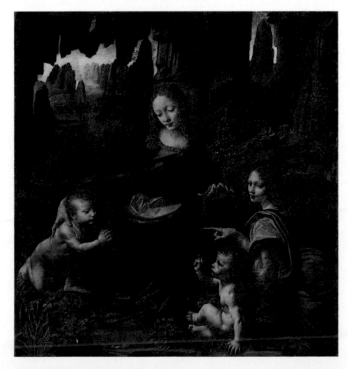

THE VIRGIN OF THE ROCKS. This painting reveals Leonardo's interest in the variety of human faces and facial expressions and in natural settings.

The figures are arranged geometrically, with every stone and plant depicted in accurate detail. In *The Last Supper*, painted on the refectory walls of a monastery in Milan (and now in an advanced state of decay), he displayed his equally keen studies of human psychology. In this image, a serene Christ has just announced to his disciples that one of them will betray him. The artist succeeds in portraying the mingled emotions of surprise, horror, and guilt on the faces of the disciples as they gradually perceive the meaning of their master's statement. He also implicates the painting's viewers in this dramatic scene, since they too dine alongside Christ, in the very same room.

Renaissance Arts in Venice and Rome

The innovations of Florentine artists were widely imitated. By the end of the fifteenth century, they had influenced a group of painters active in the wealthy city of Venice, among them Tiziano Vecellio, better known as Titian (c. 1490–1576). Many of Titian's paintings evoke the luxurious, pleasure-loving life of this thriving commercial center; for although they copied Florentine techniques,

Analyzing Primary Sources

Leonardo da Vinci Applies for a Job

Few sources illuminate the tensions between Renaissance ideals and realities better than the résumé of accomplishments submitted by Leonardo da Vinci to a prospective employer, Ludovico Sforza of Milan. In the following letter, Leonardo explains why he deserves to be appointed chief architect and military engineer in the duke's household administration. He got the job and moved to Milan in 1481.

1. I have the kind of bridges that are extremely light and strong, made to be carried with great ease, and with them you may pursue, and, at any time, flee from the enemy; . . . and also methods of burning and destroying those of the enemy.

2. I know how, when a place is under attack, to eliminate the water from the trenches, and make endless variety of bridges . . . and other machines. . . .

3. . . . I have methods for destroying every rock or other fortress, even if it were built on rock, etc.

4. I also have other kinds of mortars [bombs] that are most convenient and easy to carry. . . .

5. And if it should be a sea battle, I have many kinds of machines that are most efficient for offense and defense. . . .

6. I also have means that are noiseless to reach a designated area by secret and tortuous mines. . . .

7. I will make covered chariots, safe and unattackable, which can penetrate the enemy with their artillery. . . .

8. In case of need I will make big guns, mortars, and light ordnance of fine and useful forms that are out of the ordinary.

9. If the operation of bombardment should fail, I would contrive catapults, mangonels, trabocchi [trebuchets], and other machines of marvelous efficacy and unusualness. In short, I can, according to each case in question, contrive various and endless means of offense and defense.

10. In time of peace I believe I can give perfect satisfaction that is equal to any other in the field of architecture and the construction of buildings. . . . I can execute sculpture in marble, bronze, or clay, and also in painting I do the best that can be done, and as well as any other, whoever he may be.

Having now, most illustrious Lord, sufficiently seen the specimens of all those who consider themselves master craftsmen of instruments of war, and that the invention and operation of such instruments are no different from those in common use, I shall now endeavor . . . to explain myself to your Excellency by revealing to your Lordship my secrets. . . .

Source: Excerpted from Leonardo da Vinci, *The Notebooks*, in *The Italian Renaissance Reader*, eds. Julia Conaway and Mark Mosa (Harmondsworth, UK: 1987), pp. 195–96.

Questions for Analysis

1. Based on the qualifications highlighted by Leonardo in this letter, what can you conclude about the political situation in Milan and the priorities of its duke? What can you conclude about the state of military technologies in this period and the conduct of warfare?

2. What do you make of the fact that Leonardo mentions his artistic endeavors only at the end of the letter? Does this fact alter your opinion or impression of him? Why or why not?

most Venetian painters showed little of that city's concerns for philosophical or religious allegory. Their aim was to appeal to the senses by painting idyllic landscapes and sumptuous portraits of the rich and powerful. In the subordination of form and meaning to color and elegance, they may have mirrored the tastes of the men for whom they worked.

Rome, too, became a major artistic center in this era and a place where the Florentine school exerted a more potent influence. Among its eminent painters was Raffaello Sanzio (1483–1520), or Raphael. Although influenced by Leonardo, Raphael cultivated a more spiritual and philosophical approach to his subjects. As we noted in Chapter 4, his fresco *The School of Athens* depicts both the harmony

THE LAST SUPPER. This fresco on the refectory wall of the monastery of Santa Maria delle Grazie in Milan is a testament to both the powers and limitations of Leonardo's artistry. It skillfully employs the techniques of one-point perspective to create the illusion that Jesus and his disciples are actually dining at the monastery's head table, but because Leonardo had not mastered the techniques of fresco painting, he applied tempera pigments to a dry wall that had been coated with a sealing agent. As a result, the painting's colors began to fade just years after its completion. By the middle of the sixteenth century, it had seriously deteriorated. Large portions of it are now invisible.

and the differences of Platonic and Aristotelian thought (see page 117). It also includes a number of Raphael's contemporaries as models. The image of Plato is actually a portrait of Leonardo, while the architect Donato Bramante (c. 1444–1514) stands in for the geometer Euclid, and Michelangelo for the philosopher Heraclitus.

Michelangelo Buonarroti (1475–1564), who spent many decades in Rome in the service of a papacy, was another native of Florence. Like Leonardo, he was a polymath: painter, sculptor, architect, poet—and he expressed himself in all these forms with a similar power. But if Leonardo was a naturalist, Michelangelo was an idealist—despite the harsh political and material realities of the conditions in which he worked. At the center of all of his work, as at the center of Renaissance humanism, is the male figure: the embodied masculine mind.

Michelangelo's greatest achievements in painting appear in a single location, the Sistine Chapel of the Vatican palace, yet they are products of two different periods in the artist's life and consequently exemplify two different artistic styles and outlooks on the human condition. More famous are the extraordinary frescoes painted on the ceiling from 1508 to 1512, depicting scenes from the book of Genesis. All the panels in this series, including *The Creation of Adam*, exemplify the young artist's commitment to classical artistic principles. Correspondingly, all affirm the sublimity of the Creation and the heroic qualities of humankind. But a quarter of a century later, when Michelangelo returned to work in the Sistine Chapel, both his style and mood had changed dramatically. In the enormous *Last Judgment*, a fresco completed on the chapel's altar wall in 1536, Michelangelo repudiated classical restraint and substituted a style that emphasized tension and distortion, a humanity wracked with fear, guilt, and frailty. He included himself in it—painting a grotesque self-portrait on the flayed skin of Saint Bartholomew, who was allegedly martyred by being skinned alive. One wonders whether Michelangelo intended this as a metaphor for the challenges of working in the service of the papal court.

SELF-PORTRAIT OF THE ARTIST AS A YOUNG MAN: DETAIL FROM *THE SCHOOL OF ATHENS*. We have already analyzed aspects of Raphael's famous group portrait of the Greek philosophers, with Plato and Aristotle at their center (see page 118). In addition to featuring his own contemporaries as models—including the artists Leonardo and Michelangelo and the architect Bramante—Raphael put himself in the picture, too. ▪ *What messages does this choice convey?*

Michelangelo and the Renaissance of Sculpture

Although sculpture was not a new medium for artists, as oil painting was, it became an important area of Renaissance innovation. For the first time since late antiquity, monumental

THE CREATION OF ADAM. This is one of a series of frescoes painted on the ceiling of the Sistine Chapel of the Vatican palace in Rome, executed by Michelangelo over a period of many years and in circumstances of extreme physical hardship. It has since become an iconic image. ▪ *How might it be said to capture Renaissance ideals?*

statues became figures "in the round" rather than sculptural elements incorporated into buildings or featured as effigies on tombs. By freeing sculpture from its bondage to architecture, the Renaissance reestablished it as a separate art form.

The first great master of Renaissance sculpture was Donatello (c. 1386–1466). His bronze statue of David, triumphant over the head of the slain Goliath, is the first free-standing nude of the period. Yet this *David* is clearly an agile adolescent rather than a muscular Greek athlete like that of Michelangelo's *David*, executed in 1501, as a public expression of Florentine civic life: not merely graceful but heroic. Michelangelo regarded sculpture as the most exalted of the arts because it allowed the artist to imitate God most fully in re-creating human forms. Furthermore, in Michelangelo's view,

THE POWER AND VULNERABILITY OF THE MALE BODY. Donatello's *David* (left) was the first freestanding nude executed since antiquity. It shows the Hebrew leader as an adolescent youth and is a little over five feet tall. The *David* by Michelangelo (center) stands thirteen feet high and was placed prominently in front of Florence's city hall to proclaim the city's power and humanistic values. Michelangelo's *Descent from the Cross* (right), which shows Christ's broken body in the arms of the elderly Nicodemus, was made by the sculptor for his own tomb. (The Gospels describe Nicodemus as a Pharisee who became a follower of Jesus and who was present at his death.) ▪ *Why would Michelangelo choose this figure to represent himself?* ▪ *How does his representation of David—and the context in which this figure was displayed—compare to that of Donatello?*

the most God-like sculptor disdained slavish naturalism; anyone could make a plaster cast of a human figure, but only an inspired creative genius could endow his sculpted figures with a sense of life. Accordingly, Michelangelo's sculpture subordinated reality to the force of his imagination and sought to express his ideals in ever more astonishing forms. He also insisted on working in marble—the "noblest" sculptural material—and by creating figures twice as large as life. By sculpting a serenely confident young man at the peak of physical fitness, Michelangelo celebrated the Florentine republic's own determination in resisting tyrants and upholding ideals of civic justice.

Yet the serenity seen in *David* is no longer prominent in the works of Michelangelo's later life when, as in his painting, he began to explore the use of anatomical distortion to create effects of emotional intensity. While his statues remained awesome in scale, they also communicate rage, depression, and sorrow. The culmination of this trend is his unfinished but intensely moving *Descent from the Cross*, a depiction of an old man (the sculptor himself) grieving over the distorted, slumping body of the dead Christ.

Renaissance Architecture

To a much greater extent than either sculpture or painting, Renaissance architecture had its roots in the classical past. The Gothic style pioneered in northern France (see Chapter 9) had not found a welcome reception in Italy; most of the buildings constructed there were Romanesque in style, and the great architects influenced by the Renaissance movement generally adopted their building plans from these structures—some of which they believed (mistakenly) to be ancient. They also copied decorative devices from the authentic ruins of ancient Rome. But above all, they derived their influence from the writings of Vitruvius (fl. c. 60–15 B.C.E.), a Roman architect and engineer whose multivolume *On Architecture* was among the humanists' rediscovered ancient texts. The governing principles laid out by Vitruvius were popularized by Leon Battista Alberti in his own book, *On the Art of Building*, which began to circulate in manuscript around 1450.

In keeping with these classical models, Renaissance buildings emphasize geometrical proportion. These aesthetic values were also reinforced by the interest in Pla-

ST. PETER'S BASILICA, ROME. This eighteenth-century painting shows the massive interior of the Renaissance building. But were it not for the perspective provided by the tiny human figures, the human eye would be fooled into thinking this a much smaller space.

tonic philosophy, which taught that certain mathematical ratios reflect the harmony of the universe. For example, the proportions of the human body serve as the basis for the proportions of the quintessential Renaissance building: St. Peter's Basilica in Rome. Designed by some of the most celebrated architects of the time, including Bramante and Michelangelo, it is still one of the largest buildings in the world. Yet it seems smaller than a Gothic cathedral because it is built to human scale. The same artful proportions are evident in smaller-scale buildings too, as in the aristocratic country houses later designed by the northern Italian architect Andrea Palladio (1508–1580), who created secular miniatures of ancient temples (such as the Roman Pantheon) to glorify the aristocrats who dwelled within them.

THE RENAISSANCE NORTH OF THE ALPS

Despite Italian resentment of the political encroachment of foreign monarchs, contacts between Italy and northern Europe were close throughout this period. Italian merchants and financiers were familiar figures at northern courts; students from all over Europe studied at Italian universities such as Bologna or Padua; northern poets (including Geoffrey Chaucer; see Chapter 11) and their works traveled to and from Italy; and northern soldiers were frequent; combattants in Italian wars. Yet only at the very end of the fifteenth century did the innovative artistry and learning of Italy begin to be exported across the Alps into northern Europe and across the eastern Mediterranean into Spain.

A variety of explanations have been offered for this delay. Northern European intellectual life in the later Middle Ages was dominated by universities such as those of Paris, Oxford, and Prague, whose curricula focused on the study of philosophical logic, Christian theology, and (to a lesser extent) medicine. These rigorous courses of study left little room for the study of classical literature. In Italy, by contrast, universities were more often professional schools specializing in law and medicine and were more integrally tied to the nonacademic intellectual lives of the cities in which they were situated. As a result, a more secular, urban-oriented educational tradition took shape in Italy, as we saw in our previous discussion of humanism. In northern Europe, by contrast, those scholars who *were* influenced by Italian ideas usually worked outside the university system under the private patronage of kings and princes.

Before the turn of the sixteenth century, northern rulers were also less committed to patronizing artists and intellectuals than were the city-states and princes of Italy. In Italy, as we may have seen, such patronage was an important arena for competition between political rivals. In northern Europe, however, political units were larger and political rivals were fewer. It was therefore less necessary to use art for political purposes in a kingdom than it was in a city-state—a major exception being the independent duchy of Burgundy, which surpassed even the French court in its magnificence. A statue erected in a central square of Florence would be seen by all the city's residents. In Paris, such a statue would be seen by only a tiny minority of the French king's subjects. But as royal courts became more firmly established in royal capitals and so became showcases for royal power, kings needed to impress townspeople, courtiers, and visitors—and they consequently relied more and more on artists and intellectuals to advertise their wealth and taste.

Christian Humanism and the Career of Erasmus

In general, then, the Renaissance movement of northern Europe differed from that of Italy because it grafted certain Italian ideals onto preexisting traditions, rather than sweeping away older forms of knowledge. This can be seen very clearly in the case of the intellectual development known as Christian humanism. Although Christian humanists shared the Italian humanists' scorn for scholasticism's limitations, northern humanists were more committed to seeking ethical guidance from biblical and religious precepts, as well as from Cicero or Virgil. Like their Italian counterparts, they embraced the wisdom of antiquity, but the antiquity they favored was Christian as well as classical—the antiquity of the New Testament and the early Church. Similarly, northern artists were inspired by the accomplishments of Italian masters and copied their techniques, but they depicted classical subjects less frequently and almost never portrayed completely nude human figures.

Any discussion of Christian humanism must begin with the career of Desiderius Erasmus (c. 1469–1536). The illegitimate son of a priest, Erasmus was born near Rotterdam in the Netherlands. Later, as a result of his wide travels, he became a virtual citizen of all Europe. Forced into a monastery against his will when he was a teenager, the young Erasmus found little formal instruction there—but plenty of freedom to read what he liked. He devoured all the classics he could get his hands on, alongside the writings of the church fathers (see Chapter 6). When he

ERASMUS BY HANS HOLBEIN THE YOUNGER. This is generally regarded as the most evocative portrait of the preeminent Christian humanist.

Past and Present

The Reputation of Richard III

England's King Richard III (r. 1483–1485) has been a byword for villainy since the time of his death, when Sir Thomas More and other propagandists working for his successor, Henry VII, alleged that his physically deformed body was matched by the depravity of his actions. For centuries, historians have debated the truth of both claims. Was Richard really a hunchback—and a murderer, too? In 2012, the stunning discovery of Richard's body (under a parking lot near the medieval battlefield where he died) confirmed that he had indeed suffered from severe scoliosis. The other claim has yet to be proven.

 Watch related author interview on StudySpace
wwnorton.com/web/westernciv18

was about thirty years old, he obtained permission to leave the monastery and enroll in the University of Paris, where he completed the requirements for a bachelor's degree in divinity.

But Erasmus subsequently rebelled against what he considered the arid learning of Parisian academe. Nor did he ever serve actively as a priest. Instead, he made his living from teaching, writing, and the proceeds of various ecclesiastical offices that required no pastoral duties. Ever on the lookout for new patrons, he traveled often to England, stayed for three years in Italy, and resided in several different cities in Germany and the Low Countries before settling finally, toward the end of his life, in Basel (Switzerland). By means of a voluminous correspondence with learned friends, Erasmus became the leader of a humanist coterie. And through the popularity of his numerous publications, he also became the arbiter of northern European cultural tastes during his lifetime.

Erasmus's many-sided intellectual activity may be assessed from two different points of view: the literary and the doctrinal. As a Latin prose stylist, Erasmus was unequaled since the days of Cicero. Extraordinarily eloquent and witty, he reveled in tailoring his mode of discourse to fit his subject, creating dazzling verbal effects and coining puns that took on added meaning if the reader knew Greek as well as Latin. Above all, Erasmus excelled in the deft use of irony, poking fun at everything, including himself. For example, in his *Colloquies* (Discussions) he has a fictional character lament the evils of the times: "Kings make war, priests strive to line their pockets, theologians invent syllogisms, monks roam outside their cloisters, the commons riot, and Erasmus writes colloquies."

But although Erasmus's urbane Latin style and humor earned him a wide audience on those grounds alone, he intended everything he wrote to promote what he called the "philosophy of Christ." Erasmus believed that the society of

The Renaissance North of the Alps | 403

his day had lost sight of the Gospels' teachings. Accordingly, he offered his contemporaries three different kinds of writings: clever satires in which people could recognize their own foibles, serious moral treatises meant to offer guidance toward proper Christian behavior, and scholarly editions of basic Christian texts.

In the first category belong the works of Erasmus that are still widely read today: *The Praise of Folly* (1509), in which he ridiculed pedantry and dogmatism, ignorance and gullibility—even within the Church; and the *Colloquies* (1518), in which he held up contemporary religious practices for examination, couching a serious message in the ironic tone we just noted. In these books, Erasmus let fictional characters do the talking so his own views on any given topic can only be determined by inference. But in his second mode, Erasmus spoke clearly in his own voice. In the *Handbook of the Christian Knight* (1503), he used the popular language of chivalry as a means to encourage a life of inward piety; in the *Complaint of Peace* (1517), he argued movingly for Christian pacifism. Erasmus's pacifism was one of his most deeply held values, and he returned to it again and again in his published works.

Despite the success of these writings, Erasmus considered textual scholarship his greatest achievement. Revering the authority of the earliest church fathers, he brought out reliable printed editions of works by Saints Augustine, Jerome, and Ambrose. He also used his extraordinary command of Latin and Greek to produce a more accurate edition of the New Testament. For after reading Lorenzo Valla's *Notes on the New Testament* in 1504, Erasmus became convinced that nothing was more imperative than divesting the Christian scriptures of myriad errors in transcription and translation that had piled up over the course of preceding centuries. He therefore spent ten years comparing all the early Greek biblical manuscripts he could find in order to establish an authoritative text. When it finally appeared in 1516, Erasmus's Greek New Testament, published together with explanatory notes and his own new Latin translation, became one of the most important scholarly landmarks of all time. In the hands of Martin Luther, it would play a critical role in the early stages of the Reformation (see Chapter 13).

The Influence of Erasmus

One of Erasmus's closest friends, and a close second to him in distinction among Christian humanists, was the Englishman Sir Thomas More (1478–1535). In later life, following a successful career as a lawyer and speaker of the House of Commons, More was appointed lord chancellor of England in 1529. He was not long in this position, however, before he opposed King Henry VIII's plan to establish a national church under royal control that would deny the supremacy of the pope (see Chapter 13). (He was eventually executed and is now revered as a Catholic martyr.) Much earlier, however, in 1516, More published his most famous book, *Utopia* (No Place).

Purporting to describe an ideal community on an imaginary island, the book is really an Erasmian critique of contemporary culture: disparities between poverty and wealth, drastic punishments, religious persecution, and the senseless slaughter of war. In contrast to Europeans, the inhabitants of the fictional Utopia hold all their goods in common, work only six hours a day (so that all may have leisure for intellectual pursuits), and practice the natural virtues of wisdom, moderation, fortitude, and justice. Although More advanced no explicit arguments here in favor of Christianity, he might have meant to imply that if the Utopians could manage their society so well without the benefit of Christian revelation, Europeans who knew the Gospels ought to be able to do even better.

Erasmus and More head a long list of energetic and eloquent northern humanists who made signal contributions to the collective enterprise of revolutionizing the

SIR THOMAS MORE BY HANS HOLBEIN THE YOUNGER. Holbein's skill in rendering the gravity and interiority of his subject is matched by his masterful representation of the sumptuous chain of office, furred mantle, and velvet sleeves that indicate the political and professional status of Henry VIII's lord chancellor.

study of early Christianity, and their achievements had a direct influence on Protestant reformers—as we shall see in the next chapter. Yet very few of them were willing to join Luther and other Protestant leaders in rejecting the fundamental principles on which the power of the Roman Church was based. Most tried to remain within its fold while still espousing an ideal of inward piety and scholarly inquiry. But as the leaders of the Church grew less and less tolerant of dissent, even mild criticism came to seem like heresy. Erasmus himself died early enough to escape persecution, but several of his less fortunate followers did not.

The Literature of the Northern Renaissance

Although Christian humanism would be severely challenged by the Reformation, the artistic Renaissance in the North would flourish. Poets in France and England vied with one another to adapt the elegant lyric forms pioneered by Petrarch (Chapter 11) and popularized by many subsequent poets, including Michelangelo. The sonnet was particularly influential and would become one of the verse forms embraced by William Shakespeare (1554–1616; see chapter 14). Another English poet, Edmund Spenser (c. 1552–1599), drew on the literary innovation of Ariosto's *Orlando Furioso*: his *Faerie Queene* is a similarly long chivalric romance that revels in sensuous imagery. Meanwhile, the more satirical side of Renaissance humanism was embraced by the French writer François Rabelais (*RA-beh-lay*, c. 1494–1553).

Like Erasmus, whom he greatly admired, Rabelais began his career in the Church; but he soon left the cloister to study medicine. A practicing physician, Rabelais interspersed his professional activities with literary endeavors, the most enduring of these are the twin books *Gargantua* and *Pantagruel*, a series of "chronicles" describing the lives and times of giants whose fabulous size and gross appetites serve as vehicles for much lusty humor. Also like Erasmus, Rabelais also satirized religious hypocrisy, scholasticism, superstition, and bigotry. But unlike Erasmus, who wrote in a highly cultivated classical Latin style comprehensible only to learned readers, Rabelais chose to address a different audience by writing in extremely crude French and by glorifying every human appetite as natural and healthy.

Northern Architecture and Art

Although many architects in northern Europe continued to build in the flamboyant Gothic style of the later Middle Ages, the classical values of Italian architects can be seen in some of the splendid new castles constructed in France's Loire valley—châteaux too elegant to be defensible—and in the royal palace (now museum) of the Louvre in Paris, which replaced an old twelfth-century fortress. The influence of Renaissance ideals are also visible in the work of the German artist Albrecht Dürer (*DIRR-er*, 1471–1528). Dürer was the first northerner to master the techniques of proportion and perspective, and he shared with contemporary Italians a fascination with nature and the human body. He also took advantage of the printing press to circulate his work to a wide audience, making his delicate pencil drawings into engravings that could be mass produced.

But Dürer never really embraced classical subject, drawing inspiration instead from more traditional Christian legends and from the Christian humanism of Erasmus. For example, Dürer's serenely radiant engraving of Saint Jerome seems to express the scholarly absorption that Erasmus would have enjoyed while working quietly in his study. Indeed, Dürer aspired to immortalize Erasmus himself in a major portrait, but the paths of the two men crossed only once. Instead, the accomplishment of capturing Erasmus's pensive spirit in oils was left to another northern artist, the German Hans Holbein the Younger (1497–1543). Holbein also painted an acute portrait of Erasmus's friend and kindred spirit, Sir Thomas More. These two portraits, in themselves, exemplify a Renaissance emphasis on the making of naturalistic likenesses that express human individuality.

Tradition and Innovation in Music

Like the visual arts, the gorgeous music produced during this era was nourished by patrons' desire to surround themselves with beauty. Yet unlike painting and sculpture, musical practice did not reach back to classical antiquity but drew instead on well-established medieval conventions. Even before the Black Death, a musical movement called *ars nova* ("new art") was already flourishing in France, and it had spread to Italy during the lifetime of Petrarch. Its outstanding composers had been Guillaume de Machaut (c. 1300–1377) and Francesco Landini (c. 1325–1397).

The madrigals (part-songs) and ballads composed by these musicians and their successors expanded on earlier genres of secular music, but their greatest achievement was a highly complicated yet delicate contrapuntal style adapted for the liturgy of the Church. Machaut was the first-known composer to provide a polyphonic (harmonized) version of the major sections of the Mass. In the fifteenth century, the dissemination of this new musical aesthetic combined with a host of French, Flemish, and Italian elements in the multicultural courts of Europe, particularly that of Burgundy.

THE POLITICS OF CHRISTIAN EUROPE

We have already observed how the intellectual and artistic activity of the Renaissance movement was both fueled and hindered by the political developments of the later fifteenth century—within Italy, and throughout Europe. In 1453, France had emerged victorious in the Hundred Years' War, while England plunged into a further three decades of bloody civil conflict that touched every corner of that kingdom. The French monarchy was therefore able to rebuild its power and prestige while at the same time extending its control over regions that had long been controlled by the English crown and that were now part of an enlarged kingdom of France.

In 1494, the French king Charles VIII acted on a plan to expand his reach even further, into Italy. Leading an army of 30,000 well-trained troops across the Alps, he intended to press ancestral claims to the duchy of Milan and the kingdom of Naples. This effort yielded only a tenuous hold on Naples by the time Charles left a year later, and it solidified Italian opposition to French occupation, as we noted above; in our discussion of Machiavelli.

The rulers of Spain, whose territorial claims on Sicily also extended to Naples, were spurred by this to forge an uneasy alliance among the Papal States, some principalities of the Holy Roman Empire, Milan, and Venice. But the respite was brief. Charles's successor, Louis XII, launched a second invasion in 1499. For over a generation, until 1529, warfare in Italy was virtually uninterrupted. Alliances and counteralliances among city-states became further catalysts for violence and made Italy a magnet for mercenaries who could barely be kept in check by the generals who employed them.

Meanwhile, northern Italian city-states' virtual monopoly of trade with Asia, which had been one of the chief economic underpinnings of artistic and intellectual patronage, was being gradually eroded by the shifting of trade routes from the Mediterranean to the Atlantic (Chapters 10 and 11). It was also hampered by the increasing power of the Ottoman Empire, and even by the imperial pretensions of a new Russian ruler.

The Imperial Power of Ivan the Great

In previous chapters, we noted that the Russian duchy of Muscovy had become the champion of the Greek Orthodox Church and, as such, considered itself a true heir of Rome. After the fall of Constantinople to the Ottomans, the Muscovite grand duke even assumed the imperial title *tsar* (caesar)

***SAINT JEROME IN HIS STUDY* BY DÜRER.** Jerome, the biblical translator of the fourth century (see Chapter 6), was a hero to both Dürer and Erasmus: the paragon of inspired Christian scholarship. Note how the scene exudes contentment, even down to the sleeping lion, which seems more like an overgrown tabby cat than a symbol of Christ.

By the beginning of the sixteenth century, Franco-Flemish composers came to dominate many important courts and cathedrals, creating a variety of new forms and styles that bear a close affinity to Renaissance art and poetry.

Throughout Europe, the general level of musical proficiency in this era was very high. The singing of part-songs was a popular pastime in homes and at informal social gatherings, and the ability to read a part at sight was expected of the educated elite. Aristocratic women, in particular, were expected to display mastery of the new musical instruments that had been developed to add nuance and texture to existing musical forms, including the lute, the viol, the violin, and a variety of woodwind and keyboard instruments like the harpsichord.

Although most composers of this period were men trained in the service of the Church, they rarely made sharp distinctions between sacred and secular music. Like sculpture, music was coming into its own as a serious independent art. As such, it would become an important medium for the expression of both Catholic and Protestant ideals during the Reformation and also one of the few art forms equally acceptable to all.

THE EXPANSION OF MUSCOVITE RUSSIA TO 1505. The grand duchy of Moscow was the heart of what would soon become the Russian Empire. ■ *With what other empires and polities did the Muscovites have to compete during this period of expansion?* ■ *How did the relative isolation of Moscow, compared with early Kiev, allow for the growth of Muscovite power, on the one hand, and Moscow's distinctively non-Western culture, on the other?* ■ *How might the natural direction of the expansion of Muscovite power until 1505 help to encourage attitudes often at odds with those of western European civilization?*

and borrowed the Byzantine ideology of the ruler's divine election. These claims would eventually undergird the sacred position later ascribed to the tsars. But ideology alone could not have built the Russian Empire. Behind its growth lay the steadily growing power of its rulers, especially that of Grand Duke Ivan III (1462–1505), known as Ivan the Great, the first to lay down a distinctive imperial agenda.

Ivan launched a series of conquests that annexed all the independent principalities lying between Moscow and the border of Poland-Lithuania. After invading Lithuania in 1492 and 1501, Ivan even succeeded in bringing parts of that domain (portions of modern Belarus and Ukraine) under his control. Meanwhile, he married the niece of the last Byzantine emperor, giving real substance to the claim that Muscovy was New Rome. He also rebuilt his fortified Moscow residence, known as the Kremlin, in magnificent Italianate style. He would later adopt, as his imperial insignia, the double-headed eagle of Rome and its legions. By the

IVAN THE GREAT. This modern tribute to Ivan III prominently displays the two-headed eagle of imperial Rome. ▪ *What is the significance of this symbolic choice?*

that were emerging in this era. For under the terms of these concordats, kings now received many of the revenues that had previously gone to the papacy. They also acquired new powers to appoint candidates to church offices. It was, in many ways, a drastic reversal of the hard-won reforms of the eleventh and twelfth centuries that had created such a powerful papacy in the first place.

Having given away so many sources of revenue and authority, the popes of the late fifteenth century became even more dependent on their own territories in central Italy. But to tighten their hold on the Papal States, they had to rule like other Italian princes: leading armies, jockeying for alliances, and undermining their opponents by every possible means—including covert operations, murder, and assassination. Judged by the secular standards of the day, these efforts paid off: the Papal States became one of the better-governed and wealthier principalities in Italy. But such methods did nothing to increase the popes' reputation for piety, and disillusionment with the papacy as a force for the advancement of spirituality became even more widespread.

With both papal authority and Rome's spiritual prestige in decline, kings and princes became the primary figures to whom both clergy and laity looked for religious and moral guidance. Many secular rulers responded to such expectations aggressively, closing scandal-ridden monasteries, suppressing alleged heretics, regulating vice, and prohibiting the lower classes from dressing like the nobility. By these and other such measures, rulers could present themselves as champions of moral reform while also strengthening their political power. The result was an increasingly close link between national monarchies and national churches, a link that would become even stronger after the Reformation.

time of his death in 1505, Muscovy was firmly established as a dominant power. Indeed, the power of the tsar was more absolute in this period than that of any European monarch.

The Growth of National Churches

Meanwhile, as Muscovy laid claim to the mantle of Roman imperial power, the papacy was pouring resources into the glorification of the original Rome and the aggrandizement of the papal office. But neither the city nor its rulers could keep pace with their political and religious rivals. Following the Council of Constance (see Chapter 11), the papacy's victory over the conciliarists was a costly one. To win the support of Europe's kings and princes, various popes negotiated a series of religious treaties known as "concordats," which granted these rulers extensive authority over churches within their domains. The papacy thus secured its theoretical supremacy at the expense of its real power. Reigning popes also strengthened the national monarchies

The Triumph of the "Reconquista"

The kingdoms of the Iberian Peninsula were also in constant conflict during this period. In Castile, civil war and incompetent governance allowed the Castilian nobility to gain greater control over the peasantry and greater independence from the monarchy. In Aragon, royal government benefited from the extended commercial influence of Catalonia, which was under Aragonese authority. But after 1458, Aragon too became enmeshed in a civil war, a war in which both France and Castile became involved.

A solution to the disputed succession that had caused the war in Aragon would ultimately lie in the blending of powerful royal families. In 1469, Prince Ferdinand of Aragon was recognized as the undisputed heir to that throne

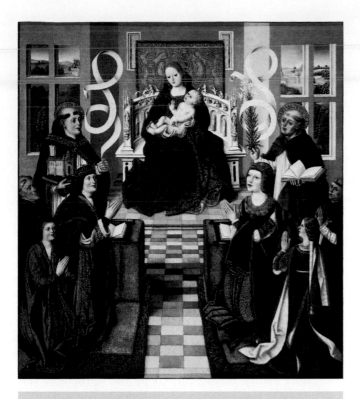

FERDINAND AND ISABELLA HONORING THE VIRGIN. In this contemporary Spanish painting, the royal couple are shown with two of their children and two household chaplains and in the company of the Blessed Virgin, the Christ Child, and saints from the Dominican order (the Dominicans were instrumental in conducting the affairs of the Spanish Inquisition). ▪ *How clear is the distinction between these holy figures and the royal family?* ▪ *What message is conveyed by their proximity?*

and, in the same year, secured this position by marrying Isabella, the heiress to Castile. Isabella became a queen in 1474, Ferdinand a king in 1479; and although Castile and Aragon continued to be ruled as separate kingdoms until 1714—there are tensions between the two former kingdoms even now—the marriage of Ferdinand and Isabella enabled the pursuit of several ambitious policies. In particular, their union allowed them to spend their combined resources on the creation of Europe's most powerful army, which was initially employed to conquer the last remaining principality of what had been al-Andalus: Muslim Spain. That principality, Granada, fell in 1492.

The End of the Convivencia and the Expulsion of the Jews

For more than seven relatively centuries, Spain's Jewish communities had enjoyed the many privileges extended by their Muslim rulers, who were also relatively tolerant of their Christian subjects. Indeed, scholars often refer to this period of Spain's history as a time of *convivencia*, a word that means "living together" or "harmonious coexistence." While relations among various religious and ethnic groups were not always uniformly peaceful or positive, the policies of Muslim rulers in al-Andalus had enabled an extraordinary hybrid culture to flourish there.

The aims of the Spanish Reconquista were diametrically opposed to those of "living together." The crusading ideology of "reconquest" sought instead to forge a single, homogenous community, based on the fiction that Spain had once been entirely Christian and should be restored to its former purity. The year 1492 therefore marks not only the end of Muslim rule in medieval Spain but also the culmination of a process of Jewish exclusion that had accelerated in the late thirteenth century (see Chapter 9). Within this history, the Spanish expulsion of the Jews stands out for the staggering scope of the displacements and destruction it entailed: at least 100,000 and possibly as many as 200,000 men, women, and children were deprived of their homes and livelihoods.

The Christian monarchs' motives for ordering this expulsion are still debated. Tens of thousands of Spanish Jews had converted to Christianity between 1391 and 1420, many as a result of coercion but some from sincere religious conviction. And for a generation or so, it seemed possible that these converts, known as *conversos*, might successfully assimilate into Christian society. But the same civil wars that led to the union of Ferdinand and Isabella made the *conversos* targets of discriminatory legislation. Conflict may also have fueled popular suspicions that these converts remained Jews in secret. To make "proper" Christians out of the *conversos*, the "Most Catholic" monarchs—as they were now called—may have concluded that they needed to remove any potentially seditious influences that might stem from the continuing presence of a Jewish community in Spain.

What became of the Spanish Jews? Some traveled north, to the Rhineland towns of Germany or to eastern Europe, but most settled in Muslim regions of the Mediterranean and Middle East. Many found a haven in the Ottoman Empire. As we already noted, there were many opportunities for advancement in the Ottoman imperial bureaucracy, while the Ottoman economy benefited from the highly skilled labor of Jewish artisans and the vast trading networks of Jewish merchants. In time, new forms and expressions of Jewish culture would emerge, and new communities would form. And although the extraordinary opportunities afforded by the *Convivencia* could never be revived, the descendants of these Spanish Jews—known as

Sephardi Jews, or Sephardim—still treasure the traditions and customs formed in Spain over a thousand years ago.

The Extension of the Reconquista

Although the Christian kingdoms of Iberia had been devoted, for centuries, to the reconquest of territory, the victory over the Muslims of Granada and the expulsion of the Jews in 1492 were watershed events. They mark the beginning of a sweeping initiative to construct a new basis for the precariously united kingdoms of Aragon and Castile, one that could transcend rival regional identities. Like other contemporary monarchs, Ferdinand and Isabella sought to strengthen their emerging nation-state by constructing an exclusively Christian identity for its people and by attaching that new identity to the crown and promoting a single national language, Castilian Spanish. They also succeeded in capturing and redirecting another language: the rhetoric of crusade.

The problem with the crusading ethos, as we have seen, is that it always seeks new outlets. Having created a new exclusively Christian Spanish kingdom through the defeat of all external enemies and internal threats, where were the energies harnessed by the Reconquista to be directed? The answer came from an unexpected quarter and had very unexpected consequences. Just a few months after Ferdinand and Isabella marched victoriously into Granada, the queen granted three ships to a Genoese adventurer who promised to reach India by sailing westward across the Atlantic Ocean, claiming any new lands he found for Spain. Columbus never reached India, but he did help to extend the tradition of reconquest to the New World—with far-reaching consequences.

NEW TARGETS AND TECHNOLOGIES OF CONQUEST

The Spanish monarchs' decision to underwrite a voyage of exploration was spurred by their desire to counter the successful Portuguese ventures of the past half century. For it was becoming clear that a tiny kingdom on the northwestern tip of the Iberian Peninsula would soon dominate the sea-lanes if rival entrepreneurs did not attempt to find alternate routes and establish equally lucrative colonies. This competition with Portugal was another reason why Isabella turned to a Genoese sea captain when she sought

to expand Spain's wealth and global influence—not to a Portuguese one.

Prince Henry the Navigator and Portuguese Colonial Initiatives

Although Portugal had been an independent Christian kingdom since the twelfth century (see Chapter 9), it was never able to compete effectively with its more powerful neighbors (Muslim or Christian) on land. But when the focus of European economic expansion began to shift toward the Atlantic (see Chapter 10), Portuguese mariners were well placed to take advantage of the trend. A central figure in the history of Portuguese maritime imperialism is Prince Henry, later called "the Navigator" (1394–1460), a son of King João I of Portugal and his English queen, Philippa of Lancaster (sister of England's Henry IV).

Prince Henry was fascinated by the sciences of cartography and navigation, and he helped to ensure that Portuguese sailors had access to the latest charts and navigational instruments. He was also inspired by the stories told by John de Mandeville and Marco Polo—particularly the legend of Prester John, a mythical Christian king dwelling somewhere at the end of the earth, whom Europeans believed would be their ally against the Muslims if only they could locate him. More concretely, Prince Henry had ambitions to extend Portuguese control into the Atlantic, to tap into the burgeoning market for slaves in the Ottoman Empire and to establish direct links with the sources of African gold.

Prince Henry played an important part in organizing the Portuguese colonization of Madeira, the Canary Islands, and the Azores—and in the process he pioneered the Portuguese slave trade, which almost entirely eradicated the population of the Canaries before targeting Africa. By the 1440s, Portuguese explorers had reached the Cape Verde Islands. In 1444, they landed on the African mainland in the area that became known as the Gold Coast, where they began to collect cargoes of gold and slaves for export back to Portugal. Prince Henry personally directed eight of the thirty-five Portuguese voyages to Africa that occurred during his lifetime. And in order to outflank the cross-Saharan gold trade, largely controlled by the Muslims of North Africa and mediated by the Genoese, he decided to intercept this trade at its source by building a series of forts along the African coastline. This was also his main reason for colonizing the Canary

OVERSEAS EXPLORATION IN THE FIFTEENTH AND SIXTEENTH CENTURIES. ▪ *What were the major routes taken by European explorers of the fifteenth and sixteenth centuries?* ▪ *What appear to be the explorers' main goals?* ▪ *How might the establishment of outposts in Africa, America, and the East Indies have radically altered the balance of power in the Old World, and why?*

Islands, which he saw as a staging ground for expeditions into the African interior.

From Africa to India and Beyond: An Empire of Spices

By the 1470s, Portuguese sailors had rounded the western coast of Africa and were exploring the Gulf of Guinea. In 1483, they reached the mouth of the Congo River. In 1488, the Portuguese captain Bartholomeu Dias was accidentally blown around the southern tip of Africa by a gale, after which he named the point "Cape of Storms." But King João II (r. 1481–95) took a more optimistic view of Dias's achievement: he renamed it the Cape of Good Hope and began planning a naval expedition to India. In 1497–98, accordingly, Vasco da Gama rounded the cape, and then, with the help of a Muslim navigator named Ibn Majid, crossed the Indian Ocean to Calicut, on the southwestern coast of India. For the first time, this opened a viable sea route between Europe and the Far Eastern spice trade. Although Gama lost half his fleet and one-third of his men on his two-year voyage, his cargo of spices was so valuable that his losses were deemed insignificant. His heroism became legendary, and his story became the basis for the Portuguese national epic, the *Lusiads*.

Now masters of the quickest route to riches in the world, the Portuguese swiftly capitalized on their decades of accomplishment. Not only did their trading fleets sail regularly to India, there were Portuguese efforts to monopolize the entire spice trade: in 1509, the Portuguese defeated an Ottoman fleet and then blockaded the mouth of the Red Sea, attempting to cut off one of the traditional routes by which spices had traveled to Alexandria and Beirut. By 1510, Portuguese military forces had established a series of forts along the western Indian coastline, including their headquarters at Goa. In 1511, Portuguese ships seized Malacca, a center of the spice trade on the Malay Peninsula. By 1515, they had reached the Spice Islands (East Indies) and the coast of China. So completely did the Portuguese now dominate the spice trade that by the 1520s even the Venetians were forced to buy their pepper in the Portuguese capital of Lisbon.

Naval Technology and Navigation

The Portuguese caravel—the workhorse ship of those first voyages to Africa—was based on ship and sail designs that had been in use among Portuguese fishermen since the thirteenth century. Starting in the 1440s, however, Portuguese shipwrights began building larger caravels of about 50 tons

displacement equipped with two masts, each carrying a triangular (lateen) sail. Columbus's *Niña* was a ship of this design, although it was refitted with two square sails in the Portuguese-held Canary Islands to enable it to sail more efficiently before the wind during the Atlantic crossing. Such ships required much smaller crews than did the multi-oared galleys that were still commonly used in the Mediterranean. By the end of the fifteenth century, even larger caravels of around 200 tons were being constructed, with a third mast and a combination of square and lateen sails.

Europeans were also making significant advances in navigation during this era. Quadrants, which could calculate latitude in the Northern Hemisphere by the height of the North Star above the horizon, were in widespread use by the 1450s. As sailors approached the equator, however, the quadrant became less and less useful, and navigators instead made use of astrolabes, which reckoned latitude by the height of the sun. Like quadrants, astrolabes had been in use for centuries. But it was not until the 1480s that the astrolabe became a really practical instrument for seaborne navigation, thanks to the preparation of standard tables for the calculation of latitude whose preparation was sponsored by the Portuguese crown. Compasses, too, were coming into more widespread use during the fifteenth century. Longitude, however, remained impossible to calculate accurately until the eighteenth century, when the invention of the marine chronometer finally made it possible to keep accurate time at sea. In this prior age of discovery, Europeans sailing east or west across the oceans generally had to rely on their skill at dead reckoning to determine where they were.

European sailors also benefited from a new interest in maps and navigational charts. Especially important were books known as *rutters* or *routiers*. These contained detailed sailing instructions and descriptions of the coastal landmarks a pilot could expect to encounter en route to a variety of destinations. Mediterranean sailors had used similar portolan charts since the thirteenth century, mapping the ports along the coastlines, tracking prevailing winds and tides, and indicating dangerous reefs and shallow harbors (see Chapter 10). In the fifteenth century, these mapmaking techniques were extended to the Atlantic Ocean; by the end of the sixteenth century, the accumulated knowledge contained in rutters spanned the globe.

Artillery and Empire

Larger, more maneuverable ships and improved navigational aids made it possible for the Portuguese and other European mariners to reach Africa, Asia, and—eventually—

into the Indian Ocean in 1498, but the Portuguese did not gain control of that ocean until 1509, when they defeated combined Ottoman and Indian naval forces. Portuguese trading outposts in Africa and Asia were essentially fortifications, built not so much to guard against the attacks of native peoples as to ward off assaults from other Europeans. Without this essential military component, the European maritime empires that were emerging in this period could not have existed.

Atlantic Colonization and a New Kind of Slavery

Although slavery had effectively disappeared in much of northwestern Europe by the early twelfth century, it continued in parts of the Mediterranean world and had been introduced into some regions of eastern Europe after the Black Death. But this slavery existed on a very small scale. There were no slave-powered factories or large-scale agricultural systems in this period. The only major slave markets and slave economies were in the Ottoman Empire, and there slaves ran the vast Ottoman bureaucracy and staffed the army. And in all these cases, as in antiquity, no aspect of slavery was racially based. In Italy and elsewhere in the medieval Mediterranean world, slaves were often captives from an array of locales. In eastern Europe, they were functionally serfs. Most Ottoman slaves were European Christians, predominantly Poles, Ukrainians, Greeks, and Bulgarians. In the early Middle Ages, Germanic and Celtic peoples had been widely enslaved. Under the Roman Empire, slaves had come from every part of the known (and unknown) world.

What was new about the slavery of the late fifteenth century was its increasing racialization—an aspect of modern slavery that has made an indelible impact on our own society. To Europeans, African slaves were visible in ways that other slaves were not, and it became convenient for those who dealt in them to justify the mass deportation of entire populations by claiming their racial inferiority and their "natural" fitness for a life of bondage. This nefarious practice, too, has had long-lasting and tragic consequences that still afflict the civilizations of our own world.

In Lisbon, which became a significant market for enslaved Africans during Prince Henry's lifetime, something on the order of 15,000 to 20,000 African captives were sold within a twenty-year period. In the following half century, by about 1505, the numbers amounted to 150,000. For the most part, the purchasers of these slaves regarded them as

SPANISH GALLEON. The larger, full-bottomed ships that came into use during the fifteenth century would become engines of imperial conquest and the vessels that brought the riches of those conquests back to Europe. This wooden model was made for the Museo Storico Navale di Venezia (Naval History Museum) in Venice, Italy.

the Americas. But fundamentally, these European commercial empires were military achievements that capitalized on what Europeans had learned in their wars against each other. Perhaps the most critical military advance was the increasing sophistication of artillery, a development made possible not only by gunpowder but also by improved metallurgical techniques for casting cannon barrels. By the middle of the fifteenth century, as we observed in Chapter 11, the use of artillery pieces had rendered the stone walls of medieval castles and towns obsolete, a fact brought home in 1453 by the successful French siege of Bordeaux (which ended the Hundred Years' War), and by the Ottoman siege of Constantinople (which ended the Byzantine Empire).

Indeed, the new ship designs (first caravels, and then the heavier galleons) were important in part because their larger size made it possible to mount more effective artillery pieces on them. European vessels were now conceived as floating artillery platforms, with scores of guns mounted in fixed positions along their sides and swivel guns mounted fore and aft. These guns were vastly expensive, as were the ships that carried them, but for those rulers who could afford them, such ships made it possible to back mercantile ventures with military power. As we already noted, Vasco da Gama had been able to sail

Analyzing Primary Sources

The Ottomans' Army of Slaves

Although the growing African slave trade was creating a newly racialized idea of slavery in the Caribbean and the Americas, slavery in Europe was not tied to race. Indeed, slavery could be a path to upward mobility in the Ottoman Empire. The following account is from a memoir written by Konstantin Mihailovic, a Serbian Christian who was captured as a youth by the army of Sultan Mehmet II. For eight years, he served in the Ottoman janissary ("gate-keeper") corps. In 1463, the fortress he was defending for the sultan was captured by the Hungarians, after which he recorded his experiences for a Christian audience.

henever the Turks invade foreign lands and capture their people, an imperial scribe follows immediately behind them, and whatever boys there are, he takes them all into the janissaries and gives five gold pieces for each one and sends them across the sea [to Anatolia]. There are about two thousand of these boys. If, however, the number of them from enemy peoples does not suffice, then he takes from the Christians in every village in his land who have boys, having established what is the most every village can give so that the quota will always be full. And the boys whom he takes in his own land are called *cilik*. Each one of them can leave his property to whomever he wants after his death. And those whom he takes among the enemies are called *pendik*. These latter after their deaths can leave nothing; rather, it goes to the emperor, except that if someone comports himself well and is so deserving that he be freed, he may leave it to whomever he wants. And on the boys who are across the sea the emperor spends nothing; rather, those to whom they are entrusted must maintain them and send them where he orders. Then they take those who are suited for it on ships and there they study and train to skirmish in battle. There the emperor already provides for them and gives them a wage. From there he chooses for his own court those who are trained and then raises their wages.

Source: Konstantin Mihailovic, *Memoirs of a Janissary* (Michigan Slavic Translations 3), trans. Benjamin Stolz (Ann Arbor, MI: 1975), pp. 157–59.

Questions for Analysis

1. Why might the Ottoman emperor have established this system for "recruiting" and training janissaries? What are its strengths and weaknesses?

2. Based on your knowledge of Western civilizations, how unusual would you deem this method of raising troops? How does it compare to the strategies of other rulers we have studied?

status symbols; it became fashionable to have African footmen, page boys, and ladies' maids. In the Atlantic colonies—Madeira, the Canaries, and the Azores—land was still worked mainly by European settlers and sharecroppers. Slave labor, if it was employed at all, was generally used only in sugar mills. On Madeira and the Canaries, where sugar became the predominant cash crop during the last quarter of the fifteenth century, some slaves were introduced as agricultural laborers. But even sugar production did not lead to the widespread introduction of slavery on these islands.

However, a new kind of slave-based sugar plantation began to emerge in Portugal's eastern Atlantic colonies in the 1460s, starting on the Cape Verde Islands and then extending southward into the Gulf of Guinea. These islands were not populated when the Portuguese began to settle them, and their climate generally discouraged most Europeans from living there. They were ideally located, however, along the routes of slave traders venturing outward from the nearby West African coast. It was this plantation model that would be exported to Brazil by the Portuguese and to the Caribbean islands of the Americas by their Spanish conquerors, with incalculable consequences for the peoples of Africa, the Americas, and Europe (see Chapter 14).

EUROPEANS IN A NEW WORLD

Like his contemporaries, Christopher Columbus (1451–1506) understood that the world was a sphere. But like them, he also thought it was much smaller than it actually is. (As we saw in Chapter 4, the accurate calculation of the globe's circumference made in ancient Alexandria had been suppressed centuries later by Roman geographers.) Furthermore, it had long been accepted that there were only three continents, Europe, Asia, and Africa—hence Columbus's decision to reach Asia by sailing west, a plan that seemed even more plausible after the discovery and colonization of the Canary Islands and the Azores. The existence of these islands reinforced a new hypothesis that the Atlantic was dotted with similar lands all the way to Japan. This emboldened Columbus's royal patrons, who became convinced that the Genoese mariner could reach China in about a month, after a stop for provisions on the Canaries. This turned out to be a kind of self-fulfilling prophecy, for when Columbus reached the Bahamas and the island of Hispaniola after only a month's sailing, he reported that he had reached the outer islands of Asia.

The Shock of Discovery

Of course, Columbus was not the first European to set foot on the American continents. As we have already learned, Viking sailors briefly settled present-day Newfoundland, Labrador, and perhaps even portions of New England around the year 1000 (see Chapter 8). But knowledge of these Viking landings had been forgotten or ignored outside of Iceland for hundreds of years. It wasn't until the 1960s that the stories of these expeditions were corroborated by archaeological evidence. Moreover, the tiny Norwegian colony on Greenland—technically part of the North American landmass—had been abandoned in the fifteenth century, when the cooling of the climate (see Chapter 10) destroyed the fragile ecosystems that had barely sustained the lives of Norse settlers there.

Although Columbus brought back no spices to prove that he had found an alternate route to Asia, he did return with some small samples of gold and a few indigenous people—whose existence gave promise of entire tribes that might be "saved" by conversion to Christianity and whose lands could provide homes for Spanish settlers seeking new frontiers after the Reconquista. This provided sufficient incentive for the "Most Catholic" monarchs to finance three further expeditions by Columbus, and many more by other adventurers, missionaries, and colonists.

Meanwhile, the Portuguese, who had already obtained a papal bull granting them (hypothetical) ownership of all lands south of the Canaries, rushed to establish their own claims. After two years of wrangling and conflicting papal pronouncements, the Treaty of Tordesillas (1494) sought to demarcate Spanish and Portuguese possession of as-yet-undiscovered lands. The Spanish would ultimately emerge as the big winners in this gambling match. Within a decade, the coasts of two hitherto unknown continents were identified, as were clusters of new islands, most on the Spanish side of the (still disputed) meridian.

Gradually, Europeans reached the conclusion that the voyages of Columbus and his immediate successors had revealed an entirely "New World." And—shockingly—this world had not been foretold either by the teachings of Christianity or the wisdom of the ancients. Among the first to champion the fact of two new continents' existence was the Italian explorer and geographer Amerigo Vespucci (1454–1512), whose name was soon adopted as a descriptor for them. Eventually, those who came to accept this fact were forced to question the reliability of the key sources of knowledge on which Western civilizations had hitherto hinged (see Chapter 14).

At first, the realization that the Americas (as they were now called) were not an outpost of Asia came as a disappointment to the Spanish: two major land masses and two vast oceans disrupted their plans to beat the Portuguese to the Spice Islands. But new possibilities gradually became clear. In 1513, the Spanish explorer Vasco Núñez de Balboa first viewed the Pacific Ocean from the Isthmus of Panama, and news of the narrow divide between two vast oceans prompted Ferdinand and Isabella's grandson to renew their dream. This young monarch, Charles V (1500–1556), ruled not only Spain but the huge patchwork of territories encompassed by the Holy Roman Empire. In 1519, he accepted Ferdinand Magellan's proposal to see whether a route to Asia could be found by sailing around South America.

But Magellan's voyage demonstrated beyond question that the world was simply too large for any such plan to be feasible at that time. Of the five ships that left Spain under his command, only one returned, three years later, having been forced to circumnavigate the globe. Out of a crew of 265 sailors, only 18 survived. Most had died of scurvy or starvation; Magellan himself had been killed in a skirmish with native peoples in the Philippines.

This fiasco ended all hope of discovering an easy southwest passage to Asia—although the deadly dream

America as an Object of Desire

Under the influence of popular travel narratives that had circulated in Europe for centuries, Columbus and his fellow voyagers were prepared to find the New World full of cannibals. They also assumed that the indigenous peoples' custom of wearing little or no clothing—not to mention their "savagery"—would render their women sexually available. In a letter sent back home in 1495, one of Columbus's men recounted a notable encounter with a "cannibal girl" whom he had taken captive in his tent and whose naked body aroused his desire. He was surprised to find that she resisted his advances so fiercely that he had to tie her up—which of course made it easier for him to "subdue" her. In the end, he cheerfully reports, the girl's sexual performance was so satisfying that she might have been trained, as he put it, in a "school for whores."

The Flemish artist Jan van der Straet (1523–1605) would have heard many such reports of the encounters between (mostly male) Europeans and the peoples of the New World. This engraving, based on one of his drawings, is among the thousands of mass-produced images that circulated widely in Europe, thanks to the invention of printing. It imagines the first encounter between a male "Americus" (like Columbus or Amerigo Vespucci himself) and the New World, "America," depicted as a voluptuous, available woman. The Latin caption reads: "America rises to meet Americus; and whenever he calls her, she will always be aroused."

Americen Americus retexit, & *Semel vocauit inde semper excitam.*
AMERICA.

Questions for Analysis

1. Study the details of this image carefully. What does each symbolize, and how do they work together as an allegory of conquest and colonization?

2. On what stereotypes of indigenous peoples does this image draw? Notice, for example, the cannibalistic campfire of the group in the background or the posture of "America."

3. The New World itself—America—is imagined as female in this image. Why is this? What messages might this—and the suggestive caption—have conveyed to a European viewer?

of a northwest passage survived and motivated many European explorers of North America into the twentieth century. It has been revived today: in our age of global warming, the retreat of Arctic pack ice has led to the opening of new shipping lanes, and in 2008 the first commercial voyage successfully traversed the Arctic Ocean.

The Dream of Gold and the Downfall of Empires

Although the unforeseen size of the globe made a westward passage to Asia untenable, given the technologies then available, Europeans were quick to capitalize on the sources of wealth that the New World itself could offer. What chiefly fired the imagination were those small samples of gold that Columbus had initially brought back to Spain. While rather paltry in themselves, they nurtured hopes that gold might lie piled in ingots somewhere in these vast new lands, ready to enrich any adventurer who discovered them. Rumor fed rumor, until a few freelance Spanish soldiers really did strike it rich beyond their most avaricious imaginings.

Their success, though, had little to do with their own efforts. Within a generation after the landing of the first ships under Columbus's command, European diseases had spread rapidly among the indigenous peoples of the Caribbean and the coastlines of the Americas. These diseases—especially measles and smallpox—were not fatal to those who carried them, because Europeans had developed immunities over many generations. But to the peoples of this New World, they were deadly in the extreme. For example, there were probably 250,000 people living on Hispaniola when Columbus arrived; within thirty years—a single generation—70 percent had perished from disease.

Moreover, the new waves of *conquistadores* (conquerors) were assisted by the complex political, economic, and military rivalries that already existed among the highly sophisticated societies they encountered. The Aztec Empire of Mexico rivaled any European state in its power, culture, and wealth—and like any successful empire it had subsumed many neighboring territories in the course of its own conquests. Its capital, Tenochtitlán (*ten-och-tit-LAN*, now Mexico City), amazed its European assailants, who had never seen anything like the height and grandeur of its buildings or the splendor of its public works. This splendor was itself evidence of the Aztecs' imperial might, which was resisted by many of the peoples from whom they demanded tribute.

The Aztecs' eventual conqueror, Hernán Cortés (1485–1547), had arrived in Hispaniola as a young man, in the wake of Columbus's initial landing. He had received a land grant from the Spanish crown and acted as magistrate of one of the first towns established there. In 1519, he headed an expedition to the mainland, which had been the target of some earlier exploratory missions that had not resulted in any permanent settlements—owing largely to the tight control of the Aztecs, whose imperial domain extended far beyond Tenochtitlán.

When Cortés arrived on the coast of the Aztec realm, he formed an intimate relationship with a native woman known as La Malinche. She became his consort and interpreter in the Nahua language, which was a lingua franca among the many different ethnic groups within the empire. With her help, he discovered that some peoples subjugated by the Aztecs were rebellious, and so he began to form stra-

THE AZTEC CITY OF TENOCHTITLÁN. The Spanish conquistador Bernal Díaz del Castillo (1492–1585) took part in the conquest of the Aztec Empire and later wrote a historical account of his adventures. His admiring description of the Aztec capital at Tenochtitlán records that the Spaniards were amazed to see such a huge city built in the midst of a vast lake, with gigantic buildings arranged in a meticulous urban plan around a central square and broad causeways linking the city to the mainland. This hand-colored woodcut was included in an early edition of Hernán Cortés's letters to Emperor Charles V, printed at Nuremberg (Germany) in 1524.

tegic alliances with their leaders. Cortés himself could only muster a force of a few hundred men, but his native allies numbered in the thousands.

These strategic alliances were crucial: although Cortés and his men had potentially superior weapons—guns and horses—these were more effective for their novelty than their utility. In fact, the rifles were of inferior quality, while gunpowder dampened by the humid climate had a tendency to misfire or fail to ignite altogether. So Cortés adopted the tactics and weaponry of his native allies in his dealings with the Aztec king, Montezuma II (r. 1502–1520), and in his final assaults upon the fortification of Tenochtitlán. In the end, though, it was European bacteria (not European technology or cunning) that led to his victory: the Aztecs were devastated by an outbreak of the plague virus that had arrived along with Cortés and his men. In 1521, their empire fell.

In 1533, another lucky conquistador, Francisco Pizarro, would manage to topple the highly centralized empire of the Incas, based in what is now Peru, by similar voluntary and involuntary means. In this case, he took advantage of an ongoing civil war that had weakened the reigning dynasty. He was also assisted by an epidemic of smallpox. Like Cortés, Pizarro promised his native allies liberation from an oppressive regime. Those formerly subject to the Aztecs and Incas would soon be able to judge how partial these promises were.

The Price of Conquest

The astonishing conquests of Mexico and Peru gave the conquistadors access to hoards of gold and silver that had been accumulated for centuries by Aztec and Inca rulers. Almost immediately, however, a search for the sources of these precious metals was launched by agents of the Spanish crown. The first gold deposits were discovered in Hispaniola, where surface mines were speedily established using native laborers, who were already dying in appalling numbers from disease and were now further decimated by brutality and overwork. The population dwindled further, to a mere 10 percent of its Pre-Columbian strength.

The loss of so many workers made the mines of Hispaniola uneconomical to operate, so European colonists turned instead to cattle raising and sugar production. Modeling their sugarcane plantations on those of the Cape Verde Islands and St. Thomas (São Tomé) in the Gulf of Guinea, colonists began to import thousands of African slaves to labor in the new industry. Sugar production was, by its nature, a capital-intensive undertaking. The need to import slave labor added further to its costs, guaranteeing that control over the new industry would fall into the hands of a few extremely wealthy planters and financiers.

Despite the establishment of sugar production in the Caribbean and cattle ranching on the Mexican mainland—whose devastating effects on the fragile ecosystem of Central America will be discussed in Chapter 14—it was mining that would shape the Spanish colonies most fundamentally in this period. If gold was the lure that had initially inspired the conquest, silver became its most lucrative export. Even before the discovery of vast silver deposits, the Spanish crown had taken steps to assume direct control over all colonial exports. It was therefore to the Spanish crown that the profits of empire were channeled. Europe's silver

SPANISH CONQUISTADORS IN MEXICO. This sixteenth-century drawing of conquistadors slaughtering the Aztec aristocracy emphasizes the advantages that plate armor and steel swords gave to the Spanish soldiers.

A Spanish Critique of New World Conquest

Not all Europeans approved of European imperialism or its "civilizing" effects on the peoples of the New World. One of the most influential contemporary critics was Bartolomé de las Casas (1484–1566). In 1502, when Bartolomé was eighteen years old, he and his father joined an expedition to Hispaniola. In 1510, he became the first ordained priest in the Americas and eventually became bishop of Chiapas (Mexico). Although he was a product of his times—he owned many slaves—he was also prescient in discerning the devastating effects of European settlement in the West Indies and Central America, and he particularly deplored the exploitation and extermination of indigenous populations. The following excerpt is from one of the many eloquent manifestos he published in an attempt to gain the sympathies of the Spanish crown and to reach a wide readership. It was printed in 1542 but draws on the impressions and opinions he had formed since his arrival in New Spain as a young man.

od made all the peoples of this area, many and varied as they are, as open and as innocent as can be imagined. The simplest people in the world—unassuming, long-suffering, unassertive, and submissive—they are without malice or guile, and are utterly faithful and obedient both to their own native lords and to the Spaniards in whose service they now find themselves.... They are innocent and pure in mind and have a lively intelligence, all of which makes them particularly receptive to learning and understanding the truths of our Catholic faith and to being instructed in virtue; indeed, God has invested them with fewer impediments in this regard than any other people on earth....

It was upon these gentle lambs ... that from the very first day they clapped eyes on them the Spanish fell like ravening wolves upon the fold, or like tigers and savage lions who have not eaten meat for days. The pattern established at the outset has remained unchanged to this day, and the Spaniards still do nothing save tear the natives to shreds, murder them and inflict upon them untold misery, suffering and distress, tormenting, harrying and persecuting them mercilessly....

When the Spanish first journeyed there, the indigenous population of the island of Hispaniola stood at some three million; today only two hundred survive. The island of Cuba, which extends for a distance almost as great as that separating Valladolid from Rome, is now to all intents and purposes uninhabited; and two other large, beautiful and fertile islands, Puerto Rico and Jamaica, have been similarly devastated. Not a living soul remains today on any of the islands of the Bahamas ... even though every single one of the sixty or so islands in the group ... is more fertile and more beautiful than the Royal Gardens in Seville and the climate is as healthy as anywhere on earth. The native population, which once numbered some five hundred thousand, was wiped out by forcible expatriation to the island of Hispaniola, a policy adopted by the Spaniards in an endeavour to make up losses among the indigenous population of that island....

At a conservative estimate, the despotic and diabolical behaviour of the Christians has, over the last forty years, led to the unjust and totally unwarranted deaths of more than twelve million souls, women and children among them....

The reason the Christians have murdered on such a vast scale and killed anyone and everyone in their way is purely and simply greed.... The Spaniards have shown not the slightest consideration for these people, treating them (and I speak from first-hand experience, having been there from the outset) not as brute animals—indeed, I would to God they had done and had shown them the consideration they afford their animals—so much as piles of dung in the middle of the road. They have had as little concern for their souls as for their bodies, all the millions that have perished having gone to their deaths with no knowledge of God and without the benefit of the Sacraments. One fact in all this is widely known and beyond dispute, for even the tyrannical murderers themselves acknowledge the truth of it: the indigenous peoples never did the Europeans any harm whatever....

Source: Bartolomé de las Casas, *A Short Account of the Destruction of the Indies*, trans. Nigel Griffin (Harmondsworth, UK: 1992), pp. 9–12.

Questions for Analysis

1. Given his perspective on the behavior of his countrymen, how might Bartolomé de las Casas have justified his own presence in New Spain (Mexico)? What do you think he may have hoped to achieve by publishing this account?

2. What comparisons does the author make between New Spain (Mexico) and the Old, and between indigenous peoples and Europeans? What is he trying to convey?

3. Compare this account with the contemporary engraving on page 000. What new light does this excerpt throw on that visual allegory? How might a reader-viewer of the time have reconciled these two very different pictures of European imperialism?

shortage, which had been acute for centuries, therefore came to an end.

Yet this massive infusion of silver into the European economy created more problems than it solved, because it accelerated an inflation that had already begun in the late fifteenth century. Initially, inflation had been driven by the renewed growth of the European population, an expanding colonial economy, and a relatively fixed supply of food. Thereafter, thanks to the influx of New World silver, inflation was driven by the hugely increased supply of coinage. As we shall see, this abundance of coinage led to the doubling and quadrupling of prices in the course of the sixteenth century and the collapse of this inflated economy—paradoxically driving a wave of impoverished Europeans to settle in the New World in ever greater numbers.

CONCLUSION

The expansion of the Mediterranean world into the Atlantic, which had been ongoing since the thirteenth century, was the essential preliminary to Columbus's voyages and to the rise of European empires in Africa, India, the Caribbean, and the Americas. Other events and innovations that we have surveyed in this chapter played a key role, too: the relatively rapid communications facilitated by the printing press; the tussle for power in Italy that led to the development of ever deadlier weapons; the navigational and colonial initiatives of the Portuguese; and the success of the Spanish Reconquista, which displaced Spain's venerable Jewish community and enabled Spanish rulers and adventurers to seek their fortunes overseas.

After You Read This Chapter

Visit StudySpace for quizzes, additional review materials, and multimedia documents. **wwnorton.com/web/westernciv18**

REVIEWING THE OBJECTIVES

- The artists of Italy were closely tied to those with political and military power. How did this relationship affect the kinds of work these artists produced?
- What aspects of Renaissance artistry and learning were adopted in northern Europe?
- What was the Reconquista, and how did it lead to a new way of thinking about Spanish identity?
- Europeans, especially the Portuguese, were developing new technologies and techniques that enabled exploration and colonial ventures in this period. What were they?
- The "discovery" of the New World had profound effects on the indigenous peoples and environment of the Americas. Describe some of these effects.

For the indigenous peoples and empires of the Americas, the results were cataclysmic. Within a century of Europeans' arrival, between 50 and 90 percent of some native populations had perished from disease, massacre, and enslavement. Moreover, Europeans' capacity to further their imperial ambitions wherever ships could sail and guns could penetrate profoundly destabilized Europe and its neighbors, sharpening the divisions among competing kingdoms and empires.

The ideals of the humanists and the artistry associated with the Renaissance often stand in sharp contrast to the harsh realities alongside which they coexisted and in which they were rooted. Artists could thrive in the atmosphere of competition and one-upmanship that characterized this period, but they could also find themselves reduced to the status of servants in the households of the wealthy and powerful—or forced to subordinate their artistry to the demands of warfare and espionage. Meanwhile, intellectuals and statesmen looked for inspiration to the precedents and glories of the past. But to which aspects of the past? Some humanists may have wanted to revive the principles of the Roman Republic, but many of them worked for ambitious despots who modeled themselves on Rome's dictators. The theories that undergirded European politics and colonial expansion were being used to legitimize many different kinds of power, including that of the papacy. All of these trends would be carried forward in the sixteenth century and would have a role to play in the upheaval that shattered Europe's fragile religious unity. It is to this upheaval, the Reformation, that we turn in Chapter 13.

PEOPLE, IDEAS, AND EVENTS IN CONTEXT

- Why was **GUTENBERG**'s invention of the **PRINTING PRESS** such a significant development?
- How did **NICCOLÒ MACHIAVELLI** respond to Italy's political situation within Europe? In what ways do artists like **LEONARDO DA VINCI** and **MICHELANGELO BUONARROTI** exemplify the ideals and realities of the Renaissance?
- How did northern European scholars like **DESIDERIUS ERASMUS** and **THOMAS MORE** apply humanist ideas to Christianity? How were these ideas expressed in art?
- What is significant about **IVAN THE GREAT**'s use of the title **TSAR**? In what other ways did the Russian emperor claim to be the heir of Rome?
- How did **ISABELLA OF CASTILE** and **FERDINAND OF ARAGON** succeed in creating a unified Spain through the **RECONQUISTA**?
- How does **PRINCE HENRY THE NAVIGATOR** exemplify the motives for pursuing overseas expansion? Why were the Portuguese so successful in establishing colonies in this period?
- What were the expectations that launched **COLUMBUS**'s voyage? What enabled the Spanish **CONQUISTADORS** to subjugate the peoples of the **AMERICAS**?

THINKING ABOUT CONNECTIONS

- Phrases like "Renaissance man" and "a Renaissance education" are still part of our common vocabulary. Given what you have learned in this chapter, how has your understanding of such phrases changed? How would you explain their true meaning to others?
- How do the patterns of conquest and colonization discussed in this chapter compare to those of earlier periods, for example the era of the Crusades or the empires of antiquity? How many of these developments were new?
- Although the growth of the African slave trade would result in a new racialization of slavery in the Atlantic world, the justifications for slavery had very old roots. How might Europeans have used Greek and Roman precedents in defense of these new ventures? (See Chapters 4 and 5.)

STORY LINES

- The movement catalyzed by Martin Luther's challenge to the Church grew out of much earlier attempts at reform, but it was also a response to more recent religious and political developments.

- Within a decade after Luther's break with Rome, religious dissent was widespread and a number of different Protestant faiths were taking hold in various regions of Europe.

- Protestantism transformed not only the political landscape of Europe but also basic structures of the family and the attitudes toward marriage and sexuality which still shape our lives today.

- These changes also affected the structures and doctrine of the Roman Catholic ("universal") Church, which reemerged as an institution different in many ways from the medieval Church and more similar to that of today.

CHRONOLOGY

Before
You
Read
This
Chapter

Rulers of Principal States

THE CAROLINGIAN DYNASTY

Pepin of Heristal, Mayor of the Palace, 687–714
Charles Martel, Mayor of the Palace, 715–741
Pepin III, Mayor of the Palace, 741–751; King, 751–768
Charlemagne, King, 768–814; Emperor, 800–814
Louis the Pious, Emperor, 814–840

West Francia

Charles the Bald, King, 840–877; Emperor, 875–877
Louis II, King, 877–879
Louis III, King, 879–882
Carloman, King, 879–884

Middle Kingdoms

Lothair, Emperor, 840–855
Louis (Italy), Emperor, 855–875
Charles (Provence), King, 855–863
Lothair II (Lorraine), King, 855–869

East Francia

Ludwig, King, 840–876
Carloman, King, 876–880
Ludwig, King, 876–882
Charles the Fat, Emperor, 876–887

HOLY ROMAN EMPERORS

Saxon Dynasty

Otto I, 962–973
Otto II, 973–983
Otto III, 983–1002
Henry II, 1002–1024

Franconian Dynasty

Conrad II, 1024–1039
Henry III, 1039–1056
Henry IV, 1056–1106
Henry V, 1106–1125
Lothair II (Saxony), 1125–1137

Hohenstaufen Dynasty

Conrad III, 1138–1152
Frederick I (Barbarossa), 1152–1190
Henry VI, 1190–1197
Philip of Swabia, 1198–1208 ⎫
Otto IV (Welf), 1198–1215 ⎭ Rivals

Frederick II, 1220–1250
Conrad IV, 1250–1254

Interregnum, 1254–1273

Emperors from Various Dynasties

Rudolf I (Habsburg), 1273–1291
Adolf (Nassau), 1292–1298
Albert I (Habsburg), 1298–1308
Henry VII (Luxemburg), 1308–1313
Ludwig IV (Wittelsbach), 1314–1347
Charles IV (Luxemburg), 1347–1378
Wenceslas (Luxemburg), 1378–1400
Rupert (Wittelsbach), 1400–1410
Sigismund (Luxemburg), 1410–1437

Habsburg Dynasty

Albert II, 1438–1439
Frederick III, 1440–1493

Maximilian I, 1493–1519
Charles V, 1519–1556
Ferdinand I, 1556–1564
Maximilian II, 1564–1576
Rudolf II, 1576–1612
Matthias, 1612–1619
Ferdinand II, 1619–1637
Ferdinand III, 1637–1657

Leopold I, 1658–1705
Joseph I, 1705–1711
Charles VI, 1711–1740
Charles VII (not a Habsburg), 1742–1745
Francis I, 1745–1765
Joseph II, 1765–1790
Leopold II, 1790–1792
Francis II, 1792–1806

RULERS OF FRANCE FROM HUGH CAPET

Capetian Dynasty

Hugh Capet, 987–996
Robert II, 996–1031
Henry I, 1031–1060
Philip I, 1060–1108
Louis VI, 1108–1137
Louis VII, 1137–1180
Philip II (Augustus), 1180–1223
Louis VIII, 1223–1226
Louis IX (St. Louis), 1226–1270
Philip III, 1270–1285
Philip IV, 1285–1314
Louis X, 1314–1316
Philip V, 1316–1322
Charles IV, 1322–1328

Valois Dynasty

Philip VI, 1328–1350
John, 1350–1364
Charles V, 1364–1380
Charles VI, 1380–1422
Charles VII, 1422–1461
Louis XI, 1461–1483
Charles VIII, 1483–1498
Louis XII, 1498–1515
Francis I, 1515–1547

Henry II, 1547–1559
Francis II, 1559–1560
Charles IX, 1560–1574
Henry III, 1574–1589

Bourbon Dynasty

Henry IV, 1589–1610
Louis XIII, 1610–1643
Louis XIV, 1643–1715
Louis XV, 1715–1774
Louis XVI, 1774–1792

After 1792

First Republic, 1792–1799
Napoleon Bonaparte, First Consul, 1799–1804
Napoleon I, Emperor, 1804–1814
Louis XVIII (Bourbon dynasty), 1814–1824
Charles X (Bourbon dynasty), 1824–1830
Louis Philippe, 1830–1848
Second Republic, 1848–1852
Napoleon III, Emperor, 1852–1870
Third Republic, 1870–1940
Pétain regime, 1940–1944
Provisional government, 1944–1946
Fourth Republic, 1946–1958
Fifth Republic, 1958–

RULERS OF ENGLAND

Anglo-Saxon Dynasty

Alfred the Great, 871–899
Edward the Elder, 899–924
Ethelstan, 924–939
Edmund I, 939–946
Edred, 946–955
Edwy, 955–959
Edgar, 959–975

Edward the Martyr, 975–978
Ethelred the Unready, 978–1016
Canute, 1016–1035 (Danish Nationality)
Harold I, 1035–1040
Hardicanute, 1040–1042
Edward the Confessor, 1042–1066
Harold II, 1066

House of Normandy

William I (the Conqueror), 1066–1087
William II, 1087–1100
Henry I, 1100–1135
Stephen, 1135–1154

House of Plantagenet

Henry II, 1154–1189
Richard I, 1189–1199
John, 1199–1216
Henry III, 1216–1272
Edward I, 1272–1307
Edward II, 1307–1327
Edward III, 1327–1377
Richard II, 1377–1399

House of Lancaster

Henry IV, 1399–1413
Henry V, 1413–1422
Henry VI, 1422–1461

House of York

Edward IV, 1461–1483
Edward V, 1483
Richard III, 1483–1485

House of Tudor

Henry VII, 1485–1509
Henry VIII, 1509–1547
Edward VI, 1547–1553
Mary, 1553–1558
Elizabeth I, 1558–1603

House of Stuart

James I, 1603–1625
Charles I, 1625–1649

Commonwealth and Protectorate, 1649–1659

House of Stuart Restored

Charles II, 1660–1685
James II, 1685–1688
William III and Mary II, 1689–1694
William III alone, 1694–1702
Anne, 1702–1714

House of Hanover

George I, 1714–1727
George II, 1727–1760
George III, 1760–1820
George IV, 1820–1830
William IV, 1830–1837
Victoria, 1837–1901

House of Saxe-Coburg-Gotha

Edward VII, 1901–1910
George V, 1910–1917

House of Windsor

George V, 1917–1936
Edward VIII, 1936
George VI, 1936–1952
Elizabeth II, 1952–

RULERS OF AUSTRIA AND AUSTRIA-HUNGARY

*Maximilian I (Archduke), 1493–1519
*Charles V, 1519–1556
*Ferdinand I, 1556–1564
*Maximilian II, 1564–1576
*Rudolf II, 1576–1612
*Matthias, 1612–1619
*Ferdinand II, 1619–1637
*Ferdinand III, 1637–1657
*Leopold I, 1658–1705
*Joseph I, 1705–1711
*Charles VI, 1711–1740
Maria Theresa, 1740–1780

*Joseph II, 1780–1790
*Leopold II, 1790–1792
*Francis II, 1792–1835 (Emperor of Austria as Francis I after 1804)
Ferdinand I, 1835–1848
Francis Joseph, 1848–1916 (after 1867 Emperor of Austria and King of Hungary)
Charles I, 1916–1918 (Emperor of Austria and King of Hungary)
Republic of Austria, 1918–1938 (dictatorship after 1934)
Republic restored, under Allied occupation, 1945–1956
Free Republic, 1956–

*Also bore title of Holy Roman Emperor

RULERS OF PRUSSIA AND GERMANY

*Frederick I, 1701–1713
*Frederick William I, 1713–1740
*Frederick II (the Great), 1740–1786
*Frederick William II, 1786–1797
*Frederick William III,1797–1840
*Frederick William IV, 1840–1861
*William I, 1861–1888 (German Emperor after 1871)
Frederick III, 1888

*Kings of Prussia

*William II, 1888–1918
Weimar Republic, 1918–1933
Third Reich (Nazi Dictatorship), 1933–1945
Allied occupation, 1945–1952
Division into Federal Republic of Germany in west and German Democratic Republic in east, 1949–1991
Federal Republic of Germany (united), 1991–

RULERS OF RUSSIA

Ivan III, 1462–1505
Vasily III, 1505–1533
Ivan IV, 1533–1584
Theodore I, 1534–1598
Boris Godunov, 1598–1605
Theodore II,1605
Vasily IV, 1606–1610
Michael, 1613–1645
Alexius, 1645–1676
Theodore III, 1676–1682
Ivan V and Peter I, 1682–1689
Peter I (the Great), 1689–1725
Catherine I, 1725–1727
Peter II, 1727–1730

Anna, 1730–1740
Ivan VI, 1740–1741
Elizabeth, 1741–1762
Peter III, 1762
Catherine II (the Great), 1762–1796
Paul, 1796–1801
Alexander I,1801–1825
Nicholas I, 1825–1855
Alexander II,1855–1881
Alexander III, 1881–1894
Nicholas II, 1894–1917
Soviet Republic, 1917–1991
Russian Federation, 1991–

RULERS OF UNIFIED SPAIN

Ferdinand { and Isabella, 1479–1504
and Philip I, 1504–1506
and Charles I, 1506–1516
Charles I (Holy Roman Emperor Charles V), 1516–1556
Philip II, 1556–1598
Philip III, 1598–1621
Philip IV, 1621–1665
Charles II, 1665–1700
Philip V, 1700–1746
Ferdinand VI, 1746–1759
Charles III, 1759–1788
Charles IV, 1788–1808

Ferdinand VII, 1808
Joseph Bonaparte, 1808–1813
Ferdinand VII (restored), 1814–1833
Isabella II, 1833–1868
Republic, 1868–1870
Amadeo, 1870–1873
Republic, 1873–1874
Alfonso XII, 1874–1885
Alfonso XIII, 1886–1931
Republic, 1931–1939
Fascist Dictatorship, 1939–1975
Juan Carlos I, 1975–

RULERS OF ITALY

Victor Emmanuel II, 1861–1878
Humbert I, 1878–1900
Victor Emmanuel III, 1900–1946

Fascist Dictatorship, 1922-1943 (maintained in northern
   Italy until 1945)
Humbert II, May 9–June 13, 1946
Republic, 1946–

PROMINENT POPES

Silvester I, 314–335
Leo I, 440–461
Gelasius I, 492–496
Gregory I, 590–604
Nicholas I, 858–867
Silvester II, 999–1003
Leo IX, 1049–1054
Nicholas II, 1058–1061
Gregory VII, 1073–1085
Urban II, 1088–1099
Paschal II, 1099–1118
Alexander III, 1159–1181
Innocent III, 1198–1216
Gregory IX, 1227–1241
Innocent IV, 1243–1254
Boniface VIII, 1294–1303
John XXII, 1316–1334
Nicholas V, 1447–1455
Pius II, 1458–1464

Alexander VI, 1492–1503
Julius II, 1503–1513
Leo X, 1513–1521
Paul III, 1534–1549
Paul IV, 1555–1559
Sixtus V, 1585–1590
Urban VIII, 1623–1644
Gregory XVI, 1831–1846
Pius IX, 1846–1878
Leo XIII, 1878–1903
Pius X, 1903–1914
Benedict XV, 1914–1922
Pius XI, 1922–1939
Pius XII, 1939–1958
John XXIII, 1958–1963
Paul VI, 1963–1978
John Paul I, 1978
John Paul II, 1978–2005
Benedict XVI, 2005–2013
Francis, 2013–

Further Readings

CHAPTER 1

Aldred, Cyril. *The Egyptians.* 3d ed. London, 1998. An indispensable, lively overview of Egyptian culture and history by one of the great masters of Egyptology.

Baines, J., and J. Málek. *Atlas of Ancient Egypt.* Rev. ed. New York, 2000. A reliable, well-illustrated survey, with excellent maps.

Bottéro, Jean. *Everyday Life in Ancient Mesopotamia.* Trans. Antonia Nevill. Baltimore, MD, 2001. A wide-ranging, interdisciplinary account.

Bottéro, Jean. *Religion in Ancient Mesopotamia.* Chicago, 2001. An accessible, engaging survey.

Dodson, Aidan. *Amarna Sunset: Nefertiti, Tutankhamun, Ay, Horemheb, and the Egyptian Counter-Reformation.* Cairo, 2009. A provocative study of the resistance to Akhenaten's religious "reformation," this book argues that Nefertiti was not only queen but also a kind of "joint-pharaoh," the mother of Tutankhamun, and the leader of the movement toward a return to traditional forms of worship.

Foster, Benjamin R. and Karen Polinger Foster. *Civilizations of Ancient Iraq.* Princeton, 2011. A critically-acclaimed survey that charts the history of this region from the earliest Sumerian civilization to the Arab conquests of the seventh c. C.E.

Geller, Markham J. *Ancient Babylonian Medicine: Theory and Practice.* Malden, MA, 2010. Makes use of previously unstudied cuneiform sources to tell a new story about the relationship between medicine and magic.

George, Andrew, trans. *The Epic of Gilgamesh: A New Translation. The Babylonian Epic Poem and Other Texts in Akkadian and Sumerian.* New York and London, 1999. A reliable translation which carefully distinguishes the chronological "layers" of this famous text; also includes many related texts.

Hodder, Ian. *The Leopard's Tale:Revealing the Mysteries of Çatalhöyük.* London and New York, 2006. The most up-to-date account of this fascinating archaeological site, written for general readers by the director of the excavation.

Kemp, Barry. *The City of Akhenaten and Nefertiti: Armana and Its People.* London, 2012. A cutting-edge study of this ancient site, based on decades of archeological research.

Leick, Gwendolyn. *The Babylonians: An Introduction.* London and New York, 2002. A wide-ranging survey of Babylonian civilization across the centuries.

McDowell, A. G. *Village Life in Ancient Egypt: Laundry Lists and Love Songs.* Oxford, 1999. A fascinating collection of translated texts recovered from an Egyptian peasant village, dating from 1539 to 1075 B.C.E.

McGregor, Neil. *A History of the World in 100 Objects.* London, 2011. Based on an acclaimed BBC Radio program, this book features a range of artifacts from the collections British Museum, embeds them in their historical contexts, and explores the ways that that still hold meaning today.

Pollock, Susan. *Ancient Mesopotamia.* Cambridge, 1999. An advanced textbook that draws on theoretical anthropology to interpret Mesopotamian civilization up to 2100 B.C.E.

Redford, Donald B., ed. *The Oxford Encyclopedia of Ancient Egypt.* 3 vols. New York, 2001. An indispensible reference work, intended for both specialists and beginners.

Roaf, Michael. *Cultural Atlas of Mesopotamia and the Ancient Near East.* New York, 1990. An informative, authoritative, and lavishly illustrated guide, with excellent maps.

Robins, Gay. *The Art of Ancient Egypt.* London, 1997. An excellent survey, now the standard account.

Shafer, Byron E., ed. *Religion in Ancient Egypt: Gods, Myths, and Personal Practice.* London, 1991. A scholarly examination of Egyptian belief and ritual, with contributions from leading authorities.

Shaw, Ian, ed. *The Oxford History of Ancient Egypt.* Oxford, 2000. An outstanding collaborative survey of Egyptian history from the Stone Age to c. 300 C.E., with excellent bibliographical essays.

Shryock, Andrew and Daniel Lord Smail. Berkeley, 2012. *Deep History: The Architecture of Past and Present.* A fascinating fusion of historical, anthropological, and scientific research on what it means to be human.

Smail, Daniel Lord. *On Deep History and the Brain.* Berkeley, 2008. A pioneering introduction to the historical uses of neuroscience and evolutionary biology.

Snell, Daniel C., ed. *A Companion to the Ancient Near East.* Oxford, 2005. A topical survey of recent scholarly work, particularly strong on society, economy, and culture.

Wengrow, David. *The Archaeology of Early Egypt: Social Transformations in North-East Africa, 10,000 to 2650 B.C.* Cambridge, 2006. An authoritative account of archeological evidence and its interpretation.

CHAPTER 2

Aubet, Maria Eugenia. *Phoenicia and the West: Politics, Colonies, and Trade.* Trans. Mary Turton. Cambridge, 1993. An intelligent and thought-provoking examination of Phoenician civilization and its influence.

Boardman, John. *Assyrian and Babylonian Empires and Other States of the Near East from the Eighth to the Sixth Centuries* B.C. New York, 1991. Scholarly and authoritative.

———. *Persia and the West.* London, 2000. A great book by a distinguished scholar, with a particular focus on art and architecture as projections of Persian imperial ideologies.

Boyce, Mary. *Textual Sources for the Study of Zoroastrianism.* Totowa, NJ, 1984. An invaluable collection of documents.

Bryce, Trevor. *The Kingdom of the Hittites.* Oxford, 1998. And *Life and Society in the Hittite World.* Oxford, 2002. An extraordinary synthesis, now the standard account of Hittite political, military, and daily life.

Curtis, John. *Ancient Persia.* Cambridge, MA, 1990. Concise, solid, reliable.

Dever, William. *Who Were the Early Israelites and Where Did They Come From?* Grand Rapids, MI, 2003. A balanced, fair-minded account with excellent bibliographical guidance to recent work.

Dickinson, O. T. P. K. *The Aegean Bronze Age.* Cambridge, 1994. An excellent summary of archaeological evidence and scholarly argument concerning Minoan, Mycenaean, and other cultures of the Bronze Age Aegean basin.

Dothan, Trude, and Moshe Dothan. *Peoples of the Sea: The Search for the Philistines.* New York, 1992. The essential starting point for understanding Philistine culture and its links to the Aegean basin.

Drews, Robert. *The End of the Bronze Age: Changes in Warfare and the Catastrophe ca. 1200 B.C.* Princeton, NJ, 1993. A stimulating analysis and survey, with excellent bibliographies.

Finkelstein, Israel, and Nadav Na'aman, eds. *From Nomadism to Monarchy: Archaeological and Historical Aspects of Early Israel.* Jerusalem, 1994. Scholarly articles on the Hebrews' transformation from pastoralists to a sedentary society focused on the worship of Yahweh.

Fitton, J. Lesley. *Minoans: Peoples of the Past* (British Museum Publications). London, 2002. A careful, reliable debunking of myths about the Minoans, written for nonspecialists.

Kamm, Antony. *The Israelites: An Introduction.* New York, 1999. A short, accessible history of the land and people of Israel up to 135 C.E., aimed at students and general readers.

Kuhrt, Amélie. *The Ancient Near East, c. 3000–330 B.C.* 2 vols. London and New York, 1995. An outstanding survey, written for students, that includes Egypt and Israel as well as Mesopotamia, Babylonia, Assyria, and Persia.

Marinatos, Nannos. *Minoan Kingship and the Solar Goddess: A Near Eastern Koine.* Champaign, IL, 2010. A rich new interpretation of Minoan culture and its wider connections and influence within the world of the late Bronze Age.

Metzger, Bruce M., and Michael D. Coogan, eds. *The Oxford Companion to the Bible.* New York, 1993. An outstanding reference work, with contributions by leading authorities.

Niditch, Susan. *Ancient Israelite Religion.* New York, 1997. A short introduction designed for students, emphasizing the diversity of Hebrew religious practices.

Prezioso, Donald and Louise A. Hitchcock. *Aegean Art and Architecture.* Oxford, 2000. Archaic Greek artistic forms in their broader geographic and cultural context, from the fourth millennium to 1000 B.C.E.

Redford, Donald B. *Egypt, Canaan, and Israel in Ancient Times.* Princeton, NJ, 1992. An overview of the interactions between these peoples from about 1200 B.C.E. to the beginning of the Common Era.

Renfrew, Colin. *Archaeology and Language: The Puzzle of Indo-European Origins.* Cambridge, 1987. A masterful but controversial work by one of the most creative archaeologists of the twentieth century.

Sandars, Nancy K. *The Sea Peoples: Warriors of the Ancient Mediterranean.* Rev. ed. London, 1985. An introductory account for students and scholars.

Tubb, Jonathan N., and Rupert L. Chapman. *Archaeology and the Bible.* London, 1990. A good starting point for students that clearly illustrates the difficulties in linking archeological evidence to biblical accounts of early Hebrew history and society.

Wood, Michael. *In Search of the Trojan War.* New York, 1985. Aimed at a general audience, this carefully researched and engagingly written book is an excellent introduction to the late–Bronze Age context of the Trojan War.

CHAPTER 3

Penguin Classics and the Loeb Classical Library both offer reliable translations of Greek literary, philosophical, and historical texts.

Beard, Mary. *The Parthenon.* Cambridge, MA, 2003. A book that traces the successive stages of this monument's construction, deconstruction, reconstruction, and restoration.

Boardman, John, Jaspar Griffin, and Oswyn Murray, eds. *Greece and the Hellenistic World.* Oxford, 1988. A reprint of the Greek and Hellenistic chapters from *The Oxford History of the Classical World,* originally published in 1986. Excellent, stimulating surveys, accessible to a general audience.

Brunschwig, Jacques, and Geoffrey E. R. Lloyd. *Greek Thought: A Guide to Classical Knowledge.* Translated by Catherine Porter. Cambridge, MA, 2000. An outstanding work of reference.

Buckley, Terry, ed. *Aspects of Greek History, 750–323 B.C.: A Source-Based Approach.* London, 1999. An outstanding collection of source materials.

Cartledge, Paul A. *The Spartans: An Epic History.* New York, 2003. A lively and authoritative history of Sparta from its origins to the Roman conquest.

Dover, Kenneth J. *Greek Homosexuality.* Cambridge, MA, 1978. The standard account of an important subject.

Fantham, Elaine, Helene Foley, Natalie Kampen, Sarah B. Pomeroy, and H. A. Shapiro. *Women in the Classical World: Image and Text.* Oxford, 1994. Wide-ranging analysis drawing on both visual and written sources, covering both the Greek and the Roman periods.

Fornara, Charles W., and Loren J. Samons II. *Athens from Cleisthenes to Pericles.* Berkeley, CA, 1991. An excellent narrative history of Athenian politics during the first half of the fifth century B.C.E.

Garlan, Yvon. *Slavery in Ancient Greece.* Ithaca, NY, 1988. Now the standard account.

Hanson, Victor Davis. *The Other Greeks: The Family Farm and the Agrarian Roots of Western Civilization.* New York, 1995. Polemical and idiosyncratic, but convincing in its emphasis on smallholding farmers as the backbone of Greek urban society.

Havelock, Eric A. *The Literate Revolution in Greece and Its Cultural Consequences.* Princeton, 1982. A now-classic account of the wide-ranging effects of writing on Greek society.

Jones, Nicholas F. *Ancient Greece: State and Society.* Upper Saddle River, NJ, 1997. A concise survey from the Minoans up to the end of the Classical Period that emphasizes the connections between the social order and politics.

Krentz, Peter. *The Battle of Marathon.* New Haven, 2011. A fresh analysis of this landmark battle, paying special attention to the conditions in which hoplite warriors fought.

Lefkowitz, Mary, and Maureen Fant. *Women's Life in Greece and Rome: A Source Book in Translation.* 3rd ed. Baltimore, MD, 2005. A remarkably wide-ranging collection, topically arranged, invaluable to students.

Nevett, Lisa C. *Domestic Space in Classical Antiquity.* Cambridge, 2010. Reassesses what we can know about the architecture of households in antiquity through a fresh assessment of archeological evidence and material culture.

Pomeroy, Sarah B., Stanley M. Burstein, Walter Donlan, and Jennifer Tolbert Roberts. *Ancient Greece: A Political, Social, and Cultural History.* Oxford, 1999. An outstanding textbook; clear and lively.

Pomeroy, Sarah. *Goddesses, Whores, Wives, and Slaves: Women in Classical Antiquity.* New York, 1995. The first historical survey of antiquity to place women at the center of the narrative, and still unrivaled in scope.

Price, Simon. *Religions of the Ancient Greeks.* Cambridge, 1999. Concise and authoritative, this survey extends from the Archaic Period up to the fifth century C.E.

Seaford, Richard. *Money and the Greek Mind: Homer, Philosophy, Tragedy.* Cambridge, 2004. A provocative study of portable wealth and its far-reaching effects.

Strassler, Robert B., ed. *The Landmark Thucydides.* New York, 1996. Reprints the classic Richard Crawley translation with maps, commentary, notes, and appendices by leading scholars.

Thomas, Carol G., and Craig Conant. *Citadel to City-State: The Transformation of Greece, 1200–700 B.C.E.* Bloomington, IN, 1999. A lucid and accessible study that examines developments at a number of different Dark Age sites.

Thomas, Rosalind. *Oral Tradition and Written Record in Classical Athens.* Cambridge, 1989. A fascinating look at how oral epic, lyric, and drama were transmitted over time.

CHAPTER 4

Penguin Classics and the Loeb Classical Library both offer reliable translations of scores of literary and historical texts from this period. Particularly important are historical works by Arrian (*Anabasis of Alexander*), Plutarch (*Life of Alexander*), and Polybius (*The Histories*).

Austin, M. M. *The Hellenistic World from Alexander to the Roman Conquest: A Selection of Ancient Sources in Translation.* Cambridge, 1981. A good collection of primary documents.

Bagnall, R. S., and P. Derow. *Greek Historical Documents: The Hellenistic Period.* Chico, CA, 1981. Another useful collection.

Borza, Eugene N. *In the Shadow of Olympus: The Emergence of Macedon.* Princeton, NJ, 1990. The standard account of the rise of Macedon up to the accession of Philip II.

Bosworth, A. B. *Conquest and Empire: The Reign of Alexander the Great.* Cambridge, 1988. A political and military analysis of Alexander's career that strips away the romance, maintaining a clear vision of the ruthlessness and human cost of his conquests.

——. *The Legacy of Alexander: Politics, Warfare, and Propaganda under the Successors.* Oxford, 2002. The most recent survey of the half century following Alexander's death and of the people who created the Hellenistic kingdoms of Egypt, Persia, and Macedon.

Burstein, Stanley M., ed. and trans. *The Hellenistic Age from the Battle of Ipsos to the Death of Kleopatra VII.* Cambridge, 1985. An excellent collection, with sources not found elsewhere.

Cartledge, Paul. *Agesilaus and the Crisis of Sparta.* Baltimore, MD, 1987. A thorough but readable analysis of the social and political challenges besetting Sparta in the fourth century B.C.E.

——. *Alexander the Great: The Hunt for a New Past.* Woodstock, NY, 2004. A compelling account of Alexander's life, times, and influences.

Green, Peter. *Alexander to Actium: The Historical Evolution of the Hellenistic Age.* Berkeley, CA. 1990. An outstanding, comprehensive, and wide-ranging history of the period.

——. *Alexander of Macedon, 356–323 B.C.* Berkeley, CA, 1991. Revised edition of the author's earlier biography; entertainingly written, rich in detail and insight.

——. *The Hellenistic Age: A Short History.* New York, 2007. An authoritative synthesis that carries the history of Greek influence into the fourth century C.E.

Hansen, Mogens H. *The Athenian Democracy in the Age of Demosthenes.* Oxford, 1991. An examination of the political institutions of Athens in the fourth century B.C.E.

Holt, Frank. L. *Into the Land of Bones: Alexander the Great in Afghanistan.* Berkeley, 2012 repr. ed. A vivid, charged narrative that places the beginning of a current war in the distant past.

Lloyd, Geoffrey, and Nathan Sivin. *The Way and the Word: Science and Medicine in Early China and Greece.* New Haven, CT, 2002. An extraordinary comparative study.

McGing, Brian. *Polybius' Histories.* Oxford, 2010. A critical dissection of this influential ancient historian's techniques and historical philosophy.

Nicholas, G. L. *The Genius of Alexander the Great.* Chapel Hill, NC, 1998. A clear, authoritative, admiring account, distilling a lifetime of research on the subject.

Ober, Josiah. *Mass and Elite in Democratic Athens: Rhetoric, Ideology, and the Power of the People.* Princeton, NJ, 1989. An excellent study of the ideology of democracy in Athens that borrows from the insights of modern social science.

Pollitt, Jerome J. *Art in the Hellenistic Age.* New York, 1986. The standard account, blending cultural history with art history.

Sherwin-White, Susan, and Amélie Kuhrt. *From Samarkhand to Sardis: A New Approach to the Seleucid Empire.* London, 1993. A stimulating examination of the relationship between rulers and ruled in the vast expanses of the Seleucid Empire.

Shipley, Graham. *The Greek World after Alexander, 323–30 B.C.* New York and London, 2000. A study of the social, intellectual, and artistic changes in the Hellenistic era.

Thomas, Carol G. *Alexander the Great in His World.* Oxford and Malden, MA, 2007. A study of the contexts—familial, political, and social—that shaped Alexander's career.

Tripolitis, Antonia. *Religions of the Hellenistic-Roman Age.* Grand Rapids, MI, 2002. Survey of the variety of religious experience, ritual, and belief in the centuries before the emergence of Christianity.

Tritle, Lawrence A., ed. *The Greek World in the Fourth Century: From the Fall of the Athenian Empire to the Successors of Alexander.* New York, 1997. A wide-ranging collection of scholarly essays.

CHAPTER 5

Translations of Roman authors are available in both the Penguin Classics series and in the Loeb Classical Library.

Arnason, Johann P. and Kurt A. Raaflaub, eds. *The Roman Empire in Context: Historical and Comparative Perspectives.* Malden, MA, 2011. One of the few books to place the formation of the Roman Empire in a comparative, global perspective.

Barker, Graeme, and Tom Rasmussen. *The Etruscans.* Oxford and Malden, MA, 1998. A fine survey, from the Blackwell *Peoples of Europe* series.

Beard, Mary. *Pompeii: The Life of a Roman Town.* A fascinating, cutting-edge study of daily life.

Boardman, John, Jasper Griffin, and Oswyn Murray. *The Oxford History of the Roman World.* Oxford, 1990. Reprint of relevant portions of the excellent *Oxford History of the Classical World* (1986). Stimulating, accessible topical chapters by British specialists.

Cornell, T. J. *The Beginnings of Rome: Italy and Rome from the Bronze Age to the Punic Wars (c. 1000–264 B.C.).* London, 1995. An ambitious survey of the archaeological and historical evidence for early Rome.

Crawford, Michael. *The Roman Republic,* 2d ed. Cambridge, MA, 1993. A lively, fast-paced survey of republican Rome. An excellent place to start.

Fantham, Elaine, Helene Peet Foley, Natalie Boymel Kampen, Sarah B. Pomeroy, and H. Alan Shapiro. *Women in the Classical World.* Oxford, 1994. An expert survey of both Greece and Rome.

Garnsey, Peter, and Richard Saller. *The Roman Empire: Economy, Society, and Culture.* Berkeley, CA, 1987. A straightforward short survey.

Gruen, Erich S. *The Hellenistic World and the Coming of Rome.* 2 vols. Berkeley, CA, 1984. A massive survey, focused on the unpredictable rise of Rome to a position of dominance within the Mediterranean world.

Harris, William V. *War and Imperialism in Republican Rome, 327–70 B.C.* Oxford, 1979. A challenging study arguing that Rome's need for military conquest and expansion was deeply embedded in the fabric of Roman life.

Krebs, Christopher. *A Most Dangerous Book: Tacitus's "Germania" from the Roman Empire to the Third Reich.* A history of this ancient ethnography's transmission and reception, and especially the political uses to which was put in Nazi Germany.

Lancel, Serge. *Carthage: A History.* Trans. Antonia Nevill. Oxford, 1995. An account of Rome's great rival for control of the Mediterranean world.

Millar, Fergus G. B. *The Emperor in the Roman World, 31 B.C.–A.D. 337.* London, 1977. A classic work that showed (among much else) the importance of emperor worship to the religious outlook of the Roman Empire.

———. *The Crowd in Rome in the Late Republic.* Ann Arbor, MI, 1999. A revisionist account that emphasizes the reality of Roman democracy in the late republic, against those who would see the period's politics as entirely under the control of aristocratic families.

Ward, Allen M., Fritz Heichelheim, and Cedric A. Yeo. *A History of the Roman People,* 3d ed. Upper Saddle River, NJ, 1999. An informative, well-organized textbook covering Roman history from its beginnings to the end of the sixth century C.E.

Watkin, David. *The Roman Forum.* London, 2009. A history of the successive buildings and archeological excavations of this central Roman space.

Wells, Colin. *The Roman Empire,* 2d ed. Cambridge, MA, 1992. An easily readable survey from the reign of Augustus to the mid-third century C.E., particularly useful for its treatment of the relationship between the Roman central government and its Italian provinces.

Wiseman, T. P. *Remembering the Roman People.* Oxford, 2009. A collection of studies devoted to popular politics in the late republic.

Woolf, Greg. *Becoming Roman: The Origins of Provincial Civilization in Gaul.* Cambridge, 1998. An exemplary study of how provincial elites made themselves "Roman."

———. *Rome: An Empire's Story.* Oxford, 2012. A masterful account of Rome's reconfiguration of the ancient world and enduring impact; critically acclaimed by scholars and general readers.

———. *Tales of the Barbarians: Ethnography and Empire in the Roman West.* Malden, MA, 2011. Applies modern ethnographic methodologies to a dissection of Romans applied their own ethnographic theories to contemporary "others."

CHAPTER 6

Augustine. *The City of God.* Trans. Henry Bettenson. Baltimore, MD, 1972.

———. *Confessions.* Trans. Henry M. Chadwick. Oxford, 1991.

———. *On Christian Doctrine.* Trans. D. W. Robertson Jr. New York, 1958.

Boethius. *The Consolation of Philosophy.* Trans. R. Green. Indianapolis, IN, 1962.

Bowersock, G. W., Peter Brown, and Oleg Grabar. *Late Antiquity: A Guide to the Postclassical World*. Cambridge, MA, 1999. An authoritative compilation. The first half is devoted to essays on the cultural features of the period; the second half is organized as an encyclopedia.

Brown, Peter. *Augustine of Hippo*. Berkeley, CA, 1967. A great biography by the great scholar of late antiquity.

———. *The Body and Society: Men, Women and Sexual Renunciation in Early Christianity*. New York, 1988. A revealing study of the fundamental transformations wrought by Christianity in the late antique world.

———. *Power and Persuasion in Late Antiquity: Toward a Christian Empire*. Madison, WI, 1992. An important account of Christianity's effects on the political culture of the later Roman Empire.

———. *The Rise of Western Christendom: Triumph and Diversity, 200–1000*, 2d ed. Oxford, 2002. An evocative picture of Christianity's spread eastward and northward from the Mediterranean world.

———. *The World of Late Antiquity*. New York, 1971. Still the best short survey of the period, with excellent illustrations.

———. *Through the Eye of a Needle: Wealth, the Fall of Rome, and the Making of Christianity in the West, 350–550 AD*. Princeton, NJ, 2012. The most recent of this historian's magisterial dissections of late antiquity, focused on the relationship between religion, culture, power, and wealth (or its lack).

Cameron, Averil. *The Later Roman Empire, A.D. 284–430*. London, 1993. Now the standard account of its period, with an emphasis on imperial politics.

———. *The Mediterranean World in Late Antiquity, A.D. 395–600*. London, 1993. Masterful, with excellent, succinct bibliographical essays.

Cassiodorus. *An Introduction to Divine and Human Readings*. Trans. L. W. Jones. New York, 1946.

Chadwick, Henry M. *Augustine*. Oxford, 1986. A short introduction to Augustine's thought.

———. *Boethius*. Oxford, 1981. An intellectual biography of this important thinker.

Clark, Gillian. *Christianity and Roman Society*. Cambridge, 2004. A short, stimulating survey that places early Christianity firmly in its Roman social context.

———. *Women in Late Antiquity*. Oxford, 1993. A clear, compact account of an important subject.

Coogan, Michael, ed. *The Oxford History of the Biblical World*. Oxford, 1998. A reliable but rather traditional account of the historical events recounted in the Hebrew Bible and the New Testament.

Ehrman, Bart D. *The New Testament: A Historical Introduction to the Early Christian Writings*, 4th ed. Oxford, 2008. The standard textbook by a leading authority.

Ehrman, Bart D. and Zlatko Pleše, eds. *The Aprocryphal Gospels: Texts and Translations* Oxford, 2011. The first scholarly edition and translation of all the apocryphal gospels, including Latin, Greek, and Coptic texts.

Eusebius. *The History of the Church*. Trans. G. A. Williamson. Baltimore, MD, 1965. A contemporary account of Constantine's reign, written by one of his courtier-bishops.

———. *Eusebius' Life of Constantine*. Trans. Averil Cameron and Stuart Hall. Oxford, 1999. An admiring biography that reflects Constantine's own vision of his religious authority.

Hopkins, Keith. *A World Full of Gods: The Strange Triumph of Christianity*. New York, 1999. An imaginative study of religious pluralism in the Roman world and the context in which Christianity emerged.

Kulikowski, Michael. *Rome's Gothic Wars: From the Third Century to Alaric*. Cambridge, 2007. An authoritative and critical account.

Lawrence, Clifford Hugh. *Medieval Monasticism*, 3d ed. London, 2000. Concise, perceptive survey of monasticism from its beginnings to the end of the Middle Ages.

Pagels, Elaine. *The Gnostic Gospels*. New York, 1979. A pathbreaking study of the noncanonical gospels and the history of their exclusion from the Bible.

Potter, David. *The Roman Empire at Bay, A.D. 180–395*. London and New York, 2004. The most up-to-date account of the empire's reorganization and transformation in this era.

Rebillard, Éric. *Christians and Their Many Identities in Late Antiquity, North Africa, 200–450 CE*. Ithaca, 2012. In this book, as in his earlier works, the author argues that there was no special importance attached to being a "Christian" in late antiquity, and that religious identities are better understood as fluid and hybrid.

Sanders, E. P. *The Historical Figure of Jesus*. London and New York, 1993. A fine study of Jesus in his first-century Jewish context.

Shanks, Hershel, ed. *Christianity and Rabbinic Judaism: A Parallel History of Their Origins and Early Development*. Washington, DC, 1992. Accessible chapters written by top authorities, describing both Jewish and Christian developments from the first to the sixth centuries C.E.

Sherwin-White, A. N. *Roman Society and Roman Law in the New Testament*. Oxford, 1963. A fascinating reading of the New Testament in its historical context.

Traina, Giusto. *428 AD: An Ordinary Year at the End of the Roman Empire*. Princeton, NJ, 2011. An enlightening glimpse into the world of late antiquity, from the vantage point of a single "average" year.

Wallace-Hadrill, John Michael. *The Barbarian West*, 3d ed. London, 1966. A classic analysis of the hybrid culture of the late Roman West.

Whittaker, C. R. *Frontiers of the Roman Empire: A Social and Economic Study*. Baltimore, MD, 1994. A convincing picture of the frontiers of the Roman Empire as zones of intensive cultural interaction.

Williams, Stephen. *Diocletian and the Roman Recovery*. New York, 1997. Thorough and authoritative.

CHAPTER 7

Bede. *A History of the English Church and People*. Trans. Leo Sherley-Price. Baltimore, MD., 1955. The fundamental source for early Anglo-Saxon history.

Campbell, James, ed. *The Anglo-Saxons*. Oxford, 1982. An authoritative and splendidly illustrated volume.

Collins, Roger. *Early Medieval Europe, 300–1000*. 2d ed. New York, 1999. Dry and detailed, but a useful textbook nonetheless.

Conant, Jonathan. *Staying Roman: Conquest and Identity in Africa and the Mediterranean, 439–700*. Cambridge, 2012. An exploration of what it meant to be "Roman" and the sources of identity in this tumultuous period.

Donner, Fred. *The Early Islamic Conquests*. Princeton, NJ, 1981. A scholarly but readable narrative and analysis.

Einhard and Notker the Stammerer. *Two Lives of Charlemagne*. Trans. Lewis Thorpe. Baltimore, MD, 1969. Lively and entertaining works of contemporary biography.

Fletcher, Richard A. *The Barbarian Conversion: From Paganism to Christianity*. Berkeley, CA, 1999. Slow paced but informative and perceptive.

———. *Moorish Spain*. Berkeley, CA, 1993. The best short survey in English.

Geanakoplos, Deno John, ed. *Byzantium: Church, Society and Civilization Seen through Contemporary Eyes*. Chicago, 1984. An outstanding source book.

Gregory, Timothy E. A *History of Byzantium*. Malden, MA, and Oxford, 2005. The most accessible of the recent textbooks on Byzantium. An excellent place to start.

Herrin, Judith. *Byzantium: The Surprising Life of a Medieval Empire*. Princeton, 2009. An accessible and comprehensive history of the eastern Roman Empire.

———. *The Formation of Christendom*. Princeton, NJ, 1987. A synthetic history of the Christian civilizations of Byzantium and western Europe from 500 to 800, written by a prominent historian.

Hodges, Richard, and David Whitehouse. *Mohammed, Charlemagne and the Origins of Europe*. London, 1983. A critical analysis of the "Pirenne thesis," reexaming the relationship between the Mediterranean world and northern Europe.

Hourani, Albert. *A History of the Arab Peoples*. New York, 1992. A sympathetic and clear survey written for nonspecialists.

Kazhdan, Alexander P., ed. *The Oxford Dictionary of Byzantium*. 3 vols. Oxford, 1991. An authoritative reference work.

Kennedy, Hugh. *The Prophet and the Age of the Caliphates*. 2d ed. Harlow, UK, 2004. A lucid introduction to the political history of the Islamic world from the sixth through the eleventh centuries.

Krautheimer, Richard. *Early Christian and Byzantine Architecture*. 4th ed. New York, 1986. A classic work by one of the greatest Byzantine art historians of the twentieth century.

Little, Lester K., ed., *Plague and the End of Antiquity: The Pandemic of 541–750*. Cambridge, 2006. The first full-length scholarly history of the first global pandemic.

Mango, Cyril, ed. *The Oxford History of Byzantium*. Oxford and New York, 2002. Full of sharp judgments and attractively illustrated.

McCormick, Michael. *The Origins of the European Economy: Communications and Commerce A.D. 300–900*. Cambridge, 2002. An astonishing reinterpretation of the evidence for the myriad contacts between Christian Europe and Islam.

McKitterick, Rosamond. *Charlemagne: The Formation of a European Identity*. Cambridge, 2008. A history of Charlemagne's career and its lasting impact by an eminent scholar of the Carolingian world.

———, ed. *The Uses of Literacy in Early Medieval Europe*. New York, 1990. A superb collection of essays.

McNamara, Jo Ann, and John E. Halborg, eds. *Sainted Women of the Dark Ages*. Durham, NC, 1992. Translated saints' lives from Merovingian and Carolingian Europe.

Murray, A. C., ed. *From Roman to Merovingian Gaul: A Reader*. Toronto, 2000. An excellent collection of sources.

Pelikan, Jaroslav. *The Christian Tradition*. Vol. II, *The Spirit of Eastern Christendom*. Chicago, 1974. An outstanding synthetic treatment of the doctrines of Byzantine Christianity.

Procopius. *The Secret History*. Trans. G. A. Williamson. Baltimore, MD, 1966. An "unauthorized" account of Justinian's reign, written by the emperor's offical historian.

Reuter, Timothy. *Germany in the Early Middle Ages, 800–1056*. New York, 1991. The best survey in English.

Treadgold, Warren. *A History of the Byzantine State and Society*. Stanford, CA, 1997. A massive, encyclopedic narrative of the political, economic, and military history of Byzantium from 284 until 1461.

Wallace-Hadrill, John Michael. *Early Germanic Kingship in England and on the Continent*. Oxford, 1971. A classic analysis of changing ideas about kingship in early medieval Europe, emphasizing the links between Anglo-Saxon and Carolingian cultures.

———. *The Frankish Church*. Oxford, 1983. A masterful account that links the Merovingian and Carolingian churches.

Watt, W. Montgomery. *Islamic Philosophy and Theology*, 2d ed. Edinburgh, UK, 1985. The standard English account.

Wemple, Suzanne Fonay. *Women in Frankish Society: Marriage and the Cloister, 500–900*. Philadelphia, PA, 1981. An influential account of changing attitudes toward marriage among the early Franks.

Whittow, Mark. *The Making of Orthodox Byzantium, 600–1025*. London, 1996. Emphasizes the centrality of orthodoxy in shaping Byzantine history. Particularly good on Byzantine relations with the peoples outside the empire.

Wickham, Chris. *Framing the Middle Ages: Europe and the Mediterranean, 400–800*. Oxford, 2007. An eye-opening history that spans the transitional periods of late antiquity and the early Middle Ages, paying careful attention to regional differences.

Wood, Ian. *The Merovingian Kingdoms, 450–751*. New York, 1994. A detailed study, but difficult for beginners.

CHAPTER 8

Amt, Emily, ed. *Women's Lives in Medieval Europe: A Sourcebook*. New York, 1993. An excellent collection of primary texts.

The Song of Roland. Trans. Robert Harrison. Penguin, 1970. A lively translation.

Arnold, Benjamin. *Princes and Territories in Medieval Germany*. Cambridge and New York, 1991. The best such survey in English.

Blumenthal, Uta-Renate. *The Investiture Controversy*. Philadelphia, 1988. A clear review of a complicated subject.

Boswell, John E. *Christianity, Social Tolerance, and Homosexuality: Gay People in Western Europe from the Beginning of the Christian Era to the Fourteenth Century*. Chicago, 1980. A pioneering account, hotly debated but highly respected.

Burman, Thomas E. *Reading the Qur'ān in Latin Christendom, 1140–1560*. Philadelphia, 2007. A fascinating account of the Qu'ran's reception in medieval Europe.

Colish, Marcia. *Medieval Foundations of the Western Intellectual Tradition, 400–1400*. New Haven, CT, 1997. An encyclopedic work, best used as a reference.

Dunbabin, Jean. *France in the Making, 843–1180,* 2d ed. Oxford and New York, 2000. An authoritative survey of the disparate territories that came to make up the medieval French kingdom.

Dyer, Christopher. *Making a Living in the Middle Ages: The People of Britain 850–1520*. New Haven, 2002. A splendid new synthesis that combines social, economic, and archaeological evidence.

Fossier, Robert. *The Ax and the Oath*: *Ordinary Life in the Middle Ages*. Princeton, 2010. A quirky, personal, and often insightful look at the daily lives and worldview of this era by a leading French historian.

Frankopan, Peter. *The First Crusade: The Call from the East*. Cambridge, MA, 2012. Analyzes the causes and catalysts of the crusading movement.

Hicks, Carola. *The Bayeux Tapestry: The Life Story of Masterpiece*. London, 2006. An art historian's engrossing account of the making, reception, and interpretation of this amazing artifact.

Horden, Peregrine and Nicholas Purcell. *The Corrupting Sea: A Study of Mediterranean History*. Malden, MA, 2000. An extraordinary attempt to encompass the history of the Mediterranean World over a span of three millennia.

Leyser, Henrietta. *Medieval Women: A Social History of Women in England, 440–1500*. New York, 1995. Although limited to one country, this is the best of the recent surveys treating medieval women.

McLaughlin, Megan. *Sex, Gender, and Episcopal Authority in an Age of Reform, 1000–1122*. Cambridge, 2010. A new interpretation of gendered discourse and politics during the Investiture Controversy.

Miller, Maureen C. *Power and the Holy in the Age of the Investiture Conflict. A Brief History with Documents*. Boston, 2005. A stimulating approach to the eleventh-century conflicts over temporal and spiritual power, with many newly translated sources.

Moore, Robert I. *The First European Revolution, c. 970–1215*. Oxford and Cambridge, MA, 2000. A remarkable description of the ways in which European society was fundamentally reshaped during the eleventh and twelfth centuries.

Peters, F. E. *Aristotle and the Arabs*. New York, 1968. Well written and engaging.

Raffensperger, Christian. *Reimagining Europe: Kievan Rus' in the Medieval World*. Cambridge, MA, 2012. An exciting new study of early Rus' and its neighbors.

Reilly, Bernard F. *The Medieval Spains*. New York, 1993. A succinct account that covers the entire Iberian peninsula from 500 to 1500.

Reynolds, Susan. *Fiefs and Vassals: The Medieval Evidence Reinterpreted*. Oxford and New York, 1994. A detailed revisionist history of "feudalism."

Rubenstein, Jay. *Armies of Heaven: The First Crusade and the Quest for Apocalypse*. New York, 2011. An accessible narrative of the First Crusade, written for a general audience and arguing for a new interpretation of crusaders' motives.

Sawyer, Peter, ed. *The Oxford Illustrated History of the Vikings*. Oxford, 1997. The best one-volume account, lavishly illustrated.

Sheingorn, Pamela, trans. *The Book of Sainte Foy*. Philadelphia, 1995.

Stillman, Norman A. *The Jews of Arab Lands: A History and Source Book*. Philadelphia, PA, 1979. An essential resource.

Stow, Kenneth R. *Alienated Minority: The Jews of Medieval Latin Europe*. Cambridge, MA, 1992. An excellent survey.

Tierney, Brian. *The Crisis of Church and State, 1050–1300*. Toronto, 1988. An indispensable collection for both teachers and students.

Winroth, Anders. *The Conversion of Scandinavia: Vikings, Merchants, and Missionaries in the Remaking of Northern Europe*. New Haven, 2012. Argues that the peoples of Scandinavia were active participants in the cultural, economic, and political processes that accompanied their conversion to Christianity.

CHAPTER 9

Abelard and Heloise. *The Letters and Other Writings*. Trans. William Levitan. Indianapolis, 2007. A beautiful and accurate translation of the correspondence and related documents, with a full introduction and notes.

Abulafia, David. *Frederick II: A Medieval Emperor*. London and New York, 1988. A reliable biography that strips away much of the legend that has hitherto surrounded this monarch.

Baldwin, John W. *The Government of Philip Augustus*. Berkeley and Los Angeles, CA, 1986. A landmark scholarly account.

Barber, Malcolm. *The Crusader States*. New Haven, 2012. A new and comprehensive history by an esteemed historian.

Bartlett, Robert. *The Making of Europe: Conquest, Colonization and Cultural Change, 950–1350*. Princeton, NJ, 1993. A wide-ranging examination of the economic, social, and religious expansion of Europe, full of stimulating insights.

Bisson, Thomas N. *The Crisis of the Twelfth Century: Power, Lordship, and the Origins of European Government*. Princeton, NJ, 2009. A new interpretation of the evidence.

Bynum, Caroline Walker. *Holy Feast and Holy Fast: The Religious Significance of Food to Medieval Women*. Berkeley and Los Angeles, 1988. One of the most influential and important works of scholarship published in the late twentieth century.

Camille, Michael. *Gothic Art: Glorious Visions*. New York, 1996. A succinct and beautifully illustrated introduction.

Chrétien de Troyes. *Arthurian Romances*. Trans. W. W. Kibler. New York, 1991.

Clanchy, Michael T. *Abelard: A Medieval Life*. Oxford and Cambridge, MA, 1997. A great biography.

———. *From Memory to Written Record: England, 1066–1307*. Oxford, 1992. A fascinating and hugely influential account of this revolutionary shift.

Cobban, Alan B. *The Medieval Universities*. London, 1975. The best short treatment in English.

Fassler, Margot. *Gothic Song: Victorine Seqeunces and Augustinian Reform in Twelfth-Century Paris*. Cambridge, UK, 1993. The emergence of new musical genres and their cultural context.

Gillingham, John. *The Angevin Empire,* 2d ed. Oxford and New York, 2001. The best treatment by far of its subject, brief but full of ideas.

Gottfried von Strassburg. *Tristan.* Trans. A. T. Hatto. Baltimore, MD, 1960.

Hallam, Elizabeth, and Judith Everard. *Capetian France, 987–1328,* 2d ed. New York, 2001. A clear and well-organized account.

Haskins, Charles Homer. *The Renaissance of the Twelfth Century.* Cambridge, MA, 1927. A classic and influential study.

Jones, P. J. *The Italian City-State: From Commune to Signoria.* Oxford and New York, 1997. A fundamental reinterpretation of the evidence.

Jordan, William C. *Europe in the High Middle Ages: The Penguin History of Europe.* Vol. III. New York and London, 2003. An outstanding new survey.

Kaeuper, Richard W. *Chivalry and Violence in Medieval Europe.* Oxford and New York, 1999. A darker view of chivalry than Keen's.

Keen, Maurice. *Chivalry.* New Haven, CT, 1984. A comprehensive treatment of chivalry from its origins to the sixteenth century.

Lawrence, Clifford Hugh. *The Friars: The Impact of the Early Mendicant Movement on Western Society.* London and New York, 1994. The best short introduction to the early history of the Franciscans and the Dominicans.

Leclerq, Jean. *The Love of Learning and the Desire for God,* 3d ed. New York, 1982. A beautiful interpretation of twelfth-century monastic culture and the influence of Bernard of Clairvaux.

Little, Lester. *Religious Poverty and Profit Economy in Medieval Europe.* Ithaca, 1978. A fascinating study of the relationship between religious practice and economic reality.

Lopez, Robert S., and Irving W. Raymond, eds. *Medieval Trade in the Mediterranean World.* New York, 1990. A pathbreaking collection of source material.

Madden, Thomas F. *The New Concise History of the Crusades.* New York, 2005. An acclaimed and accessible survey for students.

Marie de France. *Lais.* Trans. Glyn S. Burgess and Keith Busby. Harmondsworth, UK, 1999. A compelling and entertaining prose translation.

Moore, R. I. *The War on Heresy.* Cambridge, MA, 2012. A courageous and searching revisionist history, based on decades of research and reflection. Moore argues for a radical reassessment of what "heresy" consisted of, and why those branded as "heretics" were persecuted during the Middle Ages.

Morris, Colin. *The Papal Monarchy: The Western Church from 1050 to 1250.* Oxford, 1989. An excellent scholarly survey; part of the Oxford History of the Christian Church series.

Newman, Barbara, ed. *Voice of the Living Light: Hildegard of Bingen and Her World.* Berkeley and Los Angeles, CA, 1998. An introduction to Hildegard's life and work.

Otto, Bishop of Freising. *The Deeds of Frederick Barbarossa.* Trans. C. C. Mierow. New York, 1953. A contemporary chronicle interesting enough to read from start to finish.

Smalley, Beryl. *The Study of the Bible in the Middle Ages,* 3d ed. Oxford, 1983. The standard work, gracefully written and illuminating.

Strayer, Joseph R. *On the Medieval Origins of the Modern State.* With new forewords by Charles Tilly and William Chester Jordan. Princeton, 2005. This new edition of Strayer's series of lectures places them in their scholarly context.

Swanson, R. N. *The Twelfth-Century Renaissance.* Manchester, UK, 1999. An updated survey of the intellectual developments of the twelfth century.

Symes, Carol. *A Common Stage: Theater and Public Life in Medieval Arras.* Ithaca, NY, 2007. A study of a vibrant cultural hub.

Wakefield, Walter, and Austin P. Evans, eds. and trans. *Heresies of the High Middle Ages.* New York, 1969, 1991. A comprehensive collection of sources.

Wilhelm, James J., ed. and trans. *Medieval Song: An Anthology of Hymns and Lyrics.* New York, 1971. An excellent collection of sacred and secular poetry that illustrates the connections between them.

Wolfram von Eschenbach. *Parzival.* Trans. H. M. Mustard and C. E. Passage. New York, 1961.

CHAPTER 10

Abu-Lughod, Janet L. *Before European Hegemony: The World System* A.D. *1250–1350.* Oxford and New York, 1989. A study of the trading links among Europe, the Middle East, India, and China, with special attention to the role of the Mongol Empire; extensive bibliography.

Allsen, Thomas T. *Culture and Conquest in Mongol Eurasia.* Cambridge and New York, 2001. A synthesis of the author's earlier studies, emphasizing Mongol involvement in the cultural and commercial exchanges that linked China, Central Asia, and Europe.

Christian, David. *A History of Russia, Central Asia and Mongolia.* Vol. 1, *Inner Eurasia from Prehistory to the Mongol Empire.* Oxford, 1998. The authoritative English-language work on the subject.

Cole, Bruce. *Giotto and Florentine Painting, 1280–1375.* New York, 1976. A clear and stimulating introduction.

Crummey, Robert O. *The Formation of Muscovy, 1304–1613.* New York, 1987. The standard account.

Dante Alighieri. *The Divine Comedy.* Trans. Mark Musa. 3 vols. Baltimore, MD, 1984–86.

Dunn, Ross E. *The Adventures of Ibn Battuta: A Muslim Traveler of the Fourteenth Century.* Berkeley, rev. ed. 2005. Places the writings and experiences of this far-reaching Muslim traveler in their historical and geographical contexts.

Dyer, Christopher. *Standards of Living in the Later Middle Ages: Social Change in England, c. 1200–1520.* Cambridge and New York, 1989. Detailed but highly rewarding.

Foltz, Richard. *Religions of the Silk Road: Premodern Patterns of Globalization.* New York, 2nd ed. 2010. A compelling and thought-provoking study of the varieties of religious experience and cross-cultural interaction in medieval Eurasia.

The History and the Life of Chinggis Khan: The Secret History of the Mongols. Trans. Urgunge Onon. Leiden, 1997. A newer version of *The Secret History,* now the standard English version of this important Mongol source.

Horrox, Rosemary, ed. *The Black Death.* New York, 1994. A fine collection of documents reflecting the impact of the Black Death, especially in England.

Jackson, Peter. *The Mongols and the West, 1221–1410.* Harlow, UK, 2005. A well-written survey that emphasizes the interactions among the Mongol, Latin Christian, and Muslim worlds.

Jordan, William Chester. *The Great Famine: Northern Europe in the Early Fourteenth Century.* Princeton, NJ, 1996. An outstanding social and economic study.

Keen, Maurice, ed. *Medieval Warfare: A History.* Oxford and New York, 1999. The most attractive introduction to this important subject. Lively and well illustrated.

Kitsikopoulos, Harry, ed. *Agrarian Change and Crisis in Europe, 1200–1500.* London, 2011. An up-to-date collection of scholarly essays that addresses a classic and complicated set of historical questions.

Komaroff, Linda and Stefano Carboni, eds. *The Legacy of Ghenghis Khan: Courtly Art and Culture in Western Asia, 1256–1353.* New York, 2002. An informative and lavishly illustrated catalog of an acclaimed exhibition.

Larner, John. *Marco Polo and the Discovery of the World.* New Haven, CT, 1999. A study of the influence of Marco Polo's *Travels* on Europeans.

Mandeville's Travels. Ed. M. C. Seymour. Oxford, 1968. An edition of the *Book of Marvels* based on the Middle English version popular in the fifteenth century.

Memoirs of a Renaissance Pope: The Commentaries of Pius II. Abridged ed. Trans. F. A. Gragg, New York, 1959. Remarkable insights into the mind of a particularly well-educated mid-fifteenth-century pope.

Nicholas, David. *The Transformation of Europe, 1300–1600.* Oxford and New York, 1999. The best textbook presently available.

Rossabi, M. *Khubilai Khan: His Life and Times.* Berkeley, CA, 1988. The standard English biography.

Swanson, R. N. *Religion and Devotion in Europe, c. 1215–c. 1515.* Cambridge and New York, 1995. An excellent study of late-medieval popular piety; an excellent complement to Oakley.

The Travels of Marco Polo. Ed. Peter Harris. London, 2008 repr. A new edition of a classic translation.

Vaughan, Richard. *Valois Burgundy.* London, 1975. A summation of the author's four-volume study of the Burgundian dukes.

CHAPTER 11

Alberti, Leon Battista. *The Family in Renaissance Florence (Della Famiglia).* Trans. Renée Neu Watkins. Columbia, SC, 1969.

Allmand, Christopher T., ed. *Society at War: The Experience of England and France During the Hundred Years' War.* Edinburgh, 1973. An outstanding collection of documents.

———. *The Hundred Years' War: England and France at War, c. 1300–c. 1450.* Cambridge and New York, 1988. Still the best analytic account of the war; after a short narrative, the book is organized topically.

Boccaccio, Giovanni. *The Decameron.* Trans. Mark Musa and P. E. Bondanella. New York, 1977.

Brucker, Gene. *Florence, the Golden Age, 1138–1737.* Berkeley and Los Angeles, CA, 1998. The standard account.

Bruni, Leonardo. *The Humanism of Leonardo Bruni: Selected Texts.* Trans. Gordon Griffiths, James Hankins, and David Thompson. Binghamton, NY, 1987. Excellent translations, with introductions, to the Latin works of a key Renaissance humanist.

Burke, Peter. *The Renaissance.* New York, 1997. A brief introduction by an influential modern historian.

Burkhardt, Jacob. *The Civilization of the Renaissance in Italy.* Many editions. The nineteenth-century work that first crystallized an image of the Italian Renaissance, and with which scholars have been wrestling ever since.

Canning, Joseph. *Ideas of Power in the Late Middle Ages, 1296–1417.* Cambridge, 2011. An old fashioned but nonetheless original synthesis.

Cassirer, Ernst, et al., eds. *The Renaissance Philosophy of Man.* Chicago, 1948. Important original works by Petrarch, Ficino, and Pico della Mirandola, among others.

Chaucer, Geoffrey. *The Canterbury Tales.* Trans. Nevill Coghill. New York, 1951. A modern English verse translation, lightly annotated.

Cohn, Samuel K., Jr. *Lust for Liberty: The Politics of Social Revolt in Medieval Europe, 1200–1425. Italy, France, and Flanders.* Cambridge, MA, 2006. An important new study.

Coles, Paul. *The Ottoman Impact on Europe.* London, 1968. An excellent introductory text, still valuable despite its age.

Dobson, R. Barrie. *The Peasants' Revolt of 1381,* 2d ed. London, 1983. A comprehensive source collection, with excellent introductions to the documents.

Fernández-Armesto, Felipe. *Before Columbus: Exploration and Colonisation from the Mediterranean to the Atlantic, 1229–1492.* London, 1987. An indispensible study of the medieval background to the sixteenth-century European colonial empires.

Froissart, Jean. *Chronicles.* Trans. Geoffrey Brereton. Baltimore, MD, 1968. A selection from the most famous contemporary account of the Hundred Years' War to about 1400.

Goffman, Daniel. *The Ottoman Empire and Early Modern Europe.* Cambridge and New York, 2002. A revisionist account that presents the Ottoman Empire as a European state.

Hankins, James. *Plato in the Italian Renaissance.* Leiden and New York, 1990. A definitive study of the reception and influence of Plato on Renaissance intellectuals.

———, ed. *Renaissance Civic Humanism: Reappraisals and Reflections.* Cambridge and New York, 2000. An excellent collection of scholarly essays reassessing republicanism in the Renaissance.

Hobbins, Daniel, ed. and trans. *The Trial of Joan of Arc.* Cambridge, MA, 2007. A new and excellent translation of the transcripts of Joan's trial.

Inalcik, Halil. *The Ottoman Empire: The Classical Age, 1300–1600.* London, 1973. The standard history by the dean of Turkish historians.

———, ed. *An Economic and Social History of the Ottoman Empire, 1300–1914.* Cambridge, 1994. An important collection of essays, spanning the full range of Ottoman history.

John Hus at the Council of Constance. Trans. M. Spinka, New York, 1965. The translation of a Czech chronicle with an expert introduction and appended documents.

Kafadar, Cemal. *Between Two Worlds: The Construction of the Ottoman State.* Berkeley and Los Angeles, 1995. An important study of

Ottoman origins in the border regions between Byzantium, the Seljuk Turks, and the Mongols.

Kempe, Margery. *The Book of Margery Kempe*. Trans. Barry Windeatt. New York, 1985. A fascinating personal narrative by an early-fifteenth-century Englishwoman who hoped she might be a saint.

Lane, Frederic C. *Venice: A Maritime Republic*. Baltimore, MD, 1973. An authoritative account.

Morgan, David. *The Mongols*. 2d ed. Oxford, 2007. An accessible introduction to Mongol history and its sources, written by a noted expert on medieval Persia.

Ormrod, W. Mark. *Edward III*. New Haven, 2012. A new biography of this English monarch by a leading social historian.

Saunders, J. J. *The History of the Mongol Conquests*. London, 1971. Still the standard English-language introduction; somewhat more positive about the Mongols' accomplishments than is Morgan.

Shirley, Janet, trans. *A Parisian Journal, 1405–1449*. Oxford, 1968. A marvelous panorama of Parisian life recorded by an eyewitness.

Sumption, Jonathan. *The Hundred Years' War*. Vol. 1: *Trial by Battle*. Vol. 2: *Trial by Fire*. Philadelphia, 1999. The first two volumes of a massive narrative history of the war, carrying the story up to 1369.

The Four Voyages: Christopher Columbus. Trans. J. M. Cohen. New York, 1992. Columbus's own self-serving account of his four voyages to the Indies.

CHAPTER 12

Baxandall, Michael. *Painting and Experience in Fifteenth-Century Italy*. Oxford, 1972. A classic study of the perceptual world of the Renaissance.

Castiglione, Baldassare. *The Book of the Courtier*. Many editions. The translations by C. S. Singleton (New York, 1959) and by George Bull (New York, 1967) are both excellent.

Cellini, Benvenuto. *Autobiography*. Trans. George Bull. Baltimore, MD, 1956. This Florentine goldsmith (1500–1571) is the source for many of the most famous stories about the artists of the Florentine Renaissance.

Erasmus, Desiderius. *The Praise of Folly*. Trans. J. Wilson. Ann Arbor, MI, 1958.

Fernández-Armesto, Felipe. *1492: The Year the World Began*. London, 2010. A panoramic view of the world in a pivotal year, putting the voyage of Columbus in a broad historical perspective.

Flint, Valerie I. J. *The Imaginative Landscape of Christopher Columbus*. Princeton, NJ, 1992. A short, suggestive analysis of the intellectual influences that shaped Columbus's geographical ideas.

Fox, Alistair. *Thomas More: History and Providence*. Oxford, 1982. A balanced account of a man too easily idealized.

Grafton, Anthony, and Lisa Jardine. *From Humanism to the Humanities: Education and the Liberal Arts in Fifteenth- and Sixteenth-Century Europe*. London, 1986. An account that presents Renaissance humanism as the elitist cultural program of a self-interested group of pedagogues.

Grendler, Paul, ed. *Encyclopedia of the Renaissance*. New York, 1999. A valuable reference work.

Jardine, Lisa. *Worldly Goods*. London, 1996. A revisionist account that emphasizes the acquisitive materialism of Italian Renaissance society and culture.

Kanter, Laurence, Hilliard T. Goldfarb, and James Hankins. *Botticelli's Witness: Changing Style in a Changing Florence*. Boston, 1997. This catalog for an exhibition of Botticelli's works, at the Gardner Museum in Boston, offers an excellent introduction to the painter and his world.

King, Margaret L. *Women of the Renaissance*. Chicago, 1991. Deals with women in all walks of life and in a variety of roles.

Kristeller, Paul O. *Renaissance Thought: The Classic, Scholastic, and Humanistic Strains*. New York, 1961. Very helpful in defining the main trends of Renaissance thought.

Machiavelli, Niccolò. *The Discourses* and *The Prince*. Many editions. These two books must be read together if one is to understand Machiavelli's political ideas properly.

Mallett, Michael and Christine Shaw. *The Italian Wars, 1494–1559: War, State, and Society in Early Modern Europe*. Boston, 2012. Argues that the endemic warfare of this period within Italy revolutionized European military tactics and technologies.

Mann, Charles. C. *1491: New Revelations of the Americas Before Columbus*. New York, 2006.

———. *1493: Uncovering the New World Columbus Created*. New York, 2012. Written for a popular audience, these are also engaging and well-informed syntheses of historical research.

Martines, Lauro. *Power and Imagination: City-States in Renaissance Italy*. New York, 1979. Insightful account of the connections among politics, society, culture, and art.

More, Thomas. *Utopia*. Many editions.

Olson, Roberta, *Italian Renaissance Sculpture*. New York, 1992. The most accessible introduction to the subject.

Parker, Geoffrey. *The Military Revolution: Military Innovation and the Rise of the West (1500–1800)*. 2d ed. Cambridge and New York, 1996. A work of fundamental importance for understanding the global dominance achieved by early modern Europeans.

Perkins, Leeman L. *Music in the Age of the Renaissance*. New York, 1999. A massive new study that needs to be read in conjunction with Reese.

Phillips, J. R. S. *The Medieval Expansion of Europe*. 2d ed. Oxford, 1998. An outstanding study of the thirteenth- and fourteenth-century background to the fifteenth-century expansion of Europe. Important synthetic treatment of European relations with the Mongols, China, Africa, and North America. The second edition includes a new introduction and a bibliographical essay; the text is the same as in the first edition (1988).

Phillips, William D., Jr., and Carla R. Phillips. *The Worlds of Christopher Columbus*. Cambridge and New York, 1991. The first book to read on Columbus: accessible, engaging, and scholarly. Then read Fernández-Armesto's biography.

Rabelais, François. *Gargantua and Pantagruel*. Trans. J. M. Cohen. Baltimore, MD, 1955. A robust modern translation.

Reese, Gustave. *Music in the Renaissance*, rev. ed. New York, 1959. A great book; still authoritative, despite the more recent work by Perkins, which supplements but does not replace it.

Rice, Eugene F., Jr., and Anthony Grafton. *The Foundations of Early Modern Europe, 1460–1559,* 2d ed. New York, 1994. The best textbook account of its period.

Rowland, Ingrid D. *The Culture of the High Renaissance: Ancients and Moderns in Sixteenth-Century Rome.* Cambridge and New York, 2000. Beautifully written examination of the social, intellectual, and economic foundations of the Renaissance in Rome.

Russell, Peter. *Prince Henry "The Navigator": A Life.* New Haven, CT, 2000. A masterly biography by a great historian who has spent a lifetime on the subject. The only book one now needs to read on Prince Henry.

Scammell, Geoffrey V. *The First Imperial Age: European Overseas Expansion, 1400–1715.* London, 1989. A useful introductory survey, with a particular focus on English and French colonization.

1973 OPEC oil embargo Some leaders in the Arab-dominated Organization of the Petroleum Exporting Countries (OPEC) wanted to use oil as a weapon against the West in the Arab-Israeli conflict. After the 1972 Arab-Israeli war, OPEC instituted an oil embargo against Western powers. The embargo increased the price of oil and sparked spiraling inflation and economic troubles in Western nations, triggering in turn a cycle of dangerous recession that lasted nearly a decade. In response, Western governments began viewing the Middle Eastern oil regions as areas of strategic importance.

Abbasid Caliphate (750–930) The Abbasid family claimed to be descendants of Muhammad, and in 750 they successfully led a rebellion against the Umayyads, seizing control of Muslim territories in Arabia, Persia, North Africa, and the Near East. The Abbasids modeled their behavior and administration on that of the Persian princes and their rule on that of the Persian Empire, establishing a new capital at Baghdad.

Peter Abelard (1079–1142) Highly influential philosopher, theologian, and teacher, often considered the founder of the University of Paris.

absolutism Form of government in which one body, usually the monarch, controls the right to make war, tax, judge, and coin money. The term was often used to refer to the state monarchies in seventeenth- and eighteenth-century Europe. In other countries the end of feudalism is often associated with the legal abolition of serfdom, as in Russia in 1861.

abstract expressionism The mid-twentieth-century school of art based in New York that included Jackson Pollock, Willem de Kooning, and Franz Kline. It emphasized form, color, gesture, and feeling instead of figurative subjects.

Academy of Sciences This French institute of scientific inquiry was founded in 1666 by Louis XIV. France's statesmen exerted control over the academy and sought to share in the rewards of any discoveries its members made.

Aeneas Mythical founder of Rome, Aeneas was a refugee from the city of Troy whose adventures were described by the poet Virgil in the *Aeneid,* which mimicked the oral epics of Homer.

Aetolian and Achaean Leagues These two alliances among Greek poleis formed during the Hellenistic period in opposition to the Antigonids of Macedonia. Unlike the earlier defensive alliances of the classic period, each league represented a real attempt to form a political federation.

African National Congress (ANC) Multiracial organization founded in 1912 whose goal was to end racial discrimination in South Africa.

Afrikaners Descendants of the original Dutch settlers of South Africa; formerly referred to as Boers.

agricultural revolution Numerous agricultural revolutions have occurred in the history of Western civilizations. One of the most significant began in the tenth century C.E., and increased the amount of land under cultivation as well as the productivity of the land. This revolution was made possible through the use of new technology, an increase in global temperatures, and more efficient methods of cultivation.

AIDS Acquired Immunodeficiency Syndrome. AIDS first appeared in the 1970s and has developed into a global health catastrophe; it is spreading most quickly in developing nations in Africa and Asia.

Akhenaten (r. 1352–1336 B.C.E.) Pharaoh whose attempt to promote the worship of the sun god, Aten, ultimately weakened his dynasty's position in Egypt.

Alexander the Great (356–323 B.C.E.) The Macedonian king whose conquests of the Persian Empire and Egypt created a new Hellenistic world.

Tsar Alexander II (1818–1881) After the Crimean War, Tsar Alexander embarked on a program of reform and modernization, which included the emancipation of the serfs. A radical assassin killed him in 1881.

Alexius Comnenus (1057–1118) This Byzantine emperor requested Pope Urban II's help in raising an army to recapture Anatolia from the Seljuk Turks. Instead, Pope Urban II called for knights to go to the Holy Land and liberate it from its Muslim captors, which launched the First Crusade.

Algerian War (1954–1962) The war between France and Algerians seeking independence. Led by the National Liberation Front (FLN), guerrillas fought the French army in the mountains and desert of Algeria. The FLN also initiated a campaign of bombing and terrorism in Algerian cities that led French soldiers to torture many Algerians, attracting world attention and international scandal.

Dante Alighieri (c. 1265–1321) Florentine poet and intellectual whose *Divine Comedy* was a pioneering work in the Italian vernacular and a vehicle for political and religious critique.

Allied Powers The First World War coalition of Great Britain, Ireland, Belgium, France, Italy, Russia, Portugal, Greece, Serbia, Montenegro, Albania, and Romania.

al Qaeda The radical Islamic organization founded in the late 1980s by former mujahidin who had fought against the Soviet Union in Afghanistan. Al Qaeda carried out the 9/11 terrorist

A17

attacks and is responsible as well for attacks in Africa, Southeast Asia, Europe, and the Middle East.

Ambrose (c. 340–397) One of the early "fathers" of the Church, he helped to define the relationship between the sacred authority of bishops and other Church leaders and the secular authority of worldly rulers. He believed that secular rulers were a part of the Church and therefore subject to it.

Americanization The fear of many Europeans, since the 1920s, that U.S. cultural products, such as film, television, and music, exerted too much influence. Many of the criticisms centered on America's emphasis on mass production and organization. The fears about Americanization were not limited to culture. They extended to corporations, business techniques, global trade, and marketing.

Americas The name given to the two great landmasses of the New World, derived from the name of the Italian geographer Amerigo Vespucci. In 1492, Christopher Columbus reached the Bahamas and the island of Hispaniola, which began an era of Spanish conquest in North and South America. Originally, the Spanish sought a route to Asia. Instead they discovered two continents whose wealth they decided to exploit. They were especially interested in gold and silver, which they either stole from indigenous peoples or mined using indigenous peoples as labor. Silver became Spain's most lucrative export from the New World.

Amnesty International Nongovernmental organization formed in 1961 to defend "prisoners of conscience"—those detained for their beliefs, color, sex, ethnic origin, language, or religion.

Anabaptists Protestant movement that emerged in Switzerland in 1521; its adherents insisted that only adults could be baptized Christians.

anarchists In the nineteenth century, they were a political movement with the aim of establishing small-scale, localized, and self-sufficient democratic communities that could guarantee a maximum of individual sovereignty. Renouncing parties, unions and any form of modern mass organization, the anarchists fell back on the tradition of conspiratorial violence.

Anti–Corn Law League This organization successfully lobbied Parliament to repeal Britain's Corn Laws in 1846. The Corn Laws of 1815 had protected British landowners and farmers from foreign competition by establishing high tariffs, which kept bread prices artificially high for British consumers. The league saw these laws as unfair protection of the aristocracy and pushed for their repeal in the name of free trade.

anti-Semitism Anti-Semitism refers to hostility toward Jewish people. Religious forms of anti-Semitism have a long history in Europe, but in the nineteenth century anti-Semitism emerged as a potent ideology for mobilizing new constituencies in the era of mass politics. Playing on popular conspiracy theories about alleged Jewish influence in society, anti-Semites effectively rallied large bodies of supporters in France during the Dreyfus Affair, and then again during the rise of National Socialism in Germany after the First World War. The Holocaust would not have been possible without the acquiescence or cooperation of many thousands of people who shared anti-Semitic views.

apartheid The racial segregation policy of the Afrikaner-dominated South African government. Legislated in 1948 by the Afrikaner National Party, it existed in South Africa for many decades.

appeasement The policy pursued by Western governments in the face of German, Italian, and Japanese aggression leading up to the Second World War. The policy, which attempted to accommodate and negotiate peace with the aggressive nations, was based on the belief that another global war like the First World War was unimaginable, a belief that Germany and its allies had been mistreated by the terms of the Treaty of Versailles, and a fear that fascist Germany and its allies protected the West from the spread of Soviet communism.

Thomas Aquinas (1225–1274) Dominican friar and theologian whose systematic approach to Christian doctrine was influenced by Aristotle.

Arab-Israeli conflict Between the founding of the state of Israel in 1948 and the present, a series of wars has been fought between Israel and neighboring Arab nations: the war of 1948 when Israel defeated attempts by Egypt, Jordon, Iraq, Syria, and Lebanon to prevent the creation of the new state; the 1956 war between Israel and Egypt over the Sinai peninsula; the 1967 war, when Israel gained control of additional land in the Golan Heights, the West Bank, the Gaza strip, and in the Sinai; and the Yom Kippur War of 1973, when Israel once again fought with forces from Egypt and Syria. A particularly difficult issue in all of these conflicts has been the situation of the 950,000 Palestinian refugees made homeless by the first war in 1948 and the movement of Israeli settlers into the occupied territories (outside of Israel's original borders). In the late 1970s, peace talks between Israel and Egypt inspired some hope of peace, but an ongoing cycle of violence between Palestinians and the Israeli military have made a final settlement elusive.

Arab nationalism During the period of decolonization, secular forms of Arab nationalism, or pan-Arabism, found a wide following in many countries of the Middle East, especially in Egypt, Syria, and Iraq.

Arianism A variety of Christianity condemned as a heresy by the Roman Church, it derives from the teaching of a fourth-century priest called Arius, who rejected the idea that Jesus could be the divine equal of God.

aristocracy From the Greek word meaning "rule of the best." By 1000 B.C.E., the accumulated wealth of successful traders in Greece had created a new type of social class, which was based on wealth rather than warfare or birth. These men saw their wealth as a reflection of their superior qualities and aspired to emulate the heroes of old.

Aristotle (384–322 B.C.E.) A student of Plato, his philosophy was based on the rational analysis of the material world. In contrast to his teacher, he stressed the rigorous investigation of real phenomena, rather than the development of universal ethics. He was, in turn, the teacher of Alexander the Great.

Asiatic Society A cultural organization founded in 1784 by British Orientalists who lauded native culture but believed in colonial rule.

Assyrians A Semitic-speaking people that moved into northern Mesopotamia around 2400 B.C.E.

Athens Athens emerged as the Greek polis with the most markedly democratic form of government through a series of political struggles during the sixth century B.C.E. After its key role in the defeat of two invading Persian forces, Athens became the preeminent naval power of ancient Greece and the exemplar of Greek culture. But it antagonized many other poleis, and became embroiled in a war with Sparta and her allies in 431 B.C.E. Called the Peloponnesian War, this bloody conflict lasted until Athens was defeated in 404 B.C.E.

atomic bomb In 1945, the United States dropped atomic bombs on Hiroshima and Nagasaki in Japan, ending the Second World War. In 1949, the Soviet Union tested its first atomic bomb, and in 1953 both superpowers demonstrated their new hydrogen bombs. Strategically, the nuclearization of warfare polarized the world. Countries without nuclear weapons found it difficult to avoid joining either the Soviet or American military pacts. Over time, countries split into two groups: the superpowers with enormous military budgets and those countries that relied on agreements and international law. The nuclearization of warfare also encouraged "proxy wars" between clients of superpowers. Culturally, the hydrogen bomb came to symbolize the age and both humanity's power and vulnerability.

Augustine (c. 354–397) One of the most influential theologians of all time, Augustine described his conversion to Christianity in his autobiographical *Confessions* and articulated a new Christian worldview in *The City of God*, among other works.

Augustus (63 B.C.E.–14 C.E.) Born Gaius Octavius, this grandnephew and adopted son of Julius Caesar came to power in 27 B.C.E. His reign signals the end of the Roman Republic and the beginning of the Principate, the period when Rome was dominated by autocratic emperors.

Auschwitz-Birkenau The Nazi concentration camp in Poland that was designed to systematically murder Jews and Gypsies. Between 1942 and 1944 over 1 million people were killed in Auschwitz-Birkenau.

Austro-Hungarian Empire The dual monarchy established by the Habsburg family in 1867; it collapsed at the end of the First World War.

authoritarianism A centralized and dictatorial form of government, proclaimed by its adherents to be superior to parliamentary democracy. Authoritarian governments claim to be above the law, do not respect individual rights, and do not tolerate political opposition. Authoritarian regimes that have developed a central ideology such as fascism or communism are sometimes termed "totalitarian."

Avignon A city in southeastern France that became the seat of the papacy between 1305 and 1377, a period known as the "Babylonian Captivity" of the Roman Church.

Aztecs An indigenous people of central Mexico; their empire was conquered by Spanish conquistadors in the sixteenth century.

baby boom (1950s) The post–Second World War upswing in U.S. birth rates; it reversed a century of decline.

Babylon An ancient city between the Tigris and Euphrates Rivers, which became the capital of Hammurabi's empire in the eighteenth century B.C.E. and continued to be an important administrative and commercial capital under many subsequent imperial powers, including the Neo-Assyrians, Chaldeans, Persians, and Romans. It was here that Alexander the Great died in 323 B.C.E.

Babylonian captivity Refers both to the Jews' exile in Babylon during the sixth century B.C.E. and the period from 1309 to 1378, when papal authority was subjugated to the French crown and the papal court was moved from Rome to the French city of Avignon.

Francis Bacon (1561–1626) British philosopher and scientist who pioneered the scientific method and inductive reasoning. In other words, he argued that thinkers should amass many observations and then draw general conclusions or propose theories on the basis of these data.

balance of powers The principle that no country should be powerful enough to destabilize international relations. Starting in the seventeenth century, this goal of maintaining balance influenced diplomacy in western and central Europe for two centuries until the system collapsed with the onset of the First World War.

Balfour Declaration A letter dated November 2, 1917, by Lord Arthur J. Balfour, British foreign secretary, that promised a homeland for the Jews in Palestine.

Laura Bassi (1711–1778) She was accepted into the Academy of Science in Bologna for her work in mathematics, which made her one of the few women to be accepted into a scientific academy in the seventeenth century.

Bastille The Bastille was a royal fortress and prison in Paris. In June 1789, a revolutionary crowd attacked the Bastille to show support for the newly created National Assembly. The fall of the Bastille was the first instance of the people's role in revolutionary change in France.

Bay of Pigs (1961) The unsuccessful invasion of Cuba by Cuban exiles, supported by the U.S. government. The rebels intended to incite an insurrection in Cuba and overthrow the communist regime of Fidel Castro.

Cesare Beccaria (1738–1794) An influential writer during the Enlightenment who advocated for legal reforms. He believed that the only legitimate rationale for punishments was to maintain social order and to prevent other crimes. He argued for the greatest possible leniency compatible with deterrence and opposed torture and the death penalty.

Beer Hall Putsch (1923) An early attempt by the Nazi party to seize power in Munich; Adolf Hitler was imprisoned for a year after the incident.

Benedict of Nursia (c. 480–c. 547) Benedict's rule for monks formed the basis of western monasticism and is still observed in monasteries all over the world.

Benedictine Monasticism This form of monasticism was developed by Benedict of Nursia. Its followers adhere to a defined cycle of daily prayers, lessons, communal worship, and manual labor.

Berlin airlift (1948) The transport of vital supplies to West Berlin by air, primarily under U.S. auspices, in response to a blockade of the city that had been instituted by the Soviet Union to force the Allies to abandon West Berlin.

Berlin Conference (1884) At this conference, the leading colonial powers met and established ground rules for the partition of Africa by European nations. By 1914, 90 percent of African territory was under European control. The Berlin Conference ceded control of the Congo region to a private company run by King Leopold II of Belgium. They agreed to make the Congo valleys open to free trade and commerce, to end the slave trade in the region, and to establish a Congo Free State. In reality, King Leopold II's company established a regime that was so brutal in its treatment of local populations that an international scandal forced the Belgian state to take over the colony in 1908.

Berlin Wall The wall built in 1961 by East German Communists to prevent citizens of East Germany from fleeing to West Germany; it was torn down in 1989.

birth control pill This oral contraceptive became widely available in the mid-1960s. For the first time, women had a simple method of birth control that they could take themselves.

Otto von Bismarck (1815–1898) The prime minister of Prussia and later the first chancellor of a unified Germany, Bismarck was the architect of German unification and helped to consolidate the new nation's economic and military power.

Black Death The epidemic of bubonic plague that ravaged Europe, Asia, and North Africa in the fourteenth century, killing one third to one half of the population.

Black Jacobins A nickname for the rebels in Saint-Domingue, including Toussaint L'Ouverture, a former slave who in 1791 led the slaves of this French colony in the largest and most successful slave insurrection.

Blackshirts The troops of Mussolini's fascist regime; the squads received money from Italian landowners to attack socialist leaders.

Black Tuesday (October 29, 1929) The day on which the U.S. stock market crashed, plunging U.S. and international trading systems into crisis and leading the world into the "Great Depression."

William Blake (1757–1827) Romantic writer who criticized industrial society and factories. He championed the imagination and poetic vision, seeing both as transcending the limits of the material world.

Blitzkrieg The German "lightning war" strategy used during the Second World War; the Germans invaded Poland, France, Russia, and other countries with fast-moving and well-coordinated attacks using aircraft, tanks and other armored vehicles, followed by infantry.

Bloody Sunday On January 22, 1905, the Russian tsar's guards killed 130 demonstrators who were protesting the tsar's mistreatment of workers and the middle class.

Giovanni Boccaccio (1313–1375) Florentine author best known for his *Decameron*, a collection of prose tales about sex, adventure, and trickery written in the Italian vernacular after the Black Death.

Jean Bodin (1530–1596) A French political philosopher whose *Six Books of the Commonwealth* advanced a theory of absolute sovereignty, on the grounds that the state's paramount duty is to maintain order and that monarchs should therefore exercise unlimited power.

Boer War (1898–1902) Conflict between British and ethnically European Afrikaners in South Africa, with terrible casualties on both sides.

Boethius (c. 480–524) Member of a prominent Roman family, he sought to preserve aspects of ancient learning by compiling a series of handbooks and anthologies appropriate for Christian readers. His translations of Greek philosophy provided a crucial link between classical Greek thought and the early intellectual culture of Christianity.

Bolsheviks Former members of the Russian Social Democratic Party who advocated the destruction of capitalist political and economic institutions and started the Russian Revolution. In 1918, the Bolsheviks changed their name to the Russian Communist Party. Prominent Bolsheviks included Vladimir Lenin and Josef Stalin. Leon Trotsky joined the Bolsheviks late but became a prominent leader in the early years of the Russian Revolution.

Napoleon Bonaparte (1769–1821) Corsican-born French general who seized power and ruled as dictator from 1799 to 1814. After the successful conquest of much of Europe, he was defeated by Russian and Prussian forces and died in exile.

Boniface VIII During his pontificate (1294–1303), repeated claims to papal authority were challenged by King Philip IV of France. When Boniface died in 1309 (at the hands of Philip's thugs), the French king moved the papal court from Rome to the French city of Avignon, where it remained until 1378.

Sandro Botticelli (1445–1510) An Italian painter devoted to the blending of classical and Christian motifs by using ideas associated with the pagan past to illuminate sacred stories.

bourgeoisie Term for the middle class, derived from the French word for a town-dweller, *bourgeois*.

Boxer Rebellion (1899–1900) Chinese peasant movement that opposed foreign influence, especially that of Christian missionaries; it was finally put down after the Boxers were defeated by a foreign army composed mostly of Japanese, Russian, British, French, and American soldiers.

Tycho Brahe (1546–1601) Danish astronomer who believed that the careful study of the heavens would unlock the secrets of the universe. For over twenty years, he charted the movements of significant objects in the night sky, compiling the finest set of astronomical data in Europe.

British Commonwealth of Nations Formed in 1926, the Commonwealth conferred "dominion status" on Britain's white settler colonies in Canada, Australia, and New Zealand.

Bronze Age (3200–1200 B.C.E.) The name given to the era characterized by the discovery of techniques for smelting bronze (an alloy of copper and tin), which was then the strongest known metal.

Brownshirts Troops of young German men who dedicated themselves to the Nazi cause in the early 1930s by holding street marches, mass rallies, and confrontations. They engaged in beatings of Jews and anyone who opposed the Nazis.

Lord Byron (1788–1824) Writer and poet whose life helped give the Romantics their reputation as rebels against conformity. He was known for his love affairs, his defense of working-class movements, and his passionate engagement in politics, which led to his death in the war for Greek independence.

Byzantium The name of a small settlement located at the mouth of the Black Sea and at the crossroads between Europe and Asia, it was chosen by Constantine as the site for his new imperial capital of Constantinople in 324. Modern historians use this name to refer to the eastern Roman Empire that persisted in this region until 1453, but the inhabitants of that empire referred to themselves as Romans.

Julius Caesar (100–44 B.C.E.) The Roman general who conquered the Gauls, invaded Britain, and expanded Rome's territory in Asia Minor. He became the dictator of Rome in 46 B.C.E. His assassination led to the rise of his grandnephew and adopted son, Gaius Octavius Caesar, who ruled the Roman Empire as Caesar Augustus.

caliphs Islamic rulers who claim descent from the prophet Muhammad.

John Calvin (1509–1564) French-born theologian and reformer whose radical form of Protestantism was adopted in many Swiss cities, notably Geneva.

Canary Islands Islands off the western coast of Africa that were colonized by Portugal and Spain in the mid-fifteenth century, after which they became bases for further expeditions around the African coast and across the Atlantic.

Carbonari An underground organization that opposed the Concert of Europe's restoration of monarchies. They held influence in southern Europe during the 1820s, especially in Italy.

Carolingian Derived from the Latin name Carolus (Charles), this term refers to the Frankish dynasty that began with the rise to power of Charlemagne's grandfather, Charles Martel (688–741). At its height under Charlemagne (Charles the Great), the dynasty controlled what is now France, Germany, northern Italy, Catalonia, and portions of central Europe. The Carolingian Empire collapsed under the combined weight of Viking raids, economic disintegration, and the growing power of local lords.

Carolingian Renaissance A cultural and intellectual flowering that took place around the court of Charlemagne in the late eighth and early ninth centuries.

Carthage The great maritime empire that grew out of Phoenician trading colonies in North Africa and rivaled the power of Rome. Its wars with Rome, collectively known as the Punic Wars, ended in its destruction in 146 B.C.E.

Cassidorus (c. 490–c. 583) Member of an old senatorial family, he was largely responsible for introducing classical learning into the monastic curriculum and for turning monasteries into centers for the collection, preservation, and transmission of knowledge. His *Institutes*, an influential handbook of classical literature for Christian readers, was intended as a preface to more intensive study of theology and the Bible.

Catholic Church The "universal" (catholic) church based in Rome, which was redefined in the sixteenth century, when the Counter-Reformation resulted in the rebirth of the Catholic faith at the Council of Trent.

Margaret Cavendish (1623–1673) English natural philosopher who developed her own speculative natural philosophy. She used this philosophy to critique those who excluded her from scientific debate.

Camillo Benso di Cavour (1810–1861) Prime minister of Piedmont-Sardinia and founder of the Italian Liberal party; he played a key role in the movement for Italian unification under the Piedmontese king, Victor Emmanuel II.

Central Powers The First World War alliance between Germany, Austria-Hungary, Bulgaria, and Turkey.

Charlemagne (742–814) As king of the Franks (767–813), Charles "the Great" consolidated much of western Europe under his rule. In 800, he was crowned emperor by the pope in Rome, establishing a problematic precedent that would have wide-ranging consequences for western Europe's relationship with the eastern Roman Empire in Byzantium and for the relationship between the papacy and secular rulers.

Charles I (1625–1649) The second Stuart king of England, Charles attempted to rule without the support of Parliament, sparking a controversy that erupted into civil war in 1642. The king's forces were ultimately defeated and Charles himself was executed by act of Parliament, the first time in history that a reigning king was legally deposed and executed by his own government.

Charles II of England Nominally King of England, Ireland, and Scotland after his father Charles I's execution in 1649, Charles II lived in exile until he was restored to the throne in 1660. Influenced by his cousin, King Louis XIV of France, he presided over an opulent royal court until his death in 1685.

Chartists A working-class movement in Britain that called for reform of the British political system during the 1840s. They were supporters of the "People's Charter," which had six demands: universal white male suffrage, secret ballots, an end to property qualifications as a condition of public office, annual parliamentary elections, salaries for members of the House of Commons, and equal electoral districts.

Geoffrey Chaucer (1340–1400) English poet whose collection of versified stories, *The Canterbury Tales*, features characters from a variety of different classes.

Christine de Pisan (c. 1364–c. 1431) Born in Italy, Christine spent her adult life attached to the French court and, after her husband's death, became the first laywoman to earn her living by writing. She is the author of treatises in warfare and chivalry as well as of books and pamphlets that challenge long-standing misogynistic claims.

Church of England Founded by Henry VIII in the 1530s, as a consequence of his break with the authority of the Roman pope.

Winston Churchill (1874–1965) British prime minister who led the country during the Second World War. He also coined the phrase "Iron Curtain" in a speech at Westminster College in 1946.

Cicero (106–43 B.C.E.) Influential Roman senator, orator, Stoic philosopher, and prose stylist. His published writings still form the basis of the instruction in classical Latin grammar and usage.

Cincinnatus (519–c. 430 B.C.E.) A legendary citizen-farmer of Rome who reluctantly accepted an appointment as dictator. After defeating Rome's enemies, he allegedly left his political office and returned to his farm.

Civil Constitution of the Clergy Issued by the French National Assembly in 1790, the Civil Constitution of the Clergy decreed that all bishops and priests should be subject to the authority of the state. Their salaries were to be paid out of the public treasury, and they were required to swear allegiance to the new state, making it clear they served France rather than Rome. The Assembly's aim was to make the Catholic Church of France a truly national and civil institution.

civilizing mission An argument made by Europeans to justify colonial expansion in the nineteenth century. Supporters of this idea believed that Europeans had a duty to impose western ideas of economic and political progress on the indigenous peoples they ruled over in their colonies. In practice, the colonial powers often found that ambitious plans to impose European practices on colonial subjects led to unrest that threatened the stability of colonial rule, and by the early twentieth century most colonial powers were more cautious in their plans for political or cultural transformation.

Civil Rights Movement The Second World War increased African American migration from the American South to northern cities, intensifying a drive for rights, dignity, and independence. By 1960, civil rights groups had started organizing boycotts and demonstrations directed at discrimination against blacks in the South. During the 1960s, civil rights laws passed under President Lyndon B. Johnson did bring African Americans some equality with regard to voting rights and, to a much lesser degree, school desegregation. However, racism continued in areas such as housing, job opportunities, and the economic development of African American communities.

Civil War (1861–1865) Conflict between the northern and southern states of America that cost over 600,000 lives; this struggle led to the abolition of slavery in the United States.

classical learning The study of ancient Greek and Latin texts. After Christianity became the only legal religion of the Roman Empire, scholars needed to find a way to make classical learning applicable to a Christian way of life. Christian monks played a significant role in resolving this problem by reinterpreting the classics for a Christian audience.

Cluny A powerful Benedictine monastery founded in 910 whose enormous wealth and prestige would derive from its independence from secular authorities as well as from its wide network of daughter houses (priories).

Cold War (1945–1991) Ideological, political, and economic conflict in which the USSR and Eastern Europe opposed the United States and Western Europe in the decades after the Second World War. The Cold War's origins lay in the breakup of the wartime alliance between the United States and the Soviet Union in 1945 and resulted in a division of Europe into two spheres: the West, commited to market capitalism, and the East, which sought to build Socialist republics in areas under Soviet Control. The Cold War ended with the collapse of the Soviet Union in 1991.

collectivization Stalin's plan for nationalizing agricultural production, begun in 1929. Twenty-five million peasants were forced to give up their land and join 250,000 large collective farms. Many who resisted were deported to labor camps in the Far East, and Stalin's government cut off food rations to those areas most marked by resistance to collectivization. In the ensuing man-made famines, millions of people starved to death.

Columbian Exchange The widespread exchange of peoples, plants, animals, diseases, goods, and culture between the African and Eurasian landmass (on the one hand) and the region that encompasses the Americas, Australia, and the Pacific Islands (on the other); precipitated by voyage of Columbus in 1492.

Christopher Columbus (1451–1506) A Genoese sailor who persuaded King Ferdinand and Queen Isabella of Spain to fund his expedition across the Atlantic, with the purpose of discovering a new trade route to Asia. His miscalculations landed him in the Bahamas and the island of Hispaniola in 1492.

Commercial Revolution A period of economic development in Europe lasting from c. 1500–c.1800. Advances in agriculture and handicraft production, combined with the expansion of trade networks in the Atlantic world, brought new wealth and new kinds of commercial activity to Europe. The commercial revolution prepared the way for the industrial revolution of the 1800s.

Committee of Public Safety Political body during the French Revolution that was controlled by the Jacobins, who defended the revolution by executing thousands during the Reign of Terror (September 1793–July 1794).

commune A community of individuals who have banded together in a sworn association, with the aim of establishing their independence and setting up their own form of representative government. Many medieval towns originally founded by lords or monasteries gained their independence through such methods.

The Communist Manifesto Radical pamphlet by Karl Marx (1818–1883) that predicted the downfall of the capitalist system and its replacement by a classless egalitarian society. Marx believed that this revolution would be accomplished by workers (the proletariat).

Compromise of 1867 Agreement between the Habsburgs and the peoples living in Hungarian parts of the empire that the Habsburg state would be officially known as the Austro-Hungarian Empire.

Concert of Europe (1814–1815) The body of diplomatic agreements designed primarily by Austrian minister Klemens von Metternich between 1814 and 1848 and supported by other European powers until 1914. Its goal was to maintain a balance of power on the Continent and to prevent destabilizing social and political change in Europe.

conciliarism A doctrine developed in the thirteenth and fourteenth centuries to counter the growing power of the papacy, conciliarism holds that papal authority should be subject to a council of the Church at large. Conciliarists emerged as a dominant force after the Council of Constance (1414–1418) but were eventually outmatched by a rejuvenated papacy.

Congress of Vienna (1814–1815) International conference to reorganize Europe after the downfall of Napoleon and the French Revolution. European monarchies restored the Bourbon family to the French throne, agreed to respect each other's borders and to cooperate in guarding against future revolutions and war.

conquistador Spanish term for "conqueror," applied to the mercenaries and adventurers who campaigned against indigenous peoples in central and southern America.

Conservatives In the nineteenth century, conservatives aimed to legitimize and solidify the monarchy's authority and the hierarchical social order. They believed that change had to be slow, incremental, and managed so that the structures of authority were strengthened and not weakened.

Constantine (275–337) The first emperor of Rome to convert to Christianity, Constantine came to power in 312. In 324, he founded a new imperial capital, Constantinople, on the site of a maritime settlement known as Byzantium.

Constantinople Founded by the emperor Constantine on the site of a village called Byzantium, Constantinople became the new capital of the Roman Empire in 324 and continued to be the seat of imperial power after its capture by the Ottoman Turks in 1453. It is now known as Istanbul.

contract theory of government A theory of government written by Englishman John Locke (1632–1704) which posits that government authority was both contractual and conditional; therefore, if a government has abused its given authority, society had the right to dissolve it and create another.

Nicholas Copernicus (1473–1543) Polish astronomer who advanced the idea that the earth moved around the sun.

cosmopolitanism Stemming from the Greek word meaning "universal city," the culture characteristic of the Hellenistic world challenged and transformed the more narrow worldview of the Greek polis.

cotton gin Invented by Eli Whitney in 1793, this device mechanized the process of separating cotton seeds from the cotton fiber, which sped up the production of cotton and reduced its price. This change made slavery profitable in the United States.

Council of Constance (1417–1420) A meeting of clergy and theologians in an effort to resolve the Great Schism within the Roman Church. The council deposed all rival papal candidates and elected a new pope, Martin V, but it also adopted the doctrine of conciliarism, which holds that the supreme authority within the Church rests with a representative general council and not with the pope. However, Martin V himself was an opponent of this doctrine and refused to be bound by it.

Council of Trent The name given to a series of meetings held in the Italian city of Trent (Trento) between 1545 and 1563, when leaders of the Roman Church reaffirmed Catholic doctrine and instituted internal reforms.

Counter-Reformation The movement to counter the Protestant Reformation, initiated by the Catholic Church at the Council of Trent in 1545.

coup d'état French term for the overthrow of an established government by a group of conspirators, usually with military support.

Crimean War (1854–1856) War waged by Russia against Great Britain and France. Spurred by Russia's encroachment on Ottoman territories, the conflict revealed Russia's military weakness when Russian forces fell to British and French troops.

Cuban missile crisis (1962) Diplomatic standoff between the United States and the Soviet Union that was provoked by the Soviet Union's attempt to base nuclear missiles in Cuba; it brought the world closer to nuclear war than ever before or since.

Cuius regio, eius religio A Latin phrase meaning "as the ruler, so the religion." Adopted as a part of the settlement of the Peace of Augsburg in 1555, it meant that those principalities ruled by Lutherans would have Lutheranism as their official religion and those ruled by Catholics must practice Catholicism.

cult of domesticity Concept associated with Victorian England that idealized women as nurturing wives and mothers.

cult of the Virgin The beliefs and practices associated with the veneration of Mary, the mother of Jesus, which became increasingly popular in the twelfth century.

cuneiform An early writing system that began to develop in Mesopotamia in the fourth millennium B.C.E. By 3100 B.C.E., its distinctive markings were impressed on clay tablets using a wedge-shaped stylus.

Cyrus the Great (c. 585–529 B.C.E.) As architect of the Persian Empire, Cyrus extended his dominion over a vast territory stretching from the Persian Gulf to the Mediterranean and incorporating the ancient civilizations of Mesopotamia. His successors ruled this Persian Empire as "Great Kings."

Darius (521–486 B.C.E.) The Persian emperor whose conflict with Aristagoras, the Greek ruler of Miletus, ignited the Persian Wars. In 490 B.C.E., Darius sent a large army to punish the Athenians for their intervention in Persian imperial affairs, but this force was defeated by Athenian hoplites on the plain of Marathon.

Charles Darwin (1809–1882) British naturalist who wrote *On the Origin of Species* and developed the theory of natural selection to explain the evolution of organisms.

D-Day (June 6, 1944) Date of the Allied invasion of Normandy, under General Dwight Eisenhower, to liberate Western Europe from German occupation.

Decembrists Russian army officers who were influenced by events in France and formed secret societies that espoused liberal governance. They were put down by Nicholas I in December 1825.

Declaration of Independence (1776) Historic document stating the principles of government on which the United States was founded.

Declaration of the Rights of Man and of the Citizen (1789) French charter of liberties formulated by the National Assembly during the French Revolution. The seventeen articles later became the preamble to the new constitution, which the assembly finished in 1791.

democracy In ancient Greece, this form of government allowed a class of propertied male citizens to participate in the governance of their polis; but excluded women, slaves, and citizens without property from the political process. As a result, the ruling class amounted to only a small percentage of the entire population.

René Descartes (1596–1650) French philosopher and mathematician who emphasized the use of deductive reasoning.

Denis Diderot (1713–1784) French philosophe and author who was the guiding force behind the publication of the first encyclopedia. His *Encyclopedia* showed how reason could be applied to nearly all realms of thought and aimed to be a compendium of all human knowledge.

Dien Bien Phu (1954) Defining battle in the war between French colonialists and the Viet Minh that secured North Vietnam for Ho Chi Minh and his army and left the south to form its own government, to be supported by France and the United States.

Diet of Worms The select council of the Church that convened in the German city of Worms and condemned Martin Luther on a charge of heresy in 1521.

Diocletian (245–316) As emperor of Rome from 284 to 305, Diocletian recognized that the empire could not be governed by one man in one place. His solution was to divide the empire into four parts, each with its own imperial ruler, but he himself remained the dominant ruler of the resulting tetrarchy (rule of four). He also initiated the Great Persecution, a time when many Christians became martyrs to their faith.

Directory (1795–1799) Executive committee that governed after the fall of Robespierre and held control until the coup of Napoleon Bonaparte.

Discourse on Method Philosophical treatise by René Descartes (1596–1650) proposing that the path to knowledge was through logical deduction, beginning with one's own self: "I think, therefore I am."

Dominican Order Also called the Order of Preachers, it was founded by Dominic of Osma (1170–1221), a Castilian preacher and theologian, and approved by Innocent III in 1216. The order was dedicated to the rooting out of heresy and the conversion of Jews and Muslims. Many of its members held teaching positions in European universities and contributed to the development of medieval philosophy and theology. Others became the leading administrators of the Inquisition.

Dominion in the British Commonwealth Canadian promise to maintain their fealty to the British crown, even after their independence in 1867; later applied to Australia and New Zealand.

Dreyfus Affair The 1894 French scandal surrounding accusations that a Jewish captain, Alfred Dreyfus, sold military secrets to the Germans. Convicted, Dreyfus was sentenced to solitary confinement for life. However, after public outcry, it was revealed that the trial documents were forgeries, and Dreyfus was pardoned after a second trial in 1899. In 1906, he was fully exonerated and reinstated in the army. The affair revealed the depths of popular anti-Semitism in France.

Alexander Dubček (1921–1992) Communist leader of the Czechoslovakian government who advocated for "socialism with a human face." He encouraged debate within the party, academic and artistic freedom, and less censorship, which led to the "Prague spring" of 1968. People in other parts of Eastern Europe began to demonstrate in support of Dubček and demand their own reforms. When Dubček tried to democratize the Communist party and did not attend a meeting of the Warsaw Pact, the Soviets sent tanks and troops into Prague and ousted Dubček and his allies.

Duma The Russian parliament, created in response to the revolution of 1905.

Dunkirk The French port on the English Channel where the British and French forces retreated after sustaining heavy losses against the German military. Between May 27 and June 4, 1940, the Royal Navy evacuated over 300,000 troops using commercial and pleasure boats.

Eastern Front Battlefront between Berlin and Moscow during the First and Second World Wars..

East India Company (1600–1858) British charter company created to outperform Portuguese and Spanish traders in the Far East; in the eighteenth century the company became, in effect, the ruler of a large part of India. There was also a Dutch East India Company.

Edict of Nantes (1598) Issued by Henry IV of France in an effort to end religious violence. The edict declared France to be a Catholic country but tolerated some forms of Protestant worship.

Edward I of England King of England from 1272 to his death in 1307, Edward presided over the creation of new legal and bureaucratic institutions in his realm, violently subjugated the Welsh, and attempted to colonize Scotland. He expelled English Jews from his domain in 1290.

Eleanor of Aquitaine (1122–1204) Ruler of the wealthy province of Aquitaine and wife of Louis VII of France, Eleanor had her marriage annulled in order to marry the young count of Anjou, Henry Plantagenet, who became King Henry of England a year later. Mother of two future kings of England, she was an important patron of the arts.

Elizabeth I (1533–1603) Protestant daughter of Henry VIII and his second wife, Anne Boleyn, Elizabeth succeeded her sister Mary as the second queen regnant of England (1558–1603).

emancipation of the serfs (1861) The abolition of serfdom was central to Tsar Alexander II's program of modernization and reform, but it produced a limited amount of change. Former serfs now had legal rights. However, farm land was granted to the village communes instead of to individuals. The land was of poor quality and the former serfs had to pay for it in installments to the village commune.

emperor Originally the term for any conquering commander of the Roman army whose victories merited celebration in an official triumph. After Augustus seized power in 27 B.C.E., it was the title born by the sole ruler of the Roman Empire.

empire A centralized political entity consolidated through the conquest and colonization of other nations or peoples in order to benefit the ruler and/or his homeland.

Enabling Act (1933) Emergency act passed by the Reichstag (German parliament) that helped transform Hitler from Germany's chancellor, or prime minister, into a dictator, following the suspicious burning of the Reichstag building and a suspension of civil liberties.

enclosure Long process of privatizing what had been public agricultural land in eighteenth-century Britain; it helped to stimulate the development of commercial agriculture and forced many people in rural areas to seek work in cities during the early stages of industrialization.

The Encyclopedia Joint venture of French philosophe writers, led by Denis Diderot (1713–1784), which proposed to summarize all modern knowledge in a multivolume illustrated work with over 70,000 articles.

Friedrich Engels (1820–1895) German social and political philosopher who collaborated with Karl Marx on many publications.

English Civil War (1642–1649) Conflicts between the English Parliament and King Charles I erupted into civil war, which ended in the defeat of the royalists and the execution of Charles on charges of treason against the crown. A short time later, Parliament's hereditary House of Lords was abolished and England was declared a Commonwealth.

English Navigation Act of 1651 Act stipulating that only English ships could carry goods between the mother country and its colonies.

Enlightenment Intellectual movement in eighteenth-century Europe, that believed in human betterment through the application of reason to solve social, economic, and political problems.

Epicureanism A philosophical position articulated by Epicurus of Athens (c. 342–270 B.C.E.), who rejected the idea of an ordered universe governed by divine forces; instead, he emphasized individual agency and proposed that the highest good is the pursuit of pleasure.

Desiderius Erasmus (c. 1469–1536) Dutch-born scholar, social commentator, and Catholic humanist whose new translation of the Bible influenced the theology of Martin Luther.

Estates-General The representative body of the three estates in France. In 1789, King Louis XVI summoned the Estates-General to meet for the first time since 1614 because it seemed to be the only solution to France's worsening economic crisis and financial chaos.

Etruscans Settlers of the Italian peninsula who dominated the region from the late Bronze Age until the rise of the Roman Republic in the sixth century B.C.E.

Euclid Hellenistic mathematician whose *Elements of Geometry* forms the basis of modern geometry.

eugenics A Greek term, meaning "good birth," referring to the project of "breeding" a superior human race. It was popularly championed by scientists, politicians, and social critics in the late nineteenth and early twentieth centuries.

European Common Market (1957) The Treaty of Rome created the European Economic Community (EEC), or Common Market. The original members were France, West Germany, Italy, Belgium, Holland, and Luxembourg. The EEC sought to abolish trade barriers between its members and it pledged itself to common external tariffs, the free movement of labor and capital among the member nations, and uniform wage structures and social security systems to create similar working conditions in all member countries.

European Union (EU) Successor organization to the European Economic Community or European Common Market, formed by the Maastricht Treaty, which took effect in 1993. Currently twenty-eight member states compose the EU, which has a governing council, an international court, and a parliament. Over time, member states of the EU have relinquished some of their sovereignty, and cooperation has evolved into a community with a single currency, the euro.

Exclusion Act of 1882 U.S. congressional act prohibiting nearly all immigration from China to the United States; fueled by animosity toward Chinese workers in the American West.

existentialism Philosophical movement that arose out of the Second World War and emphasized the absurdity of human condition. Led by Jean-Paul Sartre and Albert Camus, existentialists encouraged humans to take responsibility for their own decisions and dilemmas.

expulsion of the Jews European rulers began to expel their Jewish subjects from their kingdoms beginning in the 1280s, mostly due to their inability to repay the money they had extorted from Jewish money-lenders but also as a result of escalating anti-Semitism in the wake of the Crusades, Jews were also expelled from the Rhineland in the fourteenth century and from Spain in 1492.

fascism The doctrine founded by Benito Mussolini, which emphasized three main ideas: statism ("nothing above the state, nothing outside the state, nothing against the state"), nationalism, and militarism. Its name derives from the Latin *fasces*, a symbol of Roman imperial power adopted by Mussolini.

Fashoda Incident (1898) Disagreements between the French and the British over land claims in North Africa led to a standoff between armies of the two nations at the Sudanese town of Fashoda. The crisis was solved diplomatically. France ceded southern Sudan to Britain in exchange for a stop to further expansion by the British.

The Feminine Mystique Groundbreaking book by feminist Betty Friedan (b. 1921), which tried to define *femininity* and explored how women internalized those definitions.

Franz Ferdinand (1863–1914) Archduke of Austria and heir to the Austro-Hungarian Empire; his assassination led to the beginning of the First World War.

Ferdinand (1452–1516) **and Isabella** (1451–1504) In 1469, Ferdinand of Aragon married the heiress to Castile, Isabella. Their union allowed them to pursue several ambitious policies, including the conquest of Granada, the last Muslim principality in Spain, and the expulsion of Spain's large Jewish community. In 1492, Isabella granted three ships to Christopher Columbus of Genoa (Italy), who went on to claim portions of the New World for Spain.

Fertile Crescent An area of fertile land in what is now Syria, Israel, Turkey, eastern Iraq, and western Iran that was able to sustain settlements due to its wetter climate and abundant natural food resources. Some of the earliest known civilizations emerged there between 9000 and 4500 B.C.E.

feudalism A problematic modern term that attempts to explain the diffusion of power in medieval Europe, and the many different kinds of political, social, and economic relationships that were forged through the giving and receiving of fiefs (*feoda*). But because it is anachronistic and inadequate, this term has been rejected by most historians of the medieval period.

First Crusade (1095–1099) Launched by Pope Urban II in response to a request from the Byzantine emperor Alexius Comnenus, who had asked for a small contingent of knights to assist him in fighting Turkish forces in Anatolia; Urban instead directed the crusaders' energies toward the Holy Land and the recapture of Jerusalem, promising those who took the cross (*crux*) that they would merit eternal salvation if they died in the attempt. This crusade prompted attacks against

Jews throughout Europe and resulted in six subsequent—and unsuccessful—military campaigns.

First World War A total war from August 1914 to November 1918, involving the armies of Britain, France, and Russia (the Allies) against Germany, Austria-Hungary, and the Ottoman Empire (the Central Powers). Italy joined the Allies in 1915, and the United States joined them in 1917, helping to tip the balance in favor of the Allies, who also drew upon the populations and raw materials of their colonial possessions. Also known as the Great War.

Five Pillars of Islam The Muslim teaching that salvation is only assured through observance of five basic precepts: submission to God's will as described in the teachings of Muhammad, frequent prayer, ritual fasting, the giving of alms, and an annual pilgrimage to Mecca (the Hajj).

Five-Year Plan Soviet effort launched under Stalin in 1928 to replace the market with a state-owned and state-managed economy in order to promote rapid economic development over a five-year period and thereby "catch and overtake" the leading capitalist countries. The First Five-Year Plan was followed by the Second Five-Year Plan (1933–1937) and so on, until the collapse of the Soviet Union in 1991.

fly shuttle Invented by John Kay in 1733, this device sped up the process of weaving.

Fourteen Points President Woodrow Wilson proposed these points as the foundation on which to build peace in the world after the First World War. They called for an end to secret treaties, "open covenants, openly arrived at," freedom of the seas, the removal of international tariffs, the reduction of arms, the "self-determination of peoples," and the establishment of a League of Nations to settle international conflicts.

Franciscan Order Also known as the Order of the Friars Minor. The earliest Franciscans were followers of Francis of Assisi (1182–1226) and strove, like him, to imitate the life and example of Jesus. The order was formally established by Pope Innocent III in 1209. Its special mission was the care and instruction of the urban poor.

Frankfurt Parliament (1848–1849) Failed attempt to create a unified Germany under constitutional principles. In 1849, the assembly offered the crown of the new German nation to Frederick William IV of Prussia, but he refused the offer and suppressed a brief protest. The delegates went home disillusioned.

Frederick the Great (1712–1786) Prussian ruler (1740–1786) who engaged the nobility in maintaining a strong military and bureaucracy and led Prussian armies to notable military victories. He also encouraged Enlightenment rationalism and artistic endeavors.

French Revolution of 1789 In 1788, a severe financial crisis forced the French monarchy to convene an assembly known as the Estates General, representing the three estates of the realm: the clergy, the nobility, and the commons (known as the Third Estate). When the Estates General met in 1789, representatives of the Third Estate demanded major constitutional changes, and when the king and his government proved uncooperative, the Third Estate broke with the other two estates and renamed themselves the National Assembly, demanding a written constitution. The position of the National Assembly was confirmed by a popular uprising in Paris and the king was forced to accept the transformation of France into a constitutional monarchy. This constitutional phase of the revolution lasted until 1972, when the pressures of foreign invasion and the emergence of a more radical revolutionary movement caused the collapse of the monarchy and the establishment of a Republic in France.

French Revolution of 1830 The French popular revolt against Charles X's July Ordinances of 1830, which dissolved the French Chamber of Deputies and restricted suffrage to exclude almost everyone except the nobility. After several days of violence, Charles abdicated the throne and was replaced by a constitutional monarch, Louis Philippe.

French Revolution of 1848 Revolution overthrowing Louis-Philippe in February, 1848, leading to the formation of the Second Republic (1848–1852). Initially enjoying broad support from both the middle classes and laborers in Paris, the new government became more conservative after elections in which the French peasantry participated for the first time. A workers' revolt was violently repressed in June, 1848, and in December 1848, Napoleon Bonaparte's nephew, Louis-Napoleon Bonaparte, was elected president. In 1852, Louis-Napoleon declared himself emperor and abolished the republic.

Sigmund Freud (1856–1939) The Austrian physician who founded the discipline of psychoanalysis and suggested that human behavior was largely motivated by unconscious and irrational forces.

Galileo Galilei (1564–1642) Italian physicist and inventor; the implications of his ideas raised the ire of the Catholic Church, and he was forced to retract most of his findings.

Gallipoli (1915) In the First World War, a combined force of French, British, Australian and New Zealand troops tried to invade the Gallipoli Peninsula, in the first large-scale amphibious attack in history, and seize it from the Turks. After seven months of fighting, the Allies had lost 200,000 soldiers. Defeated, they withdrew.

Mohandas K. (Mahatma) Gandhi (1869–1948) The Indian leader who advocated nonviolent noncooperation to protest colonial rule and helped win home rule for India in 1947.

Giuseppe Garibaldi (1807–1882) Italian revolutionary leader who led the fight to free Sicily and Naples from the Habsburg Empire; the lands were then peaceably annexed by Sardinia to produce a unified Italy.

Gaul The region of the Roman Empire that was home to the Celtic people of that name, comprising modern France, Belgium, and western Germany.

Geneva Peace Conference (1954) International conference to restore peace in Korea and Indochina. The chief participants were the United States, the Soviet Union, Great Britain, France, the People's Republic of China, North Korea, South Korea, Vietnam, the Viet Minh party, Laos, and Cambodia. The conference resulted in the division of North and South Vietnam.

Genoa Maritime city on Italy's northwestern coast, the Genoese were active in trading ventures along the Silk Road and in the establishment of trading colonies in the Mediterranean. They were also involved in the world of finance and backed the commercial ventures of other powers, especially Spain's.

German Democratic Republic Nation founded from the Soviet zone of occupation of Germany after the Second World War; also known as East Germany.

German Social Democratic party Founded in 1875, it was the most powerful socialist party in Europe before 1917.

Gilgamesh Sumerian ruler of the city of Uruk around 2700 B.C.E., Gilgamesh became the hero of one of the world's oldest epics, which circulated orally for nearly a millennium before being written down.

Giotto (c. 1266–1337) Florentine painter and architect who is often considered a forerunner of the Renaissance.

glasnost Introduced by Soviet leader Mikhail Gorbachev in June 1987, *glasnost* was one of the five major policies that constituted *perestroika*. Often translated into English as "openness," it called for transparency in Soviet government and institutional activities by reducing censorship in mass media and lifting significant bans on the political, intellectual, and cultural lives of Soviet civilians.

globalization The term used to describe political, social, and economic networks that span the globe. These global exchanges are not limited by nation-states and in recent decades are associated with new technologies, such as the Internet. Globalization is not new, however, as human cultures and economies have been in contact with one another for centuries.

Glorious Revolution The overthrow of King James II of England and the installation of his Protestant daughter, Mary Stuart, and her husband, William of Orange, to the throne in 1688 and 1689. It is widely regarded as the founding moment in the development of a constitutional monarchy in Britain, while also establishing a more favorable climate for the economic and political growth of the English commercial classes.

Gold Coast Name that European mariners and merchants gave to that part of West Equatorial Africa from which gold and slaves were exported. Originally controlled by the Portuguese, this area later became the British colony of the Gold Coast.

Mikhail Gorbachev (1931–) Soviet leader who attempted to reform the Soviet Union through his programs of glasnost and perestroika in the late 1980s. He encouraged open discussions in other countries in the Soviet bloc, which helped inspire the velvet revolutions throughout Eastern Europe. Eventually the political, social, and economic upheaval he had unleashed would lead to the breakup of the Soviet Union.

Gothic style A type of graceful architecture emerging in twelfth- and thirteenth-century England and France. The style is characterized by pointed arches, delicate decoration, and large windows.

Olympe de Gouges (1748–1793) French political radical and feminist whose *Declaration of the Rights of Woman* demanded an equal place for women in France.

Great Depression Global economic crisis following the U.S. stock market crash on October 29, 1929, and ending with the onset of the Second World War.

Great Famine A period of terrible hunger and deprivation in Europe that peaked between 1315 and 1317, caused by a cooling of the climate and by the exhaustion of over-farming. It is estimated to have reduced the population of Europe by 10 to 15 percent.

Great Fear (1789) Following the outbreak of revolution in Paris, fear spread throughout the French countryside, as rumors circulated that armies of brigands or royal troops were coming. The peasants and villagers organized into militias, while others attacked and burned the manor houses in order to destroy the records of manorial dues.

Great Schism (1378–1417) Also known as the Great Western Schism, to distinguish it from the longstanding rupture between the Greek East and Latin West. During the schism, the Roman Church was divided between two (and, ultimately, three) competing popes. Each pope claimed to be legitimate and each denounced the heresy of the others.

Great Terror (1936–1938) The systematic murder of nearly a million people and the deportation of another million and a half to labor camps by Stalin's regime in an attempt to consolidate power and remove perceived enemies.

Greek East After the founding of Constantinople, the eastern Greek-speaking half of the Roman Empire grew more populous, prosperous and central to imperial policy. Its inhabitants considered themselves to be the true heirs of Rome, and their own Orthodox Church to be the true manifestation of Jesus's ministry.

Greek independence Nationalists in Greece revolted against the Ottoman Empire and fought a war that ended in Greek independence in 1827. They received crucial help from British, French, and Russian troops as well as widespread sympathy throughout Europe.

Pope Gregory I (r. 590–604) Also known as Gregory the Great, he was the first bishop of Rome to successfully negotiate a more universal role for the papacy. His political and theological agenda widened the rift between the western Latin (Catholic) Church and the eastern Greek (Orthodox) Church in Byzantium. He also articulated the Church's official position on the status of Jews, promoted affective approaches to religious worship, encouraged the Benedictine monastic movement, and sponsored missionary expeditions.

Guernica The Basque town bombed by German planes in April 1937 during the Spanish Civil War. It is also the subject of Pablo Picasso's famous painting from the same year.

guilds Professional organizations in commercial towns that regulated business and safeguarded the privileges of those practicing a particular craft. Often identical to confraternities ("brotherhoods").

Gulag The vast system of forced labor camps under the Soviet regime; it originated in 1919 in a small monastery near the Arctic Circle and spread throughout the Soviet Union. Penal labor was required of both ordinary criminals and those accused of political crimes. Tens of millions of people were sent to the camps between 1928 and 1953; the exact figure is unknown.

Gulf War (1991) Armed conflict between Iraq and a coalition of thirty-two nations, including the United States, Britain, Egypt, France, and Saudi Arabia. The seeds of the war were planted with Iraq's invasion of Kuwait on August 2, 1990.

Johannes Gutenberg European inventor of the printing press, his shop in Mainz produced the first printed book—a Bible—between the years 1453 and 1455.

Habsburg Dynasty A powerful European dynasty which came to power in the eleventh century in a region now part of Switzerland. Early generations of Habsburgs consolidated their control over neighboring German-speaking lands; through strategic marriages with other royal lines, later rulers eventually controlled a substantial part of Europe—including much of central Europe, the Netherlands, and even Spain and all its colonies for a time. In practice, the Holy Roman Emperor chosen from a member of the Habsburg lineage. By the latter half of the seventeenth century, the Austrian Habsburg Empire was made of up nearly 300 nominally autonomous dynastic kingdoms, principalities, duchies, and archbishoprics.

Hagia Sophia The enormous church dedicated to "Holy Wisdom," built in Constantinople at the behest of the emperor Justinian in the sixth century C.E. When Constantinople fell to Ottoman forces in 1453, it became an important mosque.

Haitian Revolution (1802–1804) In 1802, Napoleon sought to reassert French control of Saint-Domingue, but stiff resistance and yellow fever crushed the French army. In 1804, Jean-Jacques Dessalines, a general in the army of former slaves, declared the independent state of Haiti. (See **slave revolt in Saint-Domingue**.)

Hajj The annual pilgrimage to Mecca; an obligation for Muslims.

Hammurabi Ruler of Babylon from 1792 to 1750 B.C.E., Hammurabi issued a collection of laws that were greatly influential in the Near East and which constitute the world's oldest surviving law code.

Harlem Renaissance Cultural movement in the 1920s that was based in Harlem, a part of New York City with a large African American population. The movement gave voice to black novelists, poets, painters, and musicians, many of whom used their art to protest racial subordination.

Hatshepsut (1479–1458 C.E.) As a pharaoh during the New Kingdom, she launched several successful military campaigns and extended trade and diplomacy. She was an ambitious builder who probably constructed the first tomb in the Valley of the Kings. Though she never pretended to be a man, she was routinely portrayed with a masculine figure and a ceremonial beard.

Hebrews Originally a pastoral people divided among several tribes, they were briefly united under the rule of David and his son, Solomon, who promoted the worship of a single god, Yahweh, and constructed the first temple at the new capital city of Jerusalem. After Solomon's death, the Hebrew tribes were divided between the two kingdoms of Israel and Judah, which were eventually conquered by the Neo-Assyrian and Chaldean empires. It was in captivity that the Hebrews came to define themselves through worship of Yahweh and to develop a religion, Judaism, that could exist outside of Judea. They were liberated by the Persian king Cyrus the Great in 539 B.C.E.

Hellenistic art The art of the Hellenistic period bridged the tastes, ideals, and customs of classical Greece and those that would be more characteristic of Rome. The Romans strove to emulate Hellenistic city planning and civic culture and thereby exported Hellenistic culture to their own far-flung colonies in western Europe.

Hellenistic culture The "Greek-like" culture that dominated the ancient world in the wake of Alexander's conquests.

Hellenistic kingdoms Following the death of Alexander the Great, his vast empire was divided into three separate states: Ptolemaic Egypt (under the rule of the general Ptolemy and his successors), Seleucid Asia (ruled by the general Seleucus and his heirs) and Antigonid Greece (governed by Antigonus of Macedonia). Each state maintained its independence, but the shared characteristics of Greco-Macedonian rule and a shared Greek culture and heritage bound them together in a united cosmopolitan world.

Hellenistic world The various Western civilizations of antiquity that were loosely united by shared Greek language and culture, especially around the eastern Mediterranean.

Heloise (c. 1090–1164) One of the foremost scholars of her time, she became the pupil and the wife of the philosopher and teacher Peter Abelard. In later life, she was the founder of a new religious order for women.

Henry IV of Germany King of Germany and Holy Roman Emperor from 1056—when he ascended the throne at the age of six years old—until his death in 1106. Henry'ss reign was first weakened by conflict with the Saxon nobility and later marked by the Investiture Controversy with Pope Gregory VII.

Henry VIII (1491–1547) King of England from 1509 until his death, Henry rejected the authority of the Roman Church in 1534 when the pope refused to annul his marriage to his queen, Catherine of Aragon; he became the founder of the Church of England.

Henry of Navarre (1553–1610) Crowned King Henry IV of France, he renounced his Protestantism but granted limited toleration for Huguenots (French Protestants) by the Edict of Nantes in 1598.

Prince Henry the Navigator (1394–1460) A member of the Portuguese royal family, Henry encouraged the exploration and conquest of western Africa and the trade in gold and slaves.

hieroglyphs The writing system of ancient Egypt, based on a complicated series of pictorial symbols. It fell out of use when Egypt was absorbed into the Roman Empire and was only deciphered after the discovery of the Rosetta Stone in the early nineteenth century.

Hildegard of Bingen (1098–1179) A powerful abbess, theologian, scientist, musician, and visionary who claimed to receive regular revelations from God. Although highly influential in her own day, she was never officially canonized by the Church, in part because her strong personality no longer matched the changing ideal of female piety.

Hiroshima Japanese port devastated by an atomic bomb on August 6, 1945.

Adolf Hitler (1889–1945) The author of *Mein Kampf* and leader of the Nazis who became chancellor of Germany in 1933. Hitler and his Nazi regime started the Second World War and orchestrated the systematic murder of over 5 million Jews.

Hitler-Stalin Pact (1939) Treaty between Stalin and Hitler, which promised Stalin a share of Poland, Finland, the Baltic States, and Bessarabia in the event of a German invasion of Poland, which began shortly thereafter, on September 1, 1939.

HIV epidemic The first cases of HIV-AIDS appeared in the late 1970s. As HIV-AIDS became a global crisis, international organizations recognized the need for an early, swift, and comprehensive response to future outbreaks of disease.

Thomas Hobbes (1588–1679) English political philosopher whose *Leviathan* argued that any form of government capable of protecting its subjects' lives and property might act as an all-powerful sovereign. This government should be allowed to trample over both liberty and property for the sake of its own survival and that of his subjects. For in his natural state, Hobbes argued, man was like "a wolf" toward other men.

Holy Roman Empire The loosely allied collection of lands in central and western Europe ruled by the kings of Germany (and later Austria) from the twelfth century until 1806. Its origins are usually identified with the empire of Charlemagne, the Frankish king who was crowned emperor of Rome by the pope in 800.

homage A ceremony in which an individual becomes the "man" (French: *homme*) of a lord.

Homer (fl. eighth century B.C.E.) A Greek rhapsode ("weaver" of stories) credited with merging centuries of poetic tradition in the epics known as the *Iliad* and the *Odyssey.*

hoplite A Greek foot-soldier armed with a spear or short sword and protected by a large round shield (*hoplon*). In battle, hoplites stood shoulder to shoulder in a close formation called a phalanx.

Huguenots French Protestants who endured severe persecution in the sixteenth and seventeenth centuries.

humanism A program of study associated with the movement known as the Renaissance, humanism aimed to replace the scholastic emphasis on logic and philosophy with the study of ancient languages, literature, history, and ethics.

human rights The belief that all people have the right to legal equality, freedom of religion and speech, and the right to participate in government. Human rights laws prohibit torture, cruel punishment, and slavery.

David Hume (1711–1776) Scottish writer who applied Newton's method of scientific inquiry and skepticism to the study of morality, the mind, and government.

Hundred Years' War (1337–1453) A series of wars between England and France, fought mostly on French soil and prompted by the territorial and political claims of English monarchs.

Jan Hus (c. 1373–1415) A Czech reformer who adopted many of the teachings of the English theologian John Wycliffe, and who also demanded that the laity be allowed to receive both the consecrated bread and wine of the Eucharist. The Council of Constance burned him at the stake for heresy. In response, his supporters, the Hussites, revolted against the Church.

Saddam Hussein (1937–2006) The former dictator of Iraq who invaded Iran in 1980 and started the eight-year-long Iran-Iraq War; invaded Kuwait in 1990, which led to the Gulf War of 1991; and was overthrown when the United States invaded Iraq in 2003. Involved in Iraqi politics since the mid-1960s, Hussein became the official head of state in 1979.

Iconoclast Controversy (717–787) A serious and often violent theological debate that raged in Byzantium after Emperor Leo III ordered the destruction of religious art on the grounds that any image representing a divine or holy personage is prone to promote idol worship and blasphemy. Iconoclast means "breaker of icons." Those who supported the veneration of icons were called iconodules, "adherents of icons."

Il-khanate Mongol-founded dynasty in thirteenth-century Persia.

Indian National Congress Formed in 1885, this Indian political party worked to achieve Indian independence from British colonial control. The Congress was led by Ghandi in the 1920s and 1930s.

Indian Rebellion of 1857 The uprising began near Delhi, when the military disciplined a regiment of Indian soldiers employed by the British for refusing to use rifle cartridges greased with pork fat—unacceptable to either Hindus or Muslims. Rebels attacked law courts and burned tax rolls, protesting debt and corruption. The mutiny spread through large areas of northwest India before being violently suppressed by British troops.

Indo-Europeans A group of people speaking variations of the same language who moved into the Near East and Mediterranean region shortly after 2000 B.C.E.

indulgences Grants exempting Catholic Christians from the performance of penance, either in life or after death. The abusive trade in indulgences was a major catalyst of the Protestant Reformation.

Incas The highly centralized South American empire that was toppled by the Spanish conquistador Francisco Pizarro in 1533.

Innocent III (1160/61–1216) As pope, he wanted to unify all of Christendom under papal hegemony. He furthered this goal at the Fourth Lateran Council of 1215, which defined one of the Church's dogmas as the acknowledgment of papal supremacy. The council also took an unprecedented interest in the religious education and habits of every Christian.

Inquisition Tribunal of the Roman Church that aims to enforce religious orthodoxy and conformity.

International Monetary Fund (IMF) Established in 1945 to ensure international cooperation regarding currency exchange and monetary policy, the IMF is a specialized agency of the United Nations.

Investiture Conflict The name given to a series of debates over the limitations of spiritual and secular power in Europe during the eleventh and early twelfth century, it came to a head when Pope Gregory VII and Emperor Henry IV of Germany both claimed the right to appoint and invest bishops with the regalia of office. After years of diplomatic and military hostility, it was partially settled by the Concordat of Worms in 1122.

Irish potato famine Period of agricultural blight from 1845 to 1849 whose devastating results produced widespread starvation and led to mass immigration to America.

Iron Curtain Term coined by Winston Churchill in 1946 to refer to the borders of Eastern European nations that lay within the zone of Soviet control.

Italian invasion of Ethiopia (1896) Italy invaded Ethiopia, which was the last major independent African kingdom. Menelik II, the Ethiopian emperor, soundly defeated them.

Ivan the Great (1440–1505) Russian ruler who annexed neighboring territories and consolidated his empire's position as a European power.

Jacobins Radical French political group during the French Revolution that took power after 1792, executed the French king, and sought to remake French culture.

Jacquerie Violent 1358 peasant uprising in northern France, incited by disease, war, and taxes.

James I (1566–1625) Monarch who ruled Scotland as James VI, and who succeeded Elizabeth I as king of England in 1603. He oversaw the English vernacular translation of the Bible known by his name.

James II of England King of England, Ireland, and Scotland from 1685–88 whose commitment to absolutism and Catholic zealotry led to his exile to France in the Glorious Revolution of 1688.

Janissaries Corps of enslaved soldiers recruited as children from the Christian provinces of the Ottoman Empire and brought up to display intense personal loyalty to the Ottoman sultan, who used these forces to curb local autonomy and as his personal bodyguards.

Jerome (c. 340–420) One of the early "fathers" of the Church, he translated the Bible from Hebrew and Greek into a popular form of Latin—hence the name by which this translation is known: the Vulgate, or "vulgar" (popular), Bible.

Jesuits The religious order formally known as the Society of Jesus, founded in 1540 by Ignatius Loyola to combat the spread of Protestantism. The Jesuits would become active in politics, education, and missionary work.

Jesus (c. 4 B.C.E.–c. 30 C.E.) A Jewish preacher and teacher in the rural areas of Galilee and Judea who was arrested for seditious political activity, tried, and crucified by the Romans. After his execution, his followers claimed that he had been resurrected from the dead and taken up into heaven. They began to teach that Jesus had been the divine representative of God, the Messiah foretold by ancient Hebrew prophets, and that he had suffered for the sins of humanity and would return to judge all the world's inhabitants at the end of time.

Joan of Arc (c. 1412–1431) A peasant girl from the province of Lorraine who claimed to have been commanded by God to lead French forces against the English occupying army during the Hundred Years' War. Successful in her efforts, she was betrayed by the French king and handed over to the English, who condemned her to death for heresy. Her reputation underwent a process of rehabilitation, but she was not officially canonized as a saint until 1920.

Judaism The religion of the Hebrews as it developed in the centuries after the establishment of the Hebrew kingdoms under David and Solomon, especially during the period of Babylonian Captivity.

Justinian (527–565) Emperor of Rome who unsuccessfully attempted to reunite the eastern and western portions of the empire. Also known for his important codification of Roman law, in the *Corpus Juris Civilis*.

Justinian's Code of Roman Law Formally known as the *Corpus Juris Civilis* or "body of civil law," this compendium consisted of a systematic compilation of imperial statutes, the writings of Rome's great legal authorities, a textbook of legal principles, and the legislation of Justinian and his immediate successors. As the most authoritative collection of Roman law, it formed the basis of canon law (the legal system of the Roman Church) and became essential to the developing legal traditions of every European state as well as of many countries around the world.

Das Kapital (Capital) The 1867 book by Karl Marx that outlined the theory behind historical materialism and attacked the socioeconomic inequities of capitalism.

Johannes Kepler (1571–1630) Mathematician and astronomer who elaborated on and corrected Copernicus's theory and is chiefly remembered for his discovery of the three laws of planetary motion that bear his name.

Keynesian Revolution Postdepression economic ideas developed by the British economist John Maynard Keynes, wherein the state took a greater role in managing the economy, stimulating it by increasing the money supply and creating jobs.

KGB Soviet political police and spy agency, first formed as the Cheka not long after the Bolshevik coup in October 1917. It grew to more than 750,000 operatives with military rank by the 1980s.

Genghis Khan (c. 1167–1227) "Oceanic Ruler," the title adopted by the Mongol chieftain Temujin, founder of a dynasty that conquered much of southern Asia.

Khanate The major political unit of the vast Mongol Empire. There were four Khanates, including the Yuan Empire in China, forged by Chingiz Khan's grandson Kubilai in the thirteenth century.

Ruhollah Khomeini (1902–1989) Iranian Shi'ite religious leader who led the revolution in Iran after the abdication of the shah in 1979. His government allowed some limited economic and political populism combined with strict constructions of Islamic law, restrictions on women's public life, and the prohibition of ideas or activities linked to Western influence.

Nikita Khrushchev (1894–1971) Leader of the Soviet Union during the Cuban missile crisis, Khrushchev came to power after Stalin's death in 1953. His reforms and criticisms of the excesses of the Stalin regime led to his fall from power in 1964.

Kremlin Once synonymous with the Soviet government, it refers to Moscow's walled city center and the palace originally built by Ivan the Great.

Kristallnacht Organized attack by Nazis and their supporters on the Jews of Germany following the assassination of a German embassy official by a Jewish man in Paris. Throughout Germany, thousands of stores, schools, cemeteries and synagogues were attacked on November 9, 1938. Dozens of people were killed, and tens of thousands of Jews were arrested and held in camps, where many were tortured and killed in the ensuing months.

Labour party Founded in Britain in 1900, this party represented workers and was based on socialist principles.

Latin West After the founding of Constantinople, the western Latin-speaking half of the Roman Empire became poorer and more peripheral, but it also fostered the emergence of new barbarian kingdoms. At the same time, the Roman pope claimed to have inherited both the authority of Jesus and the essential elements of Roman imperial authority.

League of Nations International organization founded after the First World War to solve international disputes through arbitration; it was dissolved in 1946 and its assets were transferred to the United Nations.

Leonardo da Vinci (1452–1519) Florentine inventor, sculptor, architect, and painter whose breadth of interests typifies the ideal of "the Renaissance man."

Vladimir Lenin (1870–1924) Leader of the Bolshevik Revolution in Russia (1917) and the first leader of the Soviet Union.

Leviathan A book by Thomas Hobbes (1588–1679) that recommended a ruler have unrestricted power.

liberalism Political and social theory that judges the effectiveness of a government in terms of its ability to protect individual rights. Liberals support representative forms of government, free trade, and freedom of speech and religion. In the economic realm, liberals believe that individuals should be free to engage in commercial or business activities without interference from the state or their community.

lithograph Art form that involves putting writing or design on stone and producing printed impressions.

John Locke (1632–1704) English philosopher and political theorist known for his contributions to liberalism. Locke had great faith in human reason and believed that just societies were those that infringed the least on the natural rights and freedoms of individuals. This led him to assert that a government's legitimacy depended on the consent of the governed, a view that had a profound effect on the authors of the United States' Declaration of Independence.

Louis IX of France King of France from 1226 to his death on Crusade in 1270, Louis was famous for his piety and for his close attention to the administration of law and justice in his realm. He was officially canonized as Saint Louis in 1297.

Louis XIV (1638–1715) Called the "Sun King," he was known for his success at strengthening the institutions of the French absolutist state.

Louis XVI (1754–1793) Well-meaning but ineffectual king of France, finally deposed and executed during the French Revolution.

Ignatius Loyola (1491–1556) Founder of the Society of Jesus (commonly known as the Jesuits), whose members vowed to serve God through poverty, chastity, and missionary work. He abandoned his first career as a mercenary after reading an account of Christ's life written in his native Spanish.

Lucretia According to Roman legend, Lucretia was a virtuous Roman wife who was raped by the son of Rome's last king and who virtuously committed suicide in order to avoid bringing shame on her family.

Luftwaffe Literally "air weapon," this is the name of the German air force, which was founded during the First World War, disbanded in 1945, and reestablished when West Germany joined NATO in 1950.

Lusitania The British passenger liner that was sunk by a German U-boat (submarine) on May 7, 1915. Public outrage over the sinking contibuted to the U.S. decision to enter the First World War.

Martin Luther (1483–1546) A German monk and professor of theology whose critique of the papacy launched the Protestant Reformation.

ma'at The Egyptian term for the serene order of the universe, with which the individual soul (*ka*) must remain in harmony. The power of the pharaoh was linked to *ma'at*, insofar as it ensured the prosperity of the kingdom. After the upheavals of the First Intermediate Period, the perception of the pharaoh's relationship with ma'at was revealed to be conditional, something that had to be earned.

Niccolò Machiavelli (1469–1527) As the author of *The Prince* and the *Discourses on Livy*, he looked to the Roman past for paradigms of greatness while at the same time hoping to win the patronage of contemporary rulers who would restore Italy's political independence.

Magna Carta The "Great Charter" of 1215, enacted during the reign of King John of England and designed to limit his powers. Regarded now as a landmark in the development of constitutional government. In its own time, its purpose was to restore the power of great lords.

Magyar nationalism Lajos Kossuth led this national movement in the Hungarian region of the Habsburg Empire, calling for national independence for Hungary in 1848. With the support of Russia, the Habsburg army crushed the movement and all other revolutionary activities in the empire. Kossuth fled into exile.

Moses Maimonides (c. 1137–1204) Jewish scholar, physician, and scriptural commentator whose *Mishneh Torah* is a fundamental exposition of Jewish law.

Thomas Malthus (1766–1834) British political economist who believed that populations inevitably grew faster than the available food supply. Societies that could not control their population growth would be checked only by famine, disease, poverty, and infant malnutrition. He argued that governments could not alleviate poverty. Instead, the poor had to exercise "moral restraint," postpone marriage, and have fewer children.

Nelson Mandela (b. 1918) The South African opponent of apartheid who led the African National Congress and was imprisoned from 1962 until 1990. After his release from prison, he worked with Prime Minister Frederik Willem De Klerk to establish majority rule. Mandela became the first black president of South Africa in 1994.

Manhattan Project The secret U.S. government research project to develop the first nuclear bomb. The vast project involved dozens of sites across the United States, including New Mexico, Tennessee, Illinois, California, Utah, and Washington. The first test of a nuclear bomb was near Alamogordo, New Mexico on July 16, 1945.

manors Common farmland worked collectively by the inhabitants of entire villages, sometimes on their own initiative, sometimes at the behest of a lord.

Mao Zedong (1893–1976) The leader of the Chinese Revolution who defeated the Nationalists in 1949 and established the Communist regime in China.

Marne A major battle of the First World War in September 1914, which halted the German invasion of France and led to protracted trench warfare on the Western Front.

Marshall Plan Economic aid package given to Europe by the United States after the Second World War to promote reconstruction and economic development and to secure the countries from a feared communist takeover.

Karl Marx (1818–1883) German philosopher and economist who believed that a revolution of the working classes would overthrow the capitalist order and create a classless society. Author of *Das Kapital* and *The Communist Manifesto*.

Marxists Followers of the socialist political economist Karl Marx who called for workers everywhere to unite and create an independent political force. Marxists believed that industrialization produced an inevitable struggle between laborers and the class of capitalist property owners, and that this struggle would culminate in a revolution that would abolish private property and establish a society committed to social equality.

Mary See **cult of the Virgin**.

Mary I (1516–1558) Catholic daughter of Henry VIII and his first wife, Catherine of Aragon, Mary Tudor was the first queen regnant of England. Her attempts to reinstitute Catholicism in England met with limited success, and after her early death she was labeled "Bloody Mary" by the Protestant supporters of her half sister and successor, Elizabeth I.

mass culture The spread of literacy and public education in the nineteenth century created a new audience for print entertainment and a new class of entrepreneurs in the media to cater to this audience. The invention of radio, film, and television in the twentieth century carried this development to another level, as millions of consumers were now accessible to the producers of news, information, and entertainment. The rise of this "mass culture" has been celebrated as an expression of popular tastes but also criticized as a vehicle for the manipulation of populations through clever and seductive propaganda.

Mayans Native American peoples whose culturally and politically sophisticated empire encompassed lands in present-day Mexico and Guatemala.

Giuseppe Mazzini (1805–1872) Founder of Young Italy and an ideological leader of the Italian nationalist movement.

Mecca Center of an important commercial network of the Arabian Peninsula and birthplace of the prophet Muhammad. It is now considered the holiest site in the Islamic world.

Medici A powerful dynasty of Florentine bankers and politicians whose ancestors were originally apothecaries ("medics").

Meiji Empire Empire created under the leadership of Mutsuhito, emperor of Japan from 1868 until 1912. During the Meiji period Japan became a world industrial and naval power.

Mensheviks Within the Russian Social Democratic Party, the Mensheviks advocated slow changes and a gradual move toward socialism, in contrast with the Bolsheviks, who wanted to push for a proletarian revolution. Mensheviks believed that a proletarian revolution in Russia was premature and that the country needed to complete its capitalist development first.

mercantilism A theory and policy for directing the economy of monarchical states between 1600 and 1800 based on the assumption that wealth and power depended on a favorable balance of trade (more exports and fewer imports) and the accumulation of precious metals. Mercantilists advocated forms of economic protectionism to promote domestic production.

Maria Sybilla Merian (1647–1717) A scientific illustrator and an important early entomologist. She conducted research on two continents and published the well-received *Metamorphosis of the Insects of Surinam*.

Merovingian A Frankish dynasty that claimed descent from a legendary ancestor called Merovic, the Merovingians were the only powerful family to establish a lasting kingdom in western Europe during the fifth and sixth centuries.

Mesopotamia The "land between the Tigris and the Euphrates rivers," Tigris and Euphrates where the civilization of Sumer, the first urban society, flourished.

Klemens von Metternich (1773–1859) Austrian foreign minister whose primary goals were to bolster the legitimacy of monarchies and, after the defeat of Napoleon, to prevent another large-scale war in Europe. At the Congress of Vienna, he opposed social and political change and wanted to check Russian and French expansion.

Michelangelo Buonarroti (1475–1564) A virtuoso Florentine sculptor, painter, and poet who spent much of his career in the service of the papacy. He is best known for the decoration of the Sistine Chapel and for his monumental sculptures.

Middle Kingdom of Egypt (2055–1650 B.C.E.) The period following the First Intermediate Period of dynastic warfare, which ended with the reassertion of pharonic rule under Mentuhotep II.

Miletus A Greek polis and Persian colony on the Ionian coast of Asia Minor. Influenced by the cultures of Mesopotamia, Egypt, and Lydia, it produced several of the ancient world's first scientists and sophists. Thereafter, a political conflict between the ruler of Miletus, Aristagoras, and the Persian Emperor, Darius, sparked the Persian Wars with Greece.

John Stuart Mill (1806–1873) English liberal philosopher whose faith in human reason led him to support a broad variety of civic and political freedoms for men and women, including the right to vote and the right to free speech.

Slobodan Milosevic (1941–2006) The Serbian nationalist politician who became president of Serbia and whose policies during the Balkan wars of the early 1990s led to the deaths of thousands of Croatians, Bosnian Muslims, Albanians, and Kosovars. After leaving office in 2000, he was arrested and tried for war crimes at the International Court in The Hague. The trial ended before a verdict with his death in 2006.

Minoan Crete A sea empire based at Knossos on the Greek island of Crete and named for the legendary King Minos. The Minoans dominated the Aegean for much of the second millennium B.C.E.

Modernism There were several different modernist movements in art and literature, but they shared three key characteristics. First, they had a sense that the world had radically changed and that this change should be embraced. Second, they believed that traditional aesthetic values and assumptions about creativity were ill-suited to the present. Third, they developed a new conception of what art could do that emphasized expression over representation and insisted on the value of novelty, experimentation, and creative freedom.

Mongols A nomadic people from the steppes of Central Asia who were united under the ruler Genghis Khan. His conquest of China was continued by his grandson Kubilai and his great-grandson son Ogedei, whose army also seized southern Russia and then moved through Hungary and through Poland toward eastern Germany. The Mongol armies withdrew from eastern Europe after the death of Ogedei, but his descendants continued to rule his vast empire for another half century.

Michel de Montaigne (1533–1592) French philosopher and social commentator, best known for his *Essays*.

Montesquieu (1689–1755) An Enlightenment philosophe whose most influential work was *The Spirit of Laws*. In this work, he analyzed the structures that shaped law and categorized governments into three types: republics, monarchies, and despotisms. His ideas about the separation of powers among the executive, the legislative, and the judicial branches of government influenced the authors of the U.S. Constitution.

Thomas More (1478–1535) Christian humanist, English statesman, and author of *Utopia*. In 1529, he was appointed lord chancellor of England but resigned because he opposed King Henry VIII's plans to establish a national church under royal control. He was eventually executed for refusing to take an oath acknowledging Henry to be the head of the Church of England and has since been canonized by the Catholic Church.

mos maiorum Literally translated as "the code of the elders" or "the custom of ancestors." This unwritten code governed the lives of Romans under the Republic and stressed the importance of showing reverence to ancestral tradition. It was sacrosanct and essential to Roman identity, and an important influence on Roman culture, law, and religion.

Wolfgang Amadeus Mozart (1756–1791) Austrian composer, famous at a young age as a concert musician and later celebrated as a prolific composer of instrumental music and operas that are seen as the apogee of the Classical style in music.

Muhammad (570–632 C.E.) The founder of Islam, regarded as God's last and greatest prophet by his followers.

Munich Conference (1938) Hitler met with the leaders of Britain, France, and Italy and negotiated an agreement that gave Germany a major slice of Czechoslovakia. British prime minister Chamberlain believed that the agreement would bring peace to Europe. Instead, Germany invaded and seized the rest of Czechoslovakia.

Muscovy The duchy centered on Moscow whose dukes saw themselves as heirs to the Roman Empire. In the early fourteenth century, Moscow was under the control of the Mongol Khanate. After the collapse of the Khanate, the Muscovite grand duke, Ivan III, conquered all the Russian principalities between Moscow and the border of Poland-Lithuania, and then Lithuania itself. By the time of his death, Ivan had established Muscovy as a dominant power.

Muslim learning and culture The Crusades brought the Latin West in contact with the Islamic world, which impacted European culture in myriad ways. Europeans adapted Arabic numerals and mathematical concepts as well as Arabic and Persian words. Through Arabic translations, Western scholars gained access to Greek learning, which had a profound influence on Christian theology. European scholars also learned from the Islamic world's accomplishments in medicine and science.

Benito Mussolini (1883–1945) The Italian founder of the Fascist party who came to power in Italy in 1922 and allied himself with Hitler and the Nazis during the Second World War.

Mycenaean Greece (1600–1200 B.C.E.) The term used to describe the civilization of Greece in the late Bronze Age, when territorial kingdoms like Mycenae formed around a king, a warrior caste, and a palace bureaucracy.

Nagasaki Second Japanese city on which the United States dropped an atomic bomb. The attack took place on August 9, 1945; the Japanese surrendered shortly thereafter, ending the Second World War.

Napoleon III (1808–1873) Nephew of Napoleon Bonaparte, Napoleon III was elected president of the French Second Republic in 1848 and made himself emperor of France in 1852. During his reign (1852–70), he rebuilt the French capital of Paris. Defeated in the France-Prussian War of 1870, he went into exile.

Napoleonic Code Legal code drafted by Napoleon in 1804 and based on Justinian's *Corpus Iuris Civilis*. It distilled different legal traditions to create one uniform law. The code confirmed the abolition of feudal privileges of all kinds and set the conditions for exercising property rights.

Napoleon's military campaigns In 1805, the Russians, Prussians, Austrians, Swedes, and British attempted to contain Napoleon, but he defeated them. Out of his victories, Napoleon created a new empire and affiliated states. In 1808, he invaded Spain, but fierce resistance prevented Napoleon from achieving a complete victory. In 1812, Napoleon invaded Russia, and his army was decimated as it retreated from Moscow during the winter. After the Russian campaign, the united European powers defeated Napoleon and forced him into exile. He escaped and reassumed command of his army, but the European powers defeated him for the final time at the Battle of Waterloo.

Gamal Abdel Nasser (1918–1970) Former president of Egypt and the most prominent spokesman for secular pan-Arabism. He became a target for Islamist critics, such as Sayyid Qutb and the Muslim Brotherhood, angered by the Western-influenced policies of his regime.

National Assembly of France Governing body of France that succeeded the Estates General in 1789 during the French Revolution. It was composed of, and defined by, the delegates of the Third Estate.

National Association for the Advancement of Colored People (NAACP) Founded in 1910, this U.S. civil rights organization was dedicated to ending inequality and segregation for black Americans.

National Convention The governing body of France from September 1792 to October 1795. It declared France a republic and then tried and executed the French king. The Convention also confiscated the property of the enemies of the revolution, instituted a policy of de-Christianization, changed marriage and inheritance laws, abolished slavery in its colonies, placed a cap on the price of necessities, and ended the compensation of nobles for their lost privileges.

nationalism Movement to unify a country under one government based on perceptions of the population's common history, customs, and social traditions.

nationalism in Yugoslavia In the 1990s, Slobodan Milosevic and his allies reignited Serbian nationalism in the former Yugoslavia, which led non-Serb republics in Croatia and Slovenia to seek independence. The country erupted into war, with the worst violence taking place in Bosnia, a multi-ethnic region with Serb, Croatian and Bosnian Muslim populations. European diplomats proved powerless to stop attempts by Croatian and Serbian military and paramilitary forces to claim territory through ethnic cleansing and violent intimidation. Atrocities were committed on all sides, but pro-Serb forces were responsible for the most deaths.

NATO The North Atlantic Treaty Organization, a 1949 military agreement among the United States, Canada, Great Britain, and eight Western European nations, which declared that an armed attack against any one of the members would be regarded as an attack against all. Created during the Cold War in the face of the Soviet Union's control of Eastern Europe, NATO continues to exist today and the membership of twenty-eight states includes former members of the Warsaw Pact as well as Albania and Turkey.

Nazi party Founded in the early 1920s, the National Socialist German Workers' Party (NSDAP) gained control over Germany under the leadership of Adolf Hitler in 1933 and continued in power until Germany was defeated in 1945.

Nazism The political movement in Germany led by Adolf Hitler, which advocated a violent anti-Semitic, anti-Marxist, pan-German ideology.

Neo-Assyrian Empire (883–859 B.C.E.–612–605 B.C.E.) Assurnasirpal II laid the foundations of the Neo-Assyrian Empire through military campaigns against neighboring peoples. Eventually, the empire stretched from the Mediterranean Sea to western Iran. A military dictatorship governed the empire through its army, which it used to frighten and oppress both its subjects and its enemies. The empire's ideology was based on waging holy war in the name of its principal god, Assur, and the exaction of tribute through terror.

Neoliberalism Neoliberals believe that free markets, profit incentives, and restraints on both budget deficits and social welfare programs are the best guarantee of individual liberties. Beginning in the 1980s, neoliberal theory was used to structure the policy of financial institutions like the International Monetary Fund and the World Bank, which turned away from interventionist policies in favor of market-driven models of economic development.

Neolithic Revolution The "New" Stone Age, which began around 11,000 B.C.E., saw new technological and social developments, including managed food production, the beginnings of permanent settlements, and the rapid intensification of trade.

Neoplatonism A school of thought based on the teachings of Plato and prevalent in the Roman Empire, which had a profound effect on the formation of Christian theology. Neoplatonists argued that nature is a book written by its creator to reveal the ways of God to humanity. Convinced that God's perfection must be reflected in nature, neoplatonists searched for the ideal and perfect structures that they believed must lie behind the "shadows" of the everyday world.

New Deal President Franklin Delano Roosevelt's package of government reforms that were enacted during the depression of the 1930s to provide jobs for the unemployed, social welfare programs for the poor, and security to the financial markets.

New Economic Policy In 1921, the Bolsheviks abandoned war communism in favor of the New Economic Policy (NEP). Under NEP, the state still controlled all major industry and financial concerns, while individuals could own private property, trade freely within limits, and farm their own land for their own benefit. Fixed taxes replaced grain requisition. The policy successfully helped Soviet agriculture recover from the civil war but was later abandoned in favor of collectivization.

Isaac Newton (1642–1727) One of the foremost scientists of all time, Newton was an English mathematician and physicist; he is noted for his development of calculus, work on the properties of light, and theory of gravitation.

Tsar Nicholas II (1868–1918) The last Russian tsar, who abdicated the throne in 1917. He and his family were executed by the Bolsheviks on July 17, 1918.

Friedrich Nietzsche (1844–1900) The German philosopher who denied the possibility of knowing absolute "truth" or "reality," since all knowledge comes filtered through linguistic, scientific, or artistic systems of representation. He also criticized Judeo-Christian morality for instilling a repressive conformity that drained civilization of its vitality.

nongovernmental organizations (NGOs) Private organizations like the Red Cross that play a large role in international affairs.

Novum Organum Work by English statesman and scientist Francis Bacon (1561–1626) that advanced a philosophy of study through observation.

October Days (1789) The high price of bread and the rumor that the king was unwilling to cooperate with the assembly caused the women who worked in Paris's large central market to march to Versailles along with their supporters to address the king. Not satisfied with their initial reception, they broke through the palace gates and called for the king to return to Paris from Versailles, which he did the following day.

Old Kingdom of Egypt (c. 2686–2160 B.C.E.) During this time, the pharaohs controlled a powerful and centralized bureaucratic state whose vast human and material resources are exemplified by the pyramids of Giza. This period came to an end as the pharaoh's authority collapsed, leading to a period of dynastic warfare and localized rule.

OPEC (Organization of the Petroleum Exporting Countries) Organization created in 1960 by oil-producing countries in the Middle East, South America, and Africa to regulate the production and pricing of crude oil.

Operation Barbarossa The codename for Hitler's invasion of the Soviet Union in 1941.

Opium Wars (1839–1842) War fought between the British and Qing China to protect British trade in opium; resulted in the ceding of Hong Kong to the British.

Oracle at Delphi The most important shrine in ancient Greece. The priestess of Apollo who attended the shrine was believed to have the power to predict the future.

Ottoman Empire (c.1300–1923) During the thirteenth century, the Ottoman dynasty established itself as leader of the Turks. From the fourteenth to sixteenth centuries, they conquered Anatolia, Armenia, Syria, and North Africa as well as parts of southeastern Europe, the Crimea, and areas along the Red Sea. Portions of the Ottoman Empire persisted up to the time of the First World War, but it was dismantled in the years following it.

Reza Pahlavi (1919–1980) The Western-friendly shah of Iran who was installed during a 1953 coup supported by Britain and the United States. After a lengthy economic downturn, public unrest, and personal illness, he retired from public life under popular pressure in 1979.

Pan-African Conference 1900 assembly in London that sought to draw attention to the sovereignty of African people and their mistreatment by colonial powers.

Panhellenism The "all Greek" culture that allowed ancient Greek colonies to maintain a connection to their homeland and to each other through their shared language and heritage. These colonies also exported their culture into new areas and created new Greek-speaking enclaves, which permanently changed the cultural geography of the Mediterranean world.

pan-Slavism Cultural movement that sought to unite native Slavic peoples within the Russian and Habsburg Empires under Russian leadership.

Partition of India (1947) At independence, British India was partitioned into the nations of India and Pakistan. The majority of the population in India was Hindu and the majority of the population in Pakistan was Muslim. The process of partition brought brutal religious and ethnic warfare. More than 1 million Hindus and Muslims died and 12 million became refugees.

Blaise Pascal (1623–1662) A Catholic philosopher who wanted to establish the truth of Christianity by appealing simultaneously to intellect and emotion. In his *Pensées*, he argued that faith alone can resolve the world's contradictions and that his own awe in the face of evil and uncertainty must be evidence of God's existence.

Paul of Tarsus Originally known as Saul, Paul was a Greek-speaking Jew and Roman citizen who underwent a miraculous conversion experience and became the most important proponent of Christianity in the 50s and 60s C.E.

Pax Romana (27 B.C.E.–180 C.E.) Literally translated as "the Roman Peace." During this time, the Roman world enjoyed an unprecedented period of peace and political stability.

Peace of Augsburg A settlement negotiated in 1555 among factions within the Holy Roman Empire, it formulated the principle *cuius regio, eius religio,* "he who rules, his religion": meaning that the inhabitants of any given territory should follow the religion of its ruler, whether Catholic or Protestant.

Peace of Paris The 1919 Paris Peace Conference established the terms to end the First World War. Great Britain, France, Italy, and the United States signed five treaties with each of the defeated nations: Germany, Austria, Hungary, Turkey, and Bulgaria. The settlement is notable for the territory that Germany had to give up, including large parts of Prussia to the new state of Poland, and Alsace and Lorraine to France; the disarming of Germany; and the "war guilt" provision, which required Germany and its allies to pay massive reparations to the victors.

Peace of Westphalia (1648) An agreement reached at the end of the Thirty Years' War that altered the political map of Europe. France emerged as the predominant power on the Continent, while the Austrian Habsburgs had to surrender all the territories they had gained and could no longer use the office of the Holy Roman Emperor to dominate central Europe. Spain was marginalized and Germany became a volatile combination of Protestant and Catholic principalities.

Pearl Harbor The American naval base in Hawaii that was bombed by the Japanese on December 7, 1941, bringing the United States into the Second World War.

peasantry Term used in continental Europe to refer to rural populations that lived from agriculture. Some peasants were free and could own land. Serfs were peasants who were legally bound to the land and subject to the authority of the local lord.

Peloponnesian War The name given to the series of wars fought between Sparta (on the Greek Peloponnesus) and Athens from 431 B.C.E. to 404 B.C.E., and which ended in the defeat of Athens and the loss of her imperial power.

perestroika Introduced by Soviet leader Mikhail Gorbachev in June 1987, *perestroika* was the name given to economic and political reforms begun earlier in his tenure. It restructured the state bureaucracy, reduced the privileges of the political elite, and instituted a shift from the centrally planned economy to a mixed economy, combining planning with the operation of market forces.

Periclean Athens Following his election as *strategos* in 461 B.C.E., Pericles pushed through political reforms in Athens, which gave poorer citizens greater influence in politics. He promoted Athenians' sense of superiority through ambitious public works projects and lavish festivals to honor the gods, thus ensuring his continual reelection. But eventually, Athens' growing arrogance and aggression alienated it from the rest of the Greek world.

Pericles (c. 495–429) Athenian politician who occupied the office of strategos for thirty years and who presided over a series of civic reforms, building campaigns, and imperialist initiatives.

Persian Empire Consolidated by Cyrus the Great in 559, this empire eventually stretched from the Persian Gulf to the Mediterranean and also encompassed Egypt. Persian rulers were able to hold this empire together through a policy of tolerance and a mixture of local and centralized governance. This imperial model of government would be adopted by many future empires.

Persian Wars (490–479 B.C.E.) In 501 B.C.E., a political conflict between the Greek ruler of Miletus, Aristagoras, and the Persian Emperor, Darius, sparked the first of the Persian Wars when Darius sent an army to punish Athens for its intervention on the side of the Greeks. Despite being heavily outnumbered, Athenian hoplites defeated the Persian army at the plain of Marathon. In 480 B.C.E., Darius's son Xerxes invaded Greece but was defeated at sea and on land by combined Greek forces under the leadership of Athens and Sparta.

Peter the Great (1672–1725) Energetic tsar who transformed Russia into a leading European country by centralizing government, modernizing the army, creating a navy, and reforming education and the economy.

Francesco Petrarca (Petrarch) (1304–1374) Italian scholar who revived interest in classical writing styles and was famed for his vernacular love sonnets.

pharaoh A term meaning "household" which became the title borne by the rulers of ancient Egypt. The pharaoh was regarded as the divine representative of the gods and the embodiment of Egypt itself. The powerful and centralized bureaucratic state ruled by the pharaohs was more stable and longlived than any another civilization in world history, lasting (with few interruptions) for approximately 3,000 years.

Pharisees A group of Jewish teachers and preachers who emerged in the third century B.C.E. They insisted that all of Yahweh's (God's) commandments were binding on all Jews.

Philip II (382–336 B.C.E.) King of Macedonia and father of Alexander, he consolidated the southern Balkans and the Greek city-states under Macedonian domination.

Philip II of Spain King of Spain from 1556–98 and briefly King of England and Ireland during his marriage to Queen Mary I of England. As a staunch Catholic, Philip responded with military might to the desecration of Catholic churches in the Spanish Netherlands in the 1560s. When commercial conflict with England escalated, Philip sent the Spanish Armada to conquer England in 1588, but it was largely destroyed by stormy weather.

Philip II Augustus (1165–1223) The first French ruler to use the title "king of France" rather than "king of the French." After he captured Normandy and its adjacent territories from the English, he built an effective system of local administration, which recognized regional diversity while promoting centralized royal control. This administrative pattern would characterize French government until the French Revolution.

Philip IV of France King of France from 1285 until his death, Philip's conflict with Pope Boniface VIII led to the transfer of the papal court to Avignon from 1309 to 1378.

Philistines Descendants of the Sea Peoples who fled to the region that now bears their name, Palestine, after their defeat at the hands of the pharaoh Ramses III. They dominated their neighbors, the Hebrews, who used writing as an effective means of discrediting them (the Philistines themselves did not leave a written record to contest the Hebrews' views).

philosophe During the Enlightenment, this word referred to a person whose reflections were unhampered by the constraints of religion or dogma.

Phoenicians A Semitic people known for their trade in exotic purple dyes and other luxury goods, they originally settled in present-day Lebanon around 1200 B.C.E. and from there established commercial colonies throughout the Mediterranean, notably Carthage.

Plato (429–349 B.C.E.) A student of Socrates, Plato dedicated his life to transmitting his teacher's legacy through the writing of dialogues on philosophical subjects, in which Socrates himself plays the major role. The longest and most famous of these, known as the *Republic*, describes an idealized polis governed by a superior group of individuals chosen for their natural attributes of intelligence and character, who rule as "philosopher-kings."

Plotinus (204–270 C.E.) A Neoplatonist philosopher who taught that everything in existence has its ultimate source in the divine, and that the highest goal of life should be the mystic reunion of the soul with this divine source, something that can be achieved through contemplation and asceticism. This outlook blended with that of early Christianity and was instrumental in the spread of that religion within the Roman Empire.

poleis One of the major political innovations of the ancient Greeks was the *polis*, or city-state (plural *poleis*). These independent social and political entities began to emerge in the ninth century B.C.E., organized around an urban center and fostering markets, meeting places, and religious worship; frequently, poleis also controlled some surrounding territory.

Marco Polo (1254–1324) Venetian merchant who traveled through Asia for twenty years and published his observations in a widely read memoir.

population growth In the nineteenth century, Europe experienced a dramatic population growth. During this period, the spread of rural manufacturing allowed men and women to begin marrying younger and raising families earlier, which increased the size of the average family. As the population grew, the portion of young and fertile people also increased, which reinforced the population growth. By 1900, population growth was strongest in Britain and Germany, and slower in France.

portolan charts Also known as *portolani*, these special charts were invented by medieval mariners during the fourteenth century and were used to map locations of ports and sea routes, while also taking note of prevailing winds and other conditions at sea.

Potsdam (1945) At this conference, Truman, Churchill and Stalin met to discuss their options at the conclusion of the Second World War, including making territorial changes to Germany and its allies and the question of war reparations.

Prague spring A period of political liberalization in Czechoslovakia between January and August 1968 that was initiated by Alexander Dubček, the Czech leader. This period of expanding freedom and openness in this Eastern bloc nation ended on August 20, when the USSR and Warsaw Pact countries invaded with 200,000 troops and 5,000 tanks.

pre-Socratics A group of philosophers in the Greek city of Miletus, who raised questions about humans' relationship with the natural world and the gods and who formulated rational theories to explain the physical universe they observed. Their name reflects the fact that they flourished prior to the lifetime of Socrates.

price revolution An unprecedented inflation in prices in the latter half of the sixteenth century, resulting in part from the enormous influx of silver bullion from Spanish America.

principate Modern term for the centuries of autocratic rule by the successors of Augustus, who seized power in 27 B.C.E. and styled himself *princeps* or Rome's "first man." See **Roman Republic**.

printing press Introduced in Europe by Johannes Gutenberg of Mainz in 1453–55, this new technology quickly revolutionized communication and played a significant role in political, religious, and intellectual revolutions.

Protestantism The name given to the many dissenting varieties of Christianity that emerged during the Reformation in sixteenth-century western Europe. While Protestant beliefs and practices differed widely, all were united in their rejection of papal authority and the dogmas of the Roman Catholic Church.

provisional government After the collapse of the Russian monarchy, leaders in the Duma organized this government and hoped to establish a democratic system under constitutional rule. They also refused to concede military defeat, and it was impossible to institute domestic reforms and fight a war at the same time. As conditions worsened, the Bolsheviks gained support. In October 1917, they attacked the provisional government and seized control.

Claudius Ptolomeus, called Ptolemy (c. 85–165 C.E.) A Greek-speaking geographer and astronomer active in Roman Alexandria, he rejected the findings of previous Hellenistic scientists in favor of the erroneous theories of Aristotle, publishing highly influential treatises that promulgated these errors and suppressed (for example) the accurate findings of Aristarchus (who had discovered the Heliocentric universe) and Erathosthenes (who had calculated the circumference of the earth).

Ptolemaic system Ptolemy of Alexandria promoted Aristotle's understanding of cosmology. In this system, the heavens orbit the earth in an organized hierarchy of spheres, and the earth and the heavens are made of different matter and subject to different laws of motion. A prime mover produces the motion of the celestial bodies.

Ptolemy (c. 367–c. 284 B.C.E.) One of Alexander the Great's trusted generals (and possibly his half brother), he became pharaoh of Egypt and founded a new dynasty that lasted until that kingdom's absorption into the Roman Empire in 30 B.C.E.

public sphere Between the official realm of state activities and the private realm of the household and individual, lies the "public sphere." The public sphere has a political dimension—it is the space of debate, discussion, and expressions of popular opinion. It also has an economic dimension—it is where business is conducted, where commercial transactions take place, where people enter into contracts, search for work, or hire employees.

Punic Wars (264–146 B.C.E.) Three periods of warfare between Rome and Carthage, two maritime empires who struggled for dominance of the Mediterranean. Rome emerged as the victor, destroyed the city of Carthage and took control of Sicily, North Africa and Hispania (Spain).

pyramid Constructed during the third millennium B.C.E., these structures were monuments to the power and divinity of the pharaohs entombed inside them.

Qur'an (often Koran) Islam's holy scriptures, comprised of the prophecies revealed to Muhammad and redacted during and after his death.

Raphael (Raffaelo Sanzio) (1483–1520) Italian painter active in Rome, his works include *The School of Athens*.

realism Artistic and literary style which sought to portray common situations as they would appear in reality.

Realpolitik Political strategy based on advancing power for its own sake.

reason The human capacity to solve problems and discover truth in ways that can be verified intellectually. Philosophers distinguish the knowledge gained from reason from the teachings of instinct, imagination, and faith, which are verified according to different criteria.

Reformation Religious and political movement in sixteenth-century Europe that led to a break between dissenting forms of Christianity and the Roman Catholic Church; notable figures include Martin Luther and John Calvin.

Reich A term for the German state. The First Reich corresponded to the Holy Roman Empire (9th c.–1806), the Second Reich was from 1871 to 1919, and the Third Reich lasted from 1933 through May 1945.

Renaissance From the French word meaning "rebirth," this term came to be used in the nineteenth century to describe the artistic, intellectual, and cultural movement that emerged in Italy after 1300 and that sought to recover and emulate the heritage of the classical past.

Restoration period (1815–1848) European movement after the defeat of Napoleon to restore Europe to its pre–French Revolution status and to prevent the spread of revolutionary or liberal political movements.

Cardinal Richelieu (1585–1642) First minister to King Louis XIII, he is considered by many to have ruled France in all but name, centralizing political power and suppressing dissent.

Roman army Under the Republic, the Roman army was made up of citizen-soldiers who were required to serve in wartime. As Rome's empire grew, the need for more fighting men led to the extension of citizenship rights and, eventually, to the development of a vast, professional, standing army that numbered as many as 300,000 by the middle of the third century B.C.E. By that time, however, citizens were not themselves required to serve, and many legions were made up of paid conscripts and foreign mercenaries.

Roman citizenship The rights and responsibilities of Rome's citizens were gradually extended to the free (male) inhabitants of other Italian provinces and later to most provinces in the Roman world. In contrast to slaves and non-Romans, Romans had the right to be tried in an imperial court and could not be legally subjected to torture.

Roman Republic The Romans traced the founding of their republic to the overthrow of their last king and the establishment of a unique form of constitutional government, in which the power of the aristocracy (embodied by the Senate) was checked by the executive rule of two elected consuls and the collective will of the people. For hundreds of years, this balance of power provided the Republic with a measure of political stability and prevented any single individual or clique from gaining too much power.

Romanticism Beginning in Germany and England in the late eighteenth century and continuing up to the end of the nineteenth century, Romanticism was a movement in art, music, and literature that countered the rationalism of the Enlightenment by placing greater value on human emotions and the power of nature to stimulate creativity.

Jean-Jacques Rousseau (1712–1778) Philosopher and radical political theorist whose *Social Contract* attacked privilege and inequality. One of the primary principles of Rousseau's political philosophy is that politics and morality should not be separated.

Royal Society This British society's goal was to pursue collective research. Members would conduct experiments, record the results, and share them with their peers, who would study the methods, reproduce the experiment, and assess the results. The arrangement gave English scientists a sense of common purpose as well as a system to reach a consensus on facts.

Russian Revolution of 1905 After Russia's defeat in the Russo-Japanese War, Russians began clamoring for political reforms. Protests grew over the course of 1905, and the autocracy lost control of entire towns and regions as workers went on strike, soldiers mutinied, and peasants revolted. Forced to yield, Tsar Nicholas II issued the October Manifesto, which pledged individual liberties and provided for the election of a parliament (called the Duma). The most radical of the revolutionary groups were put down with force, and the pace of political change remained very slow in the aftermath of the revolution.

Russo-Japanese War (1904–1905) Japanese and Russian expansion collided in Mongolia and Manchuria. Russia was humiliated after the Japanese navy sunk its fleet, which helped provoke a revolt in Russia and led to an American-brokered peace treaty.

sacrament A sacred rite. In the Catholic tradition, the administration of the sacraments is considered necessary for salvation.

Saint Bartholomew's Day Massacre The mass murder of French Protestants (Huguenots) instigated by Queen Catherine de' Medici of France and carried out by Catholics. It began in Paris on 24 August 1572 and spread to other parts of France, continuing into October of that year. More than 70,000 people were killed.

salons Informal gatherings of intellectuals and aristocrats that allowed discourse about Enlightenment ideas.

Sappho (c. 620–c. 550 B.C.E.) One of the most celebrated Greek poets, she was revered as "the Tenth Muse" and emulated by many male poets. Ironically, though, only two of her poems survive intact, and the rest must be pieced together from fragments quoted by later poets.

Sargon the Great (r. 2334–2279 B.C.E.) The Akkadian ruler who consolidated power in Mesopotamia.

SARS epidemic (2003) The successful containment of severe acute respiratory syndrome (SARS) is an example of how international health organizations can effectively work together to recognize and respond to a disease outbreak. The disease itself, however, is a reminder of the dangers that exist in a globalized economy with a high degree of mobility in both populations and goods.

Schlieffen Plan Devised by German general Alfred von Schlieffen in 1905 to avoid the dilemma of a two-front war against France and Russia. The Schlieffen Plan required that Germany attack France first through Belgium and secure a quick victory before wheeling to the east to meet the slower armies of the Russians on the Eastern Front. The Schlieffen Plan was put into operation on August 2, 1914, at the outset of the First World War.

scientific revolution of antiquity The Hellenistic period was the most brilliant age in the history of science before the seventeenth century C.E. Aristarchus of Samos posited the existence of a heliocentric universe. Eratosthenes of Alexandria accurately calculated the circumference of the earth. Archimedes turned physics into its own branch of experimental science. Hellenistic anatomists became the first to practice human dissection, which improved their understanding of human physiology. Ironically, most of these discoveries were suppressed by pseudo-scientists who flourished under the Roman Empire during the second century C.E., notably Claudus Ptolomeus Ptolemy) and Aelius Galenus (Galen).

second industrial revolution The technological developments in the last third of the nineteenth century, which included new techniques for refining and producing steel; increased availability of electricity for industrial, commercial, and domestic use; advances in chemical manufacturing; and the creation of the internal combustion engine.

Second World War Worldwide war that began in September 1939 in Europe, and even earlier in Asia (the Japanese invasion of Manchuria began in 1931), pitting Britain, the United States, and the Soviet Union (the Allies) against Nazi Germany, Italy, and Japan (the Axis). The war ended in 1945 with Germany and Japan's defeat.

Seleucus (d. 280 B.C.E.) The Macedonian general who ruled the Persian heartland of Alexander the Great's empire.

Semitic The Semitic language family has the longest recorded history of any linguistic group and is the root for most languages of the Middle and Near East. Ancient Semitic languages include those of the ancient Babylonians and Assyrians, Phoenician, the classical form of Hebrew, early dialects of Aramaic, and the classical Arabic of the Qu'ran.

Sepoy Mutiny of 1857 See **Indian Rebellion of 1857**.

serfdom Peasant labor. Unlike slaves, serfs are "attached" to the land they work, and are not supposed to be sold apart from that land.

William Shakespeare (1564–1616) An English playwright who flourished during the reigns of Elizabeth I and James I, Shakespeare received a basic education in his hometown of Stratford-upon-Avon and worked in London as an actor before achieving success as a dramatist and poet.

Shi'ites An often-persecuted minority within Islam, Shi'ites believe that only descendants of Muhammad's successor Ali and his wife Fatimah (Muhammad's daughter) can have any authority over the Muslim community. Today, Shi'ites constitute the ruling party in Iran and are numerous in Iraq but otherwise comprise only 10 percent of Muslims worldwide.

Abbé Sieyès (1748–1836) In 1789, he wrote the pamphlet "What is the Third Estate?" in which he posed fundamental questions about the rights of the Third Estate and helped provoke its secession from the Estates-General. He was a leader at the Tennis Court Oath, but he later helped Napoleon seize power.

Sinn Féin The Irish revolutionary organization that formed in 1900 to fight for Irish independence.

Sino-Japanese War (1894–1895) Conflict over the control of Korea in which China was forced to cede the province of Taiwan to Japan.

slave revolt in Saint-Domingue (1791–1804) In September of 1791, the largest slave rebellion in history broke out in Saint-Domingue, an important French colony in the Caribbean. In 1794, the revolutionary government in France abolished slavery in the colonies, though this act was essentially only recognizing the liberty that the slaves had seized by their own actions. Napoleon reestablished slavery in the French Caribbean in 1802, but failed in his attempt to reconquer Saint-Domingue. Armies commanded by former slaves succeeded in winning independence for a new nation, Haiti, in 1804, making the revolt in Saint-Domingue the first successful slave revolt in history.

slavery The practice of subjugating people to a life of bondage, and of selling or trading these unfree people. For most of human history, slavery had no racial or ethnic basis, and was widely practiced by all cultures and civilizations. Anyone could become a slave, for example, by being captured in war or by being sold for the payment of a debt. It was only in the fifteenth century, with the growth of the African slave trade, that slavery came to be associated with particular races and peoples.

Adam Smith (1723–1790) Scottish economist and liberal philosopher who proposed that competition between self-interested individuals led naturally to a healthy economy. He became famous for his influential book, *The Wealth of Nations* (1776).

Social Darwinism Belief that Charles Darwin's theory of natural selection (evolution) was applicable to human societies and justified the right of the ruling classes or countries to dominate the weak.

social democracy The belief that democracy and social welfare go hand in hand and that diminishing the sharp inequalities of class society is crucial to fortifying democratic culture.

socialism Political ideology that calls for a classless society with collective ownership of all property.

Society of Jesus See **Jesuits**.

Socrates (469–399 B.C.E.) The Athenian philosopher and teacher who promoted the careful examination of all inherited opinions and assumptions on the grounds that "the unexamined life is not worth living." A veteran of the Peloponnesian War, he was tried and condemned by his fellow citizens for engaging in allegedly seditious activities and was executed in 399 B.C.E. His most influential pupils were the philosopher Plato and the historian and social commentator Xenophon.

Solon (d. 559 B.C.E.) Elected archon in 594 B.C.E., this Athenian aristocrat enacted a series of political and economic reforms that formed the basis of Athenian democracy.

Somme (1916) During this battle of the First World War, Allied forces attempted to take entrenched German positions from July to mid-November of 1916. Neither side was able to make any real gains despite massive casualties: 500,000 Germans, 400,000 British, and 200,000 French.

Soviet bloc International alliance that included the East European countries of the Warsaw Pact as well as the Soviet Union; it also came to include Cuba.

soviets Local councils elected by workers and soldiers in Russia. Socialists started organizing these councils in 1905, and the Petrograd soviet in the capital emerged as one of the centers of power after the Russian monarchy collapsed in 1917 in the midst of World War I. The soviets became increasingly powerful and pressed for social reform, the redistribution of land, and called for Russian withdrawal from the war effort.

Spanish-American War (1898) War between the United States and Spain in Cuba, Puerto Rico, and the Philippines. It ended with a treaty in which the United States took over the Philippines, Guam, and Puerto Rico; Cuba won partial independence.

Spanish Armada Supposedly invincible fleet of warships sent against England by Philip II of Spain in 1588 but vanquished by the English fleet and bad weather in the English Channel.

Sparta Around 650 B.C.E., after the suppression of a slave revolt, Spartan rulers militarized their society in order to prevent future rebellions and to protect Sparta's superior position in Greece, orienting their society toward the maintenance of their army. Sparta briefly joined forces with Athens and other poleis in the second war with Persia in 480–479 B.C.E., but these two rivals ultimately fell out again in 431 B.C.E. when Sparta and her Peloponnesian allies went to war against Athens and her allies. This bloody conflict lasted until Athens was defeated in 404 B.C.E., after Sparta received military aid from the Persians.

Spartiate A full citizen of Sparta, hence a professional soldier of the hoplite phalanx.

spinning jenny Invention of James Hargreaves (c. 1720–1774) that revolutionized the British textile industry by allowing a worker to spin much more thread than was possible on a hand spinner.

SS (Schutzstaffel) Formed in 1925 to serve as Hitler's personal security force and to guard Nazi party (NSDAP) meetings, the SS grew into a large militarized organization that became notorious for their participation in carrying out Nazi policies.

Joseph Stalin (1879–1953) The Bolshevik leader who succeeded Lenin as the leader of the Soviet Union and ruled until his death in 1953.

Stalingrad (1942–1943) The turning point on the Eastern Front during the Second World War came when the German army tried to take the city of Stalingrad in an effort to break the back of Soviet industry. The German and Soviet armies fought a bitter battle, in which more than a half million German, Italian, and Romanian soldiers were killed and the Soviets suffered over a million casualties. The German army surrendered after over five months of fighting. After Stalingrad, the Soviet army launched a series of attacks that pushed the Germans back.

Stoicism An ancient philosophy derived from the teachings of Zeno of Athens (fl. c. 300) and widely influential within the Roman Empire; it also impacted the development of Christianity. Stoics believe in the essential orderliness of the cosmos, and that everything that occurs happens for the best. Since everything is determined in accordance with rational purpose, no individual is master of his or her fate, and the only agency that human beings have consists in their responses to good fortune or adversity.

Sumerians The ancient inhabitants of southern Mesopotamia (modern Iraq and Kuwait) whose sophisticated civilization emerged around 4000 B.C.E.

Sunnis Proponents of Islam's customary religious practices (*sunna*) as they developed under the first two caliphs to succeed Muhammad, his father-in-law Abu-Bakr and his disciple Umar. Sunni orthodoxy is dominant within Islam but is opposed by the Shi'ites (from the Arabic word *shi'a*, "faction").

syndicalists A nineteenth-century political movement that embraced a strategy of strikes and sabotage by workers. Their hope was that a general strike of all workers would bring down the capitalist state and replace it with workers' syndicates or trade associations. Their refusal to participate in politics limited their ability to command a wide influence.

tabula rasa Term used by John Locke (1632–1704) to describe man's mind before he acquired ideas as a result of experience; Latin for "clean slate."

Tennis Court Oath (1789) Oath taken by representatives of the Third Estate in June 1789, in which they pledged to form a National Assembly and write a constitution limiting the powers of the king.

Reign of Terror (1793–1794) Campaign at the height of the French Revolution in which violence, including systematic executions of opponents of the revolution, was used to purge France of its "enemies" and to extend the revolution beyond its borders; radicals executed as many as 40,000 persons who were judged enemies of the state.

Tetrarchy The result of Diocletian's political reforms of the late third century C.E., which divided the Roman Empire into four quadrants.

Theban Hegemony The term describing the period when the polis of Thebes dominated the Greek mainland, which reached its height after 371 B.C.E., under leadership of the Theban general Epaminondas. It was in Thebes that the future King Philip II of Macedon spent his youth, and it was the defeat of Thebes and Athens at the hands of Philip and Alexander—at the Battle of Chaeronea in 338—that Macedonian hegemony was forcefully asserted.

theory of evolution Darwin's theory that linked biology to history. Darwin believed that competition between different organisms and struggle with the environment were fundamental and unavoidable facts of life. In this struggle, those individuals who were better adapted to their environment survived, whereas the weak perished. This produced a "natural selection," or favoring of certain adaptive traits over time, leading to a gradual evolution of different species.

Third Estate The population of France under the Old Regime was divided into three estates, corporate bodies that determined an individual's rights or obligations under royal law. The nobility constituted the First Estate, the clergy the Second, and the commoners (the vast bulk of the population) made up the Third Estate.

Third Reich The German state from 1933 to 1945 under Adolf Hitler and the Nazi party.

Third World nations—mostly in Asia, Latin America, and Africa—that are not highly industrialized.

Thirty Years' War (1618–1648) Beginning as a conflict between Protestants and Catholics in Germany, this series of skirmishes escalated into a general European war fought on German soil by armies from Sweden, France, and the Holy Roman Empire.

Timur the Lame (1336–1405) Also known as Tamerlane, he was the last ruler of the Mongol Khans' Asian empire.

Marshal Tito (1892–1980) The Yugoslavian communist and resistance leader who became the leader of Yugoslavia and fought to keep his government independent of the Soviet Union. In response, the Soviet Union expelled Yugoslavia from the communist countries' economic and military pacts.

towns Centers for markets and administration. Towns existed in a symbiotic relationship with the countryside. They provided markets for surplus food from outlying farms as well as producing manufactured goods. In the Middle Ages, towns tended to grow up around a castle or monastery which afforded protection.

transatlantic triangle The trading of African slaves by European colonists to address labor shortages in the Americas and the Caribbean. Slaves were treated like cargo, loaded onto ships and sold in exchange for molasses, tobacco, rum, and other precious commodities.

Treaty of Brest-Litovsk (1918) Separate peace between imperial Germany and the new Bolshevik regime in Russia. The treaty acknowledged the German victory on the Eastern Front and withdrew Russia from the war.

Treaty of Utrecht (1713) Resolution to the War of Spanish Succession that reestablished a balance of power in Europe, to the benefit of Britain and in ways that disadvantaged Spain, Holland, and France.

Treaty of Versailles Signed on June 28, 1919, this peace settlement ended the First World War and required Germany to surrender a large part of its most valuable territories and to pay huge reparations to the Allies.

trench warfare Weapons such as barbed wire and the machine gun gave tremendous advantage to defensive positions in World War I, leading to prolonged battles between entrenched armies in fixed positions. The trenches eventually consisted of 25,000 miles of holes and ditches that stretched across the Western Front in northern France, from the Atlantic coast to the Swiss border during the First World War. On the eastern front, the large expanse of territories made trench warfare less significant.

triangular trade The eighteenth-century commercial Atlantic shipping pattern that took rum from New England to Africa, traded it for slaves taken to the West Indies, and brought sugar back to New England to be processed into rum.

Triple Entente Alliance developed before the First World War that eventually included Britain, France, and Russia.

Truman Doctrine (1947) Declaration promising U.S. economic and military intervention to counter any attempt by the Soviet Union to expand its influence. Often cited as a key moment in the origins of the Cold War.

tsar Russian word for "emperor," derived from the Latin *caesar* and similar to the German *kaiser,* it was the title claimed by the rulers of medieval Muscovy and of the later Russian Empire.

Ubaid culture An early civilization that flourished in Mesopotamia between 5500 and 4000 B.C.E., it was characterized by large village settlements and temple complexes: a precursor to the more urban civilization of the Sumerians.

Umayyad Caliphate (661–930) The Umayyad family resisted the authority of the first two caliphs who succeeded Muhammad but eventually placed a member of their own family in that position of power. The Umayyad Caliphate ruled the Islamic world from 661 to 750, modeling their administration on that of the Roman Empire. But after a rebellion led by the rival Abbasid family, the power of the Umayyad Caliphate was confined to their territories in al-Andalus (Spain).

Universal Declaration of Human Rights (1948) United Nations declaration that laid out the rights to which all human beings were entitled.

University of Paris The reputation of Peter Abelard and his students attracted many intellectuals to Paris in the twelfth century, some of whom began offering instruction to aspiring scholars. By 1200, this loose association of teachers had formed themselves into a *universitas,* or corporation. They began collaborating in the higher academic study of the liberal arts with a special emphasis on theology.

Pope Urban II (1042?–1099) Instigator of the First Crusade (1096–1099), who promised that anyone who fought or died in the service of the Church would receive absolution from sin.

urban populations During the nineteenth century, urban populations in Europe increased sixfold. For the most part, urban areas had medieval infrastructures, which new populations and industries overwhelmed. As a result, many European cities became overcrowded and unhealthy.

Utopia Title of a semi-satirical social critique by the English statesman Sir Thomas More (1478–1535); the word derives from the Greek "best place" or "no place."

Lorenzo Valla (1407–1457) One of the first practitioners of scientific philology (the historical study of language), Valla's analysis of the so-called Donation of Constantine showed that the document could not possibly have been written in the fourth century C.E., but must have been forged centuries later.

vassal A person who pledges to be loyal and subservient to a lord in exchange for land, income, or protection.

velvet revolutions The peaceful political revolutions throughout Eastern Europe in 1989.

Verdun (1916) This battle between German and French forces lasted for ten months during the First World War. The Germans saw the battle as a chance to break French morale through a war of attrition, and the French believed the battle to be a symbol of France's strength. In the end, over 400,000 lives were lost and the German offensive failed.

Versailles Conference (1919) Peace conference between the victors of the First World War; resulted in the Treaty of Versailles, which forced Germany to pay reparations and to give up its colonies to the victors.

Queen Victoria (1819–1901) Influential monarch who reigned from 1837 until her death; she presided over the expansion of the British Empire as well as the evolution of English politics and social and economic reforms.

Viet Cong Vietnamese communist group formed in 1954; committed to overthrowing the government of South Vietnam and reunifying North and South Vietnam.

Vikings (800–1000) The collapse of the Abbasid Caliphate disrupted Scandinavian commercial networks and turned traders into raiders (the word *viking* describes the activity of raiding). These raids often escalated into invasions that contributed to the collapse of the Carolingian Empire, resulted in the devastation of settled territories, and ended with the establishment of Viking colonies. By the tenth century, Vikings controlled areas of eastern England, Scotland, the islands of Ireland, Iceland, Greenland, and parts of northern France. They had also established the beginnings of the kingdom that became Russia and made exploratory voyages to North America, founding a settlement at Newfoundland (Canada).

A Vindication of the Rights of Woman Noted work of Mary Wollstonecraft (1759–1797), English republican who applied Enlightenment political ideas to issues of gender.

Virgil (70–19 B.C.E.) An influential Roman poet who wrote under the patronage of the emperor Augustus. His *Aeneid* mimicked the ancient Greek epics of Homer and told the mythical tale of Rome's founding by the Trojan refugee Aeneas.

Visigoths The tribes of "west" Goths who sacked Rome in 410 C.E. and later established a kingdom in the Roman province of Hispania (Spain).

Voltaire Pseudonym of French philosopher and satirist François Marie Arouet (1694–1778), who championed the cause of human dignity against state and Church oppression. Noted deist and author of *Candide.*

Lech Wałęsa (1943–) Leader of the Polish labor movement Solidarity, which organized a series of strikes across Poland in 1980. They protested working conditions, shortages, and high prices. Above all, they demanded an independent labor union. Solidarity's leaders were imprisoned and the union banned, but they launched a new series of strikes in 1988, which led to the legalization of Solidarity and open elections.

war communism The Russian civil war forced the Bolsheviks to take a more radical economic stance. They requisitioned grain from the peasantry and outlawed private trade in consumer goods as "speculation." They also militarized production facilities and abolished money.

Wars of the Roses Fifteenth-century civil conflict between the English dynastic houses of Lancaster and York, each of which was symbolized by the heraldic device of a rose (red and white, respectively). It was ultimately resolved by the accession of the Lancastrian king Henry VII, who married Elizabeth of York.

Warsaw Pact (1955–1991) Military alliance between the USSR and other communist states that was established as a response to the creation of the NATO alliance.

The Wealth of Nations 1776 treatise by Adam Smith, whose laissez-faire ideas predicted the economic boom of the Industrial Revolution.

Weimar Republic The government of Germany between 1919 and the rise of Hitler and the Nazi party.

Western Front Military front that stretched from the English Channel through Belgium and France to the Alps during the First World War.

Whites Refers to the "counterrevolutionaries" of the Bolshevik Revolution (1918–1921) who fought the Bolsheviks (the "Reds"); included former supporters of the tsar, Social Democrats, and large independent peasant armies.

William the Conqueror (1027–1087) Duke of Normandy who laid claim to the throne of England in 1066, defeating the Anglo-Saxon King Harold at the Battle of Hastings. He and his

Norman followers imposed imperial rule in England through a brutal campaign of military conquest, surveillance, and the suppression of the indigenous Anglo-Saxon language.

William of Ockham (d. 1349) An English philosopher and Franciscan friar, he denied that human reason could prove fundamental theological truths, such as the existence of God: he argued that there is no necessary connection between the observable laws of nature and the unknowable essence of divinity. His theories, derived from the work of earlier scholastics, form the basis of the scientific method.

Woodrow Wilson (1856–1924) U.S. president who requested and received a declaration of war from Congress so that America could enter the First World War. After the war, his prominent role in the Paris Peace Conference signaled the rise of the United States as a world power. He also proposed the Fourteen Points, which influenced the peace negotiations.

Maria Winkelmann (1670–1720) German astronomer who worked with her husband in his observatory. Despite discovering a comet and preparing calendars for the Berlin Academy of Sciences, the academy would not let her take her husband's place within the body after he died.

witch craze The rash of persecutions that took place in both Catholic and Protestant countries of early modern Europe and their colonies, facilitated by secular governments and religious authorities.

women's associations Because European women were excluded from the workings of parliamentary and mass politics, some women formed organizations to press for political and civil rights. Some groups focused on establishing educational opportunities for women while others campaigned energetically for the vote.

William Wordsworth (1770–1850) Romantic writer whose central themes were nature, simplicity, and feeling. He considered nature to be man's most trustworthy teacher and source of sublime power that nourished the human soul.

World Bank International agency established in 1944 to provide economic assistance to war-torn nations and countries in need of economic development.

John Wycliffe (c. 1330–1384) A professor of theology at the University of Oxford, Wycliffe urged the English king to confiscate ecclesiastical wealth and to replace corrupt priests and bishops with men who would live according to the apostolic standards of poverty and piety. He advocated direct access to the scriptures and promoted an English translation of the Bible. His teachings played an important role in the Peasants' Revolt of 1381 and inspired the still more radical initiatives of a group known as Lollards.

Xerxes (519?–465 B.C.E.) Xerxes succeeded his father, Darius, as Great King of Persia. Seeking to avenge his father's shame and eradicate any future threats to Persian hegemony, he launched his own invasion of Greece in 480 B.C.E. An allied Greek army defeated his forces in 479 B.C.E.

Yalta Accords Meeting among President Franklin D. Roosevelt, Prime Minister Winston Churchill, and Premier Joseph Stalin that occurred in the Crimea in 1945 shortly before the end of the Second World War to plan for the postwar order.

Young Turks The 1908 Turkish reformist movement that aimed to modernize the Ottoman Empire, restore parliamentary rule, and depose Sultan Abdul Hamid II.

ziggurats Temples constructed under the Dynasty of Ur in what is now Iraq, beginning around 2100 B.C.E.

Zionism A political movement dating to the end of the nineteenth century holding that the Jewish people constitute a nation and are entitled to a national homeland. Zionists rejected a policy of Jewish assimilation and advocated the reestablishment of a Jewish homeland in Palestine.

Zollverein In 1834, Prussia started a customs union, which established free trade among the German states and a uniform tariff against the rest of the world. By the 1840s, the union included almost all of the German states except German Austria. It is considered an important precedent for the political unification of Germany, which was completed in 1870 under Prussian leadership.

Zoroastrianism One of the three major universal faiths of the ancient world, alongside Judaism and Christianity, it was derived from the teachings of the Persian Zoroaster around 600 B.C.E. Zoroaster redefined religion as an ethical practice common to all, rather than as a set of rituals and superstitions that cause divisions among people. Zoroastrianism teaches that there is one supreme god in the universe, Ahura-Mazda (Wise Lord) but that his goodness will be constantly assailed by the forces of evil until the arrival of a final "judgment day." Proponents of this faith should therefore help good to triumph over evil by leading a good life, and by performing acts of compassion and charity. Zoroastrianism exercised a profound influence over many early Christians, including Augustine.

Ulrich Zwingli (1484–1531) A former priest from the Swiss city of Zurich, Zwingli joined Luther and Calvin in attacking the authority of the Roman Catholic Church.

Leon B. Alberti: "On the Family" from *The Family in Renaissance Florence*, trans./ed. by Renée Neu Watkins (University of South Carolina Press, 1969), pp. 208–213. Reprinted by permission of the translator.

Aristophanes: 300 words from *Lysistrata and Other Plays* by Aristophanes, translated with an introduction by Alan H. Sommerstein (Penguin Classics, 1973). Copyright © Alan H. Sommerstein, 1973. Reproduced by permission of Penguin Books Ltd.

Arrian: 300 words from *The Campaigns of Alexander* by Arrian, translated by Aubrey de Sélincourt, revised with an introduction and notes by J.R. Hamilton (Penguin Classics 1958, Revised edition 1971). Copyright © the Estate of Aubrey de Sélincourt, 1958. Introduction and Notes copyright © J.R. Hamilton, 1971. Reproduced by permission of Penguin Books Ltd.

Nels Bailkey (ed.): From Bailkey, *Readings in Ancient History*, 5th Edition. © 1996 Wadsworth, a part of Cengage Learning, Inc. Reproduced by permission. www.cengage.com/permissions.

Armand Bellee (ed.): *Cahiers de plaintes & doleances des paroisses de la province du Maine pour les Etats-generaux de 1789*, 4 vols. (Le Mans: Monnoyer, 1881-92), 2: 578–82. Translated by the American Social History Project, "Liberty, Equality, Fraternity: Exploring the French Revolution" by Jack R. Censer and Lynn Hunt. Reprinted by permission.

Bernard of Angers: "Miracles of Saint Foy" from *Readings in Medieval History*, 2nd Edition, edited by Patrick J. Geary (Toronto, Ont: University of Toronto Press, 2003). Copyright © 2003. Reprinted by permission of the publisher.

Henry Bettenson (ed.): "Obedience as a Jesuit Hallmark" from *Documents of the Christian Church*, 2nd Edition. Copyright © 1967, Oxford University Press. Reprinted by permission of Oxford University Press.

Gabriel Biel: "Execrabilis." Reprinted by permission of the publisher from *Defensorium Obedientiae Apostolicae Et Alia Documenta* by Gabriel Biel, edited and translated by Heiko A. Oberman, Daniel E. Zerfoss and William J. Courtenay, pp. 224–227, Cambridge, Mass.: The Belknap Press of Harvard University Press, Copyright © 1968 by the President and Fellows of Harvard College.

Jose Bove: *The World Is Not for Sale: Farmers Against Junk Food*, pp. 3–13, © Verso, 2001. Reprinted by permission of the publisher.

Walter Bower: "A Declaration of Scottish Independence," from *Scotichronicon*, Volume 7, by Walter Bower. Edited by B. Scott and D. E. R. Watt. Copyright © 1996 Aberdeen University Press. Reprinted with permission.

Boyer, Baker & Kirshner (eds): "Declaration of the Rights of Man and of the Citizen", "Napoleon's Letter to Prince Eugene" and "Circular Letter to Sovereigns" from *University of Chicago Readings in Western Civilization, Vol. 7*, pp. 238–239; 419–420; 426–427, Copyright © 1987 by The University of Chicago. Reprinted by permission of The University of Chicago Press.

Anna Comnena: 340 words from *The Alexiad of Anna Comnena*, translated by E.R.A. Sewter (Penguin Classics, 1969). Copyright © E.R.A. Sewter, 1969. Reproduced by permission of Penguin Books Ltd.

James Cracraft: "Alexander II's Decree Emancipating the Serfs, 1861," *Major Problems in the History of Imperial Russia*. Copyright © 1994 by D.C. Heath and Company.

David Brion Davis: From *Encyclopédie*, Vol. 16, Neuchâtel, 1765, p. 532 as cited in David Brion Davis, *The Problem of Slavery in Western Culture*. (Ithaca, N.Y.: Cornell University Press, 1966), p. 416. Copyright © 1966 by David Brion Davis. Reprinted by permission.

Simone de Beauvoir: From *The Second Sex* by Simone de Beauvoir, translated by Constance Borde & Sheila Malovany-Chevalier, published by Jonathan Cape, translation copyright © 2009 by Constance Borde and Sheila Malovany-Chevalier, Introduction copyright © 2010 by Judith Thurman. Reprinted by permission of Alfred A. Knopf, a division of Random House, Inc. and The Random House Group Ltd.

Geoffrey de Charny: From *The Book of Chivalry of Geoffrey de Charny: Text, Context, and Translation*, translated by Richard W. Kaeuper and Elspeth Kennedy, pp. 99. Copyright © 1996 University of Pennsylvania Press. Reprinted with permission.

Marie de France: "Equitan" in The Lais of Marie de France, translated by Gllyn S. Burgess and Kieth Burgess. Pp. 56–57. Copyright © 1985. Reproduced by permission of Penguin Books Ltd.

Pope Urban II: "Pope Urban II's Call at Clermont, November 1195" from *The Crusades: A Reader*, edited by S.J. Allen and Emilie Amt. © Broadview Press/UTP Higher Education. Reprinted with permission of the publisher.

Paul von Hindenburg: *From The War from Within: German Working-Class Women in the First World War,* translated by Margaret Ries. Pp. 68–69. Copyright © 1997 Bloomsbury Publishing Place. Reprinted with permission.

Peter Waldo: "The Conversion of Peter Waldo" from *The Birth of Popular Heresy*, edited/translated by Robert I. Moore (Edward Arnold, 1975). Copyright © 1975, Edward Arnold Publishers. Reproduced by permission of Edward Arnold (Publishers) Limited.

Sumner Willard and Charity Cannon Willard: From *The Book of the Deeds of Arms and of Chivalry*, pp. 11–13. Copyright © 1999 Pennsylvania State University Press. Reprinted with permission.

Xenophon: "Book I, The Anabasis" from *The Greek Historians* by M.I. Finley, copyright © 1959 by The Viking Press, Inc., renewed © 1987 by Charles Richard Whittaker. Used by permission of Viking Penguin, a division of Penguin Group (USA) Inc.

Emile Zola: "The Dangers of Consumer Culture" from *The Ladies Paradise*, trans. by Brian Nelson. Copyright © 1995, Oxford University Press, Inc. Reprinted by permission of Oxford University Press.

Photo Credits

Chapter 1: **p. 1:** The Louvre, Paris. Giraudon/Art Resource, NY; **p. 5:** The Bridgeman Art Library; **p. 7:** TAO Images Limited/Getty Images; **p. 8:** © INTERFOTO/Alamy; **p. 10 (left):** Ashmolean Museum, University of Oxford, UK/The Bridgeman Art Library; **p. 10 (right):** British Museum; **p. 14:** Bettmann Corbis; **p. 15:** Courtesy of the Oriental Institute of the University of Chicago; **p. 16 (left):** The Granger Collection, New York; **p. 16 (right):** The University of Pennsylvania Museum; **p. 17:** ©World Religions Photo Library/Bridgeman Art Library; © INTERFOTO/Alamy; **p. 19:** The Louvre, Paris/Herve Lewandowski, Réunion des Musées/ Nationaux Art Resource, NY; **p. 21 (left):** © RMN-Grand Palais/Art Resource, NY; **p. 21 (right):** © RMN-Grand Palais/Art Resource, NY; **p. 24 (left):** The Granger Collection, NYC; **p. 24 (right):** © Arterra Picture Library/Alamy; **p. 26 (left):** Werner Forman/Art Resource, NY; **p. 26 (right):** Werner Forman/Art Resource, NY; **p. 27 (left):** © Bettmann/Corbis; **p. 27 (right):** Ancient Civilizations, 2e by Scarre/Fagan, © 2003. Reprinted by permission of Pearson Education, Inc., Upper Saddle River, NJ; **p. 28:** © Gian Berto Vanni/Corbis; **p. 29:** © Charles & Josette Lenars/Corbis; **p. 30:** De Agostini Picture Library/The Bridgeman Art Library; **p. 32 (left):** © The Trustees of the British Museum/Art Resource, NY; **p. 32 (right):** © The Trustees of the British Museum/Art Resource; **p. 33:** Giraudon/Bridgeman Art Library **p. 34:** Louvre, Paris, France/Bridgeman Art Library.

Chapter 2: **p. 38:** Erich Lessing/Art Resource, NY; **p. 42:** © The Trustees of the British Museum/Art Resource, NY; **p. 44 (left):** © Travel Pictures/Alamy; **p. 44 (right):** © Ian M. Butterfield/Alamy; **p. 45 (left):** Scala/Art Resource, NY; **p. 45 (right):** © Jim Henderson/Alamy; **p. 46:** © Jose Fuste Raga/Corbis; **p. 47:** Erich Lessing/Art Resource, NY; Rue des Archives/The Granger Collection, NY; **p. 49:** © Gian Berto Vanni/Corbis; **p. 50:** Erich Lessing/Art Resource, NY; **p. 51:** © Gianni Dagli Orti/Corbis; © Gianni Dagli Orti/Corbis; **p. 58 (left):** Nimatallah/Art Resource, NY; **p. 58 (right):** Bloomberg via Getty Images; **p. 63:** Erich Lessing/Art Resource, NY; **p. 64:** © Gianni Dagli Orti/Corbis; **p. 65:** © Metropolitan Museum of Art/Art Resource, NY; **p. 67:** © The Art Gallery Collection/Alamy; **p. 70:** Courtesy of Zev Radovan; **p. 71:** Bildarchiv Preussischer Kulturbesitz/Art Resource, NY.

Chapter 3: **p. 74:** Erich Lessing/Art Resource, NY; **p. 76:** © nagelestock.com/Alamy; **p. 82:** De Agostini Picture Library/Bridgeman Art Library; **p. 83:** De Agostini Picture Library/The Bridgeman Art Library; **p. 85:** © RMN-Grand Palais/Art Resource, NY; **p. 87:** Scala/Art Resource, NY; **p. 88:** Carol Symes; **p. 93:** © Paul Lipke/Trireme Trust, Montague, MA; **p. 94 (left):** DeA Picture Library/The Granger Collection; **p. 94 (right):** Comedy Cent/Mad Cow Prod/The Kobal Collection/Art Resource; **p. 96:** National Museums of Scotland/ Bridgeman Art Library; **p. 98 (right):** Vanni/Art resource, NY; **p. 98 (left):** Clip Art ETC; **p. 99 (left):** Foto Marburg/Art Resource, NY; **p. 99 (center):** Gianni Dagli Orti/The Art Archive at Art Resource, NY; **p. 99 (right):** Nimatallah/Art Resource, NY; **p. 100:** Original model by G.P. Stevens; additions by Sylvia Hahn/Royal Ontario Museum; **p. 101:** Bildarchiv Preussischer Kulturbesitz / Art Resource, NY; **p. 106:** Erich Lessing/Art Resource, NY; **p. 107:** Gianni Dagli Orti/The Art Archive at Art Resource, NY.

Chapter 4: **p. 110:** Erich Lessing/Art Resource, NY; **p. 112:** The Art Archive/Gianni Dagli Orti; **p. 116 (left):** DeA Picture Library/ The Granger Collection, NYC; **p. 116 (right):** Vanni/Art Resource, NY; **p. 117:** Scala/Art Resource, NY; **p. 118:** Scala/Art Resource, NY; **p. 121:** © Gianni Dagli Orti/Corbis; **p. 122:** Erin Babnik/Alamy; **p. 123:** Erich Lessing/Art Resource, NY; Erich Lessing/Art Resource; **p. 126:** National Museum of Iran, Tehran, Iran/The Bridgeman Art Library; **p. 129 (left):** The Trustees of the British Museum; **p. 129 (right):** Bildarchiv Preussischer Kulturbesitz / Art Resource, NY; **p. 131 (left):** The Granger Collection, NY; **p. 131 (right):** © Reuters/Corbis; **p. 132:** Erich Lessing/Art Resource, NY; **p. 139:** Verulamium Museum, St. Albans, Hertfordshire, UK / The Bridgeman Art Library; **p. 140:** INTERFOTO/Alamy; **p. 141:** © Wolfgang Kaehler/Corbis; Scala/Art Resource, NY; **p. 142 (left):** akg-images/ CDA/Guillemot; **p. 142 (right):** Scala/Art Resource, NY.

Chapter 5: **p. 144:** © Cultura Creative/Alamy; **p. 147:** Italic, Etruscan, Late Classical or Early Hellenistic Period, about 330–300 BC; Findspot and Place of Manufacture: Italy, Lazio, Vulci; Marble, 93.3cm high x 117.4 cm width x 213.8 cm length; Museum of Fine Arts, Boston, Gift of Mrs. Gardner Brewer, 86.145a-b. Photograph (c) 2004 Museum of Fine Arts, Boston; **p. 150:** Statue of Cincinnatus, Cincinnati, OH, 2010, by Rick Dikeman; **p. 151:** WoodyStock/Alamy; **p. 152:** Scala/Art Resource, NY; **p. 155:** The Trustees of the British Museum; **p. 158 (left):** Alamy; **p. 158 (right):** AFP PHOTO/JAY DIRECTO/NEWSCOM; **p. 159:** Scala/Art Resource, NY; **p. 162:** Scala/Art Resource, NY; **p. 163:** Sandro Vannini/Corbis; Yale University Art Gallery/Art Resource, NY; The Trustees of the British Museum; **p. 166:** The Granger Collection, New York; **p. 167:** Courtesy of Carol Symes; **p. 170:** Silver Stock/Alamy; **p. 172:** © Images & Stories/Alamy; The Trustees of the British Museum; **p. 176:** Vanni/Art Resource, NY; **p. 177:** The Print Collector/Alamy.

Chapter 6: **p. 178:** Alinari/Art Resource, NY; **p. 181:** Erich Lessing/Art Resource, NY; **p. 182:** AFP Photo/Osservatore Romano/

France / Giraudon / The Bridgeman Art Library; **p. 403 (left):** DEA PICTURE LIBRARY/Getty Images; **p. 403 (right):** © University of Leicester/Corbis; **p. 404:** National Portrait Gallery, London, UK / The Bridgeman Art Library; **p. 406:** Bildarchiv Preussischer Kulturbesitz / Art Resource, NY; **p. 408:** Vova Pomortzeff / Alamy; **p. 409:** Museo del Prado, Madrid/ Art Archive; **p. 413:** Myriam Thyes / Wikimedia Commons; **p. 416:** Bibliotheque Nationale, Paris, France/ Giraudon/ The Bridgeman Art Library; **p. 417:** AKG-images; **p. 418:** The Art Archive / Biblioteca Nacional de Madrid / Dagli Orti.

Index

Page numbers in *italics* refer to illustrations, maps, and tables.

women:
in abolition movement, 644
in ancient Egypt, 33–34, 43–46
anti-feminists and, 774, *774*
in Aristotelian thought, 119
in Byzantine Empire, 219–20
in Çatalhöyük, 4
Catholic Church and, 301–3, 448, *449*
Christianity and, 184–85, 196, 203, 234, 301–3
in classical Greece, 100–101, 107
cult of courtly love and, 315–16
education of, 219–20, 308–9, 367, 773, *774*, 957
in Enlightenment, 567–68, 569, 570
equal right for, 956–57, *956*
Etruscan, 146–47
Existentialism and, 939–40
in First World War, 817–18, *819*, 820, 821
French Revolution and, 583, 588, *589*, 590, 592, 599, *599*
in gladiatorial combat, *172*
in Hellenistic Greece, 136–37
imperial culture and, 750
in Industrial Revolution, 622, 627
Islam and, 227
liberalism and, 663, 668, 692, 706–7
literary accomplishments of, 571, 678–80
Lutheranism and, 438–40
in medieval literature, 315–16, 318, 362–63, *363*
as medieval rulers, 315–16
monasticism and, 234
Napoleonic Code and, 601–4, 643
in Nazi Germany, 852, 856, 857
as "new woman," 773–74, *852*, 867, 959
nineteenth century colonial image of, *732*
in nineteenth-century middle class, 643–47, 772–74
in nineteenth-century reform movements, 673, 706–7, 771–74
in Old Babylonian Empire, 19–21
in politics, 773
and poverty, 1006–7
as producers of textiles, *19*
Protestantism and, 438–40, 448
redefining role of, 772–74
in Renaissance, 367, 368–69, 395, 406
in Roman Empire, 187
in Roman Republic, 154, 158–59
Romanticism and, 678–80
salons and, 569
in scientific revolution, 535–38, *535*
in Second World War, 902, *902*
sexuality of, 646–47
"sexual revolution" and, 955–57, 964
in Soviet work force, 847–48, 849

suffrage for, 665, 692, 706–7, *707*, 750, 762, 771–74, *772*, 781
Victorian gender roles and, 772–74
in Victorian thought, 643, 646–47, 706–7
in Weimar Germany, *852*
and the "woman question," 958–59
working class, 648–49, 772–74
Women of Algiers (Delacroix), *681*
Women's Social and Political Union, 772
Woodstock, 952
Woolf, Virginia (1882–1941), 800, 863
Wordsworth, William (1770–1850), 592, 677–78, 680
working class, nineteenth-century, 647–50, *649*, 690, 692
credit and, 765
education of, 648
factory life and, 649
illegitimacy among, 648–49
in Industrial Revolution, 623–25, 647–50
liberalism and, 662, 693, 705–6
living conditions of, 648
in Marxist theory, 672–73, 769
sexuality of, 648–49
spread of socialism and, 769–70
subgroups of, 647–50
women, 648–49, 772–74
see also labor unions
World Bank, 924, 985
World Trade Center, terrorist attacks on, 1004–6, *1005*, 1008
World Trade Organization (WTO), 983, 990
World War, First (1914–1918), 506, 720, 730, 736, 751, 753, 759, 769, 770, 774, 778, 780, 781, 782, 784, 796, 797, 798–835, 984
aerial warfare in, 813
alliances in, *801*
Allied blockade in, 807, 810, 813
assassination of Franz Ferdinand and, 800, 804
atrocities against civilians in, 829, 1008
Austrian ultimatum to Serbia before, 800–801, 805
Austrian withdrawal from, 827
casualties in, 800, 806, 807, 812, 827, 829, 832, 838
causes of, 725, 800–803
"cult of the offensive" in, 811
decline of democracy after, 838
domestic conflicts during, 816–17
Eastern Front in, 806
economic upheaval in, 817–22, 822, 834
German surrender in, 828
home front in, 817–22
legacy of, 800, 832–34, 871
"lost generation" of, 832, 863
nationalism after, 835, 837–38

from 1914–1916, *814*
from 1917–1918, *815*
peace treaties after, 829–31
propaganda in, 808–9, *808*, *809*, 819
Russian military failures in, 806, 824–26
Russian surrender in, 826
Schlieffen Plan in, 803, 806, *806*
science and technology after, 864–65
Second World War compared with, 874
stalemate in, 807, 810, 813
strikes in, 822
submarine warfare in, 807, 810, *810*, 821, 828
territorial changes after, *833*
as total war, 817, 828–29
treaties following, 840
trench warfare in, 806, 810–13
U.S. entry into, 807, 828
as war of empires, 829
weapons introduced in, 810–13, *810*, *811*, 812–13, 828–29, *828*
Western Front in, 803–6, 807, 810–13, *812*
women and, 707, 817–18, *819*, 820, 821
World War, Second (1939–1945), 759, 800, 846, 872–909, 911–12
aerial warfare in, 874, 881–83, 903, 908
Allied blockade in, 875
anti-communism and, 878, 888, 890
appeasement policy before, 876–78
atomic bomb in, 874, 903, *905*, 906–7, 908
atrocities against civilians in, 1008
Blitzkrieg warfare in, 874, 881, 904
casualties in, 909
causes of, 873–76
culture and thought after, 937–42
D-Day invasion in, 904, *904*
Dunkirk evacuation in, 882
Eastern Front in, 887–88, 890, 903–4, *905*
end of, 905–8
in Europe, *884*
European integration after, 1008
fall of France in, 881–83
First World War compared with, 874
First World War peace settlement and, 874, 876–78
as global war, 883–87
Holocaust in, *see* Holocaust
home front in, 903
imperialism and, 909
legacy of, 908, 909, 911–12, *913*, 937–42, 947–48
Lend-Lease program in, 883
mass culture after, 951–52
Middle East in aftermath of, 929–31
nationalism and, 873, 876